SOCIOLOGY

A CORE TEXT

James K. Semones
SAN JACINTO COLLEGE

Holt, Rinehart and Winston, Inc.
Fort Worth   Chicago   San Francisco   Philadelphia
Montreal   Toronto   London   Sydney   Tokyo

Publisher: Ted Buchholz
Acquisitions Editor: Christopher P. Klein
Project Manager: Ralph Zickgraf, Editing, Design & Production, Inc.

Credits appear on page 426.

Library of Congress Cataloging-in-Publication Data
Semones, James K.
    Sociology : a core text / James K. Semones.
        p.   cm.
    Includes bibliographical references.
  ISBN 0-03-026247-X
    1. Sociology.   I. Title.
    HM51.S426 1990
    301—dc20   89-19748
                                                 CIP

ISBN 0-03-026247-X

Address orders to: 6277 Sea Harbor Drive, Orlando, FL 32887
1-800-782-4479, or 1-800-433-0001 (in Florida)

Address editorial correspondence to: 301 Commerce St., Suite 3700, Fort Worth, TX 76102

Printed in the United States of America.

0 1 2 3 039 9 8 7 6 5 4 3 2 1

Holt, Rinehart & Winston, Inc.
The Dryden Press
Saunders College Publishing

To three mentors who made a difference:

Thomas Williams, who, by example, inspired in me the desire to become a master teacher;

Robert Sessions, who first instilled in me the sociological imagination and the wish to become a good sociologist; and

Watt Black, who patiently guided much of my journey in pursuit of both goals.

About the Author

James K. Semones is a sociology professor at San Jacinto College. He received his bachelor's and master's degrees in sociology from East Tennessee State University. His doctorate was earned at North Texas State University (now University of North Texas).

A dedicated teacher, Dr. Semones has taught sociology for over 15 years to many thousands of students in university, four-year liberal arts, and community college settings. In addition, he has served as consultant to many corporations, organizations, and schools including the Xerox Corporation, the American Heart Association, Phillips Petroleum, and Gibraltar Savings.

A sociologist of education (with secondary interests in family and deviance), Dr. Semones' primary research interest is in the sociology of teaching and learning. He is the author of *Effective Study Skills: A System for Academic Excellence.* He has also coauthored several books, including *Adult Education: Thoery and Practice, Adult Learning and Program Development* (coeditor), *Key Issues in Higher Education and Society* (all from Burgess/Alpha Editions), and *Recruiting, Marketing, and Retention in Institutions of Higher Education* (University Press of America).

Preface

Welcome to the fascinating world of sociology, the scientific study of human group behavior. The sociological perspective is a powerful and exciting one that, if taken seriously, can provide a person with a wealth of insight about the human condition not often perceived by those who dwell in the world of "common sense" notions. If this book begins to stir in you and others a deeper appreciation of the complexities of human behavior, I will consider it a success.

Those who take the introductory sociology course may be divided into three basic categories: (1) those who need it as a degree requirement, (2) those who take it primarily out of curiosity for personal enrichment, and (3) those from both groups who go on to take additional courses and perhaps major in the field. At the very least, the survey course should help students better understand the basic nature of the social world around them, the positions they occupy in it, and both the benefits and limitations of their culture. In a country like the United States that is undergoing the transition to an information society, a better understanding of human social behavior and what motivates it is of great benefit to everyone.

For a few students, however, exposure to the science of sociology will awaken in them the sociological imagination, a powerful intellectual perspective with which to view the social world and their place in it. This perspective, introduced in Chapter 1, will allow them to go beyond the obvious and visible aspects of social life to the deeper meanings that furnish the foundation for understanding the human experience. The challenge for the textbook author is to provide a learning resource that will meet the needs of both typical students and potential sociology majors as well as provide the quality of coverage desired by their instructors. This is not an easy task.

NEEDS ADDRESSED BY THIS TEXT

In any given year, there are perhaps two or three dozen nationally published and marketed textbooks in introductory sociology that enjoy a fair-to-good amount of success. Almost without exception, they are well researched, often are well organized and elegantly written, and sometimes represent masterpieces of the bookbinder's art with slick, hard covers and colorful illustrations.

The obvious question, then, is, Why write and publish another sociology text? The answer is just as obvious. The development of college textbooks represents an ongoing evolutionary process that is part art, part craft, and part science. Consequently, textbooks as learning tools must address the changing educational needs of faculty and students as we move toward the information society of the twenty-first century. As we become increasingly communications-sensitive, the need for clear, concise, and efficient learning delivery systems will be needed. Just as the computer has replaced the typewriter as a writing tool (this text was written on a Macintosh SE), textbooks today are evolving to meet the changing and diverse needs of faculty and students in a variety of educational settings. This text is designed with a particular set of needs in mind that are increasingly evident among faculty and students in many colleges and universities throughout the United States.

The Need for a Core Text. There is an increasing need for more concise and efficient learning resources that furnish both instructors and students with greater flexibility in teaching and learning. Core texts, which are relatively new in higher education, are designed expressly for this purpose. They are physically smaller than traditional texts and stress the core essentials of a subject (in this case sociology) rather than a broad topical survey. With the number of chapters reduced to an essential twelve to fourteen, each topic can be treated comprehensively, often with greater depth than in traditional textbooks. Increasingly, core texts are being written by academicians who identify just as strongly with the role of educator as they do with that of research scholar. Consequently, this core text is presented as a learning delivery system to make the acquisition of sociology content as efficient and effective as possible.

Today's core text approach has many learning advantages. First of all, it is designed to communicate to students within their own frame of reference. Once a student's experiential background has been tapped into, he or she can then be stretched as a learner to develop new insights and formulate new questions. Second, it contains only essential content explained in clear, concise language. Given its streamlined design and low cost to produce and purchase, the core text provides students a learning tool with which to grasp effectively and efficiently the essence of the discipline. The instructor who uses a core text also benefits, because he or she has greater flexibility to use a reader or to assign outside readings than would be the case with a bulkier and more expensive traditional text. Therefore, both teacher and student are able to use the core material as a springboard from which to explore a variety of supplemental teaching and learning activities that enrich the educational process.

The Need for Text Clarity. As a college student myself twenty years ago, I must confess, I found many of my textbooks cumbersome to use as learning tools. Although there were some notable exceptions, I read many of them with great reluctance only because it was necessary in order to pass the courses in which they were required. These books were invariably written by proven scholars who, in many cases, were prominent names in their respective fields. What I soon learned, however, was that brilliant scholarship and effective communication do not necessarily go together. Many textbooks at that time were lengthy tomes literally brimming with solid content. They were academically sound, but some were poorly written and poorly organized from a pedagogical or educational standpoint. This is because they tended to be written not to communicate effectively with undergraduates but to impress colleagues and gain exposure, reputation, and professional advancement for their authors.

Unfortunately, this approach meant that the ultimate consumers of these books—the students—were often poorly served. Consequently, generations of college students, I myself included, were forced to spend countless hours of tedium meandering through what seemed to be meaningless detail spread over many pages in an attempt to uncover a central point. Fortunately, textbooks have come a long way since then, especially during the last ten years, and many are not only well written but sound from a pedagogical standpoint as well. This is not to say that students should not learn to read and appreciate original sources written by great scholars that are difficult because of the complexity of the ideas conveyed. To master such material is an essential part of any college education. However, a textbook for a lower-division survey course is different. It should represent a compilation, a synthesis of a discipline. As such, it should be clear, concise, and written to attract students to the world of ideas, not drive them away.

When I was a college freshman, my speech professor read a quotation to the class that I have never forgotten. He said, ''Anyone can make a topic boring and difficult to understand. But the chief challenge of the effective communicator is to take a complex subject and make it interesting and understandable.'' This is true especially for those who write and even more important for authors of college textbooks. For unlike oral communicators, we who speak to you from the page are engaged in a monologue, not a dialogue. We cannot ask if you understand what is written nor can we address your questions. Therefore, we have a special responsibility to write clearly and in a manner that is interesting as well as informative. It is in this spirit that I wrote this book. In the final analysis, only you—the student or instructor—can judge the extent to which I have been successful.

The Need for an Integrated Text. This text has been designed to present the student with a coherent, integrated view of sociology as a discipline. I have made an attempt to present a balanced treatment of different theoretical perspectives as they apply to various topics within sociology. In addition, both micro (community) and macro (societal) levels of treatment are interwoven throughout the book. The text has also been developed to stress continuity both within and between chapters. Each chapter, for example, has been designed to flow logically into the next so that the student clearly understands the relationship between topics. By the end of the semester or term, the student should obtain "a big-picture view" of the discipline. This is especially important in a core text because most instructors who use such a learning resource will assign all chapters to their students, as compared with the "cafeteria strategy" used by many instructors with traditional textbooks.

Consequently, the core text you are about to use is intended to impart a cumulative and integrated view of sociology that will unfold and "gel" as more and more of the book is read. Chapter 1 ("The Sociological Perspective") and Chapter 2 ("What Sociologists Do: The Research Process") are designed to establish a firm foundation for the topical survey to follow. Chapter 3 ("Culture: A Way of Life") is the first of eleven chapters that survey the basic concepts, principles, and theoretical perspectives of social behavior generated out of the science of sociology. Chapter 4 ("Socialization: The Process of Becoming Human") builds on Chapter 3 by focusing on how culture is acquired by the individual and how he or she learns to act and interact according to the rules of society. Chapter 5 ("Social Organization") stresses how the human needs generated out of the interplay between culture (society) and socialization (individuals) are addressed and transformed into the structural building blocks of society. These include groups and relationships, associations, and institutions. Together, these elements influence how a society is organized. Chapters 6 through 13 are designed in a similar manner to create a smooth transition from topic to topic and to build a "big picture" view of sociology in the mind of the student.

TEACHING AND LEARNING AIDS

This text is designed as a core teaching and learning system for introductory sociology. It has the following features:

TBSK: A Pretest/Posttest Tool. The acronym TBSK stands for Test of Basic Sociological Knowledge. Developed by the author and included in Chapter 1, the TBSK is a useful tool for assessing "where students are" in terms of basic sociological knowledge when they begin the semester. The thirty True–False items in the test are representative examples of sociology content in the introductory course. As such, they are all referenced to course material actually covered in each of the thirteen chapters in this text. If the instructor or student wishes, the test may be repeated at the end of the semester as a posttest to assess learning. An additional copy of the TBSK has been placed in the student Study Guide for this purpose, along with the correct answers.

Chapter Learning Aids. A variety of learning aids is integrated into each chapter. A detailed chapter outline and list of important terms to know appear at the beginning of each chapter. The headings and subheadings contained in both the chapter outline and the text are designed to point the way for the student regarding the important Who, What, Where, When, Why, and How questions and issues addressed in the text. Other learning aids include boldface and italicized terms, chapter summaries, an end of chapter listing of terms to know, and a list of suggested readings.

Study Guide. In order to maximize efficient learning for the student, a Study Guide has been developed for use with this book. It is divided into thirteen sections that correspond to the thirteen chapters in the text. Each of these sections begins with a listing of Desired Student Learning Outcomes referenced to the corresponding chapter. These learning outcomes provide the student with both direction and focus to learning. The body of each section contains a comprehensive chapter outline so that the student may better understand how the various concepts, principles, theoretical perspectives, and contributions by prominent scholars contained in a chapter fit together as a whole. This is followed by a learning assessment test designed to give the student a realistic "rehearsal exercise" for an exam that will include the assigned text material.

ESS: A System for Academic Excellence (also bound into the Study Guide). The acronym ESS stands for Effective Study Skills. As such, it represents a condensed version of a copyrighted college study system developed by the author and used by thousands of students. This approach may be used in practically all college courses, not just sociology. Unlike most study systems, ESS is a skill-based system that emphasizes the development and use of a variety of study skills in a step-by-step sequence. If it is used exactly as explained as a total system, the typical college student should reach mastery of all necessary skills within a semester or two—and the "A" grades that go with them. The many skills covered by ESS include how to read a textbook for maximum comprehension and retention, how to take class notes, how to organize course material, how to budget study time, how to prepare for exams, and how to take various types of tests.

ACKNOWLEDGMENTS

While the responsibility for the contents of this book is mine alone, the efforts and talents of many people went into the development of the final manuscript. First, I am grateful for the comments and suggestions provided by the following colleagues from across the country who served as reviewers: Jerry B. Clavner, Cuyahoga Community College; Bess Cleveland, Jefferson Community College; Larry H. Frye, St. Petersburg Junior College; Gaye Holman, Jefferson Community College; Abraham Levine, El Camino Community College District; John Lynxwiler, University of Alabama at Birmingham; Purna C. Mohanty, Paine College;

Ludwig A. Petkovsek, University of Evansville; Steven Schada, Oakton Community College; William A. Schwab, University of Arkansas; Stuart Lee Shafer, Johnson County Community College; William E. Snizek, Virginia Polytechnic Institute and State University; Kathleen H. Sparrow, University of Southwestern Louisiana; Kendrick S. Thompson, Northern Michigan University; and William E. Thompson, Emporia State University.

The following individuals are also deserving of special thanks. Acquisitions editor Kirsten Olson of Holt, Rinehart and Winston understood my vision and aggressively championed the core text approach. She along with Christopher P. Klein, Anthropology and Sociology editor, spearheaded the project and provided encouragement and thoughtful guidance during the two and one-half years it took to go from project idea to printed book. Developmental editor Jane Knetzger of HRW, Karee Galloway, who did the permissions and photograph research, and Barbara Chernow, President of Chernow Editorial Services in New York, all provided the attention to detail so necessary in bringing the manuscript to its final form. Ralph Zickgraf of Editing, Design & Production, Inc. in Philadelphia also provided invaluable assistance.

The following people at San Jacinto College must be thanked as well: James Hall, Chairman of the Division of Social and Behavioral Sciences, whose encouragement and flexibility made this project possible; Carolyn Roberts, a faculty colleague who proofread major parts of the manuscript; and Kari Jackson and Glynda Cole who served as student readers. A special word of appreciation is due Sandra Corne who served as my assistant and "right arm" throughout the project. She put in many long hours researching, duplicating, formating, typing, and editing. I would also like to thank my introductory sociology students who, over the past few years, have served as the testing ground for almost all the material found in this book. The assistance of librarian Jan Crenshaw is also appreciated.

Finally, I would like to thank my partner in life during these past twenty years, my wife, Phyllis. Her love, patience, and understanding more than anything else have helped sustain me in my endeavors.

Houston, 1989   James K. Semones

Contents in Brief

Contents

Part One

The Sociological Perspective

Chapter 1
The Sociological Perspective

All the world's a stage,
And all the men and women merely players:
They have their exits and their entrances;
And one man in his time plays many parts. . .
William Shakespeare
As You Like It, Act 2, Scene 7

Émile Durkheim
Karl Marx
Max Weber
TWENTIETH-CENTURY SOCIOLOGY
American Sociology

Functionalism
Conflict Theory
Interactionism
Sociology and the Future

■ **TERMS TO KNOW**

bourgeoisie
conflict theory
cumulative knowledge
deduction
dynamics
dysfunctions
empiricism
epistemology
functionalism
functions
ideal type
induction
institutution
interactionism

latent functions
manifest functions
objectivity
physical sciences
proletariat
science
scientific theory
social action
social Darwinism
social facts
social sciences
sociological imagination
sociology
Socratic method
statics
verstehen

With the familiar words from *As You Like It*, the great bard of English literature has captured in capsule form much of the essence of the human condition. We humans are indeed social actors and our stage, for all practical purposes, is the society in which we live.

As we move through the life experience, we carry out many functions and play many roles. During childhood, we progress from self-centeredness and inexperience in social relations to learning how to show empathy for others and live according to a set of social rules. Adolescence is a time for learning how to make the transition from the dependency of childhood to the world of adult responsibility. It is also a time of sexual awakening and, for most, a serious interest in members of the opposite sex. The social rules for behavior we

learn during this period set the stage for adulthood.

During our adult years, the process of social adjustment continues. We are called on to play many parts and adapt to a variety of changing social conditions. We learn to adjust to the many demands placed on us by the various social positions we occupy. Most of us have an occupation as well as family responsibilities. Some of us go to school, as you are doing now. Often we are required by our various social responsibilities to do what seems to be the impossible—keep family, employer, and teachers all happy at once. But we seem to manage it most of the time. This is because we have acquired behaviors and skills that, in most cases, allow us to cope successfully with the social world around us. These behaviors and skills, which we often use unconsciously, are acquired largely from the society in which we live. The systematic study of how all this takes place is included in the domain of a science called sociology.

SOCIOLOGY AS A SCIENCE

Questions commonly asked by students taking the introductory sociology course include What is sociology about? Why take it? How does it work? and What do sociologists do? These and other basic issues will be addressed in the pages to follow.

In essence, **sociology** is the science of human social behavior at all levels of society. Because of the social nature of human beings, most everything people do involves group interaction. This makes sociology a particularly fascinating area of investigation. When we act, we tend to act socially, and this social behavior, along with its causes and consequences, is what sociologists study. Such an area of investigation is as broad as it is interesting and includes such wide-ranging topics as mate selection practices, the causes of crime, propaganda techniques used by politicians and advertisers, bureaucratic organization, and the head-hunting customs practiced by some simple societies (Service, 1971).

The Nature of Sociology

As the science of social behavior, sociology focuses on the examination of everyday behavior and familiar forms of social organization in a very systematic way. The human condition has long been the focus of study by the world's major religions, philosophic systems, and the other humanities, including literature, poetry, and music. All these disciplines and art forms have provided many valuable insights and observations and countless anecdotal pronouncements about human behavior that have been espoused by many people as "common sense." Such "obvious" sources of wisdom and truth are often accepted at face value by many people, but not by the sociologist. To illustrate how sociological knowledge differs from "common sense" opinions, an exercise has been included for you in Box 1-1. It is called TBSK: a Test of Basic Sociological Knowledge. If you wish, you may take this test to compare your current opinions with what has been ascertained about human social behavior through scientific research. Since the correct answers to all the statements contained in the test (along with supporting research citations) are interspersed throughout this book, you may wish to take the TBSK again at the end of the course to see how much you have learned.

The sociological perspective is a scientific one that goes beyond obvious "common sense" explanations. The sociologist studies the underlying causes that shape human behavior. This analysis is carried forth in an objective manner using the scientific rules of evidence. Consequently, the sociologist, because of the method of investigation used, is not likely to be influenced by the personal and cultural biases and emotions that often characterize the interpretations of the nonscientist.

Truth in the science of sociology is always tentative and depends on the social context under investigation. For example, in agricultural societies with low technology and high mortality rates, large families are needed for survival of the group. Large numbers of children are an economic asset in these societies because they work in the fields with the adults and contribute to the economic well-being of the family. In modern industrial societies, however, the reverse is true. Children in industrial economies are consumers, not producers, and represent a drain on family income because they must be sustained by the cash wages of adult members. This helps to explain why fertility rates in industrial societies tend to be much lower than those in nonindustrial societies.

Box 1–1

TBSK: A TEST OF BASIC SOCIOLOGICAL KNOWLEDGE

Listed below are thirty statements about American society and social behavior in general that are representative of course content in sociology. Information concerning each of these statements is contained in this book. Read each one carefully, then indicate your assessment of it by circling either **True** or **False** (*Note:* Your instructor may ask you to answer this on a machine-graded test form. If that is the case, take a Number 2 pencil and fill in either the A or 1 space for True or the B or 2 space for False). If directed to do so by your instructor, also answer items 31 through 37 to provide additional background information.

   To compare your current knowledge about your society and social behavior with what you learn from this course, you may wish to take this test again at the end of the semester. An additional copy of the TBSK has been placed at the end of the Study Guide for this purpose. The correct answers are listed there as well.

True   False   1. Capital punishment has little or no effect in deterring those who commit murder in the United States.

True   False   2. Human beings have a number of instincts that help to guide certain forms of behavior.

True   False   3. When viewed objectively, it is clear that American standards of morality, justice, and beauty are superior to those of most other cultures.

True   False   4. It is likely that a few children have been successfully reared to maturity by animals such as apes or wolves.

True   False   5. Firstborn children tend to be higher achievers than their younger brothers and sisters.

True   False   6. From early childhood through their eighteenth birthday, children in the United States spend more time in school than in any other activity except sleep.

True   False   7. In American society, the blood bond between family members is usually regarded as more important than the marriage bond.

True   False   8. The United States is now making the transition to an agrarian society.

True   False   9. Those who "make the first move" in initiating contact with others in group settings tend to be less likely to make friends.

Box 1–1 *(Continued)*

True False	10.	Personalized relations with fellow soldiers at the unit level were much less prevalent among American GIs during the Vietnamese Conflict than among American fighting men during World War II.
True False	11.	Deviants such as juvenile gang members and prison inmates rarely form close personalized relationships with others of their kind.
True False	12.	Bureaucracy as a form of social organization has existed for thousands of years.
True False	13.	The concept of brainwashing is a myth that exists mainly in movie plots and in the overactive imaginations of some people.
True False	14.	The behavior of most people is significantly influenced by the environment of the large-scale associations (schools, corporations, and so on) in which they participate.
True False	15.	For most Americans living in poverty, being poor is a temporary condition.
True False	16.	The majority of welfare families include only one or two children.
True False	17.	The most important indicator of social class prestige in the United States is wealth.
True False	18.	The biological concept of race as a ''pure type'' is of little or no use in science.
True False	19.	IQ tests do not measure innate capacity or ''intelligence.''
True False	20.	Like the Nazis' treatment of the Jews during World War II, both the use of concentration camps and attempts at extermination have occurred in America, only on a much smaller scale.
True False	21.	Urban legends—such as the story circulated nationwide in the 1980s that Elvis Presley was still alive—are common in America.
True False	22.	Propaganda methods are rarely used in democratic societies like the United States.
True False	23.	It is clear that alcoholism is a disease caused mainly by biological factors.

Box 1–1 *(Continued)*

True False 24. Astrology is of little or no scientific value in explaining human behavior.

True False 25. What is considered deviant or antisocial behavior in the United States (such as immorality or crime) is widely accepted in almost all societies throughout the world.

True False 26. The United States has the lowest infant mortality rate in the world.

True False 27. World overpopulation is now one of the most serious social problems facing humankind.

True False 28. Romantic love is regarded as the primary basis for mate selection in most societies.

True False 29. The most common form of family violence is spouse abuse.

True False 30. At least 90 percent of all women in the United States who have ever married give birth to at least one child before their thirty-fourth birthday.

ADDITIONAL BACKGROUND INFORMATION

31. AGE: 19 or less = A (1); 20–24 = B (2); 25–29 = C (3); 30–34 = D (4); 35 or older = E (5).

32. SEX: Female = A (1); Male = B (2).

33. COLLEGE STANDING: Freshman = A (1); Sophomore = B (2); Junior = C (3); Senior = D (4); Other = E (5).

34. MAJOR: Business = A (1); Education = B (2); Liberal Arts/Humanities = C (3); Physical Sciences = D (4); Other = E (5).

35. DID YOU HAVE SOCIOLOGY AS A COURSE IN HIGH SCHOOL? Yes = A (1); No = B (2).

36. IS THIS YOUR FIRST SEMESTER IN COLLEGE? Yes = A (1); No = B (2).

37. IF YOUR PREVIOUS ANSWER WAS YES, DO NOT CONTINUE. IF YOUR PREVIOUS ANSWER WAS NO, HOW MANY TOTAL COLLEGE CREDIT HOURS HAVE YOU COMPLETED? 1–15 = A (1); 16–30 = B (2); 31–45 = C (3); 46–60 = D (4); More than 60 = E (5).

ANSWERS: See the Study Guide developed to accompany this book.

In addition, the sociologist examines all aspects of social behavior, not just those seen as convenient to the popular biases expressed by certain individuals, communities, or societies. Conflict is studied as well as social harmony, deviance as well as conformity, and homosexual behavior along with heterosexual behavior. As a scientist, the sociologist enters the research arena with no preconceived ideas, only the desire to discover "What is" and "Why is it so?"

To embrace the sociological perspective is to be caught up in a special type of passion: the desire to know what lies behind the obvious and apparent human behaviors, social structures, and official policies of society at all levels. As Peter Berger (1963) has stated:

The fascination of sociology lies in the fact that its perspective makes us see in a new light the very world in which we have lived all our lives. This also constitutes a transformation of consciousness. . . . The sociologist will occupy himself with matters that others regard as too sacred or as too distasteful for dispassionate investigation. He will find rewarding the company of priests and prostitutes, depending, not on his personal preferences, but on the questions he happens to be asking at the moment. He will also concern himself with matters that others may find much too boring. He will be interested in the human interaction that goes with warfare or with great intellectual discoveries, but also in the relations between people employed in a restaurant or between a group of little girls

playing with their dolls. His main focus of attention is not . . . ultimate significance . . ., but the action in itself, as another example of the infinite richness of human conduct (p. 21, p. 19).

Areas of Specialization

Since the science of society is constantly expanding its base of knowledge, many sociologists specialize and concentrate their study and research in one or two specific areas or on one of the basic institutions in society. An **institution** is a major structural component of a society that addresses a special area of human needs. In American society, there are five fundamental institutions: family, government, the economy, education, and religion. To address these areas, there are the sociology of marriage and the family, political sociology, the sociology of economic systems, the sociology of education, and the sociology of religion.

Even though the specific subject matter in these areas is focused on an institution, many sociologists study social behavior within these structures on several different levels. For instance, a family sociologist might examine how the American family compares and contrasts with families in other societies or study child-rearing patterns used by unwed teen-aged mothers in Chicago, Illinois. Likewise, the sociologist of education might investigate aspects of the bureaucratic structure of American higher education or the group dynamics of children in a sixth grade classroom.

Other areas of specialization are much narrower. Some concentrate on forms of social behavior that relate to several institutions. The field of deviant behavior includes the study of such diverse activities as incest and spouse abuse (family), abuse of power (government), and crime, a form of behavior that cuts across all institutional areas. Other areas of sociological study are subfields within fields, such as criminology and juvenile delinquency, which are subsumed under deviant behavior. Finally, some fields of specialization are even more specific, including the sociologies of sport, work, and teaching.

THE NATURE OF SCIENCE

In almost any definition of sociology, terms such as "science," "scientific," or "study of" appear in places of prominence. Therefore, to truly understand the nature and goals of sociology, one must also understand the fundamentals of science and the scientific method and how the scientific approach differs from others. It is also important to understand how social sciences like sociology are distinct from the physical sciences.

Science as a Means of Explanation

Science means different things to different people. Some confuse it with technology and use phrases like "Science Moves Onward" as captions for pictures that illustrate space voyages to other planets. Others see science as little more than a specific body of knowledge and use phrases like "Science informs us" or "According to science." In truth, science represents far more than the products of investigation, such as spaceships and computers or everything known about cancer or crime. Instead, science is mainly a means of explana-

tion or method of investigation. It represents a way of discovering and explaining various aspects of reality (Hoover, 1988).

The word **science** comes from the Latin *sciens* which means "to know" (Nachmias and Nachmias, 1987). As a means of explanation, science represents an objective and systematic method of observing and explaining reality in a verifiable manner. Scientists, therefore, make no prejudgments about their subject matter, but seek the truth in whatever form it is revealed through a systematic process of investigation.

The scientific method is influenced by several basic assumptions about the nature of reality. Stated as propositions, they include the ideas that (1) nature (reality) can be known, (2) nature can be understood through sensory investigation, and (3) phenomena in nature are linked through cause-and-effect relationships (Goode and Hatt, 1952). Together, these propositions are key issues of discussion and study in **epistemology**—an area in the philosophy of science devoted to the study of knowledge and how it is validated. Although the ultimate truth of these assumptions cannot be demonstrated, science remains a superior method of investigation because of its objectivity and openness, its self-correcting nature, and the strict rules of evidence that govern its method and those who practice it.

Other Means of Explanation

There are several other means of explanation in addition to science. *Appeal to authority* involves trusting others—politicians, physicians, teachers, religious leaders, news commentators, for example—to discover, understand, and disseminate knowledge and truth. While it is tempting to blindly trust these "authorities," such an uncritical perspective can result in victimization by those who would abuse power and position.

Mysticism is similar to an appeal to authority, except that authority figures may or may not be consulted. For those who believe in mysticism, authority figures are those with "supernatural" knowledge, such as faith healers, prophets, and "channels" (spiritual mediums), who make use of ritual and ceremony to create the conditions necessary for the mystical experience. Mystical states may be drug-induced, as in Indians of Mexico and the American Southwest who use peyote cactus and sacred mushrooms that produce hallucinations and visions (Lingeman, 1974). Those most likely to accept mystical knowledge tend to do so "under conditions of depression, helplessness, and intoxication" (Nachmias and Nachmias, 1987, p. 5).

Tradition involves accepting what worked in the past. Advantages include feelings of connection with previous generations and one's culture, as well as security and peace of mind in using "what's tried and true." Disadvantages include undue bias and narrowness of viewpoint, particularly given changing social conditions. Some "traditional" people, for example, continue to espouse racism, male domination over women, and families' having unlimited numbers of offspring.

Religion is a means of explanation that contains elements of authority, mysticism, and tradition. Religion is easier to describe than to define, because it means different things to different people. In fact, the variety of religious beliefs and practices is almost limitless. Religion is a means of explaining the existence and purpose of human life and the universe. It usually contains elements of the sacred and divine that are acknowledged through ritual and worship. According to sociologist Elizabeth Nottingham (1971), religion

> has given rise to the most spacious products of . . . imagination, and it has been used to justify the extremest cruelty. . . . It can conjure up moods of sublime exaltation, and also im-

ages of dread and terror. Although preoccupied with the reality of a world that cannot be seen, religion has been involved in the most mundane details of daily life. It has been used to blaze new trails into the heart of the unknown, and utopias have been founded in its name; yet it has also served to shackle . . . [people] to outworn customs or beliefs (p. 8).

Philosophy is a systematic and rational method for organizing thought processes that is used to address critical questions. The philosophical method originated about 600 B.C. with Pythagoras, who saw it as the pursuit of wisdom. Today, philosophy includes such fields of study as aesthetics (art and beauty), metaphysics (reality), epistemology (knowledge), ethics (moral values), and logic (reasoning). The development of philosophy represented a tremendous step forward in the history of humankind, because it furnished a systematic way to organize thought in order to address intellectual problems. It remains a valuable tool of analysis today. However, philosophy—unlike science—does not contain a reliable means of verifying propositions in the world of human experience. This is where philosophy and science differ in approach, although science, in large measure, is built on a philosophic foundation, particularly in its use of logic (see Chapter 2).

The sociologist looks at different means of explanation—authority, mysticism, tradition, religion, and philosophy—through the eyes of science. Combinations of these perspectives, along with science, help us to perceive and interpret the world around us and our place in it. When such combinations of perspectives are commonly held by groups of human beings, they form the basis for an agreed-upon "worldview." These agreed-upon assumptions about reality in turn form much of the "common ground" or social cement that binds people together in social groups, organizations, institutions, and societies. The process by which these worldviews emerge, along with their social consequences, furnishes much of the subject matter for sociology and the other social sciences.

Characteristics of Science

Science has its own characteristics that distinguish it from other means of explanation. These are listed and explained briefly as follows:

1. Science is theoretical. As illustrated in Figure 1-1, science, first of all, is theoretical. **Scientific theory** consists of clearly stated propositions (statements) about reality that have been verified to some degree. Have you ever heard someone say, "Well, it's only a theory"? This inaccurate perception is held by many in the American public. It is almost as if

"theory" (propositions) is placed in one box and labeled unreliable, undemonstrated, and unproven, while "fact" is in another and acknowledged as reliable, demonstrated, and proven.

The truth is that in science, theory and fact are not separate, but are intertwined as two parts of the same whole. In science, the state of theory is the state of knowledge about some area of investigation, whether it is crime, cancer, or a wing design for jet aircraft. Scientific theory is often confused with theory in religion and philosophy. Both religion and philosophy also contain propositions, or theory. However, they lack the means of objective verification that is the hallmark of science. Therefore, "theory" becomes scientific theory only when there is some degree of objective evidence to support it.

Figure 1-1 The Nature of Scientific Theory

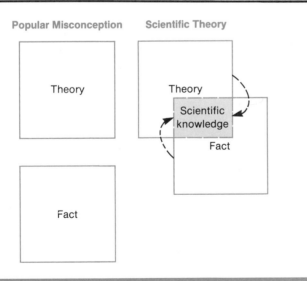

Many people have the mistaken notion that theory (propositions) and fact (verification) in science are separate concepts with little or no relation to each other. It is more accurate to say that in science, theory represents propositions about some aspect of reality that have been verified to some degree. Thus the state of knowledge in science is the state of theory.

2. Science is empirical. **Empiricism** represents the manner in which evidence in science is gathered through the organized use of the senses. We all use our senses to "verify" reality for ourselves. Yet, when sensory measurement is used without the scientific method, our senses may easily fool us. Most all of us have been betrayed by our senses from time to time. Parents often think they hear their newborn baby crying in the middle of the night, but, when they check, the child is sound asleep. In many other ways, our senses may play tricks on us. However, when the scientist is engaged in research, the senses are used for verification according to a strict system of safeguards called the rules of evidence.

3. Science is objective. **Objectivity** refers to an unbiased and unprejudiced approach aimed at determining truth. Scientists seek only the truth wherever it leads them. They carry no preconceived notions into the research process and let the facts point the way to the formulation and reformulation of theory (propositions). As practitioners of the scientific method, they are duty bound to report truth as revealed by research and acknowledge the bulk of evidence concerning a particular phenomenon regardless of personal feelings. Truth in science is always tentative, as the investigator continues to look for even more precise explanation. This self-correcting aspect of science is one of its most distinguishing hallmarks. Consequently, the scientific method is open-ended, requires no leap of faith, and can be replicated with the same results by anyone who uses it.

4. Science is cumulative. Through objectivity, knowledge in science becomes **cumulative knowledge** in that what is known is constantly added to, modified, and refined. As more precise evidence is discovered, theory is reformulated. Research being done today thus adds to what we know in all fields of en-

deavor. Take, for instance, scientific research as applied to powered flight. At the dawn of the twentieth century, the Wright brothers flew for a few brief seconds at Kitty Hawk, North Carolina. Today, given the cumulative effect of thousands of scientific studies in several related disciplines, manned flights to the moon have been made several times, and similar flights by men and women in the future to the planets and beyond seem almost a certainty.

Physical Sciences and Social Sciences

The sciences are divided into two general categories, the physical or natural sciences, and the social sciences. The **physical sciences,** which focus on physical and biological reality, include such disciplines as biology, botany, chemistry, mathematics, and physics. The **social sciences,** by contrast, study human behavior and include, in addition to sociology, such fields as anthropology, economics, political science, and psychology.

As portrayed in Figure 1-2, there are three basic distinctions between the physical and social sciences. First, the physical sciences focus on the concrete physical world, which includes such predictable things as molecules, chemical compounds, and the motion of objects. The social disciplines, by comparison, deal with the abstractions of human behavior in which no two people appear to think or react in exactly the same way. Second, the physical sciences have the luxury of universal or natural laws with which to predict with absolute certainty such things as the effects of gravity on a falling object or the boiling point of water. The social sciences, to date, have no universal laws, because human behavior varies from society to society and from one condition or social situation to another. Finally, the subject matter of the physical sciences is without will or purpose, although some non-scientists do talk to their tomatoes and play

Figure 1-2 Physical Sciences and Social Sciences: Comparative Characteristics

The Physical Sciences	The Social Sciences
1. are more concrete (with a focus on physical matter)	1. are more abstract (with a focus on human behavior)
2. contain universal laws	2. do not contain universal laws
3. examine the unpurposeful actions of matter	3. examine the purposeful behavior of human beings

Mozart concertos to their geranium plants. The social sciences deal with the purposeful behavior of human beings, who possess keen intellects with both rational and emotional dimensions (Green, 1968).

From this discussion, two related conclusions are clear. First, the physical sciences are much more advanced in development than the social sciences, because they deal with much simpler (empirically verifiable) subject matter. This is why they developed first, in some cases many hundreds of years before the emergence of the social sciences. Second, the social sciences are much less developed than their physical science counterparts, because their subject matter is infinitely more complex (in terms of verifiability). The social sciences, therefore, are the "new kids on the block" in the community of sciences and have a long way to go before they become fully developed. Sociology in this respect is only a little more than 150 years old.

THE SOCIOLOGICAL PERSPECTIVE

Sociologists use objectivity and the tools of science to look beneath the surface of the society that many of us take for granted because of our beliefs, customs, and traditions. This perspective is often referred to as the sociological imagination.

The Sociological Imagination

The expression **sociological imagination** was coined by C. Wright Mills (1959) to refer to the ability of individuals to see how interrelated their private lives are with the nature of their society. By going beyond the obvious "common sense" explanations that are readily available and convenient to use, the sociologist comes to understand that the lives of individuals and groups are significantly affected by the structural characteristics of their society. Most of us have a view of the world that is limited by our own spheres of social action. Social factors such as ethnicity, class, education, religion, income, occupation, and place of residence shape to a significant degree the way we look at the world and act in the larger community and society.

Try posing a few questions about society to your friends and acquaintances to see what types of responses you receive. One question that many people are sure to have definite opinions about is, "Why does the United States make use of capital punishment for certain violent crimes?" Although responses may vary, some people will invariably say that it deters crime. Sociological research to date, however, has shown that capital punishment in general—as it is currently structured—has little if any deterrent effect (Conrad, 1983). State execution in America has more to do with the desire for revenge, resulting from fear and emotion, than its actual deterrent value. To seek out, understand, and perhaps even conduct such research represents the sociological imagination put into practice. It represents the desire to look beyond obvious "accepted" answers to uncover the real "whys" of social behavior in a scientific way.

Perhaps more important to individuals is how their own lives are directly affected by structural policies and changes occurring in their society, and how their destinies, as well as those of their society, are intimately intertwined. A man may lose his job not because he did it poorly but because of economic issues and changes facing his company and society. If he does not see these changes coming, he is more likely to be victimized. A married couple may face serious relational problems and possible divorce not merely because of the dynamics created between their two personalities but also because of structural changes and pressures brought to bear on them by their society. If they do not see beyond their relationship and realize that the "traditional ways" of their parents may no longer apply in today's changing world, they may find themselves in a poor position to make their marriage work.

Mills (1959) saw sociology not only as a means of understanding the deeper meanings of the social world around us but as a means of personal liberation as well. By understanding the true nature of society and life in it, people can more readily avoid and free themselves from the traps created by societal change. Thus they are able, through the sociological imagination, to become more active in creating their own destinies and those of their loved ones, community, and society.

> Underlying this sense of being trapped are seemingly impersonal changes in the very nature of continent-wide societies. The facts of contemporary history are also facts about the success and the failure of individual men and women. When a society is industrialized, a peasant becomes a businessman. When classes rise or fall, a man is employed or unemployed; when the rate of investment goes up or down, a man takes new heart or goes broke. When wars happen, an insurance salesman becomes a rocket launcher; a store clerk, a radar man; a wife lives alone; a child grows up without a father. Neither the life of an individual or the history of a society can be understood without understanding both (p. 3).

What Sociologists Do: Careers in the Field

One important issue for many college freshmen is deciding on a major and planning for a career. It is common for students to change majors several times, as they take the various required survey courses during the first two years. The pursuit of a sociology major may or may not be right for you. However, one thing is clear: Whatever career you pursue, whichever occupation you decide on, will require that you work and deal effectively with people. Consequently, your job will have one or more sociological dimensions. Getting along with people, understanding their interests, motives, and needs, sizing up all kinds of social situations, and knowing how bureaucratic organizations work are among the many sociological skills possessed by most people who succeed in their chosen fields of endeavor. So, regardless of which major you choose, a few sociology courses chosen as electives could be invaluable to you.

With the Baccalaureate Degree. A common misconception among college students is that they will obtain a job after college in their major field. Often, this is not the case. A person with an undergraduate major in sociology is unlikely to obtain a position in sociology per se. Instead, a bachelor's degree in sociology may prepare a student to enter a variety of occupations and professions that require an in-depth understanding of people and social behavior (see Fig. 1-3). A few of these are listed as follows:

prelaw
high school teaching
professional sales
probation and parole
law enforcement
rehabilitation counseling
public relations
fund raising
personnel
industrial training

diplomacy
drug counseling
government administration
labor relations
health services
communications
recreation services
community development

With Graduate Training. Full professional standing as a sociologist normally requires at least a master's degree; a doctorate is preferred and often necessary for the highest-level positions. The master's degree involves at least one to two years of advanced study, depending on thesis requirements. Master's level sociologists often teach at community and junior colleges and hold professional and administrative positions in business and industry, as well as in government. The doctoral degree (normally the Ph.D. in sociology) requires at least four years of advanced study

Figure 1-3   Employment Classifications for Bachelor Degree Holders with Majors in Sociology

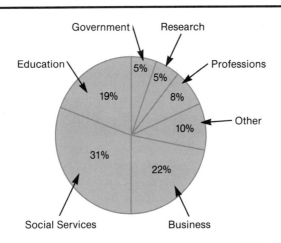

Source: Taken from Hedley, R. A., and Adams, S. M. (1982). The job market for bachelor degree holders: A cumulation. *The American Sociologist.* 17, pp. 155–163.

beyond the baccalaureate and includes the completion of a dissertation, a scholarly study resulting in an original contribution to knowledge. Sociologists with doctorates typically teach at four-year colleges and universities and, in the private sector and government, occupy professional, research, and administrative positions at the highest levels.

The occupations of professional-level sociologists are varied. About 3,000 sociologists with doctorates hold full-time teaching positions in colleges and universities, where they split their time between teaching and research and writing. Sociologists in business and industry, about 3,000, hold positions ranging from advertising and marketing analysts to human resource development executives and consultants. Governmental agencies employ approximately 2,500 sociologists. The federal government uses such professionals in the Departments of Agriculture, Defense, Health and Human Services, and Interior. Sociologists are also employed by federal agencies such as the Bureau of the Census and the Central Intelligence Agency, as well as by international organizations such as the World Bank, the World Health Organization, and the United Nations. In addition, some sociologists are in private practice as counselors, researchers, and consultants (U.S. Department of Labor, 1987).

Career Prospects for the Future

Career prospects during the next several years for degree holders in sociology look very good in some areas and only fair, at best, in others. For those with bachelor's degrees, the prospects appear very good. In contrast to the earlier trend to employ those with business and technical degrees, large corporations today are often looking for social science and liberal arts majors. They want employees who have interpersonal and communication skills and who possess the critical thinking capabilities to devise creative solutions to ever-changing work-

related problems (Watkins, 1986). Sociology also will continue to be a good major for those planning careers in law, medicine and dentistry, politics, urban planning, the ministry, and a variety of other service-related occupations and professions.

For those wishing to pursue master's and doctoral level positions as professional sociologists, the job market will be tight in some areas. In academia, positions available in sociology are expected to increase only slowly at least through the mid-1990s. The majority of available college positions will probably result from replacement needs as professors retire or otherwise leave teaching. Therefore, academic positions during the next several years will be competitive, since the supply of applicants will probably exceed the demand.

The shortage of academic positions will lead a larger percentage of sociologists with doctorates to pursue careers in government, business and industry, and private practice. Areas that look promising include demography (population research), social programs administration, and human resource management in industry. Positions in gerontology (the study of the aged) will become more plentiful as our population gets older and the aged population expands accordingly. Demand is also expected to increase in other applied sociology areas such as criminology, medical sociology, and clinical sociology.

THE EMERGENCE OF SOCIOLOGY

Sociology emerged as a formal discipline in Europe during the nineteenth century, a little more than 150 years ago. It arose as a product of the sociological imagination—that dynamic interplay between individuals and the social context in which they lived. But more than this, the arrival of sociology represented the birth of a discipline that had been gestating for more than two thousand years. During this time, the threads represented by certain key ideas, modes of inquiry, cultural perspectives, and significant historical events gradually became interwoven into a rich tapestry of intellectual and social thought that acted as the backdrop for the emergence of a science of society. How all of this came about is a very interesting story. To tell it, we begin not in Europe during the 1830s but in the ancient city-state of Athens during the time of Socrates.

Setting the Stage: Social Thought in Western Civilization

The Greeks and Presociology. By the fifth century B.C., the ancient Greek civilization in Asia Minor had reached its zenith and was actually beginning to decline because of internal strife and outside influences. Greek culture revolved around the *polis* (or city-state), with Athens at the center of the Greek world. During this time, the ideas of *rationalism* and *empiricism* arose, which, more than 2,000 years later, would combine with others to form the basis for a science of society. These ideas found their fullest expression in the contributions of three thinkers: Socrates, Plato, and Aristotle.

Socrates: Father of Rationalism. Socrates (470–399 B.C.) was the first to assert ''the supremacy of the intellect as a court from which there is no appeal'' (Becker and Barnes, 1961, p. 149). He argued that societal rules and customs as well as emotion should be seen as secondary to reason and logic. His students were taught the **Socratic method**, how to ask penetrating, logical questions about anything and everything, with nothing held back and no traditions held sacred.

Sociologists today still use this method, as do others who engage in intellectual and scientific pursuits. Perhaps you have had an instructor who used the Socratic method in teaching a class; he or she looked down the roll sheet, called on someone at random, and asked him or her to explain a point in the reading assignment. Although it often makes students feel uncomfortable at first, this method can facilitate learning and discussion. If you tried the experiment mentioned previously and asked several people the question about capital punishment or about some other aspect of society, you probably made them feel a little uncomfortable when you told them what research has found regarding the issue. In fact, you may have found yourself in a vigorous debate. This too is the Socratic method.

Socrates and his students made so many people uncomfortable that he was tried by the authorities on the charge of corrupting the morals of Athenian youth. He was found guilty and, when asked by his judges what his penalty should be, he replied that a pension and lifelong support at the expense of the city was his preference. This so angered the court that he was sentenced to death and eventually drank a concoction containing poison hemlock and died.

Plato and the Planned Society. Socrates's student Plato (428–347 B.C.) was more fortunate in that he didn't find it necessary to die for his beliefs. However, Plato lived in an age in which his society was dominated by extreme individualism. Such emphasis was placed on individual choice that the social fabric of the culture began to unravel. Social and political decadence set in, graft and bribery for individual gain became pervasive, and the basis for social order began to break down.

Plato, disturbed greatly by what was happening, used the Socratic approach to ask a series of questions about his society and the relationship of people to it. Influenced by Socrates's notion that humans could know what was good and could act on their knowledge

Socrates (470–399 B.C.) taught his students in ancient Athens to ask penetrating questions about everything including the nature of their society. He and other Greek thinkers, among whom were Plato and Aristotle, not only originated modern philosophy as a forerunner to science but, because of the social nature of their inquiry, were among the first presociologists. (The Bettmann Archive, Inc.)

for the improvement of society, Plato began to ask what were essentially sociological questions. He wanted to know why society was plagued by so much chaos and disorganization. He inquired as to the nature of the bond that held society together. The answer he arrived at was justice. How was justice to be obtained? His solution was to think carefully through and plan the structure of society. This he did in his book the *Republic,* which represented the first systematic statement of a planned society in recorded Western thought.

Aristotle: Father of Logic and Empiricism. Aristotle (384–322 B.C.), another of the first presociologists, asserted that human

beings are, by nature, social beings and that social behavior should be studied systematically. He is, however, best known for his contributions to philosophy and science in general. The Greeks developed basic forms of reasoning aimed at disciplining the thought processes. Systematic reasoning in philosophy came to be called logic and took two basic forms: deduction and induction. Aristotle contributed most to the early development of both forms of organized thinking.

Deduction (or deductive reasoning) refers to the movement from general propositions about reality to specific conclusions. This form of logic is used not only in philosophy, but is also a cornerstone of the scientific method (explained in Chapter 2). Aristotle developed the well-known form of deductive logic called the *syllogism,* an argument consisting of two propositions and a conclusion. By combining the common elements contained in each proposition, one is able to draw an inference and formulate a conclusion that represents a new piece of information. Consider this example:

General Proposition:	All humans are mortal.
Minor Proposition:	Socrates is human.
	(deductive inference)
Conclusion:	Socrates is mortal.

Aristotle is also regarded as the father of empiricism. He developed the idea that knowledge comes not from reason or logic alone but from experiences organized in a systematic way. He felt that we arrive at universal or general knowledge through our limited experiences with specific people and things. This is **induction**—the movement from specific observations of reality to general conclusions or generalizations.

Take your empirical knowledge of teachers for example. Your general view of "teachers," Aristotle would argue, is influenced by your particular experiences with individual instructors. From your experiences with teacher 1, teacher 2, teacher 3, teacher 4, and so on, you develop a general knowledge of teachers. Likewise, our experiences with all sorts of things become the components of our view of all reality. This Aristotelian mode of reasoning grounded in the world of experience—induction—acted as another cornerstone for what later became the scientific method (Miller, 1987). This is explained fully in Chapter 2.

Khaldun: "Sociologist" of the Fourteenth Century. One writer who developed sociological insights many centuries later was the Muslim historian-philosopher Ibn Khaldun (1332–1406). He agreed with Aristotle that humans were by nature social beings, and he felt that social life was governed by natural laws that needed only to be discovered. Khaldun was a pioneer in the field of human geography. He asserted that climate and geography played an instrumental role in determining whether a society developed a nomadic-rural or a sedentary-urban life for its members. Using historical and comparative approaches, he made penetrating observations comparing the cultures and life-styles of nomadic Arab tribal groups with those of sedentary city people. He found that rural tribes stressed blood bonds, group loyalty, and individual responsibility to a much greater degree than did city people, whose interpersonal relationships took the form of acquaintanceships. In urban areas, family and social bonds were weak, and people tended to be apathetic and dependent regarding their city and society (Khaldun, 1950).

Montesquieu and the Age of Reason. During the sixteenth and seventeenth centuries, the Renaissance reached full expression and the Enlightenment began. The sixteenth century was marked by the Protestant Reformation, lead by Martin Luther, and the development of such physical sciences as astronomy, biology, bontany, and zoology. With the discoveries of Copernicus and Galileo, the earth was no longer considered the center of the universe. Explorations of the new world also expanded people's view of their planet. Early ethnographers, for example, discovered the existence of preliterate people living in a state of nature. Against this backdrop, there was a spirit of adventure, of scientific curiosity, of openness to new possibilities and new ideas.

As the eighteenth century dawned, the movement gained momentum. During this period, no one better represented the thrust of "sociological" thought than Charles Montesquieu (1689–1755), the French social philosopher and historian who wrote the first descriptive treatise in "sociology." In it, Montesquieu introduced the concept of law as a key component of society and called for three sharply differentiated branches of government with a system of checks and balances—a forerunner of the American governmental system. He also asserted that there was no best society, economic system, family structure, or moral order. Instead, he took the comparative view that "best" was whatever was preferable for a given set of social circumstances faced by a social group or society.

Auguste Comte's Synthesis: A Science of Society

The Social Climate. The beginning of the nineteenth century saw Europe in a state of unprecedented change and turmoil. The Industrial Revolution was in full swing, and the tumultuous changes it wrought turned people's lives upside down. Peasant farmers, accustomed to open-air living in an agricultural society, became industrial workers in dimly lit and poorly ventilated factories. Cities sprang up almost overnight and were characterized by a cold, impersonal environment very much unlike the close-knit warmth and sense of community people were used to in rural hamlets and villages. The sudden expansion of cities with increasingly dense populations resulted in various forms of social problems, including crime, family disorganization, and disease, that were caused in part by a lack of adequate public health standards. People were confused and, because religion as the ultimate source of moral order was being called into serious question, began to look for explanations elsewhere.

The French Revolution of 1789 and its aftermath added to this confusion. The French people overthrew the monarchy in a bloody revolt, only to exchange one form of despotism for another when the military dictator Napoleon Bonaparte rose to power in 1800. During the next ten years, Napoleon depleted the French treasury in attempting to redraw the map of Europe through his military exploits. This left not only France but much of Europe in a state of turmoil.

It was in this social and political climate that Auguste Comte (1798–1857) was born and grew to adulthood. Comte is regarded today as the founding father of sociology, in part because he coined the term *sociology* in 1838. The son of a French aristocrat and government official, he was afforded the luxury of a classical education. Although he studied mainly mathematics and physics, he also read Plato and was familiar with many of the works of Western writers, including Galileo and Isaac Newton in the physical sciences and Montesquieu in social philosophy.

Comte: A Product of His Time. Comte was as much a product of his time as Plato was of his cultural milieu more than two thousand years earlier. Like Plato, he was deeply disturbed about the social unrest that plagued his society. Unlike Plato, however, who had only the rules of logic to apply to his analysis of society in the *Republic,* Comte saw the scientific method as a solution. If, he asserted, the tools of science used to describe and explain the physical world could be harnessed to study the social realm, a superior social order could be developed. His primary goal, then, was to use sociology as a means of improving society. He formulated a hierarchy of disciplines, with sociology viewed as the queen of the sciences. Perhaps too ambitiously, he felt that sociology could be used to build the perfect social order.

Comte's Sociology. Although Comte's goal was social progress, his method of analysis was historical and evolutionary. In fact, the

Social chaos in Europe, Auguste Comte, and the emergence of sociology.
**Reared in the aftermath of the French Revolution, Auguste Comte (1798–1857)
was deeply disturbed by the chaos and social disorganization that plagued much
of Europe during the first part of the nineteenth century. Taking elements from
both rational philosophy and physical science, he sought to apply the tools of
science to the study of social structure and social behavior. Comte, who coined
the term *sociology*, is regarded today as the founding father of this discipline.
(Culver Pictures, Inc.)**

evolutionary perspective was the first theoretical approach used in the emerging science of sociology. In Comte's formulation, there were three stages of societal evolution: the metaphysical stage, the theological stage, and the positive stage. In order to reach the positive stage, each society had to progress through the first two. The *theological stage,* which represented the simplest form of social system, was presided over by religion, which acted as the cohesive force in maintaining order. The *metaphysical stage* was one in which a society was dominated by speculative reasoning or philosophy as illustrated by ancient Greek society. Finally, Comte predicted that one day societies would evolve into the *positive stage,* dominated by science.

Comte saw sociology as divided into two parts: the study of social statics and the analysis of social dynamics. **Statics** was the study of how the various elements of society are structured to promote order and stability. These elements include the basic institutions of family, government, education, religion, and the economy. Stability in these and other areas of social life is necessary for the long-term survival of any society. **Dynamics** represented the study of how the various elements of society develop and change. If, for example, we applied Comte's perspective to our society today, one question we might ask in regard to dynamics might be, How has the American family changed in the last thirty years, and why?

MASTERS OF SOCIOLOGICAL THOUGHT

In the wake of Comte's synthesis, other forms of sociological analysis were developed by European theorists during the later nineteenth and early twentieth centuries. Of these, four names stand out from the rest in terms of the significance of their contributions: Herbert Spencer, Émile Durkheim, Karl Marx, and Max Weber.

Herbert Spencer

Herbert Spencer (1820–1903), an English social philosopher, was a social evolutionist who did much to popularize sociology among the masses both in Europe and in the United States. His evolutionary doctrine concerning social development was influenced mostly by Auguste Comte and Charles Darwin. Spencer echoed Comte's idea that societies evolved from the simple to the complex. He took Darwin's biological concept of the "survival of the fittest" and applied it to society. This perspective became widely known as **social Darwinism.** In his view, governments should not interfere in the lives of individuals or with the operation of organizations and institutions. This would enable the "fittest" to survive and reproduce and the "unfit" to perish. Social Darwinism became very popular in both England and the United States and was used to justify *laissez-faire* capitalism (free enterprise with no government restrictions).

Although the evolutionary doctrine represented the foundation of Spencer's sociological theory, he also espoused an *organic analogy*, in which he compared a society to a physical organism. Just as the physical body of a human or an animal (organism) is made up of separate parts or organs that function in particular ways, a society likewise contains parts (groupings of people) that function in

Herbert Spencer
"The evolutionary perspective"
(Culver Pictures, Inc.)

certain ways for the harmonious working of the social organism as a whole. In his organic analogy, Spencer was influenced heavily by Comte's concept of statics and, along with Émile Durkheim, laid much of the foundation for a perspective called functionalism which would emerge in the twentieth century (Timasheff, 1967).

Émile Durkheim

Émile Durkheim (1858–1917) was a French sociologist whose thinking, along with that of Karl Marx and Max Weber, represented one of the three great "watersheds" of sociological thought during the nineteenth century. Durkheim's position was that society, rather than the individual, should be the unit of analysis in the study of social behavior. He felt that the whole (society) was greater than the sum of its parts (individuals). Society and the social conditions it generates shapes individuals and determines to a significant degree the way they think, feel, and act. In his view, social groupings of people at various levels of society produce their own environments apart from and in addition to the individuals that make them up. These environments, in turn, shape our behavior, as in (to use modern examples) peer group pressure to smoke or not to smoke cigarettes, pressure from a crowd to stand up and cheer at a ball game, or the presence of a police car influencing us to apply less pressure to the accelerator.

Durkheim argued that sociology was the scientific study of **social facts.** Social facts represent things or events external to the individual, such as customs, that have the power to shape behavior. These phenomena are generated by groups and are, therefore, independent of individuals who may find themselves under their coercive power. Take, for example, your behavior this morning as you left your home, got in a car, and headed for school or work. Did you lock the door to your home? Do you do so regularly? Do you regularly lock your car doors as well? If you do, why do you engage in such behavior? Could it be that something called ''crime'' is in the air and custom dictates that you ''lock up'' your home and car? If Durkheim were alive today, he might say that the social fact of crime causes people to lock their homes and cars in some communities and societies, just as a social fact called the lack of crime results in people not ''locking up'' in other communities or societies.

Durkheim devoted most of his professional life to exploring and researching the nature of social facts and their impact on social behavior. He studied the nature of social order, the manner in which the division of labor in society is organized, and other diverse fields, including the nature of religion in simple societies. In *The Division of Labor in Society* (1893), he used an organic analogy similar to Spencer's to study social cohesion or solidarity in nonindustrial versus industrial societies. By doing so, he established much of the foundation for what would emerge as the functionalist perspective in the twentieth century.

In his book *Suicide,* first published in 1897, Durkheim was the first sociologist to make use of statistical analysis. As a result of this seminal research, he was awarded the first sociology professorship to be established by a university in France. In both his methodology and theoretical contributions, Durkheim appears to ''embody what has proved to be conceptually most distinctive in the field and most fertile in its contribution to other disciplines. Durkheim, it might be said, is the complete sociologist'' (Nisbet, 1965, p.1).

Karl Marx

Another key figure in nineteenth-century sociology was Karl Marx (1818–1883), the German philosopher and political economist. Marx was a controversial figure in his time, as he is today, and, though German by birth, he lived in several countries before settling in England. Since he wrote in many subject areas—history, economics, philosophy, political science, and sociology—he did not accept the title ''sociologist'' or any other academic label. Instead, Marx saw himself primarily as a social activist dedicated to using the tools of science not only to understand the social world but also to change it for the better. He was particularly critical of what he felt was the ''evil'' and ''exploitative'' nature of capitalist institutions and societies. His most fervent wish was to see the capitalist system undermined and replaced with more humane institutions.

Marx was essentially an economic determinist who viewed all human history as a series of class struggles related to the economic means of production. In two works primarily, *The Communist Manifesto* (1848), cowritten with Friedrich Engels, and *Das Kapital* (1867–1894), completed by Engels after Marx's death, he set forth his main ideas. Throughout human history, he asserted, perpetual conflict had existed between the "haves" (those with economic and political power) and the "have-nots" (those lacking in economic resources and power). During the Middle Ages in Europe, this conflict was between the feudal lords and landed gentry, and the peasant serfs who sharecropped the land. In the industrial age of the nineteenth century, the haves and have nots were represented by the bourgeoisie and proletariat respectively. The **bourgeoisie** consisted of the capitalist owners of industry who made profits from exploiting the labor of the workers. The **proletariat** consisted of the workers, the exploited class, who subsisted on wages that were no higher than necessary for survival.

Marx predicted revolution. In his view, the proletariat would become alienated from the capitalist system of production, develop class consciousness, and overthrow the bourgeoisie in a revolution that might be violent in some societies while relatively bloodless in others. This, in turn, would usher in a new era in human history in which, because of the sheer efficiency of industrial production, conflict would no longer be necessary. Consequently, a classless form of society would ultimately emerge, which would be devoid of class conflict. In such a society, Marx envisioned a social system in which people would work according to their ability and receive according to their needs.

He was wrong in his predictions for several countries, particularly for the United States. Marx failed to anticipate, among other things, the rise of the labor movement in America and the eventual success of labor unions in gaining economic and social benefits for workers. Nonetheless, his preoccupation with the questions of power and conflict furnished a firm foundation for the emergence of the conflict perspective in modern-day sociology.

Max Weber

The last of the three great theorists of classical sociology was Max Weber (1864–1920), a German legal scholar and economist. Unlike Durkheim (social facts) and Marx (class conflict), Weber concentrated on the interaction between individuals and social situations. In his view, sociology was the study of **social action**—the meaning people assign to their own behavior and their relations with others and society, and how this personal assessment of reality affects their own behavior as well that of others. According to Weber, individuals and groups interpret reality based on their previous experiences and the cultural context within which they live. To use a modern example, suppose a small dog walks by. If it is observed by an American, this animal will probably be perceived as a pet. If it is observed by a Vietnamese, the dog may be perceived as a meal. For the sociologist, Weber asserted, the challenge is to develop *verstehen*, an empathetic understanding of how individuals and groups perceive the social world and their place in it.

Weber was among the most prolific of the early sociologists in his ideas and research efforts. Like Durkheim, he felt the necessity to use statistical analysis in the study of social behavior where possible. However, he differed sharply from Comte and Marx who espoused a social activist orientation in their sociology. Weber asserted that sociological analysis should include the study of human values as part of its subject matter (value relevance), but that the sociologist as scientist must remain value-free or ethically neutral in matters of research methods and social policy and reform. In one of Weber's prominent works, *The Protestant Ethic and the Spirit of Capitalism* (1904–1905), he correlated the development

Émile Durkheim
"Social facts"
(The Bettmann Archive, Inc.)

Karl Marx
"Class conflict"
(Culver Pictures, Inc.)

Max Weber
"Social action"
(Culver Pictures, Inc.)

of capitalism as an economic system with the tenets of Protestant religion, particularly the work ethic contained in Calvinism. In his last book, *Economy and Society* (1922), published two years after his death, he traced the historical development of authority or leadership forms and the development of modern bureaucracies. Weber's ideas acted as forerunners of those developed by both Charles H. Cooley (interactionism) and Talcott Parsons (functionalism) during the twentieth century (Timasheff, 1967).

One of Weber's most valuable contributions was his development of the ideal type concept. An **ideal type** is a conceptual model of something used as a basis for comparing phenomena as they actually exist. Take "urban" as an ideal type for example. In this sense, urban is used in its ideal form as a mental or pure type to which to compare real societies and communities. If one were to use this device to analyze communities in the United States, Chicago, Illinois would be plotted much closer to the ideal type of "urban"

than would Bristol, Tennessee or Weatherford, Texas.

TWENTIETH-CENTURY SOCIOLOGY

While sociology as a formal discipline had its theoretical beginnings in Europe, it developed into a full-fledged science in the United States during the twentieth century.

American Sociology

During the nineteenth and early twentieth centuries, American sociology had its beginnings in the work of such individuals as Harriet Martineau (1802–1876), William Graham Sumner (1840–1910), and Lester Frank Ward (1841–1913). The first of these founders, Harriet Martineau, was not an American, but an Englishwoman (see Box 1-2). She is best known as the English translator of Comte's work and as the author of *How to Observe*

Box 1–2

THE DEVELOPMENT OF SOCIOLOGY: TWO FOUNDING MOTHERS

Harriet Martineau

Jane Addams

From its earliest beginnings, sociology has benefited from the contributions of women, both as scholars (pure sociology) and as activists (applied sociology). Two notable early contributors to the emerging science of society were Harriet Martineau and Jane Addams.

A contemporary of Auguste Comte, Harriet Martineau (1802–1876) was an English sociologist best known for her translation of Comte's work into English. However, she was a capable scholar in her own right. Martineau made extensive observations of social life both in her native England and in the United States. Her travels and studies in America served as the basis for her highly detailed *Society in America,* a book about American social customs. Another of her works, *How to Observe Manners and Morals* (1838), is considered the first book ever written on sociological research methods. In honor of Martineau, a professorship in sociology has been established in her name at the University of Massachusetts.

American sociologist Jane Addams (1860–1935), although a capable scholar, preferred the role of social activist, for which she was awarded the Nobel Peace Prize in 1931. An early and active member of the American Sociological Society, she published in the *American Journal of Sociology* and was offered a position in sociology at the University of Chicago. Instead, she cofounded Hull House in 1889, a Chicago commune consisting of women intellectuals and activists who provided housing for the disadvantaged and depressed, and worked for various social reforms, using sociological data in an applied fashion. Largely because of her efforts, social legislation was passed that improved the juvenile court system, created safer work environments, provided social services for the poor, and improved public sanitation.

Box 1–2 *(Continued)*

Yet she faced an uphill battle on two counts. First, she was a woman in a male-dominated culture that considered it "unladylike" and perhaps abnormal for a woman to be a social activist. Second, during a time when sociology was trying to gain legitimacy in the scientific community as a "respectable" science, applied research and social activism were not seen as appropriate activities by most in the academic establishment.

Sources: Lipset, S.M. (Ed.).(1962). *Harriet Martineau: Society in America,* New York: Doubleday; Deegan, M.J. (1987). *Jane Addams and the Men of the Chicago School, 1892–1918.* New Brunswick, N.J.: Transaction.

Manners and Morals (1838), the first book ever published on social science research methods. However, she also wrote *Society in America,* a detailed examination of social life in the United States (Lipset, 1912). William Graham Sumner taught the first sociology course offered at an American university (1875) and authored *Folkways* (1906), an influential early treatise on comparative cultures. Lester Frank Ward, the first president of the American Sociological Society (1906), did much to popularize sociology through his writings, including *Dynamic Sociology* (1883), and through his lectures. These early sociologists, particularly Sumner and Ward, tended to be the spiritual descendants of Comte in that they stressed a social reform orientation focused on solving social problems at organizational and community levels.

Since that time, the discipline of sociology has experienced significant growth and change. The first graduate programs in sociology were established at the University of Chicago. There, a unified school of thought in the spirit of Sumner and Ward developed in the 1920s—the "*Chicago School.*" This orientation, which focused on the study of everyday life and community and urban problems, dominated sociology until about 1940. From 1940 through the mid-1960s the emphasis shifted away from reform toward the development of comprehensive theoretical perspectives. As this occurred, orientations such as structural functionalism, conflict theory, and symbolic interactionism reached full expression through the contributions of sociologists at a dozen major universities. The 1970s and 1980s have witnessed the diversification of sociological research and practice. Whereas the significant majority of sociologists as late as the 1960s were academics engaged in teaching and research, recent trends have resulted in many social scientists pursuing careers in applied fields such as human resource development and career planning, and in clinical areas, including counseling and crisis intervention.

Functionalism

Structural functionalism, or **functionalism** as it is often called, refers to the analysis of the various parts of society (family, government, education, and so forth) in terms of the way they function to promote social order and harmony. This orientation, which originated in the work of Spencer and Durkheim, became the dominant perspective in sociology through much of the twentieth century. Both Spencer and Durkheim used the organic analogy in which they compared a society to a living organism. A society as a structure has specialized parts that function and interrelate for the smooth operation of the whole, just as specialized organs function to create equilibrium in the physical organism. This approach was developed in large part by Talcott Parsons in *The Structure of Social Action* (1937) and *Toward a General Theory of Action* (1951) and was later refined by his student Robert Merton in several works, most notably *Social Theory and Social Structure* (1968).

According to this approach, each of the various parts of society contains **functions,** or benefits, that help to maintain the social system in a state of order and harmony. There are two basic types of functions: manifest and latent. **Manifest functions** are intended and recognized consequences or benefits that characterize certain parts of society, such as the family (reproduction, socialization, the satisfaction of affectional needs) and education (career preparation and personal growth). Others are **latent functions,** which are unintended and unrecognized consequences that result from the various parts of society. Latent functions usually are not obvious and occur as an extra benefit from participation in certain aspects of society. For instance, mate selection may occur at college although higher education was never designed for this purpose. In similar fashion, the family as an economic unit of consumption supports the toy industry. Sometimes there are **dysfunctions,** or negative and disruptive consequences, that stem from a structural component of society, such as deficit spending within government or violence in the family. When such disruptions occur, modifications in the way such parts of society are structured may be used to reestablish order and equilibrium.

As the historically dominant approach, functionalism has come under a great deal of criticism. Some argue that it is far too conservative in orientation and thus convenient to those wishing to maintain the status quo. This argument centers on the assertion that what is seen as positive and harmonious for one segment of society may be seen as negative and dysfunctional for another. The functionalists counter with the assertion that in any society there is basic consensus concerning what is seen as important, such as "family" in Mexican culture and "equal opportunity" in American society. Another related criticism accuses functionalism, with its emphasis on consensus, of being inadequate in accounting for social change, particularly in highly technological societies such as the United States. Functionalists attempt to defend their perspective by saying that order and harmony in society take the form of a dynamic equilibrium. Consequently, there is order in society which evolves and adjusts constantly as society changes.

Conflict Theory

Whereas the emphasis in functionalism is social order and how it is maintained, **conflict theory** focuses on change. Specifically, the conflict perspective analyzes conflict and power as they relate to social policy and change within society. Although many social observers over the centuries have written on conflict and power, conflict theory as a sociological perspective originated in large part from the nineteenth-century work of Karl Marx and his emphasis on class conflict.

Since that time, Marx's economic determinism has been broadened to include the analysis of conflict in all its basic dimensions—economic, political, and social—at all levels of society. Sociologists use this perspective today to examine a variety of issues, from types of social conflict and the forms they take to the ways in which power is acquired and concentrated in society. Conflicts, for example, may exist between basic institutions such as church and state, between and within organizations such as political parties or major corporations, or between different subcultural groups including those distinguished by age, sex, race or ethnicity, sexual preference, or position on social issues. In addition, some societies contain many interest groups, each of which competes with others for power and influence in shaping the social policies that affect the lives of all society members.

While the conflict approach has long dominated sociology in certain portions of Europe, it has gained prominence in the United States only since the 1950s and 1960s, stimulated in part by the tumultuous events taking place in American society during that time. C. Wright Mills is credited with establishing the conflict perspective in the mainstream of American sociological thought through his controversial book, *The Power Elite* (1956), and other works. Mills, among his other contentions, argued that power in America was concentrated in the hands of a few leaders in the military, business, and government. Because of the work of Mills and other conflict theorists, including Lewis Coser (1956) and Ralf Dahrendorf (1959), conflict theory is now regarded as an increasingly viable approach in examining social behavior at all levels of society.

Interactionism

Symbolic interactionism, or **interactionism** as it is more commonly called, focuses on the personal meaning people assign to the social world around them and how they communicate these perceptions to others through language. This orientation was foreshadowed to some extent by the contributions made by Weber and his emphasis on the subjective nature of social life. Weber asserted that each of us look at social life through our own perceptual screen which is shaped by unique personal experiences with the outside world.

The two most prominent founders of the interactionist approach were Charles Horton Cooley (1918) and George Herbert Mead (1934). Cooley, a sociologist at the University of Michigan, developed a concept that has been called the "looking-glass self." In his view, human beings, through their social encounters, develop personal identities. We constantly assess and reassess how we imagine others see us. Our "identification" of how we think others see us then impacts on our own

Talcott Parsons
"Functionalism"

C. Wright Mills
"The power elite"
(AP/Wide World Photos.)

George Herbert Mead
"Interactionism"

self-image and how we then project to others in our social relations. Mead, a member of the "Chicago School," stressed how our acquisition and use of language affects our development of a self-image as well as our ability to interact successfully with others. He argued that our thoughts and perceptions can be shared with others only through the use of language. This capacity to think and communicate symbolically is what separates us from the lower animals. Through symbolic communication with others, we develop a self-concept and learn to accept the way others view the world and how we must act to succeed in it.

As the twentieth century has progressed, other interactionists have added to the perspectives furnished by Cooley and Mead. Herbert Blumer (1957), for instance, studied crowd behavior and how people have a tendency to redefine a social situation and act in certain ways when exposed to various types of crowds. Through a process called social contagion, crowds often spread their perceptions of reality to others, who then become caught up in the spirit of the moment. Erving Goffman (1961, 1967) studied how the social roles people play, along with the scripted behaviors that go with them, affect the way they perceive reality and then act as a result of those perceptions. Consistent in the work of later twentieth-century interactionists is the view that life in a society represents a "constructed reality" in which people share essentially the same worldview, interpretation of symbols, and definition of reality.

Sociology and the Future

With the twenty-first century only a few years away, the future of sociology promises to be one of increased growth and change. Sociological theory will continue to grow and diversify as we come to know more about the social world in which we live. Methods of sociological investigation and measurement will become increasingly sophisticated. The role of the sociologist will also continue to evolve. As sociologists become more secure in their status as scientists, the issue raised by Weber of remaining value-free and ethically neutral probably will become less a debate. The sociologist as researcher must, of necessity, remain value-free in his or her role as research scientist. However, the use of applied and clinical sociology at various levels will also become more prevalent, and more sociologists may become involved in matters of public policy and social reform.

Ultimately, the future of the science of society will depend on the development of great theorists in the tradition of Durkheim, Marx, and Weber, and, more recently, Mead, Parsons, and Mills. It is probable that some of these future theorists are already in school. Who knows? One of them might be you or one of your classmates taking this course. It all begins with something called the sociological imagination.

CHAPTER SUMMARY

1. Sociology, the science of human social behavior, goes beyond "common sense" explanations and examines the underlying causes of human behavior. As such, it represents one of several disciplines—anthropology, psychology, economics, political science, and sociology—that comprise the social sciences.

2. Science—an objective and systematic means of observing and explaining reality in a verifiable manner—differs from other means of explanation, such as appeal to authority, mysticism, tradition, religion, and philosophy. In this regard, science has four basic components or characteristics: (1) Scientific theory (verified propositions), (2) Empiricism (sensory measurement), (3) Objectivity (lack of bias), and (4) Cumulative knowledge (continual growth).

3. There are two general categories of science, the physical (or natural) sciences and the social sciences. The physical sciences deal with the concrete natural world of physical and biological matter, while the social sciences are concerned with abstract human behavior. Since the physical sciences possess universal laws and deal with phenomena (inanimate and biological matter) that, for the most part, have no will or the ability to engage in purposeful action, they developed long before the social sciences. Consequently, the subject matter of the physical sciences is far simpler (in terms of verification) than that of the social sciences, which have no universal laws and deal with the purposeful behavior of human beings.

4. The "sociological imagination" refers to the ability to recognize how intertwined our lives are with the characteristics of the society in which we live. By studying and understanding the nature of society and social behavior, we can more readily affect our own destinies as well as make a greater impact on society.

5. Some of the conditions and factors that led to the emergence of sociology in the late 1830s can be traced back to ancient Greek civilization and the ideas of such philosophers as Socrates (rationalism), Plato (the *Republic*), and Aristotle (logic and empiricism). Of particular importance are two types of logic—deduction and induction—which were developed during this time. Both deductive reasoning and inductive reasoning ultimately became incorporated into the scientific method as it emerged many centuries later.

6. Auguste Comte coined the term *sociology* in 1838 and is regarded as the "father of sociology." He used an evolutionary perspective (the first school of thought to be developed in sociology) in studying social behavior and saw sociology as the study of statics (order) and dynamics (change). He was followed by Herbert Spencer, whose evolutionary approach to the study of social behavior became known as social Darwinism. Spencer's analysis also made use of an organic analogy in which he compared a society as a structure to the body of a living organism.

7. The three greatest theorists of classical sociology during the nineteenth century were Émile Durkheim, Karl Marx, and Max Weber. Durkheim asserted that society shapes the way people think, feel, and act through the development of social environments made up of social facts. Marx took the position that history consisted of a continuous series of class struggles between the "haves" and "have-nots" and argued that economic conflict and power were the key factors in explaining social behavior. Weber felt that sociology should focus attention on social action, the meaning that people assign to their behavior and their relationship to society, and how this personal assessment affects their own behavior and that of others.

8. During the twentieth century, several sociological perspectives have developed, including functionalism, conflict theory, and interactionism. Functionalism, influenced by the foundation established by Spencer and Durkheim, examines the various parts of society in terms of how they function to promote order and stability. Conflict theory, which originated with Marx, focuses on conflict and power and how these factors impact on social policy and change. Interactionism examines the way people perceive reality and communicate these perceptions to others through the use of language.

TERMS TO KNOW

bourgeoisie: Marx's term for the capitalist owners of industry, the "haves," who made profits from exploiting the labor of the workers.

conflict theory: a modern sociological perspective that analyzes conflict and power as they relate to social policy and change in society.

cumulative knowledge: a characteristic of science in which knowledge is constantly being added to, modified, and refined.

deduction: a form of logic that involves the movement from general propositions about reality to specific conclusions.

dynamics: the study of how the various parts of society develop and change.

dysfunctions: negative or disruptive consequences (problems) that result from certain structural parts of society (for example, child abuse in the family or deficit spending in government).

empiricism: the manner in which evidence in science is gathered through the organized use of the senses.

epistemology: an area in the philosophy of science devoted to the study of knowledge and how it is validated.

functionalism: a modern sociological perspective that analyzes the various parts of society (family, government, education, and so forth) in terms of the ways they function to promote social order and stability.

functions: benefits that derive from a social structure or activity that help to promote social order and harmony.

ideal type: a conceptual model or pure type of something used as a basis for comparing phenomena as they actually exist.

induction: a form of logic that involves movement from specific observations of reality to general conclusions or generalizations.

institution: a major structural component of a society that addresses a special area of human needs (family, education, and so on).

interactionism: a modern sociological perspective that studies the personal meaning people assign to the social world around them and how they communicate these perceptions to others through the use of language.

latent functions: unintended and unrecognized benefits that result from certain structural parts of society.

manifest functions: intended and recognized benefits that result from certain structural parts of society.

objectivity: an unbiased and nonprejudiced approach aimed at determining truth, which is a characteristic of science.

physical sciences: those sciences that study the physical and biological world.

proletariat: Marx's term for the industrial workers, the "have-nots," who were paid only enough to barely survive.

science: an objective and systematic method of observing and explaining reality in a verifiable manner.

scientific theory: propositions about some aspect of reality that have been verified to some degree; the state of scientific knowledge.

social action: Weber's term for the meaning people assign to their own behavior and their relationship to society, and how this personal view of reality affects their own behavior as well as that of others.

social Darwinism: the nineteenth-century view that governments should not interfere in the lives of individuals or the operation of organizations, so that the fittest can survive and the unfit perish.

social facts: Durkheim's term for things or events external to the individual, such as customs, that have the power to shape behavior.

social sciences: those sciences that examine human behavior.

sociological imagination: the ability of individuals to see how interrelated their private lives are with the nature of their society.

sociology: the science of human social behavior at all levels of society.

Socratic method: the asking of penetrating logical questions.

statics: the study of how the various parts of society are structured to promote order and stability.

verstehen: a German term used by Weber for empathetic understanding of how individuals and groups perceive the social world and their place in it.

SUGGESTED READINGS

Invitation to Sociology: A Humanistic Perspective (Peter Berger; New York: Doubleday, 1963). A well-written and inspiring introduction to the sociological perspective.

The Sociological Imagination (C. Wright Mills; New York: Oxford University Press, 1959). An articulate case for the use of sociology as a vehicle for better understanding the human condition and how the social environment that surrounds us impacts on our thoughts, dreams, and behavior.

The Sociological Tradition (Robert A. Nisbet; New York: Basic Books, 1966). A brief history of the development of sociology and its classical theorists.

Sociology for Pleasure (Marcello Truzzi; Englewood Cliffs, NJ.: Prentice-Hall, 1974). A classic and entertaining treatment of the sociological perspective and how it can impact on people's lives.

The Student Sociologist's Handbook, 4th ed. (Pauline Bart and Linda Frankel; New York: Random House, 1986). A valuable resource for the undergraduate student that includes basic concepts, areas of study, and methods used by sociologists.

Chapter 2

What Sociologists Do: The Research Process

■ TERMS TO KNOW

applied research
biased sample
clinical sociology
content analysis
control group
cross-sectional study
dependent variable
evaluation research
experiment
experimental group
field research
Hawthorne effect
hypothesis

independent variable
longitudinal study
participant observation
policy research
population
PR-HD-OAR
pure research
random sample
research design
review of the literature
sampling error
scientific research cycle
statistics
stratified random sample
survey
variable

Two social scientists, one a sociologist and the other an anthropologist, embark on a study of American funeral rituals. They use as their key contacts some employees of "funeral parlors," who inform them as to what types of funerals are scheduled and where and when they will take place. The two researchers, using an approach called participant observation, attend these funerals, blend in with the mourners, and make their observations. Not only do they discover how varied funeral practices are in America, but they also observe that a small number of "professional mourners" exist who, for a variety of reasons, often attend the funerals of people they did not even know.

Late one night, a sociologist and his research assistant participate in a stakeout with vice officers of a police department in a large metropolitan city. The suspects being watched engage in a major drug buy, and the stakeout team closes in and makes several arrests. The sociologist and his assistant observe and record many things, including police procedure, interaction patterns of the police officers before and after a successful vice squad operation, and the "street smarts" exhibited by experienced felons caught in the act. As a bonus, the rapport established between the sociologist and the officers yields an unexpected result. The officers are quite willing to discuss the issue of police corruption within the department, the way honest cops feel about "dopers" who sell confiscated drugs back to drug pushers from their patrol cars, and the bureaucratic problems within the department in dealing effectively with crooked cops.

A sociologist completes a study on high school sociology teachers in the Southern Appalachian region, using the survey approach. The results of the research establish the extent to which sociology is offered as a high school subject in this region, the background and training of the teachers, the theoretical perspectives in sociology they identify with and use (if any), their teaching methods and techniques, and other pieces of information.

A sociology professor, after obtaining proper clearance, takes a group of undergraduate students on a day-long visit to a maximum security prison in Texas. Before the day of the visit, the students are given an orientation seminar on the prison as a separate society, how to act in such a cultural environment, and how to formulate research questions to ask the warden, the prison guards, and the prisoners themselves. In this manner, students using the interview approach are able to gather data on the various perceptions of "prison" held by people placed in different prison roles and to acquire, in an objective and systematic way, insights about crime as a form of behavior.

Each of these sociological research situations just described was conducted or participated in by the author of this book. They serve to illustrate the variety of research methods used by sociologists as well as the diversity of sociological subject matter. In this chapter, we will build on the foundation established in Chapter 1 on sociology as a science and examine what sociologists do when they engage in the research process.

TYPES OF SOCIOLOGICAL RESEARCH

The research enterprise in sociology takes two basic forms: pure and applied research. Many sociologists seek to extend the frontiers of knowledge and add to what is known about the nature of society around us. Others seek to link research to the world of social action and to related issues of social need, public policy, and social reform.

Pure Research

The first and foremost task of sociology is to develop a constantly expanding body of reliable knowledge about the social behavior of human beings at all levels of society. This is **pure research,** scientific investigation aimed at expanding the base of knowledge. In his 1930 presidential address to the American Sociological Society, William F. Ogburn emphatically stated the rationale for pure research and his position concerning sociology's proper role.

> Sociology as a science is not interested in making the world a better place in which to live, in encouraging beliefs, in spreading information, in dispersing news, in setting forth impressions of life, in leading the multitudes, or in guiding the ship of state. Science is interested directly in one thing only, to wit, discovering new knowledge (1930, p. 301).

The desire to seek knowledge for the sake of knowledge, in the view of many traditional sociologists, represents the true spirit of the scientific method. During the early twentieth century, some in the sociological community were afraid that this young discipline might not be accepted as a legitimate science if it allowed itself to be associated with addressing practical issues and solving social problems. In those early days, when sociological knowledge was sparse and the complexity of social issues was great, it was also politically expedient for sociologists to sidestep what some have called "social responsibility" by wrapping themselves in the robes of academic respectability and claiming the need to keep science "pure."

However, as sociology matured and gained legitimacy in the academy of sciences, the distinctions between pure and applied research became less of an issue in the minds of many practitioners. Today, pure and applied research are seen as complementary, rather than at odds with each other. Whether or not sociological knowledge is to be used is no longer an issue. The question now is, For what purpose?

Applied Research

In 1906 Lester F. Ward, the first president of the American Sociological Society, stated his position on the applied approach in sociology in the following manner.

> Just as pure sociology aims to answer the questions, What, Why, and How, so applied sociology aims to answer the question, what for? . . . Applied sociology is essentially practical. It appeals directly to interest. It has to do with social ideals, with ethical considerations, with what ought to be. . . . It does not apply sociological principles; it seeks only to show how they may be applied. . . . The most that it claims to do is to lay down certain general principles as guides to social and political action (as quoted in Wilkinson, 1980, p. 3).

Today, almost a century later, applied sociology is seen as a legitimate area of investigation and practice within the mainstream of the sociology profession. **Applied research** is the study of how sociological principles and knowledge might be applied to social issues, programs, and problems. Many involved in "sociological practice" are employed by or act as consultants to organizations and institutions in business and industry, government, health and human services, and education. Others are in private practice as counselors and clinical sociologists. Areas of applied research in sociology are becoming increasingly diverse and include corporate marketing, consumer and advertising research, human resource research in industry, studies of the legal and criminal justice systems, and research

on aging (Freeman, Dynes, Rossi, and Whyte, 1983).

Three areas of applied sociology in particular are receiving much attention today: policy research, evaluation research, and clinical sociology.

Policy research refers to studies related to social issues and problems whose results may be used as a basis for the formation of public policy. During the past twenty-five years, social scientists have participated in government research and served on presidential committees devoted to various issues including civil disorders, the Vietnam conflict, pornography, population growth, drug abuse and law enforcement.

Evaluation research examines the consequences of various public policies by evaluating their degree of effectiveness or ineffectiveness. In recent years, sociologists have investigated the effects of such policies as the busing of school children to achieve racial balance, the Federal Communications Commission (FCC) standards regarding violence on television and its impact on children, and the consequences and implications of certain laws ranging in scope from abortion to gun control.

A third area of sociological practice, **clinical sociology,** is an applied profession within sociology dedicated to helping people better cope with their social identities and social relations through the use of sociological principles. Clinicians in sociology have their own international organization (the Sociological Practice Association) and certification credentials (certified clinical sociologist, or C.C.S.). They engage in professional practice in several areas ranging from counseling and therapy to public health care and human resource development in industry.

Sociological Research in Perspective

Today pure research and applied research represent two halves of the same whole, the sociological enterprise. Both pure and applied

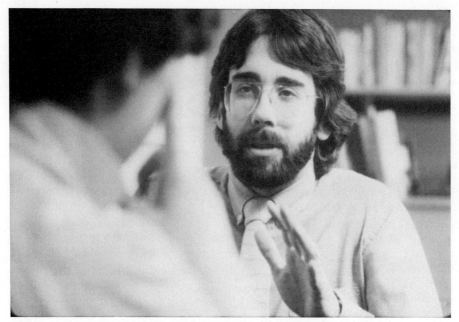

Clinical sociologists use the knowledge generated from sociological research in applied settings. (Copyright Alvis Upitis, 1985/The Image Bank.)

sociologists use the process of discovery and analysis called the scientific method. As introduced in Chapter 1, science is a means of explanation that is theoretical, empirical, objective, and cumulative. Science produces verifiable knowledge and, in this way, differs from explanations based on authority, tradition, belief, and simple logic. The scientific approach is a formal one involving a series of steps that must be carried out according to a specified set of rules. Yet science, like most forms of discovery, offers an exciting and intriguing adventure for the practitioner who yearns to see what others have not seen and know what others have not known. Just how the scientific method works, the steps involved in conducting research, and the ways in which the sociologist makes observations are the main subjects of this chapter.

GETTING STARTED

As a research scientist, the sociologist operates somewhat like a detective with a crime or mystery to solve. Conversely, the great detectives of both fact and fiction use tools of analysis very similar to those used in science.

> Raymond Chandler once called murder a "simple art." Maybe so, but detection is a decidedly elegant one, elegant in the way a mathematician calls a tidy solution to a particularly knotty problem elegant. Sherlock Holmes used logic, Father Brown an ability to put himself in the murderer's skin, Lord Peter a knack for intuitive bursts of inspiration, . . . Lew Archer a belief that more crimes can be explained by Freud than Blackstone. But more central than the methods and mannerisms of the great detectives is the fact that they cut

Because of the diversity of human behavior, every form of social experience is of interest to the sociologist—professional wrestling, for example. What are the similarities and differences between those who attend wrestling events and those who go to basketball games or modern art exhibits? What are the backgrounds of those who become wrestlers? These are but two of many questions the sociologist might explore. (Bob Daemmrich Photo.)

through confusion and chaos, solve puzzles, and set things right to make the world seem a logical place after all. They restore order. As for those methods and mannerisms—there, for the readers of detective stories, is where the fun lies (McCullough, 1984, pp. ix–x.).

As in detective work, there is a fascination and excitement that accrues to the use of the scientific method in sociological research.

Both sociologists and detectives study people and their motives, operate from clues provided by close observation of past and present social behavior, and never really know what they will find until the evidence is in and is strong enough to support conclusions. They both make use of a variety of investigative techniques to discover what behaviors people engage in and why. In this sense then, the sociologist also is a detective using the tools of science to solve the mystery of cause-and-effect relationships in human social behavior.

The Scientific Research Cycle

Scientific detection involves seven essential steps that are normally followed in chronological order to complete an investigation or study. These are the seven steps, which will be explained in detail as we proceed through this chapter:

> **Step 1.** Statement of the Research **P**roblem
>
> **Step 2.** **R**eview of the Literature
>
> **Step 3.** Statement of **H**ypotheses
>
> **Step 4.** Research **D**esign
>
> **Step 5.** Making **O**bservations
>
> **Step 6.** **A**nalysis of the Findings
>
> **Step 7.** **R**eporting the Results

Every educated person should know and understand the seven steps used in the scientific method in proper order and how they work. To help you remember, use the acronym PR-HD-OAR as a device for quick recall. **PR-HD-OAR** stands for problem, review, hypotheses, design, observations, analysis, and reporting.

As shown in Box 2-1, scientific studies in sociology and in the other sciences make use of these seven steps in a cyclical fashion that researchers refer to as the **scientific research cycle** (Wallace, 1972). Visualize, if you will, a circle that represents the process of scientific investigation. At the top of the circle, which is our starting point, we have the state of theory or knowledge in science about something as it currently exists. If, for instance, we were to draw an analogy between this scientific circle and a watch, the state of present theory or knowledge would be at twelve o'clock, or the top of the watch.

To carry the analogy further, a scientific study is conducted much in the same manner as the minute hand moves around the face of a watch in a sixty-minute period. At the beginning of the hour (state of theory/knowledge), we begin the study. The quarter-past-the-hour point is represented by hypotheses, or educated predictions concerning what we think we might find when observations are made. At the half-hour point, located at the bottom of the watch face or circle, we make observations and gather data. The three-quarters-hour point is when we make generalizations drawn from what we have observed.

As the hand of the watch moves back up to the top of the hour again, we add our findings to the state of theory or knowledge, and the cycle or study is complete. In this manner the seven essential steps in carrying out research are completed as we move through the cycle, or around the watch face. Consequently, science represents a never-ending series of such research cycles, just as time accumulates with the completion of each hour in a day, a month, or a year. This process results in the constant expansion of the scientific knowledge base and, in the case of sociology, an ongoing refinement of what is understood about human behavior.

To demonstrate the universality of the scientific method, let us first look at an overview of the scientific research cycle as applied to the physical sciences. Then we will go through the process again more slowly and in greater detail using sociological examples.

Two aerospace scientists decide to conduct research on wing design for the next generation of jet aircraft or space shuttle. They begin by examining the state of general knowledge (theory on flight), develop a specific research problem (Step 1) which relates to the need for improved wing design, and review the literature (Step 2) to see what others doing similar research have found. They then use deduction (see Chapter 1), borrowed from philosophy, to arrive at a specific conclusion called a hypothesis (Step 3). They apply this hypothesis

Box 2–1

THE SCIENTIFIC METHOD

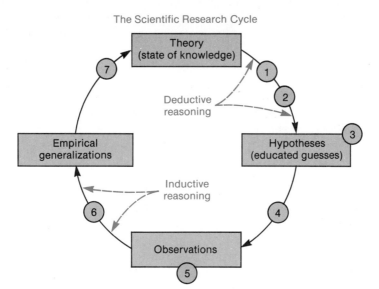

The Scientific Research Cycle

Most scientific studies involve the completion of a series of steps or stages. The researcher typically begins with the state of knowledge (theory) about the phenomenon to be investigated. The project ends with the discovery of additional information that, when integrated with what is already known, acts to reinforce, modify, and extend the state of knowledge. Each study thus represents the completion of a scientific research cycle. The scientific enterprise itself, whether in sociology, psychology, physics, chemistry or any other discipline, represents a neverending series of such cycles.

The Seven Basic Steps in Conducting a Scientific Study

Step 1: Statement of Research Problem. The researcher begins by taking what is generally known (the state of knowledge or theory) about a phenomenon and, using deduction, narrows the focus to a specific research instance. This provides direction for the study.

Step 2: Review of the Literature. The scientist next takes into full account the previous research (the state of existing knowledge) concerning the phenomenon under investigation. This aids in prediction, maintains objectivity, and maximizes efficiency. Scientists and scholars have the additional respon-

Box 2–1 *(Continued)*

sibility of remaining current with the literature (research) in their respective fields as knowledge is expanded.

Step 3: Statement of Hypotheses. Based upon the review of the literature, hypotheses are stated. They represent specific predictions (derived from deductive reasoning) about what the researcher expects to find when observations are made.

Step 4: Research Design. The research design represents the method or methods to be used in making observations (a survey, experiment, case study, content analysis, and so on).

Step 5: Making Observations. Once the research design is decided upon, it is closely followed as the study is carried out and all observations are made.

Step 6: Analysis of the Findings. Findings are then analyzed to see whether or not the hypotheses are supported. Once the findings have been fully interpreted, the researcher can make empirical generalizations from them through the use of inductive reasoning. In other words, specific observations, once analyzed, can be generalized to have application to a larger reality or population.

Step 7: Reporting the Results. To conclude the study, research results are reported in scientific and professional journals, books, and popular publications and thus become added to the state of knowledge or theory. Future researchers will then take these results and conclusions into account when they review the literature and conduct subsequent research.

The diagram ''The Scientific Research Cycle'' is adapted with permission from: Wallace, W. (1972). *The Logic of Science in Sociology.* Chicago: Aldine-Atherton, p. 18.

to predict what should occur if a wing is built to *X* specifications. Whereas in philosophy the deductive conclusion typically is the ending point in the use of logic, in science it becomes the springboard for implementing the study.

The scientists then plan their study by deciding on a research design (Step 4). In science, a variety of research designs may be used, depending on the nature of the study and the type of observations that need to be made. In this case, the two aerospace scientists decide on a research design that involves building a model plane and subjecting it to wind tunnel tests to duplicate real atmospheric conditions. The wings on the model plane are built to the same specifications as

stated in the hypothesis. Then the study is carried forth and observations are made (Step 5).

Next, the aerospace scientists analyze the findings (Step 6) to see if the hypothesis is supported. They then make empirical generalizations from the specific observations conducted on the model in the wind tunnel. At this point in the research cycle, they use a form of logic called induction, which also originated in philosophy (see Chapter 1). Unlike philosophy, however, which has no adequate mechanism for knowing when specific observations are sufficiently representative to draw generalizations from, science uses certain rules for making objective and representative observations.

By building the wings of the model plane

The same essential steps are used in the scientific research process whether one tries to develop improved designs for the next generation of aircraft or attempts to uncover the reasons for successful, long-term marriages or high rates of violent crime. (AP/World Wide Photos.)

to the same specifications as for the wings of a real plane and by duplicating real atmospheric conditions in the wind tunnel, the scientists can generalize their findings to the world of real planes and the real atmosphere. In this sense, they move from the specific observations made in the study to general conclusions or generalizations. The scientists then report the findings of the study (Step 7), and the findings become a part of the existing state of theory or knowledge on wing design.

If the research results showed the wing design to be superior, this study and others like it could be used to justify the building of an experimental aircraft costing tens of millions of dollars. By conducting thousands of such research cycles in related scientific fields, aero-

space scientists have built a cumulative knowledge base concerning flight technology. Consequently, we have moved from the Wright brothers flight of 1903 to today's world of supersonic transports and space shuttles.

The Research Problem

Sociological researchers use the scientific research cycle in similar fashion, taking the same seven steps. The first of these is the development of a research problem or question. Many questions about reality are not amenable to scientific investigation and verification; for instance, "Does God exist?" "Are there

UFOs from outer space?" "Will the United States and the Soviet Union engage in nuclear war?" These and other similar topics have to do with subjective beliefs, value judgments, and unpredictable variables. Other questions, however, can be investigated scientifically, such as, "Does the amount of education influence an individual's degree of racial prejudice and, if so, how, and how much?" "What factors contribute to child abuse?" These are the types of questions addressed by scientists called sociologists.

A scientific study normally begins with the statement of a specific *research problem* that is related to a general scientific theory. In this sense, research problems usually are designed to test, extend, and refine existing theories. To illustrate this, suppose a sociologist wants to test the theory that "amount of education influences the degree of racial prejudice people may exhibit." This is general scientific theory, because previous research has demonstrated a relationship between these two factors. In deriving a testable research problem from such a theory, however, the sociologist has to narrow his or her focus to identify needed specifics, such as the target population to be studied (the who), the type of racial prejudice to be investigated (the what), and the geographical area to be used (the where). These specifics are necessary for a research problem to be testable.

Review of the Literature

The second step in conducting scientific research is the **review of the literature,** a thorough examination of previous research concerning the scientific theory that is to be tested. By examining previous research, the sociologist is able to weigh the evidence and then make predictions concerning what might be found in the study about to be carried out. In sociology, as well as in other sciences, investigators must keep abreast of the latest developments in their research fields. The responsibility to stay current with the scientific literature, in light of rapidly expanding knowledge, largely accounts for the necessity for sociologists and other scientists to specialize.

The review of the literature is necessary for several reasons. First, a properly conducted literature review aids in *prediction*. It gives the researcher a firm foundation on which to base predictions or hypotheses. Thus, it aids in making the scientific method coherent and systematic. Second, it promotes *efficiency*. A review of the literature may show that the behavior or event the sociologist wants to observe or explain has already been thoroughly researched. As a result, needless and unproductive repetition can be prevented. The review of the literature, therefore, aids in making science cumulative. The state of reliable knowledge is continuously added to and refined, and scientists can avoid "reinventing of the wheel." Finally, this process ensures that the research is conducted with *objectivity*. The researcher cannot legitimately be accused of being biased or unscientific if hypotheses concerning expected findings are based on or grounded in the body of previous research findings.

By contrast, the scientific community looks with great disdain on those who use the language and imagery of science to make facts fit into their own preconceived "theories." This is pseudoscience, which takes many forms in its attempt to befuddle and sometimes defraud the public. Practicioners today abound in many places and take several forms, from the psychic surgeons of the Philippines with their sleight-of-hand trickery, to some authors of popular books who masquerade as social scientists by publishing biased reports on various forms of social behavior (see Box 2-2). Such devices prey on the innocent, the ignorant, and those desperate for assistance of some kind. The best defense against

Box 2–2

PSEUDOSCIENCE: THE "RESEARCH" OF SHERE HITE

She goes in with prejudice and comes out with a statistic.
Ellen Goodman, Pulitzer-prize-winning columnist

One problem faced by legitimate behavioral scientists is the large volume of material published each year that misleads and misinforms the public in the name of science. Many Americans do not know and understand the basic steps and approaches used in scientific research. Consequently, they are easily duped by authors who, masquerading as scientists, claim to report the results of valid research. These writers use the imagery and language of science but, in reality, exploit the ignorance of their readers by pandering to their gullibility and, in some cases, their vulnerability. They often have a cause to promote, an "ax to grind," or they are motivated by money. In the case of feminist author Shere Hite, all three factors appear to be present.

In 1987, Hite's third book on sex and love in America, *Women and Love: A Cultural Revolution in Progress*, was published amid a cloud of controversy. Her findings and conclusions—basically that American women as a whole are unhappy in their love and sexual relationships—were based upon 4,500 responses (4.5 percent) from 100,000 questionnaires sent to various women's and church groups. Specifically, her findings included revelations that, among American women, (1) 70 percent of those married five or more years have engaged in extramarital affairs, (2) 76 percent frequently engage in sex on the first date, (3) 95 percent are emotionally and psychologically harassed by men, and (4) 98 percent want to make basic changes in their relationships with men.

While it is clear that both marriage and male-female relations in general today are undergoing some difficulties in light of tremendous cultural change, Hite's book sheds little light on the problems of love and sex as we move into and through the 1990s. Instead, it is characterized by blatant "man-bashing," dubious findings at odds with legitimate sociological research (Hite has an M.A. in history), and patently sloppy and unscientific research methods. Nonetheless, *Women and Love* has sold fairly well among an unsuspecting and unsophisticated readership.

Despite her commercial success, Hite has been criticized severely by both the journalistic and scientific communities. According to Helen Gurley Brown, editor of *Cosmopolitan* magazine, "the report is so man-hating, so man-denigrating, and that's so easy to do. . . . What are we going to do, dump on all the men in the world?" Psychologist and author Charles Melvyn

Box 2–2   *(Continued)*

Kinder says, "If there is a growing lack of communication between men and women, it is precisely because of books like Hite's." Yale-educated sociologist Janet Lever goes on "to illustrate how unscientific Hite's report is" by discussing some of the techniques used in legitimate social research: "Social-scientific reports are typically based on a 60-to-65 percent return of questionnaires. A return rate of less than 50 percent prohibits the research from being published in respected journals. The Hite study is based on a four-and-one-half-percent response rate—truly an abysmal rate of return." This assessment is underscored by behavioral scientists nationwide. According to researcher Regina Herzog of the University of Michigan's Institute for Social Research, "Five percent could be any oddballs. We get nervous if respondents in our own surveys go under 70 percent."

Newsweek (November 23, 1987, p. 76) perhaps best captured the essence of the Shere Hite phenomenon in the following excerpt: "One can't publish a study subtitled 'A Cultural Revolution in Progress' and then expect readers to believe its sole subject is 4,500 people. The picture that has emerged of Shere Hite . . . is that of a pop-culture demagogue caught in the glare of public scrutiny and frantically dithering away whatever credibility she may once have had."

Sources: Barol, B. with Brailsford, K. (1987, November 23). Men Aren't Her Only Problem: A Bizarre Month for Sex Researcher Shere Hite. *Newsweek,* p. 76; Lever, J. (1988, February). A Sociologist Looks at Woman and Love. *Playboy,* pp. 42–43; Wallis, C. (1987, October 12). Back Off Buddy: A New Hite Report Stirs Up a Furor Over Sex and Love in the '80s. *Time,* pp. 68–73.

such "flimflam" is maturity and a sound understanding of the scientific method.

Statement of Hypotheses

After completing the review of the literature, the sociologist next makes educated guesses or predictions about what he or she expects to find when the study is carried forth. These predictions are called hypotheses. In scientific research, a **hypothesis** is a formal statement of an expected cause-and-effect relationship between two variables, which can be tested.

In science, a variable is anything subject to change or variation, such as rain in meteorology, soil erosion in geography, or rates of cancer in medicine. In sociology, a **variable** is any social characteristic or form of social behavior that may differ in some regard, or change. The family sociologist, for example, might examine variables such as marital satisfaction, family violence, and sex roles, while the demographer (one who studies population characteristics) might focus attention on such variables as fertility, mortality, and rates of immigration.

A hypothesis contains both an independent and a dependent variable. They represent the two basic types of variables included in scientific research. The **independent variable** is the causal or influencing variable. It causes or influences to some extent the occurrence of a variable called the dependent variable. Sociological research has shown, for instance, that violence in the home while a person is growing up is one independent variable which may influence him or her to engage in family violence (dependent variable) as an adult.

The **dependent variable** is the effect variable that is the subject of research. In science, investigation focuses on the dependent variable, the factor the researcher wants to account for or explain. For example, to the sociologist specializing in criminology who wishes to investigate recidivism (the rate at which released felons engage in new crimes and return to prison), recidivism is the dependent variable. It is dependent on certain causes or explanations. These causes or explanations are the independent variables that the sociologist must search for, make predictions or hypotheses about, and then test to see if expected relationships between such independent variables and the dependent variable are indeed the case.

The modern sociological method of hypothesis formation and testing was pioneered by Émile Durkheim in his research on suicide conducted late in the nineteenth century. Durkheim's basic theory was that the industrialization and rapid urbanization people experienced as the Industrial Revolution took hold had weakened their loyalty and attachment to their communities and group affiliations. As a result of these changes, he contended, some of these people became somewhat dehumanized, detached from the community and the group support mechanisms they had previously enjoyed. They became confused and alienated and were more likely to engage in various forms of behavior harmful to themselves including, in extreme cases, suicide.

Durkheim's general hypothesis was that the degree of social integration in a society or group (independent variable) was inversely related to suicide rates (dependent variable). In other words, the higher the degree of social integration in a society or social group, the lower would be suicide rates. As specific indi-

cators of social integration, he used measurable independent variables such as religious affiliation, marital status, degree of economic stability, and parental status. Some of the hypotheses he developed are summarized below:

> Catholics (who have stronger church affiliation) should have lower suicide rates than Protestants.
> Married persons should have lower suicide rates than single people.
> Married persons with children should have lower suicide rates than married persons without children.
> Times of economic prosperity should be accompanied by lower suicide rates than times of economic instability.

When the data Durkheim gathered were statistically analyzed, the results confirmed many of his hypotheses, including the examples given. He concluded that the social bonds people have or do not have in their social affiliations affect the way they act in times of personal crisis. In some cases, those with the strongest social affiliations are least likely to take their own lives, because they have more social supports than those with weak affiliations. In addition, the social norms under which they operate are more clearly defined. Not only were Durkheim's findings significant in furthering our understanding of such factors as social integration and suicide, but the way in which he stated his hypotheses, gathered his data, and analyzed the findings have furnished us with a model for conducting much of what makes up sociological research today (Durkheim, 1966).

PLANNING THE STUDY

So far we have examined the first three steps involved in moving through the scientific research cycle: the statement of the research problem, the review of the literature, and the formation of hypotheses. Step 4 is research design, one of the most fascinating and crucial aspects of scientific research.

The Concept of Research Design

In the process of conducting a sociological study, the **research design** represents the decision by the researcher to use a particular method in making scientific observations. The scientist, like the average citizen and consumer, wants simply to "find out" and will use a variety of strategies in order to do so. Earl Babbie (1983) in addressing this topic has this to say:

> Suppose, for example, that you want to find out whether a particular automobile—say the new Burpo-Blasto—would be a good car for you. You could, of course, buy one and find out that way. You could talk to a lot of B-B owners, or talk to people who considered buying one and didn't. You might check the classified ads to see if there were a lot of B-Bs being sold cheap. You could read a consumer magazine's evaluation of Burpo-Blastos, or you could find out in a number of other ways. The same situation occurs in scientific inquiry (p. 72).

The particular method used in a sociological study depends on a variety of factors. What is the nature of the research problem? How much time and money are available as resources to be used in the study? Where does the research need to be conducted—locally, two thousand miles away, or perhaps in another country? How accessible and cooperative are the people being studied likely to be? These and several other questions must be considered when developing a plan for how observations are to be made. Although there are several types of research designs that may be used, three of the most prevalent ones used by sociologists are the survey, the experiment, and field research.

The Survey

The **survey** approach uses questionnaires to gather information about people's attitudes and their social behavior. Sociological surveys take a variety of forms, including face-to-face and telephone interviews (in which typically a questionnaire is read to a respondent) and questionnaires mailed to large numbers of people with stamped return envelopes. Advantages include (1) efficiency and low cost; (2) the gaining of information that can easily be generalized to a larger population; and (3) flexibility, in that several different kinds of questions can be asked. Disadvantages may include (1) a format that does not allow in-depth answers and (2) a "snap-shot" view of reality, in that answers to questionnaires often portray largely what the subjects were feeling at the time of the study (Black and Champion, 1976). Sociological surveys are used in a variety of applications, including certain forms of demographic research such as census taking, public opinion polls on social, economic, and political issues, and studies conducted on employee morale and job satisfaction in industry.

When sociologists use the survey approach, they are very careful to examine the research instrument (questionnaire) for validity and reliability. A questionnaire or survey has *validity* if it measures what the researcher hopes to measure. *Reliability* has to do with the consistency or repeatability of the information gathered. Thus, a questionnaire would be reliable if each time it was administered to the same or a similar group of research subjects, the results were about the same.

In survey research, the total group of people, events, or things being examined or observed is called the universe or population. A population could be represented by all registered voters in a county, all civil disturbances in the United States between 1960 and 1970, or all marriage records contained in a municipal courthouse. In most cases, however, the

The survey approach sometimes involves face-to-face or telephone interviews. At other times, a questionnaire may be administered in person to a group of research subjects or sent to them through the mail. (Bob Daemmrich Photo.)

population is the total group of people being studied that meets a specified set of characteristics. The characteristics that define the boundaries of a research population usually include such factors as geographical location and time frame. For instance, a population that a criminologist uses for research purposes might consist of all males between eighteen and twenty-five years of age convicted of felony property offenses in the state of Ohio between 1985 and 1990.

In some studies, it is feasible to use an entire research population as a source of observation, particularly when the numbers of people involved are less than four or five hundred. In these cases, many researchers prefer to use the entire population. However, in instances where numbers are large and an entire population is not readily accessible, it is permissible to use a *sample,* a smaller number of people taken from the larger population being studied.

In scientific research, it is essential to use a **random sample,** one chosen in such a way that every member of the larger population being studied has an equal chance of being included. If, for example, a sociologist conducted research on all public school teachers in the state of Texas during the 1990–1991 school year, the largeness of the population (over 100,000) would necessitate the use of some sort of random sample. Through the use of random sampling, findings could be generalized to the total population from which the sample was drawn. By contrast, a similar study of teachers in Lewisville, Texas (less than 400) would make use of the entire population.

When carried out correctly, survey research can be a sophisticated method of anal-

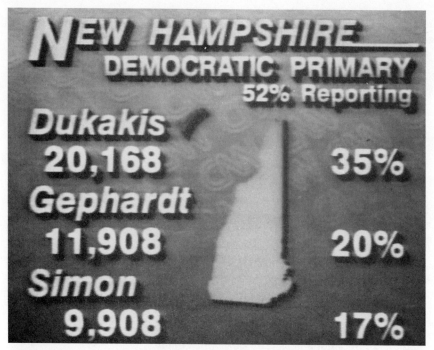

NEW HAMPSHIRE
DEMOCRATIC PRIMARY
52% Reporting

Dukakis
20,168   35%
Gephardt
11,908   20%
Simon
9,908   17%

The major television networks use the results of stratified random sampling to predict which presidential candidate will carry certain states on election night. (CNN.)

ysis. In this regard, there are several different types of random sampling approaches. One is the **stratified random sample,** a random sample chosen in such a way that certain characteristics of the population being studied are represented in accurate proportions. In network coverage of the presidential election returns on election night every four years, news commentators will project winners in certain states with only 1 or 2 percent of the votes counted. This is done through stratified random samples taken of certain precincts in each state which accurately reflect the different constituencies within the voting population.

When sampling is not carried out with precision, there are usually significant amounts of bias and error. An unscientific or **biased sample** is one that involves a lack of random selection and, in some cases, self-selection by the participants. Such things as straw polls, on-the-street interviews, phone-in responses, and letters to the editor, while sometimes interesting, have little or no scientific value because their findings cannot be generalized to a larger population. They are representative only of the people who participated by furnishing information. In Alfred Kinsey's research on sexual behavior, conducted in the 1940s, there was significant sample bias because he solicited volunteers, who responded to newspaper ads and who were paid for furnishing their sexual histories. About one-half of the men he used in his survey of males were from only one state, Indiana, and were predominantly well-educated and middle- to upper-middle-class. Consequently, his subjects were not representative of Americans in general (Kinsey, Pomeroy, and Martin, 1948).

Another problem that can occur in survey research is **sampling error,** the degree to which characteristics of a sample do not represent those of the population from which it was drawn (Borg and Gall, 1979). In the 1948 presidential election, Harry Truman, the Democratic incumbent, ran against Thomas Dewey, a formidable Republican. The major polls listed Dewey as ahead, and on election night, with the final results undecided, some newspapers (including the *Chicago Tribune*) printed headlines announcing Dewey's victory. The next morning, many people were surprised to learn that Truman had been reelected as president. The pollsters had stopped sampling voters far too soon before the election to account for shifts in attitudes in the closing weeks of the campaign. They had also used telephone surveys. Since in 1948 a significant proportion of the American population still did not have phones, the predictions were skewed and the margin of sampling error was significant. Today, however, sampling techniques are greatly improved with a margin of error, in most cases, of only 2 or 3 percent.

The Experiment

The Greek philosopher Aristotle, whom you will recall from Chapter 1, once argued that a heavy object, when dropped from a great height, would fall at a much greater speed than would a much lighter object. Yet, for almost two thousand years, no one, including Aristotle himself, ever bothered to test this idea. During this long period, mathematicians developed a formula that basically said that the speed at which an object fell was largely a function of weight. Consequently, a two-pound object would fall at twice the rate of a one-pound object, and a five-pound object would fall five times as fast. Finally, as legend has it, a young Italian professor named Galileo (1564–1642) climbed the leaning tower of Pisa one day in 1591 and dropped a one-hundred-pound cannon ball and a one-pound cannon ball from the top of it at the same time. This experiment and others that followed proved that objects fall through space at about the same rate of speed, regardless of weight. Such studies by scientists during the seventeenth century marked the beginning of the experimental method (Butterfield, 1957).

Sociologists today occasionally use the experiment as a research design. However, instead of comparing the actions of two cannonballs or other objects, they compare the behavior of two groups of people. Specifically, an **experiment** consists of a study in which two matched groups of people are compared in terms of how they act in a specially designed social situation. Both groups are examined to see how they act or perform in relation to a dependent variable which is the focus of the study. One group, called the **experimental group,** is exposed to a particular independent variable that the researcher thinks might be a causal influence on behavior in regard to the dependent variable. The other group, called the **control group,** is not exposed to the independent variable. The two groups are then compared with each other to determine whether the variable that was supposed to change, the dependent variable, did so in terms of the behavior of the experimental group.

Suppose a sociologist decides to study the grade performance of four hundred randomly chosen students enrolled in their first semester at college. In this case, grade performance would represent the dependent variable. One-half of these students (the experimental group) are then randomly chosen to be exposed to a study skills seminar called "Effective Study Skills: A Skill-Based System for

Academic Excellence." This is done after midterm grades are computed, which are then used as a basis of comparison. The other students (the control group) are not exposed to this independent variable. At the end of the semester, the grade performance of the two groups are compared to see if exposure to and implementation of the ESS study system made a difference in the experimental group.

Research similar to this actually was conducted by the author in 1979 and 1980. Students randomly chosen to attend the seminar in ESS (the experimental group) were further divided into two subgroups after the seminar and tracked to measure their end of semester performance. Experimental group 1 (EX-1) consisted of those who merely attended the ESS seminar and who showed no evidence afterward of having implemented the entire system. Experimental group 2 (EX-2) consisted of students who demonstrated implementation of the entire study system, through a special tracking mechanism built into the system called Diagnostic Follow-up. The results showed that those in EX-1 had only marginal improvement at best. However, students in EX-2 generally reported significant and, in some cases, dramatic improvement in their grades. *Note: A condensed version of ESS is included with the Study Guide that accompanies this book. Please use it. It is likely that your grade performance will also improve if you implement all of ESS as a total study system.*

Experiments are often used by sociologists to test how the structure of social environments impact on human behavior. In a much-publicized experiment, social psychologist Phillip Zimbardo (1972) and colleagues at Stanford University conducted an experiment to see how the social environment of a prison affected the behavior of guards and prisoners. They placed an advertisement in a local newspaper for students willing to work as research subjects at $15 a day for two weeks. Twenty-four "mature, emotionally stable" students

were chosen for the experiment and, at the flip of a coin, were divided into two groups, "prison guards" and "prisoners." The basement of a campus building was converted into a "prison," and those chosen to be prisoners were unexpectedly "arrested" at their homes by "police officers," handcuffed, then transported to the "prison" on campus by "patrol car."

The experiment had to be abandoned after only six days, however, because the students were so affected by the "prison" environment that they lost the capacity to differentiate between role-playing and reality. They actually turned into guards and prisoners. Zimbardo, in commenting on this, said,

> There were dramatic changes in virtually every aspect of their behavior, thinking, and feeling. In less than a week the experience of imprisonment undid (temporarily) a lifetime of learning; human values were suspended; self-concepts were challenged, and the ugliest, most . . . pathological side of human nature surfaced. We were horrified because we saw some boys (guards) treat others as if they were despicable animals, taking pleasure in cruelty, while other boys (prisoners) became servile, dehumanized robots who thought only of escape, of their own individual survival, and of their mounting hatred for the guards (1972, p. 243).

The experimental approach has certain advantages as well as some potential drawbacks. Unlike the survey, which gathers information about the social world as it exists naturally, the experiment involves intentional manipulation of one or more independent variables. This makes the experimental approach superior in some situations because of its ability to measure more precisely the cause-and-effect relationships between specified independent and dependent variables (Simon and Burstein, 1985). In addition to its ability to be controlled, the experiment has the added advantage of being easy to replicate, should a re-

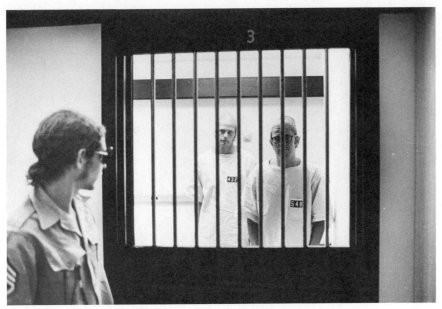

Phillip Zimbardo set up a mock prison at Stanford University and, using college students as research subjects, conducted an experiment to test how the environment of a prison affected "guards" and "prisoners."

searcher find it useful to do so. Disadvantages include the probable overuse of college students, who are readily available as research subjects, and the problem of artificiality in some experimental situations.

One potential problem in experimental research with human subjects is the **Hawthorne effect,** a temporary change in the behavior of people in a group because of the presence and influence of outsiders. During the 1920s and 1930s, Elton Mayo and his associates (Roethlisberger and Dickson, 1939) conducted research at the Western Electric Company to study the effect of working conditions on employee productivity and morale. At the company's Hawthorne plant in Chicago, they first set out to ascertain the workers' normal rate of output in what was called the bank wiring room. A ''bank'' was a set of switchboards, and it was determined that the work standard

for each worker involved completely wiring two banks per day.

Once this standard of expected output had been established by the scientists as a control, an experimental group consisting of several women was separated from the larger group of bank wirers. While working conditions for the larger control group remained the same, several changes—one at a time—were introduced into the work environment of the experimental group. However, no matter in what area change was made—work breaks, lighting conditions, the length of working hours, the length of work week, production goals—production increased with each change.

This puzzled the researchers at first and they thought the study had failed. It had failed in its original intent, because the research design was flawed. The presence of the researchers "tainted the data," in that it emphasized to members of the experimental group that they were being studied and were therefore "special." By being segregated from the other workers and made to feel special, members of the experimental group developed greater degrees of cohesion and friendship, which in turn led to mutual reinforcement and greater productivity. In addition, the special way they were treated influenced them to want to please the researchers by being "good" research subjects. While managers in large-scale organizations can use insights derived from this and other related research to maintain and improve morale and productivity among participants, the results of the Hawthorne studies also have implications for social research. Consequently, sociologists and other social scientists must take care that their presence does not influence research results. By being as unobtrusive as possible in conducting social research—especially with experiments and field research—they minimize the Hawthorne effect.

Field Research: The Example of Participant Observation

Field research involves the study of certain forms of social behavior within their natural settings. Field research techniques take a variety of forms and are referred to by such names as the case study, the in-depth interview, the community study, and participant observation. Field studies are largely descriptive or qualitative in nature, whereas surveys and experiments typically are more explanatory and stress quantitative measurement. The field approach is particularly useful when little is known about certain social phenomena or when certain forms of behavior do not lend themselves easily to quantification through surveys or experiments. Areas examined through field research include deviant behav-

ior, nonliterate foreign cultures, and "campus demonstrations, courtroom proceedings, labor negotiations, public hearings, or similar events taking place within a limited area and time" (Babbie, 1983, p. 245). These forms of social behavior are perhaps best studied, at least initially, within their natural settings.

One of the most fascinating forms of field research is **participant observation,** an approach in which the researcher actually joins the group being studied in order to obtain an inside view of social behavior. By gaining admittance to and actually participating in the group under investigation, the sociologist is able to obtain both a depth and breadth of understanding not possible with many surveys and experiments. This technique allows the sociologist the intimacy of an inside view in gaining knowledge of how people perceive their social world, and how they think, feel, and act in it.

Playing the role of imposter and sometimes even disguising one's true identity is neither new nor limited to the field of sociology. During ancient Muslim times, it was rumored that Harun al-Rashid, the caliph (king) of Baghdad, often wore the disguise of an average citizen, and sometimes a beggar, in order to observe firsthand the mood and behavior of his subjects. A story in modern literature familiar to many is *The Prince and the Pauper,* in which the little prince swaps identities with the street urchin. Novelist John Steinbeck (1939) lived for a time in migrant worker camps in order to understand more fully the people he wrote about in *The Grapes of Wrath.* In the world of modern espionage, both the Americans and the Soviets have agents posing in the guise of diplomats and embassy workers, who live and work in the country of the "enemy" to gather information about the other side.

Other scientific disciplines also make use of participant observation. The late anthropologist Margaret Mead was a pioneer in the use of this research approach. During the 1920s and 1930s, she lived among and studied several non-Western tribal cultures in portions of the North and South Pacific. Her comparative studies of family structures and sex roles in simple societies in the Admiralty Islands, New Guinea, and Samoa are regarded as classics in anthropological literature. More recently, the research of primate anthropologist Jane Goodall has given us much of what is now known about the social behavior of lower primates, particularly chimpanzees. During the last quarter century, she has devoted her professional life to living among and gathering data on chimpanzees at great sacrifice and, at times, risk to her personal safety. A colleague of Goodall's, Dian Fossey, was murdered in Africa while pursuing similar research on gorillas.

In sociology, participant observation has its roots in Max Weber's concept of *verstehen*, or empathetic understanding. By "walking in the shoes" of different types of people in various social situations, the sociologist is able to understand what Weber called social action at the individual, group, and community levels. This approach was also used in the pioneering research of "Chicago school" sociologists during the 1920s, which included Nel Anderson's (1923) study of hoboes and Frederic Thrasher's (1927) analysis of gang behavior.

More recently, there have been other classic studies, such as Erving Goffman's (1961) study of the "underlife" that patients in a mental institution experienced apart from the conventional roles played out in doctor-patient relationships. Goffman essentially went underground and worked for a year as an assistant athletic director in a mental hospital where he could "snoop" around the wards, get to know the patients, and study the hospital as a "total institution" without interference. He found that patients in such a totally controlled environment developed their own subculture, through which they were able to manipulate and deceive the staff and gain some personal control over their own lives.

Obviously, participant observation research can be both intriguing and potentially dangerous. Two studies in modern sociological literature that illustrate this involved two Caucasian journalists, a man and a woman, who each conducted separate observations. In different parts of the country and at different times, both underwent medical treatment to temporarily darken their skin in order to pose as black people.

John Howard Griffin (1961), on assignment for *Sepia* magazine, was assimilated into the black subculture of the deep South during the fall of 1959 and lived and traveled through the region as a black man for several weeks. He documented in a daily journal his experiences at the hands of white society and furnished a penetrating portrait of the pervasiveness of white racism in *Black Like Me*. When his research became known, his life was threatened, racists hung his effigy from a streetlight on the main street in his hometown, and a cross was burned in his yard.

Almost a decade later, Grace Halsell (1969) replicated Griffin's study and spent time living as a black woman in both Harlem and the deep South. She too kept a journal and made numerous observations about what it was like to be black and live in a white-dominated society during the late 1960s. During much of this experience, she worked as a maid in white households and was once sexually assaulted by "the man of the house."

Like surveys and experiments, participant observation studies have their pluses and minuses. This approach is very useful in studying social behavior among people who either lack the sophistication to draw sociological insights about their own behavior or are unwilling to share such information because of their own

John Howard Griffin, a white journalist, used the participant observation approach to pose as a black man in the deep South and wrote a book about his experiences. (AP/Wide World Photos.)

vested self-interests or deviant status. In addition, because of the large amount of time and energy spent by the researcher in making contact with the subjects of the study, a picture of group processes can be obtained in greater depth than through other types of studies that tend to take place over a relatively short period of time.

However, these very advantages pose certain problems, such as maintaining scientific objectivity in light of such intense contact, and the ethical problems that sometimes occur. For instance, should subjects be told that their new member is a sociologist conducting research? In some cases, this should be done, while in others, to do so would result in al-

tered or uncooperative behavior by those being investigated. In all instances, however, the sociologist must guard against any individual's or group's being injured or damaged by such research.

Research Design in Perspective

For the sake of clarity, two points should be made. First, the research designs just mentioned—the survey, the experiment, and field research (participant observation)—are only representative, not exhaustive, in describing the richness and diversity of sociological research. Other approaches are also used.

Some sociologists, for instance, make use of **content analysis,** a research design in which the content of communication is studied to assess its impact on social attitudes and behavior. Like the historian, the sociologist may examine a variety of existing sources including governmental records (census data, laws, court decisions, and reports), popular written communications (newspapers, magazines, and advertisements), and literary, artistic, and entertainment media (novels, plays, paintings and sculpture, motion pictures and television, and so on). Data derived from content analysis may tell us much about the nature of a given society as well as how it changes over time. Take television programming for example. How is its content today similar to or different from that of television in the 1950s? What does this tell us about American society? Which values, priorities, issues, and social patterns have remained essentially the same? Which have changed, and why?

In addition, the various research designs used in scientific research are not mutually exclusive. Instead, they sometimes overlap with two or more approaches being used in the same study or different phases of the same study. The basic principle here is that sometimes two or more research methods, when used together, may yield more precise results than one method used alone. Consequently, it is not uncommon for sociologists to use a broad-based survey involving hundreds of people in combination with a few in-depth interviews or case studies (Simon and Burstein, 1985).

CONDUCTING THE STUDY

The scientific enterprise is much like building a house. The first three steps—research problem, review of the literature, and statement of hypotheses—are analogous to planning and preparing the site of the project in terms of what is to be built (or studied), where it will be constructed, and who will be involved. Step 4, the research design, answers the "how" question by providing the blueprint for the completion of the project.

Making Observations

Once the research design is fully decided on, the planning phase is over and it is time to carry out the study by *making observations.* This data collection phase represents Step 5 in the scientific research cycle and, in most cases, must be carried out as designated in the research design for the results to be valid.

One important consideration in implementing any study is its time frame. How much time is going to be required to complete the study and make all necessary observations?

If a study is broad-based and takes place over a brief period of time, it is a **cross-sectional study.** Many surveys and experiments are cross-sectional studies. Observations in such studies are usually gathered in a period ranging from a day or two to a few weeks. In the middle 1970s, for example, a team of sociologists conducted a national survey of life satisfaction in a sample of 2,702 American

households, which found that among other things, married people were happier than single individuals (Campbell, Converse, and Rogers, 1976).

A **longitudinal study** is focused on a single group of people over an extended period of time. Many such studies take several years to complete. In a study completed in the late 1970s, sociologists spent nine years tracking two thousand randomly chosen high school freshmen to study the factors that accounted for their career choices five years after graduation from high school (Bachman, O'Malley, and Johnson, 1978).

Analysis of the Findings

Once the observations have been made and all data collected according to the specifications of the research design, it is time to *analyze the findings* in terms of whether or not the hypotheses are supported, Step 6 in the scientific research cycle. In sociological research, this usually involves the use of **statistics,** mathematical procedures that describe the characteristics of variables and explain or measure the relationships between them. Statistical analysis in survey research typically involves establishing the degree to which an independent variable is associated or correlated with the dependent variable.

However, the appearance or correlation of one variable with another does not mean, in and of itself, that the two are causally related. Therefore, it is also important to determine the probability that a correlation between two variables is due to chance. In social research, if there are more than five chances out of one hundred that the relationship (correlation) between an independent and dependent variable is due to chance or sampling error, the results are typically seen as inconclusive. This high standard of acceptability in statistics is referred to as the *.05 level of statistical significance.*

In addition to determining whether or not

the hypotheses in a study are supported, the analysis also involves *summary and presentation of the data* and empirical generalizations. The findings of sociological research, particularly with surveys and experiments, are often summarized and presented in the form of tables, graphs, and charts. Use of these devices furnishes the reader with a logical and visually clear means of fully understanding what was found. The results of statistical analysis are also summarized at the bottom of such graphic displays. *Empirical generalizations* refer to the process by which inductive reasoning (Chapter 1) is used to move from the specific observations made in the study to general conclusions or generalizations concerning a larger social process or group of people and their behavior. By using a random sample, for example, the findings of a study can be generalized to apply to the entire population from which the sample was drawn.

REPORTING THE RESULTS

Do you remember the analogy we used in which the scientific research cycle was compared to the face of a watch? Just as the minute hand of a watch approaches the twelve at the top of the circle to begin the hour-long journey again, reporting the results of research (Step 7) signals the completion of the scientific research cycle. This, in turn, adds to the state of theory (knowledge) and sets the stage for future research.

Sharing the Findings of Research

The results of sociological research are reported in a variety of ways. The results of doctoral research in sociology are reported in *Dissertation Abstracts,* an index resource available in every major university library in the United States as well as other research libraries, such as the Library of Congress. In addition, much of the most important sociological research is summarized in article form and published by a variety of professional journals in sociology. Some of the more prominent publications are the *American Journal of Sociology,* the *American Sociological Review, Social Problems,* and the *Journal of Marriage and the Family.* In addition, the American Sociological Association and other regional sociological societies hold annual conventions where the results of research are presented as professional papers and discussed and critiqued at round table discussions and group forums.

The Impact on the State of Knowledge

With the completion of each scientific research cycle, a new page is added to the library of sociological knowledge. The results of some studies represent "blind alleys" that add nothing per se to what is known about a certain aspect of social behavior. Yet, they tell us where not to look next time and aid sociologists in narrowing down the possibilities in terms of getting at cause-and-effect relationships. Other studies are ground-breaking in significance, such as Durkheim's work on suicide and Goffman's research on "total institutions," as previously mentioned. They act as powerful beacons that point the way for others to follow. Most research efforts, however, add tiny increments of information in creating a grand mosaic of understanding about the human condition. In this sense, sociological research is truly cumulative, with those engaged in science today building on the legacy created by those who came before.

RESEARCH ISSUES AND TRENDS

As exciting and rewarding as sociological research is and can be, it carries with it some serious and sober responsibilities. Unlike the geologist who studies rocks, the chemist who works with chemical compounds, and others in the physical sciences, the sociologist (1) is a part of the subject matter he or she studies and (2) deals with human beings instead of physical matter. This means that special care must be taken to ensure objectivity in the research process and that certain safeguards are used to protect the rights and sensibilities of human research subjects.

Ethical Issues

Much has been said about the medical experiments conducted on Jewish prisoners in concentration camps by the Nazis during World War II. Yet on a much smaller scale, similar research has occurred in the United States. The U. S. Public Health Service between 1932 and 1972 conducted biomedical research on 400 black males with syphilis living in poverty in Alabama. The purpose of the study was to examine the long-term effects of the disease. During this forty- year period, the government provided these men (and 200 nonsyphilitic black males used as controls) with free "medical" treatment.

However, they were never told they had syphilis nor were they ever treated for it, even though penicillin had been available as an effective treatment since the 1940s. Approximately one-third of these men died of the dis-

ease while the study was in progress. This research was finally brought to light by the Alabama advisory committee to the U. S. Commission on Civil Rights, which characterized it as involving "violations of basic human rights" (*Los Angeles Times,* May 13, 1973; Part 1A, p. 6).

During the early 1960s, the U. S. Army budgeted over six million dollars to study conditions relating to social and political unrest in Latin American countries. Several sociologists, economists, and political scientists were employed to do much of this research which became known as Project Camelot. The strong implication given by the name "Camelot" was that the United States was trying to find ways of encouraging progress in certain South American countries without violence and possible human rights violations.

When it became obvious that the results of this research would be shared with military dictators like General Pinochet of Chile and used to quell dissension and unrest, a public outcry arose in Chile and other South American countries and among social scientists in the United States. The results of this furor led to a cancellation of the project by the U. S. government in 1965 (Horowitz, 1967; Sjoberg, 1967).

In the wake of "Camelot," a debate developed among many in the social science com-

"Tumbleweeds" drawing by Tom K. Ryan. © King Features Syndicate.

munity about the propriety of conducting certain types of research without specified safeguards. In 1968, a committee of the American Sociological Association developed a code of ethics to govern social research, which was formally adopted in 1971 and revised in 1980. Among its many provisions, which are ethically binding on all sociologists, are such requirements as maintaining the confidentiality of participants' identities by the researcher and honest and accurate reporting (American Sociological Association, 1968; 1980).

Even given the guidelines furnished by a code of ethics, sociological research can involve some delicate choices between the rights of individuals, the rights of society, and the need to know by the social scientist. The rights of individual privacy and anonymity must be acknowledged and protected. However, some forms of sociological research, such as experiments and participant observation studies, usually require some degree of deception on the part of the researcher. To do otherwise would invalidate the findings, because people would not act and interact naturally. In this regard, sociological researchers generally agree that any behavior carried out in public may be studied (even if those being studied do not like it) so long as the researcher maintains confidentiality by not revealing the identities of those being studied.

> Some of the richest material in the social sciences has been gathered by sociologists who were true participants in the group under study but who did not announce to other members that they were employing this opportunity to collect research data. . . . It would be absurd . . . to insist as a point of ethics that sociologists should always introduce themselves as investigators everywhere they go and should inform every person who figures in their thinking exactly what their research is about (Erikson, 1967, p. 368).

The Challenge of Scientific Sociology

To study human social behavior systematically and do it well is not an easy task. Sociologists as scientists must stay abreast of the latest developments in their fields of specialization and in sociology as a whole. They must also maintain their objectivity in working with human subjects, yet at the same time hold fast to a code of ethics through which the fundamental rights of those same research subjects are protected. Social scientists working for agencies and organizations as employees or consultants must also guard against the pressure to endorse blindly the self-serving positions or policies of such employers in how they plan their research, carry it out, and report the findings. The danger here is co-optation. The sociologist, more than anyone else, understands the power of organizations to shape behavior and, therefore, must strive to maintain the integrity of objective science.

Sociologists as researchers are often placed in the position of being "damned if they do and damned if they don't." Indeed, Robert K. Merton (1959, pp. xv–xvi) maintains that sociologists are often placed in a four-way bind. When their research shows that what many people think to be "obvious truth" is indeed supported by the evidence, they are seen by some as terrible bores who do little more than place fancy names on simple things that people already know about and understand. When the results of their investigations support an unpopular view, they are sometimes lambasted as heretics or troublemakers. When their studies prove that what was unlikely to be the case is indeed not true, they may be perceived as fools for questioning "common sense." And when their findings result in facts that appear to be unbelievable, they are denounced by some as charlatans whose aim it is to deceive.

In spite of all this, sociologists as scientists have no foreknowledge of what is true or untrue, and what is popular or unpopular is of little or no concern. Their task is to find out "what is" in an objective and systematic way and to disseminate this knowledge to others. This is their primary imperative or mission, which is accomplished basically through the process outlined in this chapter.

As a science, sociology consists of a never-ending series of research cycles in a variety of specialty fields. Through the seven steps of **P**roblem, **R**eview, **H**ypotheses, **D**esign, **O**bservations, **A**nalysis, and **R**eporting, each sociological study is completed. What we now know about human social behavior has come about through the completion of thousands of such cycles. Consequently, sociologists engaged in research today are standing on the shoulders of those who, through their research efforts, laid the foundation for what is now known. Those engaged in sociological investigation today will be the pathfinders who will take us into the twenty-first century.

The sociological pilgrimage is bound to involve traveling some rocky roads at times for those who sign on for the trip. However, the scenery and experiences along the way promise to be very exciting. And the destination—an increased understanding of the human condition—is the magnificent obsession of all who call themselves sociologists.

CHAPTER SUMMARY

1. Pure research and applied research represent the two basic forms of sociological inquiry. Pure research focuses on expanding the frontiers of knowledge concerning what is known about human social behavior. Applied research (policy research, evaluation research, and clinical sociology) involves studies aimed at applying sociological principles and knowledge to social issues, programs, and problems.

2. Sociological research is much like detective work and, in each case, involves the comple-

tion of seven basic steps in what is called the scientific research cycle. An effective way to remember these steps involves the use of the acronym PR-HD-OAR, which stands for problem, review, hypotheses, design, observations, analysis, and reporting.

3. Getting started with a sociological study involves the completion of the first three stages in the research cycle, namely the statement of the research problem, the review of the literature, and the statement of one or more hypotheses. The research problem (Step 1) usually is designed to test, extend, or refine an existing theory about some aspect of social behavior. The review of the literature (Step 2) is a thorough examination of previous research concerning the scientific theory to be tested. The development of the hypothesis (Step 3) involves a formal statement of the expected cause-and-effect relationship between two variables that can be tested. In some studies there may be several hypotheses.

4. In planning how a study will be done, it is important to develop a research design (Step 4). Of the several types used in sociological research, three of the most prevalent research designs are the survey (use of the questionnaire), the experiment (use of two matched groups), and field research (the study of certain forms of social behavior within their own settings). Among the various field research approaches is participant observation (involvement by the sociologist in the group being studied).

5. To conduct or implement a sociological study involves two key tasks, making observations and analyzing the findings. Making observations or gathering data (Step 5) consists essentially of implementing the study according to the specifics decided in the research design, such as administering the survey, conducting the experiment, or engaging in participant observation of the group or social activity under investigation. Once all observations have been made, then analysis of the findings (Step 6) can take place which, in sociology, normally involves the use of statistics.

6. The last step in the sociological research process involves reporting the results (Step 7). This is accomplished in a variety of ways including publication in scholarly sociological journals, the presenting of papers at sociological conferences, and the publication of summary findings in periodicals such as newspapers and magazines.

TERMS TO KNOW

applied research: the study of how sociological principles and knowledge might be applied to social issues, programs, and problems.

biased sample: a sample that lacks random selection and, in some cases, involves self-selection by participants (for example: straw polls, letters to the editor).

clinical sociology: an applied profession within sociology dedicated to helping people better cope with their social identities and social relations through the use of sociological principles.

content analysis: a research design in which the content of communication is studied to assess its impact on social attitudes and behavior.

control group: the group in an experiment not exposed to the independent variable.

cross-sectional study: a broad-based study that takes place over a brief period of time.

dependent variable: in science, the effect, or variable that research attempts to account for or explain.

evaluation research: a form of research that examines the consequences of various public policies by evaluating their degree of effectiveness or ineffectiveness.

experiment: a research design in which two matched groups of people are compared in terms of how they act in a specially designed social situation.

experimental group: the group in an experiment that is exposed to the independent variable.

field research: a research design in which certain forms of social behavior are studied within their natural settings.

Hawthorne effect: a temporary change in the behavior of people in a group due to the presence and influence of outsiders.

hypothesis: in science, a formal statement of an expected cause-and-effect relationship between two variables that can be tested.

independent variable: in science, the causal or influencing variable that affects to some extent the occurrence of another variable (the effect).

longitudinal study: a study focused on a single group of people over an extended period of time.

participant observation: a form of field research in which the investigator actually joins the group being studied in order to obtain an inside view of social behavior.

policy research: studies related to social issues and problems whose results may be used as a basis for the formation of public policy.

population: the total group of people with specific characteristics being studied.

PR-HD-OAR: an acronym useful in learning the seven steps of the scientific research cycle which are problem, review, hypotheses, design, observations, analysis, and reporting.

pure research: scientific investigation aimed at expanding the base of knowledge.

random sample: a sample chosen in such a way that every member of the population being studied has an equal chance of being included.

research design: a particular method used in making scientific observations.

review of the literature: a thorough examination of previous research concerning the scientific theory about to be tested.

sampling error: the degree to which characteristics of a sample do not represent those of the population from which it was drawn.

scientific research cycle: the process by which the seven steps in scientific research are completed in a circular or cyclical manner (just as the minute hand moves around the face of a watch in the course of an hour).

statistics: mathematical procedures that describe the characteristics of variables and explain or measure the relationships between them.

stratified random sample: a random sample chosen in such a way that certain characteristics of the population being studied are represented in accurate proportions.

survey: a research design that involves the use of questionnaires to gather information about people's attitudes and their social behavior.

variable: any social characteristic or form of social behavior that may differ in some regard or change.

SUGGESTED READINGS

Basic Research Methods in Social Science, 3rd ed. (Julian L. Simon and Paul Burstein; New York: Random House, 1985). A popular and well-written text on basic research methods in social science.

The Logic of Science in Sociology (Walter L. Wallace; Chicago: Aldine-Atherton, 1972). A classic treatment of the scientific method as applied to sociological research, particularly in Wallace's use of the research-cycle approach in explaining the research process.

The Practice of Social Research, 3rd ed. (Earl Babbie; Belmont, Calif.: Wadsworth, 1983). One of the best sources regarding the ''how tos'' of sociological research.

Research Methods in the Social Sciences, 3rd ed. (David Nachmias and Chava Nachmias; New York: St. Martin's Press, 1987). A valuable resource for any student of sociology regarding the nature of scientific investigation.

Part Two

Elements of Social Life

Chapter 3

Culture: A Way of Life

■ TERMS TO KNOW

acculturation
artifacts
assimilation
beliefs
counterculture
craze
cultural relativity
cultural universals
culture
culture shock
drive
ethnocentrism
fad

fashion
folkways
instinct
knowledge
language
laws
mores
norms
reflex
sanctions
subculture
symbols
technicways
values
xenocentrism

In some parts of the world, people worship cows. The homage paid to these animals in some countries even extends to politics and law. For example, a group of holy men in India staged a demonstration in 1966 before the Indian Parliament, involving 120,000 people, to lend support to the All Party Cow Protection Campaign Committee. In addition, a U. S. government official working in Nepal once killed a cow accidentally by striking it with his car. In that country—a neighbor to India—murder is a crime against cows as well as people. To avoid the diplomatic problems that surely would have followed the arrest of this unfortunate American, the Nepalese government ruled that "the cow had committed suicide" (Harris, 1987, p. 208).

During the 1970s, the Peace Corps began experiencing problems with their volunteers in the south African nation of Botswana. Among other things, these Americans were experiencing burnout and hostility toward the Botswana people. A social scientist sent to investigate the situation found that much of the problem resulted from different cultural perceptions of "appropriate" behavior between the Americans and the Botswana. For instance, each time an American would try to go sit alone or otherwise obtain some privacy, he or she would be quickly joined by one or more Botswana. This made the Americans angry, because of the high premium placed on privacy in American culture. The Botswana, however, believe that only witches and the insane wish to be alone, because of the social nature of human life. So every time they saw an American alone, they would rush to make social contact, to avoid breaching the rules of hospitality in their country (Schultz and Lavenda, 1987).

Each of these accounts serves to illustrate the arbitrary and ambiguous nature of human social behavior. The Americans and the British speak the same language, but drive on opposite sides of the road. Americans eat with their mouths closed in order to be polite; in India, people eat with their mouths open for the same reason. In cities throughout Mexico, it is common for adolescent girls to demonstrate friendship by holding hands as they walk together; in American society, similar behavior might be interpreted as homosexual in nature. In these and in hundreds of other ways, behavior—or the interpretation of similar behaviors—may vary from one society to another.

Such variability in our actions and perceptions is due in large part to the culture in which we live and the meaning and structure it provides to our lives. **Culture,** in the sociological sense, refers to the socially established patterns of perceiving and acting that one acquires as a member of society. A person's culture thus represents a way of life as furnished by the society in which he or she lives. This way of life is passed from parent to child and consists of many elements, including a means of symbolic communication called language, a particular set of beliefs about the world and one's place in it, a history or ethnic heritage, and a set of socially standardized rules to live by. Indeed, it is largely this blueprint for living that gives our lives meaning and substance.

For this reason, after having established a foundation in the first two chapters concerning what sociology is and how the sociological enterprise is conducted, we now begin our topical survey of the key areas of knowledge generated from the science of society. Central to the systematic study of social behavior is the concept of culture.

CULTURE: THE BASIS FOR HUMANITY

It is largely culture that separates human beings from the lower animals. "Human nature" is extremely variable because of the wide diversity of cultures in different parts of the world. Humans speak different languages, eat different foods, wear different clothes, and pray to different gods. The lower animals, by contrast, have a much more specific nature that is shaped to a large degree by inborn, biological factors.

The Nature of Lower Animals

Behavior in the lower animals is governed to a large extent by instincts. An **instinct** is a genetically determined imperative for complex behavior. The animal in possession of these mechanisms is biologically "programmed" to engage in a multitude of fairly complex behavior patterns which, depending on the species, might include mating, migrating with the seasons, food getting, building a nest or home, or caring for the young. These instincts are necessary in the lower animals since they have no culture to teach them how to survive.

Three criteria must be met before any specific form of behavior can be considered "instinctive." First, the behavior must be *unlearned.* That is to say, it must be inborn or genetically inherited. Second, it must be *universal.* It must be present in all members of a particular species in the same or similar form. Third, an instinct must manifest itself as a *complex* behavior pattern (DeFleur, D'Antonio, and DeFleur, 1981). In this sense, the behavior must possess both the characteristics of "drive arousal," which tells the animal there is a need to be satisfied, plus "tension release," through which the drive is satisfied. An instinct thus completes the cycle in satisfying a basic animal need whether it is food acquisition, procreation, or protection of the young.

The mechanism that triggers the instinctive response depends in large part on the complexity of the animal species. Ants and other insects, for example, appear fairly low on the complexity scale and thus tend to be "profoundly stupid," with most behaviors determined in large part by reflex and instinct. In these creatures, the trigger that invokes the instinctive response is inborn and largely automatic.

In the more complex mammals and lower primates, however, instinct is combined with learned behavior. In this sense, the launching of the instinctive response may require an environmental trigger as represented by learned behavior. Cheetahs reared in zoos and released into the wild as adults, for instance, must be exposed to environmental circumstances similar to those that would have occurred had they been reared in nature by their mothers. So, in order to provide the environmental trigger for the release of the predatory instinct, zoologists take a very hungry cheetah to the wild, place the animal in the presence of its natural prey (such as a herd of Grant's gazelles), and motivate it to run in the direction of these animals. This triggers the instinct to kill, and the cheetah responds accordingly.

The Nature of Humans

Compared to that of the lower animals, human behavior is largely free of instinctual control. In fact, according to available research, humans have no definite instincts. The human infant is virtually helpless at birth, is equipped with only a few reflexes, and would surely perish if not cared for by parents or other adults. By contrast, lower animal species often are able to achieve independence from their parents and become completely self-reliant within minutes or hours after birth. The salmon, for instance, never meets its parents, carries out its life cycle guided largely by instincts alone, and then, guided by an instinctive imperative, ultimately goes upriver to spawn and die. Humans, lacking such inborn mechanisms, must rely on culture to equip them with the strategies for survival.

Nonetheless, the term instinct has become one of the most misused terms in the English language. It is used by many in popular society as a catchall term to describe any behavior that cannot readily be explained otherwise. Therefore, some people claim to have instincts for baking bread or gardening, and others say that they can instinctively dance, play chess, or make love.

Early in the twentieth century, the anthro-pologist Franz Boas (1911) asserted that since *Homo sapiens* represented a single species, any genuine instincts would have to be universally present in all humans. In his research as well as that of scientists since his time, no universals that could be called human instincts have been found or agreed on by the scientific community. Thus, the so-called "maternal instinct" is contradicted by child abuse and child-killing parents, the "aggressive instinct" by pacifists, and the "survival instinct" by the many thousands who commit suicide each year.

Two behaviors often confused with instincts are reflexes and drives. Both are unlearned and universally present in all humans. However, they both fail to meet the criterion of complexity necessary to be regarded as an instinct.

A **reflex** is an automatic physical response to an external stimulus by the nervous system. The child whose hand is jerked back automatically after touching a hot stove is engaged in a reflex action, as is the person whose knee jerks when hit by a physician's rubber mallet during a medical exam. Reflexes are simple reactive responses for the most part. They serve mainly as protective mechanisms to avoid pain or injury.

A **drive** represents a physiological state in the form of internal tension which signals the individual that a particular need demands satisfaction. The drives for hunger and sex serve as notable examples. Both tend to manifest themselves in the form of tension, excitement, and discomfort. However, neither the hunger drive nor the sex drive tells the human being what to do next to complete the cycle. In lower animals, instincts for food acquisition or mating would take over. We humans must look to culture to provide the answers to how such drives can and should be satisfied.

In addition to the lack of definite instincts, human beings differ from the lower animals in several other ways. Humans have a *greater intellectual capacity* because of a brain that is more complex—with about ten billion nerve cells—than that of other species. This makes it possible to think both rationally and abstractly and to develop, among other things, the technology to overcome the limitations of the natural environment. The *upright posture* of humans frees the hands for grasping and manipulating physical objects. In addition, *sophisticated hands with opposable thumbs* allow people to grasp tools, to handle and manipulate a wide variety of objects with a fine dexterity. With this capability, our ancestors were able not only to construct weapons with which to kill animals for food and defend themselves, but to develop a wide variety of technologies in the form of sophisticated tools and machines. Finally, humans have *vocal chords of a refined nature.* This permits them to produce the thousands of words necessary for articulate speech. The use of symbolic language is essential to the social sharing of thoughts, feelings, and goals and the building of culture.

These characteristics, along with the lack of rigid instincts, allow humans a flexibility unique among Earth's many species. With such capabilities, humans have devised various cultures and social systems that have functioned to provide social order and stability as well as social change and progress.

Characteristics of Culture

First of all, culture is *learned* rather than instinctive or innate. Thus, a person is born *into* a culture instead of being born *with* one. Culture is a social invention created by people to lend order and predictability to their lives. It is acquired by the individual as a result of membership in a society. Largely because of the lack of biological imperatives for human behavior, societies throughout the world have very diverse cultures that often differ from one another in fundamental ways.

Second, culture is *socially shared.* Such cultural elements as beliefs, norms, values, sym-

Lower animals acquire food and engage in other complex behaviors largely through biological imperatives called instincts. Humans, by contrast, engage in such behaviors in ways learned from their particular culture. (*Left:* Pete Turner/Image Bank. *Center:* James R. Holland/Stock, Boston. *Right:* Copyright Steve Dunwell/Image Bank.)

bols, and means of communication are passed down from parents to children and are shared in general by people in the larger community and society. The process by which culture is passed from person to person is called *socialization,* the subject of Chapter 4 to follow. Through the transmission of culture to others made possible by socialization, people are able to live in relative harmony with one another.

Because it is passed from generation to generation, culture also is subject to change and is therefore *cumulative.* This characteristic is particularly apparent in modern societies like the United States that are affected by new technology and other developments that continue to alter the way we live. Recent innovations like electronic synthesizers and compact discs have changed our music and how we listen to it; microcomputers, the way we work; automated teller machines, the way we bank; and microwave ovens and fast foods, the manner in which we prepare and eat food. Many other developments in recent years have likewise changed the way we live, such as the disease AIDS and its impact on sexual behavior. Another example is the influence of Japanese productivity on American business. As a result of these and other influences, our culture is constantly changing, adapting to new conditions that arise in society. Think, for example, of the many changes that have occurred in American culture during the last century. We now drive cars rather than ride horses, our children attend modern schools rather than little one-room country schoolhouses, and we can now shop at home by phone for some items, ordered by numbers flashed on our television screens.

In addition, culture consists of *expected patterns of behavior.* For the most part, these patterns for living are socially agreed on and accepted by members of a society. They represent mainly the social rules we live by.

These rules are kept fairly uniform and stable by social pressures to conform and are made visible by group habits. Sociologists study these habitual forms of social behavior that make up much of the subject matter for the scientific study of culture.

Finally, because of the learned, socially shared patterns of behavior that comprise culture, the *satisfaction of basic human needs* is assured. Culture satisfies our needs by giving structure and predictability to our everyday lives. Most people acquire the means to feel relatively secure and comfortable in most social situations because their lives are patterned after the cultural habits of family, friends, community, and society. Take your day-to-day activities for example. Your life probably revolves around a continuous cycle of socially acquired habits focused on family, school, and work. Your daily routine probably begins in the morning when you rise from a particular side of a bed and ends when you crawl into the same side of the bed at night. Much of what you do in between involves a group of regular behavioral patterns, such as the likelihood that you sit in the same seat (by choice or assignment) each time your sociology class meets.

By contrast, most people feel quite anxious when everyday habits and routines are unexpectedly disrupted and they have their "cultural rugs" yanked out from under them. For example, most Americans over forty remember with vivid clarity much of what they did on November 22, 1963, the day President John F. Kennedy was assassinated. It was a day of much confusion for many Americans. To avoid various forms of confusion, anxiety, and mistakes, culture provides security for society members in hundreds of different ways by showing them just what to do in most social situations. Public school children throughout the country, for instance, are put through fire drills each year so they will have a pattern to follow in case of a real emergency.

Cultural Identification

From our exposure to society while growing up (socialization), we develop our own special view of the world and how we should relate to it. For most people, this cultural identification takes the form of **ethnocentrism,** the tendency to regard one's own culture as superior and other cultures as inferior. This form of cultural bias is common to all cultures. So, whether one is American, Italian, Nigerian, or any other nationality, there is a marked tendency to perceive one's own culture as best. In fact, many if not most people regard their culture as the only really important one and are largely oblivious to the different life-styles and perspectives of those who live in other parts of the world.

Ethnocentric frames of reference also affect how people perceive their relationships with different groups at various levels within their own society. For instance, many high school students exhibit school pride at pep rallies and ball games by cheering on the "best" team. Many people also claim that their neighborhood, town, state, or region is the best in the country. Some Texans, among the most ethnocentric of all Americans, place bumper stickers on their cars that say "Native Texan" and "Love New York? Take I-10 East." In similar fashion, some Southerners still identify with the Confederate flag as a symbol of Southern pride and refer to those from the North as "Yankees." In some of the hilly regions of rural Vermont, people who have not lived there for at least twenty years are sometimes called "flatlanders" and are not quite as acceptable as "long-timers," or those who are native born.

Used as a standard to evaluate social life, ethnocentrism can have both beneficial and disruptive consequences for the individual and so-

Ethnocentrism takes a variety of forms and occurs at all levels of society. (Copyright Joel Gordon, 1987.)

ciety. On the positive side, it often furnishes the individual with a sense of belonging or "connection" with his or her community or society, which promotes stability and happiness. It also fosters social cohesion and stability at the societal level by encouraging people to take pride in their cultural heritage and way of life. In times of peace, nationalistic loyalty often promotes the intense focus needed for a country to better compete in an international marketplace or, for that matter, the world of international politics and social policy. In war, ethnocentrism may take the form of patriotism so essential in sustaining the effort needed to vanquish a foe. During times of emergency and crisis like a natural disaster or economic depression, it can serve as the basis for social assistance and cooperation.

Ethnocentrism in some forms, however, can result in problems. Some individuals become so culture-bound and intolerant because of ethnocentrism that they develop *xenophobia,* a fear of cultures or life-styles different from their own. If taken to the extreme, ethnocentrism can result in conflict between two or more parties at various levels and even violence and a breakdown of social order. Within a society, conflict between groups can lead to discrimination and denied opportunity for smaller or weaker groups, as illustrated by the historical treatment accorded blacks and Native Americans in the United States. Likewise, the nationalistic bias of representatives of two countries in conflict over key issues can result in a cessation of diplomatic relations and, in some cases, even war.

The opposite of ethnocentrism is **xenocentrism,** a preference for the ways of a foreign culture or cultures and a rejection of part or all of one's native way of life (Wilson et al., 1976). For some people, this reverse ethnocentrism takes only mild forms which might include an attraction to the exotic or unfamiliar. Many middle-class and upper-class Amer-

icans, for instance, are drawn to foreign films and vacations as well as foreign consumer goods including cars and clothing because they seem more exclusive or distinctive. In both Europe and Japan, the more affluent likewise have a tendency to be attracted to the glamour of American television shows and music and often take vacations to see places like the Grand Canyon and Disney World. However, xenocentric orientations can become quite extreme, as evidenced by the hatred and rejection some members of ethnic and social minorities exhibit toward their own groups. In some cases, individuals will have such a strong desire to identify with or belong to the dominant group that, when placed in a position of responsibility in the larger society, will actively discriminate against their own people.

Cultural identification is also influenced by ancestral background and geographical mobility. In several European and Asian countries, for instance, most people have a similar ethnic heritage because their parents and ancestors have lived in the same city or village for many generations. Consequently, a country like Japan or West Germany referred to as a *homogeneous society.* By comparison, the United States is a *heterogeneous society* because it consists of people with diverse ethnic backgrounds who tend to be geographically mobile.

Heterogeneous societies are most likely to contain what sociologists call subcultures. A **subculture** represents the heritage and life-style of a particular group in society that, though in basic harmony with the dominant culture, has some distinctive characteristics of its own. Some subcultures are regional, including those in California, the Midwest, or the deep South, while others are occupational, as illustrated by physicians and college professors with their jargon and professional standards, or rodeo cowboys and rock musicians with their special modes of dress, lan-

Some young people referred to by many as "Hippies" represented a counterculture of the late 1960s and early 1970s. (Gregg Mancuso/ Stock, Boston.)

guage, and mannerisms. Some sociologists would also designate special subcultures by age or marital status, as illustrated by the adolescent subculture or the singles subculture. Others might identify specific subcultures by social class, or by hobbies like stamp collecting, hunting, or making quilts.

However, the most visible, multifaceted, and influential subcultures are those based on the ethnic heritage of their members. In the United States, these groups include Americans with African, Italian, Mexican, Greek, Chinese, and Native American backgrounds, to mention only a few. They tend to be distinguished by characteristics that include family structure, language patterns, religious beliefs, holiday observances, and other life patterns.

Although subcultures typically are in basic agreement with society in general, countercultures usually are in disagreement or opposition. A **counterculture** is a type of subculture that is in basic conflict with the dominant culture of a society (Robertson, 1974; Yinger, 1982). During the 1960s, many college youths essentially dropped out of mainstream society and subscribed to a "hang loose" ethic. These young people, generally called "hippies," practiced alternative lifestyles characterized by the taking of mind-altering drugs and permissive sexual practices. They were alienated against many of the underlying tenets of middle-class society, including the work ethic, deferred gratification, materialism, and individual responsibility (Suchman, 1968). Since this time, countercultures have typified the life-styles of such diverse groups as the Hare Krishna, the "Moonies" and other religious sects, some factions of the "Skin Heads," the Weathermen and other extremist groups, and the recent "punk" groups in Great Britain and the United States (Brake, 1985). Groups whose activities revolve around criminal activity, including delinquent gangs and drug rings, are also considered countercultures.

Culture Shock

When some of us are exposed to an unfamiliar cultural environment, it is not unusual to experience **culture shock**, a disorientation that occurs when one is placed in a cultural setting significantly different from one's own. Most Americans, for instance, are taught that certain body noises are inappropriate in a public place. Yet, in some Mid-Eastern countries, custom encourages a guest at dinner to

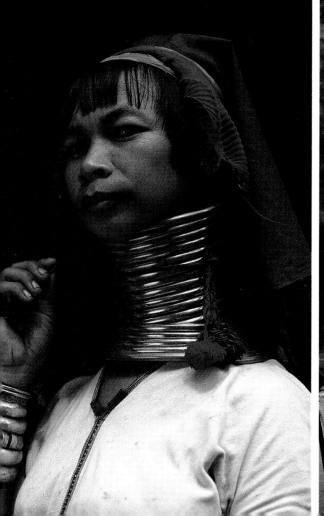

Standards of physical attractiveness vary from culture to culture.

The United States is a society of diverse subcultures.

give forth boisterous belches to show the host that the meal was fully enjoyed. When Americans travel in certain parts of Europe, they are often surprised, if not dismayed, by such things as body odor brought on by infrequent bathing, women who do not shave their legs and underarms, and topless or nude sunbathing at many parks and beaches. Visitors to the United States are likewise shocked at many American practices including (in the European view) the crass commercialism involved in littering the landscape with billboards and neon signs, and (for the Japanese) the cruel and inhuman practice of placing the elderly in nursing homes.

In a pluralistic society like the United States, a citizen can experience culture shock within the borders of his or her own country. Those from Northeastern cities including New York and Washington, D.C., who relocate to cities like Atlanta and San Antonio, often must adjust to a much slower pace of life and people who are "laid back" and much less harried. Similarly, those accustomed to the friendly, slow-paced environment of a quiet village in a rural area can find the anonymity of urban life, coupled with the hustle and bustle of rush hour traffic on the freeway, very unsettling.

It is also possible for the trained social scientist to experience culture shock when exposed to a culture drastically different from his or her own. Anthropologist Napoleon Chagnon (1983), after receiving his research training, decided to do a participant observation study of a South American tribal group called the Yanomamo. These Indians live in the rain forests of Brazil and are extremely

Most Americans would experience culture shock if exposed to a cultural perspective regarding the role of women such as that in Iran. (Jean Gaumy/ Magnum.)

fierce and warlike. They regularly raid other tribes to steal women and often have the same done to them. The men proudly wear their battle scars, which are often hideous, as badges of masculinity. Because they rarely bathe, they sometimes can be detected before they are seen in the thick jungle. In addition, they make a fermented soup from bananas which they crush with their bare feet in large vats and offer to visitors as a sign of friendship.

When the anthropologist first met the Yanomamo, a dozen men greeted him with drawn arrows. They had green tobacco stuck behind their lower lips and large amounts of green mucous hanging from their noses, the product of a green hallucinogenic powder that they regularly ingested by sniffing. Chagnon (1983) found all of this quite repugnant and reports that he

> . . . pondered the wisdom of having decided to spend a year and a half with this tribe before I had even seen what they were like. I am not ashamed to admit that had there been a diplomatic way out, I would have ended my fieldwork then and there. I did not look forward to the next day when I would be left alone with the Indians. I did not speak a word of their language, and they were decidedly different from what I had imagined them to be. The whole situation was depressing, and I wondered why I had ever decided to switch from civil engineering to anthropology in the first place (p. 10).

Cultural Relativity

Early explorers and missionaries from the 1500s through the 1800s gave us the first modern descriptions of simple, nonliterate societies. Limited by the cultural blinders of their ethnocentrism, they saw the cultures of these people as barbaric, uncivilized, and heathen. Indeed, even the highly trained social scientist today, as evidenced by the previous description of culture shock experienced by Chagnon, is hard pressed to remain objective when faced with a culture drastically different from his or her own.

Nonetheless, anthropologists and sociologists today make every effort to put into practice **cultural relativity,** the principle that requires each culture to be seen and understood in its own context apart from a biased comparison with others. Taken out of its cultural context, any behavior can seem strange or unacceptable to the outsider, as evidenced by Chagnon's reaction to the chest-pounding duels practiced by the Yanomamo. A visitor to the United States or Canada, however, might find the body-punishing contests carried out by football and ice hockey players to be equally strange and unsettling.

Social scientists have established that there are no universally agreed-upon standards for morality, religion, justice, beauty, art, or most anything else. Instead, each society develops its own cultural adaptation necessary for survival and prosperity regardless of how distasteful it may appear to outsiders. Sexual expression provides one example of cultural variability. Tibetan monks remain celibate for life, while the machismo orientation in some Latin American countries encourages the compulsive seduction of women. Among the Nayar of India, adolescent girls are encouraged to take lovers and later, as adults, "visiting husbands." By comparison, Sudanese girls in West Africa undergo surgical amputation of the clitoris in an attempt by their culture to prevent sexual relations before marriage (Saxton, 1972). Some of these practices might seem strange or even barbaric to most Americans, but sociologists and anthropologists attempt to understand them within their respective cultural contexts.

Despite tremendous variations in cultures, there are some general elements found in all societies. These are called **cultural universals,** patterns and practices common to all cultures. Every culture, for instance, has one or more specific forms of religion, although religion varies greatly in different parts of the world. Likewise, all societies prohibit murder, although what constitutes unjustified killing differs greatly from culture to culture. In fact, the list of cultural universals is quite long. It includes the following practices: athletics, body decoration, cooking, courtship, dancing, division of labor, family, folklore, funerals, games, incest taboos, medicine, music, sexual restrictions, and tool-making (Murdock, 1945).

ELEMENTS OF CULTURE

As portrayed in Figure 3-1, the culture of any society is divided into four basic elements: (1) cognitive culture, (2) normative culture, (3) material culture, and (4) language, which

Figure 3-1   **The Four Major Elements of Culture**

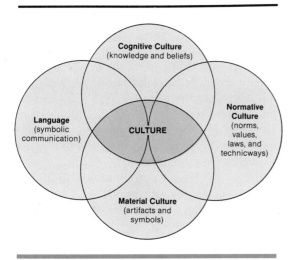

Culture is comprised of four overlapping elements. Together they form the basic social support system which gives our lives order, security, and some predictability.

contains aspects of the other three. Together, they represent the building blocks that constitute the patterns for living we use to survive successfully and prosper in society.

Cognitive Culture

Cognitive culture refers to the ways in which a culture defines what is real or what exists. One form of cognitive culture is **knowledge,** propositions about reality that can be scientifically supported. Knowledge (or the state of scientific theory) is based on demonstrated facts that have been objectively gathered and empirically demonstrated. As such, it takes several forms. These range from *pure knowledge* (information for its own sake) generated out of scientific research to *practical knowledge* (technology) aimed at improving the quality of life in such areas as horticulture, medicine, and industry.

Beliefs represent the other basic form of cognitive culture. They are represented by propositions about reality that either are not based on scientific evidence or cannot be demonstrated through scientific means. Within the United States, beliefs that are not based on scientific evidence are often held by people who tend to be poorly educated or who appear to have an anti-intellectual bias. Through their beliefs, they sometimes seem to be saying, ''Don't confuse me with the facts. I believe this way.'' Examples include the notion of members of the Flat Earth Society that our planet is flat and the belief of thousands of Americans that manned flights to the moon have never occurred.

The other type of belief—namely, propositions about reality that cannot be demonstrated or have not been verified (so far) through scientific means—are also diverse. Those of this type include the other-worldly aspects of religion, such as the concepts of heaven, hell, and reincarnation, and a multitude of other beliefs including those relating to UFOs and visits from alien life-forms, ghosts or poltergeists, and mythical creatures such as unicorns, the Loch Ness monster, and Big Foot.

When a group of beliefs becomes strongly held, an ideology may form. An *ideology* is a set of ideas aimed at promoting the interests of a particular segment of society. In *The German Ideology* (1846), Karl Marx and Friedrich Engels argued that the ideology of the ruling class—its basic set of social, political, religious, and economic ideas—was used to underpin existing social policy and maintain the status quo. In their view, it operated mainly to reinforce and perpetuate the existing class structure. Therefore, they argued, the ideology of the ruling class mandated for all what behavior was seen as lawful or unlawful, moral or immoral, and otherwise acceptable or unacceptable.

Modern sociologists, particularly conflict theorists, view this concept from a much broader perspective. The various classes and segments of society are seen to have their own ideologies aimed at promoting their interests. This is particularly evident in a pluralistic society like the United States that is comprised of many interest groups. Today, for example, there are conservative versus liberal ideologies in politics, Catholic versus Protestant ideologies regarding religion, and various other forms of ideology related to class, race and ethnicity, sex roles, and other social characteristics and issues.

Normative Culture

Another important cultural element is normative culture, which many sociologists consider to be the most important in maintaining social order and stability. *Normative culture* consists of socially agreed-upon standards for thinking, feeling, and acting in society. These standards include norms, values, laws, and technicways.

Norms. Much of the foundation for normative culture lies in the concept of **norms,** cultural rules that specify appropriate and inappropriate behavior. There are literally thousands of norms that comprise the standards we are expected to live by. Some are explicit while others are implied. Some are seen as very important and are strongly reinforced by a formal system of rewards and punishments, while others seem almost trivial by comparison and are generally followed but not taken seriously. Some apply to everyone, while others guide the behavior of only a few. Taken together, they constitute much of the blueprint for survival that is culture and, therefore, furnish each of us with a fairly detailed map for negotiating our journey through life.

Among the most important of norms are **mores.** These are norms with a compelling moral connotation whose violators meet with general condemnation and sometimes severe punishment. As children, we are taught mores as moral imperatives that specify both what must be done in many circumstances and, likewise, what is forbidden. These notions of right and wrong later become internalized in us as our most cherished, if not sacredly held, values. Consequently, most of us would find it repugnant to kill and eat the family dog, not simply because of its impracticality in a society full of food or the threat of legal punishment, but because mores in American culture have elevated the dog to the position of family member. Therefore, many if not most of us would be emotionally incapable of doing such a thing. By contrast, in portions of China where different mores are practiced, dogs are considered a delicacy and are often raised for food. Indeed, mores are often structured in an opposite manner in different cultures. For instance, American women often bare their legs but must cover their breasts, while Balinese women must hide their legs, but are free to expose their breasts (Stevens, 1970).

Folkways are broad-based norms in the forms of customs and social conventions that, when violated, carry with them only mild punishment, if any. They hold little or no moral connotation but instead represent the habitual or customary ways in which things are done. For instance, if you traded your car for a bicycle, gave up meat to become a vegetarian, and quit watching television, you would be violating several American folkways. Although your friends and neighbors might see you as a little strange or eccentric, you would not be the subject of general condemnation or severe punishment. Some folkways, however, do carry a slight "ought to" connotation, with some pressure to conform along with the likelihood of mild but emotionally significant punishment. If, for instance, you forgot the birthday of a parent, spouse, or child or suddenly decided on the day before Thanksgiving or another important holiday not to celebrate it, the consequences might be emotionally hurtful for others and for you if there was not an acceptable explanation. Folkways are the most pervasive form of norms and cover practically everything we do, from standards of social etiquette and personal hygiene to compliance with community standards and observance of cultural traditions and holidays.

Some of the most interesting types of folkways—fads, crazes, and fashions—are those limited to particular time frames and certain groups of people within a culture. These folkways are particularly important in urban high-technology cultures like the United States because they provide insights into how people form and adapt to customs in light of rapid cultural change.

A **fad** is a folkway popular for only a brief period of time among a limited group of people in a society. Recent fads in American culture have included Davy Crockett coonskin caps and hula hoops for children in the 1950s, "streaking" and disco dancing for college-aged youth in the 1970s, and "mall walking" for fitness and hot tubs for middle-class people over fifty in the 1980s. These norms usually run their course within a few weeks to several months, although occasionally they may last longer and become fashionable.

A **craze** is a fad that becomes obsessive for a brief period of time among a limited segment of society. Like most fads, crazes take a variety of forms. During the twentieth century, they have varied from get-rich-quick schemes like the Florida land boom in the 1920s to the CB radio craze of the 1970s and the video games craze of the late 1970s and early 1980s. Some crazes even focus on the hero worship of a cult personality, for example, those associated with Frank Sinatra during the 1940s, Marilyn Monroe and Elvis Presley in the 1950s, and the Michael Jackson phenomenon among preteens and young adolescents during the 1980s.

A **fashion** is a folkway more durable than a fad and may gain widespread acceptance among a large proportion of society for a fairly substantial period of time. Blue jeans, traditionally worn by the working class a few decades ago, have become fashionable in recent years for most of society. The six-passenger, domestically produced automobile popular a few years ago has been exchanged for today's fuel-efficient, four- or five-passenger car that is often manufactured in a foreign country. This particular change in fashion has been brought about partially by higher gasoline prices, a smaller American family, and higher production costs.

Ceremonial or ritualistic folkways such as rules of deference and rules of demeanor are also important in that they tell us mainly how to act rather than why we should do so. These two types of norms are constantly with us as forms of handed-down tradition and appear in every interaction we have with others (Goffman, 1967).

Rules of deference specify how and under

what conditions people may show respect for the rights and sensibilities of one another. Children and young people, by addressing adults as "sir" and "madam" (now the shortened "ma'am"), show respect for their age and social position. An employer, by deferring to the wish of an employee to be excused from work to attend the funeral of a close relative, demonstrates respect for the feelings of another to a degree which, under normal circumstances, would not be necessary. According to Erving Goffman, the ceremonial and pervasive nature of rules of deference provides each of us with constant opportunities to demonstrate respect for others in socially approved ways. We attempt to treat people with respect and expect to be treated accordingly. Consequently, the practice of these norms becomes almost a sacred obligation in that it acts to confirm the moral code each of us lives by, as well as that of our culture.

Rules of demeanor specify the socially approved ways of presenting oneself in a social situation in terms of such things as carriage, dress, and language. Regarding carriage and dress, it would be totally inappropriate for a person to dance into a business meeting wearing only a swimsuit. However, it would also be inappropriate to attend a pool party at a friend's house in a business suit. In addition, the "proper" attire at an interview will not, in and of itself, guarantee applicants a position, but inappropriate dress will automatically ruin their chances in most cases.

The proper use of language in a variety of circumstances is also socially specified. Those in professional occupations in the United States are expected to use "professional English" with proper subject and verb agreement, professional jargon when appropriate, and formal language as opposed to slang or colloquial expressions. Indeed, the manner in which a person uses language causes his or her social class background to be instantly rec-

ognizable in many if not most cases. Profanity and coarse language are also socially unacceptable in many situations. A professional teaching a sex education class would almost never use common but often derogatory sexual terms, but would opt for the more neutral and precise professional terms instead. In these and countless other ways, our demeanor in face-to-face encounters with others reflects the degree to which we are seen as normal and acceptable or abnormal and unacceptable to others in our culture.

Values. The norms of any culture are often a reflection of the values held by its members. In this sense, **values** represent the standards used by people to evaluate the relative desirability and worth of practically everything in their lives and in the society around them. This includes people, objects, ideas, acts, and feelings. Values occur at all levels of culture and thus are held by individuals, groups, and even whole societies. They define for us what is good and bad, moral and immoral, artful and in poor taste, beautiful and ugly, worthwhile and worthless.

Values, however, differ from norms in three fundamental ways. First, they are very general and abstract, while norms are specific and concrete. For instance, we may value the general concepts of marriage and freedom, but norms specify the concrete conditions under which both take place. In addition, values can be held by one person while norms cannot. Values reflect individual feelings; norms are social rules for behavior. Finally, values in and of themselves cannot be rewarded or punished, whereas norms include a system of sanctions. The way one thinks or feels (one's values) is internal and cannot be sanctioned one way or another. However, when values become transferred into behavior, this action, like any other behavior, is subject to the rewards and punishments attached to the norms one is expected to live by.

Because the United States is a heterogeneous society with a large number of subcultures, it is somewhat difficult to identify in specific terms an American value system. The fact is, some subcultures hold certain values while others have different priorities. Mexican Americans place a high premium on family cohesion, and Vietnamese Americans on the work ethic. However, both of these traditional value orientations have declined in American society as a whole during the last half century. This condition of cultural pluralism is further complicated by rapid cultural change brought about, in significant part, by changes in social and economic conditions and technology. Consequently, value orientations regarding the roles of women and minorities, consumer behavior, sexual practices, the size of families, recreation, and many other things have experienced significant change in recent decades.

Nonetheless, sociologist Robin Williams (1970) has identified several general value orientations in American culture that remain prevalent today. They include orientations toward achievement and success, activity and work, humanitarianism, practicality, material comfort, equality, freedom, democracy, and individuality.

Laws. Officially recorded norms formulated and enforced by government are **laws.** While other norms vary in terms of the proportion of people in a society to which they apply, everyone is obligated to obey laws. Most are codified mores which act to reinforce and protect the maintenance of social order. Those who choose not to conform are subject to a penalty which, for minor offenses, may be only a traffic fine or a court judgment in a civil suit. In some extreme cases, however, punishment may take the form of imprisonment or even execution. Most people conform to laws simply by knowing what they are. Others who might be tempted to deviate are at times deterred by the threat of legal punishment.

Sometimes laws correspond closely to norms regarded as important in the larger culture. In other cases, they reflect the political power of certain segments of society to have their agendas officially formulated as public policy for all to follow. Although the 55-mile-per-hour federal speed limit passed during the 1970s contributed to the reduction of the number of highway deaths, it was highly unpopular and largely ignored by many Americans during the first few years it was in effect. The felony statutes mandating harsh prison terms for possession of small amounts of marijuana were equally unpopular during the same period when at least twenty-five to thirty million Americans were using the drug recreationally. This resulted in the laws being changed so that possession of small amounts of this drug constituted a misdemeanor rather than a felony.

In addition to law representing a mechanism of social control, it also acts as a vehicle for social reform. When laws become outmoded and no longer reflect the mores of society, people in the United States have the right to sue, and the courts rule on whether or not a law is constitutional. In this manner, laws that are no longer in accord with the dominant mores are changed or abolished. During the 1960s, for instance, the U. S. Supreme Court struck down miscegenation laws, which forbade interracial marriage, as unconstitutional. In similar fashion, the rulings by the high court established the legal right to abortion during the 1970s. Legislative bodies can also write new laws that correspond to changing conditions, as illustrated by the Civil Rights Act of 1964 passed by Congress.

Technicways. A special category of norms important to survival and prosperity in high-technology societies is represented by **technicways.** These are rules for carrying out skills or habits associated with the use of technology (Hoult, 1969). Think of the culture shock a Yanomamo tribesman would face if he came to the United States and had to learn to drive a car and successfully master the rules of the road. Yet most of us are exposed to the technical aspects of driving gradually in our culture and come to take it for granted. In like manner, we acquire the skills and habits associated with microwave ovens, videocassette players, personal computers, and a myriad of other things.

In addition, some technicways we acquire are related specifically to our particular location in our culture. Traditionally, women have known more about grocery shopping, cooking, making beds, and ironing clothes than men, though changes in American culture during the last twenty years have made these skills much less sex-specific than before. Many technicways are also associated with specific occupations, such as the ability to use a crane by a heavy equipment operator or a heart-lung machine by a specially trained nurse. Others we acquire through participation in a hobby or avocation; for instance, some hunters reload their own ammunition and some antique collectors refinish their own furniture.

Material Culture

Another key cultural element is *material culture*, which consists of cultural aspects that, for the most part, are physical and tangible in form. The two basic types of material culture are artifacts and symbols.

Artifacts. Physical objects that represent a specific culture are **artifacts.** Archaeologists study the remnants of artifacts in trying to piece together the characteristics of an ancient culture. If you were to go to a museum to see an exhibit of artifacts from colonial America during the 1600s and 1700s, you would probably notice things like floor-length dresses, plows, axes, butter churns, candle molds, and spinning wheels, which would tell you a great deal about the way people lived during that time.

Suppose ten thousand years from now archaeologists are sifting through the remains of American culture left from the last two decades of the twentieth century. What do you think they would find, and how would they interpret these artifacts? They might discover, for example, huge circular structures with seating capacity for tens of thousands of people with a small rectangle of earth in the center. At first they might think that these were huge cathedrals, houses of worship where people paid homage to their god or gods. Then they would realize that they had found a huge sports stadium or the remnants of one. They might also find thousands of huge golden arches and eventually arrive at an understanding of the later twentieth-century phenomenon of "fast food."

Obviously, material things have no objective meaning based solely on their physical characteristics, but must be understood chiefly in terms of their cultural settings and how they were or are used. To Americans, a railroad car is an artifact that is used to transport people and freight from one place to another. However, among impoverished Indians in North Central Mexico, abandoned rail cars are used as homes.

Symbols. **Symbols** are acts or objects that have a special meaning within a specific culture. Many symbols are also artifacts, in that they have tangible properties and have meaning within a specific cultural context. However, what separates a symbol from an artifact is its ability to stir emotions or communicate a special meaning. Take a country's flag for example. Its presence has the ability to stir strong emotions of love, pride, patriotism—and even hatred if it is the flag of an acknowledged enemy. The flag is used in various rituals, and certain norms specify when it is to be raised or lowered, how it is to be handled physically, and how it is to be accorded respect. This expresses the special meaning attached to a cultural symbol that, physically, is no more than a rectangle of bright-colored cloth (Turner, 1967).

Many symbols have special meaning in American culture. They include the bald eagle as the national bird, the Statue of Liberty, the Liberty Bell in Philadelphia, and numerous other patriotic symbols. The wedding ring and the cross, too, evoke strong emotions. Symbols may also have commercial meaning, such as logos for television networks or for such brand-name consumer goods as soft drinks, automobiles, and designer clothes. Clothing itself is often symbolic of occupations, as evidenced by uniforms worn by police officers, nurses, and postal workers. Clothing may also symbolize social class, particularly when one looks at extremes like the society matron in her mink coat compared to the "bag lady" in her ragged attire. Additionally, symbols often take nonmaterial form such as gestures or "body language" that indicates saying hello and good-bye, flirting, or even signifying insults.

Language

Anyone who has traveled in a foreign country knows how difficult it is to function in a culture where a different tongue is spoken. Indeed, language is "the storehouse of culture" (Harroff, 1962) and represents for each of us the primary means through which we receive, understand, and pass on our way of life to others. In this sense, **language** is a learned system of symbolic communication that fur-

"Dressing up" is one of the symbolic ways in which people perceive their location in society and project themselves to others. (*Left:* Carl Purcell/Words & Pictures. *Center:* Copyright G. Colliva/The Image Bank. *Right:* Sygma.)

nishes the framework for the sharing of meaning and culture with others. Without understanding the language of a culture, it is not possible to participate in it in a meaningful way (Fishman, 1985).

Humans are unique in the animal kingdom because, unlike all other species, they use language, which furnishes them with a history and a means of passing on their thoughts and experiences to others after they die. In preliterate societies, culture is passed on through oral tradition. Societies with greater material technology are also able to make use of the written word and electronic media which allow thoughts and feelings to be permanently recorded for posterity.

In addition to acting as the primary channel through which culture is transmitted, language serves several other functions. First, it acts as the main vehicle of thought. We think in symbolic terms using the words furnished us by our culture. If reared in a Spanish-speaking culture, we think in Spanish. If taught English as a child, it furnishes the primary structure for our thoughts. Second, language allows us to transcend the world of concrete experiences. By talking to a person about a place they visited or by reading about an event of a hundred years ago in a book, we can transcend space and time and experience these things vicariously. In addition, language allows us to assign meaning to abstract or nebulous ideas or concepts. Consequently, we are able to conceptualize our feelings about love, hate, beauty, God, and other intangibles.

Although language is liberating in many respects, it can also be limiting, because it restricts the manner in which we view reality. In addressing this issue, the linguist Edward Sapir (1929) said that "the worlds in which different societies live are distinct worlds, not merely the same world with different labels attached." Some languages stress the masculine or feminine genders, showing a bias in the culture as illustrated by the masculine bias

in traditional English up until about twenty years ago. Other languages, in how they are used, reflect additional concerns and themes prevalent in given cultures. For example, the late Margaret Mead (1971), in her research on the Arapesh of New Guinea, found that they counted in terms of dogs probably because dogs have four legs. Thus, the number five was expressed as "dog and one," eight was "two dog," and twenty-four was "two dog, two dog, two dog."

The perspective that language structures the way people in different cultures think and perceive reality was developed by Edward Sapir and Benjamin Whorf and is often referred to as the *Sapir-Whorf hypothesis.* Cross-cultural examples are abundant. While English-speaking people are very time conscious, see time in a linear fashion of past, present, and future, and have numerous time concepts in their language, the Hopi have no words in their language for time or concepts related to time such as days, months, or years. Everything in their view has "become" or is "becoming." Americans generally have only one word for "snow." Eskimos, by contrast, have between twenty and thirty different terms for snow because weather conditions are important in their world. Whether language strictly determines how we see reality as Sapir and Whorf contended or basically reflects existing realities of the larger culture, as some argue (Eastman, 1975), is a matter of debate. However, one thing is clear. Language as taught to the inhabitants of any society determines in large part how they conceptualize reality and then act on such conceptions.

CONFORMITY AND SOCIAL ORDER

So far, you have learned basically what culture is, why humans alone have a definite way of life that varies from society to society, and how the basic elements of culture are structured. Now we turn to an examination of how certain mechanisms of social control act to maintain cultural conformity and social order and how cultures change.

The Need for Social Control

In ancient Babylonia over four thousand years ago, its ruler, Hammurabi, developed a system of law called the Code of Hammurabi. This code consisted of 282 laws which the king required be written on huge tablets and placed in the center of the city for all to see. The purpose of these laws, as stated in the code's prologue, was "to cause justice to prevail in the land . . . and to further the welfare of the people." These laws were comprehensive and covered the spectrum of social issues from political and military affairs to social relations with one's family and neighbors (Browne, 1946). In addition, each law contained prescribed punishments for its violation.

Ever since the time of Hammurabi, a rationalistic tradition has emerged in many cultures which has recognized the need for social control over human behavior rather than a dependence on divine intervention to control behavior. The promise of otherworldly pleasure or pain in the afterlife was found to have little or no impact on the behavior of many people whose lives were guided by the "here and now" rather than the distant future. What was needed was a culturally designed and enforced system of social control aimed at maintaining conformity to the dominant norms of society.

Among the first scholars to inquire systematically into the origins of systems of social control and the complex issue of conformity were the social contract theorists of the seventeenth and eighteenth centuries. The English philosopher Thomas Hobbes (1588–1679) was an early proponent of the *social contract* idea. In *Leviathan*, Hobbes (1651/1881) attempted to explain the origins of both society and government. He asserted that

early humans lived in nature and pursued their selfish desires as best they could. This ultimately led to conflict and chaos and a war of "all against all." In order to ensure survival, peaceful coexistence, and social order, people entered into a social contract with one another in which they agreed to give up some freedom in order to live under a system of enforced social rules.

The social contract school continued to be popular during the eighteenth century and had several European exponents, such as John Locke (1632–1704) and Jean-Jacques Rousseau (1712–1778). Both argued that the people of any society, when faced by authoritarian rule that usurped their "inalienable rights" and ceased to address their needs, had a right to overthrow this type of government and form a new contract that was more equitable (Locke, 1690; Rousseau, 1762). Locke maintained that governments had a sacred trust to guarantee and protect the freedoms of their people. Whenever a government violated this trust, the people had a right to set it aside. Thomas Jefferson, the primary author of the Declaration of Independence, was deeply influenced by Locke. Therefore, the work of John Locke formed much of the ideological basis for the American Revolution, as may be seen in this brief excerpt from the Declaration:

> We hold these truths to be self-evident, that all men are created equal, that they are endowed by their Creator with certain inalienable rights, that among these are life, liberty, and the pursuit of happiness. That to secure these rights, governments are instituted among men, deriving their just powers from the consent of the governed. . . . That whenever any form of government becomes destructive of these ends, it is the right of the people to alter or abolish it and to institute new government, laying its foundation on such principles and organizing its power in such form as to them shall seem most likely to effect their safety and happiness.

The social contract idea represented an important benchmark in the development of social thought pertaining to the nature of social order and how it should be maintained. As such, it represented a rational explanation for the origin of society and government that provided many useful insights. However, its basic propositions concerning people "wandering around alone in nature" and "deciding suddenly on forming a comprehensive social contract" are largely unsupported by modern science and are dismissed as myth. Humans have always been social creatures, and mechanisms for social control have evolved gradually in step with general cultural evolution. Nonetheless, the social contract theorists were correct in regard to one fundamental issue. Effective mechanisms for social control must be put into place in every culture to ensure social order and stability.

Mechanisms for Social Control

Social control in any culture is maintained primarily through the application of a system of **sanctions.** These are socially recognized and enforced rewards and punishments that are applied to conforming and nonconforming behavior. Sanctions may be positive or negative, informal or formal. In addition, they are usually flexible in that the norms they relate to prescribe a certain *range of tolerance* before sanctions are invoked. For instance, if a child strays momentarily from expected behavior, but then returns to conformity after acknowledging a look of disapproval on the face of a parent, no application of a sanction will be necessary in most cases. In like manner, motorists are usually given a leeway of five miles per hour before being ticketed for speeding. The range of tolerance varies from situation to situation and from one group or culture to another. College students, for example, are treated with more tolerance by their professors than high school students by their teachers in terms of personal freedom of action (they are adults), but generally with less tolerance regarding work assignment deadlines and other academic responsibilities.

Positive sanctions are rewards given for compliance with norms. Since the most effective form of social control involves voluntary conformity, most people will conform if provided a set of positive rewards that are meaningful for them. In small rural societies and in our relations with family, friends, and co-workers, *informal positive sanctions* usually are sufficient to reinforce conformity. Informal sanctions may range from a smile or nod of approval to a declaration of support and appreciation or even physical affection. Informal positive sanctions are particularly important when given to or received from a close family member, because of the emotional bond present and the wish to be appreciated by a loved one. In school and career settings and in the larger society, *formal positive sanctions* are also very necessary in motivating people to conform and achieve. They too take several forms and occur in various degrees. For example, a person may receive a raise or promotion at work, earn an "A" or make the dean's list in school, or receive a formal award or honor from his or her profession, community, or nation.

Negative sanctions are punishments given for violation of norms. They usually indicate incomplete or inadequate socialization and, like positive sanctions, take both informal and formal forms. *Informal negative sanctions* are often applied to children who are learning how to become successful social beings. However, some parents overuse them and fail to understand that a balance of rewards and punishments would be more effective. As adults, most of us have a large variety of informal negative punishments we can apply to others, just as we do with informal rewards. We can frown, scowl, be sarcastic or critical, voice displeasure or anger, ridicule and belittle, give the "silent treatment," and even slam doors or make someone sleep on the couch. These types of sanctions are often quite effective because of the emotional bond between the parties and because it is emotionally painful when we displease or upset our friends and loved ones. Sometimes, however, negative sanctions must be applied formally. This usually occurs in organizations and in the relationships of people with the larger community and society. *Formal negative sanctions* range from official reprimands, demotion, dismissal from a job or failing marks at school, to arrest and imprisonment in extreme cases for violations of criminal law.

HOW CULTURES CHANGE

Cultures do not exist in a vacuum. Instead, they are in a constant state of evolution and adaptation brought about by a variety of different factors. Three of the most fundamental causes of cultural change are technology, acculturation, and assimilation. Together they help to explain why many cultures today, the United States included, are so different in many aspects from the way they were a few decades ago.

The Role of Technology

In 1922, sociologist William F. Ogburn first stated his cultural lag hypothesis. According to Ogburn, *cultural lag* is a condition in which material culture (technology) changes more rapidly than normative or adaptive culture, causing a period of strain between the two. He asserted that material culture as represented by technology tends to change first. The first automobiles, for example, were called "horseless carriages" and, as they became mass produced, the engines were placed in front where the horse had been in relation to the wagon or buggy. To further illustrate that people's social perceptions were still rooted in the "horse and buggy" era, the engine's capacity to produce energy was called horsepower. It took decades before adaptive culture as represent-ed by norms, values, laws, and technicways could catch up or adapt in terms of highway systems, auto insurance, and repair facilities.

Emerging technology continues to change the way we live, particularly in "high-tech" societies like the United States. During the 1960s, heart bypass surgery and other innovations in medical technology were giving middle-aged and elderly people suffering from a variety of afflictions a new and more vigorous life as well as increased life expectancy. Today the computer revolution and emerging superconductor technology promise to have as great an impact on culture during the next century as the automobile and television have had during this one.

Acculturation

Acculturation involves cultural change brought about through direct contact of two cultures (or more) in which certain traits of one are borrowed by the other. Sometimes this cultural borrowing is forced on a conquered society by a conquering one. When this occurs, the primary intent by the stronger society is to subdue the subordinate one by weakening or destroying its culture.

In most cases, however, acculturation is voluntary and represents an attempt by one culture to copy or emulate another. Examples abound. When American GIs returned from World War II, those who served in Italy told their girlfriends and wives about this wonderful Italian food called "pizza" and tried to get them to duplicate it. This culture contact by American soldiers created a demand for pizza that ultimately lead to its current popularity.

During the late 1950s and early 1960s, four young men from Liverpool, England, named John, Paul, George, and Ringo became influenced by the rock music of American entertainers like Elvis Presley, Carl Perkins, and Little Richard. They in turn developed their own "sound," became known as the Beatles, and sparked the "British invasion" in rock music that influenced a generation of American youth, not just in music but in hairstyle and dress as well.

Today the results of acculturation are widely evident in many cultures. Americans use French terms in reference to food, play the Scottish game of golf, and often drive Japanese cars. The Japanese have likewise adopted the American game of baseball, often dress ''Western,'' and are becoming addicted to fast food. In West Germany, cities like Hamburg and Munich have both country and Western style ''honky-tonks'' and Japanese sushi bars.

Assimilation

When acculturation takes place within a subculture of a larger society, it often becomes part of a larger process called **assimilation.** This is a process whereby an immigrant or minority group changes its cultural patterns to conform and adapt to the ways of a dominant culture. In this manner, such a group may become largely absorbed into the larger culture over a period of several generations, and many of its original cultural traits may disappear. In the United States, the languages of several Native American tribal groups are disappearing because they are not being passed on to the younger generation. The younger people see them as impractical in an English-speaking world.

Some immigrant groups, like those from Northwestern Europe with Protestant backgrounds, have given some credibility to the *melting-pot theory* that immigrant groups basically merge into mainstream American society over a period of three or more generations (Peterson, 1969). According to this proposition, the first generation retains the ways of the country of birth while learning how to survive and make a living in the new one. The

Many aspects of culture are borrowed from other societies. Golf, a popular sport in the United States, originated in Scotland. The American game of baseball is now a popular sport in Japan. (*Left:* Copyright John P. Kelly/The Image Bank. *Right:* Focus on Sports.)

second generation, raised in the new country, has a different cultural experience and rejects most of the old ways. Finally, in both the second and third generations, young people often Anglicize their names, marry members of the dominant culture, and move away from traditional ethnic neighborhoods.

While this assimilation model does appear to apply to some immigrant groups, including those from Scandinavian countries, it does not accurately describe the experiences of others. The Amish of Pennsylvania, for example, provide a good case for the other extreme. Although the numbers of strictly orthodox Amish have declined in recent years, they have remained almost completely unassimilated by virtue of their tight-knit and self-sufficient way of life and their strongly held religious beliefs which remain at the center of their life-style. Thus assimilation is a relative concept that occurs in differing degrees and at differing rates for distinct and separate groups of people.

In addition, assimilation is a two-way process. Just as the dominant society places pressure on immigrants and minorities to adopt its ways, the reverse is also true, particularly when the subordinate group is large in number or has a significant base of political or economic influence. Canada, for instance, is a country where dominant institutions are influenced by British traditions. However, because large numbers of French immigrants also came to Canada, the language and customs of French culture are a persuasive influence in some parts of that country and many people regard themselves as French-Canadians. In the southwestern United States, there is a definite Latin flavor to the culture and many Mexican customs are visibly practiced. They range from food, dress, and architecture to the acknowledgement of holidays such as Cinco de Mayo and others. Consequently, America, if taken as an example, is a pluralistic, constantly changing society with diverse traditions and practices.

CHAPTER SUMMARY

1. Culture refers to a way of life, the patterns of perceiving and acting that we acquire as members of a society. Unlike the lower animals which must rely on instinct for survival, human beings have a definite culture, which is what separates them from the rest of the animal kingdom. Equipped with the special characteristics of superior intellect, upright posture, a sophisticated hand with opposable thumb, and refined vocal chords, humans are able to devise and use culture both as a means for maintaining social order and stability and as a vehicle for creating beneficial social change and progress.

2. Culture has several characteristics. First, it is learned rather than innate or instinctive. It is also socially shared and, in this sense, passed from parents to children and from person to person in the general population through a process called socialization. Third, culture is cumulative in that it is constantly changing and adapting to new social conditions. It also represents expected patterns of behavior by virtue of the social rules that are put into place for society members to live by. Finally, culture satisfies basic human needs by providing people with stable and predictable patterns within which to structure their lives.

3. People identify with their own culture and those of others in a variety of different ways. Most people exhibit ethnocentrism, the attitude that their culture is superior to all others. This cultural bias can result in positive consequences by promoting social cohesion and a sense of social identity among society members. However, it can also produce negative results by encouraging insensitivity toward and sometimes conflict with different groups and cultures. Some people, because of a partial or complete alienation from their own culture, manifest a very different attitude called

xenocentrism, a preference for the ways of a foreign culture or cultures. The sociologist tries to avoid both ethnocentrism and xenocentrism. Instead, the social scientist attempts to exhibit cultural relativity, the attitude that each culture should be seen and understood in its own context apart from a biased comparison with others.

4. There are several elements that act as the structural building blocks of culture. Among the most important are cognitive culture (the manner in which reality is defined) and normative culture (agreed-upon social standards for thinking, feeling, and acting). Cognitive culture is comprised of knowledge and beliefs, while normative culture consists of norms, values, laws, and technicways.

5. Two other basic cultural elements are represented by material culture and language. Material culture has to do with the physical and tangible aspects of culture as represented by artifacts and symbols. Language refers to a learned system of symbolic communication through which people receive, understand, and pass on their way of life to others.

6. Social control in any culture is maintained primarily through the use of sanctions, a system of rewards and punishments. Sanctions may be positive or negative, informal or formal. Usually, however, they are somewhat flexibly applied because of a culturally prescribed amount of leeway built into most norms, which sociologists call the range of tolerance.

7. Cultures are constantly in a state of evolution and adaptation brought about by a variety of different factors. Among the most important of these are technology, acculturation, and assimilation. The introduction of new technology often sparks cultural change. This is evidenced by innovations brought about

within American society during the twentieth century, including mass-produced automobiles, televisions, and microcomputers. Likewise, cultures often borrow from each other through cultural contact or acculturation, as seen in recent years by the Japanese love of American baseball and the similar interest Americans have in the Scottish game of golf. Finally, through assimilation, some immigrant groups and minorities adapt and conform to the ways of the larger culture by becoming at least partially absorbed by the dominant society.

TERMS TO KNOW

acculturation: cultural change brought about through direct contact of two cultures (or more) in which certain traits of one are borrowed by the other.

artifacts: physical objects that represent a specific culture.

assimilation: a process whereby an immigrant or minority group changes its cultural patterns to conform and adapt to the ways of a dominant culture.

beliefs: propositions about reality that either are not based on scientific evidence or cannot be demonstrated through scientific means.

counterculture: a type of subculture that is in basic conflict with the dominant culture.

craze: a fad that becomes obsessive for a brief period of time among a limited segment of society.

cultural relativity: the principle that each culture should be seen and understood in its own context apart from a biased comparison with others.

cultural universals: social patterns and practices common to all cultures.

culture: the socially established patterns of perceiving and acting that one acquires as a member of society.

culture shock: a disorientation that occurs

when one is placed in a cultural setting significantly different from one's own.

drive: a physiological state in the form of internal tension which signals the individual that a particular need demands satisfaction.

ethnocentrism: the tendency to regard one's own culture as superior and others as inferior.

fad: a folkway popular for only a brief period of time among a limited group of people in a society.

fashion: a folkway more durable than a fad that may gain widespread acceptance among a large proportion of society for a substantial period of time.

folkways: broad-based norms in the form of customs and social conventions that, when violated, are only mildly punished if at all.

instinct: a genetically determined imperative for complex behavior.

knowledge: propositions about reality that can be scientifically supported.

language: a learned system of symbolic communication that furnishes the foundation for the sharing of meaning and culture with others.

laws: officially recorded norms formulated and enforced by government.

mores: norms with a compelling moral connotation, the violation of which is met with general condemnation and sometimes severe punishment.

norms: cultural rules that specify appropriate and inappropriate forms of behavior.

reflex: an automatic physical response to an external stimulus by the nervous system.

sanctions: socially recognized and enforced rewards and punishments that are applied to conforming and nonconforming behavior.

subculture: the heritage and life-style of a particular group in society that, though in harmony with the dominant culture, has some distinctive characteristics of its own.

symbols: acts or objects that have a special meaning within a particular culture.

technicways: rules for carrying out skills or habits associated with the use of technology.

values: the standards used by people to evaluate the relative desirability and worth of practically everything in their lives and in the society around them.

xenocentrism: the preference for the ways of a foreign culture.

SUGGESTED READINGS

Cannibals and Kings: The Origins of Culture (Marvin Harris; New York: Random House, 1977). Through the use of the ecological perspective, the author provides a thought-provoking look at some very unconventional practices in different cultures, of which the origins of some remain a mystery.

Countercultures (J. Milton Yinger; New York: Free Press, 1982). An excellent and comprehensive portrayal of countermovements by New Left groups during the 1960s, which includes topics from drugs, sex, and back-to-nature communes to religious cults of various types and alternative styles in art.

Extraordinary Groups: The Sociology of Unconventional Life-Styles, 3rd ed. (William Kephart; New York: St. Martin's, 1987). An interesting look at alternative life-styles and countercultures within nineteenth- and early twentieth-century America, including a discussion of the Amish, the Father Divine movement, the Gypsies, the Mormons, and the Shakers.

Patterns of Culture (Ruth Benedict; Boston: Houghton Mifflin, 1934). An early and classic treatment of culture from the perspective of the social scientist.

Yanomamo: The Fierce People (Napoleon A. Chagnon; New York: Holt, Rinehart and Winston, 1983). A penetrating examination of a fierce tribal society in South America by an anthropologist who reluctantly lived among this group for an extended period of time.

Chapter 4

Socialization: the Process of Becoming Human

Peer Groups
Mass Media
ADULT SOCIALIZATION
Anticipatory Socialization

Resocialization
The Middle Years and Becoming Elderly

■ TERMS TO KNOW

anticipatory socialization
bonding
cognitive development
concrete operations
conventional morality
ego
feral child
formal operations
game stage
generalized other
id
imitative stage
looking-glass self
mass media

peer groups
personality
play stage
postconventional morality
preconventional morality
preoperations
resocialization
rites of passage
role taking
self-concept
self-fulfilling prophecy
sensorimotor stage
significant others
socialization
sociobiology
superego
youth subculture

In Chapter 3, we began our survey of the key topics in sociology by examining culture, the way of life one acquires as a member of society. Through culture, a person is provided with a set of socially accepted patterns for thinking and acting that give life order and predictability. Next we turn our attention to the process through which culture is transmitted to the individual, and the personality and self-concept are developed. Sociologists refer to this as **socialization.** To begin, we will examine a long-standing controversy in science, the nature-nurture debate.

THE NATURE OR NURTURE ISSUE

The crux of this debate is the question of how personality is determined. **Personality** refers

to the sum total of a person's unique yet consistent patterns of thought, feeling, and action. Are humans equipped at birth with a set of traits that largely direct and shape their personality development? Or are they instead shaped and influenced primarily by their experiences with the social environment that surrounds them? Proponents on both sides of this issue have argued vigorously for their respective viewpoints for well over a century.

The Nature Argument

Those who subscribe to the "nature" position maintain that human beings possess a definite set of qualities determined largely by inborn traits. One's environment, therefore, represents only the background against which these inherited characteristics are played out (Adams, 1974). The notion of an "innate human nature" was proposed by social contract theorists of the seventeenth and eighteenth centuries. Some, like Jean-Jacques Rousseau, argued that humans are basically good but tend to become corrupted by modern civilized society. Others, like Thomas Hobbes, maintained that humans by nature are essentially untrustworthy and selfish, characteristics that necessitated the formation of a society with rules to keep them under control.

In 1859 Charles Darwin published *On the Origin of Species,* which gave the nature argument a great deal of scientific legitimacy. He argued that human beings, like the lower animals, are products not of divine creation but of evolution through natural selection. Those with the genes for environmental adaptation tend to survive, while those without such genes tend to perish. Consequently, environment influences the genetic diversity present in all species, including *Homo sapiens,* and traits that are most adaptable emerge through natural selection.

The social Darwinists, led by Herbert Spencer, expanded this argument to include the nature of human societies. They argued that European societies were more civilized and dominant in the world than other societies because they were more highly evolved. Other social systems, such as agricultural societies in Asia and tribal societies in Africa, were biologically and socially inferior because they were at an earlier, and thus more primitive, stage of evolution. The social Darwinists also used the natural selection argument to explain why certain individuals within European societies and the United States were affluent, successful, and more "fit," while others, struggling in the throes of poverty were, therefore, "unfit."

Other scientists during the late nineteenth and early twentieth centuries attributed human behavior to other inherited predispositions. Some subscribed to the "bad blood" or "bad seed" theory to explain deviant behavior

such as crime, drug addiction, and homosexuality. However, the most prevalent approach was used by those who attempted to explain behavior largely in terms of "instincts." Some were very liberal with the number of instincts they claimed as causes for specific types of behavior. Thus, people got married because of a "mating" instinct, fought wars because of a "killing" instinct, lived in homes and societies because of "nesting" and "herding" instincts, and birthed and raised children because of the "maternal" or "parenting" instinct. One researcher, in documenting the increasing popularity of the instinct theory during this period, reviewed the academic and popular literature and found that over ten thousand alleged instincts had been claimed to exist (Bernard, 1924). Nonetheless, by the 1930s researchers like anthropologist Margaret Mead and others were finding that while some individuals and cultures had traits some called "instinctive," others did not. Therefore, instinct by this time had become a useless concept with which to explain human behavior in a meaningful way.

Although most of the twentieth century has been dominated by "nurture" or environmental explanations of human behavior, a new discipline has recently emerged called **sociobiology,** the "systematic study of the biological basis of social behavior, in all kinds of organisms, including man. . ." (Wilson, 1978). The founder of this perspective is Edward O. Wilson, an entomologist (one who studies insects) who originated the term *sociobiology.* Wilson and his followers have attempted to integrate or synthesize the research results of both the biological and social sciences. They argue that although culture rather than genetics is the prime cause of specific human behavior (Wilson, 1975), some forms of social behavior in general have a genetic foundation. They claim, for instance, that there are tendencies toward the exhibition of male dominance, territoriality, the incest taboo, the eating of meat, and religion that are genetically encoded in humans at birth.

Sociobiologists argue that a basic biological foundation for behavior exists in both the lower animals and humans and is used to ensure the survival of the species through the passing of genes on to the next generation. Thus, in some species, one animal will exhibit altruism by placing itself at risk to protect others. A wolf will come to the aid of its mate, a mother gazelle will create a diversion to draw a hungry lion away from her offspring, and several bird species will do the same to divert an enemy from the rest of the flock. Humans engage in the same self-sacrificing behavior, as illustrated by the soldier who dies in combat to save his buddies or a mother who plunges into a fire to save her child. These and other forms of altruistic behavior, sociobiologists claim, are biologically determined and serve to ensure that the species will survive and the gene pool will be passed on to the next generation.

This biological explanation, particularly as applied to human behavior, has come under a barrage of criticism. In a debate with Wilson over a decade ago, Marvin Harris, an anthropologist, categorically rejected the idea that traits such as aggressiveness, territoriality, and male dominance were inherited. He argued that there is tremendous variability in all these traits from culture to culture and that even if there are certain biological tendencies for behavior, they are so weak and general as to be meaningless, because they are so easily overridden by culture (Harris, 1980). Others argue that even some human behaviors long thought to be primarily biological—such as sexuality—are now being shown to be greatly influenced by cultural factors (Lauer and Handel, 1983). In short, there is little, if any, hard evidence to support the contention that most behaviors specific to individuals are determined significantly by genetic factors.

The Nurture Argument

During the late nineteenth century, researchers began to discover the impact of learning on behavior that previously was thought to be purely instinctive or otherwise inherited. At that time the Russian physiologist Ivan Pavlov demonstrated that, even among dogs, much behavior is subject to environmental conditions. Pavlov observed that dogs salivated any time food was present, a condition that appeared instinctive or reflexive. Through a process later referred to as classical conditioning, he conducted experiments with dogs in which, each time they were presented with food, a bell was rung. Gradually, he taught the dogs to salivate at the sound of the bell alone even when food was not present.

These and other experiments cast such a serious shadow on the biological explanations of human behavior that by the 1920s and 1930s, the idea of human instincts ceased to be a meaningful concept in mainstream social science. The dominance of the "nurture" argument became fully established in the scientific community, where it has remained during most of the twentieth century. In 1924 psychologist James B. Watson made his famous statement about the primacy of "nurture" over "nature" in human behavior.

> Give me a dozen healthy infants, well-formed, and my own specific world to bring them up in and I'll guarantee to take any one of them at random and train him to become any type of specialist I might select—a doctor, lawyer, artist, merchant, chief, yes even a beggarman and thief, regardless of his talents, penchants, tendencies, abilities, vocations, and the race of his ancestors (p. 104).

While Watson perhaps overstated the case, instances of children suffering extreme isolation from social contact with others provide a good illustration of the importance of socialization. Consider, for example, an experiment in which children were systemati-

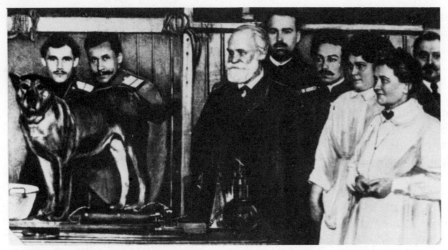

In his experiments in classical conditioning, Russian physiologist Ivan Pavlov demonstrated that even among lower animals, much behavior is learned. (The Bettmann Archive.)

cally isolated from certain socialization experiences and then observed to see how they developed. Such research, of course, would be condemned by present-day social scientists because of humane and ethical considerations. Nonetheless, this type of experiment was ordered by Emperor Frederick II during the thirteenth century. The emperor wanted to find out what types of speech patterns children would exhibit when they became adults if they had no interaction with others while growing up.

> So he bade foster mothers and nurses to suckle the children, to bathe and wash them, but in no way to prattle with them or to speak to them, for he wanted to learn whether they would speak the Hebrew language, which was the oldest, or Greek, or Latin, or Arabic, or perhaps the language of their parents, of whom they had been born. But he labored in vain because the children all died. For they could not live without the petting and joyful faces and loving words of their foster mothers (Ross and McLaughlin, 1949).

The cases of Anna and Isabelle reported by Kingsley Davis (1940, 1947, 1948) provide twentieth-century examples. Both were illegitimate children discovered and rescued by the authorities during the 1930s when they were about six years old. They both had been hidden away from view in small attic rooms by their mothers because they were unwanted.

Although the cases of these two little girls were unrelated and they were found nine months apart, their lack of socialization and states of physical condition were similar. Neither showed any human characteristics; they could only grunt and groan and were extremely ill from lack of diet and exercise. Anna could not walk, and Isabelle could only shuffle around, because her legs were so bowed. Anna was placed in a county home and later in a school for the retarded where, by the time she was seven, she had advanced to the level of an average two-year-old. When she died at age ten from an extreme case of jaundice, she was toilet trained, could dress herself, and was able to show affection for a doll. The girl known as Isabelle was more fortunate. She had experienced greater social contact with her mother and, in contrast to Anna's limpness and total lack of expression when found, was often fearful and hostile around strangers. Her care and treatment were supervised by specialists who provided her with a much more intensive learning environment as well. Consequently, she made extremely fast progress so that by age eight-and-a-half, she was functioning almost at a normal level and eventually was able to enter school.

In a more recent case involving a social isolate, the results were not as successful. Genie, a thirteen-year-old girl, had been locked naked in a room and tied to an infant's toilet seat by her father since before her second birthday. When rescued by the authorities, she could not utter a sound because her father had severely beaten her every time she tried to vocalize. In addition, she could not stand or straighten her arms and legs and could not chew because she had never been given solid food. When tested, she had the social development of a one-year-old. Placed in a special developmental program at UCLA, she made limited progress with speech over the course of four years yet never learned to behave according to social norms. She learned to speak in short phrases but never learned to read. Her social behavior, however, was manifested by such acts as grabbing strangers she liked and refusing to let go, peering into people's faces from a distance of only a few inches, and near compulsive public masturbation (Curtiss, 1977).

The cases of Anna, Isabelle, and Genie serve to illustrate clearly what can happen to children deprived of adequate social contact and stimulation. Research conducted on groups of socially deprived children in institutional settings have yielded similar results.

Rene Spitz (1945), in a two-year study,

compared populations of infants in two different types of institutions, an orphanage and a women's prison. Both groups had their physical needs attended to adequately, including food, clothing, cleanliness, and room temperature. In addition, each child in the orphanage saw a physician daily. In the prison, the children's mothers were with them regularly and were allowed to play with their babies for hours at a time. The children at the orphanage never saw their mothers and were rarely given any affection or emotional support from anyone, largely because the staff was small and overworked. They were also kept socially isolated from one another, whereas the children in the prison were in a collective nursery. Consequently, all the children in the orphanage were deficient both emotionally and socially by age two, and some were retarded. Most startling of all was that by age four, slightly over one-third of the children in the orphanage had died. When examined over the same period, the children in the prison had developed normally and not one had died.

Despite this, the notion of a **feral child**—an alleged child of nature isolated from social contact from others and perhaps raised by wild animals—has retained its romantic fascination in the minds of many people. In Roman mythology, Romulus and Remus, the founders of Rome, were suckled and raised by a wolf. In this century, several generations of Americans have been entertained by the fictional exploits of Tarzan the Ape Man, a boy from the British nobility who, after his parents died in Africa when he was an infant, was reared by Kala, an ape.

While these accounts make interesting stories, few if any social scientists feel that a human being could survive alone or in the care of animals during early childhood, much less develop into a fully functional adult. Malson (1972), in reviewing the literature of fifty-three alleged cases of feral children claimed between the 1940s and early 1960s, found

The fictional exploits of Tarzan the Ape Man have been enjoyed by generations of Americans. In reality, however, it is highly unlikely that a human child, virtually helpless in infancy, could be raised to maturity by animals. (The Museum of Modern Art/Film Stills Archive.)

that almost all such persons had significant to severe problems of functioning and in adapting in a social environment. Most, for example, could not adequately work or communicate verbally with others. Therefore, it appears that so-called feral children are unfortunate children who are lost, abandoned, or cast out by their parents with very negative consequences for their emotional and social development (Ogburn, 1959).

Each of us represents a unique combination of biological heritage and environmental experiences. From our biological backgrounds, we each are born with a genetic blueprint that includes a wide range of inborn traits and predispositions. Genes contained in this blueprint determine our complexion, our eye and hair colors, our body build and general size, our sex and blood type, and a variety of other characteristics. They also contain certain biological triggers that govern the aging process by signaling the onset of puberty, young adulthood, middle age, and old age. Biological factors also influence our level of intelligence, our personality, and our native talents. However, unlike the lower animals, we are provided by nature with only the platform or the foundation necessary to reach our potential as the most advanced and sophisticated creatures on this planet. To actually reach this potential, to become a person and develop into a fully functioning human being, each of us must rely on the environmental influences provided by socialization.

NEEDS SERVED BY SOCIALIZATION

The human infant is virtually helpless at birth and is born as a *tabula rasa*, a social blank without any experiences. Many lower animal species develop mainly in the womb and are fully capable of taking care of themselves within hours, weeks, or months after birth. The human infant, by contrast, cannot stand alone for the first year, cannot sexually reproduce for well over a decade beyond this, and cannot be totally self-sufficient for still another ten or twelve years in many societies. Acquiring the skills and information necessary to get along with others and survive in society begins at birth and continues throughout the life cycle. How this process of acquiring culture and developing a personality takes place is one of the most fascinating topics within social science. To explore it, we begin with a brief examination of the basic needs served by socialization.

Bonding and Emotional Support

Humans are social creatures who require regular and satisfying contact with others in order to develop and adjust normally to their environment. We have already seen the debilitating effects of social deprivation in small children that leads to dramatic maladjustment and, in some cases, even death. Although comprehensive studies to measure the effects of deprivation cannot be carried out on human subjects for obvious reasons, research of this type has been conducted on some of the more sociable lower animals.

Psychologist Harry Harlow and associates conducted experimental research to study the effects of social deprivation on rhesus monkeys (Harlow and Zimmerman, 1959; Harlow and Harlow, 1966; and Novak, 1979). The researchers reared baby monkeys in total isolation from other monkeys, including their mothers. Instead, each monkey was given two artificial surrogate mothers made of wire. One "mother" was equipped with a bottle for feeding and was constructed of plain wire. The other "mother" was covered in terry cloth but contained no bottle. The monkeys became attached to the terry cloth mother and would cling to it most of the time, and went to the plain wire mother with the bottle only for food.

Invariably, these animals grew up extremely maladjusted. When approached, they would bite themselves repeatedly and cower in corners. They exhibited fear and hostility when exposed to others of their kind. The females, after reaching maturity, would not mate and, when artificially inseminated, refused to care for or nurse their offspring. In a few cases, they even killed their babies before their caretakers could save them. Although one must be careful in generalizing from the behavior of lower primates to that of humans, it is clear that even with these animals, both sexual and maternal behavior are learned to a remarkable degree. Perhaps more important is the fact that monkeys, like humans, need love and nurturance in order to grow into functioning adults. Also, like humans, they may grow into neglectful and abusive parents if they themselves are neglected and abused while growing up (Kempe and Kempe, 1978; Polansky et al., 1981).

In humans, emotional needs are met primarily through **bonding**, the process of forming close personal relationships with other people, such as the relationship between a parent and a child. There are three major types of bonded relationships: (1) parent-child, (2) cross-sex, such as a married couple and (3) same-sex, as typified by two close friends (Beach, 1973). Of these, the parent-child relationship is most crucial in setting the

Bonding takes place early in life and sets the stage for later emotional and social development. (Copyright Maria Taglienti/The Image Bank.)

stage for the development of a well-adjusted personality in the child.

A growing body of research shows that bonding important to the child's later social development may take place immediately after birth (Klaus et al., 1972; Kennell, Voos, and Klaus, 1979; Klaus and Kennell, 1982). Marshall Klaus and his associates, for instance, compared the bonding effects of two groups of women with their newborns. Those women in the control group had the typical level of contact with their newborns during the first few days after birth. Women in the experimental group had much more intensive contact with their newborns and, in addition to regular feeding times, spent at least one hour with their babies immediately after birth and an additional five hours each day with them during the first ten days. In longitudinal research conducted on these women over five years, it was found that children in the "extended contact" group developed more readily than the other children in several ways. As a result of more intensive bonding, these children were healthier physically, received more physical, emotional, and verbal contact from their mothers and, at the age of five years, performed better on IQ and language exams than did the other children.

Behavioral Boundaries

In addition to meeting emotional needs, socialization also teaches the individual how to behave in a disciplined manner by placing behavior within certain boundaries. Undisciplined behavior is self-centered behavior that operates for the most part on impulse. Small children are self-centered or egocentric in orientation and, because they lack significant socialization, tend to see the world as revolving around them. However, living in a society requires that the individual learn to control impulses and act according to social rules. To do so, the child must learn to take the needs and wishes of others into consideration. Socialization, therefore, is a cultural process through which the individual becomes equipped with guidelines for acceptable behavior that allow the person to survive and prosper as a member of society.

Goal Setting

It is also important for the individual to learn how to set goals. Disciplined behavior simply for its own sake can be very unrewarding. The individual needs goals and aspirations in life so that disciplined behavior will have meaningful and beneficial consequences. Goals, therefore, act as rewards that reinforce disciplined behavior. It has been said that life essentially is concerned with setting goals, achieving them, and then setting new ones. Some goals are short-term, like getting out of bed in the morning, mowing the yard, or going out to dinner and a movie on Friday night. Others may be long-term goals, such as completing a college degree, reaching a certain career level, or raising a family. In either case, the quality of socialization experiences affects an individual's ability to set and achieve meaningful goals.

Social Survival Skills

To succeed in society, the individual must acquire a variety of coping skills. Some are general and needed by everyone, such as the skill to speak a language or get along well with others. Other skills are more specialized, such as occupational skills, which are acquired primarily through formal education and training, or experience. Some socialization skills are gradually acquired as we learn the role demands that are required of the social positions we occupy. For instance, during the course of a day a person may have to carry out the obligations that accrue to being a family member, an employee, a student, a neighbor, and

a consumer. Sometimes, given the limitations of time and energy, it can be quite a challenge to balance all of these demands.

Self-Concept

Socialization also provides the individual with a sense of identity in terms of Who am I? What am I worth? and Where am I going? The self-perception acquired may be positive or negative, depending on the types of social experiences a person has and how he or she decides to react to them. Ideally, socialization should equip a person with a positive self-image with which to become a happy, well-adjusted, and productive member of society.

This identity or self-image we all possess, which sociologists call the **self-concept**, forms much of the foundation for the personality. It represents a person's assessment of identity and self-worth and how he or she fits into the larger community and society. Self-concept is a complex area of study for the sociologist because it has many dimensions and is constantly evolving as the result of a dynamic interplay between the individual and his or her social environment.

A person's self-image contains several basic elements. First, there is the psychological dimension of how the person feels about him- or herself. Then there are the socialization influences that tend to shape that personal assessment. Finally, a person's social environment is constantly in a state of change, which requires the individual to adapt to a variety of influences as he or she moves through the life cycle.

EARLY SOCIALIZATION THEORISTS

How the personality and self-concept are formed and how we acquire culture and learn to adapt as members of society have been investigated by socialization theorists throughout the twentieth century. In the next two sections of this chapter, we will examine the pioneering work of several researchers who have greatly enlarged our understanding of the socialization process. We begin by discussing the work of two interactionists, George Herbert Mead and Charles Horton Cooley. Then we will survey the work of a psychoanalytic theorist, Sigmund Freud.

Mead: An Interactionist Perspective

George Herbert Mead (1863–1931) was a philosopher and social psychologist who served on the faculty at the University of Chicago for many years. Regarded as the father of social psychology and a founder of symbolic interactionism, he disagreed strongly with the atomistic view of humans popularized by the social contract theorists and other "scientific" philosophers of the seventeenth and eighteenth centuries. These views assumed that humans could have a self-concept and reason in nature apart from the influences of society.

Mead noted that while we have many potentialities at birth, it is only through contact with society that we develop our humanity as manifested by the personality and self-concept. In this regard, he felt that the important thing to be studied and understood is how society gets into the individual, shapes personality or "self-hood," and determines to a great degree a person's social behavior. This takes place essentially during childhood as we acquire the norms of society and learn to engage in **role taking**, the ability to imagine ourselves in the social roles of other people and act them out in order to learn the social standards that will be applied to our behavior.

The Three Stages of Role Taking. In Mead's view (1934), we learn to take on the roles of others and become social beings in three general stages.

In the **imitative stage** (the first three years), we learn to imitate the behavior of others in our immediate environment such as parents and other close family members. Small children will indiscriminately imitate the behavior of parents, for instance, some attempting to read the paper, dress up, shave, or talk like Mom or Dad.

As children become older, they move into the **play stage** in which they begin seriously to act out the roles of adults. Children from three or four through nine or ten years of age typically go through periods of wanting to be a parent or a nurse, a doctor or astronaut, or any one of a myriad of fantasy figures like cowboys, Indians, Tarzan, Wonder Woman, Superman, and so forth. Although children at this stage do not fully understand the obligations that go with certain roles, the role taking itself facilitates social development.

Finally, in middle to late childhood and early adolescence, children enter the **game stage** in which they learn to play the game of society according to the rules, in terms of role obligations. As part of this process, children typically become significantly aware of the impersonal sanctions that increasingly will be applied to their behavior by the larger society as they grow to maturity.

The Emergence of Self. As children progress through these three stages of role taking, two components of the self emerge, which Mead called the "I" and the "me." The "I" is the acting self as represented by one's natural drives and impulses, talents, and creative energies. The *"me,"* by contrast, represents the conventional, socialized self that acts in response to the demands of society. The small child, undersocialized and dominated by the "I," acts on selfish whim and impulse. Older children and adolescents, because of the role-taking influences of socialization, become increasingly dominated by the "me."

In Mead's view, for us as adults, the "me"

normally keeps the "I" in check except in certain circumstances where it is acceptable, if not desirable, to allow the "I" to express itself. Although the "me" as the social component of the self is necessary for the purposes of conformity and social order, we must guard against the other extreme in which we become oversocialized automatons who have lost the spark and spontaneity of the "I" that we all need to reach our creative potential as unique human beings.

As the self-concept develops, it is influenced most by **significant others**, people with whom the individual has close personal ties. Parents and siblings are our first sources of intimate, personal relationships, followed by the friendship circles formed within our peer groups and important role models outside the family (a favorite teacher, a coach, or a public figure). Later, as adults, most of us typically form additional bonds with significant others such as best friends, lovers, and spouses. In addition to the specific demands placed on us by our loved ones, our social behavior is also subject to universally applied norms in the form of community and societal standards for behavior. In this regard, each of us is expected to conform to the requirements of the **generalized other**, the standards of community behavior expected of anyone placed in a given social position.

Cooley: Interactionism and the Looking-glass Self

A contemporary of Mead's who also viewed social behavior from an interactionist perspective was Charles Horton Cooley (1864–1929). This quiet, unassuming scholar, who spent his entire academic life teaching sociology at the University of Michigan, was greatly influenced by the work of William James, the nineteenth-century psychologist. James (1890) developed a concept of social self rooted in the idea that the way people see themselves is greatly influenced by how others interact with and see them. Cooley built on this foundation to argue that just as we see a physical reflection when we look at ourselves in a mirror, we also see a social reflection of how we look to others as we interact with them. This image we see of ourselves as a result of interacting with others is the **looking-glass self**.

Cooley (1902, 1909) asserted that our self-image is shaped largely by three constantly interacting elements within the personality: (1) how we think we are seen by others; (2) how we think others judge or evaluate us; and (3) how we feel about and deal with their evaluations. This process, which is largely uncon-

Charles H. Cooley
The "looking-glass self"

scious, is constantly changing as a result of our varied and changing relations with individuals and groups. However, our self-concept is continually influenced by these interactions, and we constantly "take readings" on how we appear to others by examining the image we see reflected in our social mirror.

There are a couple of notable insights stemming from the concept of the looking-glass self that seem especially worthy of note. First, our self-image is basically the product of our interactions with others and our interpretations of those interactions. This has important implications regarding the socialization of children. If a child is loved, encouraged, and consistently shown approval and affection by parents while growing up, this will set the stage for how the child sees himself or herself and expects to be seen by others when he or she gazes into the social mirror. Abuse, neglect, and discouragement will tend to have an opposite impact. As W. I. Thomas once said, if individuals "define situations as real, they are real in their consequences" (Thomas and Thomas, 1928, p. 572). Consequently, if we expect to be accepted or rejected, we often are.

Second, we as adults can choose the types of social looking-glasses we peer into, although children, because of the accidents of birth, are limited in their early years by the influences of family socialization. Those with positive self-concepts are conditioned to seek out positive people, and those with negative self-images often become caught up in the "misery loves company" syndrome. This often results in what sociologist Robert Merton has called the **self-fulfilling prophecy**, a person's prediction that a particular event or situation will take place, which is then caused by that person to come true because of his or her actions based on the prediction. Therefore, if we believe in ourselves, we often make success happen, while if we expect to fail, we often do so and then blame our shortcomings on the situation or on others.

Freud: The Psychoanalytic Perspective

Unlike interactionist theorists such as Mead and Cooley who saw socialization as largely a smooth process of merging the individual with society, Sigmund Freud (1856–1939) perceived childhood socialization quite differently. Freud, an Austrian physician and the founder of the psychoanalytic school in psychology, viewed socialization as a process of coercion in which the child's freely expressed feelings and urges came under the force and control of parents and the norms of society.

The Components of Personality.   According to Freud (1930), the personality consists of three components—the id, the ego, and the superego—which develop in the child and interact together in a constant mental process which he termed the *psyche*. The **id**, which represents

Sigmund Freud
The psychoanalytic approach
(Culver Pictures)

a person's natural urges and "instincts" for such things as sex, aggression, and food, develops first in the small child. Young children are thereby dominated by the "pleasure principle" represented by the id, and are completely self-centered and obsessed with doing whatever feels good. By three or four years of age, the rational part of the self called the **ego** begins to emerge. The child's ego, governed by the "reality principle," consciously thinks through the social consequences of acting before doing so. In the small child, the ego is aware of the power of parents to sanction behavior and, thus, learns to do what is rewarding and avoid what is punishing. The **superego**, ruled by the "principle of ideals," begins to develop in middle childhood. It represents the ideal standards of behavior we live by, an inner voice or conscience that makes us feel proud when we act properly and guilty when we do wrong.

The Relationship Between the Components of Personality. According to Freud, the ego comprises the bulk of our self-concept in terms of how we see ourselves in relation to others and the larger society. It represents the governor, or the main control mechanism, in the psyche or personality. In its role as mediator between the conflicting demands of the id and superego, it channels selfish id impulses into socially desirable forms of behavior while, at the same time, it reduces ideal expectations of the superego into realistic and manageable modes of behavior that basically conform to the standards of society. If, however, the ego becomes weakened or destroyed and either the id or superego becomes dominant in the personality, then maladjustment may set in, the result being deviant or antisocial behavior. Id-dominated individuals, in extreme cases, might commit a violent crime such as murder, assault, or rape. Likewise, people whose superegos have taken over could, in the extreme, become religious fanatics or political terrorists who become so ob-

sessed with the ideal that they lose their perspective.

LATER SOCIALIZATION THEORISTS

While social scientists like Mead, Cooley, and Freud were the pioneers, others have greatly refined and extended our modern understanding of the socialization process. Three theorists that stand out in this respect are Erik Erikson, Jean Piaget, and Lawrence Kohlberg.

Erikson: Emotional Development Throughout the Life Cycle

Erik Erikson (1902–) was a student of Freud's who followed in the psychoanalytic tradition. Like his mentor, he stressed that conflict exists between the desires of the individual (id) and the rules of society (superego). However, as a modern social psychologist, his ideas and focus differed from Freud's in several respects. First, he rejected Freud's preoccupation with the sexual and aggressive "instincts" contained in the id in favor of a more balanced approach and largely abandoned the notion of "instincts" as a meaningful concept in explaining human behavior. In addition, Erikson saw the ego not as simply the mediator between the id and superego in the personality, but as a set of emotional feelings about oneself that are constantly being challenged by maturation and change. Finally, unlike Freud, who devoted most of his energies to studying socialization in the developing child, Erikson extended his analysis over the entire life span.

As summarized in Figure 4-1, Erikson saw life as marked by eight stages of emotional development beginning with infancy and ending with old age. At each stage, a person is faced with an emotional crisis or developmental challenge. How each challenge is handled by the individual determines in significant part

Figure 4-1 Erikson's Stages of Emotional Development

Developmental Stage	Crisis to Overcome
1. Infancy	Trust vs. mistrust
2. Early childhood (1-3 years)	Autonomy vs. shame and doubt
3. Play stage (4-5)	Initiative vs. guilt
4. School stage (6-11)	Industry vs. inferiority
5. Adolescence (12-18)	Identity vs. role confusion
6. Young adulthood	Intimacy vs. isolation
7. Middle age	Generativity vs. stagnation
8. Old age	Integrity vs. despair

Sources: Erikson, E. (1963). *Childhood and society.* New York: W. W. Norton & Company; Elkind, D. (1970, April 5). *The New York Times Magazine.*

how capable or incapable that person will be in dealing with future emotional challenges. A person whose early periods of emotional development are relatively successful will tend to have the ego strength and coping skills needed to weather the crises that lie ahead. A person without such a firm foundation may carry adjustment problems in the form of "emotional baggage" into subsequent stages. Nonetheless, there is always an opportunity to "correct" and resolve earlier crises and, as a result, continue to experience growth and emotional development.

The eight stages of human growth and development proposed by Erikson (1950) are listed and briefly described here.

Stage 1: Infancy. During the first year of life, the infant is virtually dependent on adult caretakers, especially the mother, and must contend with the crisis of *trust versus mistrust.* Children who develop what Erikson calls "inner certainty," as a result of consistent care and affection, will exhibit a sense of security about the outer world, while those who do not receive such treatment will come to see the world as a frightening and frustrating place.

Stage 2: Early Childhood. Between one and three years of age, children try to gain mastery over their bodies by learning to walk and run and control the processes of elimination (bladder and bowel control). This Erikson calls *autonomy versus shame and doubt.* Children who successfully negotiate this period will develop the confidence to explore their larger surroundings, while children with problems at this stage will feel shameful and doubt their abilities.

Stage 3: The Play Stage. Between three and five, children face the challenge of *initiative versus guilt* as they attempt to extend control over their bodies to the larger environment that surrounds them. They are very curious at this stage. Consequently, parents need to impose some boundaries on their child's behavior but at the same time encourage exploration and creativity. If this is done successfully, children will tend to develop the self-confidence to seek new experiences. If children at this stage are stifled, however, they may feel guilty and unsure of themselves and withdraw.

Stage 4: School Age. From about six to eleven years of age, the crisis of *industry versus inferiority* must be addressed as children shift their sphere of social relations from the home environment to that of the school and larger society. During this stage they must learn to successfully handle relationships with teachers, peer groups, and others in their social environment.

Stage 5: Adolescence. Teenagers experience a period of transition in which they gradually leave the dependency of childhood behind and take on the responsibilities of adulthood. Erikson asserted that during this stage, young people must contend with *identity versus identity confusion.* Those who are successful enter young adulthood with a firm sense of who they are, where they have been, and where they plan to go. This coherent sense of identity and the positive self-image that goes with it are invaluable in establishing meaningful pair-bonds (such as marriage) as an adult, which require maturity, understanding, and flexibility for maximum success.

Stage 6: Young Adulthood. From eighteen until about the age of thirty-five, people are faced with the first of three adult stages of development. Young adulthood is characterized by the crisis of *intimacy versus isolation.* Those who negotiate successfully this challenge are able to establish successfully one or more ongoing relationships with others, which involve personal intimacy.

Stage 7: Middle Adulthood. The years of middle age are ones of physical and emotional maturity leading to the challenge of *generativity versus stagnation.* Those who succeed during this phase of life are individuals who feel fulfilled regarding their relationships with family, work, and community and see their lives as happy and successful. Others may feel "caught in a rut" of sameness or stagnancy with little or no growth taking place.

Stage 8: Old Age. During the last years of life, Erikson maintains, people are faced with the challenge of *integrity versus despair.* It is a time of reflection in which those who feel their lives have been positive or balanced are able to make peace with themselves and with death. By contrast, those who feel life has passed them by will tend to become self-absorbed with worry and despair.

Piaget: Cognitive Development

The Swiss psychologist Jean Piaget (1896–1980) focused his socialization studies on how children develop intellectual abilities and moral judgments. He argued that children think and set priorities differently from adults primarily because their intellectual capacities are limited and, therefore, must develop gradually in a series of observable stages. **Cognitive development** refers to changes that occur in intellectual abilities as children mature.

Piaget spent years observing thousands of children and talking to them about their thoughts, feelings, and actions. He (1929, Piaget and Inhelder, 1969) concluded that children develop cognitively in four general stages—sensorimotor, preoperations, concrete operations, and formal operations—that reinforce and add new dimension to the socialization theories of Mead and Erikson (see Figure 4-2).

The Sensorimotor Stage. During the **sensorimotor stage** (birth to two years), children develop motor intelligence and learn to distinguish different objects. By *motor intelligence,* Piaget meant the acquired ability by children to perceive their bodies as separate from the rest of their external environment. Small infants neither realize this at first nor do they understand that they can use their bodies to make things happen in their environment. For

Figure 4-2 Piaget's Stages of Cognitive Development

Developmental Stage	Characteristics
1. Sensorimotor (birth-2 years)	The child develops motor skills, perception of immediate surroundings, and object permanence (the realization that objects have their own reality apart from our ability to see or otherwise experience them directly).
2. Preoperations (2-7)	The development of symbolic functions occurs. Language is acquired gradually along with the ability to picture things in the mind. The child develops the ability to take the role of another, but only one person at a time. Nonetheless, the child is limited by egocentism during this stage.
3. Concrete operations (7-12)	The development of logical thinking begins. The child acquires the ability to rank-order objects by size and class with increasing sophistication and understand their relationships to one another by weight, mass, and volume as well. The ability to consider several points of view simultaneously also develops during this stage.
4. Formal operations (12-adulthood)	The ability to think abstractly and hypothetically is developed. The individual learns to consider several options or hypothetical solutions to a problem before acting. The maturing person is thus freed from the limitations of immediate and past experiences. He or she can operate in the world of ideas and contemplate future goals and possibilities.

Source: Adapted with permission from H. Ginsburg and S. Opper. 1969. *Piaget's theory of intellectual development.* Englewood Cliffs, N.J.: Prentice-Hall.

instance, small babies do not realize that when they shake a rattle, they cause it to make a sound. Also during this period *object permanence* develops, in which children come to realize that people or objects such as parents and toys do not cease to exist when they leave one's sight. Perhaps you have played "peek-a-boo" with a two-year-old who is learning or has newly acquired the concept of object permanence. The child realizes you will reappear, but is still somewhat mystified at how it all works and enjoys the game immensely.

Preoperations. During the stage of **preoperations** (from two to about seven) children develop the ability to think in symbolic terms and use language to communicate with others. At this stage, children imitate the use of words with little understanding of what they mean. They also live to some extent in the world of "pretend" and "make believe" and usually perceive fantasy characters as real to some degree. Since during the early part of this period they do not understand concepts like weight, size, category, and cause-and-effect, they are not capable of many simple intellectual operations. If the same amount of water or milk is placed in two glasses, one short and the other tall, most children at this level of development will tend to choose the tall glass because they think it contains more. Likewise, children who are "preoperational" are likely to think large objects weigh more than small objects. By the time a child is six or seven, he or she is beginning to learn how to sort objects by size, weight, and class and has developed to some extent the ability to see reality through the eyes of another person, although he or she can consider only one viewpoint at a time.

Concrete Operations. From seven to about twelve, children move through the stage of **concrete operations** in which cause-and-effect relationships in the real world become understood and concrete reasoning ability is developed. Children learn to "factor in" several points of view simultaneously and largely abandon the world of intuition and fantasy. At this stage, they can now test relationships between objects in a literal manner by weighing two objects or measuring the quantity of liquid in two glasses. However, at this point in their intellectual development, they are still largely limited in their perceptions to their own life experiences and what they can experience directly.

Formal Operations. According to Piaget, the stage of **formal operations** (from twelve to adulthood) represents the last of the four stages of cognitive development, characterized by the acquisition of abstract thinking abilities. During this period, adolescents develop the capability to hypothesize about possible cause-and-effect relationships and possible courses of action without the necessity of having experienced them directly. They can see the potential consequences of behavior in their "mind's eye." In terms of moral behavior, most individuals are no longer egocentric and selfish in their attitudes and behavior, but

have internalized the concept of duty in regard to obeying social norms and the need to act for the greater good of the larger society.

Kohlberg: Moral Development

Influenced strongly by Piaget, Lawrence Kohlberg (1928–   ) has proposed a theory of socialization that emphasizes three levels of moral development, each of which evolves in two stages. Like his mentor, Kohlberg (1981) acknowledges the interplay between cognitive development and moral development. Unlike Piaget, however, he contends that the use of definitive age ranges for each stage of moral development is not so meaningful, because people develop moral standards at differing rates and some continue in a state of moral immaturity for life.

First Level: Preconventional Morality. Consistent with other socialization theorists, Kohlberg's research on small children has found them to be self-centered beings who define good as "what I want." This egocentrism is apparent at the first level of moral behavior called **preconventional morality**, a preoccupation by children with the personal benefits derived from conformity. This develops in two stages. In *Stage 1*, children learn about parents' coercive power, the power to punish, which results in conformity simply to avoid punishment. During *Stage 2*, their level of sophistication increases as they learn that conformity to parental guidelines can be used to bargain with parents or can be exchanged for rewards. They come to realize that since privileges and other benefits accrue from picking up their toys, bathing regularly, not fighting with their siblings, and other forms of conformity, it is really in their best interests to comply.

Second Level: Conventional Morality. During later childhood and adolescence, people typically develop **conventional morality**, in which the focus of acceptable behavior shifts

from "benefiting myself" to "pleasing others."
This begins at *Stage 3*, when children learn to
empathize with the feelings and needs of others and seek their approval. They want to be
seen in a positive light by their family and
friends as well as avoid the feelings of guilt
and lowered self-esteem that follow disapproval. This development of altruism toward
others is needed later in life in order to form
and maintain successful adult love relationships with others that require "give and take"
and mutual consideration. As individuals
move into *Stage 4*, consideration and respect
for others extends from relationships with
family and friends to the larger community
and society. By adolescence or adulthood,
people typically feel a sense of duty or obligation toward the preservation of order in
their community and society, which is reflected in their behavior.

Third Level: Postconventional Morality. The
most advanced and sophisticated level of
moral development is **postconventional morality**. This involves the development of a personal code of behavior which may or may not
conform to the norms and laws of society, but
which stresses allegiance to a universal set of
ethical principles.

It seems apparent that relatively few people ever attain this level of morality because
of the high levels of abstract thought and education required. At *Stage 5*, individuals subscribe to a "social contract" view of social
standards and behavior that stresses "the
greatest good for the greatest number." If
norms or laws in the dominant society contra-
dict such a standard, one is justified in violating them. By contrast, those operating at the
conventional morality level (Stages 3 or 4)
would tend to follow social conventions
blindly, regardless of the consequences, in order to obtain social approval and maintain
"law and order." *Stage 6* morality, even more
rare, is, according to Kohlberg, the stage in
which individuals base their actions on an al-

legiance to abstract principles, such as how
one defines and assesses the relative value of
human life and liberty in different situations.
Joan of Arc, Mahatma Gandhi, and Martin
Luther King Jr. all serve as representative examples of individuals at the postconventional
level of morality.

Kohlberg's work has drawn some criticism, particularly from those who have found
fault with his use of only male research subjects. These critics argue that males and females are different in terms of both the quality
and levels of their cognitive and moral development (Gilligan, 1982). However, recent
research has failed to substantiate any significant differences in moral development between males and females (Walker, 1985;
Greeno and Maccoby, 1986).

AGENTS OF SOCIALIZATION

Children are influenced in their individual
and social development by a variety of factors,
particularly in modern, complex societies like
the United States. The family, peer relations,
school, church, media, and the larger community and society all play an integral part in
shaping our personalities and equipping us
with the skills for social survival and prosperity. In this portion of the chapter, we will focus on three of the most important agents of
socialization—the family and peer groups,
which represent our primary sources of significant others, and the mass media, which continue to play a significant role in shaping our
attitudes and life-styles.

The Family

Of all sources of childhood socialization, the
family is the most important. As mentioned
earlier, the human infant is virtually helpless
at birth and must rely on parents and other
family members for physical care and protection during the many years required for mat-

The family is the primary agent of child socialization. (Copyright Joel Gordon, 1982.)

uration. More important for humans, however, is that our experiences with our families shape the way we see ourselves, the larger world, and our place in it. An American child grows up with a different culture, language, and worldview than a child reared in Iran, India, or Japan. Likewise, family socialization patterns within pluralistic societies like the United States are quite diverse. Children reared in a rural farming community in the Midwest come to look at the world through a different filter than those brought up in a large industrial city in the Northeast. Children whose parents practice religious fundamentalism tend to grow up with different values and life priorities than those reared as Presbyterians or Episcopalians.

One important factor involved in the transmission of culture to a child is social class. A family's socioeconomic level is important because different class levels represent distinct subcultures. Children's class backgrounds shape to a significant degree the values and beliefs they hold, their self-concepts, and how they should relate to the rest of the world. These class subcultures are further reinforced by other factors, which include region, rural or urban residence, race and ethnicity, and religion. Children reared in lower socioeconomic circumstances, for instance, tend to be fatalistic and see success as determined largely by luck. Those reared in more affluent circumstances, on the other hand tend to have an achievement orientation and see success in terms of individual effort and hard work.

Sociologist Melvin Kohn (1963, 1977) has conducted studies that show distinct differences in how children are raised in working-class versus middle-class families. Working-class parents tend to stress strict conformity to traditional standards, punish the consequences of unacceptable behavior (what children do), and are more likely to use physical punishment. They stress to their children the importance of obeying the rules and keeping out of trouble. This parenting style, according to Kohn, is at least partially influenced by the fact that working-class parents typically have blue-collar jobs. In such occupations, they are given little, if any, discretion in how they do their work and are expected to follow instructions precisely.

Middle-class parents, by contrast, tend to have white-collar jobs that, because of their complexity, require more independent thought and discretion. This orientation is reflected in how they socialize their children. Middle-class parents tend to stress and reward their children's initiative and creativity. When punishment is given, it is for the motives behind behavior instead of what the children did. Children in middle-class families are taught the importance of self-control rather than strict obedience and are more likely to be denied privileges as punishment than to be physically disciplined.

The impact of the family on the formation of self-concept is also decisively important. As we saw earlier with the cases of Anna, Isabelle, and Genie, and in Harry Harlow's deprivation research on monkeys, the lack of adequate emotional support during the formative years of development can be devastating. Small children especially need consistent love, affection, support, and encouragement in order to develop positive self-images and the confidence necessary to deal effectively with the challenges and adversities of life (Mortimer and Simmons, 1978). For them, the family is the first social group they become members of, and parents represent their first teachers, guides, and role models.

Even so, parents tend to treat their firstborn and later-born children differently. Some research indicates that firstborn children tend to receive more attention, affection, and discipline than laterborns. These firstborns then

tend to become higher achievers than their younger siblings, who tend to be more relaxed and sociable (Forer, 1976; Dunn and Kendrick, 1983). For instance, firstborn children tend to earn better grades in school, score higher on IQ tests, and appear more likely to go to college. In addition, they are overrepresented among Rhodes scholars, those in *Who's Who in America,* and even presidents (52 percent) of the United States (Vander Zanden, 1985).

Peer Groups

By the time children are five or six years old (and younger for those in day-care situations), their relations with peers begin to play an important role in their emotional and social development. **Peer groups** consist of persons of about the same age and social position. Children are fascinated with one another because of the special standing of equality they share. This sets their relations with one another apart from the inequality inherent in their dealings with parents and other adults. Because their states of physical, emotional, and intellectual development are about the same, they have experiences in common that are not applicable in their relations with adults.

In today's fast-changing modern society, children grow up in a very different world from the one their parents knew as children. This, among other things, has resulted in a gap between generations in several respects. Most notably, the twentieth century has witnessed the emergence of a **youth subculture** consisting of life-style characteristics and preferences among children and adolescents very distinct from those of their parents. This is readily seen in their use of "pop slang," distinct modes of dress, hairstyles, music, and other special consumer preferences.

The youth subculture acts to reinforce the impact of peer group socialization and can have both functional and dysfunctional consequences. On the positive side, it supports

Peer groups influence our behavior throughout the life cycle. (*Top:* Copyright Joel Gordon, 1976. *Bottom:* Copyright Susan Lapides, 1982/Design Conceptions.)

the development of interpersonal communication skills and relationships outside the home, which become very important during adulthood in both career and recreational settings. However, overidentification with the more superficial aspects of the youth subculture can retard the development of an adult sense of responsibility. Involvement by children and adolescents with deviant elements such as the "drug scene" or delinquent groups can also have negative consequences.

Peer groups function in several ways. First, they introduce children to the *impersonality of social rules.* In the home, rewards and punishments are administered by parents in a very

personal manner, while in the peer group rules are impersonally set and sanctioned and few people if any are given "special" consideration. Second, peer groups often *test adult tolerance.* Children will attempt things in peer settings that they would not dream of doing on their own, in order to test adult authority and the strength of peer support and influence. In addition, children's peer groups *may or may not reinforce adult values.* For instance, one group of twelve-year-olds may form a lawn-mowing service to make money in the summertime, while another forms a burglary ring to rob the community (Broom and Selznick, 1968). Finally, peer relations teach children some of the more *informal aspects of the larger culture* that they cannot be, or often are not, exposed to at home. Getting along with others, acquiring the etiquette of male-female social relations, learning about sex, and even the use of profanity are often acquired in peer groups.

Mass Media

The **mass media** consist of the various methods used to transmit information to large numbers of people in an organized way. Through many sources, including books, magazines, newspapers, movies, radio, and television, both children and adults are exposed to a vast array of images and topics. Of these, television probably has the strongest impact on childhood socialization. Children in the United States spend more time watching television—four hours a day or twenty-eight hours a week—than in any other single activity except sleep (Waters, 1977). Consequently, by the time they graduate from high school, they have spent more time in front of the TV set—15,000 to 18,000 hours—than in interaction with any single group, including parents, siblings, peers, and teachers.

Of course, television and other mass media are neither positive nor negative in and of themselves. Their impact depends largely on parents and other adults who are responsible for setting quality and quantity standards for television viewed by children. In many cases, television can have a positive influence on socialization. Programs like *Nature* and *Wild Kingdom* teach geography and natural ecology to children, while *Sesame Street* teaches vocabulary and math skills. Shows like *Captain Kangaroo* in the 1950s and 1960s and, more recently, *Mr. Roger's Neighborhood* have used positive role models to stress values like cooperation, social sharing, and responsibility for one's actions. Research has shown that children exposed primarily to these types of programs are more cooperative or prosocial than children exposed to a broader cross-section of programming, which includes a great amount of violence (Friedrick and Stein, 1975; Ball-Rokeach, Rokeach, and Grube, 1984).

Television and other media, however, can also have adverse effects. Children are marketed to as little consumers almost from the time they are old enough to sit in front of the television screen. During the 1980s, for example, advertisers hawked everything from E.T. dolls and Star Wars action figures to Ronald McDonald coloring books and Smurfs cereal. The message in these promotions seemed to be that in order to be accepted among one's peers or to be happy as a child, one needed the latest gadget or toy. In addition, media often distort reality by presenting stereotypical images of families, occupations, and life situations. On *Family Ties*, the Keatons never seem to have difficulties that take more than thirty minutes to solve, the same police officers on *Miami Vice* have shootouts with the bad guys each week, and on *Golden Girls*, life for women in their fifties is one big romantic, sexy party.

Perhaps the most potentially harmful consequence of television is the exposure of children to TV violence. By the time they graduate from high school, children have seen an average of 18,000 fictional killings and several

times as many violent assaults. In a review of over 2,500 studies on the effects of television violence on actual behavior (National Institute of Mental Health, 1982), the results show quite clearly that exposure to television violence encourages aggressive behavior by both children and adolescents.

ADULT SOCIALIZATION

As Erikson and other theorists have noted, socialization does not end with adulthood but instead continues throughout the life cycle. Upon leaving childhood, we experience the transition to the world of adult responsibility and make various adaptations as we grow older and mature. These adaptations take several forms. Some have to do with the role transitions we make as we leave or continue school, obtain a job, and perhaps get married and start a family. Others involve how we adjust to our own aging process as we adapt first to being a young adult, then a middle-aged person, and finally a senior citizen.

Anticipatory Socialization

The informal preparation for future life stages and responsibilities is what Robert Merton and Alice Rossi (1968) have termed **anticipatory socialization**. As George Herbert Mead found in his observations, this process of social preparation for the future actually begins in early childhood as children first imitate and then play out social roles they see enacted by parents and other adults. When you were a child, did you look forward to becoming a ''teenager'' or getting your driver's license with eager anticipation? This is fairly typical of many children for whom growing up just cannot seem to occur fast enough. This process often continues into adolescence as teenagers prepare for entering the adult world.

These mental rehearsals for the future, however, have their greatest impact during adulthood when we experience the greatest number of life transitions. For those entering college right out of high school, the environment of a college campus and the responsibilities that come with higher education offer preparation for later adult responsibilities. Similarly, entering the work force teaches individuals the skills and credentials necessary

Resocialization carries with it a fundamental change in both life-style and the norms one is expected to obey. (AP/Wide World Photos.)

for advancement. This, in turn, helps them to anticipate where they might be or what they might be doing in five or ten years.

Anticipatory socialization is also evident in our personal relationships. Going steady allows both parties to assess their relationship to see if they are sufficiently compatible to carry it further. If the relationship continues and intensifies, the couple may become engaged. Engagement, in turn, is a special period which allows two people to prepare for and anticipate a married life together. If they do get married, the first year or two of marriage or a longer period may be needed to decide about children and prepare for the responsibilities of parenthood. Life involves a series of these transitions which, if planned carefully, soften and make easier the changes and adjustments we all make as we grow older.

Resocialization

Role transitions made in adulthood often involve **resocialization**, an abrupt and often fundamental adjustment in life-style and life priorities. Being married, for example, involves a significant shift in priorities and a very different life-style as compared to being single. A much more dramatic example is that of a person who experiences a religious conversion. The convert will sometimes claim a feeling of being cleansed or "born again" and essentially begins a new life as a believer. Resocialization is also in evidence when one joins the military. Here, an institutional process of training and conditioning act to deliberately reshape a person into a soldier with a newly acquired set of skills and purposes. The uniform, discipline, camaraderie, and the drills and training exercises are all part of this reorientation process.

Resocialization is often reinforced by **rites of passage**, formal events that signal the end of one status in life and the beginning of another. Rites of passage often take the form of ceremonies or rituals such as school graduation, marriage, completion of military training, and promotions or awards. These events, often involving the taking of photographs and attendance by close family and friends, are very special occasions that are remembered for years.

The Middle Years and Becoming Elderly

As we become older, both anticipatory socialization and resocialization have important impacts on our lives. During the middle years of the forties and fifties, people look introspectively at their previous accomplishments and their current life situations. Have I used my life productively? Am I successful? Have I made a difference in the lives of others and in society? The way these questions and others are answered affects how people see middle age and the future.

The middle years can be fulfilling and productive or fraught with stress and crisis. Many people experience some of both the positives and the negatives. This is a time in which income is highest, free time is often the greatest, and parental responsibilities are being phased out as children become adults and ultimately leave home. Although middle-aged people do not have the physical appearance and energy of their youth, health and vitality are usually good and, combined with greater maturity and affluence, often provide them with very fulfilling lives. In fact, for many, the middle years are among the best.

Others in middle age, however, may experience crisis in a variety of forms. Some feel they are caught in the "sandwich generation" between responsibilities to their adolescent and young adult children, and to elderly parents in poor economic circumstances or failing health. Others may have a mid-life crisis in which they feel trapped in a boring life with no excitement or challenge. In any case, the middle years are a period of consolidation and reflection. For most, the majority of life deci-

sions and accomplishments have been made, time is getting short, and the challenge is to make the most of what they have and use it to build the best future possible.

Becoming elderly usually begins approximately at retirement. Since 1 out of 9 Americans is now over 65 years of age (U.S. Bureau of the Census, 1985 A), the elderly population is much more visible than it once was.

Senior citizens face many challenges and problems. First, they live in a society that during most of the twentieth century, has had a "youth orientation" which viewed the elderly as second-class citizens. The trend now, however, tends to be shifting toward a more positive view regarding the elderly and their capabilities, as evidenced by an increased use of elderly role models in the media and the recent increase in the mandatory retirement age in government occupations to 70. Second, the elderly often live on fixed retirement incomes that average only about one-half the earnings they had while working. Combined with increasing health problems and the difficulty in obtaining and paying for health insurance, senior citizens often face significant financial problems. Finally, retirement often brings reduced self-esteem, and the elderly must face grief crises when friends and spouses die.

Despite these problems, those 65 and older often live happy and productive lives for at least an additional decade and, for some, much longer. As the ranks of the elderly continue to swell, with the numbers of those 85 and older increasing the fastest, positive role models are also becoming more common. At the age of 78, Ronald Reagan completed his second term as president of the United States and at 92, comedian George Burns was still making movies. According to Burns, people get old and feeble because of their attitudes. They "practice to get old. The minute they get to be 65 or 70, they sit down slow, they get into a car with trouble. They start taking small steps." His approach has been to attack life with "moxie" (Toufexis et al., 1988).

Evidently, an increasing number of senior citizens agree. Hulda Crooks, 91, has climbed ninety-seven mountains, including Japan's Mount Fuji since the age of 65. Other examples include 74-year-old Dr. James Jay who, along with fifty-five others over the age of 70, completed the New York City Marathon and author Jane Stovall, 103, who became a senior golf champion in her eighties and a student pilot at age 89 (Gibbs et al., 1988).

CHAPTER SUMMARY

1. The human personality is the product of two basic factors: nature (inherited characteristics) and nurture (social environment and experiences). Theories about the inherent nature of humans have varied from the social contract theories of the seventeenth and eighteenth centuries and social Darwinism in the nineteenth century to the notion of human instincts in the early twentieth century. More recently, sociobiology has emerged as an attempt to study scientifically the biological origins of social behavior, although it has been widely criticized. The "environmental" or nurture explanation of behavior began to emerge in the late nineteenth and early twentieth centuries with the work of researchers like Ivan Pavlov and James Watson. Recent case studies of children isolated from normal social contact and related research have demonstrated clearly that human development is significantly, if not largely, determined by socialization.

2. Because human infants are virtually helpless at birth and depend on others for a significant portion of their life span, socialization serves several basic needs. Chief among these are bonding and emotional support, the establishment of behavioral boundaries, goal setting, social survival skills, and the formation and maintenance of the self-concept.

3. Three classical socialization theorists—George Herbert Mead, Charles Horton Cooley, and Sigmund Freud—laid much of the foundation for our modern understanding of human development. Mead and Cooley were symbolic interactionists who took the position that socialization was a gradual developmental process that resulted in the smooth merging of the needs and wants of the individual with those of society. Mead stated that children learn the role-taking behavior necessary to conform to the standards of society in three stages: the imitative stage, the play stage, and the game stage. Cooley stressed how our interactions with others influence our self-concept and behavior through his concept of the looking-glass self. Freud disagreed with the interactionist view and maintained that socialization is an abrupt, coercive experience for small children, in which the expression of their natural urges is severely restricted by parents and the larger society. His theory of personality development stressed three components of the psyche—the id, the ego, and the superego.

4. Recent socialization theorists have concentrated on specific aspects of socialization as illustrated by the work of Erik Erikson (emotional development), Jean Piaget (cognitive development), and Lawrence Kohlberg (moral development). Erikson identified eight stages of emotional development from infancy through old age, each of which contains a special crisis or challenge to overcome. Piaget stressed that cognitive socialization in children occurs in four stages: sensorimotor, preoperations, concrete operations, and formal operations. Kohlberg emphasized that moral development takes place on three basic levels: preconventional morality, conventional morality, and postconventional morality.

5. Of the many agents of childhood socialization, three are stressed in this chapter: the family, peer groups, and mass media. The

family is the most important agent of early socialization. Through exposure to parents and other family members, children acquire a set of basic values and learn the norms of acceptable behavior. In peer groups (groups of those about the same age and social position), the child, among other things, learns about the impersonality of social rules and some of the more informal aspects of culture that are not acquired at home. The media are another source of influence in which the child may be exposed to images and content that reinforce societal values and themes or perhaps, on the other hand, desensitize the child to the harmful effects of violence.

6. Socialization does not end with the onset of adulthood but, instead, continues throughout the life cycle. As adults, we mature and adapt in two basic ways. First, we engage in anticipatory socialization by mentally rehearsing for upcoming life events and stages. This acts to soften and make easier the changes and adjustments we all make as we get older. In addition, most of us have one or more resocialization experiences in which abrupt and fundamental adjustments in life-style and priorities are called for. Common examples include religious conversions, marriages, parenthood, and entering the military. Through these processes of anticipatory socialization and resocialization, we also adapt to our own chronological aging process as first we experience middle-age and then the retirement years later in life.

TERMS TO KNOW

anticipatory socialization: the informal preparation for future life stages and responsibilities.

bonding: the process of forming close personal relationships with others, such as the relationship between a parent and child.

cognitive development: changes that occur in intellectual abilities and thought processes as children mature.

concrete operations: the stage of cognitive development in which children come to understand cause-and-effect relationships in the real world and develop concrete reasoning ability.

conventional morality: a level of conformity based on "pleasing others" through a sense of obligation or duty.

ego: Freud's term for the rational component of the self that acts as the governor or manager of the personality.

feral child: an alleged child of nature isolated from social contact with others and perhaps raised by animals.

formal operations: the last stage of cognitive development in which children learn to think in an abstract manner through the use of hypothetical cause-and-effect relationships.

game stage: Mead's term for middle to late childhood and early adolescence, during which the individual becomes significantly aware of impersonal sanctions that will be applied to his or her behavior by the larger society.

generalized other: Mead's term for the standards of community behavior expected of anyone placed in a given social position.

id: Freud's term for one's natural urges and "instincts," such as sex and aggression.

imitative stage: Mead's term for infancy and early childhood, during which the child learns to imitate the behavior of parents and others in his or her immediate surroundings.

looking-glass self: Cooley's term for how people see themselves as a result of their assessment of how others see them.

mass media: the various methods used to transmit information to large numbers of people in an organized manner.

peer groups: in childhood socialization, children of about the same age and social position.

personality: the sum total of a person's unique yet consistent patterns of thought, feeling, and action.

play stage: Mead's term for middle childhood, during which the child begins to seriously act out the roles of adults.

postconventional morality: the development of a personal code of behavior which may or may not conform to the norms and laws of society, but which stresses allegiance to a universal set of ethical principles.

preconventional morality: a preoccupation by children with the personal benefits derived from conformity.

preoperations: the stage of cognitive development in which children acquire the ability to think in symbolic terms and use language to communicate with others.

resocialization: abrupt and often fundamental adjustments in adult life-style and life priorities.

rites of passage: formal events that signal the end of one status in life and the beginning of another.

role taking: the ability to imagine ourselves in the social roles of other people and act them out in order to learn the social standards that will be applied to our behavior.

self-concept: the personal assessment people have of their own identity and self-worth and how they fit into the larger community and society.

self-fulfilling prophecy: a prediction by a person that something will occur which is then caused to come true because of his or her actions.

sensorimotor stage: the first stage of cognitive development in which children develop motor intelligence and learn to distinguish different objects.

significant others: Mead's term for people with whom the individual has close personal ties.

socialization: the process through which culture is transmitted to the individual, and the personality and self-concept are developed.

sociobiology: the study of the biological aspects of social behavior.

superego: Freud's term for the idealized self or conscience that makes us feel proud when we act properly and guilty when we do wrong.

youth subculture: life-style characteristics and preferences among children and adolescents very distinct from those of their parents.

Suggested Readings

Adolescent Socialization in Cross-Cultural Perspective (Irving Tallman, Ramona Marotz-Baden, and Pablo Pindas; New York: Academic Press, 1983). A cross-cultural comparison of the ways families and adolescents in the United States and Mexico adapt to changing social conditions and how this impacts on adolescent socialization.

The Child and Society: The Process of Socialization, 4th. ed. (Frederick Elkin and Gerald Handel; New York: Random House, 1984). An excellent text on childhood socialization that covers most relevant issues in a balanced and scholarly manner.

The Forbidden Experiment: The Story of the Wild Boy of Aveyron (Roger Shattuck; New York: Farrar, Strauss, Giroux, 1980). The story of a wild child found wandering alone in France in the year 1800 and his problems and accomplishments in adapting to the social world of human beings.

The Life Cycle Completed (Erik H. Erikson; New York: Norton, 1982). A brief summary of Erikson's eight stages of emotional development.

The Nature of the Child (Jerome Kagan; New York: Basic Books, 1984). A balanced use of both the nurture and nature approaches in accounting for how the child develops.

Chapter 5

Social Organization

KEY FORMS OF ORGANIZATION WITHIN SOCIETIES
Kinship
Fealty
Groups
Social Positions
Contract
Bureaucracy

PATTERNS OF SOCIAL INTERACTION
Cooperation
Exchange
Competition
Conflict
Accommodation

■ **TERMS TO KNOW**

accommodation
achieved status
affinal kinship
agrarian societies
anomie
ascribed status
bureaucracy
competition
conflict
consanguineal kinship
contract
cooperation
exchange
fealty
group
horticultural societies

hunting-gathering societies
industrial societies
kinship
macrolevel organization
master status
means of subsistence
microlevel organization
postindustrial societies
role
role ambiguity
role conflict
role set
role strain
social control
social interaction
social organization
social position
society

Concert tours for popular entertainers like Madonna and Bruce Springsteen require a tremendous amount of planning and organization. Hundreds of details must be worked out starting with the necessary time set aside in the entertainer's schedule, decisions about the cities to be included and the concert locations to be used, and negotiations concerning the "cut" of the proceeds to be received by promoters, ticket sellers, and concert halls. As the tour gets under way, "roadies" are hired to transport and set up the musical instruments and sound equipment, and advance people are sent ahead to ensure that arrangements for hotel accommodations, limousines, security, concession workers to sell programs, buttons, sweatshirts, and posters, and local publicity are all properly taken care of. Finally, a day or two before the concert series begins in each city, the performer and his or her musicians, backup singers, choreographers, and technicians arrive to rehearse, to be interviewed by local media, and to make sure all details related to the performances are complete. In addition, some concerts today are technological spectaculars sometimes requiring computer-sequenced laser lights, smoke and fireworks explosions, wires and cranes to levitate the entertainer above the stage or over the audience, or other special effects. Only after all preparations are completed do the concert performances take place—often creating the illusion of spontaneous events that just unfold naturally.

In similar fashion, practically all aspects of social life involve **social organization**, the process by which society is structured as a system of social interaction to meet the needs of its members. Just as we may watch a live concert without thinking about the organization behind the scenes, we often carry out our day-to-day lives without consciously thinking about the organization or structure at all levels of the society that surrounds us.

In this chapter, we will explore basically how social organization takes place. This structuring of society makes it possible for each generation to experience culture and socialization as the social system continues to evolve and change. To begin, we first examine how social organization is influenced by social needs.

SOCIAL NEEDS: THE BASIS FOR ORGANIZATION

The particular form a society takes depends in large part on how social needs are defined and addressed by its members. The basic categories of these needs are usually the same for most if not all societies. However, specific aspects of each need may vary from society to society, as we will see. In addition, power and conflict often play a role in determining (1) how needs are defined and (2) which needs are given the greatest priority.

Population Maintenance and Control

Simply stated, *population maintenance* refers to the reproduction of society members. Every society, for its own survival, must guarantee the maintenance of its population base. This is accomplished mainly through the family institution, the structural unit in every society charged with, among other things, the reproduction of society members. The family is reinforced by a set of cultural norms that encourage people to have children and become parents. In addition, other institutional areas like religion, school, and government, through their norms, also act to reinforce the family and, in many societies, lend support and assistance toward the socialization of children.

Although population maintenance historically has been and still is an important social need, so is the need for *population control.* Many countries today are grossly overpopulated and there is a real threat that world overpopulation could permanently destroy the delicate ecological balance of the planet Earth (see Chapter 13). This is of great concern to scientists of several disciplines. Nonetheless, the entire issue of (1) whether or not to recognize the need for population control and (2) how best to handle it remains a source of great controversy and conflict throughout the world.

Division of Labor

Every society must also address the need for a *division of labor,* a system through which essential tasks are assigned to and carried out by the necessary numbers of people. Traditionally, the division of labor was based largely on sex with needed functions allocated along the lines of "men's work" and "women's work." In modern technological societies, the trend has been toward the organizing of needed societal functions according to occupational spe-

The division of labor in American society today is based more on education, occupational training, and expertise than on sex. (*Left:* Bob Daemmrich Photo. *Right:* A. Becker/The Image Bank.)

cialization and technical competence. In this regard, the sex of the position holder is not nearly as important as it was once thought to be.

Today in modern industrial societies, technology and the need for specialized expertise have made characteristics such as size and brute strength totally obsolete as requirements for most social positions. In addition, women and their supporters throughout the twentieth century—particularly in the United States—have organized politically and socially to effect changes in law and social policy, which has assured their greater participation in society. Women today engage in practically all occupations, including such traditional male positions as police officer, construction worker, and airline pilot. They have amply demonstrated their ability to perform these functions very well, given appropriate socialization, training, and experience. Likewise, men today can be just as effective as women in providing love, affection, and emotional support as primary parents to small children. Men also perform well in traditionally female occupations like elementary school teacher and nurse. Re-

gardless of the occupations or functions carried out, people are motivated to fulfill these obligations by feelings of both accomplishment and self-satisfaction, which are reinforced by social rewards including money and social recognition.

Communication

Each society must make use of one or more learned systems of symbolic *communication* that permit and guarantee the effective functioning of socialization. In preliterate cultures, this takes the form of conventional spoken language, as well as oral histories of family and society which are memorized and handed down to each succeeding generation. Modern technological societies, by comparison, have additional means of communication, including books, other literary forms, and the electronic mass media.

The organizational apparatus needed to support and implement communication in modern societies is complex and is connected to the division of labor. The print media, for instance, require the coordination of organizations that include publishing companies, book stores and other vendors, schools, and libraries. People in occupations involved in this area include authors and writers, journalists, editors, photographers, layout and design people, printers, bookbinders, marketing representatives, booksellers, educators, and librarians. The organization needed to coordinate the electronic mass media, such as television, is even more varied and complex.

In addition, those who own or otherwise have access to the media determine in large part what is communicated, to whom, and for what purposes. In totalitarian countries, most forms of mass communication are closely controlled and monitored by their governments to ensure that the people receive the "correct" message. In the United States and other democratic societies, a free press furnishes people with varied viewpoints on most issues.

Shared Values and Goals: Consensus or Conflict?

The need for shared values and goals is also important in every society. However, there is some debate among sociologists as to whether the societal values and goals needed for social organization are formed mainly through consensus or conflict.

From the functionalist perspective, the majority of members of any society must be in fundamental agreement with or at least give their consent to basic *shared values and goals.* Social agreement concerning values forms the basis for both the formation of essential norms and the social order and cohesion that result from them. Shared values and norms, in turn, act as much of the foundation for establishing the dominant goals of a society. Often a society's future is influenced by the goals set by its people or their leaders. In 1961, President John F. Kennedy established as a national goal the landing of men on the moon by the

end of the decade. This objective, supported by the American people, was met in 1969 and helped set the agenda for the continuing U.S. space program from the 1970s to the present. During the 1960s, public support for the space program was relatively easy to obtain. This was because (1) landing men on the moon was a popular dream, (2) it did not interfere with the goals of most interest groups, and (3) the United States was in a perceived "space race" with the Russians to be first on the moon, which appealed to the nationalistic pride of most Americans.

However, social consensus regarding shared values and goals is often difficult to obtain, particularly in fast-changing, pluralistic societies. The United States is, to a significant degree, a nation of diverse subcultures and interest groups. This has resulted to some extent in **anomie**, a state of confused norms (normlessness) brought about by rapid change and social complexity (Durkheim, 1966). With so many value systems espoused by so many different groups in society, it becomes very difficult to establish what the dominant norms are or should be. For children growing up in a fast-changing, technological society, there is often confusion because the norms and values taught by parents, peers, teachers, certain subcultures, and the media often conflict with one another. As a result, individuals may become unsure of how they should act, because what is acceptable or unacceptable behavior is unclear. High crime rates, racial prejudice, and drug abuse serve as specific examples of conditions which derive from a complex social system where anomie is prevalent.

From a conflict perspective, those in political, economic, and social leadership positions often use their power and influence to impose their values and goals on society as a whole. In the political arena, this is manifested in the ability to influence legislation and public policy regardless of public sentiment. The Prohibition era of the 1920s and the 55-mile-per-hour speed limit of the 1970s and 1980s serve as notable examples. Individuals and groups with economic power may support certain candidates with "favorable attitudes" for political office, purchase the services of media to persuade the general public to their point of view, and affect the supply and demand for jobs and consumer products. Those with social power often have personal charisma or "contacts" with political and economic power holders to influence others concerning values and goals.

The Maintenance of Social Order

To guarantee its survival and maintain social order, every society must have one or more mechanisms of **social control** (see Chapter 3). This involves a process designed to maintain conformity to dominant norms. The most effective form of social control ideally occurs within the family institution as the child is socialized with a coherent set of values that correspond to the established norms of the larger society. This process is then reinforced by other institutions, including the church and the school. When socialization is successful, the developing individual internalizes societal norms as a personal code of conduct that governs behavior to a large extent throughout life. For most people in most circumstances, these *internal social controls* are adequate to get them to conform.

When conventional internal controls are not sufficient to maintain conformity, much more punitive and formal sanctions must be applied. The society is then obliged to use *external social controls*, which may range from an official reprimand at a person's job or a traffic fine for double parking to the loss of liberty through imprisonment for the commission of a crime. Extreme violations of social order are handled in an organized manner through the criminal justice system, which consists of police, the courts, and prisons. Each of these

components, in turn, has its own form of organization. Police departments in large cities, for example, are complex organizations arranged in districts or precincts, each with its own captain who typically reports to a division chief. Officers with ranks under captain are specialists who carry out designated duties in specific areas: patrol, traffic control, narcotics and vice, and homicide (Taft and England, 1966). Although societies must rely primarily on successful socialization to maintain social control, it is sometimes necessary to apply external social controls to the behavior of individuals for whom socialization has been less than effective.

LEVELS OF SOCIAL ORGANIZATION

Almost every social act we perform—from the one-minute encounter with a clerk in a department store to the complex interworkings of large-scale associations, basic institutions, and whole societies—involves structured forms of behavior. In this regard, sociologists generally distinguish between two basic levels of social organization: microlevel organization and macrolevel organization.

Microlevel Organization

Microlevel organization is concerned with the patterned ways in which people act at the local community level in social encounters, relationships, and groups. The emphasis here is on how we act, react, and interact in our everyday encounters with others and how the smallest elements of a society's social structure, such as social relationships, are structured. When we interact with others, even in the most brief and casual encounters with strangers, our behavior is usually somewhat patterned and predictable. In fact, much of what we do at the microlevel approaches social ritual. Many of us tend to get up on the same side of the bed each morning, begin on the same side of the grocery store each time we do our shopping, and sit in the same seat at the kitchen table when we eat meals with our families. While it is true that the human experience is rich with individual diversity and opportunities for spontaneity, most of us operate within the structured boundaries set by our society and the habits we have acquired from our experiences with it.

These habits take several forms. For instance, even the way we encounter people in our society is highly structured. Typically, many of us avoid making eye contact with a total stranger we pass on the sidewalk. A person we recognize but know only as a casual acquaintance is usually met with a ''Hi,'' at which point he or she will respond back with a ''Hi.'' This is a one-stroke greeting ritual. If we pass someone we know somewhat better, we will say ''Hi,'' the other person will say, ''Hi,'' we will then say, ''How are you?'' and he or she will usually respond with ''Fine.'' This is a two-stroke greeting ritual. If the interaction goes beyond two strokes, the individuals will usually have a conversation that could last for several minutes or longer.

In numerous other ways, our social behavior at the microlevel is highly organized. Many of us say ''Hello'' when answering the phone, ''Have a nice day'' in a customer service role, and ''Bless you'' when someone sneezes. Likewise, many of us learn how to use certain cues to get people to respond to us in predictable ways. Depending on one's needs or purposes, a long and silent stare will cause most people to talk, standing up after a long meeting is a useful cue to end the meeting, and placing one's coat or sweater on a theater chair will usually reserve a seat.

Our relationships with family, friends, and co-workers are also structured in particular ways. Take a person's own individual family for example. Most Americans come from a family background organized around a father, a mother, and one or more siblings. Others experience a childhood in which elderly grandparents or other relatives live in the home with them and the rest of their family members. Some, because of divorce, abandonment, poverty, or other disruptions, are reared partially or totally by grandparents or a single parent.

Individual family organization also depends to some degree on other factors including class, ethnicity, religion, and size. Some parents, because of these and other factors, may be more likely to be authoritarian, democratic, or permissive in terms of how they rear their children. Size alone can affect the dynamics of the group. Older children in large families, for instance, have often found themselves in the role of surrogate parent, responsible for the behavior of their little brothers and sisters. The eldest child with only one or two siblings rarely is expected to take on this responsibility. Other examples of microlevel organization include the structured patterns of interaction evident in a local high school, church, rock music band, grocery store, or garden club.

Macrolevel Organization

By contrast, **macrolevel organization** represents the manner in which large-scale associations (organizations), basic institutions, and societies are organized and interact with one another. Large-scale associations include large organizations like school systems or colleges, church denominations, and corporations, as well as whole industries devoted to the production and promotion of such things as cars, computers, rock music, education, defense, and health care.

To illustrate, we might compare a community college with a major university as large-scale associations. Both provide their students with a fine education but are organized differently. The community college offers two-year academic degree programs along with vocational-technical certificate programs and continuing education courses. It stresses quality teaching with faculty members who teach in small classes and use a student-centered approach. A community college is usually smaller than a university and is strictly a commuter institution that serves primarily a local population. A major university, by comparison, offers four-year academic degree programs and graduate programs leading to advanced degrees. Its faculty members are research and publishing oriented, often teach large auditorium classes, and typically use a subject-centered approach. A major university tends to be a large residential institution that attracts a regional, and often national, student body.

Institutions. As mentioned in Chapter 1, an *institution* is a major structural component of a society that addresses a special area of human needs. Some simple societies are organized around one institution, the family group or kinship clan, in which all necessary social functions are carried out. Other more complex societies have *differentiated institutions,* each with its own specialized area of focus and concern. In modern social systems, there are five of these fundamental, yet specialized, institutions—the family, the economy, education, government, and religion—which together comprise the essential structural building blocks of society.

Institutions in different societies vary in the ways they are organized. Government in the United States, for example, is structured as a representative democracy with a two-party political system and three relatively equal branches: the executive branch headed by a president, the legislative branch, and the judiciary. Cuba, by contrast, is governed by a military dictator as head of state; Western Samoa has a tribal chief; Oman, a sultan; Ku-

wait, an emir; and Jordan, a king (*World Almanac and Book of Facts, 1988*). The religious institution in some societies is predominantly Christian, while others may practice Buddhism, Islam, Confucianism, or any one or a combination of religious belief systems. In addition, the family institution is organized very differently in various societies, some allowing only monogamous marriage (one spouse) while others allow polygamous marriage (multiple spouses).

Societies and Their Characteristics. The largest and most complex system of social interaction is a **society**. A society is the largest grouping of individuals with specific characteristics in a particular system of social interaction.

Given this definition, there are two basic varieties of societies: animal societies and human societies. Many lower animal species including ants, bees, wolves, baboons, and whales have social interaction systems similar in many respects to those of humans. *Animal societies* have the characteristics of (1) occupying a definite territory, (2) perpetuating their numbers through sexual reproduction, (3) being relatively independent (like a hive of bees or a pride of lions), and (4) possessing an organized way of life determined in large part by instincts. *Human societies* have the first three characteristics in common with their animal counterparts, differing only in characteristic 4 with a way of life determined by culture rather than instinct (Biesanz and Biesanz, 1973).

One of the most interesting characteristics of human societies is territoriality. Like the lower animals, we humans are territorial creatures who use various devices at both macro- and microlevels to claim space. However, unlike lower animals who use, among other things, urine and claw scratches on trees to establish territorial boundaries, humans accomplish this politically at the macrolevel through treaty arrangements with other societies. Societal or national boundaries are taken very seriously and, if threatened, are defended under force of arms if necessary. In fact, wars between nations are often caused by disputes over territory.

At the microlevel, most of us carry an invisible bubble of personal space around with us everywhere we go. The size of this territorial bubble is influenced by one's culture and the social situation, but in America, except for things like standing in line or being in an elevator, it is normally two to four or five feet in diameter. In our culture, this is usually the minimum distance we like to keep from other people, especially strangers. Americans, for instance, will usually skip at least a seat or two, if possible, between themselves and other people in a movie theater. In addition, let us suppose that two Americans are sitting in a restaurant at a table that could seat four. Two strangers enter and sit down with them rather than occupy one of the empty tables that are available. If this indeed did occur, the original occupants at the table would probably be surprised and might feel threatened or offended. However, in Germany and other parts of Europe where other standards of territoriality apply, to sit at a separate table when two chairs are available at a table already occupied would be considered ill-mannered. Physical objects are also used to "stake a claim" to personal space "as when sunglasses and lotion claim a beach chair, or a purse a seat in an airliner" (Goffman, 1972, p. 41).

Levels of Organization in Perspective

Historically, sociologists have tended to see microlevel and macrolevel analysis as separate categories to be studied differently with distinct theoretical perspectives and research approaches. Microsociologists tended to be interactionists who examined the everyday behavior of people in relationships and groups. Macrosociologists were usually functionalists or conflict theorists interested in investigating patterns of social behavior at the institutional and societal levels. Some sociologists today, however, see the division of social organization into the micro- and macrolevels to be a false dichotomy and favor a more integrated approach.

Functionalist, Conflict, and Interactionist Applications. As shown in Figure 5-1, perhaps it is more useful to see social organization as a continuum consisting of structured patterns at all levels of society, with overlapping characteristics and influences on one another. From this perspective, social organization is evident everywhere, from the most superficial encounters between two or three people, through relationships and groups, to the structured social patterns characteristic of the largest and most stable associations, institutions, and societies.

As we have seen, even the briefest, most superficial encounters at the microlevel can involve a tremendous degree of structure and predictability. Both the functionalist and conflict perspectives can be used here in addition to the interactionist approach to describe and analyze both functional and dysfunctional aspects of social relations and how power is organized and used.

Likewise, the emphasis on meaning and perception by interactionists and the power perspective offered by conflict theorists are also helpful in studying the actions of large-scale organizations, institutions, and whole societies. Just as small groups have informal means of communication and control, so do larger organizations and institutions (Schelling, 1978). For instance, chief executive officers (CEOs) of corporations and presidents of universities can often influence the impact of formal public policy on their respective institutions by having informal conversations with key legislators. In addition, corporations, governments, colleges, and other macro-struc-

Figure 5-1 Levels of Social Organization: A Continuum

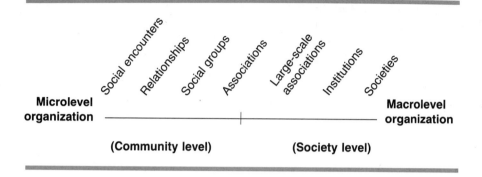

Microlevel
organization   (Community level)   (Society level)   Macrolevel
organization

tures often have organizational mind-sets caused by the perceptions and actions of small groups of key decision-makers (micro-structures) who are in control.

TYPES OF SOCIETIES

There are several ways to categorize the organization of societies as macrostructures. Perhaps the most useful form of classification is **means of subsistence**, the specific process used by a society to provide food and other resources needed by its people for survival and prosperity (see Figure 5-2). Although there are numerous types of subsistence systems, they all can be placed into four general categories for the purpose of identifying types of societies: hunting-gathering, horticultural, agrarian, and industrial. In addition, a fifth type, the postindustrial society, now appears to be emerging.

Figure 5-2 Types of Societies

Societal Type	Means of Subsistence	Examples
Hunting-gathering (Nomadic bands)	Hunting for meat and foraging for edibles (bulb roots, berries, grubs, insects, bird eggs, honey, burrowing rodents, etc.)	!Kung Bushmen of Africa; Arunta of Australia
Horticultural (Villages and tribes)	Simple slash-and-burn agriculture and the use of domesticated cattle, goats, and fowl	Yanomamo of Brazil; Nuer of Africa
Agrarian (City or nation states with large peasant class)	Advanced agricultural methods (the plow, irrigation systems, crop rotation, etc.), some mercantilism, and centralized governmental authority	People's Republic of China; much of Indochina
Industrial (Nation states)	High technology with a cash economy, mass production, and specialized occupations	United States; Japan

Hunting-Gathering Societies

The first societies, which emerged with the dawn of humankind about three or four million years ago, consisted of small bands that hunted and foraged for a living. Lacking the means to either produce food or preserve it, members of **hunting-gathering societies** lived from day to day on what they could kill or find and took life literally a meal at a time. Social organization revolved around one or a few nuclear families, the total band comprising only eight or ten to forty or fifty members. The division of labor was based largely on sex, adult males usually if not exclusively placed in the role of hunters and women usually assigned the role of gatherers who searched for roots, berries, and other edibles. In hunting-gathering cultures, private property or personal possessions were of little value because of the necessity of pursuing a nomadic way of life.

Although this type of social system was largely replaced as more advanced forms evolved, a few hunting-gathering bands still exist in some parts of the world. In the Kalahari desert region of southern Africa, the !Kung Bushmen still thrive in small wandering bands (Lee and Devore, 1976). In their society, food obtained by each family is shared communally with the rest of the band. Decision making among these peaceful and gentle people is quite egalitarian; there are no official leaders or laws. Disputes are settled by informal agreement between the parties involved, in consultation with other members of the band. The Arunta of Australia are also hunter-gatherers. These aboriginal people live in small one or two nuclear family bands and hunt animals for food, including the kangaroo and ostrich-like emu. Since they have no bows and arrows for hunting, they must rely on clubs, spears, and boomerangs (Elkin, 1954). To augment their diet, they also forage for edible roots and fungi, bird and reptile eggs, grubworms of moths and other insects, and snakes and burrowing rodents.

Horticultural Societies

Horticultural societies rely mainly for subsistence on simple slash-and-burn agriculture and the use of domesticated animals. They originated about 10,000 years ago with the *agricultural revolution*, which first made it possible to both produce food and store it for future use. With this new technology, wandering bands evolved into clans and tribes who lived in relatively permanent villages. Slash-and-burn agriculture involved cutting down all trees and foliage, burning it thoroughly, then planting primitive grains in the ashes, which acted as fertilizer. Domestication of cattle, goats, and fowl resulted in a surplus of meat which was readily available when needed, as well as secondary protein in the form of milk, cheese, and eggs. As these types of societies emerged, they became characterized by charismatic headmen (who had significant unofficial authority over the group), emphasis on blood and marriage lineage within the clan, and the development of rites of passage to reinforce lineage and a sense of belonging.

Two notable examples of horticultural societies today are the Yanomamo of Brazil and the Nuer of Sudan. The Yanomamo, as discussed in Chapter 3, are a very warlike tribal people who live in small villages ruled informally by male elders. Although there are many villages that share the Yanomamo culture, each one is a separate social unit of about sixty to ninety people in which each person is considered to be related to all village members by blood or marriage. These different village groups often engage in war with one another, alternating raids and uneasy alliances being more or less a continuous fact of life. In the Yanomamo villages, each family has its own garden, but the woman is required to do most of the work. The culture is such that "marriage does not enhance the status of the girl, for her duties as wife require her to assume difficult and laborious tasks too menial to be executed by the men" (Chagnon, 1983, p. 111).

The Nuer of the Nile river area of Sudan in southeastern Africa consist of several large tribes of about 5,000 persons each, with each tribe divided into several clans. Although they cultivate crops including millet (sorghum) and corn, the Nuer are primarily pastoral people with a subsistence system centered on the raising of cattle for milk (their number one food) and meat. Cattle are privately owned, but land for cultivation belongs to the community. Although the family of the groom pays a bride price in cattle to the bride's family for her hand in marriage, women in the Nuer culture are treated in a much more egalitarian manner (Service, 1971) than those of Yanomamo.

Agrarian Societies

About 5,500 years ago, **agrarian societies** began to develop. These were social systems organized around advanced agricultural methods and centralized governmental authority. Specifically, they were marked by the invention of the plow, the development of sophisticated irrigation systems, the rise of technologies including the development of metallurgy and the use of the wheel, and the emergence of first the city-state and, later, during and after the Middle Ages (400–1400 A.D.), the nation state. Therefore, the agricultural revolution begun earlier continued to gather momentum and was joined by a second, *the urban revolution,* which was characterized chiefly by the rise of cities and the development of formalized government.

With centralized authority placed in the hands of a few, the resources and technology of the society could be rationally coordinated, as in the planning of irrigation systems, the rotation of crops, and the terracing of fields. Crop yields per acre of ground increased manyfold over the yield of traditional slash-and-burn techniques, and food surpluses became common. The increased food supply caused populations to expand accordingly, as a result of a higher standard of living that allowed more children to survive and become adults. Because intensive agriculture required that the division of labor be taken out of the family and placed under the jurisdiction of centralized authority, the organization of societies was made much more efficient. Consequently, societies grew in size from tribal chiefdoms to major civilizations in places like Egypt, China, Greece, Rome, and Central and South America.

As time passed, civilizations rose and fell. In Europe, the decline (beginning about 400 A.D.) and ultimate demise of Greco-Roman civilization (by 900 A.D.) was accompanied by a decline in traditional political, social, and economic institutions and a corresponding rise in the feudal system of the Middle Ages. However, the land and those with the desire to work it remained, and the agrarian system survived. Intensive agriculture came under the control of an estate system administered mainly by lords who owned the land. These estates were in turn managed by supervisors appointed by the lords and were actually farmed by sharecropping peasants called serfs.

By the year 1400, the medieval period was giving way to the Renaissance, and the feudal system was being replaced by the nation-state and the reestablishment of large towns with fairly autonomous local governments. In addition, the economy was rapidly expanding from its agrarian base to include merchant and craft occupations. Other changes included growth in manufacturing, the development of modern banking and credit systems, the harnessing of water power for smelting iron and producing sheet metal, and, by the late 1400s, the printing of books (Easton, 1965). These and other developments set the stage for industrialization.

Industrial Societies

The *industrial revolution* began in England, about 1750. Its tremendous impact has shaped the way many societies have been organized ever since. Industrialization involved the development of a means of subsistence based on a factory system of mass production. The British first developed machines for mass producing textiles. Later in the 1790s, the American Eli Whitney invented the cotton gin and also developed the principle of interchangeable parts to aid in mass production. These and other innovations made it possible for machines to do the work of thousands of workers and to do it much more quickly and efficiently (Bailey, 1966).

With mass production, an almost unlimited supply of goods could be produced at lower costs. This made it possible to increase the standard of living for the average citizen.

The production process became divided into many specialized tasks and subtasks, and the concept of assembly line was ultimately developed for use in most industries. Workers were employed to carry out these specialized tasks for cash wages, which were in turn used to purchase the consumer goods—food, clothing, shelter, and other commodities—needed by the family unit. Thus, work shifted from the home and farm to the industrial factory, and the family became transformed from a unit of production (for example, the family farm or business) to a unit of consumption.

Today **industrial societies** are the most complex and technologically advanced social systems in the world. This is due mainly to factors such as mass production, specialized occupations, and accompanying urbanization. However, the very complexity and dynamism of industrial societies tend to make them more vulnerable to several types of social disorganization than many of the simpler hunting-gathering, horticultural, and agrarian societies. The contrast between the United States with its high crime and suicide rates and the Nootka Indians of British Columbia serves as

The diverse ways in which societies are organized result in very different lifestyles for their inhabitants. (*Left:* Guido Alberto Rossi/The Image Bank. *Right:* Copyright S. Punwell/The Image Bank.)

one illustration. The Nootka live on the northwest coast of North America and make their living from fishing, hunting, and gathering.

> Murder, theft, and other crimes common to organized societies are in fact very rare among the Nootka. There is no formal machinery of social control; most disputes are settled by public dressing-downs at a feast . . . if nothing else such as private counsel suffices. Revenge by an individual seems to have been rare, and suicide, the ultimate protest against society, had not occurred within the memory of any informants (Service, 1971, p. 225).

Nonetheless, the industrial organization of modern societies has resulted in an average standard of living unprecedented in human history. Inhabitants of industrial societies like Japan, the United States, and countries in Western Europe have superior standards of food, housing, medical care, public health and sanitation, and transportation.

Postindustrial Societies: Social Systems of the Future

According to sociologist Daniel Bell (1973) and several other social thinkers (Lipset, 1979; Toffler, 1980; Naisbitt, 1984), the United States and possibly other industrial societies are now making the transition to what will be the **postindustrial societies** of the future. These emerging social systems, in the view of some social scientists, will be dominated by service and information economies. This transition appears to be under way,

With the emergence of the information revolution and service-oriented economies, the United States and other technological societies appear to be making the transition to the postindustrial societies of the future. (Copyright Jeff Smith/The Image Bank.)

brought about primarily by an *information revolution* already in its first stages. With dramatic technologies being developed in computers, semiconductors, communication satellites, and other areas, societies in the twenty-first century promise to be organized very differently from those of today.

Author and consultant John Naisbitt (1984) reports that the shifting distribution of occupations is one sign that we are entering a new era.

> In 1950, only 17 percent of us worked in information jobs. Now more than 65 percent of us work with information as programmers, teachers, clerks, secretaries, accountants, stock brokers, managers, insurance people, bureaucrats, lawyers, bankers, and technicians. And many more workers hold information jobs within manufacturing companies. Most Americans spend their time creating, processing, or distributing information. For example, workers in banking, the stock market, and insurance all hold information jobs (p. 4).

KEY FORMS OF ORGANIZATION WITHIN SOCIETIES

Within the different types of societies at both the micro- and macrolevels are several forms of social organization. Among the most fundamental of these are kinship, fealty, groups, social positions, contract, and bureaucracy. Together they comprise much of the foundation for the way the process of human social interaction takes place.

Kinship

The manner in which family relations are organized is **kinship**. In all societies, blood and marriage are universal bases for kinship organization, but, in most, one or the other tends to be predominant. Most societies, particularly nonindustrial ones, have **consanguineal kinship** systems which are based primarily on

blood ties. These societies normally have an *extended family* of several generations of kin who depend on one another for mutual support and protection. Given the relatively simple division of labor in hunting-gathering and horticultural cultures, all societal functions are family-based and carried out mainly within this single institution. In these societies, male dominance is the usual pattern, women (wives and daughters) taking a secondary role, and family name and property passed from father to son. Some, however, such as the Navajo of the American Southwest, are female-focused, or matrilineal, with property being passed between generations through the women's bloodlines (Witherspoon, 1975).

Industrial societies are more likely to have **affinal kinship** systems, organized around the marriage relationship between husband and wife. Here the *nuclear family*, consisting of only the married couple and their children, tends to be the dominant family form. This transition from consanguineal to affinal kinship began with the dawn of the industrial revolution as several family functions that were once primarily family-based—like education, religion, and economic production—gradually fell within the domain of separate, specialized institutions. With the shift away from an agrarian economy to one characterized by specialized occupations and cash wages, the consanguineal kinship system, with its emphasis on the extended family as a cooperative, self-supporting unit became obsolete, at least from an economic standpoint.

Today in modern societies like the United States, extended family kin—including assorted grandparents, aunts, uncles, and cousins—tend to live in separate locations. In fact, given the demands for geographical mobility placed on many technical and professional workers in industrial societies, the nuclear family has become the only meaningful family unit in many instances because extended kin

U.S. Secret Service agents possess fealty to the point of using their bodies as shields to protect the life of the president and others in their charge. (UPI/ Bettmann Newsphotos.)

often live several hundred miles away or farther. Consequently, affinal kinship has become the standard family pattern in the United States during the twentieth century.

Fealty

The personal loyalty of a follower toward a leader is **fealty**. The leader in this regard may be an individual, a group, or a large organization or institution. Fealty involves a strong commitment to perform a service for or fulfill an obligation to the leader even, in many cases, at great risk and personal hardship. During the late Middle Ages, from the ninth through the thirteenth centuries, fealty was

an important ingredient in the organization of the feudal system. Not only did feudal lords band together in fealty to one another for mutual protection, but each lord usually had in his service a group of soldiers or knights who would take oaths of fealty to lay down their lives if necessary, to protect the lord, his lady, and their family, property, and honor.

Almost everyone is familiar with the legend of King Arthur and the Knights of the Round Table. As the story goes, the king went to fight in the Crusades and left Queen Guinevere in the care of Lancelot, his most trusted knight. While he was away, Lancelot violated his oath of fealty, he and the queen fell in love, and Arthur's trust was betrayed. While largely a fictional morality tale, it serves as a literary illustration of how fealty facilitates social cohesion and how its violation can cause social disorganization.

In modern society, fealty takes a variety of forms. Most large business organizations attempt to create a corporate climate that encourages loyalty to and identification with the organization by its employees. When this is successful, morale and productivity tend to be high, and affected employees become "company people." On the athletic field, it is called team pride and stems from a commitment to the coach, the team captain, and the team itself. The military term for fealty is *esprit de corps*, an identification with one's unit, from the squad and platoon levels to one's branch of service. Regardless of the term used, fealty acts as a cohesive binding force to promote the effective functioning of several different types of groups and organizations in society.

Groups

One of the most fundamental forms of social organization is the group. A **group** consists of two or more people with one or more characteristics in common. Most groups are easily recognizable and have clear-cut boundaries that allow us to distinguish members from nonmembers. Group boundaries are established by the characteristics of members, the norms that govern their behavior, the behavior patterns that stem from such norms, and group goals. *Social groups* (informal social interaction) and *associations* (formal organization) are types of groups largely governed by these factors. Therefore, family is easily differentiated from friends, members of a rock music group from members of a country-western band, and employees of General Motors from members of the U. S. Marines.

Other types of groups may be difficult to precisely identify or understand because of their temporary nature and constantly changing characteristics. *Physical aggregates* (crowds) and *publics* are two notable examples. Nonetheless, the groups we belong to and interact with play an important role in shaping our social behavior. More detailed information is provided in Chapter 6 to follow, which deals exclusively with groups and group behavior.

Social Positions

The term **social position** refers to a socially defined location or status a person occupies in society, along with a set of expected behavior patterns that act to regulate that person's behavior. Most of us are involved in several social positions simultaneously. In the most general sense, we are, first of all, members of a society. This position carries with it the responsibility to act in ways acceptable to the norms of our culture. We also occupy several specialized social positions that may include family member, spouse, parent, employee, supervisor, student, citizen, or consumer. Each of these positions requires some of our time and results in portions of our behavior being organized in particular ways. Take your position as college student for instance. Each week, you devote time and energy to attending class, taking notes, reading this textbook, and, it is hoped, organizing your work in preparation for successful performance on exams. Your other positions related to family and job can be demanding also. Thus, the social positions you and others occupy act to organize social behavior to a remarkable degree.

Types of Social Positions. Basic types of social positions include ascribed status, achieved status, and master status. An **ascribed status** is a social position assigned to a person at birth or otherwise imposed by society. The central point here is that the individual has little or no choice in determining the ascribed positions he or she occupies. Examples of ascribed status include being born male or female, belonging to a particular race, ethnic group, or nationality, and being an elementary school student, teenager, or a senior citizen. By contrast, an **achieved status** is a social position earned through individual effort. Being a high school or college graduate, an employee, a spouse, or parent, winning the Nobel prize, and committing murder are all examples of achieved status. In addition, most adults typically identify with one of their social positions above all others. This becomes the primary source of their social identity called the **master status**. In the United States, when two men meet for the first time at a social gathering, they will usually project a master status related to their employment or occupation. Women traditionally have identified primarily with the marital-homemaking position. Today, however, particularly for college educated professional women in a dual-career marriage, there is a similar tendency for some to see themselves primarily in terms of their jobs or careers.

Roles and Their Complications. In Chapter 4 on socialization, we saw how, according to George Herbert Mead and other interactionists, children mentally rehearse for the social positions they will carry out as adults by engaging in role-taking, the imitation and playing out of adult roles. By adulthood, when positions are actually occupied, each is characterized by a **role**—the expected forms of behavior, obligation, and privilege that go with a social position.

Roles form the building blocks that make up the structure of the social positions we hold. They also determine in large part how we behave as participants. Largely through the influence of roles and how they are sanctioned by the larger society, the social positions we occupy not only shape our behavior but determine to a significant degree who we are. As Peter Berger (1963) says:

One feels more ardent by kissing, more humble by kneeling and more angry by shaking one's fist. That is, the kiss not only expresses ardor but manufactures it. Roles carry with them both certain actions and emotions and attitudes that belong to these actions. The professor putting on an act that pretends to wisdom comes to feel wise. The preacher finds himself believing what he preaches. The soldier discovers martial stirrings in his breast as he puts on the uniform. In each case, while the emotion or attitude may have been present before the role was taken on, the latter inevitably strengthens what was there before. In many instances there is every reason to suppose that nothing at all anteceded the playing of the role in the actor's consciousness. In other words, one becomes wise by being appointed a professor, believing by engaging in activities that presuppose belief, and ready for battle by marching in formation (p. 96).

Social positions in modern societies often involve a **role set**, two or more distinct roles that relate to a single social position (Merton, 1968). The physician, for example, carries out one role in regard to patients, another in relation to nurses, and others attached to interactions with colleagues, medical students, and pharmaceutical salespeople. In similar fashion, a college baseball coach has different role obligations to players, the college he is employed by, other college coaches, coaches in high schools he recruits players from, and professional scouts who wish to recruit his players.

Sometimes the obligations associated with our various social positions cause complications for us in the form of role ambiguity, role strain, and role conflict. **Role ambiguity** occurs when the obligations attached to a social position are not clear. This often takes place in a new social position or relationship. Most of us have felt a little unsure of ourselves on a first date, in the first few days at a new job, or in the first few weeks as a college student.

Likewise, adolescence is often a confusing time for many young people with few, if any, clear-cut role demands. Role ambiguity can also occur when we are placed in an awkward situation in a social position that is normally well defined. A person might, for instance, feel very uncertain of how to proceed if a best friend asked for advice in how to handle his or her failing marriage.

Role strain occurs when (1) conflicting role demands are built into a single social position, (2) a person cannot fulfill the role demands of a given position, or both (Goode, 1960, Merton, 1976). Take the middle management supervisor in a production plant for example. Upper management wants lower labor costs and tries to freeze wages, while lower-level workers want wage increases and promotions. The conflicting role demands placed on the middle manager by these two groups can sometimes make it difficult to succeed in that social position.

The teenage marriage represents a good illustration of role strain that can occur when the role demands of a given social position simply cannot be met and the individual is overwhelmed by obligations. Young couples who marry while one or both are still in high school face role strain brought on by emotional and social immaturity, inadequate financial resources, the lack of credentials and experience to obtain adequate employment, family pressure, and a number of other problems. Taken as a whole, these elements of role strain contribute to a high teenage divorce rate. Regardless of type, unresolved role strain can lead to lowered self-esteem and, in some cases, even illness, heart attack, and premature death (Krantz, Grunberg, and Baum, 1985).

Role conflict is stress caused when conflicting role demands are built into separate social positions, each of which an individual is expected to carry out successfully. Most of us experience role conflict from time to time when the obligations of the different positions we occupy interfere with each other. The role demands of one's job may conflict with those of one's marriage. If the requirement to spend extra hours at work becomes a long-term condition, a spouse may feel neglected, and the marriage could suffer. You may have experienced role conflict as a college student, particularly if you have an outside job, are married, or both. If you do not put in sufficient study time, you may fail. But if you are not available to work when your employer needs you, you could lose your job. Obligations to a spouse or other family members may also require your attention. Consequently, many of us often feel like a juggler who must keep several balls in the air at the same time. It can be a difficult task and often requires careful planning and prioritizing. Even so, sometimes we must be wise enough to realize when we are overextending ourselves and need to cut back in certain areas.

Contract

Ever since the Middle Ages, **contract** has been an important basis for social organization. Particularly in Western societies, contracts between two or more parties that involve the exchange of one promise for another have represented an important way to structure social relations. In feudal times, free peasants would often contract with a territorial lord to exchange their services for his protection. Unlike the general and implied nature of promises made and benefits received through kinship and fealty, contractual relations, as they evolved in Western societies, were very specific and explicit. As societies became larger and more complex, the need for specific and clearly defined contracts became more important. The rise of modern business economies after the Middle Ages, followed first by the industrial revolution and later by the high technology of the twentieth century, have made them even more necessary.

Today the formal and specific nature of

The many faces of social organization.

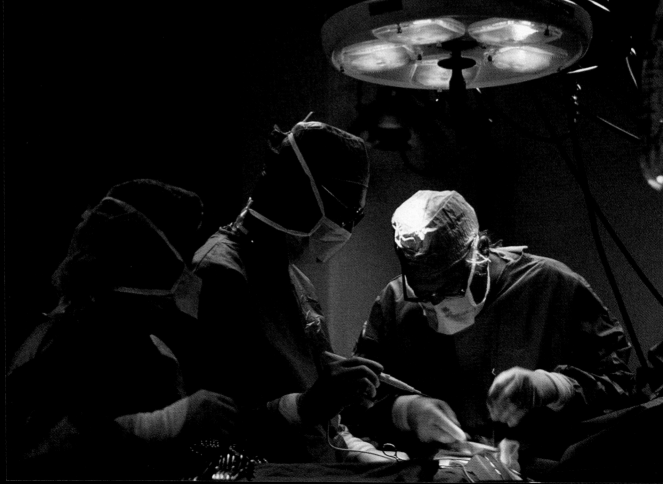

contracts has made them an indispensable form of organizing a wide variety of relationships in modern society. At the microlevel, we enter into contracts on a continuing basis each time we participate in the consumer economy by purchasing goods and services. All the activities of modern life, from charging a meal on VISA, paying college tuition to purchasing the clothes we wear, the cars we drive, or the houses we live in usually involves contracts with one or more parties. Contracts at the macrolevel of society are more likely to have political and social, as well as economic, dimensions. They may include areas as diverse as labor contracts, corporate mergers, and nuclear test ban treaties.

Bureaucracy

With the development of early civilizations like Mesopotamia and Egypt, decision making eventually came under the control of centralized authority. This was accompanied by the rise of **bureaucracy**, a form of social organization in which the work of participants in large-scale associations (organizations) is rationally organized and coordinated by professional managers. Without such leadership, the building of the pyramids in ancient Egypt, the construction of the roads and aqueducts by the Roman Empire, and similar historical developments could not have occurred.

In modern times, the emergence of industrialization in the 1800s and the development of the factory system brought revolutionary changes to the production process. Of these changes, the most important involved the problems of managing extremely large numbers of factory workers engaged in a variety of specialized occupations.

Many traditional types of leadership were ineffective in an industrial setting. Historically, those who rose to positions of authority did so as a result of personal power and charisma or were appointed on the basis of political favoritism or patronage by a king, lord, or other authority figure. The factory, however, represented a new phenomenon which had as its central purpose the mass production of economic consumer goods. In order to succeed, this type of enterprise required a rational, efficient form of management. In response to this need, professional managers were educated and trained specifically for that purpose. This process of professionalization of work roles has continued to evolve right up to the present day. Speaking to this, Max Weber has said that, in "the place of the old-type ruler who is moved by sympathy, favor, grace, and gratitude, modern culture requires for its sustaining external apparatus, the emotionally detached and hence rigorously 'professional' expert" (Bendix, 1960, p. 422).

Today most large-scale associations involve the coordination of large numbers of people engaged in diverse and specialized functions. This applies not only to industrial and business organizations in modern societies, but also to institutions such as government. In France, for instance, government consists of a huge civil service apparatus. To qualify for a high-level civil service position, one must complete a special two-year school for government training after college graduation and score high on a battery of competitive examinations (Ridley, 1979). In the United States, many occupations are becoming increasingly professionalized, including law enforcement administration, nursing administration, and hotel management. Given these trends, bureaucracy as a form of social organization appears destined to remain with us in the forseeable future.

PATTERNS OF SOCIAL INTERACTION

Although many aspects of organization vary from society to society—as in kinship structure and means of subsistence—social relations everywhere involve similar patterns of

social interaction. This process through which two or more individuals mutually influence each other's thoughts, feelings, and actions takes five basic forms: cooperation, exchange, conflict, competition, and accommodation.

Cooperation

The most common form of social interaction is **cooperation**, the sharing of responsibility by people who work together to reach a shared goal. This joint effort and teamwork represents much of the foundation for maintaining social order and stability at all levels of society. By cooperating with each other through compliance with group and societal norms, our actions contribute to social survival, harmony, and, it is hoped, progress. More specifically, social cooperation makes it feasible to achieve goals that would be difficult if not impossible for a single individual to attain. Among the Eskimos of northern Canada, hunting and fishing are conducted in groups in order to acquire enough food for subsistence. The legislative bodies of modern governments operate under systems of parliamentary procedure in order to make laws and conduct related business. Throughout history, cooperation has made it possible to accomplish feats ranging from the construction of the temples in ancient Athens to the development of space flight technology, computers, and particle accelerators today.

According to sociologist Robert Nisbet (1970), there are four basic forms of cooperation. By far the most common, in both past and modern societies, is *spontaneous coopera-*

As members of a community and society, people learn the value of many forms of cooperation. (Copyright Sobel Klonsky/Image Bank.)

tion, which takes place face-to-face at the microlevel in the form of mutual aid. Conditions that result in this type of cooperation tend to emerge from a set of situational circumstances. When a person's house catches fire, neighbors often pitch in and work together to put out the fire and provide temporary support to the affected family. Likewise, college students sometimes form study groups to prepare for an upcoming exam. *Traditional cooperation*, by comparison, takes the form of social habit that is passed from generation to generation as established custom. Americans, for example, cooperate with each other traditionally in hundreds of ways, ranging from standing in line to get a check cashed at the bank to attending the weddings and funerals of close relatives and friends.

However, modern societies—characterized by ongoing change and increasing complexity—tend to depend less on spontaneous and traditional cooperation than on two other types. One of these, *directed cooperation*, involves cooperation that is enforced by an authority figure such as an employer or teacher. The other, *contractual cooperation*, takes place when two or more parties agree to specific conditions for cooperation. This can vary in form. Contractual cooperation can be exemplified by grandparents who babysit with their grandchildren for their married children (the microlevel) or two or more countries that enter into a formal trade agreement with each other (the macrolevel).

Exchange

Cooperation is often reinforced by **exchange**, a form of interaction in which all parties expect to benefit by receiving a reward. Sociologist George Homans (1961, 1974) argues that we seek rewards in all our relations with others, and avoid negative consequences or punishments. Relationships that offer more benefits than drawbacks we tend to continue.

Those in which the negatives outweigh the positives we try to end or avoid.

Another exchange theorist, Peter Blau, asserts that what is rewarding or punishing is not always clear-cut and visible to the casual observer, but may be quite symbolic and subjective. In other words, what is meaningful as a reward may depend on the person, the situation, and the priorities or goals the individual seeks to have addressed or satisfied. For the student of behavior possessed by "the sociological imagination," Blau (1964) says that

> [s]ocial exchange can be observed everywhere once we are sensitized . . . to it, not only in market relations but also in friendship and even in love . . . as well as in many social relations between these extremes in intimacy. Neighbors exchange favors; children, toys; colleagues, assistance; acquaintances, courtesies; politicians, concessions; discussants, ideas; housewives, recipes (p. 88).

Exchange is based on the *principle of reciprocity*, the idea that people provide assistance to those who have helped them in order to maintain equality in social obligations (Gouldner, 1960). If someone comes along with jumper cables and helps you start your stalled car, you may reciprocate by offering to pay the person for his or her trouble. When you invite someone to your home for dinner or a party, that person may fulfill a felt obligation to you by returning the favor. If someone remembers your anniversary or birthday or sends you a Christmas card, you may respond in kind. In these and countless other ways, we exchange courtesies and resources with one another at all levels of society. This promotes alliances between individuals and groups and promotes cohesion and order throughout society.

Competition

Competition occurs when two or more parties attempt to reach a mutually prized goal that is limited in quantity. Unlike cooperation (shared goals) and exchange (mutual rewards), competition occurs when there can be only one winner of a ballgame, election, job promotion, or award for salesperson of the year. In these and numerous other situations, one must compete with others for scarce rewards. However, like the two previously mentioned forms of interaction, competition is governed by a set of norms (Friedsam, 1965). These norms act as rules of engagement to prevent competition from deteriorating into conflict which can be very destructive. The primary purpose of competition, therefore, is to achieve the goal, not to injure the other party or subvert the competitive process. If this process is threatened, it is sometimes necessary to apply punitive sanctions. These might include expulsion from the game for the abusive athlete or job demotion or dismissal for the unethical sales representative.

Competition, like other forms of interaction, is found in all societies to some degree, whether it involves territorial hunting rights, soil resources for farming, cattle for breeding, or markets for industrial commodities. In the United States, the competitive spirit is an underlying element in dominant traditional norms that stress individualism, capitalism, and the upwardly mobile pursuit of the American dream. In this context, the primary advantage of competition is its usefulness as a mechanism to allocate scarce resources as rewards for hard work and high achievement. However, it can also result in discouragement and a sense of failure for those who, by virtue of poverty and emotional and social deprivation brought on by the accidents of birth and childhood socialization, are not equipped to compete on an equal basis.

Conflict

When cooperation, exchange, and competition break down, there is often **conflict**, a pattern of interaction in which two or more parties seek to reach a goal by neutralizing, dominating, or destroying all adversaries against their will (Williams, 1970). Conflict occurs in all types of groups, from the most intimate to the most impersonal, and at all levels of social interaction, from the two people who bash their cars together on the freeway and pursue the matter in court to two or more countries that go to war. As the opposite of cooperation, conflict is characterized chiefly by hostility on the part of the concerned parties and a lack of norms almost to the point that "practically anything goes." Although physical confrontation and violence sometimes occur, conflict more typically involves less dramatic approaches, including verbal disagreements, written position papers, exercises in social power (for example, petitions and demonstrations), and economic sanctions.

The German sociologist George Simmel (1858–1918) argued that there were four basic types of conflict: wars, feuds, litigations, and ideological conflicts (Simmel, 1955). *Wars* represent the most destructive type of conflict from the standpoint of violence. During World War II, over 50 million people lost their lives. In the more recent Vietnam conflict, 58,000 Americans were killed and the civilian death toll for the Vietnamese numbered over 1,500,000. *Feuds* are disputes between or within groups, whereas *litigations* represent legal conflicts that are fought in the courts. *Ideological conflicts,* the last of Simmel's categories, are conflicts over ideals or principles, as illustrated by capitalism versus communism, conservatism versus liberalism, and Christianity versus agnosticism.

Accommodation

When conflict becomes disruptive, a process is needed to foster its reduction or resolution so that opposing parties can function together successfully. This is **accommodation**, which

Conflict is a pattern of interaction that may occur at any level of society in a variety of forms. (Photography by Richard Kolvar/Copyright Magnum Photos, Inc.)

takes several forms, of which compromise and toleration are among the most common. *Compromise* involves give-and-take negotiations between two parties in an attempt to find common ground sufficient to build a successful relationship. Examples might include the couple with marital conflict (the microlevel) that reaches an accommodation with or without the mediation of a professional counselor, or a labor-management dispute that is settled with or without third-party arbitration. Formal compromises often take the form of written agreements, like labor contracts or treaties. In 1987, for instance, twenty-four countries signed a treaty in Montreal, Canada, designed to protect the ozone layer in the atmosphere. The ozone layer protects us from the harmful effects of the sun's ultraviolet rays. They agreed, among other things, to freeze world production of certain chlorofluorocarbons used in refrigerators and aerosol cans, which have been destroying the ozone layer.

Toleration is an agreement between two opposing parties to coexist since neither can defeat the other. In contrast to compromise, which involves active negotiations and sometimes formal agreements, toleration usually involves an implied arrangement between two relatively equal parties. In essence, they agree that although they do not like each other, it is in their best interests not to engage each other in direct conflict. The Soviet Union and the United States are bitter ideological enemies, but, because each has sufficient nuclear armament to destroy the world several times over, they find it advantageous to avoid conflict. Although they do engage in compromise with each other in some areas and have signed treaties together, their primary relationship is one of toleration.

CHAPTER SUMMARY

1. Social organization is the process by which society is structured as a system of social interaction to meet the needs of its members. To accomplish this, particular societal needs relating to population maintenance and control (reproduction of society members), division of labor (how work is allocated), communication, shared values and goals, and social control must be addressed.

2. There are two basic levels of social organization: microlevel organization and macrolevel organization. The patterned ways people act at the local community level in social situations, relationships, and groups is microlevel organization. Macrolevel organization is concerned with the manner in which large-scale associations like school systems and corporations are organized, as well as basic institutions including the family system, government, and the economic system.

3. Although there are several ways to distinguish between different types of societies, perhaps the most useful is by means of subsistence, the process used by a society to provide food and other basic resources. In terms of subsistence, there are four basic types of societies. Hunting-gathering societies are the simplest. They consist of small bands of nomads who, because they have no means of producing or preserving food, live from day to day by hunting and foraging for food. Horticultural societies depend mainly on simple slash-and-burn agriculture and raising domesticated animals for food. Their members live in village-based clans and tribes. Agrarian societies,

which came later, developed intensive and sophisticated forms of agriculture and evolved into large civilizations, including city-states with centralized authority and, later, nation-states. Industrial societies emerged with the industrial revolution. Their characteristics include a cash economy, mass production, and specialized occupations.

4. Within the various types of societies at both the micro- and macrolevels are several key forms of social organization including kinship, fealty, and groups. Kinship has to do with the manner in which family relations are organized in given societies. As such, it occurs in two basic forms throughout the world: consanguineal kinship (based on blood ties) and affinal kinship (based on marital ties). Fealty is a form of social organization based on the personal loyalty of a follower to a leader. Common forms include loyalty of an employee to an employer, team pride in athletics, and *esprit de corps* in the military. Social behavior is also organized according to the groups to which a person belongs, along with the norms and group goals that govern behavior within such groups.

5. Other basic forms of social organization include social positions, contract, and bureaucracy. A social position is a socially defined location or status that a person occupies in society. Some of the social positions we occupy are ascribed (imposed), like sex, race, or nationality at birth; others are achieved, including education, occupation, and marriage. Each position in society also carries with it a role that consists of certain expected behaviors along with obligations and privileges. Contract, which involves the exchange of one promise for another, has been an important form of social organization since the Middle Ages. Another form of organization that has become equally important to modern societies is bureaucracy, the rational organization of work in large-scale associations coordinated by professional managers.

6. Social interaction, the process through which two or more parties mutually influence one another's thoughts, feelings, and actions, takes several basic forms. Cooperation involves the sharing of responsibility by people who work together to reach a shared goal. This is reinforced by exchange, a form of interaction in which all parties expect to benefit by receiving a reward. When a relationship is rewarding, we are motivated to maintain it. Competition, an additional type of social interaction, takes place when two or more parties attempt to reach the same desired goal that is limited in quantity. Unlike cooperation (shared goals) and exchange (mutual rewards), there can be only one winner of a competition. However, order is maintained by a commonly agreed-upon set of rules that act to govern competition (as in the rules of play in profession sports).

7. When cooperation, exchange, and competition break down, there is often conflict, a type of social interaction marked by two or more parties attempting to neutralize, dominate, or destroy all adversaries against their will. There are essentially no norms (rules) that govern conflict, as there are in competition. Consequently, its results can be very destructive. When conflict occurs, another type of social interaction is often helpful: accommodation, which involves the use of various approaches to reduce or resolve conflict.

TERMS TO KNOW

accommodation: a pattern of social interaction that fosters the reduction or resolution of conflict so that opposing parties can function together successfully.

achieved status: a social position earned through individual effort.

affinal kinship: a type of family organization based primarily on marital ties.

agrarian societies: social systems organized around advanced agricultural methods for subsistence and centralized governmental authority.

anomie: a state of confused norms (normlessness) brought about by rapid change and social complexity.

ascribed status: a social position assigned to a person at birth or otherwise imposed by society.

bureaucracy: a form of social organization in which the work of participants in large-scale associations (organizations) is rationally coordinated by professional managers.

competition: a pattern of social interaction that occurs when two or more parties attempt to reach a mutually prized goal that is limited in quantity.

conflict: a pattern of social interaction in which two or more parties seek to reach a goal by neutralizing, dominating, or destroying all adversaries against their will.

consanguineal kinship: a type of family organization based primarily on blood ties.

contract: a social bond between two or more parties that involves the exchange of one promise for another.

cooperation: a pattern of social interaction that involves the sharing of responsibility by people who work together to reach a shared goal.

exchange: a pattern of social interaction in which all parties expect to benefit by receiving a reward.

fealty: a form of social organization involving the personal loyalty of a follower to a leader.

group: two or more people with one or more characteristics in common.

horticultural societies: village-focused social systems that rely on simple slash-and-burn agriculture and the use of domesticated animals for subsistence.

hunting-gathering societies: small bands of nomadic hunters and food gatherers who, because of a lack of technology necessary to produce or preserve food, literally take life a meal at a time.

industrial societies: the most complex and technologically advanced social systems, characterized by a cash economy, mass production, and specialized occupations.

kinship: a form of social organization involving the manner in which family relations are organized.

macrolevel organization: the manner in which large-scale associations (organizations), basic institutions, and societies are organized and interact with one another.

master status: the social position held by an individual that becomes the primary source of his or her identity.

means of subsistence: the specific process used by a society to provide food and other basic resources needed by its people for survival and prosperity.

microlevel organization: the patterned ways people act at the local community level in social encounters, relationships, and groups.

postindustrial societies: emerging social systems that appear likely to be dominated by service and information economics.

role: the expected forms of behavior, obligation, and privilege that go with a given social position.

role ambiguity: a situation that occurs when the obligations attached to a social position are not clear.

role conflict: stress caused when conflicting role demands are built into separate social positions, each of which the individual is expected to carry out successfully.

role set: two or more distinct roles that relate to a single social position.

role strain: stress that occurs when (1) conflicting role demands are built into a single social position, (2) a person cannot fulfill the role demands of a given position, or both.

social control: a process designed to maintain conformity to dominant norms and ensure social order.

social interaction: the process through which two or more individuals mutually influence each other's thoughts, feelings, and actions.

social organization: the process by which society is structured as a system of social interaction to meet the needs of its members.

social position: a socially defined location or status a person occupies in society along with a set of expected behavior patterns designed to regulate that person's behavior.

society: the largest possible grouping of individuals with specific characteristics in a particular system of social interaction.

SUGGESTED READINGS

Exchange and Power in Social Life (Peter M. Blau; New York: Wiley, 1964). A comprehensive analysis of exchange as a principle in human social relations and the social processes that form much of the basis for social interaction.

The Functions of Social Conflict (Lewis Coser; New York: Free Press, 1964). A "must read" for the student who desires a basic, yet comprehensive, understanding of both the beneficial as well as the disruptive aspects of conflict in modern society.

A Poison Stronger than Love: The Destruction of an Ojibwa Community (Anastasia Shkilnyk; New Haven, Conn.: Yale University Press, 1985). An anthropological study of a Native American village in Canada that profoundly illustrates the important role played by social organization and stable relations at all levels in maintaining both societal and individual well-being.

Power and Privilege: A Theory of Social Stratification (Gerhard Lenski; New York: McGraw-Hill,

1966). A penetrating analysis of different types of societies from the standpoint of inequality, power, and change.

Social Roles (Louis A. Zurcher; Beverly Hills, Calif.: Sage Publications, 1983). An insightful treatment of the diverse social roles characteristic of modern society and the various ways in which people adapt, conform to, resist, and alter them.

Social Theory and Social Structure, Enlarged Edition (Robert K. Merton; New York: Free Press, 1968). A major contribution to our understanding of social organization from the functionalist perspective.

Part Three

Order, Rank, Opportunity, and Change

Chapter 6
Groups in Society

It was almost midnight in San Diego on February 1, 1985, and young Christopher Valva was arriving home from his second shift job at a printing company. The nineteen-year-old noticed three juveniles "hanging out" near his house, told them to go away, and, after an angry exchange of words, was attacked and stabbed in the heart with a long hunting knife. As his assailants fled, Chris stumbled into his house, and his shocked mother, seeing her blood-covered son, immediately dialed 911. Within minutes police and paramedics were on the scene and Chris was rushed by ambulance to the trauma center at Mercy Hospital and Medical Center. En route, while the driver communicated with Mercy and a surgical team was hastily assembled, paramedics continued to apply CPR to Chris although he had almost no blood, collapsed veins, no pulse, and dilated pupils.

Upon his arrival at the hospital, Dr. Eugene Rumsey, Jr., and a team of other trauma surgeons, nurses, and technicians went to work on a patient that by most traditional indications was already dead. Knowing that the young man had only a 1 percent chance for survival, the team opened his chest and, while a breathing bag forced oxygen into his lungs and IVs sent blood and solution coursing through his veins, Rumsey held Chris's heart in his hand and massaged it until it showed signs of life and finally began beating on its own. As it beat, the heart spurted blood from a one-and-a-half-inch wound, which was carefully sewn shut and repaired by a thoracic surgeon. Over the next several hours after surgery, the crises of restoring liver and kidney functions, treating heart arrhythmias, and combating the sudden drop in body temperature with blankets and blood transfusions were dealt with and successfully overcome. Thirty-five days after entering the Mercy trauma center, Chris Valva was released from the hospital in March of 1985. By Christmas, he was able to return to work and today has a second chance at life (Michelmore, 1986).

This rather dramatic incident serves to illustrate how fundamentally important groups are and can be to each of us. In Chris Valva's case, a group of delinquents almost caused his death, while the intercession of his mother and two other groups—paramedics and the trauma team—saved his life. While nothing this extreme may happen to most of us, our group contacts and relations with others nonetheless have a profound effect on our behavior, emotional and social well-being, and happiness.

As we have already seen, both culture (Chapter 3) and socialization (Chapter 4) are the products of group processes. Likewise, the way we affiliate with and interact in groups has an important impact on the social organization of a society (Chapter 5). In the discussion to follow, we shall focus our attention specifically on groups and how they operate in society.

GROUP CHARACTERISTICS AND TYPES

Although group processes form the foundation for the human experience, groups themselves represent a difficult phenomenon to classify and study. A *group,* as mentioned in Chapter 5, consists of two or more people with one or more characteristics in common. Each of us refers to groups everyday to identify and distinguish among a wide assortment of different collections of people. Depending on who we are and the particular circumstances involved, we may talk or hear about Italian-Americans, Fortune 500 companies, people with AIDS, farmers in Kansas, smokers, Democrats, country-western singers, bald-headed men, David Letterman fans, people with hemorrhoids, Baptists, widows, students, and so forth. The list becomes practically endless.

In addition, many of these groups may be divided into subgroups. Students, for example, may be classified into elementary, secondary, college, and graduate or professional students. If we then concentrate attention on one of these subcategories, such as college students, it likewise may be divided even further by class rank (freshmen, sophomores, juniors, se-

niors), college major, grade point average, and membership in school organizations.

Many groups tend to be temporary and dynamic in nature. Some, like new social relationships or business organizations, are just beginning, while others are changing in focus and composition or, in some cases, may be in the process of dissolving altogether.

Characteristics of Groups

Given the diverse, temporary, and ever-changing nature of groups, sociologists use a variety of characteristics to distinguish among their different types. Of these, four in particular—common attributes, consciousness of kind, patterned social relations, and formal organization—appear to be most useful. Some types of groups may possess only one or two of these characteristics, while others typically may have three or all four.

Common Attributes. The term **common attributes** refers to the characteristics members of a group have in common with one another. In all groups there are one or more shared characteristics among members, which act as boundaries to distinguish members from non-members. For instance, age, sex, and special activities represent characteristics that distinguish members of a Girl Scout troop from those in other groups. In similar fashion, professional basketball players may be identified by physical height and uniforms, college professors by education and academic rank, convicted felons by criminal records, and corporations by method of organization.

Consciousness of Kind. In 1906, sociologist William Graham Sumner originated the concept **consciousness of kind**, the tendency of people to recognize others like themselves and, in many cases, to feel some common sense of identification or connection as a result (Sumner, 1906, 1960). This is often evident when people find themselves in an unfamiliar social setting comprised mainly of strangers with whom they have little if anything in common. Noncommissioned military personnel, for instance, tend to congregate while waiting at large airports during layovers between flights. In an unfamiliar place full of strangers, they are immediately drawn to the uniforms of those with whom they share a common bond. In numerous other instances, consciousness of kind acts as a pervasive characteristic of many groups in society. We are continually drawn to people with whom we have things in common.

Patterned Social Relations. In many groups, members have and take the opportunity to influence the feelings, attitudes, and behavior of one another through personal social interaction and/or some indirect system of social contact. These **patterned social relations** form the foundation for human interaction at the microlevel of society. They include rules of conduct called norms (Chapter 3) and patterns of interaction including cooperation, exchange, competition, conflict, and accommodation (Chapter 5). Together these elements shape to a significant degree how we interact meaningfully with family, friends, neighbors, and co-workers. In addition, patterned social relations are also characteristic of large-scale associations and institutions at the middle range and macrolevels of society. Both General Motors and the United States government, for instance, make use of patterned social interaction both internally and in relating to other large-scale associations and institutions. This often involves more indirect and impersonal forms of social contact, such as conventions and large meetings along with newsletters, memoranda, and other means of correspondence.

Formal Organization. Some groups also have **formal organization**, the action taken by members to pursue one or more specific practical goals. Often these goals are fairly com-

plex in nature. Take, for example, a group of workers in an industrial production plant who are disenchanted with their pay, fringe benefits, and working conditions. If they form a local chapter of a labor union to address these concerns, they will be organizing themselves formally as a means of achieving a larger complex goal. Groups with formal organization tend to be larger than many social groups (like families and friendship circles). In fact, size alone can make formal organization a necessity. Consequently, large charitable organizations are organized to raise money for the needy, corporations to make profits, colleges to educate society's future leaders, and governmental agencies to serve the public at large.

Types of Groups

As mentioned earlier, some groups may have only one or two of the characteristics mentioned above, while others may have three or all four (see Figure 6-1). In this regard, sociologists generally classify groups into five general categories: physical aggregates, statistical categories, social categories, social groups, and associations.

Physical Aggregates. Sometimes we find ourselves in the midst of a collectivity of people by simply being in the same place they are at the same time. This form of social experience involves a **physical aggregate**, a group distinguished primarily by the physical proximity of its members. We briefly participate in aggregates each time we stand in a line, get on an elevator with others, attend a concert or go to a movie, and otherwise find ourselves in crowds. We normally tend to feel neutral about such groups. Although we share one or more attributes with these people, there is little else to make a lasting impression. If there is any social interaction in a crowd—such as our asking someone in front of us in a movie line when the show starts—it tends to be

Figure 6-1   Types of Groups and Their Characteristics

Type of Group	Typical Characteristics			
	Common Attributes	Consciousness of Kind	Patterned Social Relations	Formal Organization
Physical aggregate	Yes	No	No	No
Statistical category	Yes	No	No	No
Social category	Yes	Yes	No	No
Social group	Yes	Yes	Yes	No
Association	Yes	Yes	Yes	Yes

brief, superficial, and unstructured. Therefore, we usually forget our encounters with physical aggregates the moment they are over.

Statistical Categories. Another type of group to which we are largely oblivious is the **statistical category**, a group formed by researchers for the purposes of social analysis. Since it is not formed by the members themselves, it is an artificial group that holds greatest meaning for those who conduct various forms of social research. In this respect, each of us belongs to dozens, if not hundreds, of these groups, although we are not consciously aware of inclusion. We show up in census data, consumer surveys, popularity ratings for television shows, and political polls. Even the "junk mail" we receive tends to be based in significant part on our membership in statistical categories by age, marital status, income, occupation, and so forth, in which we are placed for marketing purposes. Like physical aggregates, statistical categories lack consciousness of kind, patterned social relations, and formal organization.

Social Categories. The **social category**, unlike the two previously mentioned groups, is characterized by both common attributes and con-

sciousness of kind. This is a group distinguished by its members' having one or more visible or otherwise special features or characteristics in common. The chief factor here is consciousness of kind. We tend to identify with fellow members of the social categories in which we hold membership. Men, therefore, feel a bond with other men, women an identification with other women, Mexican Americans a connection with others of Mexican descent; likewise, college students, U.S. Marines, Cherokee Indians, senior citizens, rodeo riders, Methodists, and sociologists feel an affinity with others of their kind. However, social categories as total groups typically lack both patterned social relations and formal organization. These additional characteristics may appear, however, in social groups and associations that are often formed within social categories.

Social Groups. The most important and fundamental of all group types is the **social group**, which consists of people bound together by common interests and values in a definite pattern of social interaction. A person's family, a circle of close friends, a sociology class, two couples on a picnic, and several neighborhood children at play with one an-

Physical aggregates (or crowds) are a common occurrence in modern urban societies. (William Kennedy/The Image Bank.)

other all serve as representative examples. They each possess common attributes, consciousness of kind, and patterned social relations.

Social group relations are at the core of the human experience. Culture (Chapter 3), socialization (Chapter 4), and social organization (Chapter 5) all take place within group settings. In addition, a person's basic social identity is shaped primarily through patterned interaction with others. For these reasons, this chapter is devoted largely to an exploration of the different types of social groups, the factors that shape the way they are organized, and the forms of behavior that take place within them.

Associations. The last of the five types of groups is the **association**, a group deliberately formed to pursue one or more specific practical goals. Like social groups, associations also are very important to human survival and prosperity, particularly in large technological societies with differentiated institutions and a specialized division of labor. They too are characterized by common attributes, consciousness of kind, and patterned social relations. However, unlike most social groups, associations have an additional characteristic, formal organization, which allows the most complex of human endeavors, from performing open-heart surgery to landing people on the moon, to be carried out in a highly organized and efficient manner.

Associations exist at both the micro- and macrolevels and may range in size and complexity from local garden clubs, PTAs, and professional and fraternal organizations—

some of which are local chapters of national associations—to national and multinational corporations, professional and trade associations, and governmental bodies. Larger associations make use of bureaucracy (Chapter 5) as a method of organization. In addition, they may vary in their purposes or specific practical goals. Some exist to make profit, others aim to promote a professional or social cause, and some serve the public at large. A more detailed discussion of associations and bureaucracy is contained in Chapter 7 to follow, which is devoted exclusively to this topic.

SOCIAL GROUPS

Because culture, socialization, and social organization take place largely within the framework of social relations, the bulk of this chapter is devoted to a discussion of social groups. In this regard, sociologists distinguish between two fundamental types: primary groups and secondary groups.

Primary Groups

Charles Horton Cooley (1909, 1956) originated the concept of **primary group**, a small group characterized by personalized, ongoing relationships. In his formulation of the "looking-glass self" theory related to personality, Cooley was particularly interested in examining group relationships that have the greatest impact on the developing child. He felt that the family and children's play groups are among the most important influences on a child's socialization because (1) they are the first groups a person is exposed to and (2) they represent the primary source of social and emotional support. In elaborating on primary groups, he had this to say:

> By primary groups I mean those characterized by intimate face-to-face associations and cooperation. They are primary in several senses,

Primary group relations are very personalized, with levels of emotional intimacy and social sharing that make them special for each of us. (Copyright Joel Gordon, 1980.)

but chiefly in that they are fundamental in forming the social nature and ideals of the individual. The result of intimate association, psychologically, is a certain fusion of individualities in a common whole, so that one's very self, for many purposes at least, is the common life and purpose of the group. . . . Primary groups are [also] primary in the sense that they do not change in the same degree as more elaborate relations, but form a comparatively permanent source out of which the latter are ever springing. Of course they are not independent of the larger society, but to some extent reflect its spirit. . . . These groups, then, are the springs of life, not only for the individual, but for social institutions (1956, pp. 23–29).

Characteristics of Primary Groups. Based on Cooley's initial formulation and subsequent observations by other sociologists (King and Koller, 1975), it is clear that primary groups and their relations have several distinct characteristics. Of these, eight of the most important are listed below:

1. *Relative smallness.* Given the fast-paced and relatively specialized nature of social relations in technological societies today, it is relatively rare for primary groups—such as one's family or circle of best friends—to exceed more than eight to ten individuals. Most contain only two to five people. Indeed, given the geographically mobile nature of life for many Americans, it is difficult to sustain long-term and personal relations with relatives and friends that one no longer lives near nor sees on a regular basis.

2. *Strong affectional ties.* The relationships among primary group members are personal and emotion laden. We tend to build an emotional investment with our significant others, and they with us. Given this degree of intimacy, our primary group relations serve as our basic source for emotional and social support.

3. *Strong personal identification.* As a result, in large part, of our very personal relations with our primary group members, we also identify strongly with them and desire their approval. Therefore, primary groups play an instrumental role in socialization and influence to a remarkable degree the formation of a person's self-concept.

4. *Multidimensional relationships.* Interaction among primary group members tends to be relatively open, free, and extensive. Because our fellow members care about us and accept us as we are, it is possible to interact with them as a whole person and to "be ourselves." In many social encounters, however, we share only a single facet of our personality with others because of the special role demands—such as those of an employee, student, or customer—placed on us as well as on those with whom we interact.

5. *Continuous face-to-face contact.* Members of primary groups interact with one another on a one-to-one basis frequently over a continuous period of time. We usually see and interact directly with our immediate family and best friends daily or weekly on an ongoing basis.

6. *Durability.* Primary group relations are very durable and often border on permanence. This is partially due to the fact that personal relationships, especially in modern technological societies, are difficult to form and maintain and, once established, are not easily transferable to other people. It is quite difficult, if not impossible, to replace the strong ties felt with a close relative or best friend.

7. *Trust.* As a result of the close personal nature of primary group relations and their durability, we tend to trust our fellow members and, likewise, they feel they can trust us. Most of us, for instance, would not hesitate to take the word of a close family member or friend but would be skeptical about many things told to us by acquaintances or strangers.

8. *Informal social controls.* Because of many of the preceding factors, formal or official social controls are usually unnecessary in primary groups. Informal sanctions, like praise (positive) or criticism (negative) are usually sufficient in maintaining conformity to group rules or standards.

The Scope of Primary Relations. Our interactions with others in our primary groups represent "the ties that bind." By connecting to others in a personal and ongoing manner, we not only obtain satisfaction of our basic needs for emotional intimacy and social sharing, but we also contribute to the cohesiveness of the larger community and society. Primary group relations thus furnish us with a sense of belonging, a feeling of being connected to the larger human experience. This need to belong is important to us and manifests itself throughout life not only in family and typical friendship groups but in a number of other diverse primary group circumstances as well.

People are capable of making some rather unusual informal adaptations in order to form and maintain primary group relations. Take life in the military during wartime for instance. During World War II, both German and Allied soldiers possessed a sense of fealty toward their fellow soldiers at the combat unit level that rivaled the intimacy of families (Shils and Janowitz, 1948; Shils, 1950). German infantry units were effective not so much because of their loyalty to the Nazi cause but, instead, because of their primary group affiliations with their units on a company level. Unlike the American military, the *Wehrmacht* sent men into battle who had already formed strong bonds by having trained together (Van Creveld, 1982). Whenever a German fighting unit became depleted through the taking of heavy casualties, the entire unit would be pulled back from the front, reconstituted, and then returned to action.

The Americans, by contrast, constantly added new recruits to depleted units and formed primary group bonds on the battlefront. In addition to eating, sleeping, and fighting together, they shared the most intimate details of their past lives, read each other's mail, shared their belongings and gifts from home, and generally considered each other brothers. The formation of these primary groups, above all else, contributed to their cohesiveness and fighting effectiveness during the war.

In the Korean conflict, although there was similar loyalty to one's fighting unit, the most pervasive and effective primary groups consisted of pairs of soldiers who would stick together as "buddies" and look out for each other. The buddy system in Korea became necessary, in part, as a result of a personnel rotation system that constantly changed the makeup of fighting units. Roger W. Little (1970), a sociologist who lived with an American infantry rifle company as an observer from November 1952 through February 1953, chronicled this situation. In an excerpt from one of the many interviews that Little conducted, a soldier had this to say about the buddy system:

> A buddy understands you and is interested in your story. Some big mouths talk as if everyone is interested in their story but they're not. You've got to find a guy you like and he likes you, then you're buddies and you know he will listen to you when you want to talk. A buddy shares everything; if you don't get mail, he lets you read his (p. 364).

More recent observations concerning the value of primary groups in the military have also been illuminating. Close personal relations were much less prevalent among American soldiers during the Vietnamese conflict (Moskos, 1975). This military action was officially termed a "conflict" rather than a war, had no battlefront, unclear objectives, and a rotation period of twelve to thirteen months that kept most soldiers dealing with it in their own particular fashion. Each man had his own designated departure date which marked the end of the war for him. He spent his time "in country" counting down the days until he could return to "the world." Consequently, morale in many units was low, dissension was high, and whenever a man was "short" (with less than sixty days to go), he was much less likely to be "gung ho" about anything that involved potential contact with the enemy.

The recent experiences by the Israelis are somewhat related. They have found that unless combat units are formed and trained carefully over a designated period of time, the development of *esprit de corps* will be significantly impaired. Soldiers in quickly formed units, when placed in a combat situation, do not perform well and are more likely to suffer mental breakdown compared to units characterized by primary group affiliation (Solomon, Mikulincer, and Hobfoll, 1986).

Primary group relations also develop within the context of deviant behavior. Partially because of the pressure and felt desperation of an "us" versus "them" mentality, as well as family disorganization and other factors, juvenile gangs and subgroups within them sometimes take on many of the characteristics of primary groups. The same can be said of adult criminal gangs. You probably are already familiar, for instance, with the story of Bonnie Parker and Clyde Barrow. These two lovers, commonly known as "Bonnie and Clyde," headed a gang that robbed banks in several states during the 1930s until they were finally killed from ambush by law enforcement officials. In like manner, the relationship between pimp and prostitute sometimes involves professed love and romance, although in reality it is usually one-sided, the pimp "conning" the woman in order to exploit her for money (Bryan, 1965; Harmatz and Novak, 1983).

Among the most interesting of primary group relationships among those regarded as deviant is the homosexual "marriage" that takes place in coercive institutions like women's prisons. Sociologist Rose Giallombardo (1970) has researched this phenomenon and gives the following description:

The *femme* or *mommy* is the inmate who plays the female role in a homosexual relation-

ship. . . . The complementary role to the femme is the *stud broad* or *daddy* who assumes the male role. . . . Cast in the context of a "marital" relationship, the homosexual dyad is viewed by the inmates as a meaningful personal and social relationship. From the mass of interview data it is clear, however, that this mode of behavior would be repugnant to most prisoners, but the uniqueness of the prison situation compels the inmate to redefine and attach new meanings to this behavior within the prison structure.

. . . For the vast majority of the inmates, adjustment to the prison world is made by establishing a homosexual alliance with a compatible partner as a marriage unit. Although we cannot discuss the dynamics of mate selection, courtship, and marriage in this paper, it should be pointed out that when a stud and femme have established a homosexual alliance, they are said to be "making it" or to be "tight"; *that is* to say, they are socially recognized as constituting a legitimate married pair. Since one of the important goals in establishing a homosexual marriage alliance is to strive for what is referred to as a "sincere" relationship, which is . . . one based upon romantic love, the *trick* is held in low esteem by the inmates because she allows herself to be exploited rather than to develop a relationship that is sincere (p. 404).

Secondary Groups

In contrast to the primary group is the **secondary group**, a relatively large collection of people with whom one has superficial and somewhat impersonal relations. Our interactions with secondary groups tend to be more task oriented and specialized as compared to our primary relations which are focused on friendship and personal intimacy. Although our experiences with them may be pleasant (such as discussing career possibilities with a school counselor) or unpleasant (like complaining about poor service in a restaurant), we tend to feel neutral and somewhat aloof

Secondary group relations are the most common in American society. They tend to involve brief encounters with others, superficial in nature and somewhat impersonal. (Gary Gladstone/The Image Bank.)

concerning most of our secondary group encounters.

Characteristics of Secondary Groups. Secondary groups have the following characteristics:

1. *Relatively large size.* Secondary groups are generally larger than primary groups and often include thirty, forty, or fifty people or more (for example, students in a college class, employees who work in a particular department or division of a company).

2. *Weak affectional ties.* Relationships among members tend to be relatively impersonal with little, if any, emotional investment. As a result, secondary relations are easily transferable to other people and social situations. Take the classes you enroll in each semester for example. At the end of each college term, few, if any, people feel pangs of loss at the prospect of never seeing their classmates again. Most people enroll for the next semester or term, form new secondary relations with teachers and students, and have only fleeting thoughts at most concerning the "relationships" they left behind.

3. *Little or no personal identification.* Because our secondary group relations are generally interchangeable, they tend to have much less influence on our self-concept than our relations with our family and close friends.

4. *One-dimensional relationships.* Interaction in these groups tends to be specialized and somewhat inhibited. Secondary group relations are structured primarily in terms of specialized social positions and the role demands that go with them. Therefore, especially in modern societies, people in most social situations tend to reveal to others only the single facet of themselves required by positions such as employer or employee, teacher or student, store clerk or customer, IRS representative or taxpayer. We realize that because of the highly specialized and complex nature of American society, we remain oblivious to the multidimensional nature of most people with whom we come into contact, if we pause even for a moment to think about it. However, most of us are probably so preoccupied with our own lives and priorities that we do not.

5. *Limited face-to-face contact.* Members of secondary groups tend to interact with each other rather infrequently on a one-to-one basis over a relatively short period of time.

Take yourself, for example, as a member of a sociology class. How many of your classmates have you verbally interacted with directly in a one-on-one, face-to-face manner? How often? What does this tell you about the quality of your relationships at school or, for that matter, in most social encounters?

6. *Nonpermanence*. These groups tend to last for only a relatively short period of time, in part as a result of their specialized nature and easy transferability to other people and to other situations. A secondary group transaction between a customer and a counterperson at a fast-food restaurant may last only a minute or two. A college class will meet for one quarter or semester and then disband forever.

7. *Distrust*. Because of the somewhat reserved, impersonal, and temporary nature of secondary groups, distrust often tends to replace trust as an assumption on which relationships between members are based.

8. *Formal social controls*. Conformity to group standards, in most cases, is ensured through a system of formal rules that apply equally to all members. Company employees must conform to rules related to working hours, work loads, lunch hours, and vacations. Students must contend with rules concerning attendance, curriculum requirements, grading standards, and registration procedures.

The Scope of Secondary Relations. In mass urban societies today, most social contacts with others involve secondary rather than primary relations. Most Americans, for example, spend the bulk of each weekday either at school or at work. Both schoolchildren and college students come in contact with several teachers and dozens, if not hundreds, of other students each day. Likewise, physicians,

teachers, department store cashiers, and those in numerous other occupations come in contact with many people in a variety of different specialized circumstances. In a given day, a college professor, for instance, may teach several classes, have individual conferences with students, interact with colleagues, administrators, and textbook salespeople, and sit on one or more committees. In fact, many occupations involve working with people in a variety of capacities including project groups, task forces, and committees, which are all typical secondary groups. Members usually know little about one another so that liking or disliking one another personally tends to be irrelevant as long as they can interact together successfully in the context of their jobs (Olmsted and Hare, 1978).

Regarding the scope of secondary relations, sociologist Louis Wirth commented in 1938 that

> the city is characterized by secondary rather than primary contacts. The contacts of the city may indeed be face to face, but they are nevertheless impersonal, superficial, transitory, and segmental. The reserve, the indifference, and the blasé outlook which urbanites manifest in their relationships may thus be regarded as devices for immunizing themselves against the personal claims and expectations of others (pp. 1–2).

The German sociologist Georg Simmel (1918, 1950 A), a contemporary of Wirth's, spoke of the psychological and interpersonal impact that resulted from the indifference and reserve characteristic of social relations in the modern metropolis.

> As a result of this reserve we frequently do not even know by sight those who have been our neighbors for years. And it is this reserve which in the eyes of small town people makes us appear to be cold and heartless. Indeed, if I do not deceive myself, the inner aspect of this outer reserve is not only indifference but, more often than we are aware, it is a mutual

strangeness and revulsion, which will break into hatred and fight at the moment of a closer contact, however caused (1950 A, p. 415).

Social Group Relations in Perspective

Although the concepts of primary and secondary groups are useful for discussion purposes, few social groups are strictly one type or the other. Instead, most are composites that, though they may be predominantly primary or secondary in nature, still contain elements of the other type.

Consequently, primary groups and secondary groups are perhaps best understood as ideal types at either end of a continuum. Secondary group elements may develop within primary group relationships and vice versa. Take the family for example. A young person may move back home with parents for a while after graduation from college and pay rent just like any other boarder. Likewise, a person who works for a large corporation will interact socially with most fellow employees on a secondary group basis. However, within a given department or office, people may see each other socially outside work and sometimes form strong friendships. Behavioral scientists find that one important factor leading to the forming of primary groups among relative strangers and acquaintances is continued proximity. The longer we are near people on a regular basis, the more likely it is that we will develop on ongoing pattern of interaction, get to know them, and form meaningful friendships (Gergen and Gergen, 1981).

SOCIAL STRUCTURE AND THE QUALITY OF GROUP RELATIONS

The manner in which a society is structured or organized affects to a significant degree the overall quality of social relations that occur within it. This is perhaps best illustrated in the work of two late nineteenth-century European sociologists, Ferdinand Tönnies and Émile Durkheim.

Tönnies: *Gemeinschaft* and *Gesellschaft*

Ferdinand Tönnies (1855–1936) was a German sociologist who spent his entire academic life at the University of Keil in northern Germany. His most important contribution to sociological theory, *Gemeinschaft und Gesellschaft (Community and Society)*, was published in 1887. In this ground-breaking work, which was subsequently published in six other editions, Tönnies developed a typology in which he distinguished between the social organization of village-focused societies and that of mass societies characterized by large cities and an urban way of life. His pioneering use of the **polar typology**—the placing of two dissimilar concepts as ideal types at either end of a continuum—is a tool of analysis still used by sociologists today (Timasheff, 1967). This is illustrated in Figure 6-2.

The **Gemeinschaft** *Society.* The **gemeinschaft** is a community-oriented society in which most relations are personal, informal, and tend to be based on tradition. Both horticultural and agrarian societies (Chapter 5) tend to be largely *gemeinschaft* in terms of the way social relations are organized. In speaking of this, Tönnies (1887, 1957) said:

> Family life is the general basis of life in the *Gemeinschaft.* It subsists in village and town life. The village community and the town themselves can be considered as large families, the various clans and houses representing the elementary organisms of its body. . . . Here, original kinship and inherited status remain an essential, or at least the most important condition of participating fully in property and other rights (1957, pp. 228–229).

Figure 6-2   Tönnies's Polar Typology of Societies

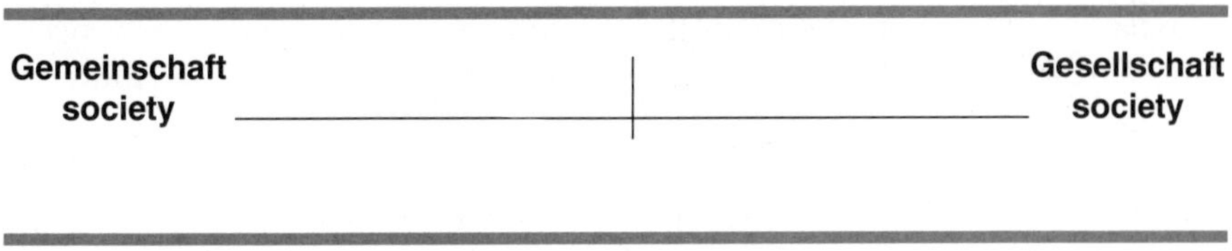

Gemeinschaft
society _____|_____   Gesellschaft
society

Based upon the discussion in this chapter, where would you plot the United States
along this continuum? What about Saudi Arabia or Mexico?

In the *gemeinschaft* environment, primary group relations abound because of a variety of factors. These nonindustrial, village-focused societies typically have *low levels of material technology* and *slow rates of change*. These attributes, coupled with *common ancestry*, combine to produce a system of *commonly held norms and values*.

In a farm-based economy, life tends to be organized around *tradition-based social positions* into which people are socialized from birth. Men, women, and children all have their own prescribed roles that govern not only how they interact within the family but also how they identify with and contribute to the community as a whole. Since most occupations and functions revolve around farming and animal husbandry, people have a great deal in common with one another and form *close-knit and long-term ties* with family and community members. In these societies, there is also *geographical stability* as many of their members grow up, get married, raise their families, and grow old and die within a few miles of their birthplace. These factors tend to create a societal climate conducive to primary group relations.

The **Gesellschaft** *Society.* By contrast, the *gesellschaft* is an urban industrial society with impersonal and somewhat formal relations that tend to be based on contract. Tönnies was concerned about the decline of primary relations and offered at least a partial explanation by identifying several key characteristics of

emerging urban societies. In his view, the intimacy and sense of community characteristic of *gemeinschaft* societies were being replaced by

> the rational will of the *Gesellschaft*. In the course of history, folk culture has given rise to the civilization of the state.
>
> The main features of this process can be described in the following way. . . . Economic control is achieved in many forms, the highest of which is planned capitalist production or large-scale industry. It is through the merchants that the technical conditions for the national union of independent individuals and for capitalist production are created. This merchant class is by nature, and mostly also by origin, international as well as national and urban, i.e., it belongs to *Gesellschaft* not *Gemeinschaft*. Later all social groups and dignitaries and, at least in tendency, the whole people acquire the characteristics of the *Gesellschaft*. . . . Simultaneously, along with this revolution in the social order, there takes place a gradual change in the law, in meaning as well as in form. The contract as such becomes the basis of the entire system, and rational will of *Gesellschaft* formed by its interests combines with the authoritative will of the state to create, maintain and change the legal system (1957, pp. 225–226).

Largely because of its size and complexity, the way a *gesellschaft* society is organized acts to create barriers to primary group relations. Given such factors as *high technology*, *rapid change*, and *diverse ancestry* among society members, *diverse and specialized norms and val-*

ues emerge. People develop very different perceptions of appropriate and inappropriate behavior, given their particular cultural heritage, occupations, and other quite diversified life situations.

An industrial economy results in *contract-based social positions* in which long-standing traditions may be of little relevance in light of changing social conditions. Personal relationships give way to business and professional relationships that are highly specialized in nature. Relationships based on friendship, trust, and good will are replaced by those which stress profit, productivity, and the achievement of other rational goals. Long-term close ties are replaced by *temporary and specialized friendships,* which are spread over several groups and tend to change in membership as time passes and conditions change. Finally, a *gesellschaft* society is characterized by *geographical and social mobility* among its members. In an industrial economy, people often must go where the jobs are, even if it means leaving extended relatives and friends behind and moving to another city or state.

Durkheim: Mechanical and Organic Solidarity

The French sociologist Émile Durkheim, a contemporary of Tönnies, was also interested in exploring the relationship between the way a society is structured and the overall manner in which social group relations take place. Like other analytical sociologists of his day, including such notables as Tönnies, Georg Simmel, and Gabriel Tarde, he favored the comparative approach, particularly that of comparing simple versus complex societies.

Durkheim's main research interest throughout his academic career was focused on the issue of social solidarity (social order) and its fundamental causes. In his first book, *The Division of Labor in Society* (1893, 1933), he sought to explain from a historical perspec-

tive the types of social solidarity characteristic of both simple rural societies and modern industrial social systems. Although he concentrated mainly on social solidarity, much of what he said had significant relevance toward explaining the quality of social relations in different types of societies.

Durkheim distinguished between simple nonindustrial societies, characterized by mechanical solidarity, and complex industrial societies, characterized by organic solidarity. He felt that social solidarity was the result of a **collective conscience**, a state of mental and moral agreement among members of a society concerning basic norms and values. Thus the collective conscience of a society, as expressed in a particular form of social solidarity, was the moral and social cement that held society together.

Mechanical Solidarity. Among the results of Durkheim's analysis was his finding that the primary group relations prevalent in simple nonindustrial societies were related to **mechanical solidarity**, the solidarity of resemblance. Most people in simple societies of the past, such as the feudal societies of preindustrial Europe, were almost identical in their occupations, interests, and values. The low level of material technology in these societies resulted in a very simple division of labor. Therefore, the actions of most people tended to take the form of automatic or mechanical responses to rather predictable life situations. With everyone engaging in the same activities and thinking similar thoughts about most things, it then followed that social relations in these small societies tended to be personal and open for the most part.

Since almost everyone knew almost everyone else in the hamlet or village, there were few obstacles to interfere with primary group relations. Durkheim found that in these societies the collective conscience was very strong and social solidarity was, therefore, relatively easy to maintain. This friendly, open sort of orientation toward others in the community can still be observed even today in rural pockets of largely industrial societies like the United States.

However, something developed in recent history to undermine mechanical solidarity, weaken the collective conscience, and alter the nature of social relations. That something was the industrial revolution, which began about 1750 but did not have a significant impact until after 1800. The factory system of production, Durkheim asserted, resulted in the emergence of a specialized division of labor and with it a different type of social cohesion, which he termed organic solidarity.

Organic Solidarity. Durkheim used the term **organic solidarity** in reference to the solidarity of differences. In modern societies, individuals are differentiated by their occupations, values, and life-styles. The result of this societal condition brought on largely by industrialization is a society composed of different types of people. These different individuals function much like the various organs of the body. They carry out different functions, but ones that complement or blend with each other for the smooth working of the society as a whole. Just as the heart, lungs, stomach, and other organs perform different yet complementary functions to maintain equilibrium in the physical organism, the same could be said for the way differentiated occupations interrelate smoothly to maintain order in the industrial society.

To carry the organic analogy further, a breakdown in one functional area can cause dislocation all across the system in either a physical organism or a human society. If, for example, a person experiences a heart attack or a serious back injury, his or her entire body is rendered incapable of functioning properly until the injured part recovers. Durkheim asserted that the same is true in a society. In the United States, for instance, coal miners produce coal; coal runs the steel mills; steelworkers produce steel; steel is used in the production of automobiles; car manufacturers distribute the cars to car dealers; the dealers then sell the cars to consumers. Hypothetically speaking, a long and unresolved coal miners' strike could create somewhat of a domino effect, which in turn could possibly impair a large part of the economy.

Durkheim was concerned because organic solidarity was more precarious than the earlier type and, given the differentiated nature of modern societies, the collective conscience was weakened. He felt that the sheer complexity of these societies resulted in a condition of *anomie* (Chapter 5), the absence or breakdown of norms.

In terms of social relations, industrial societies—composed of huge numbers of people who are different from each other in occupations, values, and life-styles—are structured in a manner that discourages primary group relations and encourages secondary group relationships. One may come into contact with so many different types of people in so many different situations that it becomes difficult to maintain anything other than secondary group relationships with most of them.

Social Relations Today

Some sociologists like Harold L. Wilensky and Charles N. Lebeaux argue that "the breakdown of primary group life and informal controls has been greatly exaggerated" (1958, p. 125). They cite studies which show that the need to form primary relations is fairly universal and manifests itself in urban as well as rural settings. Even in a geographically mobile, industrial society, people who are isolated from one source of primary relations seek out and find others.

While it is true that people everywhere desire and need primary group relations, an impressive body of research shows that the nature of urban industrial society makes it difficult for people to form and sustain primary relations. Stanley S. Guterman (1969), for instance, concluded from his research that urban dwellers are less likely to have primary group bonds with close friends than those who live in small towns. More recently, a national study asked those in the sample to identify the persons with whom they could discuss important matters. Through the use of this measure, the study found that the average person had strong personal ties with only three other people (Marsden, 1987).

GROUP DYNAMICS

To gain a basic understanding of the richness and diversity of the human experience requires an examination of groups and group processes. Because we are social creatures, our lives are shaped significantly not only by our exposure to a multiplicity of groups but by our impact on these groups as well. So far, we have devoted most of this chapter to a discussion of the architecture of groups and how the characteristics of certain types of societies shape the way they are structured. However, groups are not static things to be merely classified and cataloged in the abstract for analytical purposes. Instead, they represent dynamic processes that impact directly on each of us. Therefore, let us now focus our attention on **group dynamics**, the systematic study of small-group processes.

Basic Principles of Group Dynamics

The study of group dynamics is a relatively new development in sociology, which originated during the late 1940s and early 1950s. Although several scholars have conducted research in this area of microsociology, three names tend to stand out from the rest: Robert F. Bales, George C. Homans, and Alex Bave-

las. Together, through their research, they have formulated many of the basic principles of group dynamics. Five of these are discussed as follows:

Task-oriented Groups Use a Three-stage Process. Robert F. Bales (1950) pioneered a method for investigating small-group interaction which became known as *interaction process analysis.* Over many years, Bales and his associates studied small groups of research subjects behind one-way glass. Each group was given a task to perform, and the verbal responses of each member were recorded and a record kept as to which person each comment was directed to.

The entire interaction process for each individual and group was charted according to twelve categories of response. Examples of these categorized responses include: defends or asserts oneself, agrees, demonstrates antagonism, understands, gives help, asks for opinion. One of several findings derived from this research was that groups went through three distinct behavioral phases in addressing tasks. First, there was the *orientation phase* in which participants sought and gave information. This was followed by the *evaluation phase* in which all input was evaluated and opinions given. Finally, the group entered the *control phase* in which information was prioritized, solutions offered, and conclusions made (Bales, 1950; Bales and Strodtbeck, 1951; Bales, 1970).

Group Behavior Is Norm-based. A founding father of group dynamics research, George Homans, in his seminal book *The Human Group* (1950), set forth several basic principles of small-group processes. Among these, the most important are the principles that group behavior is norm-based, interaction encourages friendship, and initiative promotes status.

First of all, Homans found that all groups operate according to a set of norms that are established and maintained by each group. These norms provide the group with structure, order, and focus. In established groups, the new member in most cases must find out what the norms are and adapt to them in order to be accepted. Groups that are newly formed invariably go through a process of establishing what the norms will be. As this occurs, a group structure emerges that includes leadership and interaction patterns and a certain style of decision making. Think back for a moment to your first few days at college. What norms did you discover and adjust to that were different from those in high school? Which norms in your sociology class (usually set by the instructor) are similar to or different from those in some of your other classes?

Interaction Encourages Friendship. Homans also asserted the principle that interaction encourages friendship. Not only are primary relations characterized by greater interaction between members than are secondary groups, but taking the initiative in talking to others can cause friendships to develop. Stated in simple terms, there are many lonely people, just waiting to be "discovered," who are in need of a friend or friends. Sociologists like Homans have found that the most effective way to establish friendships is to muster the courage to make the first move. By thrusting ourselves into the world of social action and being the first to smile, put out a hand, introduce ourselves, and initiate conversation, we can usually satisfy our desire for friendship.

Initiative Promotes Status. Homans (1950) and others have also found that initiative promotes status. By taking the initiative in interacting with others, a person is able to promote

Those who initiate contact with others are more likely to make friends. (Sam Zarember/The Image Bank.)

himself or herself to a position of high status within the group. Those who interact least in groups tend to be low-status members. In addition, some researchers have found that the person who initiates the most interactions often is perceived as the leader by other group members. This individual, by virtue of the force of personality in both keeping the group task oriented and supporting the ideas of other members, gains their loyalty and support (Bales and Slater, 1955).

Group Communication Is Affected by the Positioning of Members. During the 1960s, sociologist Alex Bavelas (1962) conducted a series of communication experiments on task-oriented groups consisting of five persons each. He arranged these groups into different configurations including a circle, a wheel, a Y

and a chain (see Figure 6-3). Of these arrangements, the wheel—in which the leader tended to be the person in the center—was found to accomplish tasks most efficiently, although group morale suffered. By being located at the hub of the wheel, the leader could both effectively communicate his or her wishes to the group and control all communication that went to individual group members who were cut off from one another. By contrast, the circle was found to be less effective from a task-completion standpoint because there was no definite leader. It had, however, the highest morale among members because of the high level of communication that was possible. Bavelas found that both the quantity and style of communication resulted from the way members were positioned in the group, which in turn affected both leadership and morale.

Figure 6-3   Group Position and Communication

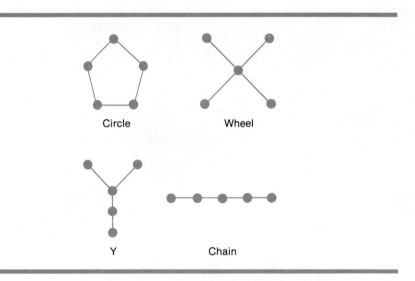

The manner in which people are positioned in groups affects their ability to communicate with other group members. If you were the leader of a five-person group, which group communication structure would you prefer, and where would you locate yourself in it? Each dot represents a person, and each line between dots represents a line of communication. *Source:* Adapted from Bavelas, A. (1962). Communication patterns in task-oriented groups. In D. Cartright and A. F. Zander (Eds.), *Group dynamics*, New York: Harper & Row.

Relating to Groups as an Individual

In-groups and Out-groups. Probably the most fundamental way each of us relates to groups as an individual is in terms of "us" versus "them." Early in the twentieth century, William Graham Sumner (1906) addressed this issue by distinguishing between in-groups and out-groups. An **in-group** is a group a person belongs to or identifies with. It is a "we" group as compared to a "they" group. In-groups have a sense of "we-ness" or consciousness of kind that is usually based on commonly shared values or experiences among group members. Nongroup members are typically viewed as outsiders or "they." Our in-groups may range in size from the smallest of social groups, such as a marriage or friendship circle, to the largest of social categories, such as "we" women, "we" Methodists, "we" New Yorkers, or "we" Americans. These types of group identifications reinforce both our need to belong and social cohesion as manifested in *ethnocentrism* (Chapter 3).

An **out-group**, by contrast, is a group a person does not belong to or identify with. It is a "they" group as compared to a "we" group. Groups distinguished according to in-groups and out-groups differ in membership and orientation and are often characterized by rivalry and tension. If one is Jewish, an out-group would be Protestants. In similar fashion, the old would represent an out-group for the young, those who like mainly classical music would be an out-group for country-western fans, and Palestinians would be an out-group for Israelis.

Social Distance. The manner in which an individual relates to groups can also be examined by measuring **social distance**. This refers to the degree of acceptance an individual feels toward those who belong to various groups to which he or she does not belong. Sociologist Emory S. Bogardus (1959) devised a seven-point system to measure social distance. When it is administered to research subjects in the form of a scale, they are asked to answer yes or no to whether they would be willing to accept a certain category of person—a member of a different ethnic group for instance—as (1) a family member by marriage, (2) a personal friend, (3) a close neighbor, (4) a co-worker, (5) a citizen in their country, (6) a visitor to their country, or if they instead (7) would ban the person from their country.

Through the use of the Bogardus Social Distance Scale and other measures, sociologists are able to ascertain how close or distant people feel toward certain groups according to certain characteristics, such as age, ethnicity, race, class, religion, sexual preference, and nationality. This allows us to predict with some accuracy the extent to which some groups will either be cooperative or antagonistic towards one another.

Reference Groups. In 1942, Herbert Hyman used the term *reference group* to describe another way people relate to the groups that surround them. A **reference group** is a group to which a person may or may not belong, which is used as a standard of comparison to evaluate his or her values, behavior, and goals. A person's primary groups, including family and close peer relations (see Chapter 4), may be reference groups in the sense that they are usually seen as models for value formation and behavior.

Many reference groups, however, are social categories that we use strictly as a basis for comparing our own attitudes and performance. Using them as benchmarks can be a valuable device for assessing our own social identities and deciding on what we wish to achieve in life. Therefore, it is important for a person serious about obtaining a college degree to identify with college graduates, just as

The reference groups we identify with help us to set goals and measure our own progress. (Copyright Susan Lapides, 1981/Design Conceptions.)

high school and college athletes often do with professional ball players, aspiring writers with published authors, and beginning employees with those in the upper ranks of management.

Both success and failure tend to be defined in terms of the groups in which we choose to participate and those with which we identify. To identify with the success of a particular reference group only as a dream, with little or no commitment or effort devoted to it, will not be sufficient to attain a wished-for standard of performance or objective. However, without beginning with a dream, as measured by the behavior and accomplishments of others, the achievement of success, regardless of how it is socially defined and measured, will usually not occur.

Size and Group Behavior: Dyads and Triads

Almost everyone is familiar with the expression "Too many cooks spoil the broth." Al-

though many clichés have little basis in truth, this one, as it relates to group complexity, appears to have some validity. For instance, sociologist John James (1951), in a classic study involving nine thousand people in both work and recreational situations, found that 71 percent of all interactions engaged in by the research subjects involved only two people, and 21 percent included only three people. Of the rest, only 2 percent of the interactions involved more than four people. Subsequent research has yielded similar results.

Much of the basis for the fact that we appear to prefer interactions that are one-on-one with others has to do with the factor of complexity. The smaller the group, the less complicated it is to establish and maintain the qualities of rapport, effective communication, and successful decision making. Thus, the size of a group plays a very important role in affecting the patterns of interaction that take place within it. Sociologist Paul Hare (1962), for instance, mentions that in a two-person group, there is only a single relationship between the two members. But with a three-person group, the number of potential relationships increases geometrically to 6. By the time we arrive at a seven-person group, there are 966 potential relationships (see Table 6-1).

This exponential rise in group complexity can be readily observed when the interaction dynamics of a **dyad** (a two-person group) are compared with those of a **triad** (a three-person group). Among the first to study these two different types of groups was the German sociologist Georg Simmel (1858–1918), who in 1905 published an analysis of dyads and triads in a seminal article entitled "Quantitative Aspects of the Group." He found the dyad, or two-person group, to be very fragile because it "depends on each of its two elements alone—in its death though not in its life; for its life it needs *both*, but for its death, only one" (1905, 1950 B, p. 124).

A dyad is at once the most intimate and the most vulnerable of groups. Since there are no others to divide time and energy among,

Table 6-1 Group Size and Potential Relationships

Number of Persons in Group	Number of Potential Relationships
2	1
3	6
4	25
5	90
6	301
7	966

As the number of people in a group increases, the number of potential relationships increases geometrically. Even in a group of only three or four people, the communication and power combinations are not only complex but are constantly subject to adjustment.
Source: Hare, A. P. (1962). *Handbook of small group research.* Glencoe, Ill.: Free Press, p. 229.

there can be a degree of rapport and mutual sharing between the two participants not possible with larger groups. Dyads, however, tend to be difficult to maintain because, unlike larger groups, individual responsibility is an "all or nothing" situation that cannot be shifted onto the group or delegated to others. In addition, conflict that may arise between the two parties is not subject to either mediation or interference by other group members. Consequently, it is normally the complete responsibility of the two members to resolve a dispute, accommodate it, or dissolve the group by parting company (Gupta, 1983).

When a dyad becomes a triad through the addition of a third party, the dynamics of the group become much more complex. A triad is a more durable group in that the leaving of any one member is not essential to group survival; the two remaining members can continue their relationship. Intimacy is not so profound as with the dyad, because each member must now divide time and energy between two persons. In addition, when conflict breaks out between two of the members, the third party can act as a mediator to help resolve the conflict.

Perhaps the most complicating aspect of all, however, is that in the triad, power coalitions of two against one are possible, whereas they are not feasible in the dyad. Thus, any member can play the role of opportunist in joining forces with another member to overwhelm the third party or act as a strategist in seizing power through the use of "divide and conquer" tactics. With the opportunity for shifts in power ever present, alignments between members can and often do change from time to time and from issue to issue (Caplow, 1969).

Nowhere is the distinction between a dyad and triad more apparent and important than in the interaction dynamics of a married couple versus a married couple with a child. Given the previous discussion, a newly married couple typically would do well to postpone having a child for at least a year or two in order to adjust to the role obligations that go with being married. With this foundation firmly established, the couple would then be in a better position to handle the increasing complexities that accrue to adding a third family member. For example, having a child ideally means that both partners are able to carry out successfully and balance the role obligations of both spouse and parent without overidentifying with or neglecting either. In addition, parenting represents an extension of the partnership established at the onset of marriage, in which both spouses work together as a team to establish consistent standards for child rearing.

THE FOCUS OF GROUP BEHAVIOR

In the last section of this chapter, we will briefly examine some of the basic factors that shape the focus of group behavior. The direction and momentum that groups exhibit are determined to a significant degree by their purposes, as well as by their types and styles of leadership.

Group Purposes

Most groups tend to be characterized by a predominance of one or the other of two basic purposes, expressive or instrumental. Primary social groups have, for the most part, an **expressive group purpose** in which the main goal is the emotional benefit derived from participation. Here, group interaction in the family and one's circle of close friends represents an end in itself; namely, the sense of intimacy, community, and belonging one receives from interacting with others on a personal level. Secondary group relations, by comparison, typically have an **instrumental group purpose** in which interaction with others is used

as a means to a practical end. In this regard, we interact with waiters and waitresses mainly to receive a meal, teachers to obtain an education, employers to earn a living, and salespeople and clerks of various types to acquire needed consumer items. Associations also make use of instrumental purposes of a much more specific and complex nature through formal organization.

Group purposes act to structure social interaction in specific ways which, although not expressly stated, are understood by practically everyone. In this regard, our primary group members are likely to feel manipulated and "used" if they discover we have ulterior motives aimed at personal gain in interacting with them. Likewise, those with whom we interact in secondary group situations may feel uncomfortable or exploited if we take up too much of their time or try to get too personal with them.

Types and Styles of Leadership

The focus of group interaction is also influenced by its type of leadership. A *leader* is a person who is able to wield more authority or power than other members in influencing the way the group functions. Some leaders influence the group by virtue of their official position of authority, while others are informal leaders who influence other members through the force of their personalities. Nevertheless, there are two basic types of leaders generally recognized by sociologists, task leaders and socioemotional leaders (Bales, 1953; Fiedler, 1981).

Task leaders focus their attention on instrumental group purposes aimed at reaching practical goals. They tend to concentrate on "getting the job done" as their first consideration. Some researchers hold that task leadership competence is the most important leadership element (Hollander, 1964). They cite findings that small groups tend to look for task competence in their leaders and appear somewhat adept in being able to identify such individuals (Firestone, Lichtman, and Calamosca, 1975). Yet, as other research indicates, members of some groups can develop, over a period of time, a significant amount of hostility and resentment toward the task leader and "taking orders," as well as toward each other, particularly when their interest in the task at hand is not high (Burke, 1967, 1968). When this occurs, another type of leadership, socioemotional leadership, is often more effective.

Socioemotional leaders concentrate their energies on expressive group purposes aimed at promoting morale and harmony among members. They focus attention on meeting people's emotional needs for acceptance and appreciation and in reducing conflict. Socioemotional leaders tend to be better liked than task leaders, especially when groups function over a long period of time and initial enthusiasm for a task has diminished (Slater, 1955). Whether the task leader or socioemotional leader is the more effective depends on several factors relating to the group situation. In most groups, both large and small, both types of leaders are present.

Another important consideration is leadership style, which takes three basic forms: authoritarian, laissez-faire, and democratic (Lewin, 1954; White and Lippitt, 1960). The leader who uses the *authoritarian* style basically gives orders and makes most if not all decisions pertaining to the group. This ap-

Different types of social situations often call for certain types of leadership. What type of leadership style would be most appropriate here? (Copyright Marc Romanelli/The Image Bank.)

proach is normally effective and efficient when the leader is present but often breaks down when the leader is absent. Members of authoritarian groups often have low morale and exhibit frustration and hostility toward the leader. Many if not most people, however, prefer an authoritarian "take charge" leader in a crisis, and some people, perhaps those with low self-esteem or those who lack competence in the area of behavior required by the group, prefer to have the leader tell them what to do. The *laissez-faire* leader occupies the other polar extreme, in that he or she remains passive and uninvolved and allows the group to proceed on its own. Consequently, there is little group productivity, and conflicts between group members are usually quite apparent.

Democratic leaders, who occupy the middle ground between the two extremes, are typically effective regardless of whether the group is a family, a local association or club, a major corporation, or any one of several other types. Participation in decision making is spread across the group, which heightens morale as a result of an increased sense among members that their ideas are appreciated. However, democratically run groups are much slower in responding to changing social conditions and are thus less efficient than authoritarian groups because of the time required to seek input from members. In addition, some groups, like military organizations in wartime, would probably be totally ineffective if they functioned democratically.

CHAPTER SUMMARY

1. There are four basic characteristics that are useful in distinguishing between different types of groups in society. One characteristic all groups possess is that of common attributes, which are used as group boundaries to distinguish members from nonmembers. Whether or not a given group has one or more of the other three characteristics—consciousness of kind, patterned social relations, and formal organization—depends on what type it represents.

2. There are five basic types of groups, the most fundamental of which is the social group. The other four types consist of physical aggregates (crowds), statistical categories (groups designated for research and comparative purposes), social categories (those with visible or special characteristics), and associations (groups with planned practical goals). Given the importance of the social group, it represents the basic focus for most of the remaining chapter.

3. Social groups are of two basic forms: primary groups and secondary groups. The primary group is a small group distinguished by personal, ongoing relations between members. Our primary group relations are very important in that they serve as our basic source of emotional and social support. The qualities of primary group relations include multidimensional relationships, continuous face-to-face contact, durability, trust, and informal social controls. Secondary groups, by comparison, involve relatively superficial and impersonal relations with large collectivities of people. Relations of this kind, which tend to be the most common form in modern societies, are one-dimensional, nonpermanent, tend to be based on distrust, and make use of formal social controls.

4. The predominance of either primary or secondary group relations is affected in large part by the way a given society is structured or organized. This is perhaps best illustrated in the pioneering work of two late nineteenth-century European sociologists, Ferdinand Tönnies and Émile Durkheim. Tönnies is best known for his *gemeinschaft-gesellschaft* typology, in which he distinguished between the social organization of small village-focused societies (*gemeinschaft*) and large urban societies (*gesellschaft*). Because the *gemeinschaft* social system has a low level of material technology, common ancestry among inhabitants, tradition-based social positions, close-knit and long-term ties, and geographical stability, it fosters a climate conducive to primary group relations. The *gesellschaft* society, with largely opposite characteristics, has a social structure more amenable to secondary relations.

5. Durkheim was also interested in studying the relationship between social structure and social relations. He sought to discover and compare the nature of social order (solidarity) in simple, nonindustrial societies with that of modern industrial systems. He found that traditional nonindustrial societies had mechanical solidarity—the solidarity of resemblance—which was more conducive to primary group relations, while modern societies possessed organic solidarity—the solidarity of differences—which was better suited for secondary relations.

6. Group dynamics is the systematic study of small-group processes. Basic principles of group interaction include the following: groups approach tasks in a three-step process, group behavior is norm based, interaction encourages friendship, initiative promotes status, and group communication is affected by the positioning of people within the group.

7. The ways in which we relate to groups as individuals, as well as the size of groups, also affect the manner in which they function. In terms of relating to groups, each of us perceives in-groups ("we" groups) with whom we feel a bond or a sense of connection. This identification promotes group solidarity and ethnocentrism. We also perceive out-groups ("they" groups) with whom we may feel a

sense of rivalry or tension. In addition, size plays an important role in group dynamics, a dyad (a two-person group) being much simpler in several respects than a triad (a three-person group).

8. The focus or thrust of group behavior is affected by a variety of factors, including group purposes and leadership types and styles. Primary relations usually involve an expressive group purpose (emotional benefit), while secondary relations typically have an instrumental purpose (practical benefit). With regard to leadership, there are two basic types of leaders: those who are socioemotional in orientation (concerned with group morale) and those who are task-oriented (focused on getting the job done). Additionally, leaders may have a leadership style that is authoritarian (high efficiency–low morale), democratic (low efficiency–high morale), and laissez-faire (low productivity–high conflict).

TERMS TO KNOW

association: a group deliberately formed to pursue one or more specific practical goals.

collective conscience: In Durkheim's view, a state of mental and moral agreement among members of a society concerning basic norms and values.

common attributes: characteristics that members of a group have in common with one another.

consciousness of kind: the tendency of people to recognize others like themselves and, in many cases, to feel some common sense of identification or connection as a result.

dyad: a two-person group.

expressive group purpose: the focus of primary group relations in which the group is seen as an end in itself for the emotional benefits of warmth and friendship it provides to members.

formal organization: the action taken by members of an association to pursue one or more specific practical goals.

gemeinschaft: Tönnies's term for a community-oriented society in which most relations are personal, informal, and based on tradition.

gesellschaft: Tönnies's term for an urban, industrial society with impersonal and somewhat formal relations that tend to be based on contract.

group dynamics: the systematic study of small group processes.

in-group: a group a person belongs to or identifies with.

instrumental group purpose: the focus of secondary group relations in which the group is used as a means to achieve a practical goal.

mechanical solidarity: Durkheim's term for the solidarity of resemblance characteristic of traditional nonindustrial societies.

organic solidarity: Durkheim's term for the solidarity of differences characteristic of modern industrial societies.

out-group: a group a person does not belong to or identify with.

patterned social relations: the process by which members of some groups have and take the opportunity to influence the feelings, attitudes, and behavior of one another through personal social interaction and/or some indirect system of social contact.

physical aggregate: a type of group distinguished primarily by the physical proximity of its members; a crowd.

polar typology: an analytical device pioneered by Tönnies in which two dissimilar ideal types are placed at either end of a continuum for the purposes of comparison.

primary group: a small social group characterized by personal, ongoing relationships between members.

reference group: a group to which a person may or may not belong that is used as a standard of comparison to evaluate his or her values, behavior, and goals.

secondary group: a relatively large collection of people with whom one has superficial and somewhat impersonal relations.

social category: a type of group characterized by its members' having one or more visible or otherwise special characteristics in common.

social distance: the degree of acceptance an individual feels toward those who belong to various groups to which he or she does not belong.

social group: a type of group consisting of people bound together by common interests in a definite pattern of social interaction.

socioemotional leaders: those who concentrate their energies on expressive group purposes aimed at promoting morale and harmony among members.

statistical category: a type of group formed by researchers for the purposes of social analysis.

task leaders: those who focus their attention on instrumental group purposes aimed at reaching practical goals.

triad: a three-person group.

SUGGESTED READINGS

Behavior in Public Places (Erving Goffman; New York: Free Press, 1963). A series of classic observations concerning the manner in which casual social encounters (secondary relations) take place in contemporary urban society.

Decision Making (Irving L. Janis and Leon Mann; New York: Free Press, 1977). A valuable resource that presents a thorough explanation of both sociological theory and research on the group decision-making process.

The Dynamics of Small Groups (Cecilia L. Ridgeway; New York: St. Martins Press, 1983). A well-balanced and comprehensive text on small groups that covers how they function as individual entities and interact within larger social structures.

The Human Group (George C. Homans; New York: Harcourt Brace Jovanovich, 1950). A classic sociological work in group dynamics by one of its founding investigators, which furnishes the student with a penetrating analysis of how small groups like the family and work groups function.

Intimate Relations (Murray S. Davis; New York: Free Press, 1973). A fascinating analysis of primary groups in terms of how love and close-friend relationships are formed, their structure, and the interaction processes that take place within them.

Social Organization: Human Nature and the Social Order (Charles H. Cooley; New York: Free Press, 1956. Originally published in 1909). A classic discussion in this early text by Cooley on the primary group and its basic characteristics.

Chapter 7
Associations and Bureaucracy

Goal Displacement
Protection of Incompetence

The Peter Principle
Parkinson's Law

■ TERMS TO KNOW

authority
bottom-up decision making
brainwashing
charismatic authority
coercive association
collectives
conformity
formal structure
goal displacement
groupthink

informal structure
iron law of oligarchy
mortification
Parkinson's law
Peter principle
power
protection of incompetence
rational-legal authority
ritualism
traditional authority
utilitarian association
voluntary association

"In general, service in America stinks." The view reflected in this quote by Thomas J. Peters, prominent management consultant and coauthor of *In Search of Excellence*, is not an isolated one. It appears to be in evidence everywhere, as shown in this fictional, yet illustrative introduction to a recent cover story in *Time* magazine:

> For Harry Hapless, it was a rough day in the service economy. His car, a Fiasco 400, started sputtering on the highway, so Harry pulled into a gas station for help. "Sorry, no mechanics, only gas!" shouted the attendant. "How can you call this a service station?" yelled Harry. He went to the bank to get some emergency cash for a tow truck, only to find the automatic teller machine out of order again. "Real nice service!" he muttered. Then Harry decided to use a credit card to buy a tool kit at the Cheapo discount store, but he couldn't find anyone to wait on him. "Service! Anyone, please! Help me!" was his cry.
>
> It had been a trying day indeed, Harry thought as he rode a bus home, but at least he could look forward to a trip to Florida the following week with his wife Harriet. That is,

until Flyway Air called: "Sorry Mr. Hapless. Due to our merger with Byway Air, your Florida flight has been cancelled." Harry got so angry he was going to call the Federal Aviation Administration immediately. But just then his phone went dead—no doubt because the Bell system had been split up, he imagined. Well, that was the last straw. A few minutes later a wild-eyed Harry burst into the newsroom of his local newspaper. "I've got a story for you!" he cried. "There is no more service in America!" (Koepp, 1987, p. 49).

Maybe you as a consumer have felt, at times, as unappreciated and poorly served as Harry Hapless. But then again, maybe you have not. "Service" is both a subjective and relative concept that varies in practice from person to person, organization to organization, and culture to culture. Nonetheless, it represents one ingredient in the makeup of large-scale associations in modern industrial societies, many of which are also bureaucracies. Americans appreciate the concept of "service" and the life-style that industrialization has made possible. Although many may

Many of us have regular contact with large-scale associations and bureaucracies in our jobs, community activities, and at school. (Copyright E. L. Simmons/The Image Bank.)

look back with fondness at "the good old days" when life was simple and relationships were more personal, few would actually elect to go back to a society devoid of air conditioning, television, and the other benefits of modern society.

We typically come in contact with associations every day in our social positions not only as consumers but as workers, students, and citizens. Indeed, most of us as workers are employed by associations. Our occupational progress and ability to provide financially for our families are greatly influenced by how well we understand and perform in large-scale organizations. Those with little understanding of how their society and the large-scale asso-

ciations within it operate are in a poor position to be very successful.

Given the tremendous impact that formal organization and associations have on modern societies today, it is important to understand (1) the nature of associations and their different types, (2) the historical development of social authority and how it is manifested in large organizations today, (3) the development and nature of bureaucracy, (4) the manner in which large-scale associations operate as social systems, and (5) some basic problems related to associations and bureaucracy. This chapter, therefore, will build on the material presented in Chapter 6 and discuss these basic issues in some detail.

TYPES OF ASSOCIATIONS

As you will recall from Chapter 6, an *association* is a group deliberately formed to pursue one or more specific practical goals. Formed from secondary social groups, associations typically possess all four of the basic group characteristics mentioned previously: common attributes, consciousness of kind, patterned social relations, and formal organization.

Sociologists have offered several classifications of associations (Parsons, 1956; Blau and Scott, 1962; Perrow, 1967; Haas and Drabek, 1973; Etzioni, 1975). Of these, the typology devised by Amitai Etzioni (1975) is one of the most useful. It clearly shows (1) the diverse manner in which associations are organized and function, (2) the reasons that people participate in various associations, and (3) the types and degrees of control that associations assert over members. As shown in Figure 7-1, Etzioni lists three types of associations—voluntary, utilitarian, and coercive—that act as a general umbrella under which most organizations can be placed. In addition, Erving Goff-

Figure 7-1 **Etzioni's Typology of Associations**

Organization Type	Form of Power Used	Degree of Control over Participants
Voluntary	Normative	Low
Utilitarian	Remunerative	Medium
Coercive	Coercive	High

Source: Etzioni, A. (1961). *A comparative analysis of complex organizations.* New York: Free Press.

man's analysis of the total institution as an extreme form of coercive association provides additional depth and insight.

Voluntary Associations

An organization people join freely as a part-time activity because they agree with its norms and goals is a **voluntary association**. Common examples include civic and fraternal organizations like Moose, Kiwanis, and Rotary clubs, professional associations such as the American Bar Association and American Sociological Association, and personal interest organizations such as those related to hobbies, political orientation, religion, age, background, and even sex (for example, Boy Scouts of America and Daughters of the American Revolution).

In America, people tend to be joiners, with about two out of every three holding membership in at least one voluntary association. This orientation for joining is socialized into children early in life as they participate in Little League ball, Girl Scouts, and a number of other organizational activities. We learn to participate in voluntary associations in our spare time perhaps because they address interests and fulfill needs not typically met through our day-to-day encounters with fam-

Most Americans belong to one or more voluntary associations, which they join out of interest and sometimes mainly for fun. (Bob Daemmrich Photo.)

ily, friends, and secondary group relations. Consequently, they represent very specialized affiliations that tend to meet very specialized needs. According to Etzioni, this type of association involves the least amount of control over the lives of participants. The influence that is exerted is due to *normative power*, effective only because members' values are in agreement with the norms and goals of the organization.

Voluntary associations are distinguished in other ways as well. First, because they consist of like-minded people, they tend to be organized along class lines. Both Pentecostals and Presbyterians worship as Christians, but their churches are organized very differently, and their memberships tend to reflect different socioeconomic strata of society, particularly in regard to types of occupations and levels and types of education represented. Income can also be a consideration. Relatively few members of the upper class belong to motorcycle and camping clubs. Likewise, few working-class people join golf and polo clubs, because sports such as bowling are much less expensive. Second, large and well-organized voluntary associations often affect public policy. Some notable examples include the National Rifle Association (NRA), Mothers Against Drunk Driving (MADD), and the National Association for the Advancement of Colored People (NAACP).

Utilitarian Associations

A **utilitarian association** is an organization in which people participate for practical gain or profit. Examples include businesses, corporations, and professional organizations such as brokerage, law, and consulting firms. While people are not coerced into affiliating with them, participation is not strictly voluntary either. Most adult members of modern society today feel some pressure to work with or for one or more utilitarian organizations in order to provide a living for themselves and their families. As a result, these organizations fall somewhere in the middle of the continuum, between the extremes of voluntarism on one end and coercion on the other. Etzioni found that these associations can exert a fair amount of control over a person's life through the use of *remunerative power*. Particularly in difficult economic times, when jobs for many people are difficult to obtain, the "tyranny of the paycheck," whether real or imagined, can significantly influence a person's behavior and life as a whole.

Coercive Associations

An organization in which people participate as a result of force or the threat of force is a **coercive association**. Conscriptive military systems, prisoner-of-war camps, prisons, custodial mental institutions, elementary schools, and some monastic religious communities and sects serve as representative illustrations. Those placed or retained in this type of organizational environment against their will or as a result of brainwashing have few if any options and little if any freedom of action. In Etzioni's analysis, these associations exert high to complete control over their members through the use of *coercive power*. This can range from notes of disapproval sent home to parents of elementary school children to psychological and physical torture, starvation, and even death in a prisoner-of-war camp.

Total Institutions: Mortification and Brainwashing

Erving Goffman's (1961) term for an extreme form of coercive association is *total institution*. In his research, he found that although these organizations exist for different purposes, they tend to have one characteristic in common. They encapsulate their "recruits" or "inmates" by cutting them off from the outside world. Then they resocialize their new members through **mortification**, a process in which a person's old identity is stripped away through a systematic program of degradation and humiliation, and a new self more suitable to the organization is substituted in its place. Mortification is often made possible by *degradation rituals,* procedures and activities intentionally designed to disorient emotionally and shock new members into submitting to the demands of the new environment. The army recruit may be cursed at by his sergeant, made to do demeaning and self-effacing tasks, and is called only "soldier" in most instances. The prison inmate is stripped, deloused, subject to strip searches and periodic shakedowns, and is often referred to only by number.

Mortification is facilitated through a variety of environmental devices aimed at destroying the individuality of people, so that they can be easily "programmed" and thus controlled. First, the organization maintains *twenty-four-hour-a-day control* over inmates (or recruits). Participants are monitored on a constant, ongoing basis. Second, members are kept in *isolation* from the outside world. In prisons and mental hospitals, this is accomplished by walls and other physical barriers, whereas in POW camps it may also include the monitoring and censoring of mail. During the Korean conflict in the early 1950s, North Korean captors, as part of their mortification program, did not allow warm, reassuring letters from loved ones back home to "get through" to American prisoners of war. However, all the bad news—the "Dear John" letters, divorce notices, and news of family illnesses and deaths—were delivered.

Mortification is aided in other ways as well. Some coercive associations use the *confiscation of personal effects* such as clothing and jewelry to discourage individuality and maximize efficient control over participants. In some religious orders all priests or nuns must wear identical habits, in the military all recruits wear identical uniforms, and in most prisons all inmates must wear the same type of clothing. Life in a coercive association also involves *comprehensive scheduling* and *effective sanctions.* Members are told when to do everything—eat, sleep, work, recreate, bathe—so that all important decisions concerning how their time is spent are taken out of their hands. Violations of any kind are met with swift and effective sanctions such as solitary confinement, exercise, missing meals, or doing penance.

In some cases, the use of these devices can result in **brainwashing**, a process of almost complete thought control in which the victim's existing values and beliefs are made useless and replaced with those desired by the agent of influence. This most extreme form of mortification renders the individual helpless and dependent on captors for satisfaction of basic emotional and psychological needs. Peers who have already been brainwashed are often enlisted to aid in applying pressure to make the individual feel even more worthless and guilty. Then, when the victim begins to exhibit the "right" attitudes, rewards including praise, encouragement, and affection are given (Muller, 1974).

A classic example of brainwashing is evident in the story of the "People's Temple" sect that ended tragically in 1978. This group, affiliated with the Disciples of Christ, was headed by a mentally disturbed but charismatic "bishop," named Jim Jones, who appealed mainly to the poor and uneducated. Alienated from society and fearing that secular authorities were plotting against his group, he ultimately moved his flock of followers to the jungles of Guyana where they founded a settlement called Jonestown.

Once there, Jones and his close disciples confiscated all passports and kept his followers isolated from contact with their relatives and friends in the United States, who became increasingly worried. During their last several

Brainwashing can result in tragedy, as illustrated by the 900 followers of religious leader Jim Jones who committed mass suicide in 1978. (AP/World Wide Photos.)

months, he kept these people preoccupied with religious activities and rituals and had them write him letters of self-deprecation addressed to "Daddy." After an investigation by outsiders from America, some of whom he had murdered as they were trying to depart, he had his followers prepare large quantities of Kool-Aid to which was added cyanide. Believing that Jones either talked with God or was the messiah himself, his nine hundred followers drank the lethal Kool-Aid, lay down in the grass in fairly neat groups and rows, and died, many with their arms wrapped around one another. Jones himself died from a gunshot wound to the head, apparently administered by a loyal follower under his direction, who subsequently committed suicide as well (Reiterman, 1982).

FORMS OF SOCIAL AUTHORITY

The power and authority of their leaders significantly affect the functioning of both small groups and large associations. Power and authority, as we will see, come in different forms. The juvenile gang leader, for instance, has little in common with the high school teacher, although they may affect the behavior of the same people. In similar fashion, an Iranian ayatollah, a European monarch, and an American president lead the people of their countries in very different ways.

The Nature of Power and Authority

Power is the ability to influence or control the behavior of others with or without their consent. Leaders everywhere exert power by actively influencing if not determining how group and organizational decisions are made and the particular forms they take. Some are very direct and blunt about how they exercise their prerogatives, while others are quite indirect and subtle. Leaders can also use power to guide gently or to dominate totally; they may be kind or cruel, noble or dishonorable, lawful or unlawful, competent or incompetent.

There are five basic sources of power which, in turn, result in five corresponding power types: reward, coercion, referent power, expert power, and legitimate power (French and Raven, 1968). These power types may be used singly or in combination with one another. The first mentioned, *reward power*, results from the ability of a person to provide others with something of value that they desire. The employer, for instance, rewards the employee with a paycheck and the incentive for a bonus or promotion if the individual performs accordingly.

The opposite of reward power is *coercive power*, which derives from the ability of an individual to punish those whose behavior does not meet expected standards. Employers have this type of power as well and can freeze wages, demote, or fire an employee who performs below acceptable levels. The arrest powers of police and the prosecution powers of governmental agencies provide additional illustrations.

Power comes in several forms. What type of power is being exhibited by this performer? (Michael Ochs Archives.)

Referent power stems from the ability of a person personally to attract or appeal to others. The source of attraction may be that of parent figure, sex object, mentor, or other form of personal influence or inspiration. The leader of the People's Temple sect, Jim Jones, for instance, had a magnetic personality that drew hundreds of followers and gave him ultimate control over their lives.

Expert power results from people's belief that a particular type of individual possesses more knowledge than they do in a certain area of expertise. Doctors, lawyers, teachers, accountants, and other professionals have this type of power because of the respect accorded them by those they serve.

The final type of power, *legitimate power*, is usually referred to as authority. It is derived from people's belief that it is right and proper to do what a certain individual or organization directs them to do. **Authority**, therefore, is legitimated power generally recognized and supported by those over whom it is exercised. It is formal or official power held by certain individuals, organizations, and their representatives. A tribal chief, a dictator, and a king all have authority, as do governmental agencies and their representatives, corporations and their managers, schools and their teachers.

Types of Authority

Max Weber (1922, 1968), one of the early masters of sociological thought, died unexpectedly of pneumonia in 1920 before he could finish his most ambitious book, *Economy and Society* (Coser, 1971, p. 242). The manuscript, which was published posthumously in 1922, included his classic analysis of authority and bureaucratic organization (see Chapter 5). Here, Weber developed a typology of three forms of legitimate authority: charismatic, traditional, and rational-legal authority.

Charismatic Authority. Historically, some of the simplest societies have been characterized by **charismatic authority**. This authority form is based on the commonly accepted belief by followers that the leader possesses special qualities or unique characteristics. Cultures and organizations that subscribe to this authority system have participants who "believe" the charismatic leader to have a special destiny, unusual vision, divine grace, or special heroic qualities that, though scientifically unmeasurable, are "self-evident." Weber elaborates as follows:

> The charismatic leader gains and maintains authority solely by proving his strength in life. If he wants to be a prophet, he must perform miracles; if he wants to be a war lord, he must perform heroic deeds; Above all, however, his divine mission must "prove" itself in that those who faithfully surrender to him must fare well. If they do not fare well, he is obviously not the master sent by the gods (1947, p. 249).

The term *charisma* originates from the Greek language, meaning "gifts of grace," and sometimes is used in reference to divinity. Both historically and in recent times, some charismatic leaders have been regarded as divine or representatives of God or the gods. Examples include Buddha, Jesus, the Ayatollah Khomeini, and the pope in Rome. In other instances, followers have believed in the heroic qualities of their leaders, as illustrated by Alexander the Great, George Washington, Napoleon, and, more recently, Theodore Roosevelt and Franklin Roosevelt. Those who have derived their large following due to a magnetic, forceful personality or special vision include, during the twentieth century, individuals like Adolf Hitler, Winston Churchill, Martin Luther King, Jr., and John F. Kennedy.

Especially in simple societies of the past, the greatest disadvantage associated with charismatic authority was instability and the problem of succession. Who was to take over the responsibilities of leadership when the charismatic leader became too old and feeble to lead, or died? How was the new leader to be chosen? Beyond the charismatic leader himself—who alone made decisions, ruled on disputes, and provided order solely by virtue of his presence—there were no traditions, laws, or rules to look to for guidance. Although many societies tried to work out a succession system, societal decline, chaos, and even civil war between competing factions often marked the period between effective charismatic regimes. This dilemma was finally resolved historically when the charismatic grace of a leader became institutionalized into a family bloodline and stable traditions. This *routinization of charisma,* as Weber termed it, marked the transition from charismatic authority to other forms.

Traditional Authority. Although societies marked by charismatic authority may be routinized into either traditionalism or bureaucratization (Gerth and Mills, 1946), in most cases, historically, they evolved into traditional authority, a premodern form of leadership. **Traditional authority** is a type of authority based on followers' acceptance of the legitimacy contained in long-standing traditions and customs. With this type of leadership, the concept of monarchy developed, and many kings and/or queens, by virtue of accepted custom, ruled by "divine right." Because of the accepted belief that the monarch possessed charismatic grace and was thus the intermediary between God or the gods and the people, his or her authority was solidified.

Succession under traditional authority was established through accepted custom. Most societies historically were characterized by patriarchy, or rule by males. At the macrolevel, a royal line of succession was established by custom so that in many societies, the firstborn

son inherited the throne and was given total comprehensive authority to rule for life. At the microlevel, the authority structure of the family mirrored that of the government. The father was the "ruler" of the family and, on his death, his sons inherited his lands or business, with the firstborn son, in some societies, entitled to most or all of the estate. Women were usually accorded "second-class citizen" status and played only a minor role in decision making.

Few people living under a traditional system of authority questioned such laws and customs, which were rarely if ever written down. The people simply accepted them because that was what they were accustomed to. Little is changed in today's traditional societies, and people still revere old customs, which are seen as "normal" because "things have always been done this way." While in a sense this represents an irrational system of authority based largely on an accident of birth, it nonetheless has provided societies with a means of stability and continuity not possible under the charismatic system.

Rational-Legal Authority. Under traditional authority, there was no guarantee that a newly crowned monarch or a son with a newly inherited farm or business would be competent or capable of learning the responsibilities that lay ahead. While this did not appear to be an insurmountable problem before the nineteenth century, the industrial revolution brought with it a different economic system that required a rational system of authority. Weber termed this **rational-legal authority**, a type of authority based on the legitimacy of a formal system of laws and procedures that define the scope of a leader's rights and responsibilities. With the substitution of a system of laws for one of rulers, loyalty and obedience shifted away from personalities to a system of rationally determined procedures.

"I almost fell off the treadmill."

Reprinted with permission from: *The New Yorker* (1978, October 5), Vol. 63, No. 33, p. 51.

This became necessary during the 1800s because of the tremendous complexity of the emerging factory system, a more specialized division of labor, and a cash economy.

Rational-legal authority is the cornerstone of modern bureaucracy. It is rational in the sense that specialized positions occupied by workers, professionals, and management officials are carefully planned and specified in terms of the types of education and training required and the levels of performance required. It is legal in the sense that the state and political bodies within it often set, moni-

tor, and enforce the standards of performance required of those who occupy the particular positions. Corporations and other organizations that employ various workers and specialists also have their own "legal" requirements in terms of company policies and procedures, position requirements, and job descriptions.

Women in modern rational-legal systems often find themselves relatively free from the tyranny of patriarchy so characteristic of earlier charismatic and traditional systems. Particularly in societies like the United States, they are increasingly able to compete with men for high status positions on a relatively equal basis.

During the last hundred years, the United States has steadily become more rational-legal in terms of the way authority is structured and work is performed. Physicians, lawyers, teachers, beauticians, electricians, police officers, and many other individuals must meet both educational standards and legal licensing or certification requirements in order to function in their respective occupations. As we approach the dawn of the twenty-first century, this trend continues to become increasingly pronounced. Therefore, those without specialized skills and a positive orientation toward continuing education, which are both needed for a person to remain marketable in an ever-changing economic and social environment, may find themselves joining the ranks of dislocated workers.

As we reflect on these three types of authority—charismatic, traditional, and rational-legal—it is important to note that Weber saw these concepts as ideal types (Chapter 1). They represent conceptual models that are useful in assessing and comparing phenomena as they actually exist. In most societies, a single type of authority tends to be dominant. However, many social systems and institutions represent composites of two or even all three forms of authority. The United Kingdom, for instance, is officially a monarchy with established and revered customs and traditions that specify, among other things, how succession will take place. Nonetheless, its authority is grounded in basically rational-legal institutions related to government and the economy. Iran is presided over by a charismatic leader. Yet the dominant religion contains traditional elements passed down for thousands of years. In addition, Iran, in recent years, has fought a "high-tech" war with Iraq that, operationally speaking, has been largely rational-legal or bureaucratic in nature.

THE NATURE OF BUREAUCRACY

As noted earlier in Chapter 5, bureaucracy as a form of social organization

> . . . is not a new phenomenon. It existed in simple forms thousands of years ago in Egypt and Rome. But the trend toward bureaucratization has greatly accelerated during the last century. In contemporary society bureaucracy has become a dominant institution, indeed the institution that epitomizes the modern era. Unless we understand this institutional form, we cannot understand the social life of today (Blau and Meyer, 1971, p. 10).

Michels's Iron Law of Oligarchy

Robert Michels (1876–1936), a friend and colleague of Max Weber, argued that bureaucracy is incompatible with democracy and, therefore, is oligarchic by nature. In his classic book *Political Parties* published in 1911, he set forth his **iron law of oligarchy**, the principle that power in organizations invariably becomes concentrated in the hands of a few people who use it to further their own self-interests. Michels studied emerging socialist political parties and labor unions in Europe. He found that though they stressed broad-based, democratic participation by rank-and-file members, the result was a monopoly of power by the few who, it appeared, paid little attention to the opinions of the masses.

Michels sought to explain this apparent contradiction by examining the interworkings of large-scale associations. He found that as a practical matter, the extremely complex and diversified nature of such organizations required a hierarchical structure of authority with day-to-day decision making and control placed in the hands of a managerial elite. Even when ultimate authority was held by the rank-and-file membership, who could attend periodic meetings and vote on designated issues, those in the upper levels of management held certain advantages that allowed them to consolidate their power and ultimately control the organization.

First of all—in the political parties and labor unions Michels examined—leaders were full-time paid employees and elected officials. They could devote their full energies to running the organization, unlike the general membership who participated only on a part-time voluntary basis.

Leaders also had complete access and control over all information concerning the organization. This allowed them to manipulate the rank-and-file members by deciding what and how much information to provide them and what to withhold in order to further their own interests. Control over information gave upper management the ability to craft propaganda with which to control the perception of the organization and important issues by the general membership. This, combined with other political devices such as speech making, disseminating information through newsletters, setting times and agendas for general meetings, and designing committees and other activities for "active" members gave management almost full if not total control.

Add to all this the fact that democracy can be a cumbersome process in large-scale associations. Michels found that active participation by general members requires an independent assessment and commitment to what is best for the organization. These requirements, coupled with the members' willingness to attend meetings, gain some control over setting agendas, research important issues, and have their voices heard, are some of the necessary ingredients for democracy.

Instead, Michels found among the associations he examined that members tended to be apathetic regarding active participation. They were more than willing to delegate all responsibilities to elected officials. This apathy, combined with their general lack of edu-

cation and sophistication, part-time involvement because of other life priorities, and their tendency to blindly trust and respect those in authority, resulted in what Michels called "the incompetency of the masses." As a result, his most succinct assessment of bureaucracy was this brief statement: "Who says organization, says oligarchy" (p. 365).

Sociologists have vigorously debated Michels findings throughout the twentieth century. Serious questions have been raised about the extent to which oligarchic tendencies in some types of organizations can be generalized to bureaucracies as a whole. Nonetheless, recent research tends to support Michels's views.

Weber's Ideal Model of Bureaucracy

Max Weber (1922, 1968) disagreed with the position of colleague Robert Michels that bureaucracies were, by nature, oligarchic. He took the position that many could be, and in some instances were, democratic in nature. Weber asserted that if an association is structured properly, advancement within it is indeed democratic in that promotion to top-level positions is based on competence and merit. He was concerned, however, by the way some large-scale associations he observed were being managed. As a result, he developed a model based on his assessment of what constituted the ideal bureaucracy (see Figure 7-2). Bureaucracy as a pervasive form of social organization emerged with the industrial revolution and the corresponding necessity for rational-legal authority. *Rationalization,* therefore, represents the dominant force in modern society not only in the present but in the foreseeable future as well.

In Weber's view, the ideal bureaucracy contains the following characteristics:

1. *Specialized division of labor.* Participants in large-scale associations are assigned posi-

Figure 7-2 Weber's Model of
Bureaucracy

1. Specialized division of labor
2. Hierarchical authority
3. Written rules
4. Impartial performance of duties
5. Reward based upon techical competence
6. Careers

tions that center on specific, specialized functions. By dividing work into small, specialized tasks, the greatest output can be generated. If the only automobiles available for purchase, for instance, were hand crafted like the Rolls Royce or Ferrari, most of us would be riding bicycles. However, given the efficiency of mass production, we can enjoy a higher standard of living.

2. *Hierarchical authority.* It is not enough that tasks be simply specialized. They must be managed or coordinated as well. Weber saw the ideal organization as one in which "offices" or positions are arranged vertically in terms of authority and responsibility; the higher the position in the organization, the greater the area of jurisdiction. In this structure, officials are responsible to the person directly above them and responsible for the performance of others below them in the organization. To carry out responsibility effectively, each bureaucratic official must have the necessary amount and type of authority. The authority of each official is clearly defined and limited in scope so that duplication of effort and avoidance of responsibility will not occur. In addition, authority is positional, not personal. It is rational-legal in that requirements and duties accrue to the position and not the person placed in it. The individual who occupies it may come and go, but the position will remain and be perpetuated.

3. *Written rules.* Management of the bureaucracy is based on a system of written policies and procedures. These rules of operation are permanently recorded and remain fairly stable. They provide the formal structure within which the very complex and diversified activities conducted by the association can be managed and coordinated smoothly.

4. *Impartial performance of duties.* In contrast to the conduct of authority in nonindustrial societies in which relations in groups and associations are based on such factors as inheritance and personal favor, the bureaucratic official is ideally neutral and attempts to treat everyone impartially and fairly. Personal feelings are not allowed to prejudice the manner in which the official administers his or her position. Subordinates are to be treated solely on the basis of how well they perform their jobs. In Weber's words, the official operates in "a spirit of formalistic impersonality . . . without hatred or passion and hence without affection or enthusiasm" (Gerth and Mills, 1946, p. 340).

5. *Rewards based on technical competence.* Weber was adamant in stressing the importance of rewarding only technical competence. *Objective measures* are to be used both in hiring people and in judging their performance. In the bureaucracy, it is assumed that trained individuals are more likely to perform their jobs well than are those whose positions, like those in nonindustrial societies, are based largely on personality, political favors, family ties, or personal friendship. The ideal bureaucracy allocates people to positions purely on the basis of technical qualifications as measured by education, training, and experience and retains and promotes them on the basis of job performance.

6. *Careers*. In Weber's assessment, managerial and professional officials in the bureaucracy, in exchange for adequate and loyal performance, are rewarded with the security of permanent employment and the opportunity for advancement within the organization. In a career position, the official is paid a *salary instead of wages*. Under a salary arrangement, an organization purchases competence rather than a certain amount of work as measured by an hourly wage. The career individual is also accorded *a distinct degree of social esteem* by the bureaucracy. As the individual moves up through the ranks, esteem is increased as measured by several indicators, many of them concrete and visible. They include, in addition to salary and fringe benefits, such ''perks'' as titles, expense accounts, and offices. Finally, the career path of the bureaucrat is made possible through *promotion by superior officials*. A person's record of performance is periodically examined, and, if it is found to be acceptable, he or she may qualify for advancement within the organization.

Weber sought to explain how bureaucracy could best be used to ''rationalize'' human societies. He asserted that widespread bureaucracy was an inevitable outgrowth of the industrial revolution and expressed serious concern about its potential for misuse and harm. However, he also felt that it possessed ''technical superiority over any other form of organization'' (1946, p. 214). His bureaucratic model represented an attempt to show how bureaucracy could be most efficiently and effectively harnessed to serve humankind and, in the process, improve the quality of life for all.

Weber has not been without his critics. Some have argued that while he gave a classic and penetrating analysis to the formal side of bureaucracy, he overlooked the importance of the informal or human side of large-scale associations. Others note that Weber's bureaucratic model is not the only rational way to organize large-scale associations (Parsons, 1947; Gouldner, 1954; Blau and Scott, 1962). Alternatives, including the Japanese system, may function just as well, given different cultural contexts, goals, and technologies.

Criticisms aside, Weber's contributions represent a pioneering benchmark in the analysis of large-scale associations. His bureaucratic model is still taught to those majoring in business and management in colleges and universities around the world. Indeed, most large-scale organizations in the United States still reflect several of Weber's characteristics, and the trend is toward more bureaucracy rather than less. If recent growth in government and trends in the corporate sector toward increased consolidation, mergers, and multinational corporations are any indication, the twenty-first century promises to be even more ''bureaucratic'' than previous ones.

Conformity

Conformity is behavior that is in agreement with the basic norms of society or one of its smaller structural elements. As with other types of groups, bureaucratic associations can place a great deal of pressure on participants to conform through the use of both formal and informal mechanisms for social control called ''sanctions'' (Chapters 3 and 5). In large-scale organizations, this pressure to conform can occur at all levels, from the most superficial interactions of participants in formal work settings to the highest levels of decision making.

Conformity in Formal Work Settings. The extent to which individuals may succumb to group pressure is well documented. Work-related conformity in organizational settings can occur, first of all, as a result of pressure from peers.

In a series of classic experiments, Soloman Asch (1955) tested college students to see how susceptible they were to group pressure. The research subjects were told that they would participate in groups of seven to nine people in which a series of fifteen trials would be conducted to measure visual perception. Each trial involved the members of a group being shown two cards placed next to each other. Then each group participant was asked by the researcher to compare the visual image or images on card A with those on card B and announce verbally to the group the correct answer. What the actual research subject was not told was that the other members of the research group were paid stooges who were in on the experiment.

As the experiment got under way, the research confederates gave the correct answers as they had been told to do. The research subject, of course, gave the right answer as well, and the votes were unanimous. Then, midway through the trials, the other group members all started giving the wrong answers and did so for several trials. For instance, in one trial, card A had a single vertical line, card B had three vertical lines, and the task was to choose the line on card B that was the same length as the one on the other card (Figure 7-3). The paid students all gave the same wrong answer. Asch found that in the trials involving the wrong answers being given by the rest of the group, the naive students agreed with a wrong answer in 37 percent of all instances.

When Asch interviewed the actual subjects several days later, most reported that they felt anxious and uncomfortable but went along with the group in order not to cause trouble or stand out. However, some claimed that they gave honest answers based on what they actually saw. For these people, it seemed that the group pressure they experienced was strong enough to cause them not to see what was plainly evident. But the larger issue is this: If such a large proportion of people can be pressured by total strangers into compliance, or beguiled into doubting the evidence seen with their own eyes in simple matching

Figure 7-3 Comparison Cards in the Asch Experiments

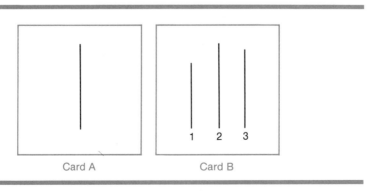

Card A   Card B

How would you react if everyone in your group agreed that line 1 or line 3 on Card B matched the length of the line on Card A? Would you go along with the group, or express disagreement even under peer pressure? *Source:* Adapted from Asch, S. 1965. Effects of group pressure upon the modification and distortion of judgments. In H. Proshansky and B. Seidenberg, Eds., *Basic studies in psychology.* New York: Holt, Rinehart and Winston, 393–401.

tests, think of the influence on behavior that might be generated if they had ongoing contact with fellow participants in large-scale associations (such as at work, at church, at school).

Some insight here is provided by the controversial yet revealing experiments conducted by social psychologist Stanley Milgram during the 1960s. Milgram (1965) sought to find out how much pain, as measured by electric shock, people would be willing to inflict on others if ordered to do so by an authority figure. The research subjects, who were paid for their participation, were led to believe that the experiments had to do with the effect of punishment on memory. Milgram (1965) gives the following description of the procedures he used:

> A rigged drawing is held so that the naive subject is always the teacher, and the accomplice becomes the learner. The learner is taken into an adjacent room and strapped into an "electric chair."
>
> The naive subject is told that it is his task to teach the learner a list of paired . . . [terms], to test him on the list, and to administer punishment whenever the learner errs in the test. Punishment takes the form of electric shock, delivered to the learner by means of a shock generator controlled by the naive subject. The teacher is instructed to increase the intensity of electric shock one step on the generator on each error. The learner, according to plan, provides many wrong answers, so that before long the naive subject must give him the strongest shock on the generator. Increases in shock level are met by increasingly insistent demands from the learner that the experiment be stopped because of the growing discomfort to him. However, in clear terms the experimenter orders the teacher to continue with the procedure in disregard of the learner's protests. Thus the naive subject must resolve a conflict between two mutually incompatible demands. . . . He may continue to follow the

orders of the experimenter and continue to shock the learner with increasing severity, or he may refuse to follow the orders of the experimenter and heed the learner's pleas (pp. 59–60).

No actual shocks were given by the research subjects, and the screams of pain and agony by the "learner" in the adjacent room were, in reality, tape recordings made especially for the experiments. Nonetheless, the "teachers" in the experiments thought everything was real, and, in one series of experiments, 65 percent of the research subjects administered what they thought were 450 volts of punishment (Milgram, 1974).

Conformity at the Highest Levels of Decision Making. Many of the factors that influence conformity at the lower levels of organizations can also be observed at policy-making levels. Compliance with group norms is, of course, a desirable outcome of social interaction at all levels of society. Without it, social order and group cohesion would be impossible to maintain.

In large-scale associations, however, conformity for conformity's sake sometimes becomes overconformity, which can be very dysfunctional, especially among groups of high-level decision makers. When conformity reaches this extreme, it becomes what Irving Janis (1982 A) calls **groupthink**, conformity in which, for the sake of cohesion and "good relations," group decisions are made uncritically with little if any conflict.

This "all for one and one for all" mentality, according to Janis, emerges out of several conditions, resulting from high cohesion, that members of the group come to exhibit as characteristics. These include members' unanimous belief that they as a group are superior, morally right, and invulnerable. Add to this their collective ability to rationalize the group position and apply simplistic negative stereotypes to those perceived as the enemy. Finally, there is strong pressure from both the group and the individual's sense of duty to keep reservations and possible criticisms to a minimum. To do otherwise would be interpreted by the group as disloyalty. Consequently, ideas, information, and suggestions that do not conform with the group's predetermined mind-set are largely ignored.

Groupthink among high-level governmental officials in the executive branch of American government contributed to both the cover-up of "Watergate" and, more recently, the Iran-Contra affair. In the business sector, automakers in the United States—the same country that landed men on the moon—exhibited groupthink by claiming during the early 1970s that it was "technologically impossible" to produce small, high quality, fuel-efficient cars that met the Environmental Protection Agency's (EPA) emission standards for pollution control. Japanese automakers like Honda did so with ease, which set the stage for their capture of a large share of the American auto market.

Janis examined numerous foreign policy decisions made by the United States after World War II. He found that of nineteen international crises identified, the American government used groupthink decision making to a significant degree in 87 percent of them. Included in these were both the Bay of Pigs fiasco by the Kennedy administration and behavior of the Johnson administration that led to the escalation of U.S. involvement in Vietnam during the 1960s.

The Kennedy administration, for instance, covertly sponsored an ill-fated invasion of Cuba in 1961 at the Bay of Pigs. The invasion by Cuban rebels, trained and equipped by the CIA, was a total failure, and most of the rebels were either killed or captured. Kennedy's advisers completely overlooked the strength of Fidel Castro's forces and failed to seek out other relevant intelligence. In the meetings between Kennedy and his advisers on this subject, the atmosphere was one of "assumed consensus," and the vote to support the project was unanimous. This fiasco further alienated the Castro regime from the United States, reinforced the already growing relationship between Cuba and the Soviet Union, and ultimately influenced the attempt by the Russians to place nuclear missiles in Cuba. The confrontation between the two superpowers that followed in October 1962, called the "Cuban missile crisis," brought the United States and the Soviet Union to the brink of nuclear war.

Several steps can be taken by groups at all levels of an organization to avoid groupthink. According to Janis (1982 B), they include, first of all, educating members as to the nature and dangers of groupthink. Members should also be encouraged to "speak their minds" critically on all issues and express their true feelings without fear of personal condemnation or reprisal. The responsibility for creating this type of group atmosphere rests with the leader or leaders, who must attempt to remain impartial. At least one group member should be assigned the responsibility for taking an alternate viewpoint that challenges the most popular position.

Another valuable tool is the use of "independent" outside experts who attend meetings and feel free to challenge any and all opinions. Although this may appear on the surface to encourage chaos and disruption, critical analysis of key issues and give-and-take among conscientious professionals lead to more effective decisions. Research has demonstrated that superior decisions usually are made when minority views are strongly and consistently voiced, causing the majority to rethink and reevaluate its position (Nemeth, 1985).

Alternative Forms of Organization

The Collective. For America, the decade of the 1960s was a tumultuous time in which many traditions were challenged and many ideas were shared. It was also a time in which many young people experienced alienation from modern society and searched for viable alternatives through social experimentation and the formation of countercultures (Chapter 3). Some of these alternative groups espoused an "anti-establishment" and "anti-bureaucratic" view of the world. To them, bigger was not better and the bureaucracy was impersonal, exploitative, and dehumanizing. Although most of these groups faded with the times, some of their ideas remain and have been incorporated by others.

One of the visible results of that generation and era has been an increase in the popularity of **collectives**. These are alternative organizations consisting mainly of small businesses and nonprofit volunteer groups that function on nonbureaucratic principles. Examples include community service organizations such as free schools, legal aid groups, and food cooperatives along with small businesses such as alternative newspapers, health food stores, and bookstores. These organizations operate for the most part as collective partnerships. They are intentionally antibureaucratic in organization and make use of consensus instead of authority, few rules, personal as opposed to "bureaucratic" relations, few status distinctions, and little or no specialization (Rothschild-Whitt, 1979). When things need to be done, members just "pitch in."

The collective appears to work well on a small scale when the number of participants is small, time and energy commitments among members are high, and profits are small. However, as the number of people increases to more than ten or twelve, primary group rela-

tions tend to break down and the group may dissolve or be taken over by a small coalition of "elites" (Rothschild, 1986). For these reasons, the collective, by its very nature, does not seem to represent a viable alternative to bureaucracy as a means of organizing large-scale associations.

The Japanese Corporation. Unlike collectives, Japanese corporations compete very well with Western bureaucracies in the world marketplace although they are structured

The Japanese corporation is often characterized by lifelong employment, concern for the employee as a total person, emphasis on group performance, and bottom-up management. (Copyright Obremsky/The Image Bank.)

somewhat differently. As recently as the late 1950s, the words "Made in Japan" conjured up images of poor quality goods and shoddy workmanship in the minds of American consumers. Those same words today, in association with brand names like Nikon for cameras, Mitsubishi for television sets, and Toyota for automobiles result in very different perceptions.

Although Japanese organizations appear similar to American corporations, the underlying foundation of the Japanese corporation is the cultural emphasis on loyalty to the group. By contrast, American society stresses individuality and individual choice (Zandu, 1983). The Japanese orientation toward the group is based on several important customs including the centuries-old tradition of bringing honor to one's family through one's deeds.

In Japan, the company becomes the "second family" for workers through the practice by corporations of furnishing employees with *lifetime employment.* For the Japanese worker, this results in an ethic of lifelong commitment to the company. The employee, therefore, wishes to bring as much honor to the second family as to the first. Life in the second family (the company) begins, as described by one Japanese steel company executive, with a "company birth" which, as an event, "has the same importance as our crying birth" (Abegglen, 1958, pp. 569–570).

Companies reinforce the family ethic by exhibiting a *concern for the employee as "total person."* Recruited immediately after graduation from school, workers are employed by companies that provide them with housing and food, medical benefits, continuing education, and various types of recreational facilities in addition to their wages. After retirement, which usually takes place at age fifty-five, the company continues to help take care of former employees until they die (Noda, 1975).

By comparison, the American system stresses a "strictly business" relationship between company and employee (Ouchi, 1981).

From an operations standpoint, the Japanese company has additional features which include an emphasis on group performance and bottom-up decision making. In contrast to the American system, which stresses and rewards individual achievement, the Japanese emphasize *group performance.* Employees are typically divided into performance groups or work teams and are evaluated on the performance of the entire group. Such a system requires both cooperation and collective decision making even at the lowest levels of the organization.

It also acts to reinforce **bottom-up decision making** in which information and decisions travel from bottom to top, rather than from top to bottom in the organization. Since the Japanese stress consensus at all levels—which they feel promotes group loyalty and productivity—top-level executives provide the general goals and guidance but leave much of the practical how-to aspects of operation to the lower-level employees. In the Japanese view, this arrangement promotes a sense of personal pride and responsibility in the employees, which reinforces both loyalty and productivity (Vogel, 1979).

Despite these characteristics, Japanese organizations can seem somewhat regimented from an American perspective. Japanese employees in many companies wear company uniforms and perform physical exercises and sing company songs in groups before starting each workday. In addition, they are expected to attend several company-sponsored functions. While Americans, with their individualistic orientation, would find these activities paternalistic and restrictive, they work well for the Japanese whose particular brand of bureaucracy produces impressive results in the international marketplace.

THE ASSOCIATION AS A SOCIAL SYSTEM

Large-scale organizations may be divided into two major structural components, the formal structure and the informal structure. Together they make up the social interaction system of an association.

The Formal Structure

One of the remarkable results of modern society is that in some respects, "the more things change, the more they remain the same." If you travel by car on a cross-country trip, you can spend the night at a Holiday Inn, eat at McDonald's or Pizza Hut, buy camera film at Eckerds or Walgreens, fill up with gas at Exxon, shop at Sears, and get a few groceries at Kroger or AppleTree with almost the identical cultural experience you would have experienced back home. A Big Mac looks and tastes exactly the same whether you are in Princeton, New Jersey; Greenville, South Carolina; Las Cruces, New Mexico; or San Diego, California. What makes this paradox of uniformity in an ever-changing society possible is the formal structure of large-scale associations.

Formal structure refers to the official set of goals, policies, and procedures of an organization that specify the behavior of its members. The formal structure of an association, therefore, is the product or result of the process called *formal organization* (Chapter 6). Since many of the stores and other service facilities we come in contact with as consumers are small parts of larger national corporations, the "sameness" we experience with them is largely due to their being part of a larger formal structure.

Weber's bureaucratic model is the most widely accepted standard against which the formal structure of most organizations is measured. The Japanese approach represents an interesting alternative. Regardless of which is preferred, however, both are models of formal structure that are quite effective within their respective cultural spheres. The fact remains that the formal structure is a rational, effective, and indispensable element in efficiently organizing the specialized work of large numbers of people in highly complex associations. Without it, it does not appear possible that most inhabitants of industrial societies could enjoy the affluent life-style of convenience that is an ongoing characteristic of modern life.

As essential as the formal structure is, however, it alone is not sufficient for the effective operation of a large-scale association. Although overlooked in Max Weber's analysis, it is also necessary to examine and understand the importance of another key component in all bureaucracies, the informal structure.

The Informal Structure

Organizations consist of people, not merely company policies, organizational charts, job descriptions, and other formal aspects. This human side of the organization, which can be observed in any bureaucracy, is the **informal structure**. It consists of the nonofficial norms and interaction patterns that emerge from the relations among participants.

The informal structure serves several functions. First of all, it acts to create a *personalized work setting*. The rules and positions in large-scale associations are, by necessity, impersonal. Everyone must abide by them and be held equally accountable for their actions under them. However, morale and the motivation to do a good job are also important and can best be kept at a high level through an informal means of interaction that allows for personal contact and friendship within the organization. This human side of the organization also contributes to *flexible decision making*.

The informal structure of a large-scale organization can contribute to higher morale and greater productivity by creating a personalized work setting. (Copyright David Frazier/Photo Researchers, Inc.)

Formal policies and procedures cannot anticipate every possible contingency. Therefore, some reliance must be placed on the informal structure to make spontaneous adjustments and changes when needed. There is also a system of informal interaction, often called the "grapevine," which creates *streamlined communications.* The "rumor mill," as it is sometimes called, can be very effective in disseminating information much more quickly than would be possible through official channels.

In addition, the informal structure is useful in the *promotion of personal interests.* This can help or hurt an organization, depending on the situation and the ability by top management to create an organizational climate conducive to high morale and productivity. Highly motivated participants, in an informal manner, can reinforce each other's morale be-

cause they feel positive about the organization. Likewise, poorly motivated and alienated workers can informally agree to perform at a minimum level, withhold creativity, and even sabotage the organization in extreme cases. Consequently, it is in the best interests of large-scale associations to create an organizational climate conducive to the successful management of human resources.

According to Thomas J. Peters and Robert H. Waterman, Jr. (1982) in their book *In Search of Excellence,* a "people orientation" by management is one of the key principles that creates organizational effectiveness. Their message to top-level managers on this topic is excerpted as follows:

Treat people as adults. Treat them as partners; treat them with dignity; treat them with respect. Treat *them*—not capital spending and automation—as the primary source of productivity gains. These are the fundamental lessons from the excellent companies research. In other words, if you want productivity and the financial reward that goes with it, you must treat your workers as your most important asset. . . .

The orientation toward people in these companies often started decades ago—full employment policies in times of recession, extraordinary amounts of training when no training was the norm, everybody on a first-name basis in times much more formal than ours, and so on. Caring runs in the veins of the managers of these institutions. People are why those managers are there, and they know it and live it. . . .

Perhaps surprisingly, the people orientation also has a *tough* side. The excellent companies are measurement happy and performance oriented, but this toughness is borne of mutually high expectations and peer review rather than emanating from table pounding managers and complicated control systems. The tough side is, in fact, probably tougher than that found in the less excellent and typically more formal systems-driven companies, for nothing is more enticing than the feeling of being needed, which is the magic that produces high expectations. What's more, if it's your peers that have those high expectations of you, then there's all the more incentive to perform well (pp. 238–240).

The Association in Perspective

The formal structure and the informal structure represent two halves to the same whole, namely, the association or organization. Neither can function well without the other in most cases, and the association as a total interaction system requires both in order to function with maximum effectiveness. In this sense, these two components are closely related to the two basic types of leadership discussed in Chapter 6. Effective management of the formal structure in an organization requires *task leadership,* while successful coordination of the informal structure necessitates

socioemotional leadership. While most groups and organizations have leaders of both types, they, like the organizational components they represent, should not be seen as mutually exclusive. Rather, the challenge for organizations in the future, as intimated in the preceding quote by Peters and Waterman, is to integrate these elements effectively. Ideally, organizations should represent an ever-changing and flexible blend of both formal and informal structures and leaders who incorporate both task and socioemotional skills to maintain a dynamic equilibrium. To be successful in creating such a balance—which varies depending on the organization, its goals, and its circumstances—is not easy. Yet, particularly for private sector corporations which must compete in a constantly evolving world marketplace, this balance is increasingly necessary and will be even more important in the future.

PROBLEMS OF LARGE-SCALE ASSOCIATIONS

Too great an emphasis on either rules and ritual (formal structure/task leadership) or on members' feelings and interpersonal relations (informal structure/socioemotional leadership) can be a contributing factor which leads to organizational problems. In this regard, we will briefly examine five common problems that plague some organizations: ritualism, goal displacement, protection of incompetence, and the dilemmas that have been described by the Peter principle and Parkinson's law.

Ritualism

One of the most pervasive problems found within bureaucracies is **ritualism**, an overconformity to the rules of the organization by an individual participant. Most of us have had experiences with ritualists. There is the clerk who cannot help you because of "company policy," although the slightest demonstration of flexibility would solve your problem; the police officer who tickets you for going four miles per hour over the speed limit, or the teacher who appears more interested in grades than in whether learning takes place. Participants in bureaucracies are socialized to see rules and regulations as important elements of the organization that should be taken seriously. Since many organizations reward their workers and officials more for following rules than for providing effective service, overconformity often occurs.

Goal Displacement

When ritualism is carried to the organizational level, it becomes **goal displacement**, a situation in which the means (rules) of an organization become substituted for the goals and participants lose sight of their original objective. Although ritualism usually occurs with lower-level workers who have responsibility but little or no authority or with the the occasional high-level bureaucrat in a similar situation, goal displacement can permeate an entire organization or one of its smaller elements. Usually, for goal displacement to occur, at least tacit agreement must flow from the highest echelons of decision making at the departmental or organizational levels. Some charitable organizations that spend much if not most of their income on "administrative costs" rather than on their stated purposes represent one example. Governmental agencies that offer contrived excuses to justify their existence long after their stated purposes have been achieved or otherwise made obsolete serve as an added illustration.

Protection of Incompetence

The **protection of incompetence** occurs when an organization fails first to identify and then to develop, reassign, or remove inadequate performers. While group morale is important

and high turnover is to be avoided in most cases, these considerations should not take precedence over the goals of the organization. Incompetence often becomes prevalent in an association in which formal goals have become sacrificed to the extremes of socioemotional leadership. In other cases, policies that were designed to provide rewards and job security to those who have given faithful service also act to insulate and protect the mediocre and incompetent. Aspects of the U. S. civil service system of employment and the seniority system in some companies provide examples. It is also apparent that the informal structure of organizations can create a condition of poor performance when workers decide informally on a relatively low rate of production. Under this arrangement, any worker who exceeds this level of production is considered a "rate buster" and is severely ostracized by fellow workers (Semones, 1977).

The Peter Principle

Lawrence Peter and Raymond Hull (1969) have identified another bureaucratic problem which they describe as the **Peter principle**. The Peter principle states that people tend to keep rising within an organization until they eventually reach their level of incompetence. An excellent classroom teacher, for instance, may become an assistant principal because of the incentives of higher pay and increased status. However, if this person is a poor administrator, advancement to a principalship over a school will probably not occur. Since this individual normally would not return to teaching, he or she becomes "locked in" at a level of incompetence.

Parkinson's Law

As associations expand and grow more complex, it becomes more difficult to manage and coordinate the diverse activities of all participants. This creates a condition ripe for a problem related to waste and inefficiency, described by **Parkinson's law** (named after its originator, British historian C. Northcote Parkinson). In its simplest form, Parkinson's law states that "Work expands to fill the time available for its completion" (Parkinson, 1957). When people in organizations have very little to do, they may try to keep this from being detected by appearing busy and engaging in "make-work." They shuffle papers, duplicate their efforts, and develop a whole array of empty rituals in order to seem productive. In some cases, this can go on for years if the perpetrators are good at it and their supervisors are preoccupied with other matters.

In closing, this chapter has attempted to build on the material in Chapter 6 to present you with an overview of associations and bureaucracy. While it is not an exhaustive treatment of the subject by any means, it is hoped that some of your questions about large-scale associations have been answered and that your curiosity has been sparked concerning many others. Since most of us will spend the majority of our adult lives working in and dealing with associations and bureaucracy, it is in our best interests to understand "from whence they came," how they operate, and where they are likely to be going. This brief treatment has been aimed to help you in these regards.

CHAPTER SUMMARY

1. As originally defined in Chapter 6, an association is a group deliberately formed to pursue one or more specific practical goals. Some associations also involve bureaucracy, a form of social organization in which the work of participants in large-scale organizations is rationally organized and coordinated by professional managers.

2. Sociologist Amitai Etzioni has developed one of the most useful means of classifying as-

sociations based on the reasons people participate in them and, in turn, the degree of control certain organizations can exert on their lives. In this respect, the voluntary association is one people join freely as a part-time activity because they agree with its norms and goals. It has low control over the individual and may take the form of a civic, professional, or personal interest organization. The utilitarian association is one organized for gain or profit. It can be a business, a corporation, or a professional firm and exercises a fair amount of control over the lives of individuals, as in the case of one's job. Finally, the coercive association involves force or the threat of force. It exercises high control over the individual, as illustrated by prisons, mental hospitals, prisoner of war camps, and some religious orders. Extreme forms of coercive associations, total institutions, often make use of mortification and brainwashing techniques to control and manipulate participants.

3. Power is the ability to influence or control others, whereas authority is legitimated power which is generally recognized and supported by those over whom it is exercised. Max Weber identified three basic forms of authority that occur in societies: charismatic, traditional, and rational-legal authority. Charismatic authority (personality) is based on followers' belief that the leader possesses divine grace, heroism, or other special qualities. Traditional authority (monarchy) involves followers' acceptance of the legitimacy of long standing traditions. Rational-legal authority (objective qualifications), the most prevalent form in modern societies, is based on the legitimacy of a formal system of laws and procedures that define the scope of a leader's authority and responsibility.

4. Regarding the nature of bureaucracy, sociologist Robert Michels argued that bureaucracy is incompatible with democracy. His iron law of oligarchy, for which he is most

There are many ingredients that go into the development of a life-style. They include where we live, how we dress and adorn ourselves, and our many tastes and preferences, ranging from favorite foods to music, hobbies, and other forms of recreation.

noted, states that power in organizations invariably becomes concentrated in the hands of a few people who use it to further their own self-interests.

5. Max Weber disagreed with Michels oligarchic perspective and felt that large-scale organizations could be democratic. He developed an ideal model of bureaucracy which consists of six basic elements: a specialized division of labor, hierarchical authority, written rules, impartial performance of duties, reward based on technical competence, and careers. He felt that if these characteristics were emulated by actual organizations, the "rationalization" of modern societies could best be realized.

6. Conformity is an essential ingredient of any large-scale association. It occurs at all levels, from the smallest of formal work settings involving people low in authority to the highest echelons of decision making. When conformity is carried to an extreme, it can result in groupthink, a situation in which group decisions are made uncritically, with little or no conflict, for the sake of cohesion and "good relations."

7. There are alternatives to bureaucracy as both Michels and Weber envisioned it. The collective and the Japanese corporation serve as notable examples. A collective is a small business or nonprofit volunteer group that functions on nonbureaucratic principles, including consensus decision making and little or no specialization. While it sometimes works well with small numbers of participants, the collective does not appear to represent a viable alternative to bureaucracy as a means of organizing large-scale associations. The Japanese corporation, however, with a system based on lifetime employment, concern for the "total person," group performance, and bottom-up decision making, func-

tions very successfully in the international marketplace.

8. Complex organizations often experience a wide variety of problems. Five of the most common include ritualism, goal displacement, protection of incompetence, and the situations described in the Peter principle and Parkinson's law. An organizational imbalance created by too great an emphasis on either the formal structure or the informal structure can contribute to most if not all of these problems.

TERMS TO KNOW

authority: legitimated power that is generally recognized and supported by those over whom it is exercised.
bottom-up decision making: a characteristic of Japanese corporations in which information and decisions based on group consensus travel from bottom to top, rather than from top to bottom in the hierarchy.
brainwashing: a process of almost complete thought control in which the victim's existing values and beliefs are replaced with those desired by the influencing agent.
charismatic authority: Weber's term for authority based on the commonly accepted belief by followers that a leader possesses special qualities or unique characteristics. (for example, the authority possessed by a tribal medicine man or shaman).
coercive association: Etzioni's term for an organization in which people participate because of force or the threat of force.
collectives: small businesses and volunteer groups that function on nonbureaucratic principles.
conformity: behavior that is in agreement with the basic norms of society.
formal structure: the official set of goals, policies, and procedures that specify the behavior of participants in an association.

goal displacement: a problem in which the means (rules) of an organization become substituted for the goals and participants lose sight of their original objective.

groupthink: a form of conformity in which, for the sake of cohesion and "good relations," group decisions are made uncritically, with little if any conflict.

informal structure: the nonofficial norms and interaction patterns that emerge among participants in an association.

iron law of oligarchy: Michels's principle that power in organizations invariably becomes concentrated in the hands of a few people who use it to further their own self-interests.

mortification: a process used in coercive associations in which a person's old identity is stripped away through a systematic process of degradation and humiliation, and a new self more suitable to the organization is substituted in its place.

Parkinson's law: a description of the problem in organizations in which "work expands to fill the time available for its completion."

Peter principle: a description of the problem involving the tendency for officials to keep rising within an organization until they eventually reach their level of incompetence.

power: the ability to influence or control the behavior of others with or without their consent.

protection of incompetence: a problem that occurs when an organization fails first to identify and then to develop, reassign, or remove inadequate performers.

rational-legal authority: Weber's term for authority based on the legitimacy of a formal set of laws or rules which define the nature and scope of a leader's rights and responsibilities (for example, authority possessed by a corporate manager or police officer).

ritualism: a problem involving overconformity to the rules of an organization by an individual participant.

traditional authority: Weber's term for authority based on followers' acceptance of the legitimacy contained in long-standing traditions and customs (for example, authority possessed by a king or queen).

utilitarian association: Etzioni's term for an organization in which people participate for practical gain or profit.

voluntary association: Etzioni's term for an organization people join freely as a part-time activity because they agree with its norms and goals.

SUGGESTED READINGS

The Art of Japanese Management: Applications for American Executives (Richard Tanner Pascale and Anthony G. Athos; New York: Warner Books, 1981). A comprehensive look at the management approach in the Japanese corporation—staff, skills, style, and superordinate goals—as compared with the traditional American emphasis on strategy, structure, and systems.

A Comparative Analysis of Complex Organizations (Amitai Etzioni; New York: Free Press, 1975). A brief but comprehensive sociological treatment of large-scale associations that includes Etzioni's typology of voluntary, utilitarian, and coercive organizations.

Complex Organizations, 3rd ed. (Charles Perrow; New York: Random House, 1986). A thorough coverage of large-scale organizations, including their nature, functions, various forms, and implications for modern societies today and in the near future.

Patterns of Industrial Bureaucracy (Alvin W. Gouldner; New York: Free Press, 1954). A classic sociological treatment of bureaucratic authority in its basic forms and how it is manifested in modern industrial society.

In Search of Excellence: Lessons from America's Best-Run Companies (Thomas J. Peters and Robert H. Waterman, Jr.; New York: Warner Books, 1982). A well-written, entertaining, and disturbing look at the American corporation, along with eight principles for organizational success and detailed examples from successful corporations including Frito-Lay, Hewlett-Packard, IBM, and others.

The Peter Principle: Why Things Always Go Wrong (Lawrence J. Peter and Raymond Hull; New York: Morrow, 1969). An often humorous but fairly accurate discussion of incompetence in the hierarchical structure of modern organizations.

Theory Z : How American Business Can Meet the Japanese Challenge (William Ouchi; Reading, MA: Addison-Wesley, 1981). A penetrating analysis of the Japanese style of management and how its major elements can be adapted to the American corporation.

Chapter 8

Social Stratification

CLASS IN AMERICA: ELEMENTS OF RANK
Power
Prestige
Wealth
Life-style
Social Class in Perspective

THE ANALYSIS OF STRATIFICATION
The Subjective Approach
The Reputational Approach
The Objective Approach

■ TERMS TO KNOW

absolute poverty
caste system
class system
conflict perspective
culture of poverty hypothesis
estate system
evolutionary perspective
felt poverty
functionalist perspective
horizontal mobility
intergenerational mobility
intragenerational mobility
life chances

life-style
objective approach
objective poverty
pluralistic theory
power-elite theory
prestige
relative poverty
reputational approach
social class
social mobility
social stratification
status inconsistency
structural unemployment
subjective approach
vertical mobility
wealth

For Prince Andrew of England and his bride, Sarah, it was a beautiful storybook wedding. For high society both in Europe and in the United States, the marriage of the second son of Queen Elizabeth II to Sarah Margaret Ferguson on July 23, 1986, was the social event of the year. Although much smaller in scale than the wedding of Prince Charles and Lady Diana Spencer five years earlier, this nonetheless was a royal spectacle. The processional route to Westminster Abbey was lined with 250,000 well-wishers along with 2,000 police and additional security personnel. The bride and groom arrived for the ceremony in separate horse-drawn carriages, he in the dress uniform of a Royal Navy officer and she in a satin gown with a seventeen-foot train. The

ceremony in Westminster Abbey, attended by 1,800 notables including Prince Albert of Monaco, assorted aristocrats and movie stars, and the then First Lady Nancy Reagan, was seen on television by an estimated 300 million people worldwide. Among the elite who comprised the guests, Mrs. Reagan alone arrived in England with a reported entourage of twenty Secret Service agents and nine staff people including her hairdresser and personal maid. As for the married couple, their wedding (which cost a reported $350,000) was brightened by wedding gifts estimated at $1.5 million in value and the titles Duke and Duchess of York as a wedding present from the queen (Iyer, 1986; Wallace, 1986).

Viewed from a sociological perspective,

the pomp and pageantry of a royal wedding plus the elegance and privilege accorded those who live the aristocratic life must be studied in direct contrast to the abject poverty and deprivation experienced by those who barely subsist at the other end of the social spectrum. Social inequality has existed in one form or another from time immemorial. Today it remains a fundamental feature of human social life.

How is it that one couple can have a $350,000 wedding while another will not earn that much money in a lifetime? What forces and factors make it possible for many Americans to own second homes while others live on the streets with no homes at all? Why does there seem to be a need for different levels of social position? What are the major elements of social rank? How is social inequality organized in different societies? These are some of the basic questions and issues to be addressed in this chapter.

STRATIFICATION AND LIFE CHANCES

Some form of structured inequality exists in most places throughout the world. Sociologists refer to this as **social stratification**, a system in each society that defines how social rank is determined and social rewards are distributed. Within a society, people are ranked in a hierarchy of social respectability and worth. This vertical arrangement of rank involves two or more layers or strata, which sociologists call "classes" in some societies and "castes" in others. In the United States, for example, there is a class system of stratification with three general levels: upper, middle, and lower class. The occupants of each class tend to think, feel, and act somewhat differently from those in other classes regarding religion, politics, recreation, and many other areas of preference and behavior. Likewise,

each stratum represents an unequal distribution of social rewards in the form of power, prestige, and wealth. For instance, a physician in America tends to enjoy a great deal more of all these benefits compared with a postal worker or plumber.

Indicators of Differential Life Chances

Social rank profoundly influences both our general attitudes and our behavior. This process begins with early childhood socialization in which, because of the accident of birth, the social stratum of our family significantly affects how we come to view the world and our place in it. In American society, children from different social classes develop distinctive value orientations. Working-class adolescents, for example, must decide whether or not to go to college after high school graduation. Among upper-middle-class teenagers, not going to college is rarely considered an option. Instead, their key decision has to do with which college to attend.

Stratification also affects what Max Weber termed **life chances**, the opportunities for survival and prosperity in society. In the United States and elsewhere, life chances impact significantly on both the length and quality of life. The higher one's social class, the longer one's *life expectancy* tends to be, according to numerous studies. Infant mortality, for example, is much higher among the poor (Gortmaker, 1979; Mare, 1982), and overall mortality rates as well as rates of specific diseases like cancer are also higher among the poor (Shai, 1986). Americans in the middle and upper classes are better fed, housed, and educated, and this contributes to longer life expectancy. They also have much better access to adequate *health care* than their less affluent counterparts. Although public assistance programs, like Medicaid, have helped narrow the health care gap significantly, these programs tend to serve only those living in the most dire circumstances, such as the elderly, the disabled, and those living in single-parent households. The underemployed "working poor," who constitute the majority of people living in poverty, tend to have little or no health insurance and, consequently, receive only sporadic medical attention at best.

Another indicator of differential life chances is *nutrition*. Families with middle-class incomes spend about 15 percent of their income on food as compared with 35 percent spent by families with incomes far below the poverty line (Gallo, Zellner, and Smallwood, 1980). The more affluent also pay less for food items than the poor because they can shop around for bargains in suburban chain grocery stores that buy foodstuffs in bulk. By contrast, the urban poor often have no personal transportation and are, especially the disabled and elderly, limited to small neighborhood markets where prices are higher and perishable goods like bread, produce, and dairy products are often stale, overripe, or semispoiled. Consequently, the diets of those in the lower strata of society are substandard, and this contributes to high infant mortality, low birth weight in babies, and millions of malnourished children.

In terms of social policy, the 1980s under the Reagan administration was a period of declining support for several forms of public assistance, including maternal and child health care programs. These cutbacks were made in order to reduce the federal bureaucracy and governmental costs (Aldous, 1986). Yet a growing body of research shows that public programs designed as preventive measures to enhance life chances actually save money in the long run, not to mention the social costs involved. In a study conducted at Harvard University, for instance, it was found that the incidence of low birth weight in babies of mothers who did not receive supplemental nutrition benefits during their pregnancies was three times higher than in babies of mothers who did receive such assistance. As a result, it was estimated that each dollar spent on such preventive prenatal care for poor mothers would net a savings of three dollars in long-term costs of health care for the children of these women (Amidei, 1981).

Poverty

Those who exhibit the lowest levels of life chances—not only in terms of life expectancy, health care, and nutrition, but also in such areas as housing, education, fertility rates, and income—are the poor. Sometimes referred to as the *underclass* (Myrdal, 1962), those experiencing *poverty* in America and elsewhere are people who lack the resources necessary for long-term survival and prosperity.

Sociologists define poverty in several different ways (Light and Keller, 1982). First, there is a distinction made between absolute and relative poverty. **Absolute poverty** exists when people lack essential resources, such as food and shelter, necessary for survival. Compared to some societies, relatively few people in the United States starve to death or die from exposure to the elements. When these things do happen, they occur mainly among abandoned infants, the elderly poor, and "street people." In the world's poorest countries, however, absolute poverty is a reality for a large proportion of their populations. During the 1984-1985 drought in Africa, for example, 2 million people died of malnutrition and disease.

Relative poverty, by comparison, refers to a standard of living that is substandard in relation to that of the majority of society members. Using this definition, millions of Americans, including the underemployed and those in steady but unskilled occupations, may have the essentials such as food, shelter, and basic health care but do not have the purchasing power to acquire many of the nonessential

Poverty takes several forms. Although the urban poor are highly visible in the media today, there are many like this rural Appalachian family who also suffer impaired life chances. (Copyright Bill Strode/Woodfin Camp and Associates.)

imum but adequate nutrition under temporary circumstances. Researchers use an elaborate formula to establish this cut-off point, based on the type of family, the number of adults and children under eighteen years living in the household, the sex of the head of household, the type of residence (farm or nonfarm), and other factors. They then calculate these factors in terms of the consumer price index. In 1987, the poverty line for a nonfarm family of four was $11,611. Consequently, about 14 percent of all Americans, slightly over 32 million, were officially poor in 1987 (U. S. Bureau of the Census, 1988). This is illustrated in Figure 8-1.

Families that fall slightly above the poverty line experience felt poverty and may indeed be worse off in terms of standard of living because they cannot qualify for public assistance programs that are open to the "official" poor. Felt poverty, however, not to be confused with relative poverty, has to do more with the psychological and emotional dimension of deprivation than with actual standard of living. A very affluent upper-class family could conceivably lose the family business, have to declare bankruptcy, and be forced to live a middle-class life-style. While perhaps many people would not feel sorry for them, members of this family nonetheless might perceive themselves as poor and experience a great deal of emotional distress.

The Poor in America

Those at the bottom of America's socioeconomic ladder vary widely in circumstances. Some are dislocated workers temporarily out of work who are "down on their luck." Although they and their families often suffer significantly and lose homes, cars, and other possessions, many if not most are able to return to work or retrain for other jobs. Others are marginal workers engaged in seasonal or unskilled jobs that offer low pay and often little

"luxury" items most people in the middle class seem to take for granted.

There is also a distinction between objective and felt poverty. **Objective poverty** is a state of official deprivation as determined by an agreed-upon standard of measurement. Since 1964, the U.S. government has used a poverty index developed by Mollie Orshansky (1965) of the Social Security Administration. This index, now known as the "poverty line," is set yearly, based on the amount of money needed each year per person to maintain min-

Figure 8-1 The Proportion of Americans in Poverty, 1960–1987.

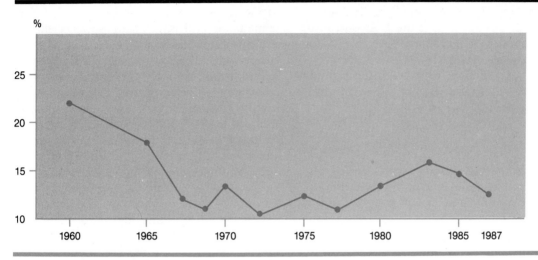

Source: U.S. Bureau of the Census, 1988.

job security, such as farm workers and manual laborers, domestics, dishwashers, car washers, and shoe shiners.

As many as 10 to 12 million (approximately one-third), however, form the "hardcore" poor who appear destined for permanent poverty. Of these, an estimated 1 to 3 million are the homeless of various types, including those with mental disorders, who help make up the ranks of the "street people." An additional several million are undocumented aliens who live on the fringes of society and continually face deportation. A few million more are single women with dependent children caught up in a long-term cycle of poverty (Harrington, 1984).

Regardless of whether the experience of deprivation is temporary or long-term, poverty appears to be a growing problem for the most vulnerable people in society. Most of America's poor occupy one or more of the following overlapping categories: women, children, minorities, the elderly, and the disabled (U.S. Bureau of the Census 1986 A; Pear, 1986).

Of these groups, the large majority of the poor are women, children, and minorities. A trend toward the feminization of poverty is obvious since most adults living in poverty today are *women*. As a result of such factors as teenage pregnancy, divorce, desertion, and widowhood, 48.6 percent of households headed by women without partners suffer from poverty. More than one-half of all poor *children* in the United States live in these households. One out of every five Americans under eighteen years of age lives in poverty— 16 percent of white children, 39 percent of Hispanic children, and 43 percent of black children. As indicated by these statistics, *minorities* in general are much poorer proportionally than whites. Fifteen percent of all black Americans, for instance, exist on less than one-half of the designated "poverty line" income, as compared with 4 percent of white Americans (U. S. Bureau of the Census, 1986 A). Overall, only 11 percent of white Americans are poor as contrasted with 29 percent of Hispanics and 31 percent of blacks.

The rates of poverty among the elderly

and disabled are also significant. Twelve percent of the *elderly* live in poverty. For those who are *disabled* of working age, the figure is 33 percent. According to the U.S. Bureau of the Census (1988), the three categories of the poor unable to work—the elderly, the disabled, and children—also constituted more than one-half (53 percent) of those Americans living in poverty in 1987.

The Culture of Poverty Hypothesis

Perhaps the most popular explanation of poverty in recent decades has been the **culture of poverty hypothesis** developed by anthropologist Oscar Lewis (1961, 1966, 1968). Using data gathered from field observations made primarily among the impoverished in Mexico and the United States, he maintains that poverty involves a subculture that socializes its children with attitudes of despair and acceptance of being poor as natural and normal for them. The poor, Lewis asserts, tend to have little sense of what is going on in the larger society and remain socially isolated from it in their own neighborhoods and communities. They appear relatively unaware of opportunities for improving their lot and fail to see how collective organization on their part could help to diminish their problems as well as influence public policy in the larger community and society. Poverty, then, can become a self-perpetuating cycle. On an individual level, the child reared in this environment tends to develop a set of values and personality characteristics very different from those of the middle-class child in the suburbs. As Lewis explains,

> The individual who grows up in this culture has a strong feeling of fatalism, helplessness, dependence and inferiority; a strong present-time orientation with relatively little disposition to defer gratification and plan for the future, and a high tolerance for psychological pathology of all kinds (Lewis, 1966, p. 23).

While Lewis's hypothesis may help to explain poverty at least in part among segments of the chronically poor (Kerbo, 1981), it has come under criticism by some social scientists. Perhaps most important is the fact that for most who experience poverty in the United States, being poor is a temporary situation from which they recover in a few months or years (Duncan, 1984). Consequently, the majority of the poor are represented by an ever-changing pool of unfortunates caught up in the throes of temporary deprivation. Some are single mothers with young children who, because of teenage pregnancy, separation or divorce from their husbands, and other factors, experience poverty and must seek public assistance for a time until they can obtain jobs. Others are displaced workers victimized by **structural unemployment**, the loss of employment as a result of changes in the economy that render certain occupations obsolete. In recent years, for example, changes in demand and technology have affected the oil, gas, steel, auto, and farm industries, which in turn has resulted in millions of "new poor."

Some sociologists, Garth Massey (1975) and others, argue that the culture of poverty is not so much the cause as it is a consequence of or adaptation to the condition of being poor. Ian Robertson (1980), in summarizing much of the literature on this point, reports that from the perspective of some writers,

> any distinctive culture of the poor is the result, not the cause, of their continuing poverty, and their characteristics and attitudes are a realistic and understandable response to their situation. The poor have to abandon the attitudes, values, and expectations of the predominantly middle-class society around them, because middle-class culture is irrelevant to their circumstances. For example, middle-class culture emphasizes "deferred gratification"—saving income and postponing pleasures today in order to reap greater benefits tomorrow. The

The poor are often victims of structural unemployment who want to work. (Bob Daemmrich Photo.)

culture of the poor, however, tends to emphasize "instant gratification"—spending one's money and enjoying what one has while it lasts. Clearly, the value of deferred gratification makes no sense to someone who does not have money to save and is pessimistic about the future. Instant gratification is a rational response to this situation, but it is the result not the cause of poverty. Indeed, empirical studies of impoverished ghetto residents show that if they do manage to get jobs that offer a stable income, they become "mainstreamers," concerned about such middle-class values as deferred gratification and respectability (p. 189).

The Poor and Welfare: Myth and Reality

There are several commonly held myths about the poor and the amount of public assistance they receive in the United States. First and

perhaps most prevalent of the misconceptions at the microlevel (family, group, and community) is the *myth of able-bodied recipients.* So-called welfare chiselers, while they do exist, are the exception rather than the rule. Most public assistance dollars go to help children, the ill, the elderly, and the disabled. To use the Aid to Families with Dependent Children program (AFDC) as an illustration, only 6 percent of AFDC families include a husband or father who is capable of working, and two-thirds of AFDC recipients are children eleven years of age or younger.

In addition, more than 60 percent of these families have only one or two children. This fact should dispel the *myth of large welfare families* that continue to grow larger in order to get additional benefits (*Statistical Abstract of the United States*, 1987, p. 358; p. 382). Actually, only 43 percent of poor families receive food stamps, and only one-third of these families receive other forms of public assistance (O'Hare, 1986).

There are also myths concerning the manner in which the American welfare system is administered at the macrolevel. One frequently held misconception is the *myth of exploding welfare costs.* While the number of poor increased by more than one-third between 1978 and 1986 and governmental expenditures in general rose dramatically over the same period, median benefits for AFDC recipients declined 33 percent in purchasing power from 1972 through the middle 1980s. On the other hand, social programs benefiting the more affluent and the elderly were funded at levels generally matching the inflation rate (Nasar, 1986).

Another faulty perception of the welfare system is the *myth that benefits discourage working.* In fact, welfare payments alone in all fifty states are not sufficient to raise a recipient family's income above the poverty line. During 1984, for instance, the average AFDC monthly payment ranged from a high of only $501 in Alaska to $91 in Mississippi. Only ten states had average payments of $400 or more, while the bottom ten averaged $188 a month or less (*Statistical Abstract of the United States,* 1987, p. 365).

SOCIOLOGICAL EXPLANATIONS OF STRATIFICATION

How is it that a royal couple in Europe can have a wedding that costs an estimated $350,000 while a poor person in the United States may subsist on $350 a month and an agricultural laborer in India or the Philippines may not earn the equivalent of that much in a year? Why is there such disparity between those with power, prestige, and wealth and the very poor in practically all societies? Soci-

ologists address these questions from several perspectives.

The Functionalist Perspective

As you will recall from Chapter 1, the functional approach studies basic structures in society in terms of the ways they function to promote social order and harmony. In 1945 Kingsley Davis and Wilbert Moore made the classical application of functionalism to stratification. The **functionalist perspective**, as stated by Davis and Moore, holds that stratification is necessary and beneficial to society because it uses a system of rewards to motivate people to acquire the skills necessary to obtain the most valued positions. They maintain that society, in effect, "dangles social carrots" in front of people in the form of social rewards such as power, prestige, and monetary gain to provide them with the incentive to seek and obtain positions that call for scarce skills and lengthy training.

Davis and Moore argue that since not all people have the same levels of ability and motivation, and some societal positions require more or less skill, training, and discipline, social inequality is inevitable. If, they assert, physicians were rewarded at the same level as laborers, it would make little sense to expect them to undergo the expensive, arduous, and time-consuming process of acquiring a medical education. Since society needs physicians and others with rare talents in order to function properly, social inequality is needed to ensure that a sufficient number of people will have the motivation to gain qualification for all the necessary positions.

The functionalist explanation of stratification is based primarily on economic incentives and other forms of extrinsic rewards. Davis and Moore and others of the functionalist school subscribe to the concept of *meritocracy,* the idea that society is dominated by the most talented who, therefore, deserve most of the social rewards. The poor, in contrast, tend to have the least talent and skill, but, nonetheless, their existence benefits certain segments of society in a "functional" way (Gans, 1972, 1973). For example, the existence of poverty creates a need for certain service occupations which include social work, public health and housing administration, and law enforcement. The poor also create markets for a variety of goods and services including pawnbroking, secondhand clothing and furniture, and a variety of other used and inferior consumer goods. Finally, poverty functions to ensure that the jobs in society the affluent do not want to do—the menial, undignified, uncomfortable, dirty, and dangerous jobs—will be filled.

While some sociologists adhere to this approach (Cullen and Novick, 1979), others have criticized it on a variety of grounds. One apparent shortcoming of functionalism is that it ignores the preexisting inequities and differential opportunities that many inherit simply because of an accident of birth (Bottomore, 1966). The poor, women, and many minorities, because of their "place" in the existing social system, face obstacles rarely encountered by white middle-class males. Women, for example, were not allowed to vote until the 1920s, and blacks were segregated from any significant participation in the mainstream of society until the late 1960s. Such barriers built into the structure of society tend to render the talents and abilities of certain groups invisible and of no consequence. The concept of a true meritocracy, therefore, is a myth. Functionalism, as Melvin Tumin (1953) argues, serves mainly to justify the status quo, which would keep those with most of the power and prestige in their positions of privilege and encourage resentment among those with the least number of opportunities.

Another criticism of functionalism is that

the social rewards "earned" by individuals often do not match the apparent value of the contributions they make to society (Wrong, 1959). Which position is more valuable to society, that of a professional baseball player or a U.S. Supreme Court judge? The answer, of course, is obvious. Yet, some athletes are paid twenty times the annual income of any and all federal officials, including the president of the United States. Likewise, movie actors, rock music stars, and other media personalities are sometimes paid enormous sums of money and enjoy a significant amount of social visibility and prestige, although their objective contribution to society is questionable. Contrast their situation with that of the public school teacher, who, though required to have one or more college degrees and entrusted with the minds of society's next generation of leaders, is the lowest paid of all professionals.

The Conflict Perspective

While functionalists argue that stratification is beneficial to society because it matches individuals with the greatest skills to positions requiring the greatest expertise, conflict theorists take an opposite view. The **conflict perspective** sees stratification as potentially harmful to society because it allows those with the most power, prestige, and wealth to dominate and exploit the less advantaged and maintain a condition of unequal opportunity.

The conflict approach originated with the work of Karl Marx in the nineteenth century. As you will recall from our discussion in Chapter 1, Marx argued that human history is largely a chronicle of class struggles that have existed in every age between two basic groups, the "haves" and the "have nots." The "haves," whether they are represented by the feudal lords of the Middle Ages or capitalists in modern times, comprise the ruling class, which possesses most of the power and wealth. The "have-nots," as represented by feudal serfs and modern factory workers, are the economically dispossessed with little or no hope for the future. In Marx's view, history was seen as a continuous cyclical process in which the tyranny and exploitation practiced by each ruling class ultimately led to its overthrow by the "have-nots," who then became the new ruling class.

Marx viewed social class strictly in economic terms as related to the means of production. Those who owned the means of production were the ruling class, and those who worked for the owners were the "have-nots" who sold their labor as their sole source of support. He predicted for modern industrial societies that the "have-nots," whom he named the *proletariat*, would realize that they were being exploited, develop *class consciousness*, and overthrow the ruling class or *bourgeoisie* in a revolution. Then, he asserted, the sheer efficiency of industrial production would create such abundance that further class conflict over scarce resources would be unnecessary, the public would own the means of production, and a truly classless society would emerge. Although Marx's notion of a proletarian revolt did not materialize and his ideas were oversimplified by modern standards, his perspective was a powerful one and his concepts established an important foundation for further sociological exploration.

Since the 1960s, American sociologists have greatly expanded Marx's narrow economic perspective on conflict. One characteristic that distinguishes conflict theory from functionalism is its emphasis on the impact of social structure on stratification, rather than on individual factors like training and talent. Some conflict theorists, for instance, might argue that no woman or black person, regardless of ability, could have been nominated for president of the United States, much less elected, before the 1980s because of the social and political structure of American society. Others, like Ralf Dahrendorf (1959), have examined how various groups such as unions, companies, and a multitude of interest groups compete with one another for political as well as economic power. Organizations like Mothers Against Drunk Driving (MADD) and the National Education Association (NEA), for instance, have no ownership in the means of production (as in Marx's view), but nonetheless wield a significant amount of political power.

The Evolutionary Perspective: An Integrated View

Both the functionalist and conflict approaches provide us with valuable insights and, therefore, should not be seen as mutually exclusive. Instead, a synthesis of the two is perhaps the most useful perspective, as societies in general exhibit a basic stability yet contain elements of conflict and discord. Sociologist Gerhard Lenski (1966) has developed an **evolutionary perspective** that attempts to integrate the two views. He argues that societies initially try to match rewards to the skills required for particular positions, but as technology evolves and surpluses develop, those in power attempt to retain control over this wealth. Lenski's basic thesis goes something like this: The functionalist perspective holds true initially as societies attempt to provide the most substantial rewards to those willing to undergo training and develop skills needed for important positions. However, as social systems evolve over time and develop additional technology, they may produce surpluses in highly valued goods and services. When this occurs, conflicts may develop over who should control or own this additional wealth. Those already in positions of political and economic power develop a vested interest in using whatever leverage they can to ensure that they retain control over these resources. Lenski maintains that, in general, as societies become more technological and complex, the level of control appears to rise as well.

TYPES OF STRATIFICATION SYSTEMS

Societies tend to have one or any combination of three different types of stratification systems: estate, caste, or class. A variety of factors, including characteristics of the economic system, forms of political organization, levels of technology, and even the nature of religions, may influence the particular form of ranking that becomes dominant in a given society.

The Estate System

An **estate system** of stratification is based on family membership along with the family's relationship to land and related property. During the Middle Ages in Europe (A.D. 900–A.D. 1400), for instance, a feudal estate system emerged that stratified people into three basic levels: lord, vassal, and serf. With the fall of the Roman Empire, there developed a powerful military aristocracy which consisted of lords who governed conquered lands on a local or regional level.

These nobles would grant land to their most trusted knights and soldiers (vassals) in exchange for loyal military service. The vassals, in turn, sometimes became lords by granting some of their land to their most loyal followers. In this way, a hierarchy of nobility was established in which relations between lords was governed primarily by fealty bond and contract. At the bottom of the hierarchy were serfs (peasants) who were forced to farm the land in exchange for being allowed to live on the estate under the lord's protection. In most respects, the lord controlled the lives of serfs and, among other things, received a portion of everything they produced as payment for living on his land (Rosenberg, 1974). Nonetheless, this system of social ranking did allow for some mobility. Serfs were sometimes freed by their lords and vassals, through meritorious service, and could become a part of "the landed gentry." For most, however, social position was strictly a matter of family birth.

As feudalism declined because of such forces as urbanization, mercantilism, nationalism, and, ultimately, industrialization, social classes began to emerge. By the 1600s and 1700s these European classes, which considered economic and occupational characteristics and qualifications more important than land and a person's relation to it, became the forerunners of social class groups that exist in various parts of the world today.

However, there are still elements of feudalism in many modern and democratic class societies. In the United States, for example, "good old boy" networks of patronage in the business world remain alive and well despite the fact that they give some individuals an unfair advantage and undercut competition based on competence. Some American politicians, corporate managers, and administrators in various large-scale organizations exhibit a "feudal mentality" in hiring relatives and friends rather than the most capable, which, in a society that espouses democratic principles, is unethical at best and illegal in some instances.

Even though Great Britain today is also largely a class society, certain feudal elements remain in the social psyche of British culture as a result of longstanding tradition. Queen Elizabeth, for example, is the wealthiest woman in the world by some accounts, because of the vast land holdings acquired by the House of Windsor over several hundred

During the Middle Ages in Europe, an estate system of stratification emerged. Because of the privilege accorded them by birth, feudal lords remained dominant because they owned and controlled most of the land. The serfs (or peasants) served as sharecroppers who farmed this land in exchange for a bare subsistence living. (Culver Pictures, Inc.)

years. The pomp and circumstance associated with British royalty continues even today and includes medieval ceremonies in which the queen, on occasion, bestows titles of nobility and knighthood on selected individuals.

Today, however, such elements of feudalism are largely only remnants of the past. In contrast to previous European and Asian societies that practiced the estate system, contemporary societies tend to be characterized by either a closed caste system or an open class system of stratification.

The Caste System

A **caste system** is a rigid and closed system of stratification in which social position is inherited and remains the same for life. While several societies, including portions of Africa, Ceylon, and traditional Japan, have experienced caste stratification of one form or another, the traditional caste system of India perhaps serves as the best illustration. This system, practiced for more than three thousand years, was legally abolished by the Indian government in 1949. Nonetheless, while it has significantly declined in urban areas, caste ranking has continued in the rural parts of the country where laws are difficult to enforce (Robertson, 1974).

The Indian caste system is closely intertwined with the ancient Hindu religion from which it evolved. The Hindus believe that the only life after death is through *samsara,* or reincarnation, in which the soul is reborn in the body of another. If one does not adhere strictly to the *dharma*, or behavior specified for the caste one is born into, then one may be downgraded in caste during the next reincarnation. Hindus believe that the only way to improve one's caste level is by strictly adhering to the dharma of one's present caste, which may bring a rebirth to a higher station as a reward in the next life.

Traditionally, this system of ranking included four main *varnas*, or castes: the *Brahmans* (priests and teachers), the *Kahatriyas* (princes and warriors), the *Vaisyas* (merchants and craftsmen), and the *Sudras* (laborers). Below these were many subcastes of *untoucha-*

Traditionally, those considered outcasts or untouchables in the Hindu caste system of India have been avoided and shunned. Often members of these subcastes have been forced to live in separate sections of a town or village and have been required to drink water from a separate well. (Ira Kirschenbaum/Stock Boston.)

bles, or "outcasts," that constituted about 20 percent of the population. These lower caste members were to be avoided at all costs and were therefore shunned by those of higher castes. Rituals related to one's caste governed practically every aspect of life: which occupations were allowed, whom one could have as a friend or marry, the proper way to enter a town, diet, and so forth (Rossides, 1976). In recent years, however, Indian leaders have been pushing for industrialization, scientific farming, and a more diversified economy, and India has increasingly become a class society (Weisman, 1986).

By comparison, the apartheid system practiced today in South Africa represents a caste system that in some ways is as rigid as that practiced in traditional India. *Apartheid* is a strict system of racial segregation. South Africans are divided into four caste-like categories: white, African, Asian, and colored (mixed racial background). Each group must be strictly segregated into separate districts of each town, and anyone who visits different racial districts must possess a pass that is periodically inspected by officials. South African whites display an attitude of overt, up-front racism not unlike that exhibited by Southern whites in the United States during the nineteenth and early twentieth centuries.

It should be noted that even in the United States, historical conditions of caste have existed as applied to certain categories of people. Originally, the freedoms espoused by the founding fathers in the Constitution and Bill of Rights applied, for the most part, only to white, property-holding males. It has taken two hundred years for the caste limitations placed on blacks, Native Americans, women, and other groups to finally be openly addressed and, to a significant degree, put aside. Consequently, class and caste are not mutually exclusive; elements of both usually exist to some degree in all societies.

The Class System

A **class system** of social ranking is relatively open and is based on achievement in terms of occupation, education, and wealth. Class systems are the product of industrialization and, although they take several different forms, can be found in all industrial societies. The number and characteristics of classes in a given society are determined in part by the productivity of its economic system. Because of the capacity of nations like the United States and Japan to generate surpluses, they tend to have more class levels and more complex stratification systems than "classless" societies, like the Soviet Union, with very sluggish economies.

Class in the United States remains a somewhat elusive concept to define precisely. This is due in part to the diverse and ever-changing nature of American society. Many sociologists, however, agree that within the three major subdivisions of upper, middle, and lower class, there are five major class groups identifiable by occupation, education, and degree of wealth: (1) the upper class (high achievement and/or inherited wealth), (2) the upper-middle class (degreed professionals with substantial incomes), (3) the lower-middle class (lower-level white-collar workers), (4) the working class (skilled and semiskilled blue-collar workers paid hourly wages), and (5) the underclass (unskilled workers, the underemployed, and the unemployed poor).

Regardless of how we define these general categories, however, there are problems and contradictions. How, for instance, should the three variables of occupation, education, and wealth be weighted? While sociologists today tend to weight occupation and education higher than mere income in assessing social rank, it is indeed ironic that many blue-collar workers have higher incomes than some in professional occupations, such as social workers and public school teachers. Even so, rating social class is much more complex than merely considering income. Therefore, a **social class** consists of a grouping of people on the socioeconomic continuum who share similar types and levels of occupation, education, wealth, and life-style.

The chief characteristic of a class system is **social mobility**, the ability to move from one social location or level of society to another. There are several ways to discuss social mobility, one of which is to distinguish between its two basic types: vertical mobility and horizontal mobility. **Vertical mobility** refers to any upward or downward change that occurs in a person's social class level. American society encourages upward mobility. Some working-class parents, for example, encourage their children to go to college, for most the surest and most direct route to middle class status. However, vertical mobility can also go the other way. The son or daughter of a research chemist who fails to finish college and elects instead to become a car salesperson, employee of a department store, or fashion model, will most probably experience downward mobility. **Horizontal mobility**, on the other hand, involves change in social position without any significant impact on social class level. The factory worker who becomes a store clerk or the carpenter who becomes a fire fighter would change occupations but experience little or no change in social class.

Another way sociologists analyze changes in stratification is by examining both intergenerational and intragenerational mobility. **Intergenerational mobility** is change in social class level that occurs across generations between parents and their children. Most college students twenty-five years old and younger fall at or below their parents' social class level. However, particularly for those with working-class parents, completion of a four-year degree will usually result in significant upward mo-

bility. By studying the over all trends of both upward and downward intergenerational mobility among various segments of the population, sociologists can more accurately assess such factors as inequality and opportunity. They also are interested in tracking **intragenerational mobility**, changes people experience in social rank within their own lifetimes or careers. Research tends to show that while many Americans change jobs and occupations, most experience only slight to medium gains or losses in relative status during the course of their careers (Sorensen, 1975).

CLASS IN AMERICA: ELEMENTS OF RANK

Marx saw class in economic terms as consisting of two groups, the propertied and the nonpropertied. However, another early theorist, the German sociologist Max Weber, took a multidimensional approach. Weber viewed social class as consisting of a dynamic interplay among three major elements: "political status" or *power*, "social status" or *prestige*, and "economic status" or *wealth* (Weber, 1946; Parsons, 1947). His assessment of class generally has been the most widely accepted in twentieth-century sociology and will represent the general framework from which we will next examine specific aspects of class in America. In addition, *life-style*, a factor Weber saw as related to prestige, deserves to be treated as a separate class characteristic in its own right.

Power

As defined earlier (Chapter 7), *power* is the ability to influence or control the behavior of others with or without their consent. For the purposes of social stratification, the most important types of power tend to be "referent power" or *influence* and "legitimate power" or *authority*. These factors determine how decisions are made and who makes them. In a given instance, does more power reside in a factory supervisor or a shop steward, a classroom teacher or a PTA president, a city mayor or a chief campaign contributor? Such issues are decided each day based on a constantly shifting balance of power in all sectors and at all levels of society.

Influence is the ability to affect the actions of others through the power of persuasion. This is informal power, which results from the possession of knowledge and the force of personality, rather than official prerogatives that go with a formal position or rank. Even if a person had the official title "fund-raiser," for instance, he or she would be an abysmal failure without certain interpersonal skills and personal characteristics. Many influential people, therefore, tend to operate without need of formal position, and some prefer to operate behind the scenes.

Although those with the power to persuade may not have a legitimate right to make decisions, they can influence those who do. Three notable examples of the twentieth century are Mahatma Gandhi, Martin Luther King, Jr., and Eleanor Roosevelt who, each in his or her own way, were able to influence policy makers and social policy as well.

Authority is legitimate power that results from an officially held position in society. It is formal in nature and generally recognized as valid by others. Like influence, authority is found at all levels and classes of society. Parents have authority over their children (microlevel), and the state has some authority over parents (macrolevel), particularly in cases of child neglect or abuse. We can also consider as examples of authority the police officer who has the authority to arrest and detain, the public school teacher to pass and fail, and the physician to diagnose and prescribe.

Those with the greatest authority (and in some cases, influence as well) include heads of institutions like Pope John Paul II, corporate CEOs such as David Kearns of Xerox, and heads of state like Corazon Aquino of the Philippines.

One of the most intriguing issues relating to power has to do with how it is concentrated. Is power in America limited to a small "ruling class" of elites, or is it instead more widely dispersed among a variety of specialized factions? The majority of social scientists have not reached agreement on this question. Perhaps this is partially due to the complexities of analysis brought on by the ever-changing economic and social conditions of American society. Then, too, the use of power, particularly influence, is not readily visible to the investigator. Those with power often keep it secret and exercise it as a guarded rite behind closed doors.

Some sociologists subscribe to the **power-elite theory** developed by C. Wright Mills. In his book *The Power Elite,* Mills (1959) asserted that American society is shaped largely by an informal unified group of elites from the highest levels of government, the military, and the corporate sector. These individuals of both high authority and substantial influence, Mills maintained, operate through interlocking networks to make decisions that serve their own vested interests. However, by working together, they can also largely determine the nature and direction of social policy. Large defense contractors, like General Dynamics and Honeywell, for example, must work with Pentagon officials who, in turn, must cooperate with legislators to get defense appropriations bills passed through Congress. The results serve the needs of all concerned. The defense contractors make money, the military obtain the latest combat hardware, and the legislators ensure that the needed level of national defense is maintained. The majority of these elites, although they occupy top positions in different sectors of society, are white males, graduates of the same twelve private universities, members of the same clubs, and have similar worldviews (Domhoff, 1967; Dye, 1986).

Other sociologists (Dahl, 1961; Reisman, 1961; Martin, 1977) subscribe to the **pluralistic theory** of power. They argue that no single group has a decisive advantage in being able to rule America. Instead, a wide variety of groups, each with its own vested interests, compete with one another for their own slices of the public policy pie. There are the various manufacturing and business lobbies centering on products like cigarettes, automobiles, oil and gas, and agricultural products. There are interest groups focused on furthering positions on issues that range from abortion, gun control, conservation, and religion, to civil rights for women, blacks and other minorities, the elderly, and children. Sociologist David Reisman and others argue that because of the large numbers of these interest groups and their many agendas, they ultimately cancel each other out, no single group being able to gain decisive power.

Prestige

The relative degree of honor and respect a person receives from others is **prestige.** The basis for such esteem and deference depends on the personal qualities seen as important by the members of any given society. In the estate system practiced in medieval Europe, family membership, amount of property, and demonstrated loyalty were all considered important criteria. The caste system in India traditionally stressed birth as the basis for esteem. In other societies, prestige may be based on a combination of these and other possible factors including power (heads of govern-

The different elements that constitute class do not necessarily go together. Real estate tycoon Donald Trump, for instance, has great wealth but limited prestige and power. Mother Teresa has great international prestige because of her efforts on behalf of the poor but is practically penniless and with little power. (AP/Wide World Photos.)

ments and corporations), wealth (billionaires), physical beauty (top fashion models), credibility (network anchor people), intellect (Nobel Prize recipients), dramatic ability (movie stars), athletic prowess (professional ball players), and life-style. Elements of all these variables may be seen in the American class system. Old, established families like the Rockefellers, DuPonts, and Mellons, for example, are noted for their family background, power, wealth, and life-style.

Some of these factors, however, have little or no bearing on the relative level of prestige experienced by most Americans. Few people will have an opportunity to co-star with Sylvester Stallone in the next installment of the "Rambo" chronicles, to co-anchor the evening news with Dan Rather, or to appear on the cover of *Vogue* magazine. Therefore, we will focus our discussion briefly on the factors that tend to be the most important common denominators of prestige in America: occupation and education.

As shown in Table 8-1, *occupation* generally is the most important indicator of prestige in America because, in most cases, it represents the primary means to both power and wealth. This is contrary to the common misconception that wealth is most important. Who has the greatest amount of prestige (and power), the president of the United States or the chairman and CEO of any of the top three automakers? The answer is obvious. Yet the president's annual salary is $200,000 compared to an estimated $20 million paid to the chairman of Chrysler, Lee Iococca, in 1987. According to research conducted by James Davis and Tom Smith (1984) at Michigan's Inter-University Consortium for Political and Social Research, Americans hold in highest esteem such professionals as physicians, college professors, lawyers, and scientists, who have undergone many years of intensive education and earn relatively high incomes. Those ranked at the bottom of the prestige hierarchy

are unskilled workers including farm laborers, maids, garbage collectors, and shoe shiners.

Education is also an important indicator of prestige because it represents the primary means of gaining entry into the most valued occupations and achieving overall upward social mobility. There is an increasing need for a high school diploma or equivalent by anyone wanting to gain any type of regular, full-time employment, and a four-year college degree is almost a universal minimum requirement for entry into the upper-middle class. As far as income alone is concerned, education in a "credential-oriented" society is a key ingredient to increasing one's standard of living. According to the U.S. Bureau of the Census, the median annual income for Americans over twenty-five in 1985, by level of education, was $23,863 for those who completed four years of high school as compared with $32,822 for those with four years of college. Individuals with graduate and professional training beyond college averaged $39,335 (U.S. Bureau of the Census, 1986 A).

Some research has shown that family background including, for example, occupation of parents, plays a crucial role in affecting the amount of education an individual acquires (Jencks, 1972). Middle- and upper-class parents socialize their children to see a four-year college degree as an essential ingredient in the transition to adulthood and self-sufficiency and often plan carefully for their children's college years. Most parents from the lower classes do not.

Wealth

The primary indicator of strictly economic stratification is **wealth,** the net worth of an individual or group in terms of property and income. For most Americans, however, the degree of wealth is more a reflection of their overall social class level than its central cause. In other words, increased wealth accrues es-

Table 8-1 Prestige Ratings of Occupations in the United States*

Occupation	Score	Occupation	Score	Occupation	Score	Occupation	Score
Physician	82	Registered nurse	62	Foreman	45	Baker	34
College professor	78	Pharmacist	61	Real estate agent	44	Shoe repairman	33
Judge	76	Veterinarian	60	Fireman	44	Bulldozer operator	33
Lawyer	76	Elementary school teacher	60	Postal clerk	43	Bus driver	32
Physicist	74	Accountant	57	Advertising agent	42	Truck driver	32
Dentist	74	Librarian	55	Mail carrier	42	Cashier	31
Banker	72	Statistician	55	Railroad conductor	41	Sales clerk	29
Aeronautical engineer	71	Social worker	52	Typist	41	Meat cutter	28
Architect	71	Funeral director	52	Plumber	41	Housekeeper	25
Psychologist	71	Computer specialist	51	Farmer	41	Longshoreman	24
Airline pilot	70	Stock broker	51	Telephone operator	40	Gas station attendant	22
Chemist	69	Reporter	51	Carpenter	40	Cab driver	22
Minister	69	Office manager	50	Welder	40	Elevator operator	21
Civil engineer	68	Bank teller	50	Dancer	38	Bartender	20
Biologist	68	Electrician	49	Barber	38	Waiter	20
Geologist	67	Machinist	48	Jeweler	37	Farm laborer	18
Sociologist	66	Police officer	48	Watchmaker	37	Maid/servant	18
Political scientist	66	Insurance agent	47	Bricklayer	36	Garbage collector	17
Mathematician	65	Musician	46	Airline stewardess	36	Janitor	17
High school teacher	63	Secretary	46	Meter reader	36	Shoe shiner	9
		Mechanic	35				

*Out of a possible score of 100.

Source: Davis, J. A. & Smith, T. W. (1984). *General social survey cumulative file, 1972–1982.* Ann Arbor, Mi: Inter-University Consortium for Political and Social Research.

sentially as a consequence of achieving higher levels of power, occupation, and education. Of the four hundred richest people in the United States, for example, only about one-third inherited their wealth. The majority are self-made millionaires and billionaires (Forbes, 1987). This is illustrated in Table 8-2. Nonetheless, those in the upper classes can and do use wealth to solidify their class position and provide opportunities for their children that most Americans could not hope to offer. The yearly cost in 1988, for instance, of sending a son or daughter to an elite private college or university was $16,630 for Columbia, $17,100 for Harvard/Radcliffe, and

$17,999 for Bennington (*New York Times*, May 12, 1987, p. B7).

Property refers to all material assets owned by a person, such as real estate, stocks and bonds, pension funds, antiques and art, and cash on hand. It is difficult to arrive at a precise breakdown on how property in America is distributed because assets are so easily hidden; for instance, funds held in foreign banks and art collections in private homes. However, it is clear from available estimates that property is distributed throughout the population quite unequally. Using the broad definition above, we can say that the top 10 percent of property holders own about 64 percent of all

Table 8-2 The Ten Wealthiest People in America, 1987

Name	Age	Net Worth (Estimated)	Major Source of Wealth
Samuel Walton	69	$8.5 billion	Self-made; Walmart Stores. Began as a clerk at J.C. Penney.
John W. Kluge	73	$3.0 billion	Self-made; Metromedia. Started radio station soon after WW II.
H. Ross Perot	57	$2.9 billion	Self-made; Electronic Data Systems (EDS). Began as a sales representative at IBM.
David Packard	75	$2.9 billion	Self-made; Hewlett-Packard. Began business in his garage with partner Hewlett.
Samuel Newhouse	59	$4.7 billion	Inherited; Advance Publications.
Donald Newhouse	58		
Lester Crown	62	$2.1 billion	Inherited.
Keith Murdoch	56	$2.1 billion	Inherited/Self-made. As a young man in his twenties, took over father's newspaper and built an international media empire.
Warren Buffet	57	$2.1 billion	Self-made; Stock market trading and speculation.
Leslie Wexner	50	$2.1 billion	Self-made; The Limited. Started with $5000 and built business in women's clothing.

Source: Adapted from The Forbes four hundred. (1987, October 26). *Forbes*, pp. 114–120.

wealth in the United States. The bottom half own only 3 percent of the nation's total wealth (Rose, 1986).

Income refers to all money earned through sources including wages or salaries, interest on savings, and investment dividends. For most Americans, income derives almost exclusively from their occupations in the form of wages and salaries. By contrast, the wealthy obtain most of their income from a variety of investments, including rental property, stocks and bonds, and interest on funds held in financial institutions. Income in the United States is also unequally distributed, although not so greatly as is property. In terms of annual income, the wealthiest 20 percent of the population in 1985 earned 43.5 percent of all available income, compared to the poorest 20 percent, who earned only 4.6 percent of all available income. This comparison is portrayed in Table 8-3. Income is also unequally distributed by sex and family type. In 1985, men employed full-time had a median yearly income of $24,999, while women similarly employed earned $16,252. The 1985 median income for all families was $27,735, compared to $22,622 for single-parent families headed by men and $13,660 for one-parent families headed by women (U.S. Bureau of the Census, 1986 B).

Life-Style

Power, aspects of prestige including occupation and education, and wealth are all important indicators of social class. However, an individual's membership in a given class is usually not recognized by others of similar status unless that person also exhibits the "appropriate" life-style that goes with it. To be fully accepted as belonging to a given class level by its other members, a person is expected to demonstrate to some degree that he or she identifies with and practices its culture. There are a multitude of ways a person may exhibit identification, ranging from certain forms of language, carriage, and dress to diet, consumer and recreational preferences, and preferred forms of social etiquette. Taken as a whole, these and other related characteristics affect to a significant degree how we see ourselves, our place in the community and society, whom we choose for our friends and companions, and how we relate to other people in general.

Sociologically speaking, **life-style** refers to the general value orientation, tastes and preferences, and pattern of living characteristic of those belonging to a particular group or social class. Some people prefer country and western music, cold beer in a can, jeans and baseball caps, and *TV Guide*. Others have a preference for classical music, gin and tonic, clothing from Ralph Lauren or Neiman Marcus, and the *Wall Street Journal*. Therefore, life-style represents a class subculture in which the way people feel, act, and live in general reflects their class status, along with other factors including power, prestige, and wealth. In terms of child socialization, for example, working-class parents rear their children to conform to

Table 8-3 **Distribution of Income in the United States, 1985***

Total Population (in annual yearly income)	Percentage of Total Available Income
Highest fifth	43.5%
Second highest fifth	24.2%
Middle fifth	16.9%
Second lowest fifth	10.9%
Lowest fifth	4.6%

*Total may not equal 100.0 because of rounding.
Source: U.S. Bureau of the Census. (1986). *Current population reports*, Series P-60. Washington, D.C.: U.S. Printing Office.

and respect authority and to be neat and orderly. Middle-class parents, in contrast, teach their children to develop attitudes of initiative and autonomy and tend to give them more freedom of action aimed at developing their creativity (Bell, 1979).

Nonetheless, writer Paul Fussel (1983) argues that the lower the social class, the less likely it is its people will recognize the importance of life-style in shaping the level of social esteem given them by others:

> At the bottom, people tend to believe that class is defined by the amount of money you have. In the middle, people grant that money has something to do with it, but think education and the kind of work you do almost equally important. Nearer the top, people perceive that taste, values, ideas, style, and behavior are indispensable criteria of class, regardless of money or occupation or education (p. 5).

Social Class in Perspective

Social scientists find that social class is difficult to measure precisely for a variety of reasons. First, there is the dimension of power and its complexity. While authority is related to the duties of an occupation or office and is thereby official and usually somewhat open to inspection and measurement, influence is not. Influence is more emotional and subjective in nature, and those who exert influence often do so quietly and discreetly.

Social class also has to do with prestige. Both elements of occupation and education can be correlated with relative degrees of power and wealth and with the esteem (reputation) accorded them by most Americans. However, level of education alone does not guarantee a person a certain social position or the lack of it. There are people with college degrees in working-class occupations, and there are those who have never been to college, who have been able to start and build

successful businesses and have significant impact on their communities.

Wealth too can be a complicated variable in placing people in specified social classes. An organized crime boss may live in a mansion on a large estate, drive a Rolls Royce, and have huge sums of ready cash. Likewise, high-priced call girls and even small-time drug dealers often generate six-figure incomes. How would they rank on the social class ladder compared with social workers, librarians, and nurses or, for that matter, with dentists, lawyers, and college professors?

Finally, there is class life-style that is subcultural and also difficult to measure. Dramatic differences in life-style are evident between those in the upper class versus those in the working class. However, the life-styles of adjacent social classes, like lower-middle and working classes, for example, may be distinctive in some ways but overlap in others.

These are but a few examples of **status inconsistency**, a contradiction that exists when a person appears to rank higher in one aspect of stratification than another. In the United States, occupation (and to a lesser degree, education) usually takes precedence over wealth. A person with a deviant occupation, such as a criminal, would be ranked very low regardless of wealth. Similarly, many in the working class, including truck drivers and union laborers, are paid higher wages than those in some middle-class occupations, including public school teachers, but are ranked lower in overall social class.

THE ANALYSIS OF STRATIFICATION

In an attempt to lend precision to the concept of social class and to analyze its impact on social behavior in general, sociologists use a variety of research approaches. Of these, the most important are the subjective approach, the reputational approach, and the objective approach.

The Subjective Approach

A method of stratification analysis in which people are asked to identify their own social class category is the **subjective approach**. One useful benefit of this method is that it furnishes sociologists with a means of comparing perceived social class by individuals and groups with their actual approximate positions on the stratification scale as determined by objective measures. Most Americans, regardless of their actual class ranking, identify themselves as belonging somewhere in the middle class, while only up to 8 percent perceive themselves as lower class and 1 or 2 percent see themselves as upper class (Hodge and Treiman, 1968; Jackman and Jackman, 1983). These findings tend to indicate, among other things, that people perceive their own social class level on the basis of their reference groups (whom they would like to be like). Sometimes people's perceptions tend to be at odds with the way their community and society would actually rank them. In a society like the United States dominated by middle-class values, however, for some people who are objectively working class, identification with these values is an important part of the mindset (for example, seeing a need for college education) required for upward mobility and middle-class status. Class then, for individuals engaged in self-ranking, often represents a social category they identify with as a goal, rather than one they occupy in actuality.

The Reputational Approach

While the use of subjective techniques involves getting individuals to rank themselves, the **reputational approach** is a method of analysis that asks people to identify the social class of others in their community. As such, it represents an approach that focuses on the dimension of class prestige. The best known of the early stratification studies that used this method were conducted during the 1930s and 1940s by W. Lloyd Warner and his associates in communities such as Newburyport, Massachusetts ("Yankee City") and Morris, Illinois ("Jonesville") (Warner and Lunt, 1941; Warner, 1949; Warner et al., 1949). In his "Yankee City" study of a New England community, Warner found six distinct class levels which, as shown by later research, he felt were fairly typical of communities throughout the United States. These class levels are briefly described as follows:

1. *Upper-upper class.* In Warner's research, the upper-upper class was found to be an old aristocracy of upper-class families. These families could trace their prominence in the community back at least three generations. Meeting the lineage test of birth and family name was therefore seen as more important than "mere wealth," which tended to be substantial. Nationally prominent upper-upper-class families today include the Vanderbilts, the Hearsts, and the Carnegies.

2. *Lower-upper class.* Those with newly acquired wealth and social standing comprised the lower-upper class. These people, Warner found, had acquired wealth through developing industries including shoes, textiles, and finance. They were separated from the upper-upper class only by the lack of long-term family status. Members of the lower-upper class today are sometimes referred to as "new money" by members of the general public.

3. *Upper-middle class.* The next group, the upper-middle class, consisted of college-educated professionals and successful business people. Members of this class tended to be property owners and were often quite ac-

tive in civic affairs. They lived in better neighborhoods and had substantial income, but not enough to constitute wealth.

4. *Lower-middle class.* The highest of what Warner called the "common classes" was the lower-middle class, which consisted of small business people, lower-level white-collar workers, and skilled blue-collar workers. People of this class lived in small houses in neat neighborhoods, tended to be politically conservative, and were careful with their money. Their reputation was that of good common people.

5. *Upper-lower class.* Warner identified semi-skilled and unskilled blue-collar workers as upper-lower class. These people lived in less desirable neighborhoods and had a reputation of being "poor but honest." The term "working class" is used by some sociologists today to identify essentially the same group (*Encyclopedia of Sociology,* 1974).

6. *Lower-lower class.* The underemployed and unemployed represented the lower-lower class. Its members had a reputation of being lazy, shiftless, and dependent and, therefore, were seen as not respectable. Based on what we know about poverty today from sociological research, many if not most of the poor in America are undeserving of such a reputation, although it is still prevalent.

The reputational approach has been very useful in studying stratification in small communities. However, it is difficult to use in large cities where people do not know others in their community and cannot, therefore, accurately judge their reputations.

The Objective Approach

The method most often used today in sociological research to measure stratification is the objective approach. Although both the subjective and reputational approaches have their place in stratification research, many sociologists prefer a method that makes use of standardized criteria for objectively measuring social rank. In this manner, feelings and perceptions of evaluators are exchanged for more precise scales that weigh several stratification factors. The objective approach is also more amenable to being used with large populations and in evaluating the stratification characteristics of whole societies.

The most common applications of the objective approach involve measures of *socioeconomic status* (SES), which sociologists use to rank individuals depending on a combination of occupation, education, and income. *Occupation* is ranked according to established prestige scales, which are in turn determined through research on large samples of Americans who are asked to rank most of the standard occupations from highest to lowest. Of chief concern here is the relative importance of certain occupational skills for society. Some occupations require greater responsibility and involve higher degrees of influence and control over people's lives than others. Evaluators are also interested in the likelihood that certain occupations will attract highly educated people. *Education,* as determined by years and levels obtained, is used because it reflects the difficulty and length of preparation required to qualify persons for given positions. It is generally assumed that the longer and more extensive the training, the more highly valued will be the skills that are developed. Finally, *income* is considered, as measured in yearly earnings. Here we see the unequal reward system which, generally speaking, pays more money to those in the most prestigious occupations who have the most education.

In closing, it is hoped that this chapter has helped you to appreciate further how fascinating, varied, and complex social stratification is and can be. Sociologists are interested primarily in assessing the impact of social rank at the macrolevel on the structure of society and vice versa. They are also interested in its impact at the microlevel on people's attitudes, opportunities, and behavior, as well as in identifying apparent trends for the future.

The United States, with its class system, has become—especially in light of the reforms of the twentieth century, including the civil rights and women's movements—one of the most open societies in the world. Nonetheless, structured inequalities exist in all social systems, and America is no exception. In addition to its class system, America retains a few caste-like aspects, as mentioned earlier. These are applied to a few notable categories of people—racial and ethnic minorities and, to some degree, women as well. The manner in which these elements of a caste system arose and have changed, in regard to racial and ethnic minorities in particular, represents much of the focus for the chapter to follow.

CHAPTER SUMMARY

1. Each society has some form of stratification that defines how social rank is determined and social rewards distributed. One consequence of rank is what Max Weber called "life chances," the opportunities for survival and prosperity in society. In terms of such indicators of life chances as life expectancy, availability of health care, and good nutrition, the upper classes in the United States fare much better than the poor.

2. Those with the lowest levels of life chances live in poverty, which sociologists categorize in a variety of ways. Absolute poverty describes the plight of people who lack the essentials for survival, while relative poverty indicates a standard of living below average for some when compared with the standard for most people in a given community or society.

A distinction is also made between objective poverty (official poverty as determined by agreed-upon criteria) and felt poverty (the psychological and emotional experience of deprivation).

3. Most of America's poor tend to belong to one or more of the following categories: women, children, minorities, the elderly, and the disabled. One popular explanation of deprivation is the culture of poverty hypothesis, which holds that attitudes of despair are socialized into children and passed from generation to generation. While this may hold true for some, poverty in America generally tends to be a temporary situation for most who experience it.

4. There are three dominant sociological perspectives on the causes of stratification. The functionalist approach holds that unequal rewards are necessary to motivate enough people to seek and fill the jobs requiring the most skill. The conflict approach, in comparison, sees ranking as harmful, as those with superior positions of power and wealth can keep the system structured to benefit themselves and thus continue to dominate and exploit the disadvantaged. A third perspective, the evolutionary approach, essentially combines the other two.

5. Societies tend to have one or any combination of three different types of stratification systems. An estate system of ranking is based on family membership and relationship to land (for example, the feudal system during the Middle Ages). A caste system is closed (traditional India), with few if any opportunities for mobility, while a class system is open (the United States), with many opportunities to change one's rank.

6. The primary dimensions of social class in America are power, prestige, wealth, and life-style. Power is the ability to influence or control the behavior of others and is divided into two types: authority (official position) and influence (the ability to persuade). Prestige is the honor and respect a person receives from others, as measured by occupation, education, and wealth. As a third indicator of class, wealth tends to be a reflection of over all class, rather than its prime determinant, and is divided into the categories of property (what one owns) and income (what one earns). Finally, life-style refers to the general value orientation, tastes and preferences, and pattern of living characteristic of those belonging to a particular group or social class.

7. Precise measurement of social class is complex, in part as a result of status inconsistency, a contradiction that exists when a person appears to rank higher in one aspect of stratification than another. To deal effectively with this and other related issues and difficulties, sociologists employ a variety of research strategies: the subjective approach (self-placement), the reputational approach (community studies), and the objective approach (socioeconomic status).

TERMS TO KNOW

absolute poverty: a condition that exists when people lack essential resources, such as food and shelter, necessary for survival.

caste system: a rigid and closed system of stratification in which social position is inherited and remains the same for life.

class system: a system of stratification that is relatively open in that it is based on the achievement of occupation, education, and wealth.

conflict perspective: an approach that sees stratification as harmful to society because it allows those with the most power, prestige, and wealth to dominate and exploit the less advantaged and maintain a condition of unequal opportunity.

culture of poverty hypothesis: the assertion that poverty involves a subculture that socializes its children with attitudes of despair and acceptance of being poor as natural and normal for them.

estate system: a system of stratification based on family membership and the family's relationship to land and related property.

evolutionary perspective: an approach that sees stratification as initially designed to match the most skilled with the most valued positions but later, as surpluses develop, as an opportunity for those with existing power to retain their control.

felt poverty: a sense of deprivation experienced by those who fall slightly above the poverty line.

functionalist perspective: an approach that sees stratification as necessary and beneficial to society because it uses a system of rewards to motivate people to acquire the skills necessary to obtain the most valued positions.

horizontal mobility: change in social position (usually occupation) without any significant impact on social class level.

intergenerational mobility: change in social class level that occurs across generations between parents and their children.

intragenerational mobility: changes in social rank that people experience within their own lifetimes or careers.

life chances: the opportunities for survival and prosperity in society.

life-style: the general value orientation, tastes and preferences, and pattern of living characteristic of those belonging to a particular group or social class.

objective approach: a method of stratification analysis that makes use of standardized criteria (such as occupation, education, and income) for measuring social rank.

objective poverty: a state of official deprivation as determined by an agreed-upon standard of measurement (such as annual income).

pluralistic theory: the argument that power in America is distributed among a wide variety of interest groups which tend to cancel each other out, thus preventing any one group from dominating public policy.

power-elite theory: the assertion that power in America is held largely by an informal yet unified group of elites from the highest levels of government, the military, and the corporate sector.

prestige: the relative degree of honor and respect a person receives from others.

relative poverty: a standard of living that is substandard in relation to that of the majority of society members.

reputational approach: a method of stratification analysis in which people are asked to identify the social class of others in their community.

social class: a grouping of people on the socioeconomic continuum who share similar types and levels of power, prestige, wealth, and life-style.

social mobility: the ability to move from one social location or level in society to another.

social stratification: a system in each society that defines how social rank is determined and social rewards are distributed.

status inconsistency: a contradiction that exists when a person appears to rank higher on one aspect of stratification than on another.

structural unemployment: the loss of employment as a result of changes in the economy that render certain occupations obsolete.

subjective approach: a method of stratification analysis in which people rank themselves.

vertical mobility: any upward or downward change that occurs in a person's social class level.

wealth: the net worth of an individual in terms of property and income.

SUGGESTED READINGS

The American Class Structure: A New Synthesis (Dennis Gilbert and Joseph A. Kahl; Homewood, Ill.: Dorsey Press, 1982). An insightful overview of class and mobility in America with a balanced coverage of both early and modern sociological research on stratification.

The New American Poverty (Michael Harrington; New York: Holt, Rinehart and Winston, 1984). An excellent account of trends concerning America's poor, including some emphasis on groups with increasing problems; displaced workers, single women with dependent children, and undocumented aliens.

Power and Privilege: A Theory of Social Stratification (Gerhard Lenski; New York: McGraw-Hill, 1966). An important book that examines the nature of stratification in different societies and how structured inequalities are built into their social fabric.

Social Stratification in the United States (Stephen J. Rose; New York: Pantheon, 1986). A recent comprehensive text with results of new studies on stratification.

Who Rules America Now? A View for the Eighties (G. William Domhoff; Englewood Cliffs, N.J.: Prentice-Hall, 1983). An excellent treatment of the upper class and how those in it impact on social policy.

Chapter 9
Racial and Ethnic Minorities

ETHNICITY AND ETHNIC MINORITIES
The Nature of Ethnicity
Hispanics
White Ethnics

MINORITY RELATIONS IN PERSPECTIVE
Patterns of Exclusion
Patterns of Participation

■ TERMS TO KNOW

accommodation
amalgamation
authoritarian personality
discrimination
ethnicity
ethnic minority
exploitative prejudice
genocide
individual discrimination
individual racism
institutional discrimination

institutional racism
Jim Crow laws
majority group
minority group
normative prejudice
pan-Indianism
prejudice
race
racial minority
racism
reverse discrimination
segregation
stereotypes

During 1987 in Los Angeles, more than 100 of the 387 people killed in gang-related incidents were innocent bystanders. As 1988 began, the death toll continued to mount. In January of that year, two innocent women—Karen Toshima and Alma Lee Washington—were shot to death in separate incidents. What made their deaths different from the others were the responses to them by local authorities and the press (Carlson, 1988). The double standard evident in these responses sparked a storm of controversy over the value of life in the ghetto.

Karen Toshima was a twenty-seven-year-old professional woman who made her living as a graphic artist. She was shot to death in a crossfire between two rival gangs outside a fancy restaurant in Westwood Village, a posh shopping center. Westwood is one of Los Angeles's most affluent West Side communities. Those in the city establishment, shocked by

the gang violence that had spilled over into one of their neighborhoods, reacted strongly. Toshima's death made several newspaper headlines and was spotlighted on the television news for days. Police response was vigorous and patrols in the Westwood area were tripled. The Los Angeles Police Department formed a thirty-officer antigang unit to solve this crime. In addition, a $25,000 reward was offered by the city councilman from Westwood for information leading to the arrest of Toshima's killer.

Across town in a ghetto area of South Central Los Angeles, Alma Lee Washington, a disabled black woman, sixty-seven, was killed in a similar incident. Confined to a wheelchair, Washington was sitting in the entrance to her small dilapidated house when she was fatally shot in the head by hoodlums driving by. Her death received little attention. In contrast to the coverage of Toshima's death, scenes of Washington's grieving family were not shown as a lead story on the television news. Two of Los Angeles's leading newspapers, the *Herald Examiner* and the *Times,* barely covered the story in the brief notes buried in obscure sections of the papers. The LAPD assigned two officers to investigate Washington's death.

This double standard of treatment created a furor in the black and Hispanic communities. Relations with city officials became so strained that the story was picked up in the national press. Writing for *Time* magazine, Margaret B. Carlson (February 22, 1988) commented as follows:

> Death may be the great equalizer, but in Los Angeles some deaths are more equal than others. Black and Hispanic leaders angrily contrasted the uproar over Toshima's killing to the indifference about violence in their neighborhoods. "There is a deep feeling in the community that the philosophy of the police department is to 'let them kill each other' in South Central L.A.," says State Assembly woman Maxine Waters. "The black community has known for years that a problem is not a problem until it hits the white community" (p. 21).

The recent situation in Los Angeles underscores the fact that orderly and cordial relations between minority and majority groups historically have been strained. Suspicion, tension, conflict, and oppression have been typical, and violence has sometimes occurred. Problems between groups are related to stratification (Chapter 8) and how opportunities for power, prestige, and wealth are distributed in the general population. Because of the tremendous diversity of physical and cultural characteristics among humans, opportunities for social rewards in many societies are also based on such factors as race and ethnicity. The characteristics of such minorities, the factors that contribute to how they are perceived and treated by those in dominance, and the ever-changing relations between minorities

and the over all society, are the focus of this chapter.

MAJORITY GROUPS AND MINORITY GROUPS

What Is a Majority Group?

A **majority group** is a social category comprised of those in society who are dominant in power, prestige, wealth, and culture. Its members use this advantage to have their values and cultural orientation legitimated as society's dominant norms and social policies.

As shown in Table 9-1, America was first settled by those of predominantly English and Scotch-Irish descent. The United States was originally a group of British colonies during much of the 1600s and 1700s. In the wake of a successful eighteenth-century revolt against British rule, the last two centuries in America have seen rapid industrialization and, with it, massive immigration by diverse racial and

Table 9-1 Ethnic Backgrounds of the U.S. Population, 1790*

Ethnic Background	Percent
English	60.1
Scottish, Scotch-Irish	14.0
German	8.6
Irish	3.6
Dutch	3.1
French, Swedish	3.0
Other	7.0

*Total may not equal 100.0 because of rounding.
The figures above are estimates from the first U.S. Census conducted in 1790. They do not include slaves, who comprised approximately 20 percent of the population at that time. Adapted with permission from Parrillo, V. N. (1985). *Strangers to these shores*, 2nd ed. New York: Wiley, p. 119.

ethnic groups drawn by the prospects of a better life. Some, however, did not come as paying passengers, but as commodities to be sold, packed tightly in the bowels of slave ships. Regardless of whether immigration was voluntary or forced, it created a rich diversity of racial and ethnic groups in America.

The United States today continues to be dominated largely by the Anglo-Saxon orientation of the original colonies. Such obvious examples as English language and legal traditions still dominate the norms of American culture. In addition, those in the affluent and powerful establishment and those who wish to emulate them exhibit an almost compulsive attraction to anything related to English life. It remains fashionable for the upper classes to live in English-style houses—Georgian, Tudor, and Cape Cod. Members of the majority and their imitators live in community developments with names like Wimbleton Estates and Georgetown Colony, on streets named Heather Glen and Hampton Court. They furnish their houses with antiques or reproductions of Chippendale, Queen Anne, or anything "Victorian" or "traditional" in design. Food and drink on special occasions are served on English bone china and in Irish crystal and, in the autumn of the year, British wool and tweed and tartan plaid are the fashionable materials for clothing.

What Is a Minority Group?

A **minority group** is a social category of people distinguished by their physical or cultural characteristics who are regarded as "different" and treated unequally as a result of prejudice and discrimination (Wirth, 1945). Minorities are usually smaller in number than the majority group, but not always. In South Africa, for example, nonwhites outnumber whites four to one but are dominated by the white establishment that runs the country.

Sociologists generally agree on the following five characteristics that distinguish a minority group from a majority group (Wagley and Harris, 1964; Vander Zanden, 1983):

1. *Those belonging to a minority group suffer disadvantages at the hands of those comprising the majority group.* Minorities do not experience the same life chances as those in the majority group, the "good things" in life. Their members generally rank lower in terms of power, prestige, and wealth. They are more likely to live in poverty than those in the majority, are often more poorly educated, and are underrepresented in positions of authority and influence in major institutions. In addition to experiencing deprivation, they often represent the source of the advantages enjoyed by the majority. For one group to have tremendous privilege, another must often be oppressed. As a final disadvantage, members of minorities are often made to feel inferior by certain indignities heaped on them by the majority.

2. *Members of minorities are identifiable on the basis of visible physical and/or cultural characteristics and, as a result, are treated differently by the majority group.* Some minorities are identified primarily on the basis of physical attributes such as race, gender, or age. Others are defined by the majority group primarily in terms of cultural characteristics including language, religion, family structure, dress, and mannerisms. The majority group sees as deviant and condemns the norms and practices based on these subcultural characteristics, and often makes them the subject of jokes. Differences based on physical characteristics are the basis for doctrines of supremacy leading to such attitudes as racism and sexism. The unique characteristics that make all humans different are largely invisible in members of a minority group in the eyes of the majority group. Thus, minority mem-

During January of 1989 in Miami, the shooting of a black citizen by a white police officer sparked several days of rioting in the black community. Incidences like this underscore the fact that racial tensions still exist in many communities across America. (AP/Wide World Photos.)

bership becomes the basis for judgment by majority group members, and nothing else matters.

3. *Members of minority groups possess a strong consciousness of kind.* This feeling of identification is due partly to distinctive subcultural characteristics that give minority members such things in common with each other as similar language patterns, modes of dress, and value orientations. Oppression and persecution also drive them together and cause sharpened distinctions between their group and others. This heightened self-consciousness results in a "stick together" attitude and intense loyalty to the group. Because of sensitivity brought on by years of differential treatment and denied opportunity, some mem-

bers of minorities tend to encapsulate themselves within their own group and have a suspicion or distrust of outsiders, who are held "at arm's length." In the American workplace today, this self-segregation, by blacks and Hispanics especially, while born of a mechanism for survival, is often mistaken by white workers as reverse racism. Learning to trust today's whites (the majority) in a climate of equal participation is difficult for those whose parents were reared in a "whites only" world.

4. *Minority group membership is an ascribed status.* Membership in most minorities is imposed by society on the basis of birth, not achievement. In Nazi Germany, for instance, Jews were persecuted mercilessly.

It mattered not that some Jews looked just like non-Jew Germans or had adopted the Christian religion. They were still regarded as Jews because of their ancestry. In the United States, a person who appears white but has even a single black grandparent is often viewed as black (Vander Zanden, 1983).

5. *Minority group members, by social pressure or choice, typically marry within their group.* Societies in general tend to put pressure on people for "like to marry like." Such pressure, termed "endogamy" by sociologists, is felt by members of majority and minority groups alike. This theme was explored in depth and with sensitivity in the now-classic 1967 motion picture *Guess Who's Coming to Dinner*, starring Spencer Tracy, Katharine Hepburn, and Sidney Poitier. In the story, a white liberal newspaper publisher (Tracy) comes face-to-face with his own supposedly progressive values when his daughter brings home her fiancee (Poitier) to meet her parents, who are surprised to discover he is black.

Types of Minorities

Minority groups are difficult to classify precisely because many individuals simultaneously fall into two or more groups that suffer disadvantages at the hands of the dominant society. A black Jewish woman, for example, may find herself treated differently on the basis of her race, ethnicity, gender, religion, or some or all of these characteristics. Of chief consideration, according to sociologist Louis Wirth (1945, p. 347), is that membership in a minority "carries with it the exclusion from full participation in the life of the society."

Sociologists generally distinguish between two major overlapping types of minorities: racial minorities and ethnic minorities. A **racial minority** is a social category that suffers social disadvantages because of visible physical characteristics (such as skin color) deemed inferior by the majority group. Racial minorities in the United States include blacks, Asians such as Japanese, Chinese, Korean, and Vietnamese Americans, Hawaiians, and those of East Indian descent. An **ethnic minority** is a social category of people who experience social disadvantages because of cultural characteristics, including traditional customs, which the majority group treats as inferior. There are many ethnic minorities in the United States today. They include Hispanic Americans, such as those of Mexican, Puerto Rican, and Cuban descent, and white ethnics, such as Irish and Jewish Americans.

Minority group status may also result from such diverse factors as gender, sexual preference, age (children and the elderly), and religion. For our purposes, however, we will focus our discussion on two minority issues in particular: race and ethnicity.

PREJUDICE AND DISCRIMINATION

One useful way to begin a discussion of minority relations is to concentrate on the sources of minority group members' unequal life chances in society. Racial and ethnic minorities historically have been denied full and active participation because of three primary factors: prejudice, discrimination, and racism. We will first focus on prejudice and discrimination, and then discuss racism later as a separate topic.

The Nature of Prejudice

Prejudice in general refers to judgment based on preconceived ideas. It is a biased attitude that usually stems from faulty inductive reasoning. To overgeneralize about dozens of things based on an inadequate and unrepresentative group of specific observations is quite easy (see Chapter 1). All of us do this from time to time. People often have prejudices about the best and worst of everything from brands of cars and restaurants to styles of dress. Some people, particularly those with untrained and undisciplined minds, feel that they not only have cornered the market on truth but have an obligation to impose their prejudices on others so that they will be "enlightened" as well.

Sociologists, however, are interested in a special form of **prejudice**, the negative judgment of individuals and groups because of preconceived ideas about them. The prejudiced individual, as social psychologist Gordon Allport (1954, p. 7) puts it, exhibits "an aversive or hostile attitude toward a person who belongs to a group, simply because he belongs to that group, and is therefore presumed to have the objectionable qualities ascribed to that group."

Types of Prejudice. Conflict theorists stress that often those in the majority seek to sustain an atmosphere of hostility toward a minority group as a means of maintaining their superior position. This is accomplished through **exploitative prejudice**, negative attitudes toward minority group members held by the majority group, which serve as justification for keeping them in a subordinate position. This form of prejudice is particularly useful to those with power to establish and sanction social norms. Many of the signers of the Declaration of Independence, for example, were slaveholders and property owners who used slave labor to sustain their economic position. Consequently, it was not in their best interests to condemn slavery. The forced migration of American Indians westward during the 1830s furnishes an additional illustration. The notion that Indians were "heathen savages" accustomed to hardships who could survive as readily on the plains and deserts of the West as they could in the forests of the Southeast served to justify this action of "American" whites. Some sociologists (Davis, Gardner, and Gardner, 1965) argue that these attitudes of superiority by those in power helped to create and reinforce a *caste system* for blacks and other minorities.

Normative prejudice takes the form of negative attitudes towards members of a particular group, which are accepted as "normal" through the process of socialization. Sociologists of the functionalist school maintain that children in practically all cultures are socialized with prejudices about those who comprise their out-groups. These attitudes ultimately become elements of the ethnocentrism most people exhibit. Since people in general tend to lack the sociological imagination, it is tempting for them to accept uncritically the orientations toward people and everything else taught by the family, the peer group, and other agents of socialization. Many if not most white children reared in American culture prior to the 1960s and 1970s were taught as a matter of course that blacks were inferior, women belonged in the home, and homosexuals were abnormal. Particularly in regard to homosexuals, similar deep-seated prejudices are still widespread. Children reared in Iran and Syria today are often taught that Americans are to be distrusted and hated. Consequently, prejudices of this type are built into the structures of institutions and societies. They are culture specific and vary from place to place. They are also subject to change with the passage of time.

Some behavioral scientists take the view that prejudice in some people is linked to deep-seated personality traits developed in childhood. T. W. Adorno and his colleagues (1950) at the University of California at Berkeley concluded from their research that highly prejudiced people may possess what they termed the **authoritarian personality**.

The 1970s show "All in the Family" is still popular in syndication on cable TV. In its many episodes, the main character, Archie Bunker, exhibits normative prejudice toward several different categories of people. His attitudes and actions place him in one humorous and embarrassing misadventure after another. This program portrays bigotry as increasingly inappropriate in a changing society that is striving to become more respectful regarding the rights of minorities. (CBS Photography.)

Using a personality scale designed to measure fascism, the F-scale, they found the authoritarian personality to be a highly rigid and intolerant person who tends to exhibit a group of identifiable personality characteristics. These include an oversimplistic view of reality in which almost everything is neatly compartmentalized into dichotomies of good or bad, black or white, us or them. As a child, this person tends to have extremely authoritarian parents who punish harshly, often at the slightest deviation from the ''proper way.'' The child, because of intimidation, develops a submissive attitude toward authority figures,

which carries over into adulthood. This person may also have unresolved anger, which is aimed at those who are different and less fortunate (Pettigrew, 1980). Authoritarian personalities tend to focus this anger on minorities and, when placed in positions of responsibility over others, can be very punitive. This makes them feel important and, for the moment, adequate.

These three types of prejudice often overlap and, therefore, are not mutually exclusive. The development of an authoritarian personality, for instance, is facilitated by a cultural climate in which the structural characteristics of society encourage certain forms of normative prejudice. The Ku Klux Klan, an extremist organization that contains an abundance of authoritarian personalities, developed historically in the deep South where the cultural climate encouraged prejudice towards blacks.

Stereotypes. Regardless of type, however, those with prejudices usually make use of **stereotypes**, fixed mental images about the characteristics of entire categories of people that are not tested against reality. As illustrated in Figure 9-1, these images form much of the content of prejudice. Some common examples of stereotypical thinking about racial and ethnic minorities and others are listed as follows: Mexicans are lazy, blacks have rhythm, Southerners are slow, athletes are dumb, male homosexuals are effeminate, old folks are senile, Jews are stingy. While certainly some individuals in these categories have the characteristics described, so does a percentage of the general population. To label everyone in terms of exaggerated negative characteristics is to distort reality. Nonetheless, stereotypical perceptions are often used as a rationale for unequal treatment.

The Nature of Discrimination

Whereas prejudice is a judgmental attitude, **discrimination** refers to differential treatment of people based on their membership in a particular social category. Applied to minorities, differential treatment at the hands of the majority group is negative and often based on prejudice. When established as a pattern, discrimination acts to reduce life chances for the group affected. The resulting deprivation, once visible, reinforces the prejudice that the minority group is inferior. This in turn breeds further discrimination, and the circle is complete. According to Robert MacIver (1948), discrimination thus feeds on itself in a vicious cycle which he illustrates as follows:

discrimination──────→lower income level──────→lower standards of living──────→lower education──────→lower earning capacity──────→discrimination (p. 64).

Types of Discrimination. Discrimination takes two basic forms. **Individual discrimination** results when individuals belonging to one group treat members of another group differently because of their group membership. A landlord who refuses to rent apartments to people of Iranian or Mexican descent is an example. **Institutional discrimination** involves unequal treatment of certain categories of people as a result of inequities built into basic institutions. The norms and values of the majority group take precedence over those of minorities in areas such as law, politics, education, business, and general customs. Blacks, for example, were not allowed to vote in the United States until the 1860s, and American Indians and women did not gain suffrage until the 1920s. While discrimination like this is direct and intentional, it sometimes takes indirect and often unintentional forms. The results, however, are the same. A case in point is the minimum height requirement for police officers used by the Chicago Police Department during the 1960s. This had the effect of discriminating against otherwise qualified Puerto Ricans who, as a group, are shorter than white and black Americans. The height requirements were later changed in the wake of riots in the Puerto Rican community in 1966, which included charges of police brutality. As a result, Puerto Ricans were then able to enter the field of law enforcement, and police and community relations were improved (Schaefer, 1985).

A controversial issue in recent years has been the charge, made primarily by some white males, of **reverse discrimination**. Reverse discrimination, it is alleged, occurs when individuals are given less than equal treatment because they belong to the dominant or ma-

Figure 9-1 Common Stereotypes

Blacks	Chinese	Hispanics	Italians
Great athletes	Sly, sinister, deceitful	Big on machismo	Stupid, ignorant
Sexual prowess	Learned, wise	Lazy	Distrust education
Stupid	Love to gamble	Refuse to learn English	Great singers
Musically gifted	Cruel	Don't value education	Talk with hands
Great rhythm	Strong family ties	Warm, emotional	Belong to the Mafia
Lazy, shiftless	Quiet, polite	Violent, hot-tempered	Cowards in battle
Violent criminals	Deferential	Don't mind using welfare	Great shoemakers

Irish	Japanese	Jews	Poles
Heavy drinkers	Chauvinistic	Cheap	Dumb
Good at politics	Hardworking, ambitious	Shrewd businessmen	Dirty
Sexually repressed	The "sneaky Jap"	Control Wall Street and the	Racists, bigots
Very religious	Great imitators	banks	Uneducated
Highly nationalistic	Law abiding	Pushy, aggressive	Boorish, uncultured,
Witty, gregarious	Educated, intelligent	Rich, ostentatious	low class
The "fighting Irish"		Have big noses	

Source: Excerpted with permission from Helmreich, W. B. (1982). *The things they say behind your back.* New York: Doubleday.

jority group. *Affirmative action* programs mandated by the U.S. government have provoked much of the controversy, and several lawsuits have been filed and decided by the courts. The aim of affirmative action is that organizations actively seek minority applicants for employment and use their minority status as one factor in selection. If, for example, two applicants applied for a position, and, in all other respects, their qualifications were about equal, the minority applicant would be given preference. The purpose of such a policy is to attempt to correct historical discrimination and bring minorities, as they acquire the necessary credentials, into the mainstream of society. There have been isolated cases of reverse discrimination in which affirmative action guidelines have been misinterpreted or abused by officials who employed or placed people largely or solely because of their minority membership. However, a systematic, society-wide effort to deny equal opportunity to the majority group in general, and white males in particular, simply has not occurred.

The Relationship between Prejudice and Discrimination

Prejudicial attitudes and discriminatory behavior are closely associated with each other in that prejudice often serves as the basis for discrimination and vice versa. The relationship between the two, however, is not so easily explained in some instances. Some people are prejudiced but do not discriminate, while others discriminate in ways that have little if anything to do with prejudice. In an attempt at clarification, Robert Merton (1976) has identified four ways the two concepts relate to each other:

1. *Unprejudiced nondiscrimination* involves "all-weather liberals" opposed to both prejudice and discrimination who consistently act on their principles in various social situations.

2. *Unprejudiced discrimination* is carried out by "fair-weather liberals" who, although not prejudiced themselves, will discriminate and support discrimination by others for practical gain. Although these people sometimes talk about being progressive in certain circles, they will not jeopardize business profits, reputation, or votes if pressure to discriminate is strong.

3. *Prejudiced nondiscrimination* involves "fair-weather bigots," who reluctantly engage in equal treatment of groups they dislike because of social pressure to do so. Both federal laws and recent Supreme Court decisions reaffirming such laws have made the practice of discrimination illegal in the United States.

4. *Prejudiced discrimination* is carried out by "all-weather bigots" who consistently discriminate against groups they dislike because of principles they subscribe to based on prejudice.

RACE AND RACISM

The Nature of Race

Race can be a confusing concept that often means different things to different people. Even scientists use this term in different ways.

Race as a Biological Concept. From a biological perspective, *race* refers to a social category of people (of both sexes and all age groups) with certain visible physical characteristics in common that are genetically inherited and passed on to future generations. There are numerous racial groups (called stocks or strains) throughout the world, with varying physical characteristics. Yet scientists do not agree on how many such groups exist in the world or how they should be classified. No matter what "identifiable physical characteristics" are used as criteria—skin pigmentation, hair texture, facial features, blood type—different numbers and types of "races" appear.

The three commonly used racial categories are Caucasian (fair skin/straight or wavy hair), Mongoloid (yellow to brown skin/epicanthic eye folds), and Negroid (dark skin/wooly hair) (Kroeber, 1948). As shown in Figure 9-2, the contradictions and problems in even this most general classification scheme are readily apparent. Many East Indian Hindus have Caucasian facial features, and straight hair but

Figure 9-2 **Three Major Racial Categories**

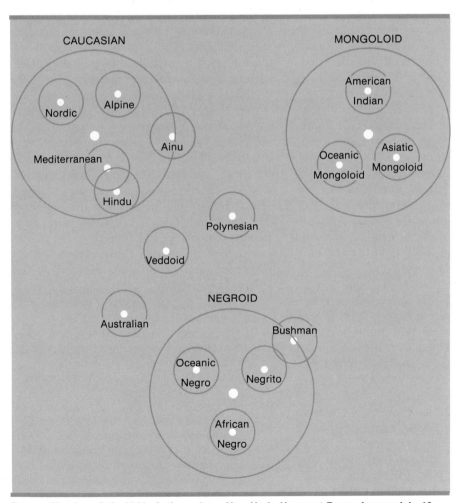

Source: Kroeber, A. L. 1948. *Anthropology.* New York: Harcourt Brace Jovanovich, 10.

dark skin like Negroes. Bushmen are classified as Negroid but have some Mongoloid features, including epicanthic folds under the eyes and light yellow-brown skin. The Polynesians of the South Pacific and the Aboriginals of Australia have so many contradictory characteristics that they cannot be placed into any of the three general categories.

Add to this complication the difficulty raised by intermarriage (and thus interbreeding) between so-called races. In the United States today, for instance, about 80 percent of black Americans have white ancestry, at least 50 percent of Mexican Americans have both Indian (Native American) and white ancestry, and approximately 20 percent of white Americans have either African or Indian ancestry (Stuckert, 1976).

Because of these considerations, the biological concept of race as a "pure type" is regarded as a social myth and is of little or no value to science (Montagu, 1972). Although physical "racial" differences do exist among humans, they are largely superficial and, by themselves, play no significant role in shaping either intellectual potential or social behavior. We are all of one species, *Homo sapiens,* and racial differences per se are of little or no consequence.

Race as a Sociological Concept. What is important about "race," however, is how various individuals, groups, and cultures perceive it. This social meaning is of particular interest to sociologists. From a sociological perspective, **race** refers to a social category of people (of both sexes and all age groups) perceived and treated in a distinct manner on the basis of certain visible physical characteristics. It represents a social invention used to assign meaning and value to people on the basis of "racial" differences (van den Berghe, 1978).

Members of one race often see themselves as distinct from others. They assume that their physical traits are related to their intellectual ability and social fortunes, whether they be high or low, positive or negative. They expect to be treated a certain way by virtue of their race and are treated as expected in many if not most cases.

The race of the majority group is often seen as superior to others, along with the lifestyle or ethnicity that goes with it. Other races and their life-styles are similarly defined as inferior in varying degrees. To some extent, the culture of the "majority" race is socialized into all offspring, including those of racial minorities. Because race and minority membership are ascribed, children of minorities are often left with a negative image of themselves because they cannot become members of the dominant racial group.

When race is equated with expectations of success or failure, privilege or hardship, and self-worth versus self-deprecation, it can have a very negative impact on the self-image of minority children. In his autobiography *Nigger,* comedian and author Dick Gregory (1967) relates what it was like growing up in the inner city of St. Louis during the 1940s. Being poor, black, and fatherless, his experiences were not unlike those experienced by many poor and minority children today.

> I never learned hate or shame at home. I had to go to school for that. I was about seven years old when I got my first big lesson . . . [and] learned to be ashamed of myself. It was on a Thursday. I was sitting in the back of the room, in a seat with a chalk circle drawn around it. The idiot's seat, the troublemaker's seat.
>
> The teacher thought I was stupid. Couldn't spell, couldn't read, couldn't do arithmetic. Just stupid. Teachers were never interested in finding out that you couldn't concentrate because you were so hungry, because you hadn't had any breakfast. All you could think about was noontime, would it ever come? Maybe you could sneak into the cloakroom and steal

a bite of some kid's lunch out of a coat pocket. A bite of something. Paste. You can't really make a meal of paste . . . but sometimes I'd scoop a few spoonfuls out of the paste jar in the back of the room. Pregnant people get strange tastes. I was pregnant with poverty. Pregnant with dirt and pregnant with smells that made people turn away, pregnant with cold and pregnant with shoes that were never bought for me, pregnant with five other people in my bed and no Daddy in the next room, and pregnant with hunger. Paste doesn't taste too bad when you're hungry.

The teacher thought I was a troublemaker. All she saw . . . was a little black boy who squirmed in his idiot's seat and made noises and poked the kids around him. I guess she couldn't see a kid who made noises because he wanted someone to know he was there (pp. 29–30).

The Nature of Racism

When an awareness of racial differences includes a higher value placed on membership in one racial group as compared to another, then racism occurs. **Racism** is a doctrine (and acts stemming from it) which holds that one racial category is superior and all others, in varying degrees, are inferior. It thus includes both prejudice and discrimination. The dominant or majority group benefits in several ways from such an ideology (Nash, 1962). First, racism serves as a convenient moral justification for unequal treatment of a minority. Second, a racist doctrine, once institutionalized, is often viewed as normal by everyone, including oppressed minorities. This, in turn, acts to discourage them from questioning the "system." Finally, racial mythology tries to justify itself on the grounds that members of the "inferior race," being untalented and helpless people, would be much worse off if major social changes occurred.

The historical treatment of blacks in Amer-

ica serves as a classic example of racism put into practice. During the summers of 1966 and 1967, racial unrest spread across America in a wave of riots and civil disturbances involving blacks and whites in dozens of cities. In places like Tampa, Atlanta, Newark, and Chicago, many black communities erupted in violence that resulted in looting, arson, assault, and several deaths. By the end of July 1967, President Lyndon Johnson had appointed a Commission on Civil Disorders to find the causes of these upheavals that were splitting the country into two polarized camps, one black and the other white. This is a brief excerpt summarizing the commission's findings:

> [T]he single overriding cause of rioting in the cities was not any one thing commonly adduced—unemployment, lack of education, poverty, exploitation—but . . . was all of these things and more, expressed in the insidious and pervasive white sense of the inferiority of black men. Here is the essence of the charge: "What white Americans have never fully understood—but what the Negro can never forget—is that white society is deeply implicated in the ghetto. White institutions created it, white institutions maintain it, and white society condones it" (*Report of the National Advisory Commission on Civil Disorders,* 1968, p.vii).

The Origins of Racism in America. To trace the roots of racism leading to the unrest of the 1960s, one must examine the early American experience. The first blacks were brought to the Jamestown settlement in Virginia in 1619 as indentured servants. By the 1660s, however, black slavery was becoming sanctioned by law and by 1700 had replaced indentured servitude as the primary source of cheap agricultural labor in the colonies (Quarles, 1969).

Slavery was justified by a doctrine of racial supremacy that consisted of several arguments. One was a biblical justification quoting various passages from the scriptures, including the Genesis account of Noah's curse on Canaan, which allegedly gave slavery God's sanction (Lincoln, 1968). A second defined the Negro as a subhuman, depraved beast. A third and somewhat more benign approach portrayed blacks as half-pathetic, half-comical creatures, simple-minded children requiring constant supervision.

This last attitude toward the Negro became the basis for a stereotypical view of black people that carried over well into the twentieth century. The following is fairly representative of the view of blacks offered by Thomas Dixon's racist novel *Leopard Spots* (1902) and other literary material of the early twentieth century:

> The Negro is an amoral creature . . . unable to discriminate between right and wrong. The power to make a free and intelligent moral choice has been denied to him by his Creator, leaving him a permanent cripple in the evolutionary struggle for existence. At his best he is a good child, for whom one may feel a genuine affection . . . akin to the love of a master for a loyal dog. But just as a dog must be told what to do if he is to be of any use in a human society, so the Negro must be guided and controlled by his Anglo-Saxon superiors, on whose shoulders rests the burden of civilizing him, so far as his limited capacities will permit (quoted in Bloomfield, 1970, p. 118).

Even as late as the 1940s, popular literature and motion pictures used images like Stepin Fetchit, a black movie character, to depict blacks as having rolling eyes, a shuffling gait, a whiny voice, and experiencing a never-ending series of predicaments brought on by simple-mindedness.

Racism and the Use of IQ Tests. By the 1930s and 1940s, some forms of racism were much more subtle and indirect. An example is the manner in which IQ tests were used and in-

terpreted. Although IQ tests were never designed with racist intentions, their use and abuse has had a discriminatory and stigmatizing effect on minority children and white children from lower socioeconomic backgrounds. In addition, supporters of white supremacy have used IQ test scores of minority children as "evidence" for racially biased arguments.

Psychological tests to measure intelligence or IQ (intelligence quotient) have been used

Movie characters like Stepin Fetchit in the 1940s portrayed blacks as simpleminded and in constant need of supervision by their white "superiors." (Culver Pictures, Inc.)

in various applications—the military, education, industry, law—since the early part of the twentieth century. Traditionally, IQ tests have been structured according to the pattern established by L. L. Thurstone (1938) to measure ability in three broad areas: verbal skills, spatial skills, and logical skills. IQ tests, such as the Stanford-Binet and Wechsler, have been administered to several generations of American school children and have been shown to be good predictors of academic success (McCall, 1975).

The extensive use of IQ tests, however, has been highly controversial in recent years and has been criticized as invalid in assessing the abilities of minority children and those from lower socioeconomic backgrounds. Such children, including blacks and Hispanics, who historically have scored 10 to 15 points behind white middle-class children, also have not done as well in school.

The term "IQ" or "intelligence test" is misleading because it implies that what is being measured is innate learning capacity. In truth, behavioral scientists are not in agreement as to precisely what intelligence is. Some see it as "adaptability," others "specific skills," and still others "scholastic aptitude" (Haber and Runyon, 1974). At best, IQ tests are imprecise measures of certain narrowly defined skills or abilities. Even these have not been measured directly but have been inferred from the behavior (scores) of children taking the tests. In partial recognition of this lack of clarity, a panel of experts appointed by the American Psychological Association's Board of Scientific Affairs in 1975 stated that IQ and other psychological tests "do not prove or disprove anyone's capacity to learn" (Roediger et al., 1984, p. 361).

In particular, the verbal and analogy sections of standardized IQ tests have been criticized for being culturally biased and representing little more than socialization keyed to a white middle-class cultural model. Many minority children and poor whites cannot be expected to "know" that cup goes with saucer, symphony with composer, or that silence is the "appropriate behavior" in church (Havighurst and Neugarten, 1967; Vander Zanden, 1972). These things are not part of their cultural experience.

As a result of such test scores, an untold number of minority and poor children have been perceived as slow learners and tracked accordingly. Consequently, some teachers have exhibited a tendency to expend less time and energy on them than on "normal IQ" and "high IQ" children with more "potential." These children also have been more likely than their white middle-class counterparts to wear the label "mentally retarded" and to be placed in special education programs (Beeghley and Butler, 1974). At the same time, ironically, children of interracial and black parentage adopted by white middle-class couples with above average education, income, and IQs consistently score 10 points above the national IQ average and 20 points above that of black children raised in poverty (Scarr and Weinburg, 1976).

Types of Racism. There are two basic forms of racism. **Individual racism** occurs when ideas and actions based on a doctrine of racial inequality are applied to members of one racial category by members of another. The individual racist may do little more than talk, gossip, or joke about members of the "inferior race" with friends of like mind. However, sometimes the individual may put these attitudes into action, as in the case of the manager who tries earnestly to hire as few members of certain racial groups as possible. **Institutional racism**, by comparison, results when ideas and actions based on a doctrine of racial inequality are built into the structure of such basic institutions as government, education, and the economic system. This very specific form of institutional discrimination may take several forms. The traditional practice of "ability grouping" and tracking minority children in school, based in large part on IQ test scores, might be considered one example. The apartheid policy practiced by the South African government, separating neighborhoods into "white," "black," and "colored," is another.

RACIAL MINORITIES

Black Americans

The largest racial minority in the United States consists of black Americans who, as of 1986, numbered 30 million and accounted for 12 percent of the total population. The black experience in this country is rooted in slavery, which lasted for more than two hundred years. The period of what has been called "the peculiar institution" might have been much shorter had Thomas Jefferson had his way. When Jefferson wrote the first draft of the Declaration of Independence in Philadelphia during June of 1776, he included a paragraph denouncing the slave trade and slavery, which was blamed on King George III (England was the primary slave trafficker). If retained, this clause would have established a foundation for emancipating the slaves. Jefferson already had a plan for this called "the Jeffersonian solution." However, the Continental Congress deleted that paragraph in the final draft (Lincoln, 1968).

In the aftermath of the Civil War (1861-1865), the Thirteenth, Fourteenth, and Fifteenth amendments to the Constitution abolished slavery and gave blacks citizenship and voting rights. Many of these freedoms were short-lived, however. The Ku Klux Klan, a white supremacist organization, brutalized black communities from the middle 1860s through the late 1870s in an attempt to keep blacks from voting and engaging in other forms of participation in "white" society. During this period, assaults, murders, and nightly cross burnings were relatively common. In a backlash of institutional racism, several Southern states began passing **Jim Crow laws** (named after a blackface minstrel dancer). These statutes denied blacks access to public facilities such as restaurants, railroad cars reserved for "whites," restrooms, and drinking fountains.

The Jim Crow policy was upheld in 1896 by the U.S. Supreme Court in *Plessy v. Ferguson*, which stated that "separate but equal" facilities for blacks was reasonable accommodation for their needs (Woodward, 1974). This ruling ushered in a sixty-year period of legally sanctioned racial segregation in which blacks sat in the back of buses, prayed in separate churches, attended separate schools, and were set apart from white society in practically all respects. The Supreme Court finally set this policy aside in 1954 in *Brown v. the Board of Education*, which overturned the "separate but equal" doctrine as it applied to school facilities. This, in part, helped set the stage for the civil rights movement of the 1960s.

In the wake of such events as the march to Selma and Dr. Martin Luther King, Jr.'s "I Have a Dream" speech in the 1960s, many changes have come for black Americans, some very positive and others not so positive. Ground-breaking federal legislation, including the Civil Rights Act of 1964, accompanied by vigorous enforcement of desegregation laws, has reduced segregation in many communities. Federal programs in the areas of education, occupational training, housing, and urban renewal have created unprecedented opportunities not only for blacks, but for other minorities as well (Farley, 1977, 1984). Re-

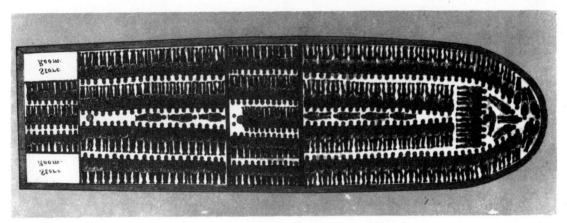

For Portuguese, English, and Dutch merchants and ship owners during the 1600s and 1700s, the African slave trade was a lucrative business. As shown in the print above, most slavers were "tight packers" who tried to cram as many slaves as possible into the holds of their ships to maximize profits. Forced to lie side by side in their own excrement with only two feet or so of crawl space, one out of every eight slaves died during the fifty days it took to make the Atlantic passage. (The Bettmann Archive.)

search indicates that attitudes in the white community have changed and that both prejudice and discrimination have declined (Farley, 1977, 1984). During the last half century, the black middle class has risen from less than 10 percent of the total black population in 1940 to 40 percent today. And the number of elected black officials—including members of Congress and mayors of several major cities— has increased to nearly 7,000 as compared to less than 100 before 1955 (Gelman et al., 1988).

Despite the rise of the black middle class and an apparent decline of "race" as an important social concept to most Americans, there are still major problems in the black community. Racism in both thought and deed still occurs, and some forms of artificial segregation and denied opportunity still exist. However, the challenge today and in the future for both the black community and Amer-

ican society as a whole has more to do with class than race (Wilson and Aponte, 1985). Largely because of the civil rights movement and the enabling legislation and governmental policies that resulted, blacks and other minorities with college degrees and specialized occupational skills are increasingly able to compete favorably with whites for middle-class jobs. Those in the ghettos and barrios, however, are not able to compete, and the poverty gap between blacks and whites seems to be widening. Families headed by women with children under eighteen serve as a good illustration, since women workers are paid less and are thus more likely to live in poverty. By the middle 1980s, 41 percent of all black families were headed by women, compared to about 13 percent of white families (U.S. Bureau of the Census, November 1985). Overall, taking into consideration indicators such as the lack of education and technical job

Today the black middle class is a growing phenomenon that accounts for 40 percent of the black population. (Copyright Elyse Lewin/The Image Bank.)

skills, black families were receiving only 57 percent of the income received by white families.

Among the poor living in urban ghettos, teenage pregnancy is at the very center of the poverty cycle.

> "A lot of the so-called feminization of poverty starts off with teenagers having babies," says Lucille Dismukes of the Council on Maternal and Infant Health in Atlanta, a state advisory group. "So many can't rise above it to go back to school or get job skills." . . . Nearly half of black females in the U. S. are pregnant by age 20. The pregnancy rate among those 15 to 19 is almost twice what it is among whites. Worse still, nearly 90% of the babies born to

blacks in this age group are born out of wedlock; most are raised in fatherless homes with little economic opportunity. "When you look at the numbers, teenage pregnancies are of cosmic danger to the black community," declares Eleanor Holmes Norton, law professor at Georgetown University and a leading black scholar. "Teenage pregnancy ranks near the very top of issues facing black people" (Wallis, 1985, pp. 79–80).

Factors such as teenage pregnancy, coupled with lack of opportunity because of residual racism, low education, and the lack of job skills, create a vicious cycle that poor blacks find difficult to break. Consequently, black Americans as a whole have made tremendous strides since the 1950s, but several social conditions require change before they will be able to participate on a par with those in the majority group.

Native Americans

American Indians, or Native Americans, were the first to settle in North America and also the first to be dominated and placed in a minority position by European immigrants. It is estimated that in the year 1500 there were approximately 12 to 15 million Indians north of the Rio Grande. They were divided into so many different tribal groups that approximately 300 languages were spoken. By 1850, however, they numbered only about 250,000, decimated by a loss of food supply and exposure to such "white man's diseases" as influenza, measles, and smallpox (Schaefer, 1988). Today, American Indians number about 1.5 million, divided into eighty-nine major tribal groups (*The World Almanac and Book of Facts, 1988*). According to the Bureau of Indian Affairs, the number of Native Americans in 1985 within states with federal reservations ranged from 745 people in Iowa (one reservation) to 166,330 in Arizona (twenty reservations).

At first, these original Americans were seen by many European colonists as "noble savages," well meaning but ignorant in the ways of civilization. Early missionaries, after some contact with Indian groups, declared that these native inhabitants of the New World "were the Ten Lost Tribes of Israel" (Deloria, 1970; p. 13). Even today, children in elementary schools are told stories—partly mythical and highly romanticized—of Squanto and the Pilgrims and how the Indians and the first white settlers shared in the feast at the first Thanksgiving in a spirit of mutual goodwill. However, by the eighteenth century, Native Americans—who had their own strongly held cultures and ethnocentric pride and who wanted nothing of the white man's civilization, including his religion—had been redefined by many in the majority group as beasts.

As European settlers demanded more and more territory for permanent settlement that had been used by Native Americans for centuries, confrontations between the two groups escalated and became increasingly hostile. The English authorities responded in the 1750s by declaring members of certain Indian tribes vermin by official proclamation and calling for their extermination.

It was the English and not the Indians, as commonly portrayed in nineteenth-century American literature and twentieth-century motion pictures, who introduced scalping to America. In 1755, for example, a proclamation was issued at Boston sanctioned by King George II which called for all Penobscot Indians to be destroyed and a bounty of forty pounds each to be paid for the scalps of all adult males and twenty pounds for the scalps of all females and children under twelve years (Deloria, 1970).

Yet, at the same time, some Indian groups were highly respected by the colonists. The Iroquois, for instance, consisted of a league of six tribes—the Cayuga, Mohawk, Oneida, Onondaga, Seneca, and Tuscarora—which, collectively, were regarded as very civilized. Portions of their system of government served as a model for some provisions incorporated into the U.S. Constitution. For example, the method used by a joint Senate-House conference committee to arrive at a compromise bill from separate bills passed in each house is based on an Iroquois concept (Parrillo, 1985).

With the formation of the United States and the end of English rule, Native Americans as a group did not fare well during the nineteenth and early twentieth centuries. Under the onslaught of western expansion and the demand for Indian territory, the U.S. government entered into treaties with various tribes for the settlement of their lands. However, many of these treaties were broken by the government, and the pressure to move from one reservation to another, sometimes with the threat of force, destroyed much of the traditional culture and food sources of many tribes. In 1871 the government ceased to make treaties with the Indians and made them wards of the government under the administration of the Bureau of Indian Affairs (BIA). The BIA did little on the Indians' behalf, and they were left basically to their own meager resources. The destruction of the buffalo by American sportsmen and hide hunters, for example, pushed the Plains Indian tribes to the brink of starvation. Some tribes reacted with violence and fought back in numerous encounters with settlers and U. S. military forces, but to no avail.

Today, Indians represent the poorest of all American minorities. Not granted full citizenship until 1924, they have suffered under many confusing and often contradictory shifts in government policy throughout the twentieth century. Most of these policies have not helped them to better their social and economic position. Indicators of poor life chances abound. Overall, 38 percent live below the poverty line and, on reservations, the figure is 48 percent. Fifty-five percent of those on reservations live in substandard housing, 70 percent must haul drinking water at least a mile to their homes, and 58 percent of their children receive less than an eighth grade education (Vander Zanden, 1983).

Nonetheless, some improvements are being made, most notably the development of what sociologist Richard T. Schaefer (1988) calls pan-Indianism. Similar in many respects to the political organization of blacks during the civil rights movement of the 1960s, **pan-Indianism** involves attempts by Indian groups to develop coalitions between several tribes to deal effectively with common problems. One perceived common problem is the insensitivity of the federal government, which, many Indians feel, treats them and their tribes as captive colonies. The most successful of the pan-Indian groups in recent years has been the Council of Energy Resource Tribes (CERT). By 1986 CERT had membership and representation from forty-two tribes. This coalition was able to negotiate a deal for the Navajos with Atlantic Ritchfield Company (ARCO) regarding gas and oil, which should bring in $78 million in revenues over a twenty-year period. If pan-Indianism is to grow into a consistent social force, the many fragmented and isolated Indian tribes must overcome their differences and mutual distrust of each other and learn to work together as a force for social change.

Asian Americans

In 1985 slightly more than 5 million Asian Americans lived within the United States. They represented several countries and regions, most notably Japan, China, the Philippines, Korea, India, and Southeast Asia (Gardner et al., 1985).

The first immigrants from Asia came in the nineteenth century, predominantly from China and Japan. As late as 1970, almost three-quarters of all Asian Americans were from these two countries. However, with the dramatic influx of Filipinos, Koreans, East Indians, and Vietnamese in recent years, those of Japanese and Chinese descent now constitute only about one-third of all Asian Americans.

Chinese Americans. The first Asians to emigrate to the United States were the Chinese who came to California in the 1840s to escape economic problems and social unrest in their own country (Kitano, 1985). At first these new inhabitants were accepted because they helped to alleviate an acute labor shortage in menial occupations. During the gold rush days of 1849 and 1850, there was a severe scarcity of women who traditionally did the cooking, laundry, and other domestic chores. Although most Chinese immigrants were male, they were glad to do this work. They also worked as laborers in the mines and, later, on the railroads.

As more and more Chinese came to the West Coast over the next three decades—at least 300,000 by 1880—their numbers, coupled with their racial and cultural characteristics, resulted in tremendous anti-Chinese sentiment. Chinese were subject to scorn and racial slurs; many were beaten and killed, and most ultimately retreated to segregated communities called "Chinatowns." Californians and, later, leaders in Congress were so fearful of unchecked Chinese immigration—often called the Yellow Peril—that Congress passed the Chinese Exclusion Act in 1882, which banned further immigration for ten years. This exclusion was later made permanent and was not repealed until World War II.

Japanese Americans. The immigration patterns of those who came to this country from Japan have been somewhat different. When

Because of a combination of war hysteria and racial bigotry, 110,000 persons of Japanese descent, most of whom were American citizens, were forcibly relocated in 1942 to the American version of "concentration camps." Once relocated, they remained in these camps for the duration of World War II. Today, greater opportunities coupled with a strong work ethic have resulted in Japanese Americans and others of Asian descent becoming among the most upwardly mobile of minority groups. (*Japanese detainees*, Culver Pictures, Inc. *Students*, Susan Lapides/Design Conceptions.)

the Japanese government ended its 200-year-old-prohibition against foreign travel in 1865, some Japanese citizens began to emigrate to the United States. However, significant numbers did not arrive before 1900 (Parrillo, 1980). Unlike the Chinese who came—almost exclusively males—the Japanese came as married couples. Once in the United States, they established families and tried to assimilate into American society. In addition, since jobs were difficult to obtain in the large cities and union members considered Asians a threat because they would work for lower wages, most Japanese Americans settled in rural outlying areas. There they worked on farms, and some ultimately became successful tenant farmers and small farm owners.

U.S. policy changed, however, on December 7, 1941, when the Japanese bombed American naval installations at Pearl Harbor.

The resulting war hysteria—many Americans feared a Japanese land invasion at California—resulted in the classification of Japanese Americans as a possible threat to national security. Consequently, 110,000 people of Japanese descent, 70,000 of whom were native-born American citizens, were uprooted from their homes and businesses and relocated to detention camps in other states. There they remained for the duration of the war. They lost their homes and farms, and were not paid reparations after the war. In an ironic twist, the most highly decorated allied fighting unit in the European theater of World War II was the 442d Regimental Combat Team, a unit of Japanese American soldiers.

In August of 1988, forty-three years after the end of the war, President Ronald Reagan signed into law a bill designed to make reparations to the survivors of the forced imprisonment. Under this legislation, the U.S. government agreed to pay each of the estimated 62,000 Japanese American detainees still alive a reparation payment of $20,000.

Asian Americans Today. In recent years, Asian immigrants have come in large numbers from Indochina, a region in Southeast Asia. During the decade following the fall of South Vietnam in 1975, more than 840,000 immigrants, mainly refugees, came to the United States from countries including Vietnam, Laos, and Thailand (Rumbaut, 1986). A large number have also immigrated from the Philippines.

Since the end of World War II, Asian Americans have become increasingly successful. Their families are typically tight-knit and stress self-discipline, hard work, and appreciation of education as the primary means of upward mobility. Because of these values, Asian Americans, including more recent arrivals from the Philippines and Indochina, are among America's most successful minority groups. Japanese Americans, for example, have a higher per capita income than any other racial minority (Wilson and Hosokawa, 1980). Asian students are more likely to take college preparatory classes in math and science while in high school, devote more time to study, and are overrepresented in the freshman classes at the nation's leading universities, in comparison with other Americans (Zigli, 1984; Butterfield, 1986).

ETHNICITY AND ETHNIC MINORITIES

The Nature of Ethnicity

Ethnicity refers to the specific cultural heritage that distinguishes one social category of people from others. In some societies, almost all inhabitants share essentially the same eth-

nicity. By comparison, the United States is a pluralistic society with citizens from dozens of different ethnic backgrounds. Nonetheless, those of European heritage, and particularly those of Anglo-Saxon descent, comprise the dominant or majority group today and have dominated both law and custom throughout American history. As a result, those with different ethnic backgrounds have been viewed as out-groups and have often been denied equal life chances. Thus, several groups have become *ethnic minorities* that are regarded differently and treated unequally because of their cultural characteristics (including traditional customs).

It should be mentioned that racial minorities, as previously discussed, also have a distinct ethnicity. However, the source of their unequal treatment has more to do with their visible physical characteristics than distinctive cultural attributes. The relocation of Japanese Americans into detention camps serves as a good example. The United States during World War II was at war with the Axis Pact, which included Germany and Italy as well as Japan. While it is true that many German and Italian Americans were harassed during this time and some Muellers became Millers and a few DiBennedettos changed their names to Bennett, there was no serious attempt to systematically quarantine these Caucasian people. Only the Japanese Americans, because of their racial visibility, were perceived as potential enemies requiring relocation and detention.

Nonetheless, several ethnic minorities have been regarded and treated differently because of their cultural characteristics. A brief discussion of some of these groups follows.

Hispanics

Today, there are over 17 million Spanish-speaking people in the United States. They comprise 7 percent of the total population.

Hispanics represent a diverse group of people whose origins are such places as Mexico, Puerto Rico, Cuba, and various Central and South American countries. They share, however, certain characteristics including language, the Roman Catholic faith, and strong ethnic identification. Today, mainly as a result of high rates of fertility and immigration, they represent one of the fastest-growing minorities and, if current trends continue, could surpass blacks as the largest minority by shortly after the end of this century (Church, 1985). Many Hispanics live in large cities like Los Angeles, Houston, and Miami, and most are concentrated in only two states, California and Texas. Arizona, New Mexico, New York, and Florida also have large Spanish-speaking populations.

Mexican Americans. The 11 million Mexican Americans, or Chicanos, represent the largest Hispanic group in the United States. This estimate, however, does not fully account for illegal immigrants from Mexico who may number millions more. Those of Spanish descent first migrated to what is now the American Southwest in the 1500s. One-time isolated Spanish missions designed to bring Christianity to various Indian groups later became settlements of significant size devoted to agriculture. When Mexico ceded one-third of its territory to the United States in 1848 following the Mexican-American War, many Mexican citizens suddenly found themselves living in the United States. Following political and economic unrest in Mexico during the late 1800s and early 1900s, many Mexicans came to America as agricultural workers or *braceros*, who were in high demand because they accepted low wages.

During the twentieth century, unstable political and economic conditions in Mexico, particularly in the last few decades, have produced a flood of illegal immigrants desperate to earn even a subsistence living. Both these

people and those of Mexican descent who are citizens have faced many problems, including the language barrier and economic and social discrimination. For example, until the 1960s, it was not uncommon for Mexican Americans to be denied service at restaurants and other businesses owned by Anglo Americans.

Since the 1960s, however, the Chicano political movement has helped to make Mexican Americans a more viable political force. Leaders include Cesar Chavez, who organized Mexican migrant farm workers in the early 1960s, and Henry Cisneros, former mayor of San Antonio who by the late 1980s had gained a national following. Mexican American and other Hispanic school children who twenty years ago were not allowed to speak Spanish on school property now have bilingual education to help them acquire formal learning more easily. Nonetheless, Mexican Americans remain far behind other Americans in terms of life chances. Almost 30 percent of all Chicanos live below the poverty line. Their plight is related to the facts that (1) many speak little or no English and (2) the majority do not finish high school.

Puerto Ricans. Governed by Spain for several hundred years, Puerto Rico was ceded to the United States in 1898 as a result of the Spanish American War. At first there was little migration of these new Americans to the mainland even after they were granted citizenship in 1917. However, the collapse of the sugar industry after World War II coupled with such factors as low airline fares and the promise of jobs triggered one of the largest voluntary migrations in recent history. During the 1950s, one-half million Puerto Ricans—one out of every six—left their native land and came to the mainland, most initially settling in New York City (Kitano, 1985). Because the majority were unskilled, poorly educated, and faced problems such as the language barrier and discrimination by labor unions, in housing, and in other areas, most were relegated to an underclass position.

Although increased opportunities in recent decades have made it possible for a larger number of Puerto Ricans to join the middle class, serious problems remain. Puerto Ricans, most of whom today live in New York and surrounding states, have problems similar to those of Mexican Americans. Fewer than one-half finish high school. As a result of this and other factors, they have the highest unemployment rate among all Hispanics, and 43 percent live below the poverty line (Parrillo, 1985; U.S. Bureau of the Census, 1986 A).

Cubans. Of all Hispanics, Cubans are closest to the American mainstream in annual family income and life chances. The majority—almost 800,000—came to the United States after 1959 to escape communism under Fidel Castro. Once here, they settled mainly in Miami, New York, and other major cities. Most of these people and their descendants are middle class, many with technical skills or college degrees (Parrillo, 1985; U.S. Bureau of the Census, 1986 B).

Although Cubans have faced both prejudice and discrimination, their class characteristics and education (as a group) have made it easier for them not only to survive but to prosper in a country with an urban business economy. Consequently, they have furnished positive role models for other Hispanics. According to sociologist Vincent N. Parrillo (1985),

> [T]he Cuban impact upon Miami, now dubbed "Little Havana," has been significant. Over half the country's Cuban-Americans live in the Miami area, where Cubans comprise 70 percent of all Hispanics. The Cuban influence has transformed Miami from a resort town to a year-round commercial center with linkages throughout Latin America and made it into a leading bilingual cultural center.

The New York City metropolitan region has the second largest concentration of Cubans. Over 80,000 Cubans live there, often near groups from other parts of Latin America. Because Cubans have had a high status throughout the Caribbean for a long time, their presence in Hispanic-American neighborhoods has brought a new dimension in intracommunity relations, expectations, and cohesion. . . . As the Cubans began to organize within their new communities, their efforts also helped other Hispanics in the neighborhood. In the Washington Heights section of New York, for example, the Hispanic-American Alliance exerts political pressure to improve local schools and increase police protection, while the Cuban-backed Capital National Bank and Latin American Chamber of Commerce work to encourage successful small business enterprises (p. 372).

White Ethnics

Those of largely non-Protestant European origin, termed "white ethnics," began emigrating to the United States in significant numbers a full half century before the following words by Emma Lazarus were inscribed on the base of the Statue of Liberty in 1886:

> . . . Give me your tired, your poor,
> Your huddled masses yearning to breathe free,
> The wretched refuse of your teeming shore.

They came primarily from Eastern and Southern Europe for a variety of reasons, some borne of desperation. Many Irish arrived in the 1840s in the wake of the potato famine in Ireland that caused economic devastation and, for some, starvation. Some Jews came to escape religious and political persecution in Europe. But mainly they came—the Italians and French, the Slavs, Greeks, Poles, and others—to seek a better life in the emerging industrial giant of a country called America.

White ethnic families such as this one had few skills and often occupied one or two rooms in "flop houses" when they first came to America early in the twentieth century. (The Bettmann Archive.)

Most white ethnics came to the United States in a great "second wave" between the 1870s and 1920s. The majority were poor and unskilled. Because of their meager resources, they settled mainly in eastern cities at or near their ports of entry. There, in places like New York and Chicago, they worked—men, women, and children—six days a week, 14 to 16 hours a day, as laborers in industrial "sweat shops" and at other unskilled and semi-skilled occupations. Many, because of low wages, were forced to live in vermin-infested tenements or "flophouses" in ethnic ghettos where whole families of six or eight often lived in one or two rooms.

Although these people provided American industry at that time with a seemingly inexhaustible supply of cheap labor and were greatly exploited before protective labor legislation began in the 1930s, they were not welcomed with open arms. Quite the contrary, they were subject to prejudice, discrimination, and even racism for a variety of reasons. First, the sheer numbers of these "foreigners" struck at the ethnocentrism of Anglo-Saxon residents, who felt their culture threatened by the strange customs and ways of the newcomers. Many Protestants, for example, rioted against Irish Catholics in the 1840s because of religious intolerance and later exhibited anti-

Semitism toward the Jews. Others displayed racism against some newcomers because their swarthy Mediterranean complexions differed from those of lighter-skinned Caucasians from Northern Europe. In addition, these people for the most part were poor and unskilled, and the more affluent Americans considered them inferior. An editorial writer in 1886, for instance, referred to them as "the very scum and offal of Europe" whom he described as "bad-smelling, . . . foreign wretches, who never did an honest hour's work in their lives" (quoted in Parrillo, 1985, p. 156).

Despite these obstacles, white ethnics as a whole have fared better than most minorities. Because they were Caucasian and understood the need to learn English, many of the first and second generations tried to assimilate into the American mainstream with some success. In addition, many white ethnics changed their family names in order to "fit-in" with the dominant Anglo-Saxon culture. As illustrated in Figure 9-3, this pattern still exists to some degree.

Jewish Americans. Jewish Americans are one example of a white ethnic group that came to this country. Although a few Jews from Spain and Portugal arrived as early as 1654, the most significant Jewish migration to America occurred around the turn of the twentieth century. Most early Jewish immigrants came voluntarily to seek a better life. However, some also came to escape religious persecution and political expulsion in Europe. By the 1930s, however, most Jews entering this country were refugees from the tyranny of Germany's Third Reich.

Today, there are about 6 million Jews in the United States, most of whom reside in or around New York City, the center for Jewish culture (Schaefer, 1988). Contrary to popular myths and stereotypes, Jewish identity is neither racial nor religious, but ethnic. Jews

Figure 9-3 Original Names of Selected White Ethnic Entertainers

Alan Alda: Alphonso D'Abruzzo	**Michael Landon:** Eugene Orotitz
Woody Allen: Allen Konigsberg	**Peggy Lee:** Norma Egstrom
Pat Benetar: Patricia Andrejewski	**Dean Martin:** Dino Crocetti
Robert Blake: Michael Gubitosi	**Harry Morgan:** Harry Bratsburg
Charles Bronson: Charles Buchinski	**Mike Nichols:** Michael Igor Peschowsky
Mel Brooks: Melvin Kaminsky	**Jack Palance:** Walter Palanuik
Tony Curtis: Bernard Schwartz	**Stephanie Powers:** Stefania Federkiewcz
Edie Gorme: Edith Gormezano	**Tony Randall:** Leonard Rosenburg
Lee Grant: Lyova Rosenthal	**Joan Rivers:** Joan Sandra Molinsky
Joel Grey: Joe Katz	**Roy Rogers:** Leonard Slye
Pee-Wee Herman: Paul Rubenfeld	**Mickey Rooney:** Joe Rule, Jr.
Barbara Hershey: Barbara Herztine	**Jane Seymour:** Joyce Frankenberg
Mary Beth Hurt: Mary Supinger	**Danny Thomas:** Amos Jacobs
Carol King: Carol Klein	**Nancy Walker:** Myrtle Swayer
Ben Kingsley: Krisna Banji	**Gene Wilder:** Jerome Silverman
Cheryl Ladd: Cheryl Stoopelmoor	**Jane Wyman:** Sarah Jane Fulks

Source: The world almanac and book of facts (1988). New York: Pharos Books, pp. 405–407.

Figure 9-4 **Minority Exclusion and Participation in Society: A Continuum**

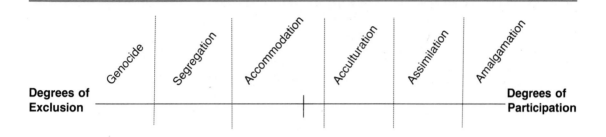

share a common cultural identity, or "people-hood," based at least partially on centuries of tradition and custom. Since most Jews who emigrated to America had been urban dwellers in Europe engaged in industrial occupations, they adapted readily to the American economic system and, as a group, have prospered.

White Ethnics Today. In addition to the Jews, many other white ethnics had also been urban dwellers in Europe. Consequently, the transition to an industrial economy in the United States was relatively smooth for many of them, especially in recent decades. Ethnic groups including the Irish, Italians, Germans, and Poles have made strong efforts to assimilate and today have family incomes competitive with those of most Americans (Greeley, 1976). Jewish Americans, for example, have higher median family incomes than Americans in general, and almost twice as many, proportionally speaking, complete four years of college. Third-generation white ethnics today are showing an ethnic pride that their parents and grandparents did not exhibit, because of the cultural climate in decades past. In 1960, an Irish Catholic named John F. Kennedy was elected president, and in 1988, Michael Dukakis, the son of a Greek immi-

grant, was nominated by the Democratic Party to run for the same office.

MINORITY RELATIONS IN PERSPECTIVE

The manner in which specific minority groups relate to the majority group and the dominant culture is perhaps best illustrated by a polar typology as shown in Figure 9-4. On one side of the continuum are patterns of exclusion in varying degrees which result in discrimination. On the other are differing degrees of participation and acceptance.

Patterns of Exclusion

As we have seen throughout this chapter, minority groups are often excluded from social participation to varying degrees. The most extreme form of exclusion is **genocide**, an intentional and systematic attempt by one group to exterminate another. Throughout much of human history, there have been attempts at genocide at both local and societal levels. The ancient Hebrews tried to eradicate the people of Canaan, the American colonists and Indians, on occasion, engaged in local massacres of one another, and Nazi Germany under Hitler systematically slaughtered six million Jews. A precondition for such barbarism is the dehumanization of the enemy (Duster, 1971). It is much easier to kill a "beast" or "vermin" than a real human being. **Segregation** involves the involuntary separation of a minority group from the majority group in terms of general social contact and participation. There are two basic forms. *De facto segregation* is separation "in fact" as established by social custom. *De jure segregation* is that mandated by law, as in the case of the current apartheid policy in South Africa. The least extreme form of exclusion is **accommodation**, in which members of a minority group attempt to coexist with the majority group without making a significant effort to adopt the norms and values of the dominant society. Some, including Jewish and Cuban Americans, have managed to gain relative prosperity while maintaining a strong ethnic identity. Others, including poor Mexican Americans, have not fared so well, in part because they still cling to portions of orthodox Roman Catholicism and the agricultural ethic that both encourage high rates of fertility.

Patterns of Participation

Minority groups may exhibit varying degrees of participation with or without the consent or encouragement of the majority group as a whole. Two of these patterns, acculturation and assimilation, were discussed earlier (see Chapter 3) and will be mentioned only briefly here. *Acculturation* is cultural change brought about through direct contact of two cultures (or more), in which certain traits of one are borrowed by the other. In the context of minority relations, acculturation is often the first step toward full participation, in that members of a minority will, for example, learn the language and develop the skills needed to improve general life chances. *Assimilation* is a process whereby an immigrant or minority group changes its cultural patterns to conform and adapt to the ways of the dominant culture. The key challenge for many minority groups is not full assimilation but equal participation without the sacrifice of cultural identity and heritage. Usually the most complete level of participation is reached with **amalgamation**, the intermarriage of minority group members with those belonging to the majority. State laws forbidding intermarriage between blacks and whites were ruled unconstitutional by the U.S. Supreme Court in 1967.

CHAPTER SUMMARY

1. Minority relations in any society depend on the interaction between a majority group and one or more minority groups. A majority group is a social category comprised of those in society who are dominant in power, prestige, wealth, and culture. Historically, the United States has been dominated by those of white Anglo-Saxon heritage. A minority group is a social category comprised of those distinguished by certain physical or cultural features who are regarded differently and treated unequally as a result of prejudice and discrimination.

2. Sociologists generally distinguish between two overlapping types of minorities: racial minorities and ethnic minorities. A racial minority is a group that, because of certain visible physical features, suffers social disadvantages at the hands of the majority group. Blacks, American Indians, and Asian Americans are representative examples. An ethnic minority is a group that experiences social disadvantages because of cultural characteristics that the majority group treats as inferior. Hispanics, Jewish Americans, and other white ethnics are typical of ethnic minorities in the United States.

3. Prejudice and discrimination are two important factors that impact on minority relations. Prejudice is the judgment of individuals and groups on the basis of preconceived ideas and takes several different forms. Three basic types of prejudice are exploitative prejudice, normative prejudice, and the authoritarian personality. Whereas prejudice is a judgmental attitude, discrimination involves differential treatment of people because of their membership in a social category. Discrimination may take both individual and institutional forms.

4. Another factor that influences minority relations is racism, which results from how race is perceived. From a biological perspective, race involves certain visible physical characteristics of a group that are passed on to future generations. Scientists generally regard biological racial differences to be superficial at best and largely meaningless, since all humans belong to one species, *Homo sapiens*. From a sociological perspective, however, race involves a category of people (of both sexes and all age groups) perceived and treated differently because of certain visible physical characteristics. In some societies, racism may become prevalent as a doctrine which holds that one racial group is superior and all others are inferior. Like discrimination, racism may take both individual and institutional forms.

5. Racial minorities in the United States include black Americans (the largest), American Indians (the poorest), and Asian Americans (one of the fastest growing). All of these groups have experienced prejudice, discrimination, and racism throughout most of their histories in the United States. Blacks were en-slaved for two hundred years and then forced to live under a system of legal and social segregation for the better part of another century. American Indians were alternately patronized and respected, vilified, slaughtered, and exploited for their lands. Asian Americans experienced economic exploitation, segregation, and, in the case of Japanese Americans, forcible detention as a group for several years. Nonetheless, conditions for racial minorities in general have improved significantly during the last several decades as a result of political activism, protective legislation, increased educational opportunities, and other factors.

6. Ethnic minorities include Hispanic Americans and white ethnics. These groups are distinguished primarily by their ethnicity or specific cultural heritage. In 1985, Hispanic Americans accounted for about 7 percent of the total U.S. population and included those of Mexican, Cuban, Puerto Rican, and Central and South American descent. If current trends continue, Hispanics could overtake black Americans as the largest minority group in the United States shortly after the turn of the century. Mexican Americans are the largest and fastest-growing group of all ethnic minorities. White ethnics are those of largely non-Protestant European origin who migrated to the United States during the nineteenth and early twentieth centuries.

7. Minority relations perhaps are best illustrated by a continuum, extreme exclusion on one side and almost if not complete acceptance and participation on the other. Patterns of exclusion range from genocide, the most extreme form, through segregation, to accommodation or tolerance. Patterns of participation begin generally with acculturation, then progress to assimilation and, finally, amalgamation.

TERMS TO KNOW

accommodation: a pattern of exclusion in which members of a minority group attempt to coexist with the majority group without making a significant effort to adopt the norms and values of the dominant society.

amalgamation: the intermarriage of minority group members with those belonging to the majority group.

authoritarian personality: a highly rigid and intolerant person who tends to possess a certain group of identifiable personality characteristics.

discrimination: differential treatment of people based on their membership in a particular social category.

ethnicity: a specific cultural heritage that distinguishes one social category of people from another.

ethnic minority: a category of people who experience social disadvantages because of cultural characteristics which the majority group treats as inferior.

exploitative prejudice: negative attitudes toward minority group members by the majority group, which serve as justification for keeping them in a subordinate position.

genocide: a pattern of exclusion that involves the intentional and systematic attempt by one group to exterminate another.

individual discrimination: a condition that results when individuals belonging to one group treat members of another group differently from others because of their group membership.

individual racism: unequal treatment that occurs when ideas and actions based on a doctrine of racial inequality are applied to members of one racial category by members of another.

institutional discrimination: unequal treatment of certain categories of people that occurs when inequities are built into basic institutions.

institutional racism: unequal treatment of members of a racial category that occurs when ideas and actions based on a doctrine of racial inequality are built into the structure of basic institutions; a specific form of institutional discrimination.

Jim Crow laws: statutes passed by Southern states after the Civil War that denied blacks access to public facilities used by whites.

majority group: a social category comprised of those in society who are dominant in power, prestige, wealth, and culture.

minority group: a social category of people distinguished by their physical or cultural characteristics who are regarded as "different" and treated unequally as a result of prejudice and discrimination.

normative prejudice: negative attitudes towards members of a particular group which are accepted as "normal" through the process of socialization.

pan-Indianism: attempts by Indian groups to develop coalitions between several tribes to deal effectively with common problems.

prejudice: the negative judgment of individuals and groups because of preconceived ideas about them.

race: a social category of people (of both sexes and all age groups) perceived and treated in a distinct manner on the basis of certain visible physical characteristics they share.

racial minority: a social category of people who suffer social disadvantages because of certain visible physical characteristics deemed inferior by the majority group.

racism: a doctrine (and acts stemming from it) which holds that one racial category of people is superior and all others, in varying degrees, are inferior.

reverse discrimination: unequal treatment of individuals because they belong to the dominant or majority group.

segregation: a pattern of exclusion in which

a minority group is involuntarily separated from the majority group in terms of general social contact and participation.

stereotypes: fixed mental images about the characteristics of entire categories of people that are not tested against reality.

SUGGESTED READINGS:

America's Jews. (Marshall Sklare; New York: Random House, 1971). A classic sociological treatment of Jews as an ethnic minority with a detailed analysis of Jewish culture, including family structure and customs, community life, and religion.

Asian Americans: Growth, Change, and Diversity. (Robert W. Gardner, Bryant Robey, and Peter C. Smith; Washington, D.C.: Population Reference Bureau, 1985). A brief but comprehensive portrait of Asian Americans today from both cultural and demographic perspectives.

Custer Died for Your Sins: An Indian Manifesto. (Vine Deloria, Jr.; New York: Avon, 1969). A dated but classic account of the treatment accorded Indians at the hands of white society written in a biting and witty style from an Indian's perspective.

From Slavery to Freedom: A History of Negro Americans, 5th ed. (John Hope Franklin; New York: Alfred A. Knopf, 1980). One of the most scholarly books ever written on the history of black Americans.

Ethnic Families in America: Patterns and Variations, 2nd ed. (Charles H. Mindel and Robert W. Habenstein, eds.; New York: Elsevier, 1981). A useful book with fifteen articles on family life of various ethnic and racial minorities including Italian, Irish Catholic, and Greek Americans.

Racial and Ethnic Groups, 3d ed. (Richard T. Schaefer: Glenview, Ill.: Scott, Foresman, 1988). An excellent comprehensive text on racial and ethnic relations in the United States from colonial times to the present.

Chapter 10

Collective Behavior

PUBLICS AND PUBLIC OPINION
Publics and Their Characteristics
Public Opinion and Factors Affecting It
SOCIAL MOVEMENTS
Characteristics

Stages
Types

■ **TERMS TO KNOW**

anonymity
bystander apathy
censorship
circular reaction
collective behavior
convergence theory
emergent norm theory
game perspective
mass behavior
mass hysteria

media
mob
propaganda
public
public opinion
rumor
social contagion theory
social movement
structural conduciveness
structural strain
urban legend
value-added theory

It was after dark when Sally, tired from a long day at work, finally shut down her word processor and left the office to go home. As she walked across the dimly lit parking lot and slowly climbed into her car, she thought of how nice it was going to be to soak in a warm tub. Five minutes later, still preoccupied with her thoughts, she was unaware that she was being followed by a large man in a pickup truck. As she reached a desolate stretch of road, she was jarred into reality by the bright lights of the pickup in her rearview mirror. Seconds later, she found herself being forced off the road by a menacing looking stranger.

In a desperate move, Sally floored the accelerator and lurched ahead of the truck and back onto the road. As she sped on through the night and passed her house, she was unable to shake the truck, which alternately held back and clung to her bumper, the driver periodically turning on and off his high beams.

Finally, she noticed a busy truck stop ahead, quickly turned in at high speed, and braked suddenly to a sliding halt with the pickup right behind her. As she ran in tears to three burly truckers for help, the stranger still on her heels, she became suddenly puzzled when she heard the stranger asking for help as well. For, you see, in the back seat of her car, there was an escaped mental patient with a butcher knife, who had been incarcerated for slashing to death his entire family, including a daughter who looked very similar to Sally. The "menacing" stranger, it turned out, had spotted the man in the car and, by following the young woman, had probably saved her life.

While this makes an interesting story, it is only one of many variations of "the killer in the backseat" legend that has little if any basis in truth (Brunvand, 1986). These stories, called urban legends, start as rumors in local communities and, in a mobile society of corporate salespeople and other travelers, are soon spread nationwide with many variations. No doubt you have heard some of them. They include such old standbys as "the escaped one-armed killer with a hook," and new legends like "the choking Doberman," "the death of little Mikey," and "the dog and the microwave." Generated spontaneously and spread in an unplanned and unstructured way, urban legends are a product of but one aspect of collective behavior, which is the focus of this chapter.

THE NATURE AND SCOPE OF COLLECTIVE BEHAVIOR

Most social behavior involves somewhat patterned responses to established norms. In our coverage of culture (Chapter 3), we discussed how its cognitive, normative, material, and language elements give our lives order and predictability. These patterns for thinking, feeling, and acting are then imparted to us through socialization (Chapter 4). In addition, the ways in which we react to and act on them form the basis for social organization (Chapter 5) at all levels of society. Together, these processes—culture, socialization, and social organization—operate in a dynamic interplay which, in large part, gives our lives structure and routine. The majority of us thus operate in most spheres of life such as family, school, and work in a fairly patterned way.

Just as there are order and structure to social life, so is there change and, at times, some unpredictability. Sociologists address the issue of social change in a variety of ways, including the study of collective behavior, a very broad area of social investigation. Briefly defined, **collective behavior** consists of people's relatively spontaneous and unstructured actions in response to ambiguous or changing social conditions (Zygmunt, 1986). Especially in situations of rapid social change, conventional norms may become blurred or nonapplicable, and habitual patterns of response may not seem appropriate. Individuals and groups in some situations are left to improvise and cope as best they can. This is typical with some crowds. A crowd is a group of people that often forms very quickly, seeks to move forward with a life of its own, may involve highly charged emotions, and may disperse as quickly as it was formed. In other circumstances, groups of people form and participate in a social movement. They impose their will on a social condition and develop norms, organization, and goals for others to follow. Those who become involved in such movements make a concerted effort to influence public opinion and are sometimes able to affect changes in public policy.

Given its unstructured, unpredictable, temporary, and often emotional nature, collective behavior represents a complex and diverse area of investigation. At one end of the continuum are the most temporary and disorganized forms, such as crowds and crowd behavior. By comparison, public opinion at times can be fairly stable. Social movements, the most organized form of collective behavior, can be durable and have been known to last for long periods of time. The civil rights movement in the United States, for example, continues after more than thirty years, although both its goals and tactics have changed considerably.

In general, sociologists divide collective behavior into four broad categories: crowds and crowd behavior, mass behavior, public opinion, and social movements. The thrust of this chapter will be to discuss each of these topics in some detail. Let us first examine some of the preconditions that lead to spontaneous and unstructured social behavior.

PRECONDITIONS OF COLLECTIVE BEHAVIOR

Sociologist Neil Smelser (1963) has developed the **value-added theory**, one of the first and most widely used approaches to understanding collective behavior. In doing so, he has attempted to combine elements of various perspectives—functionalist, conflict, and interactionist—in explaining many of the social conditions that underlie collective behavior. Through the value-added approach, Smelser argues that six conditions in society, when added together in sequential order, create a cumulative effect that increases the likelihood of relatively spontaneous group behavior. While collective behavior does not automatically follow from these conditions, each one added tends to decrease conventional options and increase the pressure on people to act out in spontaneous and unstructured ways. These six factors are briefly discussed as follows.

Structural Conduciveness

The first of Smelser's six conditions, **structural conduciveness**, refers to elements built into a society's social structure that encourage collective behavior. Simple nonindustrial societies are low in structural conduciveness because they tend to be slow-changing, tradition-based, and homogeneous regarding the life-style of their people. Life in these village-focused societies tends to be highly structured, affording little opportunity for innovation or change. Since everyone tends to have the same or similar occupations, values and beliefs, and worldview, there is little basis for conflict. Modern industrial societies on the brink of the postindustrial era, however, have a high degree of structural conduciveness. These are fast-changing urban social systems that are not bound by tradition and have very diverse populations. When this everchanging

mix of occupations, value orientations, and world perspectives among the people are combined with a burgeoning technology and increasingly sophisticated communication and information processing, conditions are ripe for collective behavior of several varieties. Consequently, the openness and flexibility of these societies, along with confusion and probable conflict, make it much easier for the emergence of crowds, fads, rumors, and even social movements.

Structural Strain

Societies with high structural conduciveness are more likely to experience **structural strain**, a situation in which (1) intergroup conflicts develop between certain segments of a population and/or (2) dramatic social changes occur. *Intergroup conflicts* serve as one source of strain. In August of 1988, Universal Studios released the movie *The Last Temptation of Christ*, creating a furor among Christian fundamentalists. Incensed by a fictionalized ''human'' portrayal of Christ, which included a dream sequence of Jesus having sex with Mary Magdalene, thousands of protestors, mainly fundamentalists, signed petitions, picketed movie theaters, and tried unsuccessfully to have the movie banned. Other conflicts have arisen among diverse groups in recent decades on issues ranging from the Vietnam conflict to abortion and gun control.

Dramatic social changes can also produce structural strain. Our behavior is governed to a significant degree by the routines or habits we acquire from our culture though socialization. If these routines are suddenly interrupted, circumstances force us to innovate or adapt to the situation. Dramatic changes might be brought on at various levels of society by such diverse events as economic downturns, industrial accidents that cause the leak of poisonous chemicals, political assassina-

Structural strain sometimes results in collective behavior because of intergroup conflicts that arise over certain social issues. (*Left:* Religious News Photo by John Lei. *Right:* AP/Wide World Photos.)

tions, and natural disasters including fires, floods, earthquakes, and hurricanes. Sometimes people are able to adapt to such things in an orderly fashion, while at other times they panic or rebel. Collective behavior resulting from such conditions might include rumors, crowd behavior, mobs, shifts in public opinion, and social movements.

Generalized Belief

For collective behavior actually to occur, however, other conditions in addition to ideal structural conditions are needed. One of these is what Smelser calls *generalized belief,* an emergent popular explanation that includes both the causes and "solutions" to a perceived social problem (structural strain). Structural strain is unsettling to many people who require an explanation or "answer" to a perceived condition that disturbs them. When the

stock market crashed in late October 1929, this dramatic event led to the generalized belief that the entire economy was going to collapse. This shared perception of reality set the stage for a run on the banks which, because of the lack of safeguards, did indeed collapse in the wake of a mass panic.

Precipitating Factors

Even with the preceding three conditions firmly in place, collective behavior does not always result. What may be needed to spark people into action are *precipitating factors,* which sharpen the focus of conduciveness and strain and create or reinforce generalized belief. During the summer of 1914, the assassination of Archduke Ferdinand of Serbia touched off a powder keg that further strained the already volatile relations between several European countries, and the explosive chain reaction that followed led to World War I. Another precipitating event, the Japanese bombing of Pearl Harbor in December of 1941, triggered American involvement in World War II. During the racial unrest of the 1960s, alleged incidents involving both "police brutality" and "inner city snipers" helped to touch off riots in several American cities.

Similar precipitating events continue to act as catalysts for collective behavior. In January 1989, intergroup conflict between native-born blacks in Miami and Hispanic immigrants exploded in violence. A Columbian-born police officer, in an attempt to stop a speeding motorcycle, shot and killed its operator in Overtown, an inner-city ghetto. The rear passenger on the motorcycle, also black, died from injuries incurred in the following crash. This event sparked two nights of rioting in which 1 participant was killed, 22 wounded, and 385 arrested for looting, arson, and random shooting. The damage to property amounted to approximately $1 million (*Time,* January 30, 1989).

Mobilization of Participants for Action

Once conduciveness and strain are in place and people feel through generalized belief and precipitating events that "the evidence is in," all that remains is to engage in collective action. To accomplish this, the leadership and activism of a few individuals will result in the *mobilization of participants.* Through such leadership, enough people with sufficient motivation can be brought together and given the focus to act. The resulting "critical mass" makes collective behavior inevitable (Oliver, Marwell, and Teixeira, 1985). At one extreme are leaders and activists in crowds, who seize the moment and urge the group to act. At the opposite end of the continuum are leaders of social movements who often develop carefully

articulated goals and the strategies designed to meet them.

Social Control

The direction collective behavior takes once it is initiated depends in part on how agents of *social control* use their power to minimize or interrupt its progress. Sometimes the actions of authorities facilitate a smooth process of spontaneous group expression, while in other cases their behavior can promote conflict and cause a tense situation to become volatile.

An example of the latter situation is the tragic incident that occurred at Kent State University in May of 1970, during a time marked by much discord over America's military involvement in Vietnam. In the wake of antiwar demonstrations on campus and rowdiness by an estimated three hundred students, which included the firebombing of the campus ROTC building, the mayor of Kent, Ohio, requested then Governor James Rhodes to send in the National Guard. Rhodes complied, declared martial law, and, to set the tone, even showed up himself on the KSU campus. There, in a public address, he attributed the situation to students "worse than the 'brown shirt' and the communist element and also the night riders in the vigilantes . . . the worst type of people that we harbor in America." He also said, "We are going to eradicate the problem. . . . It's over with in Ohio" (*Newsweek,* May 18, 1970).

The members of the Guard, mobilized under the general belief that they would be dealing with a dangerous mob of unified demonstrators, arrived on campus in force with loaded rifles and gas masks. There, during a confrontation with some demonstrators who hurled insults and rocks at the Guard, a contingent of about sixteen soldiers fired thirty-five rounds directly into the crowd which consisted mainly of spectators and students going

According to sociologist Jerry M. Lewis (1972), all six of Neil Smelser's six preconditions for collective behavior were present in the tragic events that took place at Kent State University during early May of 1970. In the wake of student antiwar demonstrations, members of the Ohio National Guard fired on some students, killing four of them and wounding several others. (*Left:* UPI/Bettmann Newsphotos. *Right:* AP/Wide World Photos.)

to and from classes. Four students were killed and ten were wounded, including one paralyzed from the waist down. None of the soldiers hit by rocks required hospitalization.

Sociologist Jerry M. Lewis (1972), in his analysis of this incident, found that all six of Smelser's preconditions had been present. He also found that the motivations of the crowd participants were diverse, that some were demonstrators and others not involved at all. *Newsweek* magazine, reporting on the incident a week after it happened, had this to say in their cover story:

> Not one of the four dead had been closer than 75 feet to the troops who had killed them— and there was not the slightest suggestion that they had been singled out as targets because of anything they had done. Indeed, all available

evidence indicated that the four dead students . . . were probably innocent bystanders.

. . . Kent State faculty members rendered a verdict of their own. Prevented from meeting on campus, they crowded into a nearby Akron Unitarian church and passed this resolution: "We hold the guardsmen acting under orders and under severe psychological pressures, less responsible than are Governor Rhodes and Adjutant General [Sylvester] Del Corso, whose inflammatory statements produced these pressures" (May 18, 1970, pp. 32, 33 f).

CROWDS AND CROWD BEHAVIOR

Some of the most spontaneous, unstructured, and short-lived forms of collective behavior occur within crowds. A crowd is a type of group that sociologists call a *physical aggregate,* a temporary and relatively unstructured group distinguished primarily by the physical proximity of its members. This term was introduced as a concept in Chapter 6 as identifying one of the five basic types of groups in society. Now we will discuss in some detail the nature of crowds, their different forms, and how they operate.

The Nature of Crowds

Crowds are emergent groups that tend to develop in response to a variety of social situations including planned events, sudden changes, and perceived injustices. They are often formed spontaneously, and, when the stimulus that attracted people ceases to be of interest, they can disperse just as quickly. Unlike other types of groups, such as social groups and associations, crowds are "now" oriented and have no history and no future. Their members have no social positions with attendant role responsibilities to perform, no division of labor, and no commonly agreed-upon goals in most cases. Members, drawn by their individual motivations based on curiosity, interest, or emotion, find themselves in crowds as spectators, active participants, or just "floaters" passing through.

One of the most pervasive characteristics of large crowds is **anonymity**, a condition in which a person's identity becomes lost in a crowd. When people feel anonymous because of their insulation by others in a large mass of people, they may also feel free to engage in behavior they would not have considered had they been acting alone. From the perspective of participants, it is almost as if rules or laws are suspended and they feel immune from conventional norms because "no one will ever know it was I." In several civil disturbances during the twentieth century, crowds involved in various antisocial activities, including lynching, looting, and the destruction of property, have often been influenced by anonymity. The sheer numbers of people involved have protected the identities of most members and furnished them with feelings of security. Some members of the Ku Klux Klan, for instance, have been prominent citizens in local communities. They often felt immune from public scrutiny and possible sanctions because, historically, they operated in secrecy and hid their identities under white robes and hoods.

Anonymity may also result in bystander apathy, according to the research of several social scientists (Darley and Latane, 1968; Schwartz and Gottlieb, 1980). **Bystander apathy** is a condition in which, during emergency situations requiring responsible action, onlookers at the scene fail to act. Most people, when alone and aware that others know of their presence, will feel some pressure to render aid to someone in need. They will often give aid in part because they do not want others to think poorly of them if they do not. However, they may be much less likely to act in a large crowd where their identity is unknown.

A dramatic illustration is the brutal murder in 1962 of a young New York woman named Kitty Genovese. Returning home late one night from her job, she was attacked in the parking lot adjacent to her apartment building by a single assailant with a knife. Stabbed repeatedly in an attack that took thirty-five minutes in three separate episodes of violence, the young woman screamed loudly for her life: "Oh, God, he stabbed me! Please help me! Please help me! . . . I'm dying! I'm dying!" In all, thirty-eight persons raised their windows and watched portions or all of the attack in which the assailant slowly took the life of his victim. One person shouted once for the attacker to stop. But no one tried otherwise to interfere. No one tried to rescue the young woman. Some went back to bed. And no one called the police. When questioned later, one of Genovese's neighbors reported that he did not want to get involved (Rosenthal, 1964).

Types of Crowds

Crowds exhibit diverse characteristics and engage in a wide variety of activities. Some are relatively calm and somewhat formal. Others are quite volatile and have little if any focus or structure. There are murderous crowds and peaceful crowds, joyous crowds and sad crowds. Sociologist Herbert Blumer (1957) developed a most useful and comprehensive system for categorizing such groups. He divided crowds into four general categories—casual, conventional, expressive, and acting—explained briefly as follows:

1. Casual Crowds. A *casual crowd* is a temporary crowd formed spontaneously with members who tend to come and go. Spectators gathered to watch a building burn or to view the effects of a car accident are representative examples. So are shoppers in a mall or people standing to watch a group of street dancers. Casual crowds are the most unstructured of all crowds, their members having little if any focus or emotional involvement. Members often pass through the group on their way to some other activity. There is very little if any interaction between members because, in this kind of crowd, there is a high degree of anonymity. It is not unusual for casual crowds to last only a few minutes.

2. Conventional Crowds. A *conventional crowd* is a fairly structured crowd that conforms to established norms. Unlike a casual crowd, this group typically has a common goal among members and acts according to an agreed-upon set of norms. Religious assemblies on Sunday morning, movie audiences, and groups in attendance at symphony concerts fall into this category.

3. Expressive Crowds. An *expressive crowd* is one that has as its primary purpose the free expression of emotions. In these groups, some allowances are made for those who want to

Crowds take a variety of forms. Casual crowds, like the one on the left, tend to be temporary, with little interaction among members. Conventional crowds (see center photo) are more structured and operate according to a set of agreed-upon norms. Expressive crowds, like the dancers on the right, make allowances for those who wish to "let go" emotionally in their own way to have a good time. (*Left:* Copyright Joel Gordon. *Center and right:* Bob Daemmrich Photog.)

"let go" emotionally in their own individual ways. Among fundamentalists, some funerals as well as religious revivals involve crowds that are particularly expressive of their emotions. Parties may involve a free release of emotions as people "unwind" and have a good time. Victory celebrations for successful political candidates are an added example.

4. Acting Crowds. An *acting crowd* is a highly aroused crowd focused on a specific situation or problem that members are willing to act on impulse to resolve. Unlike expressive crowds, which have no concentrated focus, acting crowds are usually highly charged with negative emotions that are concentrated on some source of agitation. They tend to be very volatile and thus potentially dangerous to those who might get in their way. A **mob** is the most extreme form of acting crowd. Its members are out of control and willing to engage in violence if it suits their ends. Lynch mobs and those involved in riots are typical examples.

Explanations of Crowd Behavior

In addition to Smelser's value-added theory, there are other more specific approaches that seem more suitable in helping us to understand the wide diversity of crowd behaviors and motivations. Of these, the two most prominent in recent years have been social contagion theory and emergent norm theory.

Social Contagion Theory. In 1895 French social psychologist Gustave Le Bon (1968) argued that people in crowds are so greatly influenced by the behavior of others that their own rational, decision-making capabilities are stifled. They fall under the influence of the powerful, almost hypnotic "collective mind"

of the crowd. So strong is the pull of some crowds, Le Bon asserted, that people who are typically peaceful and civilized when alone can be turned into violent barbarians under the influence of the crowd. Today Le Bon is credited as the originator of **social contagion theory**, which asserts that the mood and behavior of crowds become dominant in shaping the emotions and behavior of individual participants.

As initially formulated, contagion theory was essentially a psychological approach. It was based on the reductionist argument that the "collective mind" of the crowd influenced the minds of individuals who got caught up in a type of crowd mentality. There indeed are instances in which individuals seem to do little more than react to a crowd.

When certain crowds form, two contagion principles can sometimes be observed. First, people will often engage in *imitation*, doing what they see others doing. In a shopping mall, for example, if one hears a strange sound, such as music, and observes others going to see what it is, it is very tempting to follow them and contribute to the forming of a crowd. Second, it is also very easy to react because of *suggestibility*, the tendency of people to be influenced in their behavior by the suggestions, directions, and actions of others once a crowd is formed. Crowds are often unstructured in that conventional norms are either absent or do not seem to apply. In such a situation, people tend to look to others for clues as to how to act. Consequently, they are susceptible to following the directions of those who possess decisive leadership qualities.

Some sociologists from the interactionist school, such as Herbert Blumer (1939, 1957), however, have rejected the concept of the "collective mind" as being too simplistic. Nonetheless, some social scientists still subscribe to the contagion thesis that ordinary people in everyday situations can and do become "caught up" in crowds that alter their behavior. Blumer argues that this process is interactive as much as reactive. Through his principle of **circular reaction**, he asserts that members of crowds, particularly in conditions of unrest and heightened tension, reinforce one another's feelings and behavior in a back-and-forth or circular fashion. The emotions and behavior of a crowd in a tense situation are spread to others who not only model the original group but reinforce their actions as well. This circular process of mutual reinforcement then acts to intensify many crowd situations, producing panics, angry mobs, or looting crowds.

Emergent Norm Theory. In contrast to the contagion approach is the **emergent norm theory**, the perspective that individuals become members of crowds for numerous reasons and, through interaction with others, adopt the group norms that develop from the particular situation. The original proponents of this theory, Ralph Turner and Lewis Killian (1957, 1987), offer an approach that differs from the social contagion theory in two major respects. First, rather than having unanimity of motive for their behavior, they argue that people may have a multitude of reasons for joining a crowd (Turner, 1980; McPhail and Wohlstein, 1983). In a mob, for example, some people may be incensed about something and want retribution, while others may simply want to use the situation as a cover to loot and steal for personal gain. Still others may be spectators who do not actively participate or those just passing through the crowd to reach another destination.

Second, they argue that in most cases, people in crowds do not simply react to or even reinforce the emotions of the moment. Instead, they conform to norms that emerge from a crowd in much the same way they would in more conventional situations. Group

norms govern appropriate behavior in almost all social encounters. Emergent norm theorists maintain that the same processes occur in crowds. A few visible leaders may define norms by expression or example. Those who disagree often will not voice dissent because of the size of the group, which may be intimidating, or their fear of negative sanctions that may range from ridicule and embarrassment to the threat of physical punishment (Shibutani, 1986). Emergent norms in crowds thus say whether it is appropriate to applaud or jeer, laugh or cry, become "involved" or uninvolved, or, in some cases, whether to stand up (as in a movie ticket line) or sit down (as in the movie theater).

Other Explanations. Although a popular theory for several decades, the contagion approach in particular has drawn fire from several critics. Sociologist Richard Berk (1974) uses a **game perspective** and argues that crowds are not irrational entities that catch people up in something "bigger than they are." Instead, he asserts, crowds are often quite rational and individuals are usually in complete control. In this sense, "selling off" one's stocks in a market crash seems a logical thing to do to minimize losses. The riots that took place in the Watts section of Los Angeles during the summer of 1965 provide another illustration. In this violent upheaval in the impoverished black community, destruction was selective. Black-owned businesses were spared while white-owned stores were looted and burned (Task Force Report, 1967). In addition, some looters driving cars were observed stopping for traffic lights and stop signs.

Other social scientists subscribe to **convergence theory**. They maintain that crowds tend to draw particular types of people with definite interests and values rather than a representative cross section of people from the community. Consequently, one would not see many Episcopalians at religious revivals, country-western fans at jazz music festivals, or well-educated, professional people in lynch mobs. In essence, proponents of this approach argue that people tend to participate in many crowd situations because of their wish to do with others what they enjoy doing by themselves. What attracts them is not mere curiosity but a set of interests and values.

Placing these varied explanations of crowds in perspective—Smelser's six preconditions, social contagion theory, emergent norm theory, and others—one realizes that all have some value in explaining the extremely diverse phenomena of crowd behavior, but none is adequate in explaining all such behavior. Some crowds exhibit all six of Smelser's stages in sequence, while others do not (Milgram, 1977). Social contagion occurs in certain instances in which a crowd seems to react with unanimity, while in others, critics assert, people have a variety of motives and react in a variety of ways (Turner, 1964). In addition, these approaches are not mutually exclusive. In specific crowds, elements of two or more of these perspectives may apply.

MASS BEHAVIOR

Whereas crowd behavior occurs at the microlevel, mass behavior involves essentially the same processes extended to the macrolevel of society. Briefly defined, **mass behavior** is unstructured social behavior characteristic of large collectivities of people who operate outside one another's presence. The perspectives that are useful in explaining what happens in crowds also have some application to mass behavior. In fact, some sociologists consider "masses" as little more than diffuse crowds. Masses are, however, quite distinct. Unlike crowds, they are much larger and consist of persons "spatially dispersed and anonymous, reacting to one or more of the same stimuli but acting individually without regard for one another" (Hoult, 1969, p. 194).

Fads, Crazes, and Fashions

Fads, crazes, and fashions were introduced in Chapter 3 as variations of folkways, broadbased norms in the form of customs and social conventions. However, they also represent forms of collective behavior in that they are temporary, relatively unstructured, and often have tremendous mass appeal. *Fads* are folkways popular for a brief period among a limited segment of the population. They take a variety of forms, including slang expressions like "groovy" in the 1960s and "bad" in the 1980s. Fads are also evident in musical preferences, modes of dress, and even diets. *Crazes* are fads which, among a limited segment of society, become obsessive. They vary from the hero worship of cult personalities like athletes, motion picture stars, and musical entertainers to certain consumer preferences such as "pet rocks" in the 1970s and toys and "action figures" merchandised from the *Star Wars* trilogy of motion pictures in the 1970s and 1980s. *Fashions* are folkways more durable than fads that gain widespread acceptance among a large portion of society for a substantial period of time. Informal and varied clothing styles, driving smaller automobiles than in past decades, two-career families, not smoking cigarettes, and eating "heart healthy" foods are examples of today's fashions.

As forms of collective behavior, fads, crazes, and fashions are important for their dynamic rather than normative aspects. Although trivial and even frivolous in some instances, they sometimes serve as indicators of significant social change. In a rapidly changing mass society like the United States, what

Both jeans and small cars have become fashionable in the United States during the last few years. (Copyright Greg Meadows, 1979.)

begins as a fad or fashion can sometimes become an institutionalized part of a society's culture. Fast foods like ice cream cones, hot dogs, and hamburgers, now a permanent part of Americana, all began this way and "caught on." The same can be said of sports like golf and tennis, bras for women, radios in automobiles, and even the automobile itself.

Likewise, crazes may come and go to provide stimulation and variety for a mass culture but sometimes become institutionalized as well. During the 1630s, the Dutch developed a passion for tulips. Individuals at all levels of society wanted tulip bulbs for their gardens, and soon the demand greatly outstripped the supply. Tulip mania reached such an extreme that people were paying more for a single bulb than for a cow or a sheep, and soon bulbs were worth their weight in gold. This fever caused people to sell their farms and liq-

uidate other property to invest in tulip bulbs, and a few people became rich overnight. A rumor was started, however, that the price of tulips was about to collapse. A selling panic resulted as thousands tried to sell their bulbs and flowers all at once. The tulip market collapsed and many people were financially ruined. Nonetheless, what began at first as a prosperous and then disastrous craze gained a permanent place in the culture of Dutch society. Today, when one thinks of Holland, its world renowned tulips, which are still grown with pride in that country, often come to mind.

Rumors

Just as one unverified story set in motion a panic and the subsequent collapse of the tulip market in Holland several centuries ago, rumors today can and do help to initiate and reinforce a variety of collective behavior forms. A **rumor** is an unconfirmed story that is spread rather quickly from person to person. Such unsubstantiated stories often emerge from conditions of social strain and confusion. When authoritative information is unavailable or formal channels of communication are blocked or not functioning effectively, conditions are ripe for the spread of rumors. Given such circumstances, few people in society—even the most educated and sophisticated—are immune from the temptation at times to listen to and perhaps spread rumors. These stories tend to originate and spread most easily among people of low prestige who crave attention, those who are socially isolated, and those with little education who lack the critical thinking skills to seek verification (Buckner, 1969). Regardless of who spreads unverified stories, the central reason for rumors, sociologist Tamotso Shibutani (1966) argues, is clear:

> Rumor is a substitute for news; in fact, it is news that does not develop in institutional channels. Unsatisfied demand for news—the discrepancy between information needed to come to terms with a changing environment and what is provided by formal news channels—constitutes the crucial condition of rumor construction (p. 62).

Rumors can be very destructive; they have touched off and fueled several riots in recent years. The Watts riot of 1965 in Los Angeles was precipitated by an incident of alleged "police brutality" in which a police officer jabbed a young black youth in the stomach with his baton (Governor's Commission, 1965; Cohen, 1969). However, by the time the story was told a few times, rumor had it that the police had beaten a pregnant woman. During the Newark, New Jersey riot of 1967 a young National Guardsman fired a warning shot to scare an inner-city resident away from a window. A rumor spread among police and guardsmen alike that the shot was fired by a sniper. Shortly thereafter, some fireworks going off were mistaken for snipers and police and two columns of guardsmen riddled a housing project with intense fire (*Report of the National Advisory Commission on Civil Disorders*, 1968, pp. 3–4).

The National Advisory Commission on Civil Disorders, charged with investigating both underlying and immediate causes of the urban riots of the 1960s, reported as follows:

> Rumors significantly aggravated tension and disorder in more than 65 percent of the disorders studied by the commission. Sometimes, as in Tampa and New Haven, rumor served as the spark that turned an incident into a civil disorder. Elsewhere, notably Detroit and Newark, even where they were not precipitating or motivating factors, inflaming rumors made the job of police and community leaders far more difficult (1968, p. 326).

Rumors have also affected reputations and careers and created problems for individuals and organizations. In 1969 a rumor circulated throughout the world that Beatle Paul McCartney had died in a car accident. In the spring of 1988, the rumor spread, spurred on by a book released at the same time, that Elvis Presley was alive and had faked his own death. In 1985 Proctor and Gamble, a major producer of household products, abandoned their logo of 103 years depicting the man in the moon surrounded by thirteen stars (Salmans, 1985). For several years, fundamentalists had spread a rumor that the logo was satanic. This created more problems for the company than it thought the logo was worth.

How do rumors spread? What interpersonal dynamics take place among those who initiate and pass them along? Social scientists Gordon Allport and Leo Postman (1965) have studied rumors and found that, among several factors, leveling and sharpening seem to be of particular value. *Leveling* is a process by which, as a rumor is told and retold, it becomes more concise and retains only a few details. This makes the story easier to grasp and spread to others. The distortion is then heightened in some cases by *sharpening*, a process in which the details that are retained as the rumor is passed on increase in importance and, in essence, become the main story.

Two other processes—correcting and exaggeration—add to the development of rumors in some cases. When a story is reduced and distorted by leveling and sharpening, the details that remain and are passed on may not logically fit together anymore. The result is often *correcting*, a process in which people—either knowingly or unknowingly—make changes in an already distorted rumor so that its details seem to fit together more "logically." The addition of new details through *exaggeration* can make an interesting story even more exciting.

Urban Legends

A phenomenon similar to rumors is what Jan Harold Brunvand (1980, 1981, 1986) has called the urban legend. An **urban legend** is an unsubstantiated story, much more durable than a rumor, that is spread over an entire country or society, usually with several local variations. These stories normally contain themes consistent with issues, problems, fears, and mysteries of modern life. How such tales are spread nationwide is not known for certain, although it appears that business people who travel by plane often spread them fairly quickly from coast to coast. Brunvand (1981, p. 10) says that a rumor tends to become legend when it meets three criteria: (1) It makes for a good story, (2) it is plausible in the mind of the public, and (3) it serves as a moral object lesson.

One popular theme in urban legends is the "suppressed truth" story. "The Martians have landed" has been a very popular story in recent years, reaching urban legend status:

> Supposedly a UFO from the planet Mars with a number of humanoid creatures aboard crashed in the Midwest many years ago, and U. S. Air Force personnel recovered part of the craft and its occupants, one or two of them still alive before the rest of the spacecraft was destroyed in the resulting fire and explosion. The remaining UFO parts and the "creatures" were moved to an isolated hanger in the deserts of Arizona (Texas, New Mexico, etc.), and the men involved in the action were sworn to secrecy or lied to about the nature of their mission. . . . The occupants were described as "three-foot tall, humanlike creatures wrapped in fine metallic cloth" (Brunvand, 1986, p. 198).

Other prevalent themes include "unusual uses of technology" (microwaves, cars, freezers, and so on), "restroom legends," "unfortunate pet legends," "sex scandal legends," and "unusual forms of revenge." The following example (Brunvand, 1986) combines two of the more common urban legend themes:

> A woman went home on her lunch hour to pick up some items she needed for work, though she normally ate lunch at work. Upon her arrival home, she noticed her husband's car in the driveway. When she entered the house she heard voices coming from the bedroom and she realized what she had walked in on. She immediately left the house, returned to work, and plotted her revenge. When she went home that evening, she cooked her husband's favorite dinner, changed to a sexy negligee, lit the candles, chilled the wine, and enjoyed a romantic evening with her husband. After dinner she enticed him into the bedroom, undressed him, and sexually aroused him; and when he was fully erect, she superglued his penis to his abdomen. He required surgery for its removal (p. 146).

During the 1970s and 1980s, the story that "little Mikey" from the Life cereal commercial had died became a popular urban legend. In one version, the child actor ate a handful of Poprocks (a candy) and then drank a soft drink, the combination of which caused his stomach to explode. Despite the absurdity of such a story and the fact that John Gilchrist—the actor who played little Mikey— was alive and well, the story persisted and reached urban legend status.

Mass Hysteria

Sometimes mass behavior occurs so quickly that it becomes what sociologists call **mass hysteria**, a spontaneous excited reaction by large numbers of people to a mysterious social condition or event perceived as a threat. During May of 1981, for example, a large group of elementary school students in Massachusetts were practicing in the school auditorium for their spring concert. Suddenly, in a matter of minutes, nine children fainted. Forty children became ill with symptoms of nausea and dizziness, and six were taken to a local hospital.

When thirty children became ill at the concert later that evening, public health officials began an investigation. They concluded that the children suffered from no organic illness even though they did experience physical symptoms (Matchan, 1983). These children were probably anxious about performing before their parents and the community. Their anxiety, combined with close supervision by

During the early 1950s, Senator Joseph McCarthy led a movement to find, expose, and discredit American communists. The actions of this man and his followers created a form of mass hysteria that had many Americans worried over the "communist threat." Before McCarthy was finally discredited as an inflammatory demagogue who greatly exaggerated the communist presence and influence, hundreds of innocent Americans had had their reputations and careers destroyed. (AP/Wide World Photos.)

teachers producing a "captive audience" effect, peer pressure, and the pressure from all concerned to "get ready" for the big event, most likely produced an unbearable level of stress. Consequently, it is probable that a single child got dizzy and fainted in reaction to the pressure, which in turn provided an "escape mechanism" for others, who quickly developed similar physiological symptoms and responded accordingly.

The phenomenon of group panic, although localized at the microlevel in the preceding illustration, also takes place at the macrolevel and has occurred throughout much of history. During the Middle Ages, the bubonic plague, or "Black Death," killed millions of Europeans and produced a mass panic. In the late 1600s, a "witch scare" swept across Massachusetts. Several young women were put on trial for witchcraft and later convicted and executed by hanging (Boyer and Nissenbaum, 1974). A witch hunt of a quite different type occurred in the United States during the early 1950s. Senator Joseph McCarthy led a crusade to root out American communists, whom he and others felt were plotting to undermine the American way of life (Belfrage, 1963). Although McCarthy was finally discredited as an inflammatory demagogue, the inquisition he led produced a "Red scare" that caused the blacklisting of many people in the entertainment industry—actors, screenwriters, playwrights, and so on—and ruined the reputations and careers of hundreds of innocent Americans.

One of the most fascinating incidences of mass hysteria in the twentieth century took place in 1938. On October 30, Orson Welles broadcast a dramatic and modernized version of H. G. Wells's *War of the Worlds* from the Mercury Theater in New York City. Although Welles issued a disclaimer at the beginning of the radio program informing listeners that the story was fictional, many people tuned in during the middle of the program and thought the United States was being invaded by hostile Martians. In the story, the Martians first landed at a farm in Grover's Mill, New Jersey. After fighting a battle with U.S. troops, they moved on to New York City, where they proceeded to kill its inhabitants with poison gas. All this took place before the first thirty-minute station break. Of an estimated 6 million listeners, 1 million went into panic. They called relatives to say farewell, fled from the area by car, and many gathered in bars and other public places to await "the end." It was obvious to a careful listener that there were too many events crammed into the short time of the radio broadcast to have taken place in real life. However, radio technology was relatively new, and many people, lacking media sophistication, were convinced that a Martian

invasion was actually happening (Houseman, 1948; Cantril, 1982).

More recently, reaction to the admittedly serious AIDS epidemic has resulted in an "AIDS scare" in some sectors of society. While an estimated 3 million Americans are now carrying the virus, medical research indicates that this dreaded disease is not spread through casual social or physical contact. Nonetheless, some parents have kept their children home from schools attended by children with AIDS, and some police officers have worn rubber gloves while patrolling homosexual neighborhoods. In a few extreme cases, families of persons stricken with AIDS have had their homes destroyed by arsonists determined to drive them from their communities.

PUBLICS AND PUBLIC OPINION

Mass societies like the United States are characterized by, among other things, constantly changing policies, issues, and trends. The inhabitants of such societies often form publics which assess and react to these changing conditions in the form of public opinion. Some very visible issues that have occupied the minds of publics in recent decades include the civil rights movement and the Vietnam conflict in the 1960s, the equal rights amendment and "Watergate" in the 1970s, and the "Star-wars Defense Initiative" and increased incidence of cocaine abuse during the late 1980s. These and other concerns cause specific publics to emerge from the larger mass which, in turn, may make an impact on social policies and trends.

Publics and Their Characteristics

A **public** is a large, widely dispersed group of people who share an interest in or concern about an issue or group of issues. Modern society contains many such publics. There is a voting public, a baseball public, and an investment public, as well as those focused on concerns including abortion, ecology, women's rights, pornography, gun control, and many others. Therefore, every issue seen as significant in society tends to have its own public that is interested in how it is handled.

It is generally true that the more complex and urban a society is, the larger is its number of different publics. This is due mainly to rapid technological change and the diversity of occupations and life-styles of a society's inhabitants. These changes and varied characteristics and interests of the people create conditions ripe for the emergence of different types of publics.

Although there are several ways to describe publics, they tend to have the following three basic characteristics:

1. *The membership of a public constantly changes.* People may freely enter or leave a public at any time. Consequently, some individuals become newly intrigued or disturbed by a particular issue while others become bored, tired, or disenchanted with it and shift their interests to other issues or activities.

2. *A public is usually temporary.* Publics tend to emerge and grow with an event or issue and, likewise, lose their focus or disintegrate when the event is over or the issue dies and fades away. A viewing public for a popular television show, for instance, will form and disband during a one-hour period each week, as analyzed by polls designed to measure the audience share each show receives. Likewise, a motion picture which may take more than a year to produce, film, and edit may become a commercial success or failure based on box office receipts paid by a public over a three-

or four-week period. At best, voting publics, particularly in U.S. national elections, have a lifespan of only a few months as interest builds. Then, the day after the election, politics is suddenly a nonissue in the minds of most people.

3. *A public critically assesses the topic or issue at hand.* Members take sides on an issue and seek information about it. Moviegoers read the reviews of critics, voters listen to the candidates, and investors and business people follow the stock market and read financial columns. Publics communicate through and seek information primarily from media sources. For example, the magazines people subscribe to often identify the publics to which they belong. What publics would you guess are represented by most subscribers to the *Wall Street Journal, Ms.* magazine, *Golf Digest,* and *Field and Stream?*

Public Opinion and Factors Affecting It

Public opinion refers to the dominant attitude held by a specific public or a society's population at large. As such, it is influenced by a variety of factors. First of all, the particular stand taken by a public on an issue is affected by the organizational affiliations held by its members as well as the reference groups with which they identify (Blumer, 1948). It would be unlikely, therefore, for Republicans to favor strict gun control or for members of the National Organization of Women (NOW) to take a stand against abortion. In addition, community and national leaders exert a significant degree of influence in shaping the opinions held by members of certain publics who look to them for guidance and direction (Katz and Lazarsfeld, 1955). For example, in recent years leaders like Jesse Jackson, Jerry

Source: Bloom County, by Berke Breathed. Copyright © 1987, the Washington Post Writers Group.

Falwell, Cesar Chavez, and Jean Kirkpatrick have each had their own constituencies. However, three factors impacting on public opinion seem most worthy of expanded discussion: media, censorship, and propaganda.

Media. Media plays a dominant role in affecting public opinion. This is amply demonstrated by the billions of dollars spent each year on advertising by the producers of various consumer goods. Then, too, there are the emphasis and money spent on creating the proper "image" and gaining adequate media exposure for politicians who run for national, state, and even local office.

Media are the systematic ways used to transmit information to specific publics or the population at large. In the United States, television and newspapers furnish most adults with their primary sources of information about what is happening in the world, nation, and local community. The impact of media on public opinion is substantial. During the Vietnam conflict, the war was vividly portrayed to most Americans in living color on the television news. For the first time they were able to see the horrors of war almost as they were happening. Families saw sons and husbands being carried away on stretchers to waiting helicopters. Until that time, war had been distant and much easier to defend and even romanticize. The stark realism of media imagery no doubt had some influence on public opinion concerning U.S. involvement.

Sociologist Gary Marx (1986) argues that media are currently being used in the United States as social control mechanisms, a trend that has been on the increase in recent decades. A long list of examples includes the following: computerized databanks containing various kinds of personal information about most citizens, video surveillance cameras in public and work locations, increasingly sophisticated "eavesdropping" technology including wiretapping, satellite surveillance capability, electronic ankle devices worn by those on probation and parole that allow authorities to track their locations, and crime hotlines for reporting anonymous tips.

Marx warns that while these new uses of media may be attractive in combating crime, they could also be used to discourage free speech and most forms of nonconformity. If such a trend were to lead gradually to an insidious form of totalitarianism, which Marx fears might occur, it would have a dramatic impact on public opinion. If, as Marx asserts, such a scenario did occur, public opinion could be controlled, because people would be afraid to speak their true feelings.

Censorship. Limitations placed on the information made available to the public is **censorship**. One form of such restriction—the form usually thought of—is governmental censorship of sensitive information for national security reasons. During World War II, for instance, thousands of scientists and government employees worked on the 2-billion-dollar Manhattan Project aimed at developing the atomic bomb. Yet only a very few knew the entire story of what later turned out to be the best-kept secret of the twentieth century (Blum et al., 1973).

Limitations on information take a variety of additional forms. In the space allowed in a newspaper or the time available for a network news broadcast, those who control the media decide which information to leave in and which to exclude. Families censor the information their small children receive, especially in regard to violence and sex; motion pictures do the same within the guidelines established for the motion picture code, and manufacturers, particularly in "high-tech" industries, maintain tight security in guarding industrial secrets.

Propaganda. While censorship acts to delete all or part of a certain message, propaganda also distorts the information necessary for the public to assess an issue freely. This is accomplished by presenting only one side of an argument or otherwise engaging in a calculated attempt to persuade in a biased and often misleading manner.

Propaganda refers to the use of calculated and biased methods of persuasion based on emotional appeal. The propagandist may be a government or one of its agencies, a politician, a manufacturer or advertising executive, a church minister, or even a teacher or friend. Unlike the aims of *brainwashing,* which are to "reprogram" an individual or group with a different value orientation, those of propaganda are temporary and superficial in most cases. The goals of propagandists focus on influencing people just enough to persuade them to vote for a particular candidate, support a cause or position, sign a petition, or buy a product.

Methods of persuasion are usually aimed at a specific target population and are planned accordingly. The tobacco industry, for example, markets dozens of different brands of cigarettes. With the exception of low tar and nicotine content cigarettes, there is little difference between the various "blends" of tobacco except in the way they are packaged and marketed to specific publics. What type of targeted group is "Marlboro" aimed at? What about "Virginia Slims" or "Eve"? How do you compare what is advertised on the Sunday evening program "60 Minutes" with the products advertised on "Bugs Bunny and Tweety" seen on Saturday morning? What type of audience watches each program? Advertisers find out through *psychographic research* and carefully craft propaganda to appeal to the targeted group.

Some of the more common propaganda approaches, as identified by sociologists Leonard Broom and Philip Selznick (1968), are gaining attention, associating, concealing identity and aims, raising anxieties, and showing strength.

1. *Gaining attention*. Propagandists often use a variety of catch phrases, eye-catching devices, and other gimmicks to influence public opinion. Politicians make use of such attention getters as grand entrances, brass bands, and media exposure. Those out to discredit a politician or other public figure use a variation of the *"big lie,"* in which some half-truth about the person is spread. This is sometimes blown out of proportion by the media because it is sensational and "sells copy." When apologies are made and the negative item is put in its proper perspective, it is not real news and tends to get buried on a back page. In the mind of the public, the sensational item is often the one remembered, and the credibility of the public figure is destroyed.

   Likewise, advertisers selling a product in both print and the electronic media use a variety of attention-getting devices. Words like "free" and "sale" are very effective, as are musical jingles and catch phrases. Memorable phrases from the 1970s and 1980s include "Where's the beef?" "Be all that you can be," and "You deserve a break today." Advertisers also use sex and sexual imagery, delicious-looking food, and adorable children and animals as attention getters.

2. *Associating a cause or product with values, beliefs, or symbols held or used by the public.* Politicians, for example, may talk in *glittering generalities* about such things as home, family, God, and country as a diversionary tactic to keep away from substantive issues. Some voters, impressed with this "image" that seems to be in line with cherished values, may succumb to the orchestrated allure of such a candidate. Another associating technique used by politicians and others is to appear as *plain folks*. Advertisers and other propagandists may also use *testimonials* by motion picture stars, professional athletes, and other personalities to grace a product or cause. This again is a diversion to avoid discussing the merits of the issue at hand. Finally, propagandists use the *band wagon* technique in an attempt to convince the audience that everyone is "doing it," "buying it," "accepting it," or otherwise "jumping on the bandwagon" (Lee and Lee, 1971).

3. *Concealing real identity and goals*. Sometimes, because of prevailing attitudes in a community or society, propagandists feel they must hide their true identities and aims. Extremist groups and organized crime families, for example, may hide behind legitimate, and thus socially acceptable, "front organizations." They convince many in the public that they are acceptable when, in reality, they are engaged in covert activities (Broom and Selznick, 1968). In similar fashion, governments of countries like the United States and the Soviet Union try to convince their citizens that they are giving aid to underdeveloped

Construction crew terrified as drunk ghost staggers by

Crazed statue foams at mouth

A LADY STANDS in public foaming at the mouth, but it can't be rabies — because the 226-year-old woman is actually a solid bronze statue!

The foaming phenomenon has some residents of Carmel, NY, buzzing about spirits and other

Man disguised as a nun hides in convent 33 years

Entire town of 472 people goes into coma

Thicker, Stronger, Longer HAIR in 5 to 10 days

Woman floats out of her house in a giant soap bubble

Space creatures kidnap bride as groom watches

For Bosom Beauty

Try the one tested, trusted body creme that contains a full 40,000* units of ESTROGENIC HORMONES

Mental patient kills self by eating his arm

Teen castrates self when parents won't take him to the zoo!

Wife murderer hired by hubby was secret cop

IT'S FREE!

Mom is 9 and Dad is 13! World's youngest parents have a healthy 5 lb. baby!

Human garbage disposal boasts he'll eat anything

Housewife cooked to death by microwave

SUPERMARKET CEREAL SAVES BABY'S LIFE

Pigeon fancier attacks his neighbor

Various attention-getting devices may be used by the propagandist. Several weekly tabloids are sold at newsstands and at grocery checkout counters throughout the United States. Using lurid and sensational headlines such as those illustrated above, these "news" publications are very popular among certain segments of the population.

countries for primarily humanitarian reasons when other motivations, such as the geopolitical importance of these countries, are equally compelling.

4. *Raising fears and anxieties.* Politicians on occasion will raise fears by emphasizing *hidden enemies.* Advertisers will often attempt to raise people's anxieties concerning their health, love or sex life, breath, weight, or social standing. In television commercials, there is a standard formula. During the first few seconds, a person in the story has a life complication. Next comes the introduction of the product. This is followed immediately by an ''instant miracle'' in which the person's life is changed for the better because he or she used the product.

5. *Showing strength.* Propagandists use this persuasive technique in an attempt to show the merits of a particular point of view, cause, or product. Organized groups and social movements with few resources can impact public opinion by staging dramatic, visible events, and then using authoritative sources, such as the press, to gain maximum public exposure (Kielbowiez and Scherer, 1986). Marches, demonstrations, and sit-ins by various groups in recent years are representative examples. Advertisers also show the strength of products through the use of statistical claims, product comparisons, demonstrations, and independent tests.

Two additional points concerning propaganda should be mentioned. First, the categories mentioned above are not mutually exclusive. Instead, propagandists often incorporate several approaches in a single attempt at persuasion. For example, in 1985 the late actor Yul Brynner, who was a five-pack-per-day smoker, made an antismoking television commercial a few weeks before he died of cancer.

In this poignant attempt to persuade viewers to quit smoking, elements of associating, raising fears and anxieties, and showing strength were used. Second, propaganda is limited by several factors, including competing propagandas, the level of education and sophistication of the audience, and existing norms and cultural trends. Well-informed people are much more resistant to propaganda than the naive and poorly educated. Likewise, propaganda that drastically goes against existing cultural norms is usually ineffective.

SOCIAL MOVEMENTS

A **social movement** is a dedicated effort by a fairly large group to promote or resist change in the existing social system. Social movements represent the most highly organized form of collective behavior and are often the most long lasting. Historically, they have taken place primarily in societies characterized by complexity, growth, and change. In 1517, for example, Martin Luther set in motion one of the most significant movements of the last five hundred years when he nailed his Ninety-Five Theses to the church door in Wittenburg. The Protestant Reformation that followed helped to reshape social, political, and economic thought in Europe and affected the worldview of those who first emigrated to America in order to escape religious persecution (Bronowski and Mazlish, 1962).

Since that time, social movements have emerged for many reasons and have taken various forms. All have distinct goals. Some try to affect social values as did the recent civil rights and women's movements. Other movements attempt to gain power, such as that of the Nazis in Germany and, more recently, the Contras in Nicaragua. There are also movements focused on achieving personal benefits and psychological rewards for participants, including back-to-nature movements and religious movements like those of the Mormons of the nineteenth century and the fundamentalist evangelicals today (Turner and Killian, 1987).

Characteristics

Although social movements vary significantly in terms of goals, they usually have similar characteristics (Broom and Selznick, 1968; DeFleur, D'Antonio, and DeFleur, 1976). First, they tend to have a *different perspective* from the status quo, or existing social policy. The women's movement, as a case in point, has succeeded in helping to redefine the role and status of women in contemporary society.

Second, social movements exhibit *idealism among members.* Such idealism is particularly important as a morale booster since members of many social movements must face hardships and resistance. During the civil rights movement of the 1960s, many participants in demonstrations—often the objects of taunts, assaults, and arrests—linked arms and sang "We shall Overcome," the theme song of the movement.

In addition, members of social movements have an *action orientation.* They are dedicated to engaging in the action necessary to change some aspect of society through petitions, debates, speeches, demonstrations, and other approaches.

Finally, most movements consist of *multiple organizations.* Even though each may have its specific objectives, a coalition is often established to enable numerous organizations to work for a common cause.

Stages

According to Herbert Blumer (1939), social movements typically progress through a life cycle of four distinct stages. The first of these, the *social unrest stage,* emerges as a response to conflicts between various segments of society, unresolved social problems that sometimes appear to be getting worse, and a general state of dissatisfaction and restlessness concerning one or more issues. In such conditions of social unrest and confusion, leaders initially tend to be malcontents who do little more than heighten feelings of discontent.

Such leadership, however, tends to result in greater focus as the movement enters the *popular stage,* in which dissatisfied individuals see the need to close ranks and work together for a commonly held goal. During this period in the life span of a movement, two types of leaders may emerge—prophets and reformers. Prophets tend to be charismatic individuals with a vision, who have the ability to inspire followers to pursue a commonly held goal. Reformers are often much more pragmatic and may have an agenda for addressing specific problems and overcoming them a step at a time.

The third and fourth periods in the life of a social movement are the formalization and institutional stages. During the *formalization stage,* goals and strategies become clearly defined and standardized. The movement develops formal organization with clearly established levels and areas of leadership and authority. Policies and plans of action emerge which may resemble those of bureaucracies. Negotiators and master strategists take over the reins of leadership from the prophets and reformers. Finally, during the *institutional stage,* the movement is fully accepted and becomes part of the institutional fabric of mainstream society. Leaders become power brokers and administrators, concerned chiefly with consolidating and managing the gains that have been achieved.

Malcolm Spector and John Kitsuse (1977) suggest an additional stage—reemergence, or *renewal,* in some social movements. A portion of the original membership may feel that the movement has become too "status quo" in

Reform movements attempt to operate within the existing social system, as illustrated by these "Gray Power" activists. (AP/Wide World Photos.)

orientation or has lost its original sense of mission or purpose. Perceiving stagnation and discontent, these people may feel a need to renew efforts or perhaps begin a new movement based on the gains already achieved. The women's movements of the twentieth century furnish us with a good illustration. During the first two decades of this century, the goal for women was to achieve suffrage, the right to vote. By the late 1960s, a process of renewal was clearly evident as women focused their efforts on a much broader range of issues— abortion, pay equity, the equal rights amendment, and so on—aimed at much broader participation in society.

Types

Perhaps the most useful way to distinguish between different types of social movements is to examine their goals and the means or tactics used to achieve them. Accordingly, most social movements may be placed in one of the following categories:

1. *Reactionary movements* reject existing social policy and attempt to restore earlier values, norms, and policies, through violent means if necessary. The Ku Klux Klan historically has supported the doctrine of white supremacy and complete segregation of the

races. In attempting to reach this goal, members of the Klan and other separatist groups have periodically engaged in acts of terrorism and violence.

2. *Conservative movements* work within the system to preserve aspects of the status quo and thus resist certain forms of social change. The National Rifle Association, for instance, continues to work diligently in an attempt to preserve what it believes is the traditional right of Americans to keep and bear arms with as few restrictions as possible.

3. *Reform movements* work within the social system for changes in specific values, norms, and policies. Both the civil rights and women's movements during the twentieth century have been reform movements in that they have attempted to change customs and laws to provide minorities and women with improved opportunities and greater participation in society.

4. *Revolutionary movements* seek to replace a portion or all of an existing social system with something different, through violent means if necessary. Examples include the American Revolution of the 1770s and 1780s and the Russian Revolution of 1917. How those involved in a revolutionary struggle are perceived and characterized depends on one's vantage point and vested interest. During the American Revolution, the "Sons of Liberty" were seen as heroes by many colonists but were vilified by those still loyal to the British Crown. More recently, the Contra rebels, in their fight to overthrow the Sandinista government of Nicaragua, have been characterized as freedom fighters by some and terrorists by others.

5. *Separatist or expressive movements* find the existing social system unacceptable and seek to set up alternate organizations, communities, or societies. Some social scientists prefer to use the term "utopian" in referring to these movements (Alexander and Gill, 1984). Their members attempt to operate outside the mainstream of the host society. Their goal is the achievement of a form of personal expression and a life-style directed inward toward themselves and their group, rather than outward toward the world of social action. Some of the most notable of these isolationist movements are religious in orientation. They include, in the United States, the Shakers, the Amish, and, more recently, evangelical and Pentecostal groups.

CHAPTER SUMMARY

1. Collective behavior consists of people's relatively spontaneous and unstructured actions in response to ambiguous or changing social conditions. In general, sociologists divide investigation of this area of behavior into four broad categories: crowds and crowd behavior, mass behavior, public opinion, and social movements. This chapter is devoted primarily to a discussion of these topics.

2. We must first, however, discuss the preconditions that set the stage for collective behavior. In this regard, sociologist Neil Smelser has developed the value-added theory, the assertion that six conditions in society, when added together in sequential order, create a cumulative effect that increases the likelihood of collective behavior. These six factors are structural conduciveness, structural strain, generalized belief, precipitating factors, mobilization of participants, and social control.

3. Crowds are emergent groups that tend to develop in response to a variety of social situ-

ations, including planned events, sudden changes, and perceived injustices. One of the most pervasive characteristics of crowds is anonymity, a condition in which a person's identity becomes lost in a crowd. This, coupled with bystander apathy, can significantly influence the forms of behavior within such groupings. Crowds may be divided into four general types: casual, conventional, expressive, and acting crowds.

4. Two of the most dominant explanations of crowd behavior are provided by social contagion theory and emergent norm theory. Contagion theorists hold that the mood and behavior of crowds become dominant in shaping the emotions and behavior of the individuals who participate in them. Through such processes as imitation, suggestibility, and circular reaction, the behavior patterns of a crowd spread to include additional members. An alternative to the contagion approach is the emergent norm theory, the perspective that individuals become members of crowds for numerous reasons and, through interaction with others, adopt the group norms that develop from the situation.

5. Mass behavior is unstructured social behavior characteristic of large collectivities of people who operate outside of each other's presence. This form of collective behavior includes fads, crazes, and fashions (discussed in Chapter 3) as well as rumors, urban legends, and mass hysteria. A rumor is an unconfirmed story that is spread rather quickly from person to person. Such unverified stories tend to emerge from conditions of social strain and confusion and take form through processes of leveling, sharpening, correcting, and exaggeration. An urban legend is an unsubstantiated story, much more durable than a rumor, that is spread over an entire country or society. This kind of story usually involves themes

consistent with the issues, problems, fears, and mysteries of modern life. A third form of mass behavior is mass hysteria, a spontaneous excited reaction by large numbers of people to a mysterious social condition or event perceived as a threat.

6. Publics and public opinion represent an additional form of collective behavior. A public is a large, widely dispersed group of people who share an interest in or concern about an issue or group of issues. Every major issue in a given society has a public devoted to it. Public opinion refers to the dominant attitude held by a specific public or a society's population at large. It is influenced by several factors including media, censorship, and propaganda.

7. The most highly organized form of collective behavior is represented by the social movement, a dedicated effort by a fairly large group to promote or resist change in the existing social system. In terms of characteristics, most social movements tend to have a different perspective from the status quo, exhibit idealism among members, maintain an action orientation, and consist of multiple organizations. Specific types of social movements include the reactionary, conservative, reform, revolutionary, and separatist forms.

TERMS TO KNOW

anonymity: a condition in which a person's identity becomes lost in a crowd.
bystander apathy: a condition in which, during an emergency situation requiring responsible action, onlookers at the scene fail to act.
censorship: limitations placed on the information that is made available to the public.

circular reaction: the principle that members of crowds, particularly in conditions of unrest and heightened tension, reinforce each other's feelings and behavior in a back-and-forth or circular fashion.

collective behavior: relatively spontaneous and unstructured actions by people in response to ambiguous or changing social conditions.

convergence theory: the perspective that crowds tend to draw particular types of people with definite interests and values, rather than a representative cross section from the community.

emergent norm theory: the perspective that individuals become members of a crowd for numerous reasons and, through interaction with others, adopt the group norms that develop from the particular situation.

game perspective: the argument that crowds are often quite rational with participants who act logically under their own control in ways that benefit them.

mass behavior: unstructured social behavior characteristic of large collectivities of people who operate outside each other's presence.

mass hysteria: a spontaneous excited reaction by large numbers of people to a mysterious social condition or event perceived as a threat.

media: the systematic ways used to transmit information to specific publics or the population at large.

mob: the most extreme form of acting crowd, whose members are out of control and willing to engage in violence if it suits their ends.

propaganda: calculated and biased methods of persuasion based on emotional appeal.

public: a large, widely dispersed group of people who share an interest in or concern about an issue or group of issues.

public opinion: the dominant attitude held by a specific public or a society's population at large.

rumor: an unconfirmed story that is spread rather quickly from person to person.

social contagion theory: the position that the mood and behavior of crowds become dominant in shaping the emotions and behavior of individuals who participate in them.

social movement: a dedicated effort by a fairly large group to promote or resist changes in the existing social system.

structural conduciveness: a condition in which certain elements built into a society's social structure encourage collective behavior.

structural strain: a condition in which (1) intergroup conflicts develop between certain segments of a population and/or (2) dramatic social changes occur.

urban legend: an unsubstantiated story, much more durable than a rumor, that is spread over an entire country or society, usually with several local variations.

value-added theory: the argument that certain conditions in society, when added together in sequential order, create a cumulative effect which increases the likelihood of collective behavior.

SUGGESTED READINGS

Collective Behavior (Ralph H. Turner and Lewis M. Killian; Englewood Cliffs, N.J.: Prentice-Hall, 1987). A classic text on collective behavior now in its third edition. Chapters 2 through 12 are of particular interest.

Collective Behavior: A Sourcebook (Meredith D. Pugh; New York: West Publishing, 1980). A group of two dozen articles on various forms of collective behavior.

The Dynamics of Social Movements (Meyer N. Zald and John McCarthy; Cambridge, Mass.: Winthrop, 1979). A comprehensive examination of different types of social movements and how they develop.

The Invasion from Mars (Hadley Cantril; Princeton, N.J.: Princeton University Press, 1982). A detailed analysis and explanation of the panic that resulted from Orson Welles's radio broadcast from New York of H. G. Wells's *War of the Worlds* in 1938.

Rumor in the Marketplace: The Social Psychology of Commercial Hearsay (Fredrick Koenig; Dover, Mass.: Auburn House, 1985). An analysis of rumors and how they can have a negative impact in the corporate world.

The Vanishing Hitchhiker: American Urban Legends and Their Meanings (Jan Harold Brunvand; New York: W. W. Norton, 1981). A fascinating look at modern urban legends—their origins and variations.

Part Four

Issues
and
Institutions

Chapter 11

Deviant Behavior

The Interactionist Approach
Sociological Explanations in Perspective

■ **TERMS TO KNOW**

aberrant deviance
anomie theory
argot
astrology
atavistic theory
collective level deviance
compliant conformity
conformity
conventional conformity
cultural transmission theory
demonology
deviance
deviance by attributes

deviance resulting from an inability to conform
deviant
differential association
group level deviance
individual level deviance
innovation
labeling theory
moral entrepreneurs
nonconforming deviance
rebellion
retreatism
ritualism
socially acceptable deviance
somotype theory
XYY theory

His buddies call him Frog. At the age of thirteen, he was working the barrio areas of East Los Angeles and claims to have made $200 a week as a crack dealer (Lamar, 1988). He also claims to have rented sports cars to drive on weekends, although he can barely see over the steering wheel. He takes pride in being a newly initiated member of the Crips, a notoriously violent juvenile gang. Not long ago, Frog was busted for possession of cocaine and placed in the Los Padrinos Juvenile Detention Center. There, the four-feet-ten-inch, eighty-five-pound juvenile was twice beaten severely by older and larger inmates and had two of his teeth knocked out.

Just recently Frog was placed in a foster home, where juvenile authorities will watch his activities closely. Like thousands of youngsters across the country from impoverished and disorganized family backgrounds, he was lured into crime by the excitement and easy money to be made from the booming drug trade. These young people are no different from American adolescents everywhere in that

they are material girls and boys. They crave the glamorous clothes, cars, and jewelry they see advertised on TV, the beautiful things that only big money can buy. But many have grown up in fatherless homes, watching their mothers labor at low-paying jobs or struggle to stretch a welfare check. With the unemployment rate for black teenagers at 37%, little work is available to unemployed, poorly educated youths. The handful of jobs that are open—flipping burgers, packing groceries—pay only minimum wages or "chump change," in the street vernacular. So these youngsters turn to the most lucrative option they can find. In rapidly growing numbers, they are becoming the new criminal recruits of the inner city, the children who deal crack (Lamar, 1988, p. 20).

Danielle (Penny is her business name) works as a nude model in one of the several "studios" on Highway 121 just north of the Dallas, Texas, city limits. At establishments like "The Body Shoppe," "The Doll House," "Studio Paradise," and "The 121 Tub Club," she and several other young women make a passable though illicit living from prostitution. A striking redhead of about thirty with breasts augmented by silicone implants, Danielle has been in the "business" off and on since she was a teenager. Her mother, a staunch Baptist, divorced Danielle's father, a traveling musician, when her daughter was only two. Her mother's second husband provided some stability but began trying to molest his stepdaughter when she was fourteen. Even though his advances were unsuccessful, Danielle was afraid to tell her mother and ran away to get married two years later. After her marriage turned sour, she met an older man who "turned her out," as the expression goes, and introduced her to the world of prostitution (Semones, 1988).

Today, Danielle is a single parent with a small son to rear. She refers to herself with apparent pride as a "slut" and a "whore" and claims to have stayed in the business because the money is easy, she likes a lot of sex, and she enjoys playing the role of exhibitionist and the temporary power it gives her over some of her customers. Although she does not have plans to retire soon, she admits that she cannot tell her mother and son what she does for a living. They think she works for the phone company.

THE NATURE OF DEVIANCE

Deviance and Deviants

Both Frog and Danielle have engaged in **deviance**, behavior that violates the dominant norms of a group or society. Such norms are established and enforced by those with the power to have their perceptions of appropriate behavior instituted as social policy and custom. Taken as a whole, these standards for behavior come to define for most of us what is legal, moral, appropriate, and even "normal." Through the socialization process, which begins in infancy, most people are conditioned to accept the dominant social standards they live under as right and normal not only for themselves but for others as well.

Few if any of us abide by these standards all the time. Indeed, some people act in ways seen as socially disruptive, and a few reject socially dominant norms and live a deviant lifestyle. How deviance is defined, the forms it takes, why it arises, the consequences that stem from it, and related issues are of keen interest to sociologists and will be explored in this chapter. First of all, the analysis of deviance tells us how widely accepted a given set of norms is, along with the effectiveness of socialization and various social control mechanisms. Deviance sometimes results in serious social problems, like crime, while in other instances it may help to bring about social reform and change. The civil rights movement of the 1960s is an example of the latter.

Regardless of the form social standards take, each of us engages in minor acts of deviance from time to time. Being late for an appointment, receiving a ticket for speeding, or occasionally overdrawing a checking account are representative examples. In this sense, deviance may be seen as a continuum ranging from minor infractions of folkways and social conventions to major violations of mores and laws relating to society's most cherished values.

Those who engage in significant or extreme forms of deviance are called "deviants." There are those, like Frog and Danielle, who are regarded as deviants by most people in society. A **deviant** is a person who violates the most highly regarded norms of a group or society. Crime and delinquency, prostitution, drug abuse, and homosexuality are historically prevalent examples of behaviors perceived as extreme forms of deviance in the United States. The person defined as a deviant is often rejected as a person of value and worth and is stigmatized and subjected to ostracism, as well as severe punishment in many cases (Clinard, 1974; Schur, 1971, 1984).

Deviance as a Social Definition

One commonly held misconception about deviance is the ethnocentric notion that the "don'ts" and the "wrongs" specified by a given society are universal principles that apply everywhere. In actuality, *deviance is a social definition.* What is deemed unacceptable behavior varies according to several factors, most notably the particular society in which one lives. Three of the most important factors relating to how deviance is defined are briefly summarized as follows:

1. *Deviance and one's social context.* Émile Durkheim was one of the first sociologists to assert this principle: "It is no longer possible today to dispute the fact that law and morality vary from one social type to the next, nor that they change within the same type if the conditions of life are modified" (Durkheim, 1966, p. 70). In some societies, for example, it is not illegal to engage in public drunkenness, to take plural spouses, or to practice homosexuality. Countries such as Germany and Holland have legalized prostitution, whereas in the United States it is against the law except in certain portions of Nevada.

Deviance as a social definition: Prostitution. The practice of prostitution in the United States is a form of deviant behavior that is illegal everywhere except in certain portions of Nevada. In the photograph on the left, these women on the street are in constant danger of being arrested. By contrast, prostitution is legal in some European cities, (as shown on the right) where practitioners operate openly with little need to fear the authorities. (*Left:* Copyright Joel Gordon, 1980. *Right:* Jeroboam.)

2. *Deviance and one's position in society.* What constitutes deviance in either law or custom depends also on one's position in society. Most Americans can legally purchase and own handguns, but convicted felons cannot. Children may not vote, persons under a certain age cannot draw social security retirement benefits, and employers are not allowed to employ undocumented aliens. Even in the 1990s, women who are assertive are sometimes perceived as "argumentative" and "bitchy," while men engaged in the same behavior are seen positively as "take-charge" types and "assertive."

3. *Deviance and historical time frame.* What is viewed as deviant also depends on the historical time frame. Interracial marriage, for instance, was illegal in some states prior to 1967. In similar fashion, various countries over the last several hundred years have branded as deviant various behaviors that are not deviant by modern American standards.

> A Prussian law of 1784 prohibited mothers and nurses from taking children under two years of age into their beds. The English villein [serf] of the fourteenth century was not allowed to send his son to school, and no one lower than a freeholder was permitted by law to keep a dog. The following have at different times been crimes: printing a book, professing the medical doctrine of the circulation of blood, driving with reins, [selling] coins to foreigners, having gold in the house, buying goods on the way to market for the purpose of selling them at a higher price, [and] writing a check for less than one dollar (Sutherland and Cressey, 1970, pp. 15–16).

Social Benefits That Derive from Deviance

Most people have a tendency to view acts of deviance—particularly those that violate laws and moral codes—as "bad" or "detrimental" to society. Certainly many forms of deviance, including crime and family violence, do indeed undermine social order. However, deviance is a natural and inevitable product of social systems just as conformity is and, as such, has both positive and negative consequences for society (see Figure 11-1). Deviants and conformists spring from the same social structure (Erikson, 1966). Indeed, some forms of deviance actually may be beneficial. The following are some of the possible benefits that may be derived from antisocial behavior:

Figure 11-1 Deviance: Possible Benefits and Negative Effects

Possible Benefits	Negative Effects
1. May increase social cohesion.	1. Disrupts social order.
2. May help to clarify norms.	2. Destroys the motivation of others to conform.
3. Toleration of some forms may help to minimize more severe problems and conflicts.	3. Undermines trust in organizations and institutions (if allowed to go unpunished).
4. May help to bring about changes in social policy.	4. Is expensive to society.

1. *Deviance may increase group cohesion.* Otherwise complacent and splintered groups sometimes unify when faced with an outside threat or "enemy." In this sense, deviance facilitates a sense of "community" as people close ranks and unite under a set of commonly held beliefs and purposes. At the microlevel, a crime wave of burglary or drug pushing in a community may result in the formation of neighborhood associations and crime watch groups. This may help not only to neutralize the threat, but to bring neighbors together as well. At the macrolevel, war with another country perceived as deviant may result in the development of the necessary unity and patriotism to repel the aggressor.

2. *Deviance may help to clarify social norms.* Some norms are quite general, and deviance may serve to establish clear boundary lines of acceptable behavior. Rules of conduct are often ambiguous, relying on ill-defined standards of acceptability. Deviance confronts an issue and helps to set the outer limits concerning which behaviors will be tolerated and which will not. For example, two elementary schoolteachers each tell their students that those who talk in class will be kept after school. Teacher A keeps any student after hours who so much as whispers to another student. Teacher B allows occasional whispering but, after giving a warning or two, will punish those offenders who persist. Students test the boundaries of norms with each teacher to ascertain the limits of tolerance. Other similarly tested norms in society include unclear rules and policies and laws perceived as out-of-date or unconstitutional.

3. *The toleration of some deviance may help minimize more severe social problems and conflicts.* Although some would see this as social hypocrisy, policymakers and enforcers often find it beneficial to tolerate or "close their eyes" to certain levels and forms of deviance. To combat major crime more effectively, law enforcement agencies and prosecutors often depend on informants (usually minor criminals) and a system of plea bargaining. These officials give minor offenders special consideration so that they can deal effectively with those perceived as the more dangerous threat to social order.

   The Roman Catholic Church, with its official policies against some birth control methods and prohibitions against noncelibacy and marriage for priests, also tolerates some deviance. Many American Catholics ignore the church's orthodox stand on birth control, and some priests keep a low profile while having sexual relationships or cohabiting with women. Given the church's traditional position and the ever-changing nature of American culture, these people feel it is unwise to be open about such practices. It might create a major schism in the Catholic church. Toleration of limited deviance in these and other instances helps to preserve the social system and prevent the open rebellion that rigid enforcement would tend to produce.

4. *Deviance may help to bring about changes in social policy.* Deviance expressed as disagreement with policymakers and violation of their policies by significant numbers of people may indicate serious problems in the way a society is organized. If the needs of many, if not most, people are not being met by existing norms, a flaw in the social system may be evident and require some adjustment. The acts of civil disobedience by thousands of people during the civil rights movement of the 1960s is a case in point. Significant changes in law and social custom resulted from such "nonviolent protests."

Negative Effects of Deviance

Just as deviance, in some cases, is functional or beneficial to society, it can also have very disruptive consequences. Serious social problems, including crime and delinquency, drug abuse, suicide, and family conflict, tend to be the images most people visualize when the term "deviance" is mentioned. Here are some of the most prevalent negative effects that stem from antisocial behavior:

1. *Deviance disrupts social order.* For any society to operate smoothly, its members must cooperate with each other by obeying social norms and respecting one another's rights. When there is a lack of cooperation and mutual respect, patterned social order and the resulting security and harmony become disrupted. High crime rates, for instance, cause people in many parts of the United States to feel insecure. To protect themselves and their property, many feel it necessary to have dead-bolt locks, burglar bars, electronic alarms, handguns in bedside tables, and large dogs in order to feel safe. The social and financial costs of maintaining police organizations, the courts, and the prisons also take their toll on the society at large.

2. *Deviance destroys the motivation of others to conform.* For a child who observes that several of his or her friends have stolen toys from a department store and have not been caught, it might be tempting to engage in the same type of behavior. Similar situations occur when some students successfully cheat on an exam, delinquents vandalize a house, or criminals rob a bank. Those in the deviant's peer group and community may find it difficult to maintain their will to conform if they feel that others are not being caught and punished for their antisocial behavior.

3. *Deviance undermines trust in organizations and institutions.* How would you feel if your college instructors were chronically late or missed class, returned exam scores a month late, and the college you attend did not send your grades when promised? What if department stores did not open and close according to posted hours, mail did not arrive at appropriate destinations much of the time, and car repairs you paid for were not done properly on several occasions? Like most people, at first you would probably feel anger, indignation, and, above all, surprise. However, you might soon feel helpless and lose all confidence in these areas of society. When deviance of this sort is perceived as pervasive and ongoing, people may lose faith in the proper functioning of organizations and institutions. The Watergate scandal of 1973–1974, for instance, resulted in a significant though temporary loss of confidence by many Americans in the existing political system. A sex scandal cost Senator Gary Hart his bid for the presidency in 1988. Likewise, revelations in 1988 concerning multiple liaisons between the television evangelist Jimmy Swaggart and a prostitute resulted in the dramatic loss of revenue for his ministry and a similar decline in enrollments at his Bible college.

4. *Deviance is expensive.* The financial costs of combating and controlling deviance are high. Take crime for example. In the United States, there are over 200 million incidents of shoplifting a year that cost retail businesses at least $12 billion annually (Baumer and Rosenbaum, 1984). Most of these costs are absorbed by the consumer, who must pay higher prices for goods and services. Consumer fraud, which may be the most prevalent of all crimes, costs an additional $25 billion each year (Barlow, 1987). This figure does not include the tens

of billions in tax revenues it takes to maintain the criminal justice system comprised of law enforcement agencies and organizations, the courts, and penal institutions. Human costs are also high. During the 1980s in America, the proportion of deaths by homicide was double that of the early 1960s (Currie and Skolnick, 1988). The amount of pain and suffering inflicted on the families of these victims is incalculable.

CONFORMITY: THE OPPOSITE OF DEVIANCE

Social deviance occurs, in most cases, because of one or more of the following factors: (1) a decrease in the power and influence of certain norms in society on individuals and groups, (2) a decrease in the validity of these norms as a result of changing social conditions, or (3) a combination of both these factors. In short, deviance occurs when certain members of society have neither the ability nor the motivation to conform to the dominant norms or social rules.

Consequently, a sociological analysis of deviant behavior perhaps should begin with the issue of **conformity**, behavior that is in basic agreement with the dominant norms of society. In this regard, it is important to understand both the nature of conformity and how it is maintained.

Two Types of Conformity

Sociologists Mavis H. Biesanz and John Biesanz (1973) make the distinction between conventional conformity and compliant conformity. **Conventional conformity** is socially acceptable behavior that results from people's unconsciously following the dominant norms of society. Conventional conformists thus act from habit. They have been successfully socialized (from the standpoint of society) with

a set of socially dominant values that they have internalized as part of their identities. As a result, many if not most dominant norms are rarely questioned. If and when there are impulses or temptations to deviate, conventional conformists are usually successful in suppressing them. Most of the folkways we subscribe to would fall into the category of conventional conformity. They include the foods we eat, the language patterns we use, and most of the customs we follow. Our actions based on religious beliefs and basic moral principles are included as well.

By comparison, **compliant conformity** is socially acceptable behavior that results from external social pressures. If such pressures were suddenly removed, compliant conformists in many cases might feel they could "get away with" certain deviant acts and would not hesitate to engage in them. In other words, the primary reason for obeying norms in these instances is the fear of the consequences, not any ingrained habit or moral conviction. Compliant conformists choose not to deviate because of their fear of discovery and punishment, fear of disapproval, and sometimes simply the lack of opportunity. Therefore, some people obey the laws, submit honest tax returns, and remain faithful to their spouses primarily because of these considerations.

In actuality, the socially acceptable behavior of most people includes both types of conformity. In some instances, people engage in conventional conformity; in other circumstances, in compliant conformity. It would appear, however, that in simple rural societies with low technology, little change, and homogeneous populations, conventional conformity tends to be most prevalent. Children in such cultures are likely to have a consistent and uniformly administered set of socialization experiences. What are viewed as both appropriate and deviant forms of behavior are clearly established and widely accepted by

In many neighborhoods across America, mowing one's lawn is one of many forms of conventional conformity practiced as social custom or habit. (Copyright Greg Meadors, 1989.)

practically everyone. By comparison, it appears that compliant conformity is more likely to occur in modern, urban societies with high technology, rapid change, and heterogeneous populations. Children reared in these social systems grow up in an environment in which the norms of conduct are much more vague and ill-defined.

How Conformity Is Maintained

Sanctions and Social Controls. To the extent possible, the maintenance of conformity is ensured through social control systems that consist of sanctions and other social controls. In Chapter 3 on culture, we discussed mechanisms of social control called *sanctions,* socially recognized and enforced rewards and punish-

ments. Sanctions are applied to both conforming and deviant behavior and may be informal or formal. A smile from a loved one, for example, is an informal positive sanction, while a frown may punish a person in an equally informal way.

In Chapter 5 on social organization, we discussed how social order in society is maintained through the use of sanctions in the form of both internal and external *social controls.* Through *internal social controls* developed primarily through family socialization, the developing child acquires a personal code of conduct that shapes his or her future behavior. In other words, he or she becomes self-regulating in terms of behavior. To reinforce such conformity, society also puts into place and maintains various types of *external social controls.* These range from formally recognized rewards for socially valued acts of conformity to formally prescribed punishments for acts of deviance.

Authority Figures, Peer Pressure, and Physical Coercion. The use of sanctions and social controls to maintain conformity involves several dimensions. Many if not most people learn to conform when confronted by *authority figures* such as parents, teachers, employers, and police officers. Another source of social control is *peer group pressure*. Peer groups often shape behavior to a remarkable degree through the everpresent use of acceptance, praise, and support for conformity, and rejection, condemnation, and punishment for deviance. Since we are social creatures with a developed need for social approval and acceptance, we are very susceptible to the influence of both authority figures and peer groups. In addition, *the threat of physical coercion* represents a dimension of social control. When typical informal and formal sanctions and internal and external controls prove ineffective, the loss of liberty through imprisonment is sometimes used in the more extreme cases of crime and delinquency.

Language and Argots. Even *language* is used to distinguish conformity from deviance and to help maintain conformity within the group. Symbolic interactionists maintain that through our use of language, we structure a particular view of reality for ourselves. Our use of symbolic communication along with certain words and phrases helps us to conceptualize, among other things, our view of ourselves and our views of conformity and deviance (Harroff, 1962). Taken one step further, the way others use language allows us to identify them as conformists or deviants, according to our perceptions of these concepts in the context of our group and society. Likewise, the way we use language furnishes oth-

ers with similar perceptions of us. If a person does not use "appropriate language," he or she does not "fit in" as far as the group is concerned and may be perceived as deviant.

Sociologists have found that subcultures make use of a special form of language called an **argot**. An argot involves the use of newly constructed words along with standard words and phrases with special meanings. These forms of communication are of particular value in studying conformity and deviance in highly stratified and pluralistic societies like the United States. Their use helps to establish boundaries between various groups, since only group members tend to know the special meanings that go with certain words and phrases. A person's use or nonuse of a certain argot immediately identifies him or her to others as to whether or not the individual is a "member" of their group and thus a conformist, or an "outsider" according to their values and life-style. A person who wants to be accepted within the group learns the accepted form of language, or argot, in order to conform.

Argots are characteristic of many groups and subcultures in America. Some allow identification of the age group, social class, or ethnic background of certain segments of society. Adolescents have their own argot that changes from generation to generation. Black English is another example, as is the use of Yiddish terms and other special expressions by Jewish Americans. As illustrated in Figure 11-2, deviant groups and subcultures also use certain idiomatic expressions to establish their own sense of exclusivity and ensure internal conformity. Drug users, in their everyday speech, use such terms as "horse," "snow," "ludes," and "stash." Prostitutes have special meanings for "date," "Greek," "French," and "half-and-half." While a few argot terms find their way into the general language of a culture, they may have little or no meaning to most people in the dominant culture.

Figure 11-2   **Argots: Examples from Two Deviant Subcultures**

The Drug Subculture	Los Angeles Street Gangs
Black russian: black, potent hashish	*Benzo:* Mercedes Benz
Bag: a quantity of diluted heroin	*Breakdown:* shotgun (also *gauge*)
Blow: to inhale a drug (also *sniff*)	*Bustin':* to go out shooting
Bluebirds: amytal sodium capsules	*Dead presidents:* money
Change: a short jail or prison sentence	*Deuce-deuce:* .22 caliber gun
Clean: not carrying or using narcotics	*Do a ghost:* leave (also *Do a train*)
Chinese white: potent white heroin	*Fooled out:* made a mistake
Connect: to find source of drugs (also *score*)	*Four-five:* .45 caliber gun
Crystal palace: a place to take speed	*Glass house:* police headquarters
Flashing: glue sniffing	*Hook:* a phony person
Gorilla pills: barbituates/other sedatives	*Hoopy:* car
Juice head: a person who drinks liquor	*Jack:* hijack
Luding out: using methaqualone	*Kite:* letter from prison
Mainline: to inject drug intravenously	*Mark:* someone wanting to join gang
Narc: any narcotics officer (all levels)	*Mud duck:* an ugly girl
Off: high on a drug (also to get rid of or kill)	*Ride on:* a drive-by shooting
Peter: chloral hydrate (a sedative)	*Squab:* fight
Rifle range: withdrawal ward in hospital	*Take out of the box:* kill someone
Roach: a marijuana cigarette butt	*Talking head:* arguing
Rock: granulated heroin, cocaine, etc.	*You got four feet?:* Want to fight?

Sources: Adapted with permission from Lingeman, R. R. (1974). *Drugs from A to Z: A dictionary*, 2nd ed. New York: McGraw-Hill; The *Los Angeles Times* (1988).

LEVELS AND TYPES OF DEVIANCE

Levels of Deviance in Society

Behavior that violates the standards of social acceptability occurs at both the micro- and macrolevels of social organization. **Individual level deviance** involves acts of antisocial behavior performed by only one person at the community level. Examples include most suicides, behavior resulting from mental disorders, and many crimes of murder, rape, armed robbery, and burglary. Factors contributing to individual deviance may include faulty socialization and unequal opportunity, which produce frustration and alienation.

Group level deviance refers to socially unacceptable behavior by social groups, usually at the community level. Group deviance is often reinforced by a deviant subculture that furnishes its members with a set of socially unacceptable norms to follow. When this occurs, individuals belonging to these groups often internalize their deviant norms and values rather than those of the dominant society, especially in large urban areas of the United States. Drug addicts and juvenile gangs, connected together in such groups, contribute significantly to the incidences of burglary and violent crime. In similar fashion, prostitutes have their own social networks and emotional support groups, usually at the community level.

Sometimes, however, the distinction between group deviance and collective deviance becomes blurred. Such activities as those of organized crime, price fixing by executives in some corporations, and various types of corruption in government occur not only locally but at the macrolevel of society as well. **Collective level deviance** involves socially unacceptable behavior by large numbers of people at various levels of society. Take organized crime for instance. In the United States, there are an estimated twenty-four Mafia families spread across the country with "a formal, oath-taking national membership of some 1700" (Magnuson, 1986). Of these, about one-half are concentrated in five nationally powerful families headquartered in New York City. If we include drug trafficking as part of its activities, organized crime is even international in scope. Other examples of collective level deviance include acts of civil disobedience carried out by members of some social movements and civil wars that occasionally occur in some societies.

Sociological Types

Sociologists have categorized deviance in a variety of ways. However, a review of the literature reveals that five types in particular are useful in illustrating the diversity of deviant behavior, as well as the motivations of those who participate. In this regard, we will briefly examine the following sociological types: aberrant deviance, nonconforming deviance, socially acceptable deviance, deviance resulting from an inability to conform, and deviance by attributes.

Aberrant Deviance. According to sociologist Robert Merton (1966), **aberrant deviance** is deviant behavior in which a person violates a norm for selfish reasons and attempts to escape detection and punishment. The criminal is one obvious example. The aberrant deviant acknowledges the validity of the norms being violated, but finds it advantageous to violate them for personal gain or satisfaction. Most criminals are aberrant deviants in that they commit such acts for selfish gain, attempting at the same time to avoid detection, capture, and punishment. Those who feign illness to stay home from work and those who engage in extramarital sex might also be placed in this category.

Nonconforming Deviance. In contrast to aberrant deviance, Merton has identified **nonconforming deviance** as socially disapproved behavior in which the participant challenges the legitimacy of certain norms by violating them openly, regardless of the negative sanctions that might be imposed. This person acts out of conscience and often violates norms for unselfish reasons based on moral principles. In some cases, the nonconforming deviant is appealing to a higher moral good, an ultimate value that transcends particular norms of society. Although abortion (as of this writing) is a legal right for women that most Americans tend to support, "pro-life" demonstrators in recent years have picketed abortion clinics and many have been arrested for civil disobedience and criminal offenses. Many colonial citizens during the American Revolution were nonconforming deviants committed to certain social ideals. The same might be said for Confederate soldiers during the Civil War and the antiwar protesters and civil rights demonstrators during the 1960s and early 1970s.

Socially Acceptable Deviance. A third classification is **socially acceptable deviance**, a type of deviant behavior considered acceptable by significant portions of society (Sutherland, 1967). This sometimes occurs when laws or public policies are established because of pressure from interest groups instead of broad-based public support. Prominent twentieth-century examples in the United States include the Eighteenth Amendment (prohibition) and laws criminalizing the possession of even small amounts of marijuana. As a result of massive deviance by millions of Americans, prohibition was repealed and possession of minute quantities of marijuana has largely been decriminalized.

Sociologist Howard Becker (1963) has coined the term **moral entrepreneurs** to refer to members of some groups who wish to impose their view of morality and policy on others. What such a person sees as a "problem" or "evil" is pursued as "an absolute ethic; what he sees is truly and totally evil with no qualification. Any means is justified to do away with it" (pp. 147–148). Several other sociologists concur with Becker. They agree that socially acceptable deviance sometimes follows in the wake of laws and policies instituted on ideological and moral grounds, rather than rational or even socially popular ones. Eric Goode (1972, p. 186) has said that

> the moral entrepreneur is an ideological imperialist—it is his position that what he believes must also be right for everyone and that anyone doing what he disapproves of must be punished by the might of the law, by the state, by society as a whole. The existing rules do not satisfy him or her—some of the most influential moral entrepreneurs in history have been women, such as Carrie Nation, the alcohol prohibitionist.
>
> Naturally, all moral entrepreneurs believe that what they want to see passed into law *is good for others* and not merely a crystallization of their own personal views and prejudices. Thus antimarijuana crusaders do not see themselves as imposing their ideology and morality on the public. Rather they see themselves as *doing good*, as helping others, as lifting up the drug user to see the error of his ways, as protecting society from the damage that drug use can do to humanity. (But then, as Camus said, the welfare of humanity is always the alibi of tyrants.)

Deviance Resulting from an Inability to Conform. An additional type of antisocial behavior is **deviance resulting from an inability to conform**. This involves a situation in which an individual either cannot control his or her own behavior or is forced to commit a deviant act (Davis, 1964). In criminal cases in which the accused allegedly suffers from a mental disorder, an insanity plea may be entered, although it is used only about 4 percent of the time in the American court system (Steadman and Cocozza, 1974). John Hinkley, for example, the young man found guilty of shooting President Ronald Reagan and his Press Secretary James Brady in a 1981 assassination attempt, resides today in a mental institution rather than a prison. The standards of accountability and punishment are different for the mentally disturbed in criminal cases because, presumably, they were not in control of their faculties at the time the criminal act was committed (Bartol, 1980).

Likewise, a person forced to commit a deviant act against his or her will would not be held to the same standards of accountability. Suppose a young bank officer receives a phone call one morning from a couple of criminals holding his wife and child for ransom. If he goes to the vault and takes a large sum of money in order to get his family back safe and sound, most likely he will be met with only mild punishment, if any, from either his employer or the authorities.

Deviance by Attributes. Finally, there is **deviance by attributes** (Glaser, 1971). People with certain identifiable physical or social characteristics are often perceived and treated as deviant. The mentally retarded, midgets, those perceived as "freaks," the blind, the wheelchair bound, and other physically handicapped people are often treated in an obviously self-conscious way by some who often have more difficulty in dealing with the "special" characteristics of the handicapped than do the handicapped themselves. Others "deal" with such "different" people by simply avoiding them.

EARLY EXPLANATIONS OF DEVIANCE

Throughout history, humanity has sought to explain why certain individuals in society engage in deviant behavior. Early explanations centered on fear, myth, and superstition. Only during the past few decades have social scientists viewed deviance from a perspective of cultural relativity. This comes from a realization that most forms of deviance do not involve moral or societal absolutes, but instead are determined by such factors as cultural context, people's perceptions of reality, and historical time frame. Nonetheless, people who are unfamiliar with the scientific method and the sociological perspective continue to subscribe to an absolutist position on deviance.

Myth and Superstition: The Examples of Demonology and Astrology

The earliest explanations of deviance took the form of **demonology**. This was a system of beliefs which held that deviant behavior was caused by evil spirits or demons that possessed the body and made it act according to their will. In early societies, the witch doctor or shaman was the "law giver" who interpreted the supernatural world. Anyone who violated the laws he established was considered to be possessed by demons. He would then try to summon the good spirits to drive the demons away through such devices as the wearing of grotesque masks, dancing around the possessed victim to scare away evil spirits, the use of potions, and "grinding a hole in the per-

son's skull with a sharp stone to let the demons out" (Fox, 1976, p. 10). The expression "scaring the hell out of a person" had its origins in the demonological traditions of early societies.

Demonology has existed in numerous forms throughout the world and is still practiced (in Haiti, for example) where voodoo rituals are used to invoke or cast out demons. During the Middle Ages in Europe, rites of exorcism were used by the church to expel demons from the "possessed," and beliefs in the evil and deviant nature of witchcraft and sorcery were widely accepted. As a result of the witch trials held at Salem, Massachusetts, in 1692, nineteen women were put to death by hanging for practicing sorcery. Similar trials continued until about 1800, although no additional executions took place (Boyer and Nissenbaum, 1974).

Astrology, which originated about five thousand years ago in Mesopotamia, has also been used to explain deviance. **Astrology** refers to the notion that the movement of the planets and stars affects human behavior in general, and that the moon in particular influences deviant behavior. The concepts "lunacy" and "lunatic," part of our popular vocabulary pertaining to the mentally disturbed, had their origins in this perspective during the eighteenth century (Fox, 1976). However, astrology had already been discredited as a serious science a century earlier. In the early 1600s, the astronomer Johannes Kepler (1571–1630), himself once an astrologer, discovered that the earth, a fairly insignificant speck in the grand scheme of things, was not the center of the universe. Today social scientists see astrology as having little or no value in explaining deviance or any other form of human behavior. Nonetheless, reading their horoscopes remains a popular casual pastime for many and is still taken seriously by some people.

Explanations of deviance based on demonology were once prevalent in America. During the late 1600s, several young women were found guilty of practicing witchcraft and were hanged. (Culver Pictures, Inc.)

The Emergence of Science: Biological Explanations

By the latter half of the nineteenth century, explanations of deviance based on myth and superstition began to give way to those grounded in science. Since the behavioral sciences, including sociology, were then only in their infancy, the first scientific explanations of deviance emerged from the biological disciplines. These *biological explanations* argued that deviance was caused primarily by inborn physical traits or characteristics. Criminality and mental disorders were thus seen as genetically inherited.

Lombroso's Atavistic Theory. The father of the biological school of deviance was Cesare Lombroso (1836–1909), an Italian psychia-

trist. Lombroso developed what has been called **atavistic theory**, the argument that the criminal is an inherited type who represents a genetic throwback to primitive humans. In 1876, he published *L'Uomo Delinquente (Criminal Man)*, in which he argued that the criminal is a separate species from modern *Homo sapiens,* which he labeled *Homo delinquens.* Lombroso (1911) based his theory on data he gathered by comparing certain physical characteristics of Italian prison inmates with those of Italian soldiers. He also studied the skulls of several hundred criminals and compared them with those of prehistoric humans. He concluded that the criminal type could be identified by the presence of at least five of a large number of physical characteristics. They included a slanting forehead, prominent brow ridges, large ears, protruding lips, a heavy jaw,

The father of the biological school of deviance was Cesare Lombroso (1836–1909). Although his theory that the criminal represented a throwback to primitive man was shown to be invalid, he nonetheless paved the way for modern scientific explanations of deviance. (Culver Pictures, Inc.)

atypical eyes, a high tolerance for pain, and either excessive hairiness or a lack of body hair. The atavistic criminal lacked a sense of conscience concerning right or wrong, was egotistical and selfish, cruel and impulsive. In his later writings, Lombroso did acknowledge the influence of environment in shaping the behavior of some criminals, but his basic explanation remained a genetic one (Wolfgang, 1972).

Both Lombroso's methods of analysis and his conclusions were strongly criticized by the scientific community, although his approach was fairly well received among popular audiences. In 1913, criminologist Charles Goring (1972) tested Lombroso's assertion that genetically inherited characteristics seriously affected crime. In comparing the characteristics of three thousand English prison inmates with those of a group of English college graduates, he found no significant difference between the two groups. The findings of this study were accepted by other criminologists, and Lombroso's theory of genetic causation was essentially laid to rest.

Sheldon's Somotype Theory. Another category of biological explanation is **somotype theory**, the perspective that physique or body type is linked to both personality and deviance. Although scientific attempts to explain deviance in terms of body types have been prevalent since the 1850s, the most notable effort in recent decades has been the work of anthropologist William H. Sheldon (1949). In his classification system, Sheldon divided body types into three broad categories: the *endomorph* (fat and flabby), the *ectomorph* (thin and frail), and the *mesomorph* (muscular and athletic). Furthermore, he asserted that the endomorph was outgoing and sociable in temperament, the ectomorph was shy and withdrawn, and the mesomorph had an aggressive and adventuresome personality. In studying delinquent males incarcerated in a rehabilitation home, Sheldon found that a disproportionate number were mesomorphic in body type. Subsequent studies on juvenile offenders have yielded similar results (Glueck and Glueck, 1950; Cortes and Gatti, 1972).

While it appears clear in some studies that mesomorphic body type is associated with delinquency, most sociologists reject the idea that there is a cause-and-effect relationship between these two factors (Vold, 1958; Clinard and Meier, 1979). This would be like saying that because blacks are disproportionately represented in the prison population, "race" could be a cause of crime. A large body of sociological research suggests otherwise. It is now clearly recognized that social and environmental factors are the primary causes of both delinquency and crime. In addition, there are methodological problems associated with body type research. For example, delinquents in institutional settings are not representative of all delinquents any more than incarcerated criminals are representative of all criminals. It is just that they are the ones caught in the net of the justice system.

XYY Theory. A third type of biological explanation has attempted to link chromosomes to crime. During the 1960s, the **XYY theory** experienced some popularity. This was the assertion that the presence of an extra Y chromosome in males was associated with criminal behavior. Typically, males have both X and Y chromosomes, or XY, and females have two X chromosomes, or XX. A few males have a chromosomal anomaly in which an extra Y chromosome is present. The result is XYY, which some researchers have claimed creates a "supermale" of below average intelligence who is prone to violent criminal activity (Jacobs et al., 1965). Although XYY males are indeed overrepresented in the prison population, their records indicate a lower incidence of violence against others than those of the more typical XY inmates (Price and Whatmore, 1967; Fox, 1971). In 1969 a conference of scientists sponsored by the National Institute of Mental Health concluded that evidence for the alleged relationship between the XYY chromosomal characteristic and crime was inconclusive (Public Health Reports, October 1969). More recent research has found little or no support for XYY theory as well (Ellis, 1982).

Biological Explanations in Perspective. Biological explanations for deviance in general and, more specifically, crime and delinquency have fallen short in explaining the complexities of deviance. Sociologists Edwin H. Sutherland and Donald Cressey (1970, p. 118) have commented that it is "impossible

for criminality to be inherited as such, for crime is defined by acts of legislature and these vary independently of the biological inheritance of the violators of the law." Most sociologists agree. Donald J. Mulvihill and Melvin Tumin (1969) assess the limitations of biological explanations of deviance as follows:

> [S]ome individuals are more likely than others to become criminals or violent as a result of biological makeup. But it is never "given" in the "nature" of any individual that he will be criminal or law abiding, pacific or violent, cooperative or competitive, selfish or altruistic. All these are complex forms of social behavior, which depend upon the social and cultural milieu of the developing individual (p. 424).

Similar attempts have been made to establish a scientific basis for forms of so-called biologically derived deviance other than crime, including alcoholism, other forms of substance abuse, and mental disorders. While some of these behaviors, particularly addictive disorders, have a physiological component, the scientific evidence for biological causation is weak at best. With a few possible exceptions, physical or biological problems of deviance are little more than symptoms of larger and more fundamental social and environmental causes.

Take alcoholism for example. Medical practitioners may be able to "dry out" or "cure" the physical dependence of a patient on alcohol. However, they are ill equipped to deal with the root causes of alcoholism or "drug problems" in general, which lie deep within the fabric of society. There may be a biological predisposition toward addictive behavior. In this sense, assuming there is such a thing as an "addictive gene" or trait, one might just as easily become addicted to fast food, sex, gambling, or any one of a hundred other things that, in the extreme, could be maladaptive. However, whether an addictive predisposition becomes suppressed or indeed does manifest itself in any one of numerous possible addictions is primarily a function of socialization. Consequently, the medical community is ill equipped to deal effectively with the root causes of alcoholism or any other form of substance abuse.

Likewise, the notion of "mental illness" and "psychiatric treatment" for most mental disorders sits on shaky scientific ground. Thomas Szasz (1974), himself a physician and psychiatrist, has this to say about "mental illness":

> [P]hysicians are trained to treat bodily ills— not economic, moral, racial, religious, or political "ills." And they themselves (except psychiatrists) expect, and in turn are expected by their patients, to treat bodily diseases, not envy and rage, fear and folly, poverty and stupidity, and all the other miseries that beset man. Strictly speaking, then, disease or illness can affect only the body. Hence, there can be no such thing as mental illness. The term "mental illness" is a metaphor.
>
> . . . In other words, I maintain that mental illness is a metaphorical disease: that bodily illness stands in the same relation to mental illness as a defective television set stands to a bad television program. Of course, the word "sick" is often used metaphorically. We call jokes "sick," sometimes even the whole world "sick"; but only when we call minds "sick" do we systematically mistake and strategically misinterpret metaphor for fact and send for the doctor to "cure" the "illness." It is as if a television viewer were to send for a television repairman because he dislikes the program he sees on the screen (pp. ix, x–xi).

MODERN ANALYSIS: SOCIOLOGICAL EXPLANATIONS

Despite much research by biological scientists, a solid link between inherited factors and deviance in general has not been established. Instead, the last half century has seen a steady advance of explanations from the behavioral sciences, most notably those that stress the sociological perspective. Modern sociological explanations of deviance are divided generally into three categories that correspond to the dominant theoretical approaches of the discipline: functionalism, conflict theory, and interactionism.

The Functionalist Approach

As we discussed in Chapter 1, the *functionalist approach* in sociology maintains that society operates like an organism. That is, the various parts interact for the smooth functioning of the entire system. The resulting equilibrium forms the foundation for social order. Because deviance tends to disrupt that order, it is, in many cases, a negative and dysfunctional influence.

Anomie Theory. Perhaps the founding father of the functionalist approach was Émile Durkheim (1966) who, among his many contributions, coined the term "anomie." In his view, *anomie* represents a state of confused norms or normlessness brought on by rapid change and social complexity (Chapter 5). As societies became industrialized, developed specialized institutions and divisions of labor, and thus became more complex, different sets of norms emerged to meet the needs of diverse groups and subcultures with differing attitudes, lifestyles, and preferences. Because the norms and values stressed by different segments of modern societies tend to conflict with one another, the "rights and wrongs" and "do's and don'ts" of society tend to become blurred and unclear, or no longer relevant in light of changing social conditions.

Building on Durkheim's work, Robert Merton (1968) extended the concept of anomie to the analysis of deviant behavior. In his **anomie theory**, Merton asserts that deviance results from discrepancies that arise between culturally approved goals and access to the culturally approved means necessary to achieve them. The typical individual, the conformist, is socialized to accept both culturally prescribed goals and means. Americans in general seek a middle-class life-style. They achieve this goal by first acquiring an education and then obtaining a job to support themselves and their families. Increasingly, a middle-class life-style and such material benefits as nice clothes, cars, and houses require a good education and a well-paying job. However, the poor, minorities, the young, and other groups often do not have equal access to either culturally approved goals or the means to achieve them. The strain created by the discrepancy between a society's culture (which sets goals) and its social structure (which establishes means or opportunities to achieve them) can result in anomie or confusion. This, in turn, may cause a variety of deviant responses.

As shown in Figure 11-3, Merton identifies four different forms of deviance that may stem from anomie. He calls these innovation, ritualism, retreatism, and rebellion.

Innovation is a deviant response in which a person accepts the culturally desired goals of society, but rejects the culturally approved means of achieving those goals. A teenager living in poverty may accept the goal of having an automobile and observes that many sixteen- and seventeen-year olds have "wheels," which serve as an adolescent status symbol. However, because he or she has little access to the socially approved means to obtain a car, pushing drugs to make money or stealing a car may serve as an illegitimate means to obtain the culturally approved goal.

An individual may also react to anomie by engaging in **ritualism**. This is a deviant response in which a person rejects culturally approved goals but accepts the approved means. The ritualist responds to the confusion of anomie by grabbing onto any structured means or rules, just as a drowning person might grab for a life preserver. Culturally approved goals become secondary if not irrelevant as long as one has the security of a structured response to follow. Some bureaucrats are ritualists in that they become slaves to rules (means), while losing sight of organizational goals.

Retreatism is a deviant response in which a person rejects both culturally approved goals

Figure 11-3 Anomie Theory: Merton's Four Types of Deviance

Methods of Adaptation	Culturally Approved Goals	Culturally Approved Means
CONFORMIST	Accepts	Accepts
DEVIANT		
Innovator	Accepts	Rejects
Ritualist	Rejects	Accepts
Retreatist	Rejects	Rejects
Rebel	Rejects/Replaces	Rejects/Replaces

Source: Adapted from Merton, R. K. (1957). *Social theory and social structure*, 2nd ed. New York: Free Press, p. 140.

and means. In the wake of the stock market crash of 1929, millions of Americans during the Great Depression of the 1930s had their cultural rugs yanked out from under them in the form of economic disruption and collapse. Jobs, bank accounts, and homes were lost, and many had to struggle to survive. Thousands of men, formerly providers for their families, could not cope with this anomie and dropped out of society by hopping freight trains and living in "hobo jungles" at various train stops throughout the country. Today there are still a few hoboes, as well as other retreatists such as some of the street people, hard-core drug addicts, and teenage runaways. Participation in conventional society has become either meaningless or an extremely painful experience for such individuals. Other examples include some religious cults and other separatist groups who reject the conformity of the dominant society and seek to establish alternative life-styles or communities.

A final form of deviance resulting from anomie is **rebellion**. Merton argues that rebels reject both culturally approved goals and means and seek to replace them with other goals and means. Political extremists bent on destroying the governmental system as it presently exists and replacing it with another are representative of rebellion.

The Conflict Approach

Functionalists see deviance as a disruption of social order. Implicit in this approach is the assumption that, like physical organisms, "healthy" societies possess a certain balance or equilibrium. Deviance, like disease, can upset that balance and create harmful effects, known as social problems. Conflict theorists disagree. The *conflict approach* stresses that what is defined as "antisocial" or "deviant" arises out of a struggle for power between various groups. The group or segment of society with the most power and influence is then able to have its definitions of conformity and deviance legitimated as social policy. Those whose norms and values are not made into policy often become discontent. Out of such discontent arises antisocial behavior or deviance.

Deviance Resulting from Class Struggle. The conflict school in sociology, as discussed in Chapter 1, originated with the work of Karl Marx, the nineteenth-century German philosopher and political economist. Marx saw history as a series of class struggles between two factions, the "haves" who made and benefited from social policy and the "have-nots" who were forced to live under it.

Following in this tradition, sociologist Richard Quinney (1974, 1980) argues that not only are policies and laws made by the ruling class but, when violated by members of the privileged group, penalties tend to be minimized. If we consider just five categories of crimes committed by U.S. corporations in recent years—bribery, fraud, illegal political contributions, tax evasion, and antitrust violations—the list of violators reads like a Who's Who of American companies. Those found guilty of one or more of these crimes include Bethlehem Steel, Gulf Oil, Firestone Tire & Rubber Co., DuPont Corporation, and International Paper (Ross, 1988). Sociologist Amitai Etzioni (1985) reported that during the decade between 1975 and 1984, 62 percent of America's five hundred largest corporations had engaged in at least one form of illegal activity and 15 percent had participated in five or more types of crime. Yet, in many if not most cases, charges brought by prosecutors were for minor criminal and misdemeanor offenses, and punishments tended to be suspended sentences and monetary fines.

By contrast, those charged and found

guilty of certain other offenses including assault, burglary, drug pushing, murder, and robbery are generally punished much more severely by the criminal justice system. A burglar often is sentenced to several years in prison, while the "white-collar" criminal who embezzles $10,000 from an employer, as often as not, is never even prosecuted, much less spend any time in prison.

In addition, the poor and minorities receive the most severe punishments from the criminal justice system. Nowhere is this better illustrated than with the death penalty, the harshest punishment of all. Almost 44 percent of all those on death row are black, and 5 percent are Hispanic (Bruck, 1988). In a study published in 1980, criminologists William Bowers and Glen Pierce examined the sentencing process for homicide in three states: Florida, Georgia, and Texas.

> What they found was that in cases where white victims had been killed, black defendants in all three states were from four to six times more likely to be sentenced to death than were white defendants. Both whites and blacks, moreover, faced a much greater danger of being executed where the murder victims were white than where the victims were black. A black defendant in Florida was thirty-seven times more likely to be sentenced to death if his victim was white than if his victim was black; in Georgia, black-on-white killings were punished by death thirty-three times more often than were black-on-black killings. And in Texas, the ratio climbed to an astounding 84 to 1 (reported in Bruck, 1988, p. 502).

The Drug Issue: An Application of Conflict Theory. An illustration of how conflict theorists approach the analysis of deviance is provided by the issue of drugs and how it has been treated during the twentieth century in the United States. In the first two decades of this century, certain religious groups and their legislative counterparts in Congress waged a war against the "evils of drink." Primarily because of their lobbying efforts, they amassed enough support to secure passage of the Eighteenth Amendment to the Constitution. This prohibited the manufacture, sale, and distribution of beverages containing alcohol.

Although alcoholic beverages were banned, the prohibition amendment was an abysmal failure, in part because it focused on the use of alcohol rather than its abuse. Not only did the American public ignore prohibition, but alcohol consumption increased significantly. So did alcoholism and alcohol-related diseases and deaths (Wright and Weiss, 1980). Prohibition also enabled organized crime to establish a foothold in America by earning hundreds of millions of untaxed dollars from the sale of illegal alcohol. In 1933, after years of public controversy and debate, prohibition was repealed by the passage of the Twenty-first Amendment.

In similar fashion, recent laws prohibiting the possession of such drugs as marijuana, cocaine, and opiate-narcotics have met with little success (Julian and Kornblum, 1986). Again, the focus has centered on the morality of using certain drugs rather than the problems stemming from their abuse. Like the prohibition issue of more than a half century ago, critics argue that Congress has formulated governmental drug policy in a climate of "bipartisan hysteria," rather than by an objective and rational appraisal of the real problems (Stark, 1988). By doing so, the more substantive issues of relative harm brought about by different drugs, drug abuse, and the need for effective drug treatment have been given scant attention.

From the standpoint of objective science, it is indeed ironic that some of the most dangerous and harmful substances are more or less socially acceptable and "legal." In comparison, some of the less harmful drugs, rela-

The Eighteenth Amendment to the U.S. Constitution (called the Prohibition Amendment) went into effect in 1920. It ushered in the Roaring Twenties, a time of "speakeasies," bootleg whiskey, and bathtub gin. Because of its tremendous unpopularity and ineffectiveness, prohibition was later repealed in 1933 with the passage of the Twenty-first Amendment.

tively speaking, are socially unacceptable and "illegal." Take the practice of cigarette smoking for example. The tobacco and alcohol lobbies are powerful interest groups, which collectively spend billions of dollars annually on advertising and promotion that make their products seem relatively harmless. Yet, from the standpoint of deaths and health complications caused by harmful substances, cigarette smoking represents, by far, the number one drug problem in America. According to the U.S. Surgeon General, the effects of ciga-

rette smoking claim over 300,000 lives each year. Alcohol, another legal substance, kills another 60,000 people annually. In comparison, fewer than 6,000 deaths each year are attributable to illegal narcotics (reported in Stark, 1988).

From the conflict perspective, the argument could also be made that the manner in which resources have been allocated to combat the "drug problem" has reflected moralistic self-interest, rather an objective assessment of the issue. As of 1988, only 6 percent of the

8 billion dollars allocated annually for the Reagan administration's "war on drugs" had been spent to help support drug treatment and rehabilitation programs. In addition, about 90 percent of all people voluntarily seeking treatment at drug treatment and rehabilitation centers had been turned away because of lack of space, personnel, or resources. The typical waiting period for those turned away averaged six to eighteen months. During the same period, according to the U.S. Government Accounting Office, the Coast Guard and Navy combined forces during 1987 to spend 2,512 ship-days and $40,000,000 to search for ships transporting illegal drugs. Their efforts netted them only twenty vessels carrying such drugs and 110 suspected smugglers (reported in Stark, 1988).

The Interactionist Approach

The interactionist approach is quite distinct from those that view deviance as the product of social disruption (functionalism) or intergroup conflict (conflict theory). According to the *interactionist approach,* deviance results from certain types of interactions of a person with other people, as well as the acquisition of a deviant self-image. Two of the most prominent interactionist explanations are cultural transmission theory and labeling theory.

Cultural Transmission Theory. Some sociologists subscribe to the **cultural transmission theory**, the assertion that socialization experiences within certain groups encourage the individual to engage in deviant behavior. As applied to crime in particular, Edwin H. Sutherland (1939) has called the result of these experiences **differential association**, the principle that criminal behavior is learned in close-knit groups that encourage or condone antisocial behavior. When an individual has more contacts with these groups than with

those who favor and encourage conformity, deviance is likely to occur.

Take, for example, deviant subcultures among some criminals—organized gangsters, narcotic drug users, and juvenile gangs. These groups act as agents of socialization for their membership in several ways. First, they have their own norms, which define "right" and "wrong" differently from the dominant society. In addition, they often educate their members in how to avoid such negative sanctions imposed by "legitimate" institutions as arrest for a felony offense. Finally, exposure to deviant groups provides participants with a source of emotional and social support that, in many cases, are not provided to them in other relationships. Consequently, those engaging in deviance, by having their basic needs met through such associations, sometimes find it easy to rationalize their behavior as acceptable. In other instances, the individual may feel some pangs of guilt or remorse over what he or she does, but receives enough pressure or support from the deviant group to counterbalance and thus neutralize such influences.

The learning of deviant responses, therefore, involves a socialization process very similar in many respects to that acquired by nondeviants. The values, motives, techniques, and rationalizations of deviance are learned in primary groups for the most part. These significant others provide for the individual more motivation and reinforcement for violating socially acceptable norms than for obeying them.

Labeling Theory. Another interactionist explanation of deviance, labeling theory, is particularly useful in helping to explain why certain individuals, including prostitutes and criminals, become career deviants. Proponents of **labeling theory** assert that the manner in which people perceive social reality determines (1) what behaviors are labeled as de-

Cultural transmission theory suggests that some people adopt a deviant life-style because they associate with those who possess a deviant set of values. Through this differential association, the individual may become socialized to a deviant way of life. (Copyright Robb Kendrick Photography, 1989.)

viant and (2) how being labeled as deviant affects people's behavior. First of all, behavior viewed as deviant is not universally agreed upon but, instead, depends on such factors as the cultural context, the social situation, and "the eye of the beholder." As sociologist J. L. Simmons (1969) comments:

> [A]lmost every conceivable human . . . activity is pariah in somebody's eyes. This means that most people (you and I included) would be labelled deviant by some existing persons and groups. Anyone who moves around much from place to place or social world to social world has probably run into this. There is nothing inherently deviant in any human act; something is deviant only because some people have been successful in labelling it so. The labelling is a local matter that changes from place to place and even from time to time in the same place. To understand deviance we have to understand its environmental context. So we have to look at the people doing the labelling as much as the deviant himself (p. 4).

Those doing the labeling make the rules that define the limits of socially acceptable behavior. Individuals who violate these limits are labeled as deviant. In the United States, the development and enforcement of social norms historically have been dominated by affluent, white, Protestant, heterosexual males. Almost by definition, a person who did not fall into these categories was perceived as deviant. If a person was poor, nonwhite, non-Protestant or non-Christian, homosexual, or

Those released from prison may find it difficult to adjust successfully if the label "ex-con" and the stigma it creates are firmly placed on them by others in the larger society. (AP/Wide World Photos.)

female, that individual was perceived as "nontypical" at best, and society applied different standards to his or her behavior. Such people have been perceived as outsiders and, in many instances, have often been labeled as deviant for engaging in the same behavior as the insiders (Becker, 1963). It was not too long ago that most Americans perceived blacks as deviant for trying to use the same public facilities as whites and saw a woman's place as the home rather than the workplace.

Edwin Lemert (1951), an early labeling theorist, identified two types of deviance—primary and secondary. *Primary deviance* takes the form of impulsive episodes of socially un-

acceptable behavior that are temporary rather than habitual. Trying an illegal drug, shoplifting a record album from a department store on a dare from one's friends, or cheating on a college exam once are examples. Individuals who engaged in these types of behavior would not perceive themselves as deviant nor would they be perceived as such by society in general. *Secondary deviance*, in comparison, is ongoing and habitual antisocial behavior. Chronic drug users, thieves, prostitutes, and others who persistently violate standards of acceptability come to see themselves as deviant as a consequence of being labeled so by the dominant society. Once a label of deviance has been attached to a person by society—"pervert," "queer," "junkie," "whore," or "convict," to mention just a few—deviant status becomes the imposed master status from the standpoint of society. Other aspects of the individual's personality and life, including social positions as a family member, citizen, and employee, are ignored (Semones, 1977).

This, in turn, encourages further deviance because the deviant image is internalized as part of the individual's self-concept. For instance, convicted felons who have "served time" are often labeled in this manner by the larger society after they are released from prison. Often they find it extremely difficult to obtain a job, partially because of the stigma attached to the label "ex-con." Especially for the many who have no stable family support system when they are released, it is common to take such a stigma and rejection to heart, become alienated from society, and drift back into a pattern of criminal activity.

Sociological Explanations in Perspective

Despite their value, none of the three sociological approaches to deviance mentioned—functionalism, conflict theory, or interactionism—have escaped criticism. Functionalist explanations have been criticized on several grounds. Anomie theory, for instance, is useful in helping to explain various forms of deviance, ranging from several types of crime to retreatism. However, it does not adequately explain such other forms of deviance as mental disorders and rape. Again, not everyone in society agrees on what "socially acceptable goals" are or should be. Many of these criticisms have been leveled by conflict theorists, who argue that the natural state of society is competition and struggle between various

groups rather than order and peaceful equilibrium.

Conflict explanations have also had their critics. The value of conflict approaches in helping to explain some forms of deviance—minority deviance and lower-class property crimes included—is increasingly recognized. However, some forms of deviance, including crime in general, have increased during the twentieth century in some modern societies, while exploitation and inequality have declined (Davies, 1983). This suggests that other variables in addition to conflict may be of equal or greater importance in these cases.

Interactionist explanations, considered by themselves, also have their limitations. They are very useful in helping us understand how some career deviants, through differential socialization, come to perceive "appropriate behavior" very differently from most people. Labeling theory helps us to understand how, through the vested interests of moral entrepreneurs and those in power, certain behaviors and individuals are labeled as inappropriate and deviant. The "deviant" individual may then come to feel stigmatized and thus led to habitual deviance. However, some critics (Gove, 1980) argue that labeling theory fails to explain habitual deviants, such as shoplifters and adulterers, who have not been caught (labeled) but nonetheless continue such behavior.

The limitations inherent in any single explanation of deviance only act to underscore the immense complexity of human behavior in general and deviance in particular. There are many varieties of deviance, each with several dimensions. Each of the sociological approaches mentioned focuses on a particular aspect of this very diverse and complex phenomenon. Other courses and texts in specialized areas of sociology—social problems, deviant behavior, criminology, drugs and drug abuse, human sexuality, and so forth—address these issues specifically and in depth. In doing so, they use functionalist, conflict, interactionist, and other sociological approaches as diagnostic and explanatory tools of analysis to create a mosaic of understanding. Through the continued application of these and other sociological perspectives, those imbued with the sociological imagination will be able to build an increasingly integrated understanding of deviance and other forms of human behavior as we approach the twenty-first century.

CHAPTER SUMMARY

1. In assessing the nature of deviant behavior, sociologists make a distinction between the concepts *deviance* and *deviant*. Deviance is behavior that violates the dominant norms of a group or society. Most people engage in deviance from time to time. The deviant, however, is a person who violates the most highly regarded norms of a group or society. The criminal, for example, is stigmatized as such and is subject to ostracism, as well as severe punishment in many if not most cases.

2. From the sociological perspective, deviance is a social definition. What constitutes socially unacceptable behavior varies from culture to culture and often from situation to situation. To have multiple spouses (at the same time) is viewed as deviance in American society although it is permissible in some cultures. Likewise, to kill an "enemy" in combat during a war is acceptable, but to kill a neighbor in an argument is not. What is considered deviance also changes from one historical period to another. Behaviors such as interracial marriage and abortion, while legal today, were considered deviant and illegal in several states until the late 1960s and early 1970s.

3. Deviance involves both functions, or social benefits, and dysfunctions, or negative consequences. Potential benefits include increased group cohesion, the clarification of social norms, and significant changes in social policy. Negative consequences include the disruption of social order, the undermining of the motivation for others to conform, and the erosion of trust in organizations and institutions.

4. Any discussion of deviance should include some emphasis on conformity, behavior that is in basic alignment with the dominant norms of society. Sociologists generally agree on two basic types of conformity, conventional and compliant. Conventional conformity involves unconscious adherence to the dominant norms of society. Conventional conformists thus act out of internalized habits resulting from successful socialization. Compliant conformity, in contrast, is socially acceptable behavior that results from external social pressures. Compliant conformists are motivated to conform by the fear of discovery, embarrassment, punishment, and the like. Conformity in general is maintained through a variety of social control mechanisms. These include authority figures, peer groups, physical coercion (in extreme cases), and even language that allow us to perceive and share definitions of in-groups and out-groups and acceptable behavior versus unacceptable behavior.

5. The sociological analysis of deviance distinguishes between different types and levels of behavior perceived as socially reprehensible. Types of deviance include aberrant, nonconforming, and socially acceptable forms, as well as deviance resulting from an inability to conform and deviance defined by a person's characteristics or attributes. Deviance also occurs on individual, group, and collective levels.

6. Early explanations of deviance centered on myth and superstition. Two illustrative examples are provided by demonology and astrology. Demonology is a system of beliefs which holds that deviant behavior is caused by evil spirits or demons that possess the body and make it act according to their will. Astrology presents the notion that the movement of the planets and stars affects human behavior in general, and that the moon in particular influences deviant behavior.

7. By the end of the nineteenth century, explanations of deviance based on science began to emerge. The first scientific explanations came from the biological sciences and included atavistic theory, somotype theory, and XYY theory. Atavistic theory, developed by Cesare Lombroso, maintained that the criminal represented a throwback to primitive humans. Somotype theory, proposed by William Sheldon, asserted that deviant behavior, such as delinquency, was related to physical body type. XYY theory argued that the presence of an extra Y chromosome in males was associated with criminal behavior. Atavistic theory has been discredited altogether, somotype and XYY theories are largely without substantiation, and few social scientists today place much stock in biological approaches as primary explanations of deviance.

8. Modern explanations of deviance are largely sociological. Functionalists stress the value of such approaches as anomie theory. This approach, developed by Robert Merton, argues that some deviance stems from discrepancies that arise between culturally approved goals and access to the socially approved means necessary to achieve them. Conflict theorists stress that what is defined as "deviant" arises out of a struggle for power between various groups. The segment of society with the most power is able to have its defi-

nitions of conformity and deviance legitimated as social policy. Interactionists argue that deviance results from certain interactions of a person with others, along with the acquisition of a deviant self-image. Two of the more prominent interactionist explanations of deviance today are cultural transmission theory and labeling theory.

TERMS TO KNOW

aberrant deviance: deviant behavior in which a person violates a norm for selfish reasons and attempts to escape detection and punishment.

anomie theory: the perspective that deviance results from discrepancies between culturally approved goals and access to the culturally approved means to achieve them.

argot: a special form of language characteristic of subcultures.

astrology: the notion that the movement of the planets and stars affects human behavior in general, and that the moon in particular influences deviant behavior.

atavistic theory: a biological explanation of deviance which maintains that the criminal is an inherited type who represents a genetic throwback to primitive humans.

collective level deviance: socially unacceptable behavior by large numbers of people at various levels of society.

compliant conformity: socially acceptable behavior that results from external social pressures.

conformity: behavior that is in basic agreement with the dominant norms of society.

conventional conformity: socially acceptable behavior that results from unconsciously following the dominant norms of society.

cultural transmission theory: the perspective that socialization experiences within certain groups encourage the individual to engage in deviant behavior.

demonology: a system of beliefs which holds that deviant behavior is caused by evil spirits that possess the body and make it act according to their will.

deviance: behavior that violates the dominant norms of a group or society.

deviance by attributes: a situation in which those with certain identifiable physical or social characteristics are often perceived and treated as deviant (for example, the physically handicapped, dwarfs, the mentally retarded).

deviance resulting from an inability to conform: a situational form of deviance in which a person either cannot control his or her behavior or is forced to commit a deviant act.

deviant: a person who violates the most highly regarded norms of a group or society.

differential association: the principle that criminal behavior is learned in close-knit groups that encourage or condone antisocial behavior.

group level deviance: socially unacceptable behavior carried out by social groups, usually at the community level.

individual level deviance: acts of antisocial behavior performed by only one person at the community level.

innovation: a deviant response in which a person accepts culturally approved goals, but rejects culturally approved means.

labeling theory: the perspective that the manner in which people perceive social reality determines (1) what behaviors are labeled as deviant and (2) how being labeled deviant affects people's behavior.

moral entrepreneurs: members of some groups who attempt to impose their views of morality or policy on others.

nonconforming deviance: socially disapproved behavior in which the participant challenges the legitimacy of certain norms by violating them openly, regardless of the negative sanctions that might be imposed.

rebellion: a deviant response in which a person rejects both culturally approved goals and means and seeks to replace them with other goals and means.

retreatism: a deviant response in which a person rejects both culturally approved goals and means.

ritualism: a deviant response in which a person rejects culturally approved goals but accepts the approved means.

socially acceptable deviance: deviant behavior considered acceptable by significant portions of society.

somotype theory: a biological explanation of deviance which asserts that physique or body type is linked to both personality and deviance.

XYY theory: a biological explanation of deviance which argues that the presence of an extra Y chromosome in males is associated with criminal behavior.

SUGGESTED READINGS

Corporate and Governmental Deviance: Problems of Organizational Behavior in Contemporary Society, 3rd ed. (David M. Ermann and Richard J. Lundman; New York: Oxford University Press, 1987). A dozen concise and timely essays on the nature of corporate and governmental crime and deviance in modern society.

Deviant Behavior and Social Control (S. Kirson Weinberg; Dubuque, Iowa: William C. Brown, 1974). A brief yet comprehensive treatment of deviance including discussion of delinquency, drug addiction, sexual deviance, mental disorders, and suicide.

Explaining Delinquency and Drug Use (Delbert Elliot, David Huizinga, and Suzanne Ageton; Beverly Hills Calif.: Sage Publications, 1985). A detailed report on these two forms of deviance examined from an interactionist perspective.

Introduction to Criminology, 4th ed. (Hugh D. Barlow; Boston, Mass.: Little, Brown, 1987). An excellent and comprehensive text on criminology. Of particular interest is the chapter on crime and public policy.

Law, Order, and Power (William J. Chamblis and Robert B. Seidman; Reading, Mass.: Addison-Wesley, 1985). A comprehensive text on conformity and deviance written from a conflict perspective.

The Outsiders: Studies in the Sociology of Deviance (Howard Becker; New York: Free Press, 1963). An insightful treatment of deviance and crime from a interactionist (labeling) perspective.

Wayward Puritans: A Study in the sociology of deviance (Kai Erikson; New York: Wiley, 1966). A classic portrayal (from an interactionist perspective) of how deviance was defined and treated among the Puritans in New England.

Chapter 12

Population: An Overcrowded Planet

People at present think that five sons are not too many and each son has five sons also, and before the death of the grandfather there are already 25 descendants. Therefore people are more and wealth is less; they work hard and receive little.

Han Fei-Tzu, circa 500 B.C.

To the size of states there is a limit, as there is to other things, plants, animals, implements; for none of these retain their natural power when they are too large or too small, but they either wholly lose their nature, or are spoiled.

Aristotle, 322 B.C.

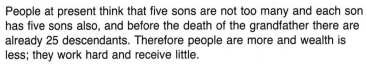

■ TERMS TO KNOW

age specific fertility rate
age specific mortality rate
agricultural revolution
census
crude birth rate
crude death rate
demographic transition
demography
dependency ratio
fecundity
fertility
fertility rate
greenhouse effect
growth rate
human ecology

industrial revolution
infant mortality rate
internal migration
international migration
life expectancy
Malthusian theory
mega-cities
migration
momentum
mortality
mortality intervention
population
population pyramid
pronatalism
sex ratio
urban revolution
vital statistics

In the minute it takes you to read this paragraph, 160 new inhabitants will be born on the planet Earth. That is 9,600 new people each hour, twenty-four hours a day, every day. By the time you wake up tomorrow morning, there will be almost a quarter million new people who were not here today. In fact, one out of every ten people who have ever lived since humanity began are alive today. And the numbers and percentages continue to grow steadily.

For thousands of years in both Eastern and Western traditions, social thinkers warned that there were limits to growth. Few heeded these warnings because the problem seemed far off in the distant future, and somehow not relevant to "here and now" realities and concerns. Consequently, the world population grew and continued to grow.

Today, many Americans are as oblivious to the dangers of overpopulation as were the citizens of ancient China and Athens during the times of Fei-Tzu and Aristotle. For those who have a relatively high standard of living, a plentiful supply of food on hand, and the technological benefits and conveniences of modern society available in the here and now, the problem of overpopulation seems distant and far away. Because of the low priority given this issue and related ecological concerns, this problem has not been of major concern in presidential campaigns, does not constitute a major component of this nation's foreign or domestic policy, and is given only passing attention in the national press. It is mainly those in the scientific community and related organizations, particularly sociologists and biological scientists, who seem concerned. Meanwhile, the world population continues to grow larger.

From a historical perspective, world population growth has perhaps had more positive than negative consequences. It has marked the transition from simple social systems with low technology to complex ones with industrial economies and advances in knowledge and technology. These changes in turn have made it possible for people in the more technologically advanced societies to enjoy a standard of living unprecedented in human history.

It is indeed ironic that overpopulation is now among the most serious social problems facing humanity, one that, along with nuclear war, threatens the very survival of our species. From 1970 to 1988, the world's population grew from 3.4 billion people to 5.2 billion, enough new inhabitants (1.8 billion) to occupy China and India, the two most densely populated nations on Earth. As of 1986, the total population was increasing by 87 million people per year, or 238,000 each day. These are enough new people during each twenty-four-hour period to create a new Akron, Ohio. At this rate of increase, there could be between 6 and 8 billion people in Asia and Africa alone by the year 2020. According to Morris K. Udall (1987, p. vii), this is "significantly more than now inhabit the entire planet. If the growth rate increases, we could be fighting for food, space, and shelter with 15 billion people within the next century."

Obviously, this tremendous upsurge in population is a relatively new phenomenon

Reprinted with permission of the *Chicago Tribune*.

Deviant behavior (as perceived by most Americans) occurs in various degrees and takes numerous forms. Some are seen as merely "in poor taste." Others may be regarded as "immoral" or "abnormal." The most severe forms of deviance are illegal and are considered heinous crimes.

that must be stopped and stopped soon. To accomplish this with a minimum of human suffering will require that people worldwide be informed about the scope of the problem as soon as possible. If birthrates worldwide are not reduced to replacement levels within the next several years, the alternative will be increased death rates from malnutrition, disease, and, perhaps, wars, along with economic instability caused at least partially by the pressure of overpopulation.

Currently, at least 10 million people starve to death each year, and another one-half to one billion go to bed hungry each night (Mayer, 1976; Ehrlich and Ehrlich, 1979). These figures can only rise in the future if nations throughout the world do not soon adopt comprehensive population control policies. Werner Fornos (1987), president of the Population Institute, comments:

> [I]f we permit the six-billion mark or the eight-billion mark to pass casually as we have the fifth, our children will pay the price. For the world they inherit from us will be one in which the nations of the developing world will have lost the struggle for economic self-sufficiency. Staggering under the weight of huge and impoverished populations, . . . many of these nations would descend into a fierce cycle of economic deterioration and political and social instability.
>
> Such conditions would have a direct and indisputable impact on the nations of the industrialized Northern Hemisphere as well. Americans, Canadians, Japanese, and Europeans would see their societies transformed by the pressures created by . . . the neighboring Third World, pressures that could well unhinge Western economies and undermine international security.
>
> This bleak scenario does not arise from any defeatism or cynicism. Rather, it is founded on the most objective and realistic demographic data available and on science's best knowledge of the relationships between population and world environment. And it is

offered in stark contrast to the striking opportunities and possibilities we have for a far brighter international future. For the fate of the world is not sealed; it is being determined by the choices and decisions we are now making (pp. 1–2).

In this chapter, we will examine the nature of population in terms of characteristics, growth, and change. When sociologists use the term **population**, they are referring to the total number of persons who inhabit a country or other politically or geographically specified territory. Because of the worldwide importance of this topic as a social issue, much of the following discussion will focus on population as a social problem. To begin, we will examine how sociologists study this area of human behavior.

DEMOGRAPHY: THE STUDY OF POPULATION

The scientific study of population characteristics and change is **demography**. Although considered a subfield of sociology, demography derives from such diverse disciplines as economics, statistics, medicine, and biology. It has been a part of sociology only during the last seventy-five years.

Specifically, demographers examine the size, composition, and distribution of human populations and how they change. They also examine the problems or potential problems associated with population growth, decline, and composition. Micro-, macro-, and international population characteristics and trends are analyzed. Some demographers, such as those employed by the U.S. Bureau of the Census, examine population factors primarily within the United States. They are interested in describing and explaining such things as rates of overall growth, trends regarding the size of the family, the ratio of rural to urban residence, which states and regions are gaining or losing population and why, and life expectancy. Others may be employed by international organizations, like the United Nations, and attempt to gather and analyze data on populations worldwide. Among other things, these scientists ascertain which countries have stable or declining populations, which have exploding populations and why, what political, social, and economic resources and solutions are needed to combat overpopulation and human suffering in certain countries, and which nations are hardest hit by the AIDS epidemic and other health problems.

The Census

One way demographers gather data on populations is through census taking. A census is a relatively complete head count of the people in a given society. The counting of populations can be traced back at least five thousand years to the ancient Sumerians and Egyptians. They most probably counted members of households along with their personal property for taxation purposes. In modern times, the taking of a formal census first emerged in democratic societies. The United States was the first modern country to make legal provision for a regular census.

The first U.S. census was taken in 1790. This initial effort showed a total U.S. population of 3.9 million people, about the same number who currently live in the metropolitan area surrounding Houston, Texas. Since then, a census has been compiled every ten years and the American population has grown dramatically. Recent census research shows a total U.S. population of 179.3 million in 1960, 203.3 million in 1970, 226.5 million in 1980, and an estimated 250 million in 1990 (*The World Almanac and Book of Facts*, 1988). The margin of error in recent census studies has involved an underestimate of from 1 to 2 percent. By compiling population data, census

takers also ascertain additional information, including each state's population by sex, race, rural or urban residence, and median age. To complete the 1990 census, which was in the final stages of preparation as this book went to press, an estimated 400,000 temporary employees were being hired by the U. S. Government.

Census data is used by many individuals and organizations for a variety of purposes. Government officials use this information to assess needs for a variety of programs including social programs aimed at assisting the poor, the disabled, the young, and the elderly. Counseling professionals use this data to better assess family trends, pressures, and potential trouble spots. During the last thirty years, census figures have documented the rise of divorce and the proportion of children living in single-parent homes. Politicians running for national office use demographic statistics to better grasp the relative size and distribution of different voter constituencies at the state, regional, and national levels. The corporate sector uses census information to assess and find markets for their products, develop advertising campaigns, and choose locations for production facilities, stores, and sales territories (Russell, 1984).

Vital Statistics

Demographers also make use of **vital statistics** to analyze population characteristics and change. These are records kept on the inhabitants of a nation or society, which include births, deaths, marriages, and incidences of disease. In early and medieval Europe, the church maintained many of these records, especially those documenting ceremonies related to births and baptisms, weddings, and burial services. However, these records documented only the ecclesiastical ceremonies that occurred after the fact, rather than the events themselves. Consequently, they were often incomplete. During the 1600s, Massachusetts became the first colony to mandate the recording of actual events rather than religious ceremonies related to them. As a result of placing record keeping in the hands of civil authorities, records became much more reliable and accurate. Not until the twentieth century, however, were comprehensive and accurate records being kept in all states. For instance, birth and death registrations in the United States were first reported and analyzed on a national basis in 1933 (Peterson, 1969).

Demographic Transition

One widely accepted explanation of population growth is the theory of **demographic transition**. This theory maintains that population growth is a three-stage process in which developing nations move from a condition of high fertility and high mortality to one of low fertility and low mortality. Before the industrial revolution began almost 250 years ago, the world's population was increasing, but stable. High fertility rates in most societies were offset by high mortality rates. With industrialization, many societies began to experience demographic transition in which their mortality rates dropped. This created a period of rapid population growth. Then as these societies modernized, their fertility rates declined as well.

Specifically, demographic transition involves the following three stages:

1. *Countries with high rates of both fertility and mortality.* Historically, this ratio between births and deaths has characterized preliterate societies before any modernization had taken place. High fertility rates were attributed to such factors as a lack of understanding concerning birth control coupled with high mortality rates that made continued childbearing necessary. The having of an unlimited number of offspring was encouraged by both family and religious norms and cultural norms in general. High mortality was chiefly due to a lack of medical technology and modern health and sanitation practices. Few societies exist at this stage today except for possible isolated tribal and village cultures in parts of Africa, Asia, and South America.

2. *Countries with high fertility rates and declining to low mortality rates.* As countries have modernized, mortality rates have dropped significantly because of access to modern medical technology and the adoption of better health practices. Historically, norms and values regarding births and family size, however, have lagged behind, sometimes for several decades. During the interim, population size often has risen dramatically. It takes time for people to realize the advantages of small families and leave old values behind. This imbalance between births and deaths characterized both Europe and the United States until the twentieth century. Today the pattern is most evident in parts of Africa, Asia, and Latin America, including such countries as Kenya, Nigeria, Zaire, India, Iran, the Philippines, Honduras, and Guatemala.

3. *Countries with declining to low fertility rates and low mortality rates.* This pattern characterizes countries near or at a state of full industrialization. In these societies, modern contraception coupled with cash economies requiring an adult labor force have made low fertility rates not only possible but economically preferable. Since children do not participate significantly in the economy and represent a drain on family resources, fertility rates have dropped accordingly. Likewise, advances in nutrition, public health and sanitation, and medical technology have resulted in lowered mortality rates. Taken together, lower rates of fertility and mortality have created a con-

dition of population stability as the demographic transition has been completed. Countries at this third stage include the United States, Canada, New Zealand, Great Britain, the Soviet Union, Japan, and Australia.

While demographic transition has characterized the history of industrial societies, demographers are divided as to whether it will accurately describe the future of today's developing countries. Unlike Europe and the United States, many of today's developing nations have higher initial rates of fertility and have experienced a much faster rate of decline in mortality (Teitelbaum, 1975). The result has been a literal "population explosion" that is unprecedented in history. The critical question is whether the complete cycle of demographic transition can be completed before many of these countries experience economic and ecological disaster. The future is beginning to look more encouraging for many of these nations, as we will see in the pages to follow. However, successful transition is far from assured, and the threat of severe dislocation and societal collapse from the pressures of overpopulation looms omnipresent on the horizon.

POPULATION IN HISTORICAL PERSPECTIVE

Malthusian Theory

The idea that the earth can become overpopulated is not new. In 1798, Thomas Malthus (1766–1834) wrote the first modern treatise on population entitled *An Essay on the Principle of Population*. In it, this English minister and economist presented a theory of population growth and, in later editions, proposed a set of solutions for the future overpopulation problem.

English economist Thomas Malthus (1766–1834) was one of the first scholars in modern times to predict a possible overpopulation crisis. (Culver Pictures, Inc.)

In setting forth what has come to be known as **Malthusian theory**, he argued that human societies increase their populations geometrically (1, 2, 4, 8, 16), while food supplies grow arithmetically (1, 2, 3, 4, 5). Malthus felt that this situation was deceptive in its initial stages because increases in food supply seemed to keep pace with the growth of human population. However, given the exponential growth of people, he predicted that biology would inevitably outdistance technology and the capacity to produce food would lag behind the numbers of people needing to be fed. This, in turn, would result in a world of misery overpopulated with malnourished people living in abject poverty.

In subsequent editions of his essay, Malthus asserted that humanity had two essential choices in dealing with the problem. Although he seriously doubted this would occur, one choice was for individuals to implement the *preventive checks* of (1) postponed marriage and (2) sexual abstinence. In lieu of such "moral restraint," the *positive checks* of (1) hunger, (2) disease, (3) war, and (4) "vice" would become the ultimate solution. He regarded artificial forms of birth control as a morally reprehensible vice. Taken as a whole, positive checks would bring the population back into balance, but at a much higher cost in terms of human suffering and degradation than the inconveniences wrought by preventive checks. Although his ideas were accepted by some, Malthus was the subject of much ridicule and criticism.

His theory of population was severely criticized for its pessimism, and many scholars regarded Malthus as the "parson of doom." In some sectors, his ideas became identified with political conservatism. Some people used them to blame overpopulation on the poor who, it was charged, were least capable of practicing "moral restraint." One of his most vehement critics was Karl Marx (1906). Marx argued that starvation, where it occurred, was caused by social policies that allowed capitalists to hoard resources and accumulate wealth. Rather than blaming the poor for the lack of food, he felt that they were victims of the unequal distribution of wealth.

Regardless of criticisms by Marx and later proponents of the conflict perspective, it is clear that Malthus was short-sighted in several respects. He failed to anticipate the rapid decline in birthrates that accompanied demographic transition in industrialized countries. He did not foresee the technological revolution in agriculture during the nineteenth and twentieth centuries which, among other things, made it possible to produce a much larger crop yield from an acre of ground. Neither did he anticipate the dramatic advances in communication and transportation that have made the distribution of vital resources, including food, less a problem. And of course, Malthus had no foresight regarding the ad-

vances in birth control during the twentieth century, which have made it much easier to plan and have small families. Consequently, his predictions of gross overpopulation and human suffering have not come to pass in Europe and the United States.

A strong case can be made, however, for the argument that the less-developed nations could become caught in a Malthusian trap. This, in turn, could have a significant impact on the stability and quality of life not only for their populations, but for modern nations and their inhabitants as well. Since the 1960s, Malthus's ideas have experienced a resurgence among those identified as the neo-Malthusian school (Morris, 1966; Ehrlich, 1970; Heilbroner, 1974). These scholars maintain that Malthus's basic thesis about runaway population growth accompanied by shortfalls in food and other vital resources was sound but premature.

Technology and Population Growth: The Three Revolutions

As discussed in Chapter 5, three technological revolutions—agricultural, urban, and industrial—have played a key role in the evolutionary development of human societies. These critical historical events have also sparked and accelerated population increase.

At the dawn of prehistory, our ancestors lived in small nomadic bands of twenty to thirty individuals and were hunters and food gatherers. Since they had no means of storing food, they literally lived from meal to meal, from hand to mouth. Life was a constant struggle for food. In some cases, these early groups followed their primary source of food—caribou, reindeer, bison, for example—on the hoof. These harsh conditions made a very large population impossible, as the food supply tended to be unstable and often relatively small. The average life span during this period ranged from thirty to forty years.

Consequently, the world's population remained small and grew very slowly.

The Agricultural Revolution. About 10,000 years ago, a great change occurred with the emergence of the **agricultural revolution.** The first technological revolution to spark population growth, it began about 8000 B.C. with the development of simple slash-and-burn agriculture. It was marked by the cultivation of grains, including wheat and corn, and by the domestication of such animals as goats and poultry. Simple farming tools, including the hoe and a primitive form of human-powered plow, were also invented during this time.

This was a monumental turning point because, for the first time in human history, a stable and surplus food supply became possible. Groups could stay in one location permanently rather than have to forage for food. With such stability, the average life span began to increase, more children could be supported, and the size of the world's population began to rise steadily. As time passed, the agricultural revolution continued to gather momentum as farming methods slowly but steadily advanced.

The Urban Revolution. The next significant boost to population growth occurred about 3500 B.C. with the rise of the cities that created the **urban revolution.** With the technological base provided by slash-and-burn farming, cities began to emerge in the Near East—Egypt, Greece, and Mesopotamia. Draft animals, such as oxen, were placed in front of a more advanced plow, and true agriculture began. Freed from depending on energy supplied by only their own muscles, farmers could plant and harvest large fields rather than small plots (Peterson, 1969). Crop rotation, the terracing of fields, the building of irrigation systems, and the development of metallurgy added to agricultural productivity.

To promote a more efficient form of agriculture and land use, soil and water resources were placed under the authority of a centralized city government. The economic and social growth of these cities was further facilitated by the establishment of trade relations with other cities. As time passed, the economic systems of these city-states became increasingly diversified and efficient, larger numbers of people could be sustained, and populations grew.

Modern civilization sprang from an urban social structure. The sheer efficiency of an urban society made it possible to institutionalize leisure time. Without having to spend every waking moment struggling for subsistence, some people were able to use their free time to ponder, to think, to imagine, to invent, and to inquire. Out of this environment came the cornerstones of modern civilization—art, music, architecture, literature, poetry, philosophy, and, ultimately, science. As these disciplines emerged and matured over a period of more than five thousand years, the stage was ultimately set for the emergence of the industrial revolution.

The Industrial Revolution. The most dramatic increase in population began about 1750 with the beginning of the **industrial revolution.** Centralized facilities for mass production (factories) began to replace the home as the location for the production of goods and services. Bureaucratic forms of management were carried out by professionals who, in successfully coordinating complex and diverse work functions, heightened efficiency and greatly improved productivity.

With more and more goods and services being produced, a much larger population could be supported. As industrialization gathered momentum and developing nations went through demographic transition, mortality rates declined dramatically as a result of advances in medicine and health practices. Fertility rates remained high for a time and then declined to much lower levels. In the interim, population growth accelerated. Many of the less-developed nations today are characterized by this high fertility/low mortality ratio that is producing the current population explosion.

World Population Growth: Past History and Future Projections

Total Numbers: Past and Future. At the beginning of the agricultural revolution, there were only about 5 million people inhabiting this planet. Over the next eight thousand years, the population grew slowly but steadily until there were approximately 250 million

people by the year A.D. 1. This figure certainly would have been much greater without wars, epidemics, plagues, and famines that kept growth at a moderate pace.

As shown in Figure 12-1, the rate of population growth has increased dramatically since that time. By the year 1650, world population had doubled to 500 million (one-half billion). Then, between 1650 and 1850, something dramatic happened. That something was the *industrial revolution.* By 1850, the world's population was 1 billion people. As industrialization continued to gather momentum, doubling times became shorter and shorter. The

Figure 12-1   World Population Growth: Past and Projected

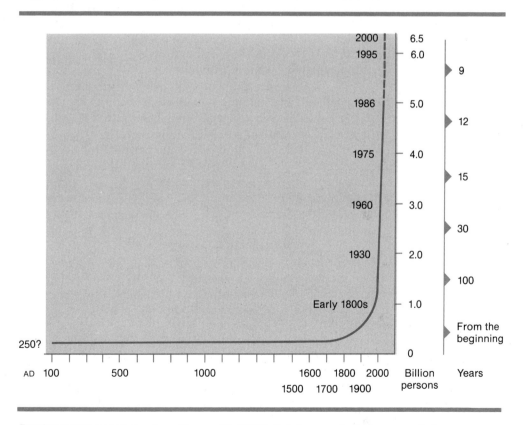

Reprinted with permission from Fornos, W. (1987). *Gaining people, losing ground: A blueprint for stabilizing world population.* Washington, D.C.: The Population Institute, p. 4.

world grew to 2 billion people by 1930 and 4 billion by 1975. In July 1986, we reached 5 billion people.

Demographers at the U.S. Bureau of the Census estimate that the world population will exceed 6 billion by the year 2000 (*World Population Data Sheet*, 1985). This will be unprecedented, because the world's population "will have tripled during a single human lifetime from two billion to six billion during the 70-year period between 1930 and 2000. No one living at any previous time has witnessed such growth" (*Popline*, April 1986, p. 4). According to demographer Phillip Hauser (1960), if these post-World War II rates of population growth were to continue for eight hundred years, the earth would indeed be a crowded place with "one person per square foot of the land surface."

Accompanying Urbanization. World population growth has been accompanied by a corresponding increase in urbanization. At first this occurred very slowly. Despite the urban revolution, ancient cities were relatively small by today's standards. Cities in early Mesopotamia and Egypt had between 5,000 and 20,000 people. Ancient Rome at its zenith had no more than 350,000. Urban areas during the Middle Ages rarely if ever contained more than 50,000 inhabitants. Even as late as 1800, less than 5 percent of the world's population was living in urban areas.

With the industrial revolution, urbanization began to accelerate. In the United States, for instance, the 1790 census showed only 5 percent of all Americans living in urban areas. By 1988, however, fully three-fourths of the population lived in areas defined as urban by the U.S. Bureau of the Census. Worldwide, the shift to cities has been much slower. Only 29 percent of the global population lived in urban areas in 1950, 40 percent in 1980, and the 50 and 60 percent marks are not expected to be reached until the years 2000 and 2025 respectively (*Popline*, October 1985, pp. 2–3).

The greatest impact of recent urbanization is being felt in less-developed nations. Traditionally rural, in 1980 these countries accounted for 54.8 percent of all urban dwellers worldwide and 75 percent of the earth's total human population. According to projections by the United Nations, 77 percent of the world's urban population and 83 percent of all people will be living in less-developed nations by the year 2025 (United Nations, 1985).

The most striking trend in world population growth has been the recent and continuing development of **mega-cities,** those with 4 million or more people (*Popline*, April 1986, p. 4). In 1950, only thirteen cities worldwide were in this category, with a combined population of 88 million people. By 1985, the number of mega-cities had more than tripled, with a total of forty-two such behemoths containing 342 million people. Estimates are that by the beginning of the twenty-first century, the world will have sixty-six mega-cities, with a combined population of almost 600 million people. As illustrated in Table 12-1, most of these cities will be in less-developed nations and, without an industrial base to provide adequate jobs, most of their inhabitants will be living in abject squalor.

According to the Population Institute (*Popline*, April 1986), this trend may be seen today as

millions of rural inhabitants no longer able to earn a living in the farm economy move to cities in quest of a better life. Lacking money for housing, they construct makeshift structures in squatter cities, often on land unsuited for human habitation—such as next to a chemical plant in Bhopal, India, or next to a large petroleum storage facility in Mexico City.

These squatter cities lack such basic amenities as sewage and water systems, electricity, police and fire protection, and, not infrequently, schools. Unremoved and untreated human excrement is everywhere. In the warm sun, the excrement dries into a fine gray pow-

Table 12-1 Population Characteristics of Selected Mega-cities

City, Country	1985 Population (in millions)	Density (population per square mile)	2000 Population (projected in millions)
Tokyo-Yokohama, Japan	25.4	23,356	23.7
Mexico City, Mexico	16.9	32,377	31.0
Sao Paulo, Brazil	14.9	33,062	25.8
New York, U.S.	14.6	11,458	14.6
Seoul, South Korea	13.7	39,956	—
Osaka-Kobe-Kyoto, Japan	13.6	27,397	—
Buenos Aires, Argentina	10.8	20,093	13.2
Calcutta, India	10.5	50,057	16.4
Bombay, India	10.1	10,620	16.8
Rio de Janeiro, Brazil	10.1	38,907	19.0

Source: Adapted from *The World Almanac and Book of Facts* (1988). Population of world's largest cities. New York: Scripps-Howard, pp. 739–740; *Popline* (1986, May). Washington, D.C.: The Population Institute, p. 7.

der which the wind scatters over the entire city. A single squatter city can be home for hundreds of thousands and even millions of human beings.

The employment sought by rural to urban migrants is more often than not, illusory. With too many people chasing too few jobs, unemployment is high and wages are depressed. If they can find a job at all, these new urban dwellers may earn a dollar or less for 8 to 10 hours of heavy labor (p. 4).

HOW POPULATIONS CHANGE

Human populations at all levels—community, society, and world—are not fixed and stable groups, but constantly changing in size, composition, and distribution because of a variety of factors. Chief among these are the variables of fertility, mortality, and migration. We next turn our attention to these concepts and how they are measured by demographers. In addition, we will also consider certain compositional characteristics of populations that bear directly on how populations change.

Fertility

In demographic research, the term **fertility** refers to the number of births that occur in a population as measured by fertility rates. As applied to an individual woman, fertility is the number of children she gives birth to during her childbearing years.

For comparison purposes, demographers sometimes use the concept of **fecundity**, the biological potential for reproduction as applied either to an individual woman or to an entire population. The fecundity for the typical woman is 20 to 25 offspring. However, because each woman would have to take motherhood very seriously from puberty through menopause to have so many children, no society has reached or is anywhere near reaching its potential for reproduction.

However, a few women in some societies have exceeded the typical fecundity level in actual number of offspring. The world's record for documented fertility in an individual woman is 69. The wife of Feodor Vassilyev, a Russian peasant, in 27 confinements between 1725 and 1765, "gave birth to 16 pairs of twins, 7 sets of triplets, and 4 sets of quadruplets'' (McWhirter, 1982, p. 28).

The Measurement of Fertility. Demographers measure fertility in several ways. The **crude birth rate** (CBR) is the total number of births per 1,000 people in a population during a given year. In 1987 the crude birth rate was 28 for the world as a whole, compared to a high of 44 in Africa and a low of 13 for European nations on the average. In comparison, the United States had a CBR of 15 during the same year (*World Population Data Sheet,* 1987). This measure of fertility is valuable in that it gives demographers on over-all picture of birth characteristics. However, it does not inform them as to the specific characteristics of average families or of the women who are giving birth.

For more precise information, demographers also compute fertility rates and age specific fertility rates. The **fertility rate** (FR) is the number of births per 1,000 women of child-bearing age (15 to 44 years) in a population during a given year. This statistic aids demographers in (1) establishing average family size in specific countries and (2) making fertility comparisons between them. The United States in 1985, for example, had a fertility rate of 65.8 compared with FRs four times as high in some less-developed countries (U.S. Bureau of the Census, 1985). The **age specific fertility rate** (ASFR) determines the number of births per 1,000 women in specific age categories during a given year. By amassing such information (what percentage of women 15-19, 20-24, 25-29, and so on, are giving birth), demographers ascertain at what ages women in a population are having their first child, their last child, and the largest number of children.

Mortality

Mortality is the number of deaths that occur in a population as measured by mortality rates. With fertility on one side, mortality is the other side of a basic equation that shapes the characteristics of a population and how it changes.

The Measurement of Mortality. Death rates are determined in several ways, the most fundamental of which is through computation of the crude death rate. The **crude death rate** (CDR) is the number of deaths per 1,000 people in a population during a given year. The world's lowest CDRs are found in the countries of North America (8), Latin America (8), and Oceania (8), while the highest occur in African countries (16). Even considering the tremendous suffering from hunger and malnutrition endured by the people of African nations and other less-developed countries, their death rates are still very low compared to their birth rates (*World Population Data Sheet,* 1985).

As with fertility, demographers employ a variety of statistical techniques to more precisely assess mortality. Different segments of a population—such as those differentiated by age, sex, social class, race, and access to health care—have varying rates of mortality. The **age specific mortality rate** (ASMR), for instance, measures the total number of deaths per 1,000 people in a population within a specific age category during a given year. By computing this statistic, demographers are able to ascertain, among other things, the life expectancy of people in various age categories, such as those in the age groups of 20-24, 40-44, 60-64, and so on.

Infant mortality is also an important indicator. The **infant mortality rate** (IMR) is the total number of deaths per 1,000 children under 12 months of age in a population within a given year. Since children are most vulnerable to disease during their first year of life, infant mortality is the most sensitive indicator of death probabilities in specific populations. In other words, infant mortality is a good predictor of **life expectancy**, the number of years a person of a certain age can be expected to live in his or her society.

This is clearly evident when one compares infant mortality rates between developed and less-developed nations. In countries like Japan and Sweden with infant mortality rates of 5.5 and 6.8 respectively, the life expectancy at birth is 77 years. The United States, with an infant mortality rate of 10.5, has an average life expectancy of 75 years (*World Population Data Sheet*, 1987). Contrast that with the relationship between infant mortality and life expectancy in less-developed countries. In India, 101 children out of each 1,000 die before their first birthday, and the average life expectancy is 55 years. Nigeria has an IMR of 124.0 (37 years), Ethiopia 152.0 (41 years), and Afghanistan 182.0 (41 years).

Migration

Migration, a factor that is more difficult to explain and precisely measure than births and deaths, also affects population change. **Migration** refers to the movement of people from one geographical location to another for the purpose of establishing residence. In countries throughout the world, there is a constant shifting of populations internationally. Some people engage in *emigration* by leaving one country to seek another. Others at the end of their journey have participated in *immigration* by coming to a new country to settle.

Types of Migration. Demographers distinguish between two general forms of migration. **International migration** involves movement of people from one country to another. During a 150-year span between 1820 and 1970, 46 million immigrants came to the United States mostly from Europe, but also from Asia and Latin America (Thomlinson, 1976). Some came to escape poverty and oppression, some to seek a better life in the spirit of adventure, and some for both reasons. More recently, significant rates of emigration

have occurred in East Germany, Korea, Vietnam, Bangladesh, Iran, and Mexico. **Internal migration** involves movement of people from one place to another within a country. In the United States, there have been significant migrations from East to West (1700 to 1900), South to North (1870 to 1940), and urban to suburban (1950 to the present). Since the 1970s, there has been some shift in U.S. population (and big business) away from the cold and heavily populated Northeast to the Southwestern region of the country, commonly known as the Sunbelt.

Why Migration Occurs. Shifts in population can be explained largely in terms of push-and-pull factors. *Push factors* are those which force people to leave their homes and communities because of conditions beyond their control. Thousands of Irish left their country during the 1840s because of the threat of starvation brought about by a potato blight. *Pull factors* are those which draw people to a new geographical location because of the promise of a better life. In 1848, the discovery of gold by James Marshall near Sutter's Fort in California sparked a gold fever that drew 80 thousand "forty-niners" to that state the next year to seek their fortune (Blum et al., 1973).

William Peterson (1975) has identified several broad categories of migration that allow us to place push-and-pull factors in perspective. Push factors are chiefly responsible for what he terms primitive migration and impelled migration. *Primitive migration* occurs when people cannot control their natural environment. Those in hunting-gathering societies, for instance, are pushed to move on in search of food and water; those in horticultural societies may migrate in response to drought, famine, and other factors. *Impelled migration* typically occurs when people are forced to leave their homeland as a result of political pressure. The exodus of Jews from Nazi Germany during the 1930s and 1940s is one example. Pull factors are more prevalent with *free migration,* in which people freely decide to migrate to another location for their own personal reasons. Both push-and-pull factors may be involved with *group migration,* in which those who share common cultural bonds migrate together to retain their group or cultural identity. Several religious groups, including the Puritans (seventeenth century) and the Hutterites (nineteenth century) came to the United States from Europe both to escape religious persecution and to preserve their way of life.

Population Growth: The Bathtub Analogy

Taken together, the factors of fertility, mortality, and migration determine the size of human populations. To measure their relationship to each other, demographers compile and compare the annual growth rates of societies throughout the world. The **growth rate** is the annual percentage of growth or loss in a population. It is measured by adding the net difference between births and deaths to the net difference between immigration and emigration per 1,000 people in a particular population.

Positive Growth Rates. Most countries experience a positive growth rate. The rate of net annual growth in turn impacts on the amount of time it takes for a country to double its population. During 1986, the United States experienced a growth rate of about 1 percent. This translates into a doubling time of 69 years. By comparison, Kenya had a growth rate of more than 4 percent, which means it will double its population in only 16 years (Holden, 1986; Fornos, 1987).

High growth rates have serious implications for the less-developed countries in which they are most prevalent (see Table 12-2). Many of these countries—Tanzania, Iran, Nigeria, Zaire, Pakistan, and the Philippines, for instance—have exploding populations with doubling times that average 20–25 years.

Think of what it means for the population of a country to double in 25 years. In order to just keep living standards at the present level, the food available to the people must be doubled. Every structure and road must be duplicated. The amounts of power must be doubled. The capacity of the transport system must be doubled. The number of trained doctors, nurses, teachers, and administrators must be doubled. This would be a fantastically difficult job in the United States—a rich country with a fine agricultural system, immense industries, and rich natural resources. Think of what this means to a country with none of these.

Remember also that in all UDCs [undeveloped countries], people have gotten the word about the better life it is possible to have. . . . They have what we like to call "rising expectations." If twice as many people are to be happy, the miracle of doubling what they now have will not be enough. It will only maintain today's standard of living. There will have to be a tripling or better. Needless to say, they are not going to be happy (Ehrlich, 1970, pp. 22–23).

Negative Growth Rates. Some countries, however, have negative growth rates and a very different population problem, that of too few rather than too many people. These countries—including Hungary, East Germany, West Germany, the Soviet Union (in eastern rural provinces) and Rumania—are beginning to experience shortages of both industrial and agricultural workers needed to maintain and expand their economies. In the Soviet Union, women who have given birth to ten children are awarded the title "Mother Heroine" by the state. Additional economic incentives by the government for increased fertility include longer maternity leaves, a cash bonus for having each child, and food allotments to help defray the costs of child rearing (Schmemann, 1985). Nonetheless, countries with underpopulation problems tend to be the exception rather than the rule.

Table 12-2 **Countries with Exploding Populations**

Country	1987 Population (in millions)	2000 Population (projected in millions)	Doubling Time (in years)
Kenya	24.0	38.3	16
Tanzania	23.5	36.6	20
Iran	50.4	73.9	21
Nigeria	108.6	159.2	23
Zaire	32.2	47.6	23
Pakistan	104.7	148.7	24
Philippines	61.5	85.5	25
Bangladesh	107.1	144.7	26
Egypt	51.9	71.2	26
Vietnam	63.6	86.3	27
Mexico	83.8	112.8	28
Ethiopia	46.0	66.5	30
India	803.0	1,000.1	31

Adapted from Fornos, W. (1987). *Gaining people, losing ground: A blueprint for stabilizing world population.* Washington, D.C.: The Population Institute, pp. 38–57.

The Bathtub Analogy. To make sense of fertility, mortality, and migration in terms of their influence on population change, the bathtub analogy is useful. Imagine for a moment that a society is like a bathtub. They are both containers of a sort. One holds water and the other contains people. In addition, both have faucets and drains, or inputs and outputs. The bathtub has two faucets (or controls), one each for hot water and cold water. A society, like a bathtub, also has two faucets, one for fertility (the primary input) and one for immigration (the secondary input). Likewise, a bathtub and a society both have drains, although the bathtub typically has only one, as compared to the two possessed by a society. A society's two drains consist of mortality (the primary output) and emigration (the secondary output).

From this brief analogy, it is relatively easy to understand the impact that fertility, mortality, and migration have on the changing size of a population. If more water goes into a bathtub than exits through the drain, the water level rises. If this condition persists long enough, the bathtub must overflow, and someone has to deal with the excess water. A similar situation occurs within a society in terms of population. If more people enter a society through fertility (and immigration) than exit through mortality (and emigration), the society as a container will overflow and will not be able to feed and care for the added numbers. If many societies have such an overflow and it persists—like so many overflowing bathtubs sitting in a giant empty swimming pool—the world itself, being a finite container like a swimming pool, is faced with a potential overflow as well.

The Composition of Populations

In addition to accounting for changes in population size, demographers also study the effects of various compositional factors on population change. In this sense, demographers are interested in how populations are composed and distributed according to such factors as age, sex, rural or urban residence, race and ethnicity, education, income, marital status, occupation, religion, national origin, and others. Of these, the composition of populations by age and sex are particularly important. This is because these two factors, taken together, largely determine the relative percentages of people who are economically productive in a given population.

Age Composition. The composition of a society in regard to the ages of most of its members plays an important role in terms of how it is structured as a social system. A population consisting mostly of children and/or the elderly has fewer options in social organization than one with smaller proportions of people in these age categories. Many less-developed countries have disproportionate numbers of children and/or the elderly. Consequently, they cannot be as economically productive and flexible, in most cases, as industrial nations. Indeed, such countries are placed under significant stress because of their age composition and, in many instances, may find it difficult to modernize. Industrial economies require an adult labor force that is educated and technically trained. Yet many less-developed nations are so burdened with the costs of just maintaining their populations that comprehensive mass education is only a dream.

One method used to measure age composition is the calculation of the **dependency ratio**. This is the number of people in a population under 15 and over 65 divided by the number of people between 15 and 65 years of age. For example, a country with a dependency ratio of 100 (100:100) has one dependent person for each productive person.

These ratios vary significantly between less-developed countries and modern nations. Dependency ratios for less-developed countries include 92.1 for Iran, 98.2 for Mexico, and 95.7 for Morocco. These countries, there-

fore, have about one dependent person for every economically productive one. By comparison, developed nations like the United States (51.1), Japan (48.4), and Canada (51.1) have roughly one dependent person for every two economically productive ones (Overbeek, 1982). The consequences in terms of both actual and potential economic productivity are obvious.

One age factor of particular concern to demographers is **momentum**, increases in a population that continue long after birth and death rates have been stabilized. The two-decade period after World War II (1946–1965) has been called the "baby boom" era in the United States. Fertility rates rose with social and economic prosperity. During this period, the average family had about 3 children. In the late 1960s, however, fertility rates began to drop, and from the middle 1970s until the present, the average American family has included only 2 children. In fact, American families today have an average of 1.9 children each, which is slightly below the replacement level.

While this is encouraging, benefits in terms of a stabilized population have been delayed as a result of the lag effect produced by momentum. Although the typical American woman today is having fewer children, there are more women having children because of the larger pool of "mothers" created during the baby boom years. Thus it takes several decades of sustained low fertility combined with other factors to produce a low- to no-growth population. When we consider the combined long-term effects of low age and high fertility in countries like Kenya, where the average woman in 1988 was having 8 children, we can understand why demographers are concerned.

Sex Composition. The sex characteristics of a society are measured by the **sex ratio**, the number of males to every 100 females in a designated population. Males initially outnumber females by significant numbers. Because females are apparently more hardy biologically, however, higher male mortality rates inevitably result in a shortage of males. At conception, there are 124 males to 100 females which, through higher rates of male fetal miscarriage, drops to 105 by birth. Until about the age of 15, there generally are more males than females. But, by that time, continuing male attrition begins to result in a surplus of females. This trend continues throughout the life cycle so that by the time people reach the 70–74 (years) age cohort, males are found in significantly fewer numbers than females. By the year 2100, when all age categories are considered, it is estimated that there will be 175 million more females in the world than males (*Popline,* July 1985).

Population Pyramids. Demographers often show the age and sex characteristics of populations as population pyramids. A **population pyramid** is a summary of age and sex compositions in a population portrayed in a graph or chart. As shown in Figure 12-2, those of less-developed countries like Kenya and Morocco look just like the name implies, an elongated pyramid. The broad base reflects high fertility rates and an overabundance of children and those under 20 years of age. The pointed top of the pyramid reflects the lower life expectancy in these countries and the very small number of both males and females over 70 years of age. Contrast this to population pyramids of more-developed nations like the United States and Sweden in which the graph, reflecting a more stable and evenly distributed population, appears more like a column.

In Kenya, the country with the world's fastest growing population, women have an average of eight children during their childbearing years. (Copyright Carl Purcell.)

Figure 12-2 Age-Sex Population Pyramids

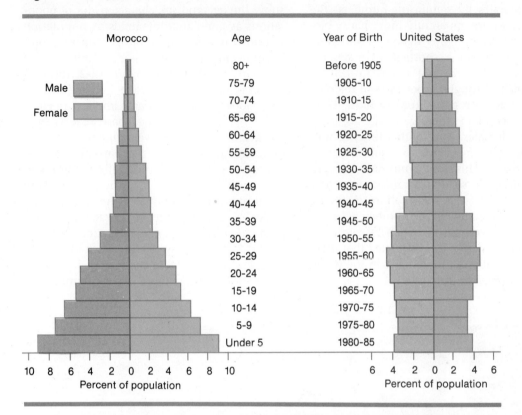

As shown in the two examples above, population pyramids in nondeveloped countries (such as Morocco) appear as a cone or pyramid that reflects such characteristics as high fertility, a larger proportion of children, and very few people in the older age categories. By comparison, population pyramids in the more developed countries (like the United States) look more like a cylinder, which reflects very different population characteristics. *Source*: Haupt, A. & Kane, T. T. (1985). *Population handbook.* Washington, D.C.: Population Reference Bureau, Inc., p. 14.

THE POPULATION DILEMMA

As evidenced from the preceding discussion, we have a problem and the problem is "us." Too many of us. The *whats* of the population dilemma are evident to most who take a rational and objective look at the major demographic and social indicators both past and present. They include exponential population growth, finite space and resources with which to support these growing numbers, and ulti-

mately, a dismal future for much if not all of humanity unless present trends are reversed within the next few decades. The broad *whys*, *implications*, and *solutions* to this problem are also relatively easy to understand. However, many of the specifics related to these concerns have themselves become controversial issues that are fiercely debated by those in both the scientific community and several other segments of society. We now turn our attention to these and related topics.

The Whys of the Population Explosion

The recent and unprecedented explosion of population in the less-developed countries may be attributed to three general factors: mortality intervention, pronatalism, and inadequate contraception.

Mortality Intervention. Eric Breindel and Nick Eberstadt (1980, p. 42), in commenting on the population crisis in less-developed nations, have stated that the rapid growth in these countries has occurred "not because their people have suddenly started breeding like rabbits but because they have finally stopped dying like flies." Most of this growth has occurred since World War II and is due primarily to **mortality intervention**. This has involved the provision of medical and health technology and assistance to less-developed nations by organizations and governments in industrialized countries. A small amount of the life-giving technology has been acquired by the less-fortunate countries themselves through the natural process of acculturation. Increased technology and aid have been furnished by religious and humanitarian organizations. However, the largest source of mortality intervention has come from industrial nations. The United States, for instance, has furnished many billions of dollars in foreign aid to less-developed countries since 1945, much of it earmarked for medical and health services and supplies. The effect has been to reduce drastically the mortality rates and double the rates of population growth in places like Latin America, Asia, Africa, and Oceania that today account for two-thirds of the world's inhabitants.

Pronatalism. Corresponding efforts and gains have not been made in terms of also reducing fertility rates in these countries. It is one thing to save the life of a sick baby through medical intervention. The child's relatives and neigh-bors appreciate this "gift of life" for years to come. However, it is quite another thing to tell people they are having too many children and should limit the number of their offspring to one or two. To do so in many cases is to attack their most cherished values, religious beliefs, traditions, and even their concepts of masculinity and femininity.

These tradition-based societies still embrace **pronatalism**, a cultural orientation that strongly encourages childbearing. Historically, the world's religions have taught their followers that procreation is a near-sacred gift from the heavens and a moral duty. Having large numbers of offspring has been regarded as a sign of fertility (femininity) in women as well as an indicator of sexual potency (masculinity) in men. Children have been necessary to carry on the family name and gene pool and to be the recipients of inherited family property. In agricultural societies, children have participated directly in the economy and have contributed to their families' well-being. Given the prevalence of these norms and values throughout much of the world, many people in several societies today simply do not want to limit their offspring. Others want to have fewer children but lack the education and resources to know how.

Lack of Contraception. While mortality rates in less-developed countries today approach those of the more technologically advanced nations, a dramatic gap still exists between them in fertility rates. Crude birth rates in LDCs (less-developed countries) are twice as high on the average as those in developed countries, and Kenya's (at 52 per 1,000 population) is more than three times as high (*Population Today*, June 1986). These disparities are caused in large part by the difference between LDCs and technological nations in levels of contraception use. As a result of such factors as pronatalist norms and policies, the lack of education, and the low availability of contraceptives, birth control is practiced by only 2 to 4 percent of families in several LDCs, including Kenya, Nepal, and Turkey. Developed nations like the United States average 65 percent (Matras, 1977; World Bank, 1985).

Implications for Human Ecology

There is a tendency for many of us to see our natural environment—the sunshine, forests, water, air, fossil fuels, and so forth—as part of the unlimited bounty of nature. For Americans, food must also be included in this equation. As a nation, we throw away and feed to our pets more food than some countries have to feed their people. However, we humans do not live in a vacuum. Our behavior impacts not only on other people and societies but on the fragile ecosystem called Earth as well. **Human ecology** is the scientific study of the relationship between human populations and their natural environments. Specifically, human ecologists are concerned with how social and cultural systems are organized within human populations to maintain harmony with the physical environment.

Population biologist Paul Ehrlich (1971) and other ecologists have warned that the accelerating growth of the world's population threatens to upset the ecological balance and pose serious problems related to long-term survival. As he has stated,

> [M]an is not only running out of food, he is also destroying the life support systems of the Spaceship Earth. The situation was recently summarized very succinctly: "It is the top of the ninth inning. Man, always a threat at the plate, has been hitting nature hard. It is important to remember, however, that NATURE BATS LAST" (p. 364).

Could it be that Ehrlich and others of like mind are alarmists who have greatly and pessimistically overstated a serious but nonthreatening problem? Many pronatalists think so.

Their numbers include high-level clergy in both the Catholic and Mormon faiths, some on the pro-life side of the abortion issue, a few from the scientific community, some government officials, and many well-intentioned citizens. They feel that, like the boy in the folktale who "cried wolf" to play a joke on the woodcutter, ecologists are exaggerating grossly the so-called "overpopulation crisis" and "ecological imbalance."

While Erhlich, other human ecologists, and demographers may have been a bit premature at times with some of their projected timetables, their basic findings are inescapable. Anyone trained in the scientific method who takes a comprehensive and objective look at existing data can hardly arrive at a different set of conclusions. If current trends of overpopulation and resource depletion are not reversed and reversed soon, an ecological crisis of dramatic proportion is inevitable. Indeed, some scientists argue that the first stages are already well upon us.

Food. Despite the promise of a "green revolution" that would yield a much larger amount of grain from an acre of farmland, food production is not keeping pace with demand. During the 1980s, this was partly due to temporary problems of internal political strife, poor crop yields as a result of drought, and distribution difficulties. Many underdeveloped countries appear to be losing the struggle for adequate food resources. The United Nations has estimated that 2,300 calories of food per day are necessary to sustain the average person under normal conditions. Yet Pakistan, which is expected to double its 100 million inhabitants in the next twenty-five years, has barely been able to produce 2,000 calories for each person per day. By 1985 several countries, including Bangladesh, Bolivia, and Chile, were generating only 1,500–1,900 daily calories per person, and Peru only 1,200 (*Popline,* June 1985).

In January of 1989, *Time* magazine broke with tradition and chose not to name a Man or Woman of the Year. Instead, Earth was named Planet of the Year in recognition of the serious dangers it faces from overpopulation and threats to its ecology.

Land Resources. One example of land resource depletion is the permanent destruction of the world's rain forests. These delicate ecosystems—located in tropical regions of Central and South America, Africa, and Asia—took 60 million years to develop. They play host to about one-half of all lower life forms on the planet, about 5 million species of insects, animals, and plants. Yet these rain forests are being destroyed at the rate of about 50,000 acres each day.

It is estimated that by the year 2000, not only will much of the world's rain forests be permanently transformed into desert, but 275,000 species of life will be extinct as well. Depleting the forests of hardwoods, such as teak and mahogany, for American and European markets is one form of the destruction. Another is the razing of forests to provide pasture land for cattle, which are raised to provide Americans with a cheap and plentiful supply of beef. The cattle completely denude the land within six to eight years and then are moved to other land to start the cycle over again. Soil nutrients, which lie near the surface, are soon washed away as tropical rains erode the soil because there are no tree roots to hold it. The result is an irreversible desert (*Popline*, September 1987).

Pollution. The press of human numbers is also creating problems of land, water, and air pollution. The accelerating effects of industrialization are producing poisonous wastes faster than the environment can absorb them. Chemical pesticides such as DDT that leak into soil and water systems are one area of concern, as are leaking chemicals from industrial sites. In 1969 several hundred families had to leave the Love Canal area in New York State because of leaking industrial chemicals that had polluted the land on which they lived. Increasing levels of toxic wastes released into the air by industrial production form acid rain which, in turn, slowly destroys forest land and kills both fresh water and sea life, an increasingly important source of food.

As much as 5 billion metric tons of carbons and other pollutants from the burning of fossil fuels and wood are released into the atmosphere each year. The result is the **greenhouse effect**, increasing cloud cover caused by pollution, which retains the warmth of the sun and produces higher temperatures. If current trends continue, icebergs could begin to melt in the twenty-first century and eventually—to use America as an example—most of Florida and much of the Gulf Coast could disappear with the melting of the polar caps.

Energy. As countries industrialize and populations worldwide become larger, the demand for energy rises rapidly. As of 1986, the most technologically developed areas—including the United States, Japan, and Western Europe—comprised about 16 percent of the world's population but consumed almost 55 percent of the planet's energy (Chirot, 1986). From 1950 to 1980, the per capita consumption of energy in the United States alone went up more than 50 percent (*Statistical Abstract of the United States*, 1984). As populations worldwide continue to increase along with "rising expectations" concerning desired life-style and affluence, such amounts of energy consumption will, of necessity, have to level off.

In the late 1960s, an international group of thirty scientists met in Rome to study the present and future predicament of humankind. This group, "the Club of Rome," studied the human ecosystem for several years and made it clear that, among other things, the ever-increasing use of energy is symptomatic of humankind's preoccupation with industrial growth (Meadows et al., 1972). They argued that this growth cannot continue forever. In 1972, another group of thirty-three noted scientists from Europe endorsed the findings of the Club of Rome. Their conclusions are excerpted as follows:

This wasteland in Brazil was a lush tropical forest only a short time ago. Razed to create pastureland for cattle, land like this is completely denuded in six to eight years from overgrazing. Then cattle are moved to other land and the cycle is repeated. Once the land has been used in this manner, there are no longer tree roots to hold nutrients in the soil. Consequently, the tropical rains quickly wash the topsoil away. This leaves a permanent, irreversible desert. (Sygma/Odinetz.)

The principle defect of the industrial way of life with its ethos of expansion is that it is not sustainable. . . . [S]ooner or later it will end (only the precise circumstances are in doubt), and . . . it will do so in one of two ways: either against our will, or in a succession of famines, epidemics, social crises and wars; or because we want it to . . . in a succession of thoughtful, humane, and measured changes.

. . . [T]he main problems of the environment do not arise from temporary and accidental malfunctions of the existing economic and social systems. On the contrary, they are the warning signs of a profound incompatibility between deeply rooted beliefs in continuous growth and the dawning recognition of the earth as a spaceship, limited in its re-sources and vulnerable to thoughtless mishandling. The nature of our responses to these symptoms is crucial. . . . If we plan remedial action with our eyes on political rather than ecological reality, then . . . very surely, we will muddle our way to extinction (Goldsmith et al., 1972, pp. 2–6).

TURNING THINGS AROUND: SOLUTIONS AND PROSPECTS

Despite the threats of overpopulation and ecological imbalance, many demographers and other scientists view the future with guarded optimism. The rate of world population increase is beginning to decline. The governmental leaders of many countries have realized the gravity of the problem and are beginning to take steps to address it directly. And some countries with historical problems of overpopulation, such as Japan and China, have already turned things around.

China: A Case Study in Population Control

China, currently the most populous country in the world with just over 1 billion people, has made tremendous strides in bringing population growth under control. Traditionally a poor, agricultural nation with a burgeoning population, China experienced a sustained drought during the late 1950s. The resulting shortfall of food created the worst famine in history. An estimated 30 million people either starved to death or died from chronic malnutrition (*Population Today,* March 1985). In response to this and related economic problems brought about by overpopulation, China instituted a two-child-per-family policy during the 1970s. To facilitate this, laws were passed prohibiting people from marrying until their late twenties (Whyte and Parish, 1984).

Although birthrates declined significantly, government officials soon realized that because of the momentum created by a baby boom in the 1950s and 1960s, the population still would not stabilize for many decades. Consequently, in 1982 China adopted a constitution which, among other things, mandated a one-child-per-family rule.

Intent on limiting growth to 1.2 billion people by the beginning of the twenty-first century, the government has instituted a set of policies that may seem harsh by American standards. Couples who have only one child are rewarded with various incentives, including periodic cash bonuses, free contraceptives, jobs and job security, and priority schooling for their child. Those who have a second child

are fined heavily, have their wages docked, are denied grain allotments and pension benefits, and experience tremendous ostracism from the community. After a couple has their first and only child, they are strongly encouraged to undergo sterilization, and those women who again become pregnant are urged to have an abortion (Beck et al., 1984; Jian, Tuan, and Jing-Yuan, 1985).

China's population control program has not been without its problems. While it has been successful in urban areas, wealthy farmers in rural provinces have sometimes paid heavy fines but continued to have several offspring because of the economic benefits of children in an agricultural economy. Less affluent Chinese, again in rural areas primarily, have practiced female infanticide if the first-born child is a girl. It is hoped that the next child will be a boy who will provide a greater economic benefit to the family. The Chinese government recently has taken several steps to stop this practice and has prosecuted and imprisoned those found guilty.

Nonetheless, crude birth rates in China have been reduced by more than half. With an annual growth rate of only 1.2 percent per year and continued low fertility, China should completely stabilize its population during the first quarter of the twenty-first century.

Needed Solutions for Population Stability

Turning the population crisis around is not only possible but probable, provided enough people with enough commitment engage in enough effort in enough time. To accomplish this, the following general solutions must be implemented.

A No-growth Cultural Orientation. To reach a stable population, societies worldwide will have to adopt a "no-growth" cultural orientation towards fertility. This will necessitate an abandonment of the pronatalist traditions of the past in favor of a two-child-per-family value orientation. This was achieved by Japan in the 1950s, China in the 1970s, and is reflected in the fertility rates of most industrial nations today. The overpopulation issue aside, most of the people in these countries have learned that by maintaining smaller families, they are better off not only economically but in quality of life as well. Given current rates of growth plus the factor of momentum, the rest of the world has perhaps thirty years to learn the same lesson, or we all will suffer the consequences.

Family Planning. To reach no-growth levels of fertility worldwide will require massive and comprehensive family planning programs.

However, providing the technology of birth control alone will not be sufficient. The approach taken by the United States government serves as a case in point. From 1965 through 1986, almost 3 billion dollars in federal aid was spent on population control, some of which was used to send 5.1 billion condoms to the people of seventy countries. About one-half, or 2.6 billion, of these devices were sent between 1980 and 1986, and in 1986 alone, $18 million was spent on 417 million condoms. Responsibility for ordering, storing, and shipping these birth control devices fell to the government's Agency for International Development (AID), a branch of the State Department (Coram, 1988).

Officials at AID thought long and hard about how best to persuade people in these

Because of a massive population control program established by the Chinese government, the average family in China today has only one child. (Magnum Photos, Inc./Eve Arnold.)

countries to use condoms for birth control. Brand names designed for cultural identification were used, including "Raja" for Bangladesh, "Moonbeam" for Sri Lanka, and "Condor" for El Salvador. The people in several of these countries, having no experience with condoms but liking colors, were sent "rubbers" in black, red, green, and assorted pastels including pink. There were some early problems: air-dropped leaflets promoting pastels fell into a mosque by mistake, the colors leached from some black and red condoms, which gave their users a few anxious moments, and some men of Kenya liked pastel condoms so well that they decided to wear them all the time as part of their attire. It was also determined that people in different countries had different coital frequency rates. So men in India were estimated to need a yearly quota of 70 condoms, while those on the island of Dominica required about 240, or five a week. Even size was calculated. Men in countries like Bangladesh, Nepal, and Mauritius were sent 49s (about 49 mm, or 1.9 inches wide by 6.2 inches long) while those in other designated countries were sent the larger 52s (Corum, 1988). Despite this program, fertility rates in most of these countries have remained about the same. Much less effort apparently has gone into teaching the people how to use birth control devices and the need for a no-growth value orientation.

For maximum effectiveness, these programs must combine a no-growth message with education about and access to the contraceptives themselves. Families with pronatalist views in several countries often will not even think of using birth control until they already have four, five, or six children and desperate circumstances drive them to it. In Ethiopia, for instance, drought, famine, and an unstable political situation in the early 1980s combined to cause many thousands of deaths from starvation, malnutrition, and disease. Massive humanitarian efforts by governments, religious groups, and even entertainers raised millions of dollars for aid. Yet that country continues to have problems feeding its people today, in large part because only 2 percent practice birth control. If a family planning program had been instituted there in 1970 with the modest goal of convincing 35 percent of the people to use contraception by 1985, conditions would have been different. Ethiopia's population would have been 1.7 million fewer and much of the suffering and starvation could have been averted (*Popline*, April 1985).

Leadership. Any societal or worldwide strategy for population control that works must include effective leadership at all levels. During the 1988 U.S. presidential campaign, for instance, both Republican candidate George Bush and Democratic candidate Michael Dukakis advocated the need for population control both in the United States (as a partial solution to poverty) and on an international level as a foreign policy issue.

However, on the issue of abortion, which was hotly debated, neither candidate stressed the fact that abortion itself is symptomatic of a larger set of problems. Many if not most of the 1.6 million abortions performed each year in the United States involve young women with inadequate information about and commitment to contraception and family planning. On a worldwide basis, about 60 million abortions are performed each year. More than a few involve desperate women living in abject poverty with little knowledge about effective birth control and little or no access to contraceptives. Effective leadership focused on comprehensive family planning education would help to alleviate much of the need for abortion.

Many national and world leaders are now taking strong stands on the need for population control. In 1987 leaders from forty-four nations issued a joint statement on population stabilization which was presented to the 100th U.S. Congress. The nations that were represented ranged from Austria and Japan to India, Kenya, and Zimbabwe. The statement urged all nations to work together "to stop population growth within the near future and for each country to adopt the necessary policies and programs to do so" (Quoted in Fornos, 1987, p. 110).

Prospects for the Future

Prospects for the future now look more promising than in previous decades. Leaders and governments in the less-developed nations are, at an increasing rate, taking aggressive steps to protect the future of their people. In 1985 Kenya, where each woman has been having an average of eight children, established a four-child-per-family goal as an intermediate step toward full population stability. India's government has instituted a series of economic incentives to encourage smaller families, and it hopes to see a two-child-per-family norm in place by the year 2000. Mexico, a success story in the Western Hemisphere, won the 1986 United Nations Population Award for, among other things, reducing its growth rate by 35 percent from 1974 to 1985. If current trends continue, the countries of the world have an excellent opportunity to stabilize the global population within the next few decades.

CHAPTER SUMMARY

1. A population is the total number of persons who inhabit a country or other specified territory. Sociologists who specialize in population engage in demography, the scientific study of population characteristics and change. Specifically, demographers examine the size, composition, and distribution of populations at micro-, macro-, and international levels. Primary resources of demographic information include periodic census and ongoing records of vital statistics.

2. In an examination of population in historical perspective, important aspects include Mathusian theory, three technological revolutions that sparked population growth, and estimates by demographers of actual population change. In 1798 Thomas Malthus proposed that populations increase geometrically (1, 2, 4, 8, 16), while food supplies increase arithmetically (1, 2, 3, 4, 5). His doomsday predictions of a future population crisis, along with his proposed solutions (deferred marriage and sexual abstinence), drew severe criticisms that have continued up to this day. Although his theory was naive and simplistic in some respects, modern scientists acknowledge that his basic premise of geometrical population growth is approximately correct. Three technological revolutions in the last 10,000 years—agricultural, urban, and industrial—have produced a rate of growth that, in the last 200 years, has been roughly geometrical. Whether Malthus's prediction of severe imbalance between people and food supply comes true remains to be seen.

3. Populations change as a result of three basic factors: fertility (births), mortality (deaths), and migration (movement of people from one place to another). Measures of fertility used by demographers include the computation of crude birth rates, fertility rates, and age specific fertility rates within designated populations. Fertility in less-developed countries remains high compared with mortality (or death rates). Mortality is measured by crude death rates, age specific mortality rates, and infant mortality rates. Migration, a third factor in assessing population change, is studied by demographers in terms of both international and internal movements of people.

4. Demographers also study the composition of society according to such factors as age and sex to ascertain how they impact on population change. The age composition of societies, as measured by the dependency ratio, informs scientists as to the percentage of people in a given population who are under fifteen or over sixty-five years of age. A country with a high dependency ratio finds it very difficult to modernize. The sex composition of a society is measured by the sex ratio, the number of males to females. When age and sex compositions are combined into a population pyramid, demographers have a graphic picture of the society compared with others regarding these characteristics.

5. The world is currently faced with the dilemma of overpopulation. The population explosion is a problem primarily in less-developed countries and stems from three general causes. The first is mortality intervention, the provision of medical and health technology and assistance to less-developed nations by organizations and governments of industrialized countries. Such aid has dramatically reduced mortality rates in these countries since 1945. However, corresponding progress has not been made in terms of reducing fertility rates. Two other factors help to account for this, pronatalism (a cultural orientation that strongly encourages childbearing) and the lack of contraception.

6. Implications for human ecology are disturbing. There are food shortages in some countries, as well as other problems including the depletion of land resources, pollution, and potential energy crises. Nonetheless, the problem of overpopulation and its threat to the natural environment is beginning to turn around. Several countries, most notably China, have begun to take significant steps to lower fertility rates and bring their populations under control. With the continued development of no-growth value orientations, family planning programs, and effective leadership, the countries of the world stand a good chance of stabilizing the global population within the next several decades.

TERMS TO KNOW

age specific fertility rate: the number of births per 1,000 women in specific age categories during a given year.

age specific mortality rate: the number of deaths per 1,000 people within particular age categories in a population during a given year.

agricultural revolution: the first technological revolution to spark world population growth, which began about 8000 B.C.

census: a relatively complete head count of the people in a given society, which is taken periodically.

crude birth rate: the number of births per 1,000 people in a population during a given year.

crude death rate: the number of deaths per 1,000 people in a population during a given year.

demographic transition: a process in which developing nations move from a condition of high fertility and high mortality to one of low fertility and low mortality.

demography: the scientific study of population characteristics and change.

dependency ratio: the number of people in a population under fifteen and over sixty-five years of age divided by the number of people between fifteen and sixty-five.

fecundity: the biological potential for reproduction.

fertility: the number of births that occur in a population as measured by fertility rates.

fertility rate: the number of births per 1,000 women of childbearing age (fifteen to forty-four years) in a population during a given year.

greenhouse effect: increasing cloud cover caused by pollution, which retains the warmth of the sun and produces warmer temperatures and climates.

growth rate: the annual percentage of population growth or loss in a given society.

human ecology: the scientific study of the

relationship between human populations and their natural environments.

industrial revolution: the third technological revolution to spark world population growth, which began about the year 1750.

infant mortality rate: the number of deaths per 1,000 infants under twelve months of age in a population within a given year.

internal migration: movement of people from one place to another within a country to establish residence.

international migration: movement of people from one country to another to establish residence.

life expectancy: the number of years a person of a certain age can be expected to live in his or her society.

Malthusian theory: An argument proposed by Thomas Malthus, which stated that human societies increase their populations geometrically (1, 2, 4, 8, 16), while food supplies increase arithmetically (1, 2, 3, 4, 5).

mega-cities: cities with 4 million or more people.

migration: the movement of people from one geographical location to another for the purpose of establishing residence.

momentum: increases in a population that continue long after fertility and mortality rates have been stabilized.

mortality: the number of deaths in a population as measured by death rates.

mortality intervention: the provision of medical and health technology and assistance to less-developed countries by developed nations.

population: the total number of persons who inhabit a country or other specified territory.

population pyramid: a summary of age and sex compositions in a population as portrayed in a graph or chart.

pronatalism: a cultural orientation that strongly encourages childbearing.

sex ratio: the number of males to every 100 females in a designated population (Example: 97 males to every 100 females or 97:100 = a sex ratio of 97).

urban revolution: The second technological revolution to stimulate world population increases, which began about 3500 B.C.

vital statistics: records maintained on the inhabitants of a society, which include births, deaths, marriages, and incidences of disease.

SUGGESTED READINGS

The Closing Circle (Barry Commoner; New York: Alfred A. Knopf, 1971). A classic in the literature of the human ecology movement in which the author presents a strong case concerning the dangers of what he calls "counter ecological" technology.

The Crowded Earth: People and the Politics of Population (Pranay Gupte; New York: W. W. Norton, 1984). A general coverage of population and ecological issues as well as the political implications involved in population and ecological control.

Gaining People, Losing Ground: A Blueprint for Stabilizing World Population (Werner Fornos; Ephrata, Penn.: Science Press, 1987). A brief yet comprehensive explanation of the current overpopulation crisis in less-developed nations and what is being done about it.

The Global 2000 Report to the President of the U.S. (Gerald O. Barney; New York: Pergamon Press, 1980). The report of a presidential commission concerning the expected long-term effects of continuing overpopulation and the poisoning and depletion of natural resources.

Malthus: An Essay on the Principle of Population (Phillip Appleman; New York: W. W. Norton, 1976). A detailed treatment of Malthusian, neo-Malthusian, and anti-Malthusian arguments.

Chapter 13

Family: Most Basic of Institutions

There is an old joke among professors who teach marriage and family courses that they can use the same tests year after year because even though the questions remain the same, the answers keep changing.

David Knox (1988, p. 1)

Marriage without Children
Nonmarital Cohabitation

■ TERMS TO KNOW

catharsis therapy
child abuse
constructive argument
dual-income family
egalitarian authority
endogamy
exogamy
extended family
family
family universals
incest taboo
latchkey children
marriage
marriage by exchange

marriage by mutual choice
matriarchal authority
monogamy
nonmarital cohabitation
norm of legitimacy
nuclear family
patriarchal authority
polygamy
role discrepancy
romantic love
rules of descent
rules of residence
single-parent family
spouse abuse
stepfamily
traditional nuclear family

As illustrated by Knox's tongue-in-cheek comment, the American family is indeed a changing institution. This is partially evident in the way it has been portrayed in the media during the last forty years. Take television programming for instance. Beginning in the early 1950s, television audiences were entertained by the exploits of families including the Ricardos on "I Love Lucy" and the Nelsons on "Ozzie and Harriet." These were followed in the 1960s by "Hazel" featuring the Baxter family and "Leave It to Beaver" with Ward and June Cleaver and their two sons. Almost without exception, these were middle- to upper-middle-class families in which the husband was the sole breadwinner and head of the household, while the wife was a homemaker. For the most part, these shows painted an idyllic, stereotypical image of the model family as reflected in the dominant cultural values of this period.

Then, also in the 1960s, the structural characteristics of television families began to change, reflecting certain emerging trends and issues in the larger society. Shows including "Julia," "The Partridge Family," and "Family Affair" spotlighted the single-parent family, while "The Brady Bunch" reflected the growing number of stepfamilies. The next decade, the 1970s, gave us the generation gap which plagued the Bunkers on "All in the Family" and the second-marriage predicaments of middle-aged Maude and Walter Finley on "Maude." From the 1980s to the present, many of us have tuned in each week to observe these and other family types, including today's dual-career family, represented by the Huxtables on "The Cosby Show."

Several recent trends are apparent. Approximately 65 percent of American families today have two breadwinners. The single-parent family has also become more prevalent as

Television programs often reflect both cultural ideals and trends regarding the American family. In "The Cosby Show," the fictional Huxtable family is headed by Dr. Cliff Huxtable (a physician) and his wife Clair (an attorney). They and their children represent a dual-income family in which both parents share equally in both the generation of income and family decision making. The Huxtables also represent an idealized model for a rising black middle class. How does this family differ from "ideal" families portrayed in the media during the 1950s and 1960s?

divorce rates have risen. The numbers of people opting for various life-style alternatives, including childlessness and unmarried cohabitation, have also risen. In contrast, the size of the American family is at an all-time low, re-

flecting lower fertility rates in recent decades. These and other developments both reflect and affect changes in the overall society as we move toward the twenty-first century.

Despite continuing change, the family remains the most basic of all social institutions. It serves as the most important and durable source of primary group relations for almost all of us. In simple societies, it often represents the only institution with all basic functions— socialization and emotional support, government, education, religion, and economic production—carried out within an extended family system. In modern societies, the family is but one of several specialized institutions, each designed to address a major area of human needs.

Regardless of the type of society, the family, in the words of the late anthropologist Margaret Mead (1953), represents

> the toughest institution we have. It is, in fact, the institution to which we owe our humanity. We know no other way of making human beings except by bringing them up in a family. . . . [W]e know no other way to bring up children to be human beings, able to act like men and women, and able to marry other men and women and bring up children, except through the family (p. 4).

By **family**, sociologists mean two or more persons related by blood, marriage, or adoption who live together and cooperate economically. Like other people in societies worldwide, Americans tend to have an ethnocentric bias concerning family that is based on their own socialization experiences. Many people assume that monogamous marriage, romantic love as a basis for marriage, and freedom of choice in selecting a mate are "normal" everywhere. They are not. Only about one-fourth of all societies insist on monogamy as the only acceptable marriage form; romantic love in general is peculiar to Western societies; and, in many cultures, the parents of prospective marrieds choose the person their child will marry. These and other issues related to the American family are explored in this chapter. To begin, let us first examine the nature of the family institution.

THE FAMILY AS A SOCIAL INSTITUTION

Several structural aspects of the family are of particular value in assessing the similarities and differences between "families" in different parts of the world. These include family universals, basic family forms, and cross-cultural differences.

Family Universals

All known societies possess some form of family system. Within each system are found at least four characteristics common to families in all societies. These are known as **family universals**. Sociologist Kathleen Gough (1986) has identified them as the incest taboo, a division of labor, marriage, and an authority system.

1. *The incest taboo.* All societies have a norm that prohibits sexual relations and marriage between close family members. This **incest taboo** varies in strength from culture to culture. All societies "forbid mother-son mating, and most, father-daughter and brother-sister. Some societies allow relations but forbid marriage between certain degrees of kin" (Gough, 1986, p. 23). Nonetheless, the results of recent research indicate that incidents of incest may take place in up to 10 percent of American families today (Gordon and O'Keefe, 1984).

2. *A division of labor.* Historically, the allocation of needed tasks to be performed in society was based largely on gender. Males essentially took care of government, hunt-

ing, and war, while females handled child care, household duties, and related crafts. Elements of a sexual division of labor still remain in societies throughout the world today. However, gender as a basis for allocating work, particularly economic functions, is becoming antiquated and may largely disappear in the future.

3. *Marriage.* All societies make some provision for **marriage**, a formally recognized relationship between one man (or more) and one woman (or more) that is durable, relatively stable, and seen as desirable. Marriage exists in various forms in different societies and, among other things, establishes the foundation for having and rearing children. Although motherhood is established biologically, fatherhood—viewed from a world perspective—is based more on the social obligations of the husband to his wife and her child, particularly his ability to provide economic and protective support.

4. *An authority pattern.* Without exception, societies make some provision for how status and authority are to be determined within the family and, for that matter, within society as well. Historically, male or **patriarchal authority** has been the dominant pattern. It is probable that early in human history, males, because of such factors as size, strength, and the lack of sex-related vulnerabilities (pregnancy, for instance), more or less gained social and economic control. Therefore, family authority is very closely related to division of labor. Many conditions in today's societies have changed. Just as gender is becoming an irrelevant factor in dividing work in modern society, so is it becoming equally irrelevant in terms of defining family and social authority.

Matriarchal authority, in which females are dominant in status and author-

Marriage is a cultural universal regarding the family that is found in some form in all societies. (Copyright Joel Gordon, 1987.)

ity, requires special consideration. Some societies—including the Hopi Indians of America, the Ashanti of Ghana, and the Nayar of India—are characterized by matrilineal descent, in which property is passed from one generation to another within the woman's blood line. The husbands in these and other matrilineal cultures have little influence over their wives. However, the male members of a woman's kin group—her older brothers and maternal uncles, for example—typically exert authority over her in terms of "managing" her property. As Gough (1986) explains:

There is in fact no true "matriarchal," as distinct from "matrilineal," society in existence or known from literature, and the chances are there never has been. This does not mean that

women and men have never had relations that were dignified and creative for both sexes, appropriate to the knowledge, skills, and technology of their times. Nor does it mean that the sexes cannot be equal in the future or that the sexual division of labor cannot be abolished. I believe that it can and must be. But it is not necessary to believe myths of a feminist Golden Age in order to plan for parity in the future (p. 24).

Egalitarian authority, in which men and women share marriage and family rights and responsibilities equally, is fast becoming the dominant family authority pattern in the United States. It has already become fairly prevalent in the middle class. However, bastions of patriarchy still linger, especially in certain segments of the working class and among certain subcultural groups, including Christian fundamentalists. However, with a growing proportion of women now participating in the work force and demonstrating increasing degrees of economic self-sufficiency, much of the traditional hold of men over women under the patriarchal system is in a state of decline.

Basic Kinship Forms

As discussed in Chapter 5, kinship organization takes two basic forms: affinal (marriage) and consanguineal (blood). The structural types of families that result are nuclear families and extended families respectively. Nuclear families are found predominantly in both hunter-gatherer and industrial societies. Extended families are found generally in agricultural social systems.

The Nuclear Family. Specifically, a **nuclear family** consists of two or more related persons, usually including a married couple, who occupy a common household. Marriage is the primary bond, as most nuclear families are married couples who may or may not have children. A nuclear family, however, can also consist of a single parent with one or more

offspring, or even two or three adult brothers or sisters who reside together.

As shown in Figure 13-1, most Americans belong to two overlapping nuclear families, the family of orientation and the family of procreation. The family we grow up in, which consists of our parents and siblings, is our *family of orientation.* This is the family of socialization that "orients" us to our society as we progress toward adulthood. Then, sometime after maturity, the majority of us marry, and most marrieds eventually have one or more children. This family we call the *family of procreation.* Making the transition from the first nuclear family to the second often involves two major adjustments. First, we must shift from the dependency of the adolescent role to the autonomy characteristic of a self-supporting adult. Then, often simultaneously, we must make the transition from single person to marriage partner, assuming the role obligations that go with this new position.

The Extended Family. Extended families are just what the name implies. That is, they are basic nuclear families that have been stretched, or extended, to include additional family members. Specifically, an **extended family** consists of two or more nuclear fami-

Figure 13-1   Nuclear Families: Orientation and Procreation

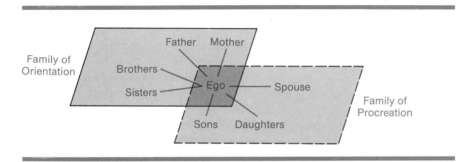

Source: **Reprinted with permission from Leslie, G. R. (1979).** *The family in social context,* **4th ed. New York: Oxford University Press, p. 15.**

lies, usually married couples of different generations, and other relatives who all reside with or near each another. Extended families are prevalent in agricultural societies and are sometimes found in the United States. You may recall "The Waltons," a popular television series of the 1970s that portrayed in nostalgic fashion the joys and struggles of a rural American family during the Great Depression. This was a time that spelled the "last hurrah" for the American extended family that, by the onset of World War II, was becoming somewhat rare. The Walton kids—John Boy, Mary Ellen, and probably several of the others as well—were lured off their mountain in rural Virginia by careers in writing, medicine, and other fields that promised a better way of life. As they moved to where their careers took them like millions of real Americans, their extended family was left "back home." Then, when they married, they formed what were usually much more isolated nuclear families.

In actuality, the incidence of the American extended family has been greatly exaggerated. This family form was never dominant in America. Most European immigrants were either single males or members of nuclear families. The American family, as it became established, was indeed patriarchal, and parents, particularly the father, influenced the marriages of their children by giving consent or approval. Most of their offspring, however, established their own relatively autonomous families. While it was common, if not expected, for elderly parents to be taken in by one of their married children, their other children had separate nuclear families.

On a cross-cultural basis, however, extended families have often been quite different from the more familiar American version. Traditionally, the blood bond was so dominant in many patriarchal societies that women were considered as little more than chattel (property). They would leave their homes and families upon marriage, go to live with their husband's extended family, and have little influence in affecting family decisions. Their influence was often diluted even further by polygyny, a marriage practice that allowed men to take multiple wives. Extreme forms of patriarchy along with various forms of plural marriage are still practiced today in such places as Africa and the Middle East.

Family Structure in Cross-Cultural Perspective

Given both nuclear and extended family forms, societies throughout the world have evolved various types of specialized norms with which to more fully organize family life. In addition to types of authority, these norms also include forms of marriage, mate selection, rules of descent, and place of residence. The structural aspects of family in different societies are summarized in Figure 13-2.

Marriage. Acceptable forms of marriage vary significantly from society to society. The most widely accepted and practiced marriage form, both traditionally and presently, is **monogamy**, the marriage of one man and one woman. Monogamy tends to be the only acceptable marriage form in societies with nuclear family systems, particularly modern societies like the United States. **Polygamy**, the other basic marriage form, refers to the taking of plural spouses.

Sociologists and anthropologists distinguish between three types of polygamy: *polygyny* (one husband, two or more wives), *polyandry* (one wife, two or more husbands), and *group marriage* (two or more husbands and wives). Of these, polyandry and group marriage are quite rare. Polyandry, for example, exists only in a handful of tribal societies and is perhaps best explained by a standard of living so low that one man cannot economically provide for a wife and offspring by himself. Polygyny, by contrast, has been quite popular and, historically, the preferred form of marriage in three-quarters of the world's societies

Figure 13-2 Family Structure in Cross-Cultural Perspective

Structural Characteristics (of the →)	Nuclear Family	Extended Family
KINSHIP ORGANIZATION: (focus of loyalty)	Affinal (marriage)	Consanguineal (blood)
FORM OF AUTHORITY:	Patriarchal (traditional) Egalitarian (modern)	Patriarchal
FORM OF MARRIAGE:	Monogamy	Monogamy or polygamy
MATE SELECTION:	Mutual choice	Exchange
RULE OF DESCENT:	Bilateral (both families equally)	Patrilineal (from males) Matrilineal (from females)
RULE OF RESIDENCE: (where couple lives upon marriage)	Neolocal (couple establishes own home)	Patrilocal (with husband's family) Matrilocal (with wife's family)

In some mideastern countries, a form of plural marriage (called polygyny) is practiced, in which a man may have more than one wife. However, it appears to be on the decline in some countries that are trying to adopt Western ways. The United Nations has condemned this practice as being exploitative of women. (Photo Ergun Cagatay/Gamma Liaison.)

(Murdock, 1965). As patriarchy has given way to egalitarianism, plural marriage has declined as a social practice, has been outlawed in many formerly polygynous societies, and has been condemned by several international organizations, including the United Nations, as being exploitative of women.

Mate Selection. **Marriage by exchange** is one of two general forms of mate selection found throughout the world. It involves marriage as a social and economic arrangement between the families of the prospective marrieds. This arrangement results in one or both parties to the marriage sacrificing their personal preferences to satisfy the needs of their blood kin. Historically, this system was rooted in extreme patriarchy, in which women were treated as little more than commodities. Valued for their labor and childbearing capabilities, daughters and sisters were often exchanged to create alliances between families. Through the marriage of one family's son with another's daughter, the fields, livestock, and other property of both families could be united and consolidated for inheritance by the next generation.

Marriages based on exchange still exist today, primarily in tradition-based agricultural societies. Anthropologists Fred Plog and Daniel Bates (1980) have summarized the practice as follows:

> In some societies, interfamily alliances are created by exchanging daughters directly. Among the Tiv of Nigeria a man may exchange one of his sisters for the sister of another man, mutually binding their families together. But such direct exchange of women is relatively rare. More commonly, a man pays the family from which he takes a daughter in marriage *(bride price)* or works for it *(bride service)*; the payment helps the family replace the daughter with a wife for one of their sons. This indirect exchange of women is found throughout the world (p. 267).

Marriage by mutual choice emphasizes freedom to commit to the needs of one's prospective spouse and those of the marital bond, rather than to those of one's blood relatives. This marriage form is characteristic of modern societies and came about primarily in response to the industrial revolution. As industrialization took hold, the extended family—once an all-encompassing institution—became less and less self-sufficient and began to lose many traditional functions. The production of goods and services became the domain of a separate, specialized economic institution which furnished jobs and cash wages. Education likewise developed into a specialized institution needed to prepare children for a future in the industrial economy. With these and other developments, young people in general, and women in particular, began to gain increasing independence from family elders. No longer rooted to the soil, they could pursue their futures with few if any restrictions.

As the family evolved from an independent unit of production to a dependent unit of consumption, the emerging nuclear family became a specialized institution in its own right. The mass urban society of the twentieth century, with its emphasis on specialized role obligations and secondary group relations, became somewhat impersonal compared to rural farm life. In this social environment, the family has become the basic source of emotional support and interpersonal intimacy for all members. In terms of mate selection, romantic love and emotional compatibility have replaced practical considerations as the bases for marriage.

Whether a spouse is selected through exchange or mutual choice, all societies have norms that attempt to regulate the pool of eligibles from which a mate is chosen. **Endogamy** is a norm that encourages or requires people to marry within certain culturally defined groups or categories. In American culture, people typically are put under some pressure by family and peers to marry a person similar to themselves according to such factors as age, race, ethnicity, religion, and class. **Exogamy** is a norm that encourages or requires people to marry outside certain culturally defined groups or categories. The most universal application of exogamy is the incest taboo that prohibits sex or marriage between certain close relatives. In all fifty states, one may not marry a parent or grandparent, child or grandchild, sibling (brother or sister), or a blood-related aunt, uncle, niece, or nephew. Most states also prohibit marriage between first cousins and half siblings (Cox, 1987).

Rules of Descent. Because of the biological potential for growth in numbers of kin, all societies have devised norms that act to reduce the number of such relatives to a manageable size. These norms, called **rules of descent**, socially define a person's relatives. This is necessary because of the fact that family obligations typically involve shared affection, economic cooperation, the provision of certain types of mutual aid when members are in need, and inheritance rights. Sociologist Gerald Leslie (1979) states that

> [t]here isn't enough affection to scatter indiscriminately over several hundred people, and to be entitled to aid from several hundred people is tantamount to receiving aid from no one. The satisfactory performance of family duties requires a group of kin of manageable size with whom orderly relationships may be maintained (p. 45).

Rules of descent take several forms. The type found in the largest number of societies is *patrilineal descent,* in which kinship and inheritance are traced through the father's bloodline (Leslie, 1979). Common in societies with an extended family system and patriarchal authority, its chief bond is one of blood between fathers, sons, and grandsons. Children are seen to have only one set of grandparents and other kin, those related to the father. Although in some cultures wives may continue relations with their blood kin, they

and their children have primary obligations to the families of their husbands. The second most prevalent form is *bilateral descent,* in which kinship and inheritance are traced through both bloodlines equally. It is common in societies with nuclear family systems, like the United States, in which children have socially defined relatives on both paternal and maternal sides of the family. Males and females inherit property and wealth equally. A relatively uncommon form is *matrilineal descent,* in which kinship and inheritance follow the mother's bloodline. Among societies that have been historically matrilineal are several American Indian groups (including the Navaho and Hopi), the Nayar of India, and the Bemba of Africa (Barnouw, 1978).

Rules of Residence. Societies also have norms called **rules of residence** that specify where a couple will go to live after marriage. Once the marriage takes place, at least one of the partners will have to change his or her residence. How this is determined is closely related to rules of descent. Societies defined by patrilineal descent tend toward *patrilocal residence,* in which, upon marriage, the couple goes to live with or near the husband's kin group. Likewise, societies of matrilineal descent tend toward *matrilocal residence,* in which, after marriage, the couple resides with or near the wife's relatives. Modern societies like the United States with nuclear family structures tend toward *neolocal residence.* This norm stresses that couples, upon marriage, should establish a residence of their own apart from both families (Clayton, 1979).

STUDYING THE FAMILY: DIFFERENT SOCIOLOGICAL APPROACHES

Most of us are experts when it comes to one family in particular, our own. It is indeed tempting sometimes to take the "facts" about our own family experience and generalize to the world of families everywhere. For some people, it is easy to assume that the way their families are structured and their members interact with each other is typical or normal for all families. It is obvious from our discussion of cross-cultural variations that this is not usually the case.

From a scientific viewpoint, facts are relatively meaningless when they lie outside some means of systematic interpretation. Family sociologists examine thousands of representative families to determine patterns and trends as well as to make comparisons. In doing so, they use a variety of different conceptual frameworks or perspectives. Some sociologists prefer the functionalist approach, while others may use conflict, interactionist, or other perspectives. Still others may employ a combination of various approaches. Each sociological approach to an examination of the family reveals but one piece of a larger puzzle. Each is valuable because it focuses on different aspects of the family. Taken together, however, these basic approaches give us a composite view and help us to understand how and why the family operates as it does.

Functionalism

As discussed in Chapter 1 and throughout this book, structural-functionalism emerged from the work of such nineteenth-century sociologists as Herbert Spencer and Émile Durkheim. Both these early theorists used an organic analogy in which they compared a human society to a biological organism. Just as the physical body as a structural system has specialized organs that work in harmony with each other to maintain biological equilibrium or homeostasis, the human society as a social structure likewise has members that carry out specialized tasks or functions for the purpose of achieving social equilibrium. During the

twentieth century, functionalism was developed most notably by Talcott Parsons, and was later refined by others, including Robert Merton. The chief proposition growing out of functionalism is that society as a structure operates or functions through its various parts to maintain social order or equilibrium. Although the equilibrium developed is dynamic and thus constantly adjusting to account for change, order and harmony characterize the natural way a society should operate. Change and conflict, especially if they are dramatic and uncontrolled, are seen by functionalists as disruptive.

One of the main structural elements or institutions that make up society is the family. Although the family varies in structure throughout the world, its main tasks or functions remain essentially the same. They include the following:

1. *Reproduction.* All societies must ensure that a sufficient number of people are produced to sustain their populations. This responsibility has always been allocated to the family institution. In the past, because of a lack of knowledge about medical treatment and health, mortality rates were very high and the survival of societies was potentially threatened. To bolster dwindling numbers and forestall possible extinction or absorption by larger and more powerful societies, it became functional or beneficial for family and societal norms to encourage parenthood. It thus became "moral" and "normal" for a family to have many children. In the overpopulated world we occupy today, the reverse is true. What was once moral is now immoral, deviant, and dysfunctional from a population-control perspective. It is now more functional to the equilibrium of family, community, society, and world to limit the parenting career to having and rearing an average of one or two children per family.

2. *Regulation of sexual expression.* The sex urge is a powerful drive that, if unregulated, can produce disruptive consequences. Since sexual behavior is closely intertwined with reproduction, societies have chosen to regulate sexual behavior primarily through the family. To protect children from sexual exploitation and the entire family from the disruptive consequences of sex between certain close family members, the *incest taboo* was instituted. To protect children further, many societies have a **norm of legitimacy** that specifies social disapproval for out-of-wedlock births. The aim is to maximize the likelihood that children will be provided with a stable and protective home environment along with rights of inheritance. Likewise, norms in some societies that discourage or prohibit sex before or outside marriage are aimed partially at protecting the rights of children and ensuring the stability of the family group.

   It must be noted, however, that in many cultures with extended family structures, children born outside marriage are amply provided for by simply being absorbed into the mother's larger family group. In addition, the stigma once attached to "illegitimate births" in the United States has been weakened significantly in recent decades.

3. *Physical care and protection.* Humans at birth are virtually helpless and, lacking basic survival instincts, must rely mainly on parents and other family members for physical care and protection (see Chapter 3). Children must be provided with the essentials necessary for survival, including food, clothing, and shelter. In most societies, this physical dependence lasts at least fifteen years and, in modern cultures, usually extends for a period of twenty or more years. Adult members incapacitated by accident or illness and the elderly no longer able to care for themselves are usually also protected to some degree by norms related to this function.

4. *Socialization.* As discussed in Chapter 4, children are born social blanks and, therefore, must be taught the culture of their society. Responsibility for this falls initially to the family, which functions as the first and most fundamental agent of childhood socialization. Through exposure to the family, the child learns and internalizes the basic norms and values of his or her culture, develops the orientation and interaction skills necessary to communicate effectively and get along with others, and acquires a self-concept. Assuming that family socialization progresses smoothly, a strong foundation is established for a person who, as an adult, will become a valuable and productive member of society.

5. *Social placement.* Transmission of culture also involves what sociologists call "social placement." As the developing individual moves through childhood, adolescence, and ultimately into adulthood, he or she must learn to deal effectively with ascribed statuses (see Chapter 5). First, the young child must learn to cope with the place he or she has been assigned within the family. During the early years of life, the individual learns to relate to parents, siblings, and other relatives. Later, the maturing child learns "place" in terms of how he or she fits into the larger community and society according to social class, race, ethnicity, religion, and other factors. Finally, the developing person must make the transition from adolescence to adulthood.

   Being placed in society ultimately means that a person has been successful in leaving behind the dependency of the child role and taking on the characteristics of autonomy and self-reliance that society requires of adults. The family in this respect functions primarily as the support system or bridge that makes the successful transition possible. From this perspective, a dysfunctional family, among other things, may impede a child's progress in making the transition to the world of adult responsibility.

6. *Emotional support*. The writer John Donne (1624) once said, "No man is an island entire of itself." As social beings, humans benefit from the emotional and social support that families provide. Adults as well as children need love, affection, recognition, encouragement, and support. Especially in modern societies, positive family relations provide a refuge of intimacy in a largely impersonal world. In this sense, the family institution facilitates order and equilibrium in society by helping to reinforce people's feelings of security, acceptance, self-worth, and general well-being.

Conflict Theory

While functionalism stresses the ways in which the family institution promotes order and stability in the society as a whole, the conflict approach focuses on opposition and change. Modern conflict theory originated during the nineteenth century with the work of Karl Marx and his colleague and co-writer Friedrich Engels (see Chapter 1). In works including *Capital* (1867, 1906), Marx and Engels argued that struggle and conflict between opposing forces were most representative of the human condition. Marx, who formulated the key ideas, argued that history was represented by a continuing series of struggles between the "haves" and the "have-nots." In modern industrial societies, the "haves" comprised the capitalist owners of industry, or the bourgeoisie, who made profits from exploiting the labor of the "have-nots," or proletariat.

Both Marx and Engels saw the family as the basic social, economic, and political unit of society. They asserted that the family represented in microcosm the class struggle taking place in the larger society. This was manifested in the historical exploitation and oppression perpetuated by men against women. Engels (1902) stated that the family is a unit in which the husband "is the bourgeois and the wife represents the proletariat."

This assessment has been reflected in the writings of several contemporary sociologists as well. Arlene S. Skolnick (1987) states that

> the history of relations between the sexes is analogous to those between different races, classes, and castes. All such relationships have involved the domination of one group, defined by birth, by members of another group, also defined by birth. Thus patriarchy—the rule of men over women—must be placed alongside of feudalism, despotism, slavery, aristocracy, and racism. In practice, however, such power arrangements appear natural and inevitable, and alternatives to them unthinkable. When religion is given as the major justification for behavior, subordination of one group by another is explained in religious terms. More recently, domination is usually justified in terms of biological necessity, irrevocable instincts, and inherent inferiority (pp. 185–186).

In addition to macrolevel issues such as sexual inequality, the conflict approach also has some application at the microlevel regarding intrafamily conflict and family disorganization. What are the basic sources of conflict between family members? How does conflict arise? What forms does it take? How can it be managed effectively? What are the major social problems arising out of family conflict, and how can they be addressed? These and other questions may be addressed by conflict sociologists using a microperspective. Summarized below are some of the key issues raised by conflict theorists today which focus on the family.

1. *The nature of family conflict*. Proponents of the conflict approach see conflict as a nat-

ural outgrowth of any relationship, particularly those within families. Conflict makes visible certain adjustments that we all have to make to each other as we and our partners in relationships grow and change over time. In this sense, the absence of all conflict would perhaps indicate that family members no longer care enough to engage each other and that true intimacy, as expressed in open communication and sharing, has been impaired or destroyed.

2. *Sources of conflict.* Sources of conflict with family members may be internal or environmental (Rice, 1983). Internal sources include physical fatigue, illness, emotional upset, and mental disorders. Environmen-

tal sources of family conflict are much more varied. They include problems outside the home which spill over into the family (such as difficulties with a supervisor at work), interference by others (including well-meaning friends and in-laws), and situational pressures (including those caused by family finances, sex, and children). All of these factors may create stress and tension that manifest themselves as conflict.

3. *Conflict management.* Most conflict theorists agree that since family discord is inevitable, normal, and not subject to complete resolution, it should be effectively and constructively managed. However, the best ap-

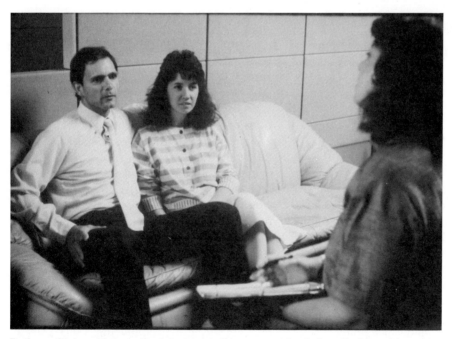

Both conflict and interactionist perspectives are particularly valuable at the micro level of society in helping people to better understand the nature of their own marriage and family relationships. The services of a professional marriage and family counselor are often helpful in learning to maintain and improve interpersonal communication and constructively manage conflicts if and when they arise. (Copyright Erik Leigh Simmons/The Image Bank.)

proach for accomplishing this is a subject of much debate, not just among sociologists, but among counselors and therapists from other disciplines as well. One method used by some therapists is **catharsis therapy**, the verbal release of hostility toward a spouse or other family member in a controlled therapeutic environment. This approach is based on the premise that such therapy acts as a safety valve to release tensions and prevent a major explosion of hostility at a later time. Critics charge that this is a myth and only encourages further aggression (Straus, 1974; Lamanna and Riedman, 1985). Another approach is **constructive argument**, a process in which family members work through a series of steps that place the focus on the problem rather than on personalities. By avoiding the destructive consequences of quarreling, the parties involved can build a "win-win" rather than a "win-lose" solution.

Interactionism

Symbolic interactionism, or interactionism, is a third approach. Developed early in the twentieth century by sociologists including Charles H. Cooley and George Herbert Mead, the interactionist perspective focuses on the meaning people assign to the social world around them (see Chapter 1). Also of importance are the ways in which people symbolically communicate their perceptions of reality to others. These unique perceptions are largely a product of our socialization experiences.

When this approach is applied to the family, it is of particular value in helping to explain the interpersonal dynamics between members. Note, as an illustration, the impact of significant others, like parents, on shaping the self-image of the child and his or her perceptions of family relations. Small children, as first explained by George Herbert Mead, look to their parents as role models for their own future family behavior. As sociologist Ira Reiss (1980) explains:

> [O]bserve them [children] playing house. The young female who plays the mother will usually indicate strong elements of her mother's role in her own play behavior. This indicates that she has learned her mother's role and, thus has role taken with her mother. The entire area of anticipatory socialization is involved here. We socialize our children ahead of time by our own behavior in the roles they will later perform. One can see this in everyday areas such as driving and drinking and smoking, but even more broadly in parental roles. The kind of parent-role conceptions children develop will be heavily influenced by their own parents' role behavior (p. 64).

As people come to maturity and look forward to establishing their own adult family roles, the perceptions they developed in childhood take the form of *role expectations*. They anticipate how they will act and should act in the roles of husband, wife, and, later, parent and how a spouse will and should act as well. Consider the situation faced by a couple who are prospective marriage partners. To increase the likelihood for marital success, they should openly communicate to each other before marriage their perceptions of married life, including the roles each person should play. To put it in blunt and metaphorical terms, they should lay all their cards on the table, hold nothing back, and assume nothing on issues of values, life goals, money matters, sex, the having of children and parenting, and in-laws. The divorce courts are full of those who did not. Doing these things, of course, is not a panacea for all marital ills, nor a guarantee of long-term marital success. It simply means that, at the point of marriage, the two people have established a sound basis for compatibility and the lines of communication are open. The challenge after marriage is to keep them that way.

Those couples who enter marriage without openly communicating their perceptions of family reality to each other are likely candidates for **role discrepancy**. This is a possible source of marital discord in which expectations about the nature and responsibilities of married life are inconsistent with its realities. Judson Landis and Mary Landis (1973) comment as follows:

> [I]n marriage, it is easy to be concerned with only one's own needs and expectations without seeing the other side of the question. . . . Couples contemplating marriage need to give thought to how well they understand each other and to what kinds of situations are tolerable or intolerable to each other. A competitive attitude toward each other during courtship may indicate conflicting role expectations. Each married couple must work out the husband-wife pattern according to the capacities and the adaptability of the partners and the circumstances of their lives. Whatever role patterns develop in any particular marriage, mutually supportive attitudes are essential to a good relationship (p. 28).

Interactionism is also useful in examining the complexities of family role relationships as they change over time (Stryker and Statham, 1985). A marriage is a process, not a "thing." To maintain a stable and growing relationship, each partner must guard against taking the other partner and the relationship for granted. Each person enters a marriage with a definition of his or her role, that of the partner, and how they should interconnect. However, these definitions change and may become more complex as couples get older, have children, and add or rearrange goals and priorities. Children bring complexity to the dynamics of a relationship. Their arrival means that the marital role must be balanced with the parental role. Careers and financial obligations may add other complications. Certain events may occur—midlife crises, loss of job, children's growing up and leaving home,

and loss of a family member through death or divorce—which call for other adjustments.

The interactionist perspective provides family counselors and clinicians with a very useful therapeutic tool in helping individual families understand, achieve, maintain, and improve successful interpersonal relations with their loved ones. In fact, it is often recommended that any couple contemplating marriage undergo premarital counseling with a professionally trained and certified family counselor. If problems and conflicts arise at any point in the marital or family relationship that family members feel they cannot handle alone, a few sessions with a professional counselor can often facilitate a resolution.

We live in a society in which many people do not hesitate to spend between ten and twenty thousand dollars for a new car. They place a high value on transportation and see this as a "necessity." Is not the most fundamental and basic human relationship we have or perhaps will ever have also a necessity? If it becomes characterized by conflict or some other impairment, is it worth the few hundred dollars for counseling that could save or improve it? Only you can answer that question.

THE AMERICAN FAMILY TODAY

Today's family is very different in its structure, in the issues facing it, and in its interpersonal dynamics than its counterpart in colonial America more than three hundred years ago. The industrial revolution is largely responsible for its transformation from a unit of economic production (for example, the farm) to one characterized by economic consumption. Other factors during the last fifty years, including World War II, the women's movement, and changes in the economy, have created diverse variations of the nuclear family as it exists today. We now turn our attention to

The idealized relationships between feudal knights and ladies during the eleventh and twelfth centuries A.D. formed much of the basis for modern romantic love. (Culver Pictures, Inc.)

an examination of these patterns as they have emerged.

Romantic Love

Romantic love as a basis for marriage is a relatively new idea. Traditionally, societies saw marriage in very practical terms as necessary for procreation, inheritance rights for children, and cementing alliances between families. Romantic love in many societies was viewed as a type of emotional disorder. Among the ancient Greeks, it "was considered a form of madness that fortunately was 'cured' by marriage" (Coleman, 1988, p. 145). In modern times, it may be traced to the concept of courtly love in the eleventh and twelfth cen-

turies. As a prevalent and institutionalized basis for marriage, romantic love first emerged in Europe among the middle and working classes during the sixteenth, seventeenth and eighteenth centuries. It was brought to America by the Puritans and other European migrants as early as the 1600s. Today, partially as a result of the reinforcing factors of industrialization and a mass impersonal society, romantic love continues as the basis for marriage in the United States.

Just what is this thing called love? **Romantic love** may be defined as the idealization of another person based on attachment, commitment, and intimacy. Three similar elements have been identified by psychologist Zick Rubin (1970). According to Rubin, *at-*

tachment involves the need to be physically near and emotionally supported by the other person. He uses the term "caring" for a second element, which involves concern for the well-being of the person loved along with a willingness to take some responsibility for maintaining and improving the relationship. The author actually prefers the term *commitment* which involves demonstrated caring. Some people think they care and say they care ("I love you") but are unable for whatever reason to follow through. *Intimacy,* according to Rubin, involves a bonding process manifested in large part by open, extensive, and confidential communication.

It is perhaps useful to distinguish between two types or stages of romantic love. *Initial romantic love* includes the elements of attachment, commitment, and intimacy along with passion and a sense of euphoria. In this context, *passion* refers to an intense physical and sexual attraction. *Euphoria* is a heightened sense of well-being. The other type of love, *mature romantic love,* typically involves increased degrees of attachment, commitment, and intimacy, and diminished levels of both passion and euphoria. Mature love relationships typically involve a mellowing process in which the intensity and excitement of initial love evolves into a deep and enduring devotion.

Dick and Jane: The Traditional Nuclear Family

During the 1940s, 1950s, and early 1960s, elementary schoolchildren learned to read in the first few grades by following the exploits of Dick and Jane in their reading primers. Dick and Jane were white middle-class children who lived in the suburbs with their parents, a little sister named Sally, and a couple of pets, Spot the dog and Puff the cat. Dad wore a suit and carried a briefcase to work in the city while Mom stayed home and engaged in domestic chores. This was a portrayal of the **traditional nuclear family**, one consisting of a full-time working husband, a homemaker wife, and one or more school-age children. The implicit message in elementary readers during the 1940s to the 1960s was that Dick and Jane would grow up, each find and marry a spouse, and live in the suburbs where they would follow their parents' pattern in the next generation.

In most cases, the family lives of young people growing up in America from the 1940s on have not turned out this way. Instead, the traditional nuclear family has become somewhat of an endangered species. According to the U.S. Bureau of the Census (1985, November), 70 percent of all U.S. households were traditional nuclear families in 1950. By 1979, however, their numbers had declined to 14 percent and today represent less than 10 percent of all households. The primary reason for this change lies in the recent rise in other family variations, including dual-income families, single-parent families, and stepfamilies.

The Dual-Income Family

The family form that has largely replaced the traditional nuclear family is the **dual-income family**, in which both partners generate income and share in home and child-rearing responsibilities. It is the dominant American family form today; approximately two-thirds of U.S. households consist of couples who both work. Even so, married life for two-income couples appears to be more complex than for traditional couples in several respects.

Authority and Careers. In a traditional marriage, if the husband's career necessitated a move to another city, the wife and children moved with him. However, in today's two-income marriage, there are two careers to consider. Whose career is more important? Should one or the other make a sacrifice?

What if the other spouse cannot find a job in his or her chosen occupation or profession in the new location? Of course, there are no ready-made solutions. Each couple has to resolve this type of problem based on their own values and priorities.

Certainly two-income families have become more egalitarian, as women in the work force today have more options than did their mothers and grandmothers. Even so, the career of the husband typically is regarded as the more important, the wife agreeing to make a move even though it may jeopardize her career (Cooper et al., 1986). This situation is probably caused, at least in part, by the lag that still exists between women's pay versus men's pay for comparable jobs. A second factor in some marriages is the effect of traditional male socialization on men who may feel their masculinity compromised if their careers are lost or inhibited. The effects of traditional childhood socialization on women who were taught the importance of a man's career may also play a part. However, at least 12 percent of all working women (6 million wives) have higher incomes than their husbands (U.S. Bureau of the Census, 1983). Among these marriages, husbands are more likely to make sacrifices in their careers.

Commuter Marriages. Sometimes career circumstances necessitate that a couple live apart in a *commuter marriage.* As a significant lifestyle element among modern couples, this is a relatively new phenomenon. Consequently, serious research on commuter marriages did not begin until the early 1970s. The United States is a highly mobile society; about 15 million families move each year, a pattern that appears likely to continue through the 1990s. With an estimated one-fourth of all American workers changing or planning to change their occupations each year, coupled with the rise in the number of two-income families, a sig-

nificant growth in the number of commuter marriages is inevitable (Porter, 1986).

These marriages, which today may number nearly 1 million, are increasingly characteristic of college-educated professionals. The fact that partners live in different cities means that they may see each other only on weekends at best. Disadvantages include loneliness, the costs of maintaining two households, and impaired marital and sexual adjustment if the situation lasts for an extended period of time. To combat these effects, one study indicated that 42 percent of commuter spouses were in contact by phone on a daily basis and more than 50 percent spent each weekend with each other (Gerstel and Gross, 1984). Nonetheless, this arrangement is seen by most couples as temporary until both can find positions in the same location.

Marriage Contracts. When a couple marries, the partners enter into a civil contract with legal rights and responsibilities specified for each person according to the laws of the state. These rights and obligations include living together as husband and wife in a common residence, property and inheritance rights, and reasonable sexual obligations (Broderick, 1988). Therefore, marriage is not simply a personal commitment but a legal contract entered into with the state as the third party. To dissolve this contract permanently, all three parties—the husband, wife, and state—become involved in a legal process called divorce.

Given the complexities of modern family life, a small but growing number of couples are electing to enter into a *personal marriage contract.* This is a written agreement between two partners that specifies the expectations, rights, and obligations of each party to the marriage, along with the conditions of the relationship. Critics argue that such contracts interfere with marital spontaneity and "natural growth" because they are calculated and based on distrust. Proponents argue just the opposite. They claim that the process of two people coming together and agreeing to the basic structure and direction of their relationship brings all important issues into the open to build a relationship on trust and open communication.

Sociologists Mary Ann Lamanna and Agnes Riedman (1985, p. 267) state that "writing a personal agreement can allow partners to understand each other's role expectations." Other family sociologists and therapists argue that a personal marriage contract facilitates a more egalitarian marriage in which the man and woman are equal participants. Sociologist F. Philip Rice (1983) has summarized the literature on this subject as follows:

> When a couple supports and signs such an agreement, husbands are more likely to share in household chores, to look upon their wives as equal partners, and to be relieved of the entire responsibility of earning family income. Advocates also point out that issues are clarified and conflicts are minimized. . . . There are even marriage counselors who use the contract principle of negotiation and reciprocity to assist couples in working out their problems (pp. 369–370).

> . . . Proponents of a personal contract emphasize that this is one way that difficulties can be avoided; the couple learn to talk about everything with one another, they enhance their decision-making capability, and they develop negotiating skills and their own personal and social identities. They derive real security from knowing what to expect in the future (p. 371).

Child Care. A familiar early morning sight today is one or more parents driving to work with their preschool child strapped into a protective seat beside them. Before the parent or parents arrive at work, the child is dropped off at a day-care facility.

Third-party day care for children under six years of age is a growing phenomenon resulting from the growing numbers of both dual-income and single-parent families. Yet, day care is increasingly expensive. At $12 to $14 a day, forty-eight weeks a year, if one deducts for holidays and vacations, costs can average $3,000 annually. Many parents pay $15 per day and more. Indications are, however, that this money is well spent. Research has found that children in the better day-care centers with low child-to-caregiver ratios and well-trained staff receive adequate care in a warm and nurturing environment (Cochran and Gunnarsson, 1985; Meredith, 1986). Parents need to be selective, nonetheless, to ensure that their child is receiving adequate care.

By some estimates, in the United States today there are more than 7 million **latchkey children**, who spend significant amounts of time alone without adult supervision. These are older school-aged children who spend an average of two and one-half hours daily without the presence of responsible adults (Turkington, 1983). This situation may pose little or no danger to some children, who may learn to be more self-reliant and responsible (Wattenberg, 1985; Collins, 1988). No doubt in other cases latchkey children have accidents and get into trouble because they are left alone too often and for too long without supervision. However, sufficient data is not available to show it to be more harmful than helpful for these children in general to be unsupervised for brief periods (Rodman and Cole, 1987).

The Single-Parent Family

According to the U.S. Bureau of the Census (1982), the proportion of one-parent families increased from 11 percent of all families in 1971 to 21 percent in 1981. By 1985, the figure was 26 percent (U.S. Bureau of the Census, 1986 C). Most projections estimate that at least one of every two children growing up today will spend at least some time in a single-parent family.

As defined by sociologists, a **single-parent family** consists of a single, separated, divorced, or widowed adult with one or more offspring. Of the 9 million such families in the United States, 8 million are headed by women and 1 million by men. Most single parents are separated or divorced, although about 25 percent are women who have never been married (Hanson and Sporakowski, 1986).

Single parents face many problems and challenges. Because of the gap in earnings between men and women, single parents who

are women face many more financial problems and are increasingly more likely to be poor (Glick, 1981). The effect of the absence of a father or mother figure for the child presents a special challenge for the single parent in trying to find surrogate role models for the absent parent. As an illustration, both young boys and girls whose fathers are absent may become too dependent on their mothers and experience problems in peer relations, as compared with fewer of these problems among children in father-present families (Santrock, 1970; Biller, 1971). Other problems include emotional overload because there is no parenting partner to "take up the slack," and responsibility overload because there is no one

About one fourth of all American families today are headed by single parents. Parenting without a partner involves special challenges and sacrifices. However, many single parents today appear able to successfully handle such responsibilities. (Copyright M. W. Peterson, 1986/The Image Bank.)

with whom to share decisions in disciplining and advising the children (Coleman, 1988). Despite these and other difficulties, many single parents appear to be successful in raising their children and report satisfaction even though their personal sacrifices are often great.

The Stepfamily

A **stepfamily** exists when two people marry and stepparent and stepsibling relationships are formed. During much of the twentieth century, divorce rates have increased significantly. Since most divorced people remarry and the majority of them are also parents, stepfamily relationships are formed in increasing numbers. Today, stepfamilies account for about one-sixth of all families, and about 35 percent of all children born today will spend some time in a stepfamily before their eighteenth birthday (Johnson, 1986). Many of these children will grow up with stepsiblings in addition to their own brothers and sisters.

The chief characteristic of stepfamilies is complexity. A person who marries a divorced person with one or more children enters a complex web of relationships. This often includes an ex-spouse who at the least must be tolerated for the sake of the children. Stepchildren must be won over in terms of love and respect, which often takes time. When two divorced people marry, each with children from a previous relationship, it is often a case of "my children, your children, and our children" if they decide to have children together. Providing equal amounts of love and consistent emotional support to all these children becomes a task few people would envy. Remarkably, marriage partners who form stepfamilies seem to be as happy in the beginning as couples in first marriages. However, their relationships tend to be more unstable

over time. According to projections, 49 percent of those in first marriages will divorce, compared to 60 percent in second marriages, many of which involve stepfamilies (Glick, 1984). This suggests that the majority of people in stepfamilies could benefit from marriage and family counseling at least periodically to help keep their relationships on a stable footing.

FAMILY CRISIS AND CONFLICT

The complexities and pressures of life in modern society often contribute to family crisis and conflict. Two of the most fundamental types of family problems today are marital breakdown and family violence.

Marital Breakdown

In terms of the *crude divorce rate*, the number of divorces each year per 1,000 people, the general trend during the last century and a third has been upward. In 1860, the crude divorce rate was about .3 per 1,000 people, compared to 1.0 in 1900 and 2.0 in 1940 (U.S. National Center for Health Statistics, March 1979). Since that time, divorce rates have more than doubled, reaching a high of 5.1 per 1,000 people in 1980 and 5.0 in 1985 (*Newsweek*, August 24, 1987). As shown in Figure 13-3, these figures indicate that about one out of two marriages will eventually end in divorce. In comparison, the projected divorce rate in 1920 was one out of seven marriages (Kenkel, 1973).

Why have divorce rates risen? Several variables account for the increases over the last several decades. First and perhaps most important have been changes in rights for women that have given them greater economic freedom. Today working women, whose mothers and grandmothers may have

Figure 13-3 Rates of Marriage and Divorce:* 1950–1987

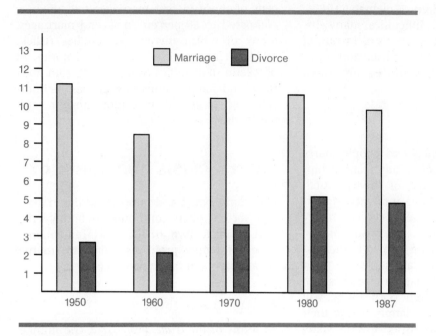

*Per 1,000 population.
Source: U.S. Bureau of the Census, 1988.

been locked into miserable marriages because of economic dependence on their husbands, have more options. They can support themselves and their children alone if necessary. In addition, the social stigma once attached to divorce by the church, the workplace, and society in general has also been largely removed. A third factor has been significant changes in the divorce process itself. A divorce may be obtained much more easily today. The old adversarial system, in which one party had to be proved "guilty" to the court, has largely been replaced by no-fault divorce. Consequently, a divorce—assuming there is no conflict over division of property and child custody—is little more than a formality in which an attorney files certain papers with the court, often for a fee of less than $200 dollars. In community-property states like California and Texas, non-

contested divorces like this are fairly commonplace.

Predictors of Divorce. Several factors can be strong predictors for the increased likelihood of marital breakdown and divorce. First, age at marriage is correlated with divorce, especially for the very young. Projections for teenage marriage show a likelihood of almost 70 percent ending in divorce (Glick and Norton, 1977). Young people under the age of twenty are more likely to be emotionally and socially immature, not prepared to settle down, and less likely to be able to financially support themselves. From an ethnic standpoint, Mexican Americans have the most stable marriages, followed by Cubans and white Anglo Americans. The least stable marriages occur among Puerto Ricans and blacks (Cherlin,

1981; Frisbie, 1986). Religious affiliation also influences divorce. Protestants have higher divorce rates than Catholics, and interfaith marriages are more likely to fail than same-faith marriages.

Trends. Indications are that divorce rates will remain relatively high in the foreseeable future. At least for now, however, they appear to have peaked and show a trend toward a slight decline. In 1986, for instance, the rate was 4.8 per 1,000 people, down .2 from 5.0 per 1,000 in 1985 (*Newsweek,* Aug. 24, 1987). Americans are also waiting longer to get married, which indicates that finishing school and establishing careers may be seen as more important than they were two decades ago. In 1970, the median age at first marriage was 20.6 for women and 22.5 for men. In 1984, it was 22.8 and 24.6 years respectively. These trends, plus indications that more Americans are seeking the professional services of marriage and family counselors, are some cause for optimism.

Family Violence

When family conflict remains unresolved, it can evolve into violence. The two most prevalent forms of family violence are spouse abuse and child abuse.

Spouse Abuse. **Spouse abuse** is the use of overt aggression by one spouse against another which produces physical injury, emotional problems, or both. In this sense, spouse abuse can take many forms, including repeated blows with either a closed fist or open palm, kicking, repeated pushing, hitting with objects, and even rape or attempted rape. Of these variations, the two most commonly used criteria in assessing what factors constitute abuse tend to be *physical injury* and *repeated acts.* Available national research indi-

cates that spouse abuse is the most common form of family violence. A violent episode occurs within 16 percent of all marriages each year (Straus, Gelles, and Steinmetz, 1980).

Spouse abuse may be initiated by either partner. However, the victims are most often wives. According to estimates by the FBI and others, 3 to 4 million women are victims of spousal assault each year, and one out of ten women will be physically abused by her husband during their marriage (Coleman, 1988). Immediate causes that trigger violence include jealousy, alcohol and drugs, and arguments about money or children (Roscoe and Benaske, 1985). Underlying causes are varied. *Socioeconomic status* is one factor, since family violence in general is more prevalent among the poor and disadvantaged. *Childhood socialization* also plays a role, as many spouse and child abusers were themselves exposed to violence or abused in their families as children. *Chronic stress* stemming from poverty, unemployment or job-related problems, and pregnancy are also associated with family violence. Although spouse abuse remains a serious social problem, it appears to be gradually declining as a result of efforts in education and treatment. The increasing availability of shelters, "safe houses," and "hotlines" for abused women is also furnishing them with resources and options (Gelles, 1980; Coleman, 1988).

Child Abuse. **Child abuse** refers to overt acts of aggression by a parent or other adult against a child that produce physical injury, emotional problems, or both. Such treatment takes several forms, including excessive verbal cruelty and intimidation, physical beatings, and sexual contact. It is difficult to estimate the incidence of child abuse, because it usually takes place behind closed doors. From reported cases, however, it is clear that up to 2 million children suffer abuse at the hands of their parents each year and close to two thousand are killed annually (Straus, Gelles, and Steinmetz, 1980).

Parents and other caretakers who abuse children usually fit a general profile. Many are very *authoritarian* and make use of few positive reinforcements in dealing with children. Abusers also tend to be *emotionally immature,* prone to impulsive outbursts of hostility when faced with frustration, and therefore have *little self-control.* They also tend toward *low self-esteem, depression,* and *dependence on alcohol and other drugs* (Gelles, 1973; Enfer and Scheewind, 1982). Like spouse abusers, those who mistreat children *often were themselves abused* as children (Coleman and Cressy, 1984). Because violence in the home was part of their own socialization, it often becomes internalized as an appropriate response to stress and frustration in adulthood. Unless this destructive cycle is broken, family violence becomes contagious and may perpetuate itself across generations.

Given the vulnerability of children caught in this web of violence, the general public is being encouraged to report all incidences of child abuse. Early intervention, in some cases, has saved children who otherwise might have been killed at the hands of their parents. As this book went to press, the toll-free phone number for the National Child Abuse Hotline was (800)-422-4453. Types of treatment include the *psychological-psychiatric approach,* which stresses individual and group therapy, and the *sociological approach,* which emphasizes education in marriage and family life, family planning, and marital and family counseling (Rice, 1983).

LIFE-STYLE ALTERNATIVES

Despite its problems, the family is an amazingly diverse and adaptable institution and in little danger of disappearing. In fact, the re-

verse seems to be true. As we move through the 1990s toward the twenty-first century, several additional family subtypes and lifestyle alternatives are emerging. To put this in perspective, the words of sociologist Suzanne Keller (1985) seem appropriate:

> [I]f we wish to understand what is happening to the family—to our own family—in our own day, we must examine and observe it in the here and now. In doing so, it would be well to keep in mind that the family is an abstraction at best serving as guide and image of what a particular society considers desirable and appropriate in family relations, not what takes place in actual fact. In reality there are always a number of empirical family types at variance with this (p. 521).

Three life-style alternatives at substantial variance from the cultural ideal of family in America are remaining single, marrying but remaining childless, and nonmarital cohabitation. While they certainly do not exhaust the possibilities, they are perhaps most representative of life-styles that are increasingly popular today.

Remaining Single

In 1985, approximately 21.5 percent of all persons over eighteen in the United States had never been married (*Statistical Abstract of the United States,* 1986). Although those considered single also include the divorced and the widowed, the never-marrieds represent the largest proportion of singles. Several factors account for this: the increasing numbers of women college students, increased peer and general social support for a person's remaining single, and greater economic opportunities for women (Knox, 1988). In addition, changing attitudes about sex, coupled with improved means of birth control, have made society more tolerant of nonmarital sexual relations. As a result, there is less pressure for

An increasing number of couples today are electing to remain childless by choice. Called DINKS (double income, no kids) by some, these couples claim benefits that include a simpler and less stressful home environment, increased affluence, and more leisure time. Nonetheless, the majority of Americans still elect to experience both the joys and challenges of parenthood. (Copyright Joel Gordon, 1979.)

most people to feel they must marry in their early to middle twenties. Given the evolution of a supportive singles subculture in recent years—singles clubs, housing, resorts, publications, and so forth—pressure to marry may decline even further in the future.

Marriage without Children

Childless or child-free couples are also on the increase. A certain percentage of couples (about 10 to 12 percent) have always remained childless involuntarily because of medical reasons. In recent decades, however, there has been a growing number of couples who make an active choice either to postpone

parenting or to not have children at all. In 1960, 1 out of 10 women between twenty-five and thirty-four years of age who were ever married had never given birth. By 1985, the figure was 1 out of 4 women (*Newsweek*, September 1, 1986).

Today, the "three's a crowd" sentiment among married couples, especially the college educated, is a growing trend. Some couples appear to drift into a state of permanent childlessness as a result of a series of postponements which often entail education, career, and material goals. Then there is the cost of rearing a child (about $135,000 from birth to college) and the hesitancy of some couples to sacrifice "the good life made possible by two incomes'' (*Newsweek,* September 1, 1986, p. 3). It is often possible for young college-educated couples or DINKS (double income, no kids) to have a standard of living unattainable by many middle-aged couples with children. Other factors include a decline in pronatalism because of overpopulation, changes in sex roles for women that offer alternatives to motherhood, and support groups, including the National Organization for Non-Parents, which use slogans like ''None is fun.'' Consequently, many couples seem quite fulfilled today by choosing not to have children. However, their numbers remain in the minority. Most couples today still want to have and rear children and experience both the joys and challenges of parenting.

Nonmarital Cohabitation

Another significant trend in recent years has been the increasing popularity of **nonmarital cohabitation** as a family alternative. This involves an intimate relationship between a man and woman who share a common residence without benefit of marriage. Between 1970 and 1985, the number of heterosexual cohabiting couples in the United States quadrupled from approximately 523,000 to 2,000,000 (U.S. Bureau of the Census, 1985 November). Research shows that perhaps one-half or more of the couples who apply for marriage licences already are living together (Gwartney-Gibbs, 1986). This indicates that cohabitation is becoming institutionalized as a form of trial marriage. Given high divorce rates and the concerns of many people today about relationships, ''living together'' is perceived as a viable alternative by couples who need intimacy but who wish to proceed with caution and keep options open. As to whether cohabitation is generally beneficial or detrimental to the building of successful relationships, reports are mixed and sociological research is inconclusive. Some couples report positive results. Others complain that because it is so easy for participants to go their separate ways, the necessary degree of initial commitment needed to build a successful relationship is often lacking.

CHAPTER SUMMARY

1. The family is the most fundamental of all institutions and exists in one form or another in all societies. Family universals (characteristics found in all societies) include the incest taboo, a division of labor, marriage, and a family authority pattern. If we examine, for example, family authority patterns throughout the world, we see that patriarchal authority has been most prevalent and egalitarian authority has become characteristic of the American family. Matriarchal authority may exist in individual families throughout the world, although it is not an institutionalized family authority form in any society.

2. There are two basic family structural types: the nuclear family and the extended family. A nuclear family consists of two or more related persons, usually including a married couple, who share a common household. The most fundamental of family types, the nuclear family represents the dominant family form in both hunter-gatherer and modern industrial societies. In the United States, most people hold membership in two overlapping nuclear families, the family of orientation (birth and socialization) and the family of procreation (marriage and children). The extended family consists of two or more nuclear families and other relatives who all reside together or near each other. These families, which usually consist of three or more generations, are most prevalent in agricultural societies.

3. From a cross-cultural perspective, societies throughout the world have devised various types of specialized norms with which to structure the family. One of these has to do with acceptable forms of marriage. Monogamy (one husband, one wife) is the most widespread form of marriage in all societies and is the only acceptable form in some, including the United States. Historically, however, some type of polygamy (the taking of plural spouses) has been the preferred marriage form in the majority of the world's societies. There are three basic types of polygamy: polygyny (one man, two or more wives), polyandry (one woman, two or more husbands), and group marriage. Other specialized family norms include those related to mate selection, rules of residence, and rules of descent.

4. Conceptual frameworks used by sociologists to study the family include functionalism, conflict theory, and interactionism. The functionalist approach examines the family as an institution in terms of how it functions to help maintain social harmony and order. The conflict perspective addresses family conflict and change. The interactionist approach focuses on the interpersonal dynamics between members of individual families and between families and their community.

5. The American family today is a diverse and changing institution. Throughout its history, romantic love has increasingly become the dominant basis for mate selection. Through the middle 1960s, the most prevalent form of American family was the traditional nuclear family. During the last few decades, it increasingly has been replaced by the dual-income family. Other recent trends regarding American families include the increasing number of both single-parent families and stepfamilies.

6. The complexities and pressures of modern life have impacted on family crisis and conflict, of which two of the most prevalent forms are marital breakdown and family violence. Divorce is usually the result of marital breakdown. Divorce rates have risen steadily during the past several decades because of a variety of social factors. Recent evidence, however, suggests that they have leveled off and declined slightly and, if current trends hold, could continue to decline in the future. Two prevalent forms of family violence, another current social problem, are spouse abuse and child abuse.

7. As we approach the twenty-first century, several life-style alternatives appear to be increasing in popularity. They include remaining single, marriage without children, and nonmarital cohabitation.

TERMS TO KNOW

catharsis therapy: the verbal release of hostility felt toward a spouse or other family members in a controlled therapeutic environment.

child abuse: overt acts of aggression by a parent or other adult against a child that produce physical injury, emotional problems, or both.

constructive argument: a process of conflict resolution in which family members work through a series of steps that focus on the problem rather than on personalities.

dual-income family: a family in which both partners generate income and share home and child-rearing responsibilities.

egalitarian authority: a pattern of family decision making in which males and females share power equally.

endogamy: a norm that encourages or requires people to marry within certain culturally defined groups or categories.

exogamy: a norm that encourages or requires people to marry outside certain culturally defined groups or categories.

extended family: two or more nuclear families, usually married couples of different generations, and other relatives who all reside together or near each other.

family: two or more persons related by blood, marriage, or adoption who live together and cooperate economically (share a common household).

family universals: characteristics common to families in all societies.

incest taboo: a norm that prohibits sexual relations and marriage between close family members.

latchkey children: children who spend significant amounts of time alone without adult supervision.

marriage: a formally recognized relationship between one man (or more) and one woman (or more) that is durable, relatively stable, and seen as desirable.

marriage by exchange: a form of mate selection involving a social and economic arrangement between the families of the prospective marrieds.

marriage by mutual choice: a form of mate selection that emphasizes the needs of the prospective spouses rather than those of extended blood kin.

matriarchal authority: a pattern of family decision making in which females are dominant in power.

monogamy: marriage involving one man and one woman.

nonmarital cohabitation: the intimate relationship between a man and woman who share a common residence without benefit of marriage.

norm of legitimacy: a norm that specifies social disapproval for out-of-wedlock births.

nuclear family: two or more related persons, usually including a married couple, who occupy a common household.

patriarchal authority: a pattern of family decision making in which males are dominant in power.

polygamy: the taking of plural spouses.

role discrepancy: a possible source of marital conflict in which expectations about the nature and responsibilities of married life are inconsistent with its realities.

romantic love: the idealization of another person based on attachment, commitment, and intimacy.

rules of descent: norms that socially define a person's relatives.

rules of residence: norms that specify where a couple will go to live after marriage.

single-parent family: a family consisting of a single, separated, divorced, or widowed adult and one or more offspring.

spouse abuse: the use of overt acts of aggression by one spouse against another, which produce physical injury, emotional problems, or both.

stepfamily: a family established when two people marry and stepparent and stepsibling relationships are formed.

traditional nuclear family: a family consisting of a full-time working husband, a homemaker wife, and one or more school-age children.

SUGGESTED READINGS

Families in Transition, 5th ed. (Arlene S. Skolnick and Jerome H. Skolnick, editors; Boston, Mass.: Little, Brown, 1986). A highly successful and popular reader with articles that cover a wide variety of issues facing the family today.

The Family: An Introduction, 5th ed. (J. Ross Eshelman; Boston, Mass.: Allyn and Bacon, 1988). A comprehensive text on the family as it exists not only in the United States but cross-culturally throughout the world.

Married People: Staying Together in the Age of Divorce (Francine Klagsburn; New York: Bantam Books, 1985). An insightful look into the nature of marital relationships and needed ingredients to make them work. The author presents various sociological approaches in clear and concise language.

Single Life: Unmarried Adults in Social Context (Peter J. Stein; New York: St. Martins, 1981). A representative compilation of research and essays on the varieties of the single life-style as represented by the never-married, the separated, the divorced, and the widowed.

Surviving the Breakup: How Children and Parents Cope with Divorce (Judith S. Wallerstein and Joan Berlin Kelley; New York: Basic Books, 1985). Explores the various psychological and sociological dimensions of divorce and its aftermath in clear language, which could be of particular value to anyone faced with the prospect of divorce.

Working Wives/Working Husbands (Joseph H. Pleck; Beverly Hills, Calif.: Sage, 1985). A discussion of changing sex roles characteristic of men and women in marriages today and of how such division of labor patterns are impacting on individuals and relationships.

References

Abegglen, J. C. 1958. *The Japanese factory*. New York: Free Press.

Adams, N. 1974. Heredity and environment. *Encyclopedia of Sociology*, 126. Guilford, Conn.: The Dushkin Publishing Group.

Adorno, T. W., E. Frenkel-Brunswick, D. J. Levinson, and R. N. Sanford. 1950. *The authoritarian personality*. New York: Wiley.

Aldous, J. 1986. Cuts in selected welfare programs: The effects on U. S. families. *Journal of Family Issues* (June).

Alexander, P. and R. Gill eds. 1984. *Utopias*. London: Duckworth.

Allport, G. 1954. *The nature of prejudice*. Reading, Mass.: Addison-Wesley.

Allport, G. and L. Postman. 1965. *The psychology of rumor*. New York: Holt, Rinehart and Winston. Originally published in 1947.

American Sociological Association, Committee on Professional Ethics. 1968. Toward a code of ethics for sociologists. *American Sociologist* 3 (November):316–318.

American Sociological Association 1980. Revised A. S. A. code of ethics. *A. S. A. Footnotes* 8 (August):12–13; 52.

————. 1982. Revised code of ethics. *A. S. A. Footnotes* 10 (March):9–10.

Amidei, N. 1981. Testimony, U. S. Congress, House Committee on Energy and Commerce, Subcommittee on Health and the Environment (October):459.

Anderson, N. 1923. *The hobo.* Chicago: University of Chicago Press.

Appleman, P. 1976. *Malthus: An essay on the principle of population.* New York: Norton.

Asch, S. E. 1955. Opinions and social pressure. *Scientific American* 193:4–8.

Babbie, E. 1983. *The practice of social research.* 3rd ed. Belmont, Calif.: Wadsworth.

Bachman, J. G., P. M. O'Malley, and J. Johnston. 1978. *Adolescence to adulthood: Change and stability in the lives of young men.* Vol. 4, *Youth in transition.* Ann Arbor, Mich.: Institute for Social Research.

Balley, T. 1966. *The American pageant: A history of the republic.* 3d ed. Boston: D. C. Heath.

Bales, R. F. 1950. *Interaction process analysis.* Reading, Mass.: Addison-Wesley.

————. 1953. The equilibrium problem in small groups. In T. Parsons et al., eds. *Working papers in the theory of action.* Glencoe, Ill.: Free Press.

————. 1970. *Personality and interpersonal behavior.* New York: Holt, Rinehart and Winston.

Bales, R. F. and P. E. Slater. 1955. Role differentiation in small decision-making groups. In T. Parsons and R. F. Bales, eds. *Family, socialization, and interaction process.* New York: Free Press.

Bales, R. F. and F. L. Strodtbeck. 1951. Phases in group problem-solving. *Journal of Abnormal and Social Psychology* 46 (October):485–495.

Ball-Rokeach, S. J., M. Rokeach, and J. W. Grube. 1984. *The great American values test: Influencing behavior and belief through television.* New York: Free Press.

Barlow, H. 1987. *Introduction to criminology.* 4th ed. Boston: Little, Brown.

Barney, G. O. 1980. *The Global 2000 report to the president of the U.S.* New York: Norton.

Barnouw, V. 1978. *Ethnology: An introduction to anthropology.* 3d ed. Homewood, Ill.: Dorsey Press.

Bart, P. and L. Frankel. 1986. *The student sociologist's handbook,* 4th ed. New York: Random House.

Bartol, C. R. 1980. *Criminal behavior: A psychosocial approach.* Englewood Cliffs, N.J.: Prentice-Hall.

Baumer, T. L. and D. P. Rosenbaum. 1984. *Combatting retail theft: Programs and strategies.* Boston: Butterworth.

Bavelas, A. 1962. Communication patterns in task-oriented groups. In *Group dynamics.* 2d ed., ed. D. Cartright and A. F. Zander, 669–682. New York: Harper & Row.

Beach, L. R. 1973. *Psychology: Core concepts and special topics.* New York: Holt, Rinehart and Winston.

Beck, M., with L. Rohter and C. Friday. 1984. An unwanted baby boom. *Newsweek,* 30 April, 47.

Bccker, H. S. 1963. *The outsiders: Studies in the sociology of deviance.* New York: Free Press.

Becker, H., and H. E. Barnes. 1961. *Social thought from lore to science:* Vol. 1. 3d ed. New York: Dover.

Beeghley, L. and E. W. Butler. 1974. The consequences of intelligence testing in the public schools before and after desegregation. *Social Problems,* 21:740–754.

Belfrage, C. 1963. *The American inquisition, 1945–1960.* New York: Bobbs-Merrill.

Bell, D. 1973. *The coming of the post-industrial society.* New York: Basic Books.

Bell, R. R. 1979. *Marriage and family interaction.* 5th ed. Homewood, Ill.: Dorsey Press.

Bendix, R., ed. 1960. *Max Weber: An intellectual portrait.* Garden City, N.Y.: Doubleday.

Benedict, R. 1934. *Patterns of culture.* New York: Houghton Mifflin

Bennett, R. and L. Nahemow. 1965. Institutional totality and criteria of social adjustment in residences for the aged. *Journal of Social Issues* 21 (October):44–78.

Berger, P. L. 1963. *Invitation to sociology: A humanistic perspective.* Garden City, N. Y.: Doubleday.

Berk, R. 1974. A gaming approach to crowd behavior. *American Journal of Sociology* 79:355–373.

Bernard, L. L. 1924. *Instinct.* New York: Holt, Rinehart and Winston.

Biesanz, M. H. and J. Biesanz. 1973. *Introduction to Sociology.* 2d ed. Englewood Cliffs, N.J.: Prentice-Hall.

Biller, H. B. 1971. *Father, child, and sex role: Paternal determinants of personality development.* Lexington, Mass.: D. C. Heath.

Black, J. A., and D. J. Champion. 1976. *Methods and issues in social research.* New York: Wiley.

Blau, P. 1964. *Exchange and power in social life.* New York: Wiley.

Blau, P. M. and M. W. Meyer. 1971. *Bureaucracy in modern society.* 2d ed. New York: Random House.

Blau, P. M. and W. R. Scott. 1962. *Formal organizations.* San Francisco: Chandler.

Bloomfield, M. 1970. Dixon's *The leopard's spots:* A study in popular facism. In *White racism: Its history, pathology and practice,* ed. B. N. Schwartz and R. Disch. New York: Dell.

Blum, J. W., et al. 1973. *The national experience: A history of the United States.* 3d ed. New York: Harcourt Brace Jovanovich.

Blumer, H. 1939. Collective behavior. In *An outline of the principles of sociology,* ed. R. E. Park. New York: Barnes and Noble.

———. 1948. Public opinion and public opinion polling. *American Sociological Review* 13, 542–549.

———. 1957. Collective behavior. In *Principles of sociology,* ed. A. M. Lee. New York: Barnes and Noble.

Boas, F. 1911. *The mind of primitive man.* New York: MacMillan.

Bogardus, E. S. 1959. *Social distance.* Yellow Springs, Ohio: Antioch Press.

Borg, W. R., and M. D. Gall. 1979. *Educational research: An introduction.* New York: Longman.

Bottomore, T. B. 1966. *Classes in modern society.* New York: Pantheon Books.

Bowers, W. J. and G. Pierce. 1983. What is the effect of executions: Deterrence or brutalization? Unpublished paper cited in E. van den Haag and J. P. Conrad, eds. *The death penalty: A debate.* New York: Plenum Press.

Boyer, P. and S. Nissenbaum. 1974. *Salem possessed: The social origins of witchcraft.* Cambridge, Mass.: Harvard University Press.

Brake, M. 1985. *Comparative youth culture: The sociology of youth cultures and youth subcultures in America, Britain and Canada.* Boston/London: Rutledge and Kegan Paul.

Breindel, E. M. and N. Eberstadt. 1980. Paradoxes of population. *Commentary* 70 (August 8):42.

Broderick, C. B. 1988. *Marriage and the Family.* 3d ed. Englewood Cliffs, N.J.: Prentice-Hall.

Bronowski, J. and B. Mazlish. 1962. *The Western intellectual tradition: From Leonardo to Hegel,* 76–85. New York: Harper Torchbooks.

Broom, L. and P. Selznick. 1968. *Sociology: A text with adapted readings.* 4th ed. New York: Harper & Row.

Browne, L. ed. 1946. *The world's great scriptures.* New York: Macmillan.

Bruck, D. 1988. Decisions of death. In *Crisis in American institutions.* 7th ed., ed. J. H. Skolnick and E. Currie. Glenview, Ill.: Scott, Foresman.

Brunvand, J. H. 1980. Urban legends: Folklore for today. *Psychology Today* 14 (June):50.

———. 1981. *The vanishing hitchhiker: American urban legends and their meanings.* New York: Norton.

———. 1986. *The choking Doberman and other new urban legends.* Paperback ed. New York: Norton.

Bryan, J. A. 1965. Apprenticeships in prostitution. *Social Problems* 12 (Winter):287–297.

Buckner, H. T. 1969. A theory of rumor transmission. In *Readings on collective behavior,* ed. R. R. Evans. Chicago: Rand McNally.

Burke, P. J. 1967. The development of tasks and socioemotional role differentiation. *Sociometry* 30 (December):379–392.

———. 1968. Role differentiation and the legitimization of task activity. *Sociometry* 31 (December):404–411.

Burt, R. 1982. *Toward a structural theory of action.* New York: Academic Press.

Butterfield, F. 1986. Why Asians are going to the head of the class. *The New York Times* (August 3):Section 12, 18–23.

Butterfield, H. 1957. *The origins of modern science.* Rev. ed. New York: Free Press.

Campbell, A., P. E. Converse, and W. L. Rogers. 1976. *The quality of life in America: Perceptions, evaluations, and satisfactions.* New York: Russell Sage Foundation.

Cantril, H., with H. Gaudet and H. Herzog. 1982. *The invasion from Mars.* Princeton, N.J.: Princeton University Press.

Caplow, T. 1969. *Two against one: Coalition in triads.* Englewood Cliffs, N.J.: Prentice-Hall.

Carlson, M. B. 1988. The price of life in Los Angeles. *Time* (February 22):31.

Chagnon, N. A. 1983. *Yanomamo: The fierce people.* 3d. ed. New York: Holt, Rinehart and Winston.

Chamblis W. J. and R. B. Seidman. 1985. *Law, order, and power.* Reading, Mass.: Addison-Wesley.

Cherlin, A. 1981. *Marriage, divorce, remarriage.* Cambridge, Mass.: Harvard University Press.

Childe, V. G. 1950. The urban revolution. *Town Planning Review* 21:3–17.

Chirot, D. 1985. The rise of the West. *American Sociological Review* 50 (April):181–195.

———. 1986. *Social change in the modern era.* 2d ed. San Diego: Harcourt Bracc Jovanovich.

Church, G. J. 1985. Hispanics: A melting of cultures. *Time* (July 8):36.

Clark, P. 1988. A drug test for members of congress. *Playboy* 49 (November):54.

Clayton, R. R. 1979. Cross cultural variations of the family. *The family, marriage, and social change.* 2d ed. Lexington, Mass.: D. C. Heath.

Clinard, M. B. 1974. *Sociology of deviant behavior.* New York: Holt, Rinehart and Winston.

Clinard, M. B., and R. F. Meier. 1979. *The sociology of deviant behavior,* 31. Holt, Rinehart and Winston.

Cochran, M. M., and L. Gunnarsson. 1985. A follow-up study of group day-care and family-based childbearing patterns. *Journal of Marriage and the Family* 47 (May):297–309.

Cohen, N., ed. 1969. *The Los Angeles Riots: A sociopsychological study.* New York: Praeger.

Coleman, J. 1988. *Intimate relationships, marriage, and family.* 2d ed. New York: Macmillan.

Coleman, J., and D. Cressey. 1984. *Social problems.* 2d ed. New York: Harper & Row.

Collins, R. 1988. *Sociology of marriage and the family: Gender, love, and property.* 2d ed. Chicago: Nelson-Hall.

Commoner, B. 1971. *The closing circle.* New York: Knopf.

Conrad, J. P. 1983. Deterrence, the death penalty and the data. In *The death penalty: A debate,* ed. E. van den Hagg and J. P. Conrad. New York: Plenum.

Cooley, C. H. 1902. *Human nature and the social order.* New York: Scribner's.

———. 1909. *Social organization.* New York: Scribner's.

———. 1956. *Social organization.* Glencoe, Ill.: Free Press. (Originally published in 1909 by Scribner's.)

Cooper, K., L. Chassin, S. Braver, K. Zeiss, and K. A. Khavari. 1986. Correlates in mood and marital satisfaction among dual-worker and single-worker couples. *Social Psychology Quarterly* 49:322–329.

Coram, R. 1987. Rubbers from Ronnie. *Playboy* (June):110–112, 150–153.

Cortes, J. B., and F. M. Gatti. 1972. *Delinquency and crime: A biopsychological approach.* New York: Seminar Press.

Coser, L. A. 1956. *The functions of social conflict.* New York: Free Press. (Later edition in 1964.)

———. 1971. *Masters of sociological thought.* New York: Harcourt Brace Jovanovich. (First published in 1956.)

Cox, F. D. 1987. *Human intimacy: Marriage, the family and its meanings.* 4th ed. New York: West.

Cullen, J. B., and S. M. Novick. 1979. The Davis-Moore theory of stratification: A further examination and extension. *American Journal of Sociology* 84 (May):1424–1427.

Currie, E., and J. H. Skolnick. 1988. *America's problems: Social issues and public policy.* 2d ed. Glenview, Ill.: Scott, Foresman.

Curtiss, S. 1977. *Genie: A psycholinguistic study of a modern-day ''wild child.''* New York: Academic Press.

Dahl, R. 1961. *Who governs?* New Haven, Conn.: Yale University Press.

Dahrendorf, R. 1959. *Class and class conflict in industrial society.* Stanford, Calif.: Stanford University Press.

Darley, J., and B. Latane. 1968. Bystander intervention in emergencies: Diffusion of responsibility. *Journal of Personality and Social Psychology* 8:377–383.

Darwin, C. 1859. *On the origin of species.* New York: Macmillan, 1927.

Davies, C. 1983. Crime, bureaucracy, and equality. *Policy Review* 23:89–105.

Davis, A., B. B. Gardner, and M. R. Gardner. 1965. *Deep South: A social anthropological study of caste and class.* Chicago: University of Chicago Press.

Davis, F. 1964. Deviance disavowal: The management of strained interaction by the visually handicapped. In *The other side.* ed. H. Becker, 119–137. New York: Free Press.

Davis, J. A., and T. W. Smith. 1984. *General social survey cumulative file, 1972–1982.* Ann Arbor, Mich.: Inter-University Consortium for Political and Social Research.

Davis, K. 1940. Extreme social isolation of a child. *American Journal of Sociology* 45:554–564.

———. 1947. Final note on a case of extreme isolation. *American Journal of Sociology* 50:432–437.

———. 1948. *Human society.* New York: Macmillan.

Davis, K. and W. Moore. 1945. Some principles of stratification. *American Sociological Review* 10 (April):242–249.

Davis, M. S. 1973. *Intimate relations.* New York: Free Press.

DeFleur, M. L., W. V. D'Antonio, and L. B. DeFleur. 1981. *Sociology: Human society.* 3d ed. Glenview, Ill.: Scott, Foresman. (Also 1976, 2d. ed.)

DeLoria, V. 1970. *Custer died for your sins: An Indian manifesto.* New York: Avon.

Domhoff, G. W. 1967. *Who rules America?* Englewood Cliffs, N.J.: Prentice-Hall.

Domhoff, G. W. 1983. *A view for the eighties.* Englewood Cliffs, N.J.: Prentice-Hall.

Duncan, G. 1984. *Times of poverty, times of plenty.* Ann Arbor, Mich.: University of Michigan Institute for Survey Research.

Dunn, J., and C. Kendrick. 1983. *Siblings: Love, envy, and understanding.* Cambridge, Mass.: Harvard University Press.

Durkheim, É. 1933. *The division of labor in society.* 2d ed. New York: Free Press. (Originally published in 1893.)

———. 1966. *Suicide.* Trans. J. A. Spaulding and G. Simpson. Ed. G. Simpson. New York: Free Press.

———. 1966. *The rules of sociological method.* Trans. S. A. Solovay and J. H. Mueller. Ed. G. E. G.

Catlin. New York: Free Press. (First published in French in 1893; in English, 1938.)

Duster, T. 1971. Conditions for a guilt-free massacre. In *Sanctions for evil: Sources of social destructiveness.* Ed. N. Sanford, C. Comsbock, and associates. Boston: Beacon Press.

Dye, T. R. 1986. *Who's running America: The conservative years.* 4th ed. Englewood Cliffs, N.J.: Prentice-Hall.

Eastman, C. M. 1975. *Aspects of language and culture.* San Francisco: Chandler and Sharp.

Easton, S. C. 1965. *The heritage of the past: From the earliest times to 1500.* Rev. ed. New York: Holt Rinehart and Winston.

Ehrlich, P. R. 1970. *The population bomb.* New York: Ballantine Books.

———, and A. H. Ehrlich. 1979. What happened to the population bomb? *Human Nature* (January):88–92.

Elkin, A. P. 1954. *The Australian aborigines.* 3d. ed. Sydney and London. Also 1964. New York: Doubleday.

Elkin, F. and G. Handel. 1984. *The child and society.* New York: Random House.

Ellis, L. 1982. Genetics and criminal behavior. *Criminology* 20 (May):42–46.

Elliot, D., D. Huizinga, and S. Ageton, 1985. *Explaining delinquency and drug use.* Beverly Hills, Calif.: Sage.

Encyclopedia of sociology. 1974. Working class, 313. Guilford, Conn.: The Dushkin Publishing Group.

Engels, F. 1902. *The origin of the family, private property and the state.* Chicago: Charles H. Kerr. (First published in 1884.)

Engfer, A., and K. A. Scheewind. 1982. Causes and consequences of harsh parental punishment. *Child Abuse and Neglect: The Interactionist Journal* 6:129–140.

Erikson, E. 1950. *Childhood and society.* New York: Norton.

Erikson, E. H. 1982. *The life cycle completed.* New York: Norton.

Erikson, K. T. 1966. *Wayward puritans: A study in the sociology of deviance.* New York: Wiley.

———. 1967. A comment on disguised observation in sociology. *Social problems* 14 (Spring):366–373.

Ermann, D. M. and R. J. Lundman. 1987. *Corporate and governmental deviance: Problems of organizational behavior in contemporary society.* 3rd ed. New York: Oxford University Press.

Eshleman, J. R. 1988. *The Family: An introduction.* 5th ed. Boston, Mass: Allyn and Bacon.

Etzioni, A. 1964. *Modern organizations.* Englewood Cliffs, N.J.: Prentice-Hall.

———. 1975. *A comparative analysis of complex organizations.* New York: Free Press.

———. 1985. Shady corporate practices. *New York Times* (November 15):204.

Farley, R. 1977. Trends in racial inequalities: Have the gains of 1960s disappeared in the 1970s? *American Sociological Review* 42 (April):189–207.

Farley, R. 1984. *Blacks and whites.* Cambridge, Mass.: Harvard University Press.

Ferrero, G. L. 1911. *Lombroso's criminal man.* New York: G. P. Putnam's Sons.

Fiedler, F. E. 1981. Leadership effectiveness. *American Behavioral Scientist* 24:619–632.

Firestone, I. J., C. M. Lichtman, and J. Calamosca. 1975. Leader effectiveness and leader conferral as determinants of helping in a medical emergency. *Journal of Personality and Social Psychology* 31 (February):345–348.

Fishman, J. 1985. *The rise and fall of the ethnic revival: Perspectives on language and ethnicity.* Berlin: Mouton.

The Forbes four hundred. 1987. *Forbes* 40 (October):114–240.

Forer, L. K. 1976. *The birth order factor.* New York: David McKay.

Fornos, W. 1987. *Gaining people, losing ground. A blueprint for stabilizing world population.* Ephrata, Penn: Science Press.

Fox, G. R. 1971. The XYY offender: A modern myth? *The Journal of Criminal Law, Criminology and Police Science* 62 (March):59–73.

Fox, V. 1976. *Introduction to criminology.* Englewood Cliffs, N.J.: Prentice-Hall.

Franklin, J. H. 1980. *From slavery to freedom: A history of Negro Americans.* 5th ed. New York: Knopf.

Freeman, H. E., R. E. Dynes, P. H. Rossi, and W. F. Whyte, eds. 1983. *Applied sociology.* San Francisco: Jossey-Bass.

French, J. R. P., Jr., and B. Raven. 1968. The bases of social power. In *Group Dynamics.* 3d ed., ed. D. Cartwright and A. Zander, 259–269. New York: Harper & Row.

Freud, S. 1930. *Civilization and its discontents.* Trans. J. Strachey. New York: Norton.

Friedrich, L. K., and A. H. Stein. 1975. Prosocial television and young people. *Child Development* 46:27–38.

Friedsam, H. J. 1965. Competition. In *A Dictionary of the Social Sciences,* ed. J. Gould and W. L. Kolb. New York: Free Press. 118–119.

Frisbie, W. P. 1986. Variations in patterns of instability among Hispanics. *Journal of Marriage and the Family* 48:99–106.

Fussel, P. 1983. *Class.* New York: Ballatine Books.

Gallo, A. E., J. A. Zellner, and D. M. Smallwood. 1980. The rich, the poor, and the money they spent for food. (Consumer Research) *National Food Review* (Summer):16–18.

Gans, H. J. 1972. The positive functions of poverty. *American Journal of Sociology* 78 (September):275–289.

———. 1973. *More equality.* New York: Pantheon.

Gardner, R. W., B. Robley, and P. C. Smith. 1985. Asian Americans: Growth, change, and diversity. *Population Bulletin* 40 (October):5, 8.

Gelles, R. J. 1973. Child abuse as psychopathology: A sociological critique and reformation. *American Journal of Orthopsychiatry* 43:611–621.

———. 1980. Violence in the family: A review of the research of the 1970s. *Journal of Marriage and the Family* 42:873–875.

Gelman, D., M. Springen, K. Brailsford, and M. Miller. 1988. Black and white in America. *Newsweek* (March 7):18–23.

Gergen, K. J., and M. M. Gergen. 1981. *Social psychology.* New York: Harcourt Brace Jovanovich.

Gerstel, N. and H. Gross. 1984. *Commuter marriage: A study of work and family.* New York: Guilford Press.

Gerth, H. H. and C. W. Mills, eds. and trans. 1946. *From Max Weber: Essays in sociology.* New York: Oxford University Press.

Giallombardo, R. 1970. Social roles in a prison for women. In *The Sociology of Organizations: Basic*

Studies, ed. O. Grusky and F. A. Miller, 393–408. New York: Free Press.

Gibbs, J. P. 1966. Sanctions. *Social Problems* 14 (Fall):147–159.

Gibbs, N. R., et al. 1988. Grays on the go. *Time* (February 22):66–75.

Giddens, A. 1985. *The construction of society: Outline of the theory of structuration.* Berkeley, Calif.: University of California Press.

Gilligan, C. 1982. *In a different voice: Psychological theory and women's development.* Cambridge, Mass.: Harvard University Press.

Glaser, D. 1971. *Social deviance.* Chicago: Markham.

Glick, P. C. 1981. Children from one-parent families: Recent data and projections. Paper presented at the Special Institute on Critical Issues in Education, sponsored by the Charles F. Kettering Foundation and held at the American University, Washington, D. C. June 20, 1981.

———. 1984. Marriage, divorce, and living arrangements. *Journal of Family Issues* 5:7–26.

Glick, P. C., and A. J. Norton. 1977. Marrying, divorcing, and living together today. *Population Bulletin* 32:1–40.

Glueck, S., and E. Glueck. 1950. *Unraveling juvenile delinquency.* New York: Harper & Row.

Goffman, E. 1961. *Asylums.* Garden City, N.Y.: Doubleday.

———. 1963. *Behavior in public places.* New York: Free Press.

———. 1967. *Interaction ritual: Essays on face-to-face behavior,* 5. Garden City, N.Y.: Doubleday. Anchor Books.

———. 1972. Territories of the self. In *Relations in public,* ed. E. Goffman. New York: Harper, Colophon.

Goldsmith, E. 1972. Blueprint for survival. *The Ecologist* 2 (January):2–6.

Goode, E. 1972. *Drugs in American society.* New York: Knopf.

Goode, W. J. 1960. A theory of role strain. *American Sociological Review* 25:483–496.

Goode, W. J. and P. K. Hatt. 1952. *Methods in Social Research.* New York: McGraw-Hill.

Gordon, L., and P. O'Keefe. 1984. Incest as a form of family violence. *Journal of Marriage and the Family* 46:27–34.

Goring, C. 1972. *The English convict: A statistical study.* Montclair, N.J.: Patterson Smith.

Gortmaker, S. 1979. Poverty and infant mortality in the United States. *American Sociological Review* 44 (April):280–297.

Gough, K. 1986. The origin of the family. In *Family in transition: Rethinking marriage, sexuality, childbearing, and family organization,* ed. A. S. Skolnick & H. H. Skolnick. Boston, Mass.: Little, Brown. 22–39.

Gouldner, A. W. 1954. *Patterns of industrial bureaucracy.* Glencoe, Ill.: Free Press.

———. 1960. The norm of reciprocity. *American Sociological Review* 25 (February):161–178.

Gove, W. R., ed. 1980. *The labeling of deviance: Evaluating a perspective.* Beverly Hills, Calif.: Sage.

Governor's Commission on the Los Angeles Riots. 1965. *Violence in the city: An end or a beginning.* Los Angeles.

Greeley, A. M. 1976. Political attitudes among American white ethnics. In *Sociological essays and research,* ed. C. H. Anderson. Homewood, Ill.: Dorsey.

Green, A. W. 1968. *Sociology: An analysis of life in modern society.* New York: McGraw-Hill.

Greeno, C. G., and E. Maccoby. 1986. How different is the different voice? *Signs* 11:310–316.

Gregory, D. 1967. *Nigger.* Simon & Shuster, Pocket Books edition.

Griffin, J. H. 1961. *Black like me.* New York: Signet Books.

Gupta, M. 1983. A basis for friendly dyadic interpersonal relationships. *Small Group Behavior* 14 (February):15–33.

Gupte, P. 1984. *The crowded earth: People and the politics of population.* New York: Norton.

Guterman, S. S. 1969. In defense of Wirth's "Urbanism as a way of life." *American Journal of Sociology* 74 (March):492–493.

Gwartney-Gibbs, P. A. 1986. The institutionalization of premarital cohabitation: Estimates from marriage license applications 1970 and 1980. *Journal of Marriage and the Family* 48 (May):423–424.

Haas, J. E., and T. E. Drabek. 1973. *Complex organizations: A sociological perspective.* New York: MacMillan.

Haber, A., and R. P. Runyon. 1974. *Fundamentals of psychology.* Reading, Mass.: Addison-Wesley.

Halsell, G. 1969. *Soul sister.* New York: Fawcett.

Hanson, S. H., and M. J. Sporakowski. 1986. Single parent families. *Family Relations* 35: 308.

Hare, A. P. 1962. *Handbook of small group research.* Glencoe, Ill.: Free Press. 229

Harlow, H. F., and M. K. Harlow. 1966. Learning to love. *Scientific American* 215:244–272.

Harlow, H. F., and R. Z. Zimmerman. 1959. Affectional responses in the infant monkey. *Science* 130:421–432.

Harmatz, M. G., and M. A. Novak. 1983. *Human sexuality.* New York: Harper & Row. 525.

Harrington, M. 1984. *The new American poverty.* New York: Holt, Rinehart and Winston.

Harris, M. 1977. *Cannibals and kings: The origins of culture.* New York: Random House.

———. 1980. *Cultural materialism.* New York: Random House, Vintage edition.

———. 1987. India's sacred cow. In *Conformity and conflict: Readings in cultural anthropology.* 6th ed., ed. J. P. Spradley and D. W. McCurdy. Boston, Mass. Little, Brown.

Harroff, P. B. 1962. On language. In *Readings in sociology.* Ed. J. F. Cuber and P. Harroff. New York: Appleton-Century-Crofts. 61–88.

Haupt, A., and T. T. Kane. 1985. *Population handbook.* Washington, D.C.: Population Reference Bureau, Inc.

Hauser, P. M. 1960. *Population perspectives.* New Brunswick, N.J.: Rutgers University Press.

Havighurst, R. J., and B. L. Neugarten. 1967. *Society and education.* 3d ed., 78–79. Boston: Allyn and Bacon.

Hedley, R. A., and S. M. Adams. 1982. The job market for bachelor degree holders: A cumulation. *The American Sociologist* 17:155–163.

Heilbroner, R. L. 1974. *An inquiry into the human prospect.* New York: Norton.

Helmreich, W. B. 1982. *The things they say behind your back.* New York: Doubleday

Hobbes, T. 1881. *Leviathan.* Oxford: James Thornton.

Hodge, R., and D. Treiman. 1968. Class identification in the United States. *American Journal of Sociology* 73:312.

Holden, C. 1986. A revisionist look at population growth. *Science* 231:1493–1494.

Hollander, G. P. 1964. *Leaders, groups, and influence,* 11–26. New York: Oxford University Press.

Homans, G. 1950. *The human group.* New York: Harcourt Brace.

———. 1951. The Western Electric researchers. In *Human Factors in Management.* Ed. S. D. Hoslett. New York: Harper & Row.

———. 1961. *Social behavior: Its elementary forms.* New York: Harcourt, Brace and World.

Homans, G. C. 1974. *Social behavior: Its elementary forms.* New York: Harcourt, Brace Jovanovich.

Hoover, K. R. 1988. *The elements of social scientific thinking.* 4th ed. New York: St. Martin's Press.

Horowitz, I. L., ed. 1967. *The rise and fall of Project Camelot.* Cambridge, Mass.: M.I.T. Press.

Hoult, T. F. 1969. *Dictionary of modern sociology,* 5. Totowa, N.J.: Littlefield, Adams and Company.

Houseman, J. 1948. The men from Mars. *Harper's Magazine* 197 (December):74–82.

Hyman, H. H. 1942. The psychology of status. *The Archives of Psychology* 37:15.

Iyer, P. 1986. From the Windsors, a down-home royal bash. *Time* 128 (August 4):42–44.

Jackman, M. R., and R. W. Jackman. 1983. *Class awareness in the United States.* Berkeley, Calif.: University of California Press.

Jacobs, P. A., M. Brunton, H. M. Melville, R. P. Brittain, and W. F. McClemont. 1965. Aggressive behavior, mental subnormality and the XYY male. *Nature* 208:1351–1352.

James. J. 1951. A preliminary study of the size determinent in small group interaction. *American Sociological Review* 16:474–477.

James, W. 1890. *The principles of psychology.* New York: Dover.

Janis, I. L. 1982 A. *Victims of groupthink: A psychological study of foreign policy decisions and fiascoes.* Boston: Houghton Mifflin.

———. 1982 B. Counteracting the adverse effects of concurrence-seeking in policy-planning groups: Theory and research perspectives. In *Group decision making.* Ed. I. H. Brandstatter, J. H. Davis, and G. Stocker-Kreichgauer. 477–501. New York: Academic Press.

Janis, I. L. and L. Mann. 1977. *Decision making.* New York: Free Press.

Jencks, C. 1972. *Inequality.* New York: Basic Books.

Jian, S., C. H. Tuan, and Y. Jing-Yuan. 1985. *Population control in China*. New York: Praeger.

Johnson, J. 1986. 90's home: Make room for stepfamilies. *USA Today* (March 6):1-A.

Julian, J., and W. Kornblum. 1986. *Social problems*. 5th ed. Englewood Cliffs, N.J.: Prentice-Hall.

Kagan, J. 1976. Day care is as good as home care. *Psychology Today* 9 (May):36–37.

———. 1984. *The nature of the child*. New York: Basic Books.

Kahl, J. A. 1982. *The American class structure: A new synthesis*. Homewood, Ill.: Dorsey Press.

Katz, E., and P. F. Lazarsfeld. 1955. *Personal influence*. New York: Free Press.

Keller, S. 1985. Does the family have a future? In *Rethinking marriage, sexuality, childbearing, and family organization*. 5th ed., eds. A. S. Skolnick and J. H. Skolnick. Boston, Mass.: Little, Brown.

Kempe, R., and H. Kempe. 1978. *Child abuse*. Cambridge, Mass.: Harvard University Press.

Kenkel, W. F. 1973. *The family in perspective*. Englewood Cliffs, N.J.: Prentice-Hall.

Kennell, J. H., D. K. Voos, and M. H. Klaus. 1979. Parent-infant bonding. In *Handbook of infant development*, ed. J. D. Osofsky, 786–798. New York: Wiley.

Kephart, W. 1987. *The sociology of unconventional life-styles*. 3d ed. New York: St. Martin's Press.

Kerbo, H. R. 1981. Characteristics of the poor: A continuing focus in social research. *Sociology and Social Research* 65 (April):323–331.

Khaldun, I. 1950. *An Arab philosophy of history; Selection of the prolegomena of Ibn Khaldun*. Trans. C. Issawi. London: John Murray.

Kielbowiez, R. B., and R. Scherer. 1986. The role of the press in the dynamics of social movements. *Research in Social Movements, Conflict and Change* 9:71–96.

King, D. C., and M. R. Koller. 1975. *Foundations of sociology*, 27–30. San Francisco: Rinehart Press/ Holt, Rinehart and Winston.

Kinsey, A. C., W. B. Pomeroy, and C. E. Martin. 1948. *Sexual behavior in the human male*. Philadelphia: Saunders.

Kitano, H. L. 1985. *Race relations*. 3d ed. Englewood Cliffs, N.J.: Prentice-Hall.

Klagsburn, F. 1985. *Married people: Staying together in the age of divorce*. New York: Bantam Books.

Klaus, M. H., et al. 1972. Maternal bonding: Importance of the first postpartum days. *New England Journal of Medicine* 286:460–463.

Klaus, M. H., and J. H. Kennell. 1982. *Parent-infant bonding*. 2d ed. St. Louis: Mosby.

Knox, D. 1988. *Choices in relationships: An introduction to marriage and the family*. 2d ed. St. Paul, Minn.: West.

Koenig, F. 1985. *Rumor in the Marketplace: The social psychology of commercial hearsay*. Dover, Mass.: Auburn House.

Koepp, S. 1987. Pul-eeze! Will somebody help me? Frustrated American consumers wonder where the service went. *Time* 129 (February 28):48–55.

Kohlberg, L. 1981. *The philosophy of moral development*. Vol. 1, *Essays on moral development*. New York: Harper & Row.

Kohn, M. L. 1963. Social class and parent-child relationships: An interpretation. *American Journal of Sociology* 68:471–480.

———. 1977. *Class and conformity*. 2d ed. Homewood, Ill.: Dorsey.

Krantz, D. S., N. E. Grunberg, and A. Baum. 1985. Health psychology. *Annual Review of Psychology* 36:349–384.

Kroeber, A. L. 1948. *Anthropology*. New York: Harcourt, Brace and World.

Lamanna, M. A., and A. Reidman. 1985. *Marriages and families: Making choices throughout the life cycle*. 2d ed. Belmont, Calif.: Wadsworth.

Lamar, J. V. 1988. Kids who sell crack. *Time* (May 9):20–33.

Landis, J. T., and M. G. Landis. 1973. *Building a successful marriage*. 6th ed. Englewood Cliffs, N.J.: Prentice Hall.

Lauer, R. H., and W. H. Handel. 1983. *Social psychology: The theory and application of symbolic interactionism*. 2d ed. Englewood Cliffs, N.J.: Prentice-Hall.

LeBon, G. 1985. *The crowd: The study of the popular mind*. London: Ernest Benn (2d ed. 1968, Dunwoody, Ga.: Norman S. Berg).

Lee, A. M., and E. B. Lee. 1971. *The fine art of propaganda*. New York: Octagon.

Lee, R. R., and I. DeVore, eds. 1976. *Kalihari hunter-gatherers: Studies of the !Kung San and their neighbors*. Cambridge, Mass.: Harvard University Press.

Lemert, E. 1951. *Social pathology.* New York: Mc-Graw-Hill.

Leslie, G. R. 1979. *The family in social context.* 4th ed. New York: Oxford University Press.

Lenski, G. E. 1966. *Power and privilege: A theory of social stratification.* New York: McGraw-Hill.

Lewin, K. 1954. Experiments of K. Lewin, R. Lippitt, and R. K. White reported by H. H. Kelley and J. W. Thibault. In *Handbook of social psychology.* Vol. 2, ed. G. Lindsey, 776–777. Reading, Mass.: Addison-Wesley.

Lewis, J. W. 1972. A study of the Kent State incident using Smelser's theory of collective behavior. *Sociological Inquiry* 42:87–96.

Lewis, O. 1961. *The children of Sanchez: Autobiography of a Mexican family.* New York: Vintage Books.

———. 1966. The culture of poverty. *Scientific American* 215 (October):19–25.

———. 1968. *A study of slum culture.* New York: Random House.

Light, D., and S. Keller. 1982. *Sociology.* 3rd ed. New York: Knopf.

Lincoln, C. E. 1968. *Chronicles of black protest.* New York: New American Library, Mentor edition.

Lingeman, R. R. 1974. *Drugs from A to Z: A dictionary.* 2d ed. New York: McGraw-Hill.

Lipset, S. M., ed. 1962. *Harriet Martineau: Society in America.* New York: Doubleday.

———. 1979. *The third century: America as a postindustrial society.* Chicago: University of Chicago Press.

Little, R. W. 1970. Buddy relations and combat performance. In *The sociology of organizations: Basic studies,* ed. O. Grusky and G. A. Miller, 361–375. New York: Free Press.

Locke, J. 1690. *Two treatises of government.*

Lombroso, C. 1911. *Crime, its causes and remedies.* Boston, Little, Brown.

Los Angeles Times. 1973. Syphilis study of 600 blacks called racist. Los Angeles: UPI Dispatch (May 13):1A, 6.

MacIver, R. M. 1948. *The more perfect union.* New York: Macmillan.

Magnuson, E. 1986. Hitting the mafia: A wave of trials is putting the nation's crime bosses behind bars. *Time* 128 (September 29):16–22.

Malson, L. 1972. *Wolf children and the problem of human nature.* New York: Monthly Review Press.

Mare, R. D. 1982. Socioeconomic effects on child mortality in the United States. *American Journal of Public Health* (June):541–543.

Marsden, P. V. 1987. Core discussion networks of Americans. *American Sociological Review* 52 (February):122–131.

Martin, R. 1977. *The sociology of power.* London: Routledge and Kegan Paul.

Marx, G. 1986. The iron fist and the velvet glove: Totalitarian potentials within democratic structures. In *The social fabric: Dimensions and issues.* Ed. J. F. Short, Jr. Newbury Park, Calif.: Sage.

Marx, K. 1906. *Capital.* Vol. 1. New York: Modern Library. First published in 1867 as *Das Kapital.*

Marx, K. and F. Engels. 1846. *The German Ideology.* New York: International Publishers edition, 1939.

Massey, G. 1975. Studying social class: The case of embourgeoisement and the culture of poverty. *Social Problems* 22 (June):595–608.

Matchan, L. 1983. *Boston Globe* (October 17):41, 43.

Matras, J. 1977. *Introduction to population.* Englewood Cliffs, N.J.: Prentice-Hall. 292–293.

Mayer, J. 1976. The dimensions of human hunger. *Scientific American* (September):40–46.

McCall, R. B. 1975. *Intelligence and heredity.* Homewood, Ill.: Learning Systems Company.

McPhail, C. and R. T. Wolstein. 1983. Individuals and collective behaviors within gatherings, demonstrations, and riots. *Annual Review of Sociology* 9. Palo Alto, Calif.

McCullough, D. W., ed. 1984. *Great detectives: A century of the best mysteries from England and America.* New York: Pantheon.

McWhirter, N. 1982. *Guinness book of world records,* 28. New York: Bantam Books.

Mead, G. H. 1934, *Mind, self, and other.* Chicago: University of Chicago Press.

Mead, M. 1953. The impact of cultural changes on the family. *The family in the urban community.* Detroit: The Merrill-Palmer School.

———. 1971. Comment. In *Discussions on child development.* Ed. J. Tanner and B. Inbelder. New York: International Universities Press.

Meadows, D. H., et al. 1972. *The limits to growth.* New York: Signet Books.

Meredith, D. 1986. Day-care: The nine to five dilemma. *Psychology Today* 20 (February):36–44.

Merton, R. K. 1959. Notes on problem-finding in sociology. In *Sociology today: Problems and prospects,* ed. R. K. Merton, L. Broom, and L. S. Cottrell, Jr., ix-xxxiv. New York: Basic Books.

———. 1968. *Social theory and social structure* Enl. ed. New York: Free Press.

———. 1976. *Sociological ambivalence and other essays.* New York: Morrow.

———. 1976. Discrimination and the American creed. *Sociological ambivalence and other essays.* New York: Free Press. 190–199.

Merton, R. K., and A. S. Rossi. 1968. Contributions to the theory of reference group behavior. In *Social theory and social structure.* Enl. ed. 319–322. New York: Free Press.

Michelmore, P. N. 1986. A knife in the heart. *Reader's Digest* (April):109–114.

Michels, R. 1966. *Political parties: A sociological study of the oligarchical tendencies of modern democracy.* New York: Free Press Paperback. (Originally published in 1911.)

Milgram, S. 1965. Some conditions of obedience and disobedience to authority. *Human Relations* 18:57–75.

———. 1974. *Obedience to authority.* New York: Harper & Row.

———. 1977. *The individual in a social world.* Reading, Mass.: Addison-Wesley.

Miller, E. L. 1987. *Questions that matter: An invitation to philosophy.* New York: McGraw-Hill.

Mills, C. W. 1959. *The sociological imagination.* New York: Oxford University Press.

Mindel, C. H. and R. W. Haberstein, eds. 1981. *Ethnic families in America: Patterns and variations,* 2d ed. New York: Elsevier.

Montague, A. 1972. *Statement on race.* New York: Oxford University Press.

Morris, J. K. 1966. Professor Malthus and his essay. *The Population Bulletin* 22 (February):7–27.

Mortimer, J. T., and R. G. Simmons. 1978. Adult socialization. *Annual Review of Sociology* 4:421–454.

Moskos, C., Jr. 1975. The American combat soldier in Vietnam. *Journal of Social Issues* (Fall):25–37.

Muller, B. 1974. Brainwashing. *Encyclopedia of sociology.* Guilford, Conn.: The Dushkin Publishing Group.

Mulvihill, D. J., and M. Tumin (with L. Curtis). 1969. *Crimes of violence,* Staff Report to the National Commission on the Causes and Prevention of Violence. Washington, D.C.: U.S. Government Printing Office.

Murdock, P. M. 1945. The common denominator of cultures. In *The science of man and the world crisis.* Ed. R. Linton. New York: Columbia University Press.

———. 1965. *Social structure.* New York: Free Press. Originally published in 1949.

Myrdal, G. 1962. *Challenge to affluence.* New York: Random House.

Nachmias, D., and C. Nachmias. 1987. *Research methods in the social sciences.* 3d. ed. New York: St. Martins Press.

Naisbitt, J. 1984. *Megatrends: Ten new directions transforming our lives.* New York: Warner Books.

Nasar, S. 1986. America's poor: How big a problem? *Fortune* (May 26):74–80.

Nash, M. 1962. Race and the ideology of race. *Current anthropology* 3:285–288.

National Institute of Mental Health. 1982. *Television and behavior: Ten years of scientific progress and implications for the eighties.* Washington, D.C.: U.S. Government Printing Office.

Nemeth, C. J. 1985. Dissent, group process, and creativity: The contribution of minority influence. *Advances in group processes.* Greenwich, Conn.: JAI Press 2:57–75.

Newsweek. 1970. 'My God! They're killing us. (May 18): 31–33, 33F.

———. 1986. (September, 1):3.

———. 1987. How to stay married (August 24):53.

New York Times. 1987. Tuitions at new peak, heating cost debate (May 12):B7.

Nisbet, R. A. 1965. *Émile Durkheim.* Englewood Cliffs, N.J.: Prentice Hall.

———. 1966. *The sociological tradition.* New York: Basic Books.

———. 1970. *The social bond.* New York: Knopf. 66–69.

Noda, K. 1975. Big business organization. In *Modern Japanese organization and decision making.* Ed. E. F. Vogel. Berkeley, Calif.: University of California Press.

Nottingham, E. K. 1971. *Religion: A sociological view:* New York: Random House.

Novak, M. A. 1979. Social recovery of monkeys isolated for the first year of life: II. Long term assessment. *Developmental Psychology.* 11:453–461.

Ogburn, W. F. 1922. *Social change: With respect to culture and original nature.* New York: Huebsch.

———. 1930. The folk-ways of scientific sociology. *Scientific Monthly.* 30 (April):300–306.

———. 1959. The wolf boy of Agra. *American Journal of Sociology.* 46 (March):499–554.

O'Hare, W. 1986. The eight myths of poverty. *American Demographics.* 8 (May):22–25.

Oliver, P., G. Marwell, and R. Teixeira. 1985. A theory of the critical mass: Interdependence, group heterogeneity, and the production of collective action. *American Journal of Sociology.* 91:522–556.

Olmsted, M. S., and A. P. Hare. 1978. *The small group.* 2d ed. New York: Free Press.

Orshansky, M. 1965. Who's Who among the poor: A demographic view of poverty. *Social Security Bulletin.* 28 (July):3–32.

Ouchi, W. G. 1981. *Theory Z: How American business can meet the Japanese challenge.* Reading, Mass.: Addison-Wesley.

Overbeek, J. 1982. *Population.* New York: Harcourt Brace Jovanovich. 232.

Parrillo, V. N. 1985. *Strangers to these shores.* 2d ed. New York: Wiley. Also 1980. 1st ed. Boston, Houghton Mifflin.

Parkinson, C. N. 1957. *Parkinson's law and other studies in administration.* Boston: Houghton Mifflin.

Parsons, T., ed. 1947. *Max Weber: The theory of social and economic organization.* New York: Oxford University Press.

Parsons, T. 1947, Introduction. In M. Weber, *The theory of social and economic organization.* Trans. A. M. Henderson and T. Parsons. Glencoe, Ill.: Free Press.

———. 1956. Suggestions for a sociological approach to theory of organizations. *Administrative Science Quarterly* 1 (June):63–85.

Pascale, R. T. and A. G. Athos. 1981. *The art of Japanese management: Applications for American executives.* New York: Warner Books.

Pear, R. 1986. Poverty rate shows slight drop for '85 census bureau says. *New York Times* (August 27):1, 9.

Perrow, C. 1967. A framework for the comparative analysis of organizations. *American Sociological Review* 32 (April):194–208.

Peter, L. J., and R. Hull. 1969. *The Peter principle: Why things always go wrong.* New York: Morrow.

Peters, T. J., and R. J. Waterman, Jr. 1982. *In search of excellence: Lessons from America's best-run companies.* New York: Warner Books.

Peterson, W. 1969. *Population,* 115. New York: Macmillan.

———. 1975. *Population.* 3d ed. New York: Macmillan.

Pettigrew, T. F. 1980. Prejudice. *Harvard encyclopedia of American ethnic groups.* Cambridge, Mass.: Belnap Press.

Piaget, J. 1929. *The child's conception of the world.* New York: Harcourt, Brace and World.

Piaget, J., and B. Inhelder. 1969. *The psychology of the child.* New York: Basic Books.

Pleck, J. H. 1985. *Working wives/working husbands.* Beverly Hills, Calif.: Sage.

Plog, F., and D. G. Bates. 1980. *Cultural anthropology.* 2d ed. New York: Knopf.

Polansky, N. A., M. A. Chalmers, E. Buttenseiser, and D. P. Williams. 1981. *Damaged parents, an anatomy of child neglect.* Chicago: University of Chicago Press.

Popenoe, D. 1971. *Sociology,* 530–531. New York: Appleton-Century-Crofts.

Popline. April 1985. A bitter struggle with millions of lives at stake, 1. Washington, D.C.: The Population Institute.

———. June 1985. Hunger: A continuing crisis. Washington, D.C.: The Population Institute.

———. July 1985. 20 million more men. Washington, D.C.: The Population Institute.

———. October 1985. 100 new mega-cities expected, 2–3. Washington, D.C.: The Population Institute.

———. April 1986. Mega-cities: New 3rd world phenomenon, 8. Washington, D.C.: The Population Institute.

———. September 1987. Population growth is contributing to rainforest decline, 3. Washington, D.C.: The Population Institute.

Population Today March 1985. China's demographic disaster of 1958–1962. 13:7.

———. June 1986. Survey report, Kenya. 14:5.

Porter, A. 1986. Work in the new information age. *The Futurist* 20 (September-October): 9–14.

Price, W. H., and P. B. Whatmore. 1967. Behavior disorders and patterns of crime among XYY males identified at a maximum security hospital. *British Medical Journal* 1:533–536.

Public Health Reports. 1969. Link between XYY syndrome and criminality not clear. 89 (October):914.

Pugh, M. D. 1980. *Collective behavior: A sourcebook.* New York: West.

Quarles, B. 1969. *The Negro in the making of America.* New York: Macmillan.

Quinney, R. 1974. *Critque of legal order: Crime control in capitalist society.* Boston: Little, Brown.

———. 1980. *Class, state and crime.* 2d ed. New York: Longman.

Reisman, D. 1961. *The lonely crowd.* New Haven, Conn.: Yale University Press.

Reiss, I. 1980. *Family systems in America.* 3d ed. New York: Holt, Rinehart and Winston.

Reiterman, T. 1982. *Raven: The untold story of the Rev. Jim Jones and his people.* New York: Dutton.

Report of the national advisory commission on civil disorders, 3–4. 1968. New York: Bantam Books.

Rice, F. P. 1983. *Contemporary marriage.* Boston: Allyn and Bacon.

Ridgeway, C. L. 1983. *The dynamics of small groups.* New York: St. Martin's Press.

Ridley, F. F., ed. 1979. *Government and administration in Western Europe.* New York: St. Martins Press.

Robertson, I. 1974. Indian caste system. In the *Encyclopedia of sociology.* Guilford, Conn.: The Dushkin Publishing Group.

———. 1974. Counterculture. In the *Encyclopedia of sociology,* 60–61. Guilford, Conn.: Dushkin Publishing Group.

———. 1980. *Social problems.* 2d ed. New York: Random House.

Rodman, H., and C. Cole. 1987. Latch-key children. A review of policy and resources. *Family Relations* 36:101–105.

Roediger, H. L., J. P. Rushton, E. D. Capaldi, and S. G. Paris. 1984. *Psychology.* Boston: Little, Brown.

Roethlisberger, F. J. and W. J. Dickson. 1939. *Management and the Worker.* Cambridge, Mass.: Harvard University Press.

Roscoe, B., and N. Benaske. 1985. Courtship violence experienced by abused wives: Similarities in patterns of abuse. *Family Relations* 34:419–424.

Rose, S. J. 1986. *The American Profile Poster.* New York: Pantheon.

———. 1986. *Social stratification in the United States.* New York: Pantheon.

Rosenberg, D. H. 1974. Feudalism. In the *Encyclopedia of sociology.* Guilford, Conn.: The Dushkin Publishing Group.

Rosenthal, A. M. 1964. *Thirty-eight witnesses.* New York: McGraw-Hill.

Ross, J. B., and M. M. McLaughlin, eds. 1949. *The portable medieval reader.* New York: Viking Press.

Ross, I. 1988. How lawless are big companies? In *Crisis in American institutions.* 7th ed., ed. J. H. Skolnick and E. Currie. Glenview, Ill.: Scott, Foresman.

Rossides, D. W. 1976. *The American class system: An introduction to social stratification.* Boston: Houghton-Mifflin.

Rothschild, J. 1986. Alternatives to bureaucracy: Democratic participation in the economy. *Annual Review of Sociology* 12:307–328.

Rothschild-Whitt, J. 1979. The collectivistic organization: An alternative to rational bureaucratic models. *American Sociological Review* 44:509–527.

Rousseau, J. J. 1762. *A treatise on the social compact.*

Ruben, Z. 1970. Measurement of romantic love. *Journal of personality and social psychology* 16: 265–273.

Rumbaut, G. R. 1986. Southeast Asian refugees in the United States: A portrait of a case of migration and resettlement, 1975–1985. Paper presented at the annual meeting of the American Sociological Association.

Russel, C. 1984. The business of demographics. *Population Bulletin* 39 (June):1–40.

Salmans, S. Man in the moon loses job at P&G. *New York Times,* 25 April, 1985.

Santrock, J. W. 1970. Influence of onset and type of paternal absence on the first four Eriksonian developmental crises. *Developmental Psychology* 3:273–274.

Sapir, E. 1929. The status of linguistics as a science. *Language* 5:207 214.

Saxton, L. 1972. *The individual, marriage, and the family.* 2d ed. Belmont, Calif.: Wadsworth.

Scarr, S., and R. A. Weinberg. 1976. IQ test performance of black children adopted by white families. *American Psychologist* 31 (April):726–739.

Schaefer, R. T. 1988. *Racial and ethnic groups.* 3d ed. Glenview, Ill.: Scott, Foresman. Also 1985. 2d ed. Boston: Little, Brown.

Schelling, T. C. 1978. *Micromotives and macrobehavior.* New York: Norton.

Schmemann, S. Russia wants a baby boom of its own. *The New York Times,* 28 July, 1985.

Schultz, E. A., and R. H. Lavenda. 1987. *Cultural anthropology: A perspective on the human condition.* New York: West.

Schur, E. M. 1971. *Labeling deviant behavior: Its sociological implications.* New York: Harper & Row.

———. 1984. *Labeling women deviant: Gender, stigma, and social control.* New York: Random House.

Schwartz, S., and A. Gottlieb. 1980. Bystander anonymity and reaction to emergencies. *Journal of Personality and Social Psychology* 39:418–440.

Semones, J. K. 1977. Associations and bureaucracy. *Introductory sociology: A core text,* 114. Dubuque, Iowa: Kendall/Hunt.

———. 1977. Deviant behavior. *Sociology: A core text.* Dubuque, Iowa: Kendall/Hunt.

———. Danielle: An unpublished interview. Part of a series of case studies on deviance in contemporary America, 3 September, 1988.

Service, E. R. 1971. *Profiles in ethnology.* Rev. ed. New York: Harper & Row.

Shai, D. 1986. Cancer mortality, ethnicity, and socioeconomic status: Two New York City groups. *Public Health Reports* (September–October):547.

Shattuck, R. 1980. *The forbidden experiment. The story of the wild boy of Aveyron.* New York: Farrar, Strauss, Giroux.

Shkilnyk, A. 1985. *A poison stronger than love: The destruction of an Ojibwa community.* New Haven, Conn.: Yale University Press.

Sheldon, W. H. 1949. *Varieties of delinquent youth: An introduction to constitutional psychiatry.* New York: Harper & Row.

Shibutani, T. 1966. *Improvised news: A sociological study of rumor,* 62. Indianapolis: Bobbs-Merrill.

———. 1986. *Social processes: An introduction to sociology,* Berkeley, Calif.: University of California Press.

Shils, E. A. 1950. Primary groups in the American army. In *Continuities in social research.* Ed. R. K. Merton and P. F. Lazarsfeld. New York: Free Press.

Shils, E. A., and M. Janowitz. 1948. Cohesion and disintegration of the Wehrmacht in World War II. *Public Opinion Quarterly* (Summer):280–315.

Simmel, G. 1950 A. The metropolis and mental life. *The sociology of Georg Simmel.* Ed. and trans. K. Wolff. New York: The Free Press. (This article was first published in 1918.)

———. 1950 B. Quantitative aspects of the group. *The sociology of Georg Simmel.* Ed. and trans. K. Wolff. New York: Free Press. (This article was first published in 1905.)

———. 1955. *Conflict and the web of group affiliations.* New York: Free Press.

Simmons, J. L. 1969. *Deviants.* Berkeley, Calif.: The Glendessary Press.

Simon, J. L., and P. Burstein. 1985. *Basic research methods in social science.* 3d ed. New York: Random House.

Sjoberg, G. 1967. Project Camelot: Selected readings and personal reflections. In *Ethics, politics, and social research,* ed. G. Sjoberg. Cambridge, Mass.: Schenkman.

Sklare, M. 1971. *America's Jews.* New York: Random House.

Skolnick, A. 1987. *The intimate environment: Exploring marriage and the family.* 4th ed. Boston: Little, Brown.

Skonick, A. S. and J. H. Skolnick, eds. 1986. *Families in Transition,* 4th ed. Boston: Mass.: Little, Brown.

Slater, P. E. 1955. Role differentiation in small groups. In *Small groups: Studies in social interaction,* ed. A. P. Hare et al. New York: Knopf.

Smelser, N. 1962. *Theory of collective behavior.* New York: Free Press.

Solomon, Z., M. Mikulincer, and S. E. Hobfoll. 1986. Effects of social support and battle intensity on loneliness and breakdown during combat. *Journal of Personality and Social Psychology* 51:1269–1276.

Sorensen, A. B. 1975. The structure of intragenerational mobility. *American Sociological Review* 40:456–471.

Spector, M., and J. I. Kitsuse. 1977. *Constructing social problems.* Menlo Park, Calif.: Cummings.

Spitz, Rene. 1945. Hospitalization: An inquiry into the genesis of psychiatric conditions in early childhood. In *The psychoanalytic study of the child,* ed. A. Freud. New York: International Universities Press.

Stark, P. 1988. A drug test for members of congress. *Playboy* (November): 49, 54.

Statistical Abstract of the United States. 1984. U.S. Bureau of the Census, 573. Washington, D.C.: U.S. Government Printing Office.

Statistical Abstract of the United States. 1987 (1986). Washington, D.C.: U.S. Government Printing Office.

Steadman, H. J., and J. J. Cocozza. 1974. *Careers of the criminally insane.* Lexington, Mass.: Lexington Books.

Stein, P. 1981. *Single life: Unmarried adults in social context.* New York: St. Martin's

Steinbeck, J. 1939. *The grapes of wrath.* New York: Viking Press.

Stevens, W. A. 1970. A cross-cultural study of modesty and obscenity. In *Technical reports of the Commission on Obscenity and Pornography.* Washington, D.C. IX.

Straus, M. A. 1974. Leveling, civility, and violence in the family. *Journal of Marriage and the Family* 36 (February):13–20.

Straus, M. A., R. J. Gelles, and S. K. Steinmetz. 1980. *Behind closed doors: Violence and the American family.* New York: Doubleday.

Stryker, S., and A. Statham. 1985. Symbolic interaction and role theory. In *Handbook of social psychology.* Vol. 1, 3d ed., ed. G. Lindsey and E. Aronson. New York: Random House.

Stuckert, R. P. 1976. "Race" mixture: The black ancestry of white Americans. In *Physical anthro-* *pology and archaeology,* ed. P. B. Hammond. New York: Macmillan.

Suchman, E. A. 1968. The "hang-loose" ethic and the spirit of drug use. *Journal of health and social behavior* (June):146–155.

Sumner, W. G. 1960. *Folkways.* New York: The New American Library. (Originally published in 1906.)

Sutherland, E. H. 1939. *Principles of criminology.* Philadelphia: Lippincott.

———. 1967. *White collar crime.* New York: Holt, Rinehart and Winston.

Sutherland, E. H., and D. R. Cressey. 1970. *Criminology.* 8th ed. Philadelphia: Lippincott.

Szasz, T. S. 1974. *The myth of mental illness.* New York: Harper & Row.

Taft, D. R., and R. W. England. 1966. *Criminology.* 4th ed. New York: MacMillan.

Tallman, I., R. Marotz-Baden, and P. Pindas. 1983. *Adolescent socialization in cross-cultural perspective.* New York: Academic Press.

Task Force Report: Crime and its impact. 1967. President's Commission on Law Enforcement and Administration of Justice. Washington, D.C.: U.S. Government Printing Office.

Teitelbaum, M. S. 1975. Relevance of demographic transition theory for developing countries. *Science* 188 (May):420–425.

Thomas, W. I., and M. Thomas. 1928. *The child in America: Behavior problems and programs.* New York: Knopf.

Thomlinson, R. 1976. *Population dynamics: Causes and consequences of demographic change.* New York: Random House.

Thrasher, F. M. 1927. *The gang.* Chicago: University of Chicago Press.

Thurstone, L. L. 1938. Primary mental abilities. *Psychometric monographs,* No. 1. Chicago: University of Chicago Press.

Timasheff, N. S. 1967. *Sociological theory: Its nature and growth.* 3d ed. New York: Random House.

Time. 1989. A brightly colored tinderbox. (January 30): 28–29.

Tönnies, F. 1957. *Community and society: Gemeinschaft and Gesellschaft.* Ed. and trans. C. A. Loomis. East Lansing, Mich.: Michigan State University Press. (Originally published in 1887.)

Toffler, A. 1980. *The third wave.* New York: Morrow.

Toufexis, A., et al. Older—but coming on strong. *Time* 22 February 1988, 76–79.

Truzzi, M. 1974. *Sociology for pleasure.* Englewood Cliffs, N.J.: Prentice-Hall.

Tumin, M. 1953. Some principles of stratification: A critical analysis. *American Sociological Review* 18:387–394.

Turkington, C. 1983. Lifetime of fear may be the legacy of latchkey children. *Monitor.* Washington, D.C.: American Psychological Association (November):19.

Turner, R. H. 1964. Collective behavior. In *Handbook of modern sociology,* ed. R. E. L. Fatis. Chicago: Rand McNally.

———. 1980. New theoretical frameworks. In *Collective behavior: A source book,* ed. M. D. Pugh, 31–41. New York: West.

Turner, R. H., and L. M. Killian, eds. 1957. Collective behavior. Englewood Cliffs, N.J.: Prentice Hall. 3d ed., 1987.

Turner, V. 1967. *The forest of symbols,* 3. Ithaca, N.Y.: Cornell University Press.

Udall, M. K. 1987. Introduction. In W. Fornos, *Gaining people; losing ground, vii.* Washington, D.C.: The Population Institute.

United Nations. 1985. *Estimates and Projections of Urban, Rural and City Population, 1950–2025.*

U.S. Bureau of the Census. 1982. Household and family characteristics, March 1981. *Current Population Reports,* Series P-20, No. 372. Washington, D.C.: U.S. Government Printing Office.

———. 1983. Wives who earn more than their husbands. *Special Demographic Analysis,* CDS-80-9. Washington, D.C.: U.S. Government Printing Office.

———. 1985. November. Marital status and living arrangements, March 1985. *Current Population Reports,* Series P-20, No. 410. Washington, D.C.: U.S. Government Printing Office.

———. 1985 A. *Current Population Reports,* Series P-60, No. 149. Washington, D.C.: U.S. Government Printing Office.

———. 1985 B. Fertility of American Women. *Current Population Reports.* Series P-20, No. 401. Washington, D.C.: U.S. Government Printing Office.

———. 1985 C. *Statistical abstract of the United States.* Washington, D.C.: U.S. Government Printing Office.

———. 1986 A. Money income and poverty status, 1985: Advance report. *Current Population Reports,* Series P-60, No. 152. Washington, D.C.: U.S. Government Printing Office.

———. 1986 B. Money income and poverty status of families and persons in the United States, 1985. *Current Population Reports,* Series P-60, No. 154:13. Washington, D.C.: U.S. Government Printing Office.

———. 1986 C. November. Households, families, marital status, and living arrangements, March 1986. Advance Report. *Current Population Reports,* Series P-20, No. 410. Washington, D.C.: U.S. Government Printing Office.

———. 1987. Money income and poverty status of families and persons in the United States, 1986. *Current Population Reports,* Series P-60, No. 157. Washington, D.C.: U.S. Government Printing Office.

———. 1988. Money income and poverty status of families in the United States: 1987. *Current Population Reports.* Washington, D. C.: U.S. Government Printing Office.

U.S. Department of Labor, Bureau of Labor Statistics. 1987. Education, social service, and related occupations (Bulletin 2250-6, reprinted from the *Occupational Outlook Handbook,* 1986–1987 ed.). Washington, D.C.: U.S. Government Printing Office.

U.S. National Center for Health Statistics. 1979, March. Department of Health, Education, and Welfare Publication No. (PHS) 78-1120. Washington, D.C.: U.S. Government Printing Office.

Van Creveld, M. 1982. *Fighting power: German and U.S. army performance, 1939–1945.* Westport, Conn.: Greenwood Press.

van den Berghe, P. 1978. *Race and racism. A comparative perspective.* 2d ed. New York: Wiley.

Vander Zanden, J. W. 1972. *American minority relations: The sociology of race and ethnic groups.* 3d ed, 46–47. New York: Ronald Press.

———. 1983. *American minority relations.* 4th ed. New York: Knopf.

———. 1985. *Human development.* 3d ed. New York: Knopf.

Vogel, E. 1979. *Japan as number one: Lessons for America.* Cambridge, Mass.: Harvard University Press.

Vold, G. 1958. *Theoretical criminology,* 74. New York: Harvard University Press.

Wagley, C., and M. Harris. 1964. *Minorities in the new world.* New York: Columbia University Press.

Walker, B. 1985. *The crone: Women of age, wisdom, and power.* New York: Harper & Row.

Wallace, C. 1986. The royal wedding. *People* 26 (4 August):23–28.

Wallace, W. 1972. *The Logic of Science in Sociology.* Chicago: Aldine-Atherton.

Wallerstein, J. S. and J. B. Kelley. 1985. *Surviving the breakup: How children and parents cope with divorce.* New York: Basic Books.

Wallis, C. 1985. Children having children: Teen pregnancies are corroding America's social fabric. *Time* 126 (9 December):78–90.

Warner, W. L. 1949. *Democracy in Jonesville.* New York: Harper & Row.

Warner, W. L., and P. S. Lunt. 1941. *The social life of a modern community.* New Haven, Conn.: Yale University Press.

Warner, W. L., M. Meeker, and K. Ells. 1949. *Social class in America.* Chicago: Science Research Associates.

Waters, H. P. 1977. What TV does to kids. *Newsweek,* 21 February, 107–112.

Watkins, L. M. 1986. Liberal arts graduates prospects in the job market grow brighter. *Wall Street Journal,* (May 6):29.

Wattenberg, B. J. 1985. *The good news is the bad news is wrong.* New York: Simon and Shuster.

Watson, J. B. 1924. *Behavior.* New York: Norton.

Weber, M. 1946. Class, status, and party. In *From Max Weber: Essays in sociology.* Ed. and trans. H. Gerth and C. W. Mills. New York: Oxford University Press. 180–195.

———. 1946. The sociology of charismatic authority. In *From Max Weber: Essays in sociology.* Ed. and trans. H. Gerth and C. W. Mills. New York: Oxford University Press, 245–252.

———. 1968. *Economy and society.* New York: Bedminster Press. (Originally published in 1922.)

Weisman, S. R. 1986. The Rajiv generation. *New York Times Magazine,* 20 April, 18–22.

Whorf, B. L. 1956. *Language, thought, and reality: Selected writings of Benjamin Lee Whorf.* Ed. J. B. Carroll. Cambridge, Mass.: MIT Press.

White, R. K., and R. O. Lippitt. 1960. *Autocracy and democracy.* New York: Harper & Row.

Whyte, M. K., and W. L. Parish. 1984. *Urban life in contemporary China.* Chicago: University of Chicago Press.

Wilensky, H. L., and C. N. Lebeaux. 1958. *Industrial society and social welfare.* New York: Russel Sage Foundation.

Wilkinson, D. 1980. Applied sociology: Is it Pure? *A. S. A. Footnotes* 8 (May):3. Quoted from Ward, L. F. 1906. *Applied sociology,* 3. Boston, Mass. Ginn.

Williams, R. M., Jr. 1970. *American society: A sociological interpretation.* 3d ed. New York: Knopf.

———. 1970. Social order and social conflict. *Proceedings of the American philosophical society* 114:217–225.

Wilson, E. O. 1975. *Sociobiology: The new synthesis.* Cambridge, MA: Harvard University Press.

———. 1978. What is sociobiology? *Society* 15 (September–October):6.

Wilson, R. A., and B. Hosokawa. 1980. *East to America: A history of the Japanese in the United States.* New York: Morrow.

Wilson, W., et al. 1976. Authoritarianism left and right. *Bulletin of the Psychonomic Society* 7 (March):271–274.

Wilson, W. J. and R. Aponte. 1985. Urban poverty. *Annual review of sociology* 11:231–258.

Wirth, L. 1938. Urbanism as a way of life. *American Journal of Sociology* 44 (July):1–2.

———. 1945. The problem of minority groups. In *The science of man in the world crisis.* Ed. R. Linton, 347–372. New York: Columbia University Press.

Witherspoon, G. 1975. *Navajo kinship and marriage.* Chicago: University of Chicago Press.

Wolfgang, M. E. 1972. Cesare Lombroso (1835–1909). In *Pioneers in criminality.* Ed. H. Mannheim. Montclair, N.J.: Patterson Smith.

Woodward, C. V. 1974. *The strange career of Jim Crow.* 3d ed. New York: Oxford University Press.

The World Almanac and Book of Facts. 1988. Nations

of the world. New York: Pharos Books, 650–738.

World Bank. 1985. *World population report, 1985.* New York: Oxford University Press.

World Population Data Sheet. 1985. Washington, D.C.: Population Reference Bureau.

———. 1987. Washington, D.C.: Population Reference Bureau.

Wrang, D. 1967. *Population and Society.* 3d ed. New York: Random House.

Wright, B., and J. P. Weiss. 1980. *Social problems.* Boston: Little, Brown.

Wrong, D. H. 1959. The functional theory of stratification: Some neglected considerations. *American Sociological Review* 24:772–782.

Yinger, J. M. 1982. *Countercultures.* New York: Free Press.

Zald, M. N. and J. McCarthy. 1979. *The dynamics of social movements.* Cambridge, Mass.: Winthrop.

Zandu, A. 1983. The value of belonging to a group in Japan. *Small Group Behavior* 14:6–14.

Zigli, B. 1984. Asian-Americans beat others in academic drive. *USA Today,* 25 April, 1D.

Zimbardo, P. G. 1972. Pathology of imprisonment. *Society* 9 (April):4–8.

Zurcher, L. A. 1983. *Social roles.* Beverly Hills, Calif.: Sage.

Zygmunt, J. E. 1986. Collective behavior as a phase of societal life: Blumer's emergent views and their implications. *Research in Social Movements, Conflicts and Change* 9:25–46.

Name Index

Abegglen, J. C., 197
Adams, N., 93
Adams, S. M., 15
Addams, J., 26–27
Adorno, T. W., 240
Ageton, S., 326
al-Rashid, H., 54
Aldous, J., 209
Alexander (the Great), 186
Alexander, P., 292
Allport, G., 240, 279
Amidei, N., 209
Anderson, N., 55
Andrew (Prince), 207
Aponte, R., 251
Appleman, P., 357
Aquino, C., 222
Aristotle, 17, 18, 19, 31, 51, 328, 329
Asch, S. E., 193
Athos, A. G., 204

Babbie, E., 48, 54, 63
Bachman, J. G., 57
Bailey, T., 132
Bales, R. F., 166, 172
Ball-Rokeach, S. J., 114
Barlow, H., 304, 327
Barnes, H. E., 15
Barney, G. O., 357
Barnouw, V., 367
Barol, B., 46
Barrow, C., 159
Bart, P., 33
Bartol, C. R., 310
Bates, D. G., 366
Baum, A., 138
Baumer, T. L., 304
Bavelas, A., 166, 168
Beach, L. R., 100
Beck, M., 352
Becker, H., 17, 310, 322, 327

Beeghley, L., 249
Belfrage, C., 283
Bell, D., 133
Bell, R. R., 228
Benaske, N., 381
Bendix, R., 139
Benedict, R., 91
Berger, P., 8, 33, 137
Berk, R., 276
Bernard, L. L., 94
Biesanz, J., 127, 305
Biesanz, M. H., 127, 305
Biller, H. B., 378
Blau, P. M., 141, 146, 180, 189, 192
Bloomfield, M., 248
Blum, J. W., 286, 341
Blumer, H., 30, 274–275, 284, 290
Boas, F., 69
Bogardus, E. S., 169
Borg, W. R., 51
Bottomore, T. B., 215
Bowers, W. J., 318
Boyer, P., 283, 311
Brady, J., 310
Brailsford, K., 46
Brake, M., 74
Breindel, E., 347
Broderick, C. B., 376
Bronowski, J., 289
Broom, L., 113, 287, 290
Brown, H. G., 45
Brown, W. C., 326
Browne, L., 85
Bruck, D., 318
Brunvand, J. H., 267, 280, 295
Bryan, J. A., 159
Brynner, Y., 289
Buckner, H. T., 279
Buffet, W., 226
Burke, P. J., 173
Burns, G., 116
Burstein, P., 52, 57, 63

Wilensky, H. L., 165
Wilkinson, D., 37
Williams, R. M., Jr., 81, 142
Wilson, E. O., 94–95
Wilson, R. A., 256
Wilson, W., 73
Wilson, W. J., 251
Wirth, L., 161, 237, 239
Witherspoon, G., 134
Wohlstein, R. T., 276
Wolfgang, M. E., 313
Woodward, C. V., 250
Wright, B., 318

Wright brothers, 12, 43
Wrong, D. H., 215

Yinger, J. M., 74, 91

Zald, M. N., 294
Zandu, A., 197
Zellner, J. A., 209
Zigli, B., 256
Zimbardo, P., 52, 53
Zimmerman, R. Z., 99
Zygmunt, J. E., 268

Subject Index

Referent power, 186
Reflex, 69, 91
Relative poverty, 209, 231, 233
Relativism, *see* Cultural relativity
Reliability, instrument, 48
Religion(s), 10
  Amish and, 292
  Calvinism, 25
  Catholics and, 303, 348, 381
  cults and sects, 74, 183–184
  Episcopalians and, 277
  fundamentalists and, 275, 279, 363
  Hindus and, 219
  Hutterites and, 342
  as a justification for slavery, 247–248
  Mormons and, 289–290, 348
  Puritans and, 342, 374
  Protestant Reformation and, 289
  Protestants and, 381
  Shakers and, 292
  world, 127
Remaining single (unmarried), 382–383
Reporting the results of research, *see* Research
Republic (Plato), 18, 20, 31
Reputational approach, stratification analysis and
    the, 229–230, 232, 233
Research
  analysis of the findings of, 40, 42, 57–58, 62
  the challenge of sociological, 60
  efficiency in, 44
  ethical issues in, 59–60
  hypotheses in, 40, 41, 42, 46–47, 48
  methods of (research design), 40, 42, 48–57
  objectivity in, 44
  prediction in, 44
  the research problem in, 40, 41, 43–44, 61
  reporting the results of, 40, 41, 42, 58, 61, 62
  review of the literature in, 40, 41–42, 44, 46,
    47, 61, 63
  steps in conducting, 40–43, 61–62
  types of social, 36–37, 61
Resocialization, *see* Socialization
Retreatism and deviance, 316–317, 326
Reverse discrimination, *see* Discrimination
Review of the literature, *see* Research
Revolution
  agricultural, *see* Agricultural revolution
  American, *see* American revolution
  and deviance, *see* Rebellion
  French, *see* French revolution
  industrial, *see* Industrial revolution
  Russian, 292
  urban, *see* Urban revolution
Riots, 247, 276, 279

Rites of passage, 115–116, 119
Ritualism
  and bureaucracy, 200–201, 203, 204
  and deviance, 316, 326
Rituals, greeting, 126
Role, 137, 138, 146
  ambiguity, 137–138, 146
  conflict, 137, 146
  discrepancy, 373, 386
  expectations, 372
  set, 137, 146
  strain, 138, 146
Role taking, 102, 117, 119
  stages of, 102
Romantic love, *see* Love
Rumania, 342
Rumor(s), 199, 278–280, 293, 294

Sacred cows of India, 67
Sample
  biased, 50, 62
  random, 49, 50, 62
  stratified random, 50, 62
Sampling error, 51, 57, 63
Sanctions, 86–87, 90, 91, 306
Sapir-Whorf hypothesis, 84
Science
  characteristics of, 11–12, 30–31
  defined, 9, 32
  as means of explanation, 9, 30
  nature of, 9–11
  physical and social, 12–13, 31
Scientific research cycle, 40–43, 47, 57, 61, 63
Scientific theory, 11, 30–31, 32
Secondary deviance, *see* Deviance
Secondary group(s), 159–162, 174, 176
  characteristics of, 160–161
  in modern urban societies, 161–162
Segregation, *see* Exclusion, patterns of minority
Self-concept, 101, 111, 117, 119, 157
  research on, 50–51
Self-fulfilling prophesy, 104, 119
Sensorimotor stage, 107–108, 117, 119
Serbia, 270
Sex composition, *see* Population
Sex ratio, 344, 356, 357
Sex scandals, 280, 304
Sexual behavior, extramarital, 309
Significant others, 103, 119
Single-parent family, *see* Family
Social action, 24, 32
Social category, 154, 174, 176
Social class, *see* Social stratification

Credits

Page 15, Figure 1-3, From Hedley, R. A. and Adams, S. M. (1982). The job market for bachelor degree holders: A cumulation. Published by permission of Transaction Publishers from *The American Sociologist*, Vol. 17, p. 158. Copyright © 1982 by Transaction Publishers.

Pages 41–2, Box 2-1, Adapted with permission from Wallace, W. (1972) *The logic of science in sociology*. Chicago: Aldine-Atherton, p. 18.

Page 59, "Tumbleweeds" drawing by Tom K. Ryan. © 1989 North America Syndicate, Inc.

Page 106, Figure 4-1, Adapted form CHILDHOOD AND SOCIETY, Second Edition, by Erik H. Erikson, by permission of W. W. Norton & Company, Inc. Copyright 1950, © 1963 by W. W. Norton & Company, Inc. Copyright renewed 1978 by Erik H. Erikson.

Page 108, Figure 4-2, Herbert P. Ginsburg/Sylvia Opper, *Piaget's Theory of Intellectual Development*, 3e, © 1988. Adapted by permisision of Prentice-Hall, Inc., Englewood Cliffs, New Jersey.

Page 168, Figure 6-3, Adapted with permission from Leavitt, H. J. (1951). Some effects of certain communication patterns on group performance. *Journal of Abnormal and Social Psychology*, vol. 46, pp. 38–50.

Page 171, Table 6-1, Adapted with permission of The Free Press, A Division of MacMillan, Inc. from *Handbook of Small Group Research* by A. Paul Hare. Copyright © 1962 by The Free Press.

Page 181, Figure 7-1, Adapted with permission of The Free Press, a Division of MacMillan, Inc. from *A Comparative Analysis of Complex Organizations* by Amitai Etzioni, Copyright © 1961 by The Free Press.

Page 188, Drawing by Handelsman; © 1978 The New Yorker Magazine, Inc.

Page 193, Figure 7-3, Adapted with permission from Asch, S. (1965). Effects of group pressure upon the modification and distortion of judgments, In H. Proshansky and B. Seidenberg (Eds.), *Basic Studies in Psychology*. New York: Holt, Rinehart and Winston, pp. 393–401

Page 225, Table 8-1, Reprinted with permission from Davis, J. A. and Smith T. W. (1984). *General social survey cumulative file, 1972-1982*. Ann Arbor, MI: Inter-University Consortium for Political and Social Research.

Page 227, Table 8-2, Adapted by permission of *Forbes* magazine, October 26, 1987. © 1987 Forbes, Inc.

Page 236, Table 9-1, Adapted with permission from Parillo, V. N. (1985). *Strangers to These Shores*, 2e, New York: John Wiley and Sons, Inc., p. 119.

Page 243, Figure 9-1, "Common Stereotypes" from *The Things They Say Behind Your Back* by William B. Helmreich, copyright © 1982 by William B. Helmreich. Used by permission of Doubleday, a division of Bantam, Doubleday, Dell Publishing Group, Inc.

Page 245, Figure 9-2, Reprinted with permission from Kroeber, A. L. (1948). *Anthropology*. New York: Harcourt Brace Jovanovich, p. 10.

Page 261, Figure 9-3, Adapted from *The World Almanac and Book of Facts, 1989 edition*, copyright © Newspaper Enterprise Assn., Inc. 1988. New York, NY 10166.

Page 285, cartoon, © 1987, The Washington Post Writers' Group. Reprinted with permission.

Page 308, Figure 11-2, Adapted with permission from Lingeman, R. R. (1974). *Drugs from A to Z: A dictionary*, 2e. New York: McGraw-Hill and from *The Los Angeles Times* throughout 1988.

Page 316, Figure 11-3, Adapted with permission of The Free Press, A Division of MacMillan, Inc. from *Social Theory and Social Structure* by Robert K. Merton. Copyright © 1957 by The Free Press, renewed 1985 by Robert K. Merton.

Page 330, Drawing by Dick Locher. Reprinted by permission: Tribune Media Services.

Page 331, Text, From Fornos, W. (1987). Gaining people, losing ground: A blueprint for stabilizing world population. Ephrata, PA: Science Press, pp. 1–2.

Page 337, Figure 12-1, Reprinted with permission from Fornos, W. (1987). *Gaining People, Losing Ground: A Blueprint for Stabilizing World Population*. Washington, DC: The Population Institute, p. 4.

Page 339, Table 12-1, Adapted from *The World Almanac and Book of Facts, 1989 edition*, copyright © Newspaper Enterprise Assn., Inc. 1988. New York, NY 10166 and from *Popline* (May, 1986). Washington, DC: The Population Institute, p. 7.

Page 343, Table 12-2, Adapted from Fornos, W. (1987). *Gaining People, Losing Ground: A Blueprint for Stabilizing World Population*. Ephrata, PA: The Science Press, pp. 38–57.

Page 346, Figure 12-2, Adapted with permissions from Haupt, A. and Kane, T. T. (1985). *Population handbook*. Washington, DC: Population Reference Bureau, Inc., p. 14.

Page 349, Copyright © 1988 The Time Inc. Magazine Company. Reprinted by permission.

Page 363, Figure 13-1, From *The Family in Social Context*, 7e, by Gerald R. Leslie. Copyright © 1967, 1973, 1976, 1979, 1982, 1985, 1989 by Oxford University Press, Inc. Reprinted by permission.